Reference Book - Room Use Only

MARK & HELEN OSTERLIN LIBRARY
NORTHWESTERN MICHIGAN COLLEGE
TRAVERSE CITY, MICHIGAN 49686-3061

WITHDRAWN

WITHDRAWN

Encyclopedia of Insurgency and Counterinsurgency

A New Era of Modern Warfare

Spencer C. Tucker,
Editor

ABC-CLIO

Santa Barbara, California • Denver, Colorado • Oxford, England

© Copyright 2013 by ABC-CLIO, LLC

All rights reserved. No part of this publication may be reproduced, stored in a retrieval system, or transmitted, in any form or by any means, electronic, mechanical, photocopying, recording, or otherwise, except for the inclusion of brief quotations in a review, without prior permission in writing from the publisher.

Library of Congress Cataloging-in-Publication Data

Encyclopedia of insurgency and counterinsurgency : a new era of modern warfare / Spencer C. Tucker, editor.

     pages cm

  Includes bibliographical references and index.

  ISBN 978-1-61069-279-3 (hardcover : alk. paper)—ISBN 978-1-61069-280-9 (ebook)

  1. Counterinsurgency—Encyclopedias. 2. Insurgency—Encyclopedias. 3. Armed Forces—Officers—Biography—Encyclopedias. 4. Guerrillas—Biography—Encyclopedias. 5. Guerrilla warfare—Encyclopedias. I. Tucker, Spencer, 1937–

  U240.E68   2013

  355.02'1803—dc23

                            2013016415

ISBN: 978-1-61069-279-3
EISBN: 978-1-61069-280-9

17 16 15 14 13   1 2 3 4 5

This book is also available on the World Wide Web as an eBook.
Visit www.abc-clio.com for details.

ABC-CLIO, LLC
130 Cremona Drive, P.O. Box 1911
Santa Barbara, California 93116-1911

This book is printed on acid-free paper ∞
Manufactured in the United States of America

For Pat Carlin,
a superb colleague
and a good friend

About the Editor

Spencer C. Tucker, PhD, has been senior fellow in military history at ABC-CLIO since 2003. He is the author or editor of 44 books and encyclopedias, many of which have won prestigious awards. Tucker's last academic position before his retirement from teaching was the John Biggs Chair in Military History at the Virginia Military Institute, Lexington, Virginia. He has been a Fulbright scholar, a visiting research associate at the Smithsonian Institution, and, as a U.S. Army captain, an intelligence analyst in the Pentagon. His recently published works include *The Encyclopedia of the Mexican-American War: A Political, Social, and Military History; The Encyclopedia of the War of 1812: A Political, Social, and Military History;* and *Almanac of American Military History,* all published by ABC-CLIO.

Contents

List of Entries

ix

Preface

The term "insurgency" is difficult to define. In general terms, an insurgency is a revolt or rebellion against a state government or other constituted authority in which the individual insurgents seek to destroy the political authority of the constituted authority over its people. The U.S. Department of Defense describes insurgency as "an organized movement aimed at the overthrow of a constituted government through the use of subversion and armed conflict." The term "insurgency" is often used pejoratively by governments and other authorities, implying that the rebel cause is illegitimate. Those taking part in an insurgency are often not recognized as belligerents. Indeed, the Hague Conference of 1899 failed to reach agreement on whether the irregular forces known as francs-tireurs during the Franco-Prussian War of 1870–1871 were lawful combatants or could be subject to immediate execution on capture. Argument over this continues, as in the case of the detainees held by the U.S. government at Guantanamo Bay.

Not all rebellions are insurgencies, for a state of belligerency may exist between a sovereign state and rebel forces. Thus, during the American Civil War, the British government chose not to recognize the Confederate States of America as a sovereign state but to accord it belligerent status, which nonetheless permitted Confederate warships access to British ports.

The term "counterinsurgency" is much easier to define. Known to the U.S. defense establishment as COIN, counterinsurgency is simply the effort to defeat an insurgency. Generally, this involves a comprehensive joint civilian-military effort that addresses and removes the core grievances feeding an insurgency, separates the population from insurgent influence, and then defeats the insurgents themselves militarily. Taken together, insurgency and counterinsurgency are included within the broad category of conflicts once identified as small wars and now known as irregular warfare or revolutionary warfare (defined as the combination of guerrilla war and political action).

This encyclopedia treats numerous selected insurgencies and counterinsurgencies and their leaders throughout history and also treats some terms as well as military theorists of insurgency and counterinsurgency. I have included selected examples from the ancient, medieval, and early modern periods, but the focus here is the modern period. Even then, this encyclopedia is very selective, for while war between sovereign states has been in decline, there has been a steady rise in the number of insurgencies and thus in counterinsurgency operations. With an absolute limit of 260,000 words, I have had to be extremely selective in choosing entry topics. I have also endeavored to emphasize insurgencies associated with American history. These include not only the most famous example of the Indian Wars but also more obscure but nonetheless important insurgencies, such as Bacon's Rebellion, the Regulator Revolt, Shays' Rebellion, and the Whiskey Rebellion.

This encyclopedia is intended as an introduction to insurgency and counterinsurgency. Hopefully readers will find in this work a useful reference as well as material that will further their own study and interest in the subject.

I am grateful to Conrad C. Crane for his excellent introduction. Dr. Crane is director of the U.S. Army Military History Institute at Carlisle Barracks, Pennsylvania, and although he has written widely on U.S. military history, he is also acknowledged as an expert in insurgency and counterinsurgency warfare.

Spencer C. Tucker

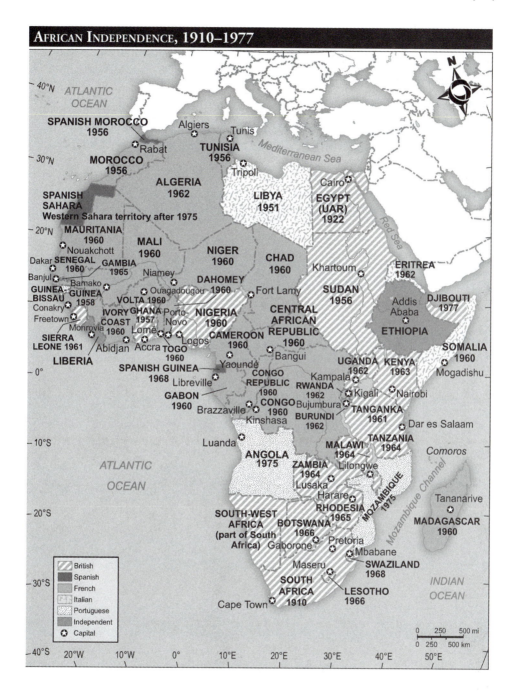

AFRICAN INDEPENDENCE, 1910–1977

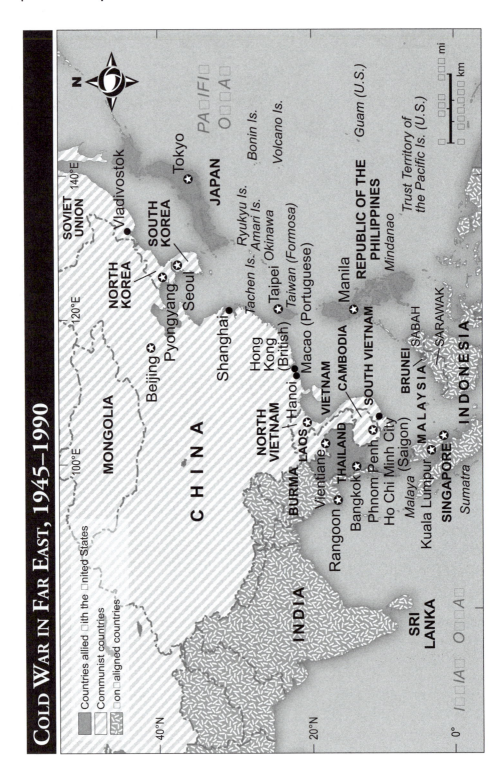

COLD WAR IN FAR EAST, 1945–1990

Countries allied with the United States

Communist countries

Nonaligned countries

EAST CENTRAL EUROPE, 1945

LATIN AMERICA AND THE CARIBBEAN POST-1945

MIDDLE EAST

Introduction

There is no word in the contemporary defense and national security lexicon that is more overused and abused than "asymmetric." There are numerous military staff and think tank cells established to focus on asymmetric warfare and tactics, and there have been myriad studies about their unique threat today, especially to Western militaries. In reality, there have been two kinds of warfare throughout history: asymmetric and stupid. Every intelligent combatant tries to get an edge on its opponent, and no military has been as asymmetric as that of the United States, whether focused on the application of overwhelming force (superior mass is about as asymmetric as you can get) or on innovative uses of technology, such as airpower and nuclear weapons. Weaker parties also choose unique paths designed to avoid enemy strengths and exploit whatever advantages are at hand. Often this results in an insurgency.

The current accepted U.S. Department of Defense definition for insurgency is "The organized use of subversion and violence by a group or movement that seeks to overthrow or force change of a governing authority. Insurgency can also refer to the group itself." The corresponding Department of Defense definition of counterinsurgency is "Comprehensive civilian and military efforts taken to defeat an insurgency and to address any core grievances." Back in the 1960s and 1970s, insurgency and counterinsurgency were seen as opposite components of revolutionary war, generally seen as an internal war for political control within a state or region.

Insurgencies can be launched against occupying forces or established governments but always incorporate tactics to negate superior resources. Chinese Communist leader Mao Zedong's theories from the 1930s exploited mass mobilization, time, and space to wear down the invading Japanese Army and recognized the need to closely coordinate political and military activities. As his ideas help spawn a series of popular uprisings in the 1950s and 1960s, a coherent body of counterinsurgency theory appeared from British and French authors trying to maintain colonial empires.

French Army officer David Galula, for instance, highlighted the unfair nature of the revolutionary wars the British and French faced, where the rules favored the insurgent in many important ways. Disorder, an insurgent goal to dislocate and embarrass ruling authorities, is much easier to create than prevent. Defending widespread targets takes many more resources than does attacking just one target. Insurgents trying to usurp power also have great advantages in the information realm, where they are judged by the promises they make, while governments must generally produce real results and deliver actual services.

Modern insurgencies tend to be loose coalitions of groups pursuing different goals and tactics, creating a complex set of problems for counterinsurgents and bringing into question the continuing relevance of Maoist theory. But such conflicts maintain characteristics far different from conventional military operations. Galula argued that revolutionary wars were 80 percent political and only 20 percent military, a useful metaphor for emphasizing the ingredients of the solution set that normally end such conflicts but not very evident to a soldier in the middle of an ambush or a firefight. The localized and mosaic nature of insurgency and counterinsurgency, which varies from country to country and village to village, makes generalizations difficult if not downright dangerous, but there are still some common attributes of these operations worth pondering by anyone studying or planning them.

By definition, the combatants on both sides of an internal war are pursuing political power. The victor will be decided by the people of the contested region, based on their own definition of legitimacy or whose governance they will accept. All governing authorities rule by a combination of consent and coercion. Those defined as legitimate rely primarily on the consent of the governed. Governance that relies basically on coercion is possible but more unstable; as soon as power is disrupted, the people cease to obey it. However, the concept of legitimacy varies by culture. Some cultures accept theocratic rule or value security over freedoms that Western societies consider essential. Abraham Maslow's hierarchy of social needs theory is often a greater determinant of legitimacy than any theory of political science.

Because behaviors and attitudes of the population play such an important role in determining outcomes, influence and information operations permeate insurgency and counterinsurgency. This is sometimes called a battle over hearts and minds, but there are many other parts of the anatomy that can also be targeted to affect results. Both sides will take actions to shape popular opinion, and the old saying "Perception is reality" is particularly relevant. Every action has an information reaction, and the side that can control the resulting immediate narrative obtains a major advantage. People respond to what they believe at the time, not to what historians write many years later. Often, operations are shaped purely to create bad publicity for an opponent or to promote an overreaction that will incur a popular backlash. Another important skill in manipulating public opinion is managing expectations. Unkept promises can create severe dissatisfaction in a population, especially for governments, which also can suffer from impressions of unfulfilled obligations. Insurgents often profit from this vulnerability of authority early in a conflict but begin to face it themselves as they become more successful and control more territory.

There are many audiences for this information warfare. Obviously, the indigenous population in the middle of the conflict is a very important target, but there are many other targets when it comes to information warfare. Although these conflicts are called internal wars, there are usually many external players. Insurgents may rely on direct support from a key foreign ally or obtain financing and recruits from international sources. A resisting government may also draw on outside aid, to include military assistance ranging from advisers to air support to significant numbers of foreign combat troops. International and nongovernmental organizations can get drawn into the conflict on both sides.

These sources of external support have popular opinions of their own to consider and organizational and national wills that can wax and wane. Just as both sides will conduct kinetic operations to reduce sources of internal and external support for their enemy, so too will they conduct information campaigns. The ability to get internal and external allies to give up or change sides can have a decisive effect.

Often, the information reaction to an activity is shaped primarily by how force is applied. Brutal repression can intimidate and terrorize but can also spark outrage and resistance. Conducting a messy military assault with great collateral damage that kills 5 insurgents while creating 50 more does not profit a counterinsurgent. Insurgent terror attacks might sap popular will or increase the willingness of the populace to tolerate increased security measures. The use of force must be carefully shaped and calibrated to achieve desired effects and to avoid unexpected backlash.

Popular support can also be gained by providing social services or a viable justice system. Military organizations and action alone are rarely enough to achieve lasting success. Insurgents will often create shadow governments to compete with existing authority. Both sides will attempt to deny access to areas they control in order to consolidate political control without competition. The goal of both insurgents and counterinsurgents is to eventually have a population that accepts their authority with the need for minimum coercion.

Sometimes the result is a compromise that gives both sides some objectives while otherwise just ending violent strife. In such cases, the real victor or loser may be hard to determine, and historians still argue over the outcome of many case studies. Internal wars sometimes appear to resemble a hockey fight, with both sides punching and grabbing until they become so exhausted that some mediator steps in and imposes or guides a settlement.

Another factor that helps make every insurgency and counterinsurgency unique is that they change over time. They vary not only from location to location also but from year to year. This is because both sides, whether from survival instincts or brilliant insight, eventually must adjust to altered conditions or lose. Learning and adapting are perhaps the most important abilities for either side to possess. When one side develops a new tactic, the other side will counter it. When one side creates a program that garners significant popular support, the other side will work to dismantle it or will develop a more attractive alternative. One of the popular myths about such conflicts is that if the insurgents are not losing, they are winning. That is not true. Time is neutral, and the will to continue can wear down on both sides. Whoever can find the innovative spark or new ally to break a stalemate or can come up with new approaches that confound their enemy can usually win in the end. The goal is to be able to learn and adapt so fast that the enemy can never catch up.

This volume highlights the rich and varied history of insurgency and counterinsurgency, which began thousands of years before Mao. The wide range of actors affected by such conflicts and who can affect them in return should provide this comprehensive work with a broad audience. Insurgency and counterinsurgency are worldwide phenomena that will always be with us as long as people feel compelled to resort to violence to resist or change governing authorities.

Conrad C. Crane

A

Abd al-Qadir

Birth Date: 1808
Death Date: 1883

Algerian political and military leader and Islamic scholar who led an insurgency against France. Abd al-Qadir, also known as Abd al-Qadir al-Jaza'iri (Abd al-Qadir the Algerian), Abd-el-Kader, and Abd-al-Kadir, is also known by the titles of emir, prince, and sheikh (shaykh). He was born near the town of Mascara near Oran in northwestern Algeria on September 6, 1808. Abd al-Qadir's father was a sheikh in the Qadiri Rafai Sufi order of Islam and a Berber who claimed descent from Muhammad. As a youth, Abd al-Qadir memorized the Qur'an (Koran) and received an excellent education. He was also well trained in horsemanship. In 1825 he undertook the Hajj (pilgrimage to Mecca) with his father and then visited religious sites in Damascus and Baghdad. This trip cemented Abd al-Qadir's own strong religious beliefs. He returned home a few months before the French invasion of Algeria in June 1830.

The French captured the city of Algiers on July 5, 1830, and then gradually expanded their hold over the rest of Algeria. In 1832, having been confirmed as emir of Mascara after his father's death that same year and with the support of a number of the tribes in western Algeria, Abd al-Qadir proclaimed a jihad (holy war) against the French. During the course of the next decade until 1842, he led a highly successful guerrilla campaign.

Despite victory at La Macta on June 28, 1934, Abd al-Qadir was unable to prevent the French sack of Mascara in December. His forces were defeated by the French under Général de Division Thomas Robert Bugeaud at Sikkah on July 6, 1836, and on June 1, 1837 Abd al-Qadir concluded with Bugeaud the Treaty of Tafna. Under its terms, Abd al-Qadir recognized French sovereignty in Oran and Algiers, while he was recognized as controlling some two-thirds of the country (chiefly the interior). Although this arrangement was justified by the situation on the ground, there was great opposition to the treaty in France and much criticism of Bugeaud as having sold out French interests. The government of King Louis Philippe now agreed to send to Algeria the troop reinforcements previously denied Bugeaud and to make a major military effort in the eastern part of the country at Constantine, which the French took by assault on October 13, 1837. Meanwhile, Abd al-Qadir organized an efficient theocratic government in the territory under his control.

When French troops crossed into territory recognized as controlled by Abd al-Qadir, fighting resumed on October 15, 1839. The French practiced a scorched-earth policy, and Abd al-Qadir was unable to secure support from important tribes in eastern Algeria. His army of 40,000 men was scattered by 2,000 French in the Battle of Smala (May 10, 1843) and then was crushed by Bugeard in the Battle of the Isly River (August 14, 1844). Although Abd al-Qadir continued to win battles, notably the Battle of Sidi Brahim (September 22–25, 1845), French military pressure forced him into Morocco, where he sought to rally the Rif tribes. Moroccan government action prompted by suspicions regarding Abd al-Qadir's intentions forced him back into Algeria, and on December 21, 1847, under the pledge that he would be allowed to go into exile in the Levant, he surrendered to French général de division Louis de Lamorcière.

The French failed to honor this pledge, and Abd al-Qadir was exiled to France, first in Toulon, then in Pau, and during 1848–1852 at the Château of Amboise. Released by French emperor Napoleon III with a pension of 200,000 francs on the pledge that he not return to Algeria, Abd al-Qadir settled first in Bursa in the Ottoman Empire (today Turkey) and then in 1855 in Damascus. There he devoted himself to the study of Muslim theology and philosophy and wrote several books.

In 1860 during fighting in Damascus, Abd al-Qadir saved some 1,200 Christians, taking them into his residence. For this the French government increased his pension and bestowed on him the Grand Cross of the Légion d'Honneur. In 1865 Abd al-Qadir became a mason, and the next year he was received by Emperor Napoleon III in Paris. Abd al-Qadir died in Damascus on May 26, 1883. His remains were returned to Algeria in 1966.

A highly effective guerrilla leader, Abd al-Qadir was also chivalrous toward his adversaries, on occasion releasing French prisoners when he did not have sufficient food for them. Many Algerians regard him today as the greatest national hero of their struggle for independence. There are a number of monuments to Abd al-Qadir in Algeria, where a university is also named for him. His green and white flag standard was adopted as the flag of the independence movement against France and is today the national flag of Algeria.

Spencer C. Tucker

See also Algeria, French Pacification of

Further Reading

Danziger, Raphael. *Abd-al-Qadir and the Algerian Resistance to the French Internal Consolidation.* New York: Holmes and Meier, 1977.

Julien, Charles-André. *Histoire de l'Algérie contemporaine: La conquête et les débuts de la colonisation* [History of Contemporary Algeria: The Conquest and the Beginnings of Colonization]. Paris: Presses universitaires de la France, 1964.

Lataillade, Louis. *Abd el-Kader, adversaire et ami de la France.* Paris: Pygmalion, 1984.

Sahli, Mohammad Chérif. *Abd el-Kader, chevalier de la foi.* Alger: Entreprise algérienne de presse, 1984.

Abd el-Krim al-Khattabi, Muhammad ibn

Birth Date: 1882
Death Date: 1963

Moroccan Berber leader and religious scholar, known as "The Wolf of the Rif," who led a liberation movement against French and Spanish rule in Morocco. Born in Ajdir, Morocco, in 1882, the son of a qadi (caid, local administrator) of the Aith Yusuf clan of the Aith Uriaghel (Waryaghar) tribe, Muhammad ibn Abd el-Krim al-Khattabi received a traditional Muslim education in addition to Spanish education. Fluent in Spanish, he became a secretary in the Bureau of Native Affairs in the protectorate government. In 1915 Abd el-Krim was appointed qadi al-qadat (chief Muslim judge) for the Melilla district, where he also taught at a Hispano-Arabic school and served as editor of an Arabic section of the Spanish newspaper *El Telegrama del Rif.*

Disillusioned with Spanish control of his country, Abd el-Krim came to speak out against Spanish policies, and in 1916–1917 during World War I (1914–1918) he was imprisoned by the Spanish for allegedly conspiring with the German consul. He returned to Ajdir in 1919.

In 1921, Abd el-Krim raised the standard of resistance against foreign control of Morocco. This marked the beginning of the Rif War (1921–1926), although some date its start to 1920. He was greatly aided by his younger brother Muhammad, who became his chief adviser and commander of the rebel army,

In late July 1921, determined to destroy the rebels, Spanish general Fernandes Silvestre moved into the Rif Mountains with some 20,000 men but failed to carry out adequate reconnaissance or take sufficient security precautions. At Annual (Anual) on July 21, the Spanish column encountered Spanish troops fleeing the next post at Abaran. In the ensuing confusion, Rif forces fell on both flanks of the Spanish column, leading to widespread panic and the death of as many as 12,000 Spanish troops. Silvestre committed suicide, and several thousand Spaniards were taken prisoner. News of this military disaster created a political firestorm in Spain and brought strongman General Miguel Primo de Rivera to power that September. With the support of King Alfonso XIII, Rivera established a virtual military dictatorship until his resignation in January 1930.

Meanwhile, in Morocco in 1923, Abd el-Krim proclaimed the Republic of the Rif, with himself as president, and began organizing a centralized administration based on traditional Berber tribal institutions but that would override tribal rivalries. Fighting continued, and by the end of 1924 the Spanish had been forced to withdraw to the coastal enclaves of Melilla and Tetuán.

On April 12, 1925, Abd el-Krim opened a major offensive against the French in their portion of Morocco. Although he had limited resources, in July French resident-general Général de Division Hubert Lyautey was able to stop the insurgents short of their objective of Fez. On July 26, representatives of the French and Spanish governments met in Madrid and agreed to set aside their rivalry over Morocco and cooperate fully against Abd el-Krim. The French were to assemble up to 150,000 men under Marshal Henri Philippe Pétain, while the Spanish put together 50,000 men under General José Sanjurjo. Facing overwhelming force and technological superiority in the form of modern artillery and aircraft, on May 26, 1926, Abd el-Krim surrendered to the French, bringing the Rif War to a close.

The French sent Abd el-Krim into exile on the island of Réunion in the Indian Ocean. Receiving permission in 1947 to live in France, he left Réunion and was granted political asylum en route by the Egyptian government. For five years he headed the Liberation Committee of the Arab West (sometimes called the Maghrib Bureau) in Cairo. With the restoration of Moroccan independence in 1956, King Muhammad V invited Abd el-Krim to return to Morocco, but he refused to do so as long as French troops remained in the Maghrib (Northwest Africa). Abd el-Krim died in Cairo on February 6, 1963.

Well educated and a skilled tactician and capable organizer, Abd el-Krim was a forerunner of the successful post–World War II wars of liberation in the Maghrib against European rule. He was defeated largely because of the size and technological superiority of the European armies sent against him. Abd el-Krim's guerrilla tactics also influenced 20th-century revolutionary leaders in Latin America and Asia.

Spencer C. Tucker

See also Rif War

Further Reading

Abdelkrim. *Mémoires d'Abd el Krim, recueillis par J. Roger-Mathieu* [Memnoirs of Abd el Krim, Collected by J. Roger-Mathieu]. Paris: Librairie des Champs Elysées, 1927.

Harris, Walter B. *France, Spain, and the Rif.* London, 1927.

Pennell, Charles Richard. *A Country with a Government and a Flag: The Rif War in Morocco, 1921–1926.* Wisbech, Cambridgeshire, UK: Menas, 1986.

Woolman, David S. *Rebels in the Rif: Abd el Krim and the Rif Rebellion.* Stanford, CA: Stanford University Press, 1968.

Abrams, Creighton Williams, Jr.

Birth Date: September 15, 1914
Death Date: September 4, 1974

U.S. Army general; commander, U.S. Military Assistance Command, Vietnam (MACV); and army chief of staff. Born on September 15, 1914, in Springfield, Massachusetts, Creighton Williams Abrams Jr. graduated from the U.S. Military Academy, West Point in 1936 and was posted to the 7th Cavalry Regiment. When World War II (1939–1945) loomed, he volunteered for armor.

Abrams rose to prominence as commander of a tank battalion that often spearheaded General George Patton's Third Army during World War II. Abrams led the forces that relieved the encircled 101st Airborne Division at Bastogne during the Battle of the Bulge and received a battlefield promotion to full colonel.

After World War II, Abrams served as director of tactics at the Armor School at Fort Knox (1946–1948), graduated from the Command and General Staff College (1949), and was a corps chief of staff during 1953–1954 at the end of the Korean War (1950–1953). He graduated from the Army War College (1953) and was promoted to brigadier general in 1956 and to major general in 1960. Abrams held a variety of staff assignments during this period, and from 1960 to 1962 he commanded the 3rd Armored Division. In 1963 Abrams was promoted to lieutenant general and made commander of V Corps in Germany.

When American involvement in Vietnam intensified, in mid-1964 Abrams was promoted to full general and made army vice chief of staff. In that assignment he was deeply involved in the army's troop buildup, a task made infinitely more difficult by President Lyndon Johnson's refusal to call up reserve forces.

In May 1967 Abrams was assigned to Vietnam as deputy commander of MACV. In that position, he devoted himself primarily to improvement of the Republic of Vietnam (RVN, South Vietnam) armed forces. During the 1968 Tet Offensive when the Army of the Republic of Vietnam (ARVN, South Vietnamese Army) forces gave a far better account of themselves than was expected, Abrams rightly received much of the credit.

Soon after the beginning of the Tet Offensive, Abrams was sent north to take command of I Corps, distinguishing himself in the fighting there and working effectively with ARVN commanders to secure the clearing of Hue. When General William C. Westmoreland was recalled to Washington, Abrams replaced him as MACV commander on July 3, 1968.

Abrams now changed the conduct of the war in fundamental ways. His predecessor's attrition strategy, search-and-destroy tactics, and reliance on body count as the measure of merit were discarded. Abrams stressed population security as the key to success. He directed a one-war approach, pulling together combat operations, pacification, and the upgrading of South Vietnamese forces into a coherent whole. For Abrams, combat operations had as their ultimate objective providing security for the population so that pacification, the most important thing, could progress.

Abrams urged his commanders to drastically reduce so-called H&I (harassment and interdiction) fires, unobserved artillery fire that he thought did little damage to the enemy and a good deal of damage to innocent villagers. He also cut back on the multibattalion sweeps that gave Communist forces the choice of terrain, time, and duration of engagement. Abrams replaced these with multiple small-unit patrols and ambushes that blocked the enemy's access to the people, interdicting their movement of forces and supplies.

Abrams understood that many enemy attacks could be preempted if their supply caches could be discovered and captured or destroyed. He also discerned that Communist main forces depended heavily on guerrillas and the Viet Cong infrastructure in the hamlets and villages, not the other way around, and that digging out that infrastructure could deprive the main forces of the guides, bearers, intelligence, locally procured food and supplies, and other wherewithal that they needed to function effectively. These insights were key to revising the tactics of the war.

After the 1968 Tet Offensive, the U.S. government sought a way out of the war. In the years that followed, Abrams's army was progressively taken away from him. Still, he did what he could to inspire, encourage, and support the remaining forces, American and Vietnamese alike.

Abrams left Vietnam in June 1972 to become army chief of staff. In that position, he set about dealing with the myriad problems of an army that had been through a devastating ordeal. He concentrated on rebuilding the army and its readiness and the well-being of the soldier, always the touchstones of his professional concern. Stricken with cancer, Abrams died in office on September 4, 1974.

Lewis Sorley

See also Vietnam War; Westmoreland, William Childs

Further Reading

Colby, William, with James McCargar. *Lost Victory: A Firsthand Account of America's Sixteen-Year Involvement in Vietnam.* Chicago: Contemporary Books, 1989.

Palmer, Bruce, Jr. *The 25-Year War: America's Military Role in Vietnam.* Lexington: University Press of Kentucky, 1984.

Sorley, Lewis. *A Better War: The Unexamined Victories and Final Tragedy of America's Last Years in Vietnam.* New York: Harcourt, Brace, 1999.

Sorley, Lewis. *Thunderbolt: General Creighton Abrams and the Army of His Times.* New York: Simon and Schuster, 1992.

Abu Sayyaf

Islamic insurgent group in the southern Philippine Islands. The name "Abu Sayyaf" comes from Arabic and is loosely translated as "father of swordsmith." Its members also call themselves Al-Harakat Al-Islamiyya (Islamic Movement). Established in 1991 and led by Khadaffy Janjalani until his death in battle with Philippine government forces in September 2006, Abu Sayyaf members seek the establishment of an independent Islamic state in the southern Philippines, where other Islamic organizations—most notably the Moro National Liberation Front (MNLF) and the Moro Islamic Liberation Front (MILF)—have been active since 1969.

With an estimated 200 fighters and an extended membership of 2,000, Abu Sayyaf is the smallest of the Islamic insurgent groups seeking autonomy or independence for the largely Muslim southern Philippines. Abu Sayyaf is also the most radical organization, wanting establishment of an Islamic fundamentalist state. Most active in the islands of Jolo and Basilan, Abu Sayyaf has been involved in bombings, drive-by shootings, kidnappings, and extortion and is also reportedly involved in drug dealing.

The U.S. government has included Abu Sayyaf on its list of international terrorist organizations, and since 2002 fighting the group has been part of the mission of the U.S. military's Operation ENDURING FREEDOM, part of the Global War on Terror. The U.S. Central Intelligence Agency has dispatched agents to help hunt down Abu Sayyaf leaders, and several hundred U.S. Army Special Forces personnel have been sent to the Philippines to assist Filipino forces in counterinsurgency training.

Spencer C. Tucker

See also Moro Islamic Liberation Front; Moro National Liberation Front; Moros

Further Reading

Banlaoi, Rommel. *Philippine Security in the Age of Terror.* New York: Taylor and Francis, 2010.

Aden Emergency

Start Date: 1963
End Date: 1967

Insurgency in the British crown colony of Aden during 1963–1967. Now part of the Republic of Yemen, Aden is located at the southern tip of the Arabian Peninsula. The port was of great interest to the British as an antipiracy station to protect shipping lanes to India, and the British East India Company landed forces there in 1839. With the opening of the Suez Canal, Aden also served as a coaling station and became a crown colony in 1937.

The British established the Federation of Arab Emirates of the South in 1959. Subsequently nine states were added, and in April 1962 the federation became the Federation of South Arabia. Aden joined this entity in January 1963. Inspired by the Pan-Arabism and socialism of Egyptian president Gamal Abdel Nasser, in June 1963 a Marxist insurgent organization was established in Aden. Known as the National Liberation Front (NLF), it enjoyed Egyptian support. Shortly thereafter, a rival insurgent group came into being, known as the Front for the Liberation of South Yemen (FLOSY).

There had been considerable unrest in Aden for a number of years, and a United Nations Observer Force had been dispatched there in June 1963. Following a December 10, 1963, grenade attack on the British high commissioner that killed 1 person and injured 50, the British declared a state of emergency.

The ensuing Aden Emergency pitted the British and local sheikhs against the NLF and FLOSY, but the situation was complicated by the fact that the two insurgent groups often fought one another. Indeed, when the NLF became more Marxist, Nasser switched Egyptian support to FLOSY. The insurgents engaged largely in hit-and-run attacks. The British moved in troops as well as aircraft, and by 1965, when the British suspended the Federation of South Arabia government and imposed direct British rule, the Royal Air Force had nine squadrons of fixed-wing aircraft and helicopters there.

The situation in Aden was exacerbated by the June 1967 Arab-Israeli War. Nasser charged that the British had assisted the Israelis during that war, and this led to a mutiny on June 20 among the South Arabian Federation Army and police in Aden's Crater District, resulting in the deaths of 23 British servicemen. Following two weeks of insurgent control, on July 5 in Operation STIRLING CASTLE, Lieutenant Colonel Colin Campbell "Mad Mitch" Mitchell's 1st Battalion, Argyll and Sutherland Highlanders, restored order in the district.

Guerrilla attacks against the British soon resumed, however. British casualties went from 2 in 1964 to 44 in 1967. In all, 382 people died as a result of terrorist incidents during 1964–1967, with 57 of them being British military personnel. Despite these relatively modest casualties, the British Labour government of Prime Minister Harold Wilson announced in February 1967 that it would quit Aden. Major fighting then occurred in Aden between the NLF and FLOSY, with heavy casualties on both sides. In November 1967 London withdrew all British troops from Aden and southern Arabia, and on November 30 the federation came to an end. The precipitous British departure occurred without agreement on governance, but the Marxist NLF, having secured the support of the Yemeni Federal Army, defeated FLOSY, now bereft of Egyptian military support as a consequence of the June 1967 Arab-Israeli War.

The NLF then proclaimed the People's Republic of South Yemen. The closure of the naval base meant hard times economically for Aden for a number of years thereafter. In 1978 the NLF changed its name to the Yemeni Socialist Party and made it the only legal political party. In May 1990 the People's Republic of South Yemen united with the Yemen Arab Republic, commonly known as North Yemen, to form the current Republic of Yemen.

Spencer C. Tucker

See also Front for the Liberation of Occupied South Yemen; Mitchell, Colin Campbell; National Liberation Front of Aden

Further Reading

Kostiner, Joseph. *The Struggle for South Yemen.* New York: St. Martin's, 1984.

Naumkin, Vitaly. *Red Wolves of Yemen: The Struggle for Independence.* Cambridge, UK: Oleander, 2004.

Walker, Jonathan. *Aden Insurgency: The Savage War in Yemen, 1962–1967.* Barnsley, South Yorkshire, UK: Pen and Sword Military, 2011.

Adwa, Battle of

Event Date: March 1, 1896

In the last decade of the 19th century, a scramble by the major European powers occurred as they sought to carve up Africa. Newly unified Italy joined the race for African colonies, and beginning in 1884, Emperor Yohannes IV of Abyssinia (present-day Ethiopia) found himself fighting a two-front war with the Mahdist state to the west in the Sudan and the new Italian colony at Massawa on the Red Sea. In the Battle of Dogali on January 26, 1887, some 7,000 Ethiopians destroyed an Italian battalion of 500 men, killing 420 and wounding 80; the wounded managed to escape. This defeat temporarily thwarted Italian expansion, but the Italians were determined to exact revenge. In 1889 Yohannes IV was killed fighting the Mahdists, and Menelek II became emperor.

Menelek sought to convince the Italians that he was their client, signing the Treaty of Uccialli in 1889. He became suspicious of the Italians, however, when they wooed pretender to the Abyssinian throne Ras Mengesha and became friendly with leaders in Tigre, which bordered Eritrea. Menelek was also angered by Italian claims to a protectorate over Abyssinia. The Treaty of Uccialli existed in both Italian and Amharic versions, with the Italian version containing a clause to that effect.

In 1889 the Italians expanded their occupation of Massawa, and on January 1, 1890, they organized the territory as Eritrea. In 1889 Italy also established a new colony in Somaliland on the east coast of Africa, southeast of Ethiopia. It was now clear to Menelek that the Italian government sought to expand its East African holdings.

In February 1893, confident in the consolidation of his authority, Menelek denounced the Treaty of Uccialli. Having acquired a fair stockpile of modern weapons from the various European colonial powers, including the Italians themselves, he commenced a military campaign across the Mareb River into Tigre in December 1894. There followed an outpouring of pro-Abyssinian nationalist and anti-Italian sentiment. Nonetheless, the governor of Eritrea and commander of Italian colonial forces, General Oreste Baratieri, with 9,000 troops crushed the rebellion. The Italians then occupied the Tigrian capital of Adwa.

Baratieri suspected that Mengesha would attempt to invade Eritrea and marched to meet him. In the Battle of Coatit in January 1895, the Italians were victorious. Pursing Mengesha's retreating forces, the Italians captured documents proving Menelek's complicity with Mengesha. Baratieri's victory over Mengesha and his early success against the Sudanese Mahdists led him to underestimate the difficulties of a war with Menelek, however.

Abyssinian forces were victorious over the defending Italians at Amba Alagi on December 7, 1895, forcing the Italians to withdraw back into Eritrea. The Abyssinians then attacked the unfinished Italian fortress at Makale, held by 200 Italians and 1,150 native Askaris under Major Giuseppe Gailliano. Following several unsuccessful Abyssinian assaults and a three-week siege, the defenders ran out of food and ammunition and were forced to surrender on January 21. The Italians were taken prisoner. The native auxiliaries were branded on the arm and released, warned not to fight against Menelek again.

Italian premier Francesco Crispi, seeking a scapegoat for the military reverses, ordered the recall of Baratieri and his replacement by General Antonio Baldissara. Goaded by his official disgrace or ordered by Crispi to advance (accounts differ) and convinced that the well-trained and effectively equipped reinforcements arriving in Massawa from Italy would be sufficient to overwhelm the Abyssinian forces opposing him, Bararieri gathered half of the Italian forces in East Africa and began a new advance into Tigre with four brigades totaling 20,000 men and 54 guns.

The decisive battle occurred near Adwa (most often known as Adowa or by the Italian name Adua) on March 1, 1896. Emperor Menelek was prepared and waiting with a force that approached 100,000 men, some 70,000 of whom were armed with rifles. They also had some 40 artillery pieces, although a number of these were antiquated. On the night of February 28, Baratieri advanced his brigades. Poor maps and faulty communication led one brigade to be some three miles in advance of the others, and early on March 1 Menelek overwhelmed it by sheer force of numbers. As the remaining Italian brigades advanced to the rescue, they were defeated in detail. The Italians were utterly routed. By the time they began their retreat that afternoon, perhaps 6,500 of the original force were dead (4,500 of them Italians), and another 2,500 (1,600 Italians) had been taken prisoner. Baratieri's army in effect ceased to exist. By order of Menelek, some 800 Askaris found to have been branded after the Battle of Maklale had their right hands and left feet amputated. Ethiopian casualties totaled some 4,000–6,000 dead and 8,000 wounded.

Adwa was the worst defeat for a European army by an African army since the time of Hannibal Barca and the Carthaginian Wars. Fortunately for the Italians, the Abyssinians did not attempt any serious pursuit. Menelek also did not try to invade Eritrea. In 1914, only Abyssinia and Liberia in Africa were free of European conquest.

William T. Dean III and Spencer C. Tucker

See also Mahdist Uprising in Sudan

Further Reading

Jonas, Raymond. *The Battle of Adwa: African Victory in the Age of Empire.* Cambridge, MA: Harvard University Press, 2011.

Lewis, David. *The Race to Fashoda: European Colonialism and African Resistance in the Scramble for Africa.* New York: Weidenfeld and Nicolson, 1987.

Marcus, Harold. *The Life and Times of Menelik II: Ethiopia, 1844–1913.* Oxford, UK: Clarendon, 1975.

Afghanistan Insurgency

Start Date: 2001
End Date: 2013

During the Afghanistan War, known as Operation ENDURING FREEDOM (OEF), the Afghan front was in 2001 the main focus in the U.S. Global War on Terror. OEF was initiated by President George W. Bush following the September 11, 2001, terrorist attacks that killed nearly 3,000 Americans and after the ruling Taliban in Afghanistan had refused to hand over the members of the Al Qaeda terrorist network responsible for the attacks. OEF called for the removal from power of the Taliban and the defeat of Al Qaeda and its leader, Osama bin Laden. OEF began on October 7, 2001, in a special operations mission that, working with Afghan opponents of the Taliban, overthrew that regime with a minimal troop commitment.

The overthrow of the Taliban was followed by humanitarian assistance, stability operations, and nation building conducted in partnership with the North Atlantic Treaty Organization (NATO) and non-NATO allied partners under the International Security Assistance Force (ISAF). Hamid Karzai took office as president of Afghanistan in December 2004. Several years into the Karzai administration, the Afghan government had little if any presence in most of the country and lacked any real ability to govern. Government officials, many of them former warlords, were inept, corrupt, and involved in the production of opium, Afghanistan's chief export. The police—functionally unreformed militiamen in uniforms—preyed on the Afghan population, and the average Afghan saw little if any government services.

The failure of Karzai's government to secure the country and the shift of U.S. attention and resources to the Iraq War meant that by 2003, life had returned to tribal infighting and competition for resources and influence by rivaling patronage networks reminiscent of the era that had ushered in the Taliban. The Taliban was thus able to capitalize on local grievances against the government, promote its own cause, and establish itself as the only authority in rural areas. Even though most Afghans did not adhere to the political ideologies and interpretations of Islam advanced by the Taliban or its affiliated groups, in the face of such a weak and predatory government, many Afghans believed that they had little choice but to support the Taliban.

Between 2002 and 2005, the Taliban allied with other militant groups and established training camps in the lawless Pakistani border region. The Quetta Shura Taliban, based at Quetta in Baluchistan and led by the Taliban emir al-mumineen ("Commander of the Faithful"), served as the political and military hub for the Afghan insurgency.

The Taliban leadership divided Afghanistan into five operational zones and by 2005 had secured sufficient fighters, training, and weapons in Pakistan to be able to launch attacks on and overwhelm Afghan government outposts and harass NATO forces.

Although insurgent groups operating in Afghanistan existed under the umbrella of the Quetta Shura Taliban, not all shared identical motivations, political ideology, or religious outlook. The Taliban leadership who fought the Soviet forces in the 1980s and emerged as a movement in the 1990s were motivated more by their desire to reestablish the Islamic Emirate of Afghanistan and Taliban rule as well as by removal of all foreign forces from Afghan soil. Propagating fundamentalist

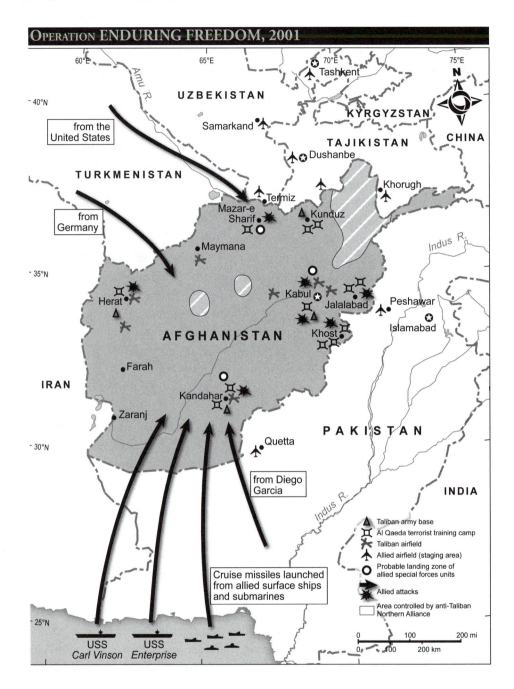

OPERATION ENDURING FREEDOM, 2001

Legend:

△ Taliban army base
⍓ Al Qaeda terrorist training camp
✳ Taliban airfield
✈ Allied airfield (staging area)
○ Probable landing zone of allied special forces units
➤ Allied attacks
✶
▭ Area controlled by anti-Taliban Northern Alliance

from the United States

from Germany

from Diego Garcia

Cruise missiles launched from allied surface ships and submarines

USS Carl Vinson

USS Enterprise

0   100   200 mi
0   100   200 km

Deobandism, a Sunni fundamentalist school, they were less interested in waging global jihad, although they used the rhetoric of jihad to justify their fight against Western forces, much as the mujahideen justified their battle with the Soviets in a religious light.

Hizb-e Islami Gulbuddin, led by Hekmatyar Gulbuddin, had similar roots as the Quetta Shura Taliban and was once a favored recipient of weapons and aid by the U.S. government in the war against the Soviets (1979–1989). Hizb-e Islami Gulbuddin had a fairly dedicated following in eastern Afghanistan and was patronized by Al Qaeda and the Pakistani Inter-Services Intelligence.

Jalaluddin Haqqani was also a former mujahideen commander and warlord. Historically based in Loya Paktia, he led what analysts refer to as the Haqqani Network, the most lethal faction currently fighting NATO and Afghan government forces largely because of its links with foreign terrorist organizations. Also in this mix were narcotics and poppy traffickers, tribal kinship networks, salafist jihadists, foreign global jihadists, and competing patronage networks, to include those of government officials. Taliban factions were further broken down according to district, tribe, mujahideen loyalties, and other factors. While Mullah Omar was the emir al-mumineen and the political figure unifying these groups and providing strategic guidance to them, for most of these groups, field commanders were relegated operational and tactical responsibilities.

Until 2005, this milieu of insurgent factions relied on classic guerrilla warfare. The summer of 2005 marked the beginning of their campaign to retake entire provinces in southern and eastern Afghanistan and to destabilize others. Having studied tactics employed by insurgent forces in Iraq and after years of working alongside more radicalized fighters, some Taliban commanders relied on increased numbers of suicide bombings, although this tactic had been scarcely employed and culturally frowned upon by most Afghans. In addition to the increased use of more sophisticated improved explosive devices (IEDs), insurgents employed more conventional tactics, such as massing upwards of 100 fighters to carry out assaults against government positions and ISAF outposts. At the time, there were insufficient coalition troops to deflect the growing numbers and operational sophistication of the Taliban, while the Afghan National Security Forces were largely impotent.

In response to the Taliban attacks, the ISAF increased troop levels throughout the country and began a more robust counterinsurgency campaign. Nonetheless, the insurgency grew stronger between 2006 and 2009, and in several instances insurgents were able to overrun U.S. military positions in remote areas.

U.S. military authorities recognized the dire situation, and a strategy review resulted in the application of the counterinsurgency framework employed in Iraq. In 2010, 33,000 American surge troops were inserted into key areas in the southern and eastern portions of the country. Eleven thousand marines were sent to Helmand Province alone and spent two years conducting operations to root out the Quetta Shura Taliban from one of their key financial hubs. Although the Taliban was dealt a serious blow in southern Afghanistan, the ever-versatile insurgents remained resilient and shifted operations to areas in western and northern provinces that had traditionally been quiescent. Taliban tactics in the south saw the widespread use of IEDs, political assassinations, and attacks on Afghan Army forces, who were deemed more vulnerable than the ISAF.

The Haqqani Network and its affiliates meanwhile transitioned to high-profile terrorist-style attacks in Kabul and assassinations of key national figures. The faction was far more extremist under its new operational leader, Sirajuddin Haqqani, who adopted tactics employed by affiliated high-value terrorist groups, such as the Islamic Movement of Uzbekistan and Lashkar-e Taiba. Unlike elements of the Quetta Shura Taliban and possibly even Hizb-e Islami Gulbuddin, the Haqqani Network was unlikely ever to reconcile with the Afghan government or ISAF and posed the most serious threat of the Afghan insurgent groups to an enduring, stable Afghanistan.

Although the Afghan insurgency continues, on June 18, 2013, in an important milestone in the now nearly 12-year-long war, President Karzai announced that the Afghan armed forces, now numbering some 352,000 men and women, had taken over responsibility from the U.S.-led NATO coalition for security nationwide. NATO military forces will now move entirely into a support and advisory role, with an expected full withdrawal of such forces in 18 months.

Larissa Mihalisko

See also Aircraft in Counterinsurgency Operations; Jihad; Soviet-Afghan War

Further Reading

Giustozzi, Antonio. *Koran, Kalashnikov, and Laptop: The Neo-Taliban Insurgency in Afghanistan, 2002–2007.* New York: Columbia University Press, 2009.

Jones, Seth G. *Counterinsurgency in Afghanistan,* Vol. 4. Santa Monica, CA: RAND, 2008.

Rashid, Ahmed. *Pakistan on the Brink: The Future of America, Pakistan, and Afghanistan.* New York: Viking, 2012.

Rubin, Barnett R. *The Fragmentation of Afghanistan: State Formation and Collapse in the International System.* New Haven, CT: Yale University Press, 2002.

Aguinaldo y Famy, Emilio

Birth Date: March 22, 1869
Death Date: February 6, 1946

Filipino insurgent leader and president of the Philippine Republic. Of Chinese and Filipino Tagalog ancestry, Emilio Aguinaldo y Famy was born in Cavite El Viejo (now Kawit) in Cavite Province, Luzon, on March 22, 1869. His father headed the town administration. Following the death of his father, Aguinaldo was forced to leave secondary school to assist his mother in running the family farm. At age 17 he was elected head of a barrio in Cavite El Viejo, and in 1895 he had charge of the town government.

Spain's once-powerful colonial empire was crumbling, with insurgencies under way in both Cuba and the Philippines, and in 1896 Aguinaldo joined the Katipunan, the Filipino revolutionary movement led by Andrés Bonifacio. The charismatic Aguinaldo quickly attracted a large following, and his victory over Spanish forces in the Battle of Imus (September 3, 1896) brought him to the forefront. Aguinaldo's followers then accused Bonifacio of planning a coup. Bonifacio's execution in May 1897 left Aguinaldo as the unchallenged leader of the Filipino revolutionary movement.

The struggle for power, however, led to the loss of many of Bonifacio's followers, and Spanish troops severely mauled Aguinaldo's forces. Wishing to avoid a protracted guerrilla war, Spanish authorities offered Aguinaldo attractive terms, which he accepted in December 1897, going into exile in Hong Kong in return for a sizable monetary settlement, which Spain was then delinquent in paying.

As the United States edged toward war with Spain, U.S. officials urged Aguinaldo to return to the Philippines, and he did so after the U.S. Navy victory in the Battle of Manila Bay (May 1, 1898). Commodore George Dewey agreed to provide Aguinaldo with arms and ammunition to fight the Spanish. On May 24 Aguinaldo announced the formation of a provisional government, and in June a Filipino assembly proclaimed an independent Philippine Republic, with Aguinaldo as president. With its own designs on the Philippines, Washington did not recognize this government, however.

Aguinaldo's forces routed isolated Spanish garrisons in the islands and soon were besieging Manila. In June 1898, however, U.S. troops began to arrive, and Washington ordered their commander, Major General Wesley Merritt, to exclude the Filipino insurgents from any peace talks with the Spanish. Relations between Aguinaldo and the U.S. military steadily deteriorated, exacerbated by the exclusion of his troops from participation in the sham First Battle of Manila (August 13, 1898), and U.S. were not allowed in the city after the Spanish garrison surrendered.

Following the end of fighting between Spain and the United States on August 12, 1898, tensions between American and Filipino forces worsened. Evidence suggests that the new U.S. military governor in the Philippines, Major General Elwell S. Otis, deliberately provoked an armed clash. In any case, fighting erupted on February 4, 1899.

With the beginning of the Philippine-American War (Philippine Insurrection) of 1899–1902, superior U.S. weaponry and training soon told. Also, although Aguinaldo was charismatic, his military and political leadership was lacking. His decision to try to engage U.S. forces in conventional warfare was a serious error, and he was soon forced to adopt guerrilla tactics. Aguinaldo's hope that William Jennings Bryan would win the U.S. 1900 presidential election and that the United States would then give the islands their independence also proved to be misplaced.

Aguinaldo quarreled with able Filipino general António Narciso Luna de St. Pedro. In June 1900, two soldiers loyal to Aguinaldo assassinated Luna. Many blamed Aguinaldo for the deed, further reducing his influence. By now, military operations against the Americans were in the hands of local commanders, not Aguinaldo.

On March 23, 1901, Aguinaldo was captured by U.S. forces under Colonel Frederick Funston and taken to Manila. Perhaps believing that further resistance against the United States was futile or simply realizing that his own influence had deteriorated too much to warrant a continuation of the struggle, Aguinaldo took an oath of allegiance to the United States and encouraged his followers to do the same.

Despite the oath, Aguinaldo felt no strong sense of attachment to the United States, and during World War II (1939–1945) he tried unsuccessfully to have the Japanese occupiers appoint him president. He died in Quezon City on February 6, 1946, and thus did not live to see the Philippines granted full independence from the United States on July 4, 1946. Although his Philippine Republic of 1899–1901 never was accorded foreign recognition, most Filipinos consider Aguinaldo their first president.

Jerry Keenan and Spencer C. Tucker

See also Funston, Frederick; Philippine Islands and U.S. Pacification during the Philippine-American War

Further Reading

Gates, John M. *Schoolbooks and Krags: The United States Army in the Philippines, 1898–1902.* Westport, CT: Greenwood, 1973.

Linn, Brian M. *The Philippine War, 1899–1902.* Lawrence: University Press of Kansas, 2000.

Linn, Brian M. *The U.S. Army and Counterinsurgency in the Philippine War, 1899–1902.* Chapel Hill: University of North Carolina Press, 1989.

Aircraft in Counterinsurgency Operations

Counterinsurgents embraced airpower while it was still in its infancy. Italian forces employed aircraft in counterinsurgency roles during the Italian-Ottoman War in Libya (1911–1913), the French deployed air assets against rebellion Moroccan tribesmen in 1913, and a squadron of observation planes accompanied the U.S. Punitive Expedition into Mexico in 1916–1917. These early applications of airpower in irregular warfare enjoyed limited effectiveness, but they did not discourage further uses of aircraft in the small wars, colonial conflicts, and guerrilla struggles of the interwar period. Beginning in the early 1920s, Britain's Royal Air Force developed the doctrine of air control, a concept that emphasized the coercive and punitive use of airpower against Britain's rebellious imperial subjects in the

Middle East and the Horn of Africa and on India's North-West Frontier. Intended to help Britain police its empire with minimum resources and manpower, air control was neither as cost-effective nor strategically prudent as its proponents claimed. Grounded in fundamentally Orientalist cultural assumptions about non-European peoples' alleged imperviousness to any arguments other than force, the concept of air control privileged kinetic effects over attempts to address the root causes of unrest. France's use of airpower to suppress the Rif War (1921–1926) and the Great Syrian Revolt (1925–1927) showcased the utility of aircraft as providers of fire support and reconnaissance, while the U.S. experience in the Nicaragua Insurgency (1927–1933) demonstrated the value of planes not only as kinetic force multipliers but also in resupplying remote garrisons.

World War II (1939–1945) refined these trends. German employment of aircraft against partisans in Yugoslavia and the Soviet Union produced only limited results. At the same time, the Allies exploited airpower in the form of short takeoff and landing (STOL) aircraft such as the versatile Westland Lysander to liaise with indigenous resistance movements in Nazi-occupied Europe. Imaginative employment of airpower for close air support, reconnaissance, airlift, and psychological operations proved critical to counterinsurgent forces' victories in the Greek Civil War (1946–1949), the Philippine Hukbalahap Insurgency (1946–1954), and the Malayan Emergency (1948–1960). Airpower gave French forces a significant advantage over the Viet Minh in the Indochina War (1946–1954) but proved quantitatively insufficient in preventing the French defeat at Dien Bien Phu. In the Algerian War (1954–1962), French forces fighting the Front de Libération Nationale (FLN, National Liberation Front) insurgents enjoyed a preponderance of air assets and pioneered a decentralized approach to command and control of airpower that was better suited to counterinsurgency operations than orthodox concepts of centralized control. In addition, the French exploited a new technology in the form of helicopters, pioneering heliborne tactics combining firepower and mobility that would be subsequently emulated by the U.S. military in the Vietnam War (1957–1975) and by the Rhodesian security forces' fire force concept in the Rhodesian Bush War (1964–1979). Helicopters would also form a central pillar of air operations in such counterinsurgency campaigns as the Dhofar Rebellion (1962–1976), the El Salvador Insurgency (1980–1992), the South African Border War (1966–1989), and the Portuguese Colonial Wars (1957–1974).

The second half of the 20th century also revealed the growing vulnerability of both fixed-wing and rotary aircraft to insurgent countermeasures. This was revealed in stark terms in the French Indochina War and the Vietnam War, where airplanes and helicopters whose performance characteristics (low stall speed, low altitude, and long loiter time) made them ideal for counterinsurgency work also rendered them highly vulnerable to ground fire. The development and proliferation of shoulder-launched antiaircraft missiles compounded the danger, as the Soviet experience during the Soviet-Afghan War (1979–1989) indicated.

At the beginning of the 21st century, airpower—both airplanes and helicopters—remains one of the most formidable tools in counterinsurgents' inventory. Recent conflicts, such as the Afghanistan War and the Iraq War, attest to the critical edge that aviation affords to counterinsurgent forces. Apart from fulfilling such traditional roles as furnishing close air support to ground troops, air assets also provide tactical and strategic mobility and airlift, rapid medical evacuation, and complex real-time intelligence. Finally, the advent of unmanned aerial vehicles (UAVs) has significantly enhanced counterinsurgents' intelligence, surveillance, and reconnaissance capabilities while facilitating their ability to selectively destroy high-value targets.

The utility of airpower as an instrument of counterinsurgency remains a subject of intense debate. Skeptics and advocates have yet to agree about the compatibility of airpower, a fundamentally blunt instrument that excels in delivering firepower, with a form of warfare whose success and failure depend less on producing kinetic effects and more on winning political legitimacy and securing the population's hearts and minds. Such recent examples as Israel's frustrating experience in its 2006 conflict with Hezbollah underscore the difficulties of using airpower to combat an elusive enemy with no discernible center of gravity that is vulnerable to direct air attack. Equally problematic is the issue of airpower's usefulness against urban insurgents and guerrillas. In particular, French air operations over Damascus (1927), German suppression of the Warsaw Uprising (1944), American experiences in Mogadishu (1993), Russian efforts to eradicate Chechen fighters in Grozny (1994–1996), and the international coalition's operations in the urban centers of Iraq (2003–2009) indicate some of the difficulties inherent in using air assets in densely populated areas. Finally, the proliferation of UAVs raises serious ethical and legal questions, challenges traditional concepts of sovereign airspace, creates potential frictions with allies and coalition partners, and risks antagonizing the international community.

Historical experience suggests that in order to remain an effective instrument of counterinsurgency, airpower must be fully integrated into holistic strategies that combine military operations with civic and police action, sociopolitical and economic reforms, and public relations initiatives. Mere emphasis on the production of maximum kinetic effects, aiming at the destruction of targets as an end in itself and divorced from the strategic and political context of the counterinsurgency, is likely to sabotage the ultimate goal of counterinsurgencies: securing political legitimacy in the eyes of the population while denying it to the insurgents.

Sebastian H. Lukasik

See also Algerian War; Dhofar Rebellion; El Salvador Insurgency; Great Syrian Revolt; Greek Civil War; Hukbalahap Rebellion; Indochina War; Iraq Insurgency; Iraq Revolt; Malayan Emergency; Mexican Expedition; Nicaragua Insurgency; Rhodesian Bush War; Rif War; Soviet-Afghan War; Vietnam War

Further Reading

Arkin, William. *Divining Victory: Airpower in the 2006 Israel-Hezbollah War.* Montgomery, AL: Air University Press, Maxwell Air Force Base, 2007.

Corum, James C., and Wray Johnson. *Air Power in Small Wars: Fighting Insurgents and Terrorists.* Lawrence: University Press of Kansas, 2003.

Omissi, David. *Air Power and Colonial Control, 1919–1939.* Manchester, UK: Manchester University Press, 1990.

Shrader, Charles R. *The First Helicopter War: Logistics and Mobility in Algeria, 1954–1962.* Westport, CT: Praeger, 1999.

Towle, Philip. *Pilots and Rebels: The Use of Aircraft in Unconventional Warfare, 1918–1988.* London: Brassey's, 1989.

Al-Aqsa Intifada.

See Intifada, Second

Algeria, French Pacification of

Start Date: 1830
End Date: 1847

On June 14, 1830, a French expeditionary force of some 34,000 men under the command of Marshal Louis Auguste Victor, Count de Ghaisnes de Bourmont, landed near the city of Algiers in North Africa and established a beachhead. The pretext for the invasion was the insult to French consul to Algiers Pierre Duval, who had been struck with a flyswatter by Dey Husain in 1827. The French sought to remove a threat to their Mediterranean trade, but the real reason behind King Charles X's plan to take Algiers was to shore up the unpopular French government headed by the Prince de Polignac and enable it to win the 1830 national elections.

Algiers was duly taken on July 5, 1830, although King Charles X's gambit to shore up his regime failed, as France experienced a revolution that same month. In the July Revolution (July 28–30), Charles X was forced to abdicate in favor of his cousin Louis Philippe, Duc d'Orléans, who nonetheless decided to continue French military operations in Algeria.

Initially, French control was largely limited to the coastal areas and cities. A succession of French commanders proceeded to fight a variety of opponents and campaigns in widely differing terrain, from the Atlas Mountains to salt marshes and the *bled* (interior). Particularly effective in opposing the French was Abd al-Qadir, the emir of Mascara in western Algeria. Capable and chivalrous, he waged a highly successful guerrilla war commencing in 1835 in which he called on the faithful to do war against Christianity. However, Abd al-Qadir was defeated by French forces under General Thomas Robert Bugeaud de la Piconnerie on July 6, 1836, in the Battle of Sikkak.

On June 1, 1837, Bugeaud and Abd al-Qadir concluded the Treaty of Taftna. The treaty recognized French sovereignty in Oran and Algiers, while Abd al-Qadir was left in control of perhaps two-thirds of the country (chiefly the interior). Although justified by the military situation on the ground, the treaty encountered a firestorm of opposition in France, and Bugeaud returned to France. A new wellspring of support for a strong military showing in Algeria led the French government to send the troop reinforcements it had previously denied its commanders and to make a major military effort in the eastern part of the country at Constantine, which fell to 20,000 French troops under General Sylvain-Charles, Comte Valée, in October 1837.

In October 1839 Abd al-Qadir, claiming that the French had broken the 1837 Treaty of Tfana by crossing into his territory, again took the field, declaring a jihad (holy war) against the French. In December 1840 Bugeaud returned to Algeria as its governor-general. Louis Philippe's government, now enjoying widespread popular support in France for its imperialist venture, supplied Bugeaud with reinforcements, which ultimately brought French strength in Algeria to some 160,000 men.

Bugeaud, the first major French African colonial administrator, proved to be an able organizer as well as an effective military commander. He greatly improved living conditions for the troops, including expanded and improved hospital care and the introduction of practical uniforms. He also created native military units and new tactical formations, including highly mobile flying columns equipped with light artillery and operating from fixed bases spread across Algeria, as well as a system of echelon square formations that facilitated supporting fire. His new troop formations of Zouaves, Spahis, Chasseurs d'Afrique, Tirailleurs Algerien, and the French Foreign Legion included native troops and excited widespread interest and enthusiasm worldwide. Bugeaud also employed night marches and converging columns and a scorched-earth policy and created a highly effective intelligence organization, the Bureau Arabe.

By 1843, Bugeaud had captured Abd al-Qadir's major strongholds, including Tlemcen, Mascara, and Tagdempt. Abd al-Qadir was also effectively isolated from assistance from eastern Algeria. Bugeaud was rewarded for his accomplishments with advancement to marshal of France.

Abd al-Qadir's army of 40,000 men was scattered in the Battle of Smala (May 10, 1843) and then crushed by Bugeaud in the Battle of the Isly River (August 14, 1844). Although Abd al-Qadir continued to win battles, notably the Battle of Sidi Brahim (September 22–25, 1845), French military pressure forced him into Morocco, where he attempted to rally the Rif tribes. Moroccan government action forced Abd al-Qadir to return to Algeria, and in December 1847 he surrendered to the French.

By 1847, there were some 100,000 Europeans living in Algeria. Only gradually did the French establish control over the Algerian interior, however. This was accomplished only during the Second Empire of Napoleon III (1852–1870).

William T. Dean III and Spencer C. Tucker

See also Abd al-Qadir; Bugeaud de la Piconnerie, Thomas Robert

Further Reading

Danziger, Rapahel. *Abd al'Qadir and the Algerians: Resistance to the French and Internal Consolidation.* New York: Holmes and Meier, 1977.

Sessions, Jennifer. *By Sword and Plow: France and the Conquest of Algeria.* Ithaca, NY: Cornell University Press, 2011.

Sullivan, Anthony. *Thomas-Robert Bugeaud: France and Algeria, 1784–1849: Politics, Power, and the Good Society.* Hamden, CT: Archon Books, 1983.

Algerian War

Start Date: 1954
End Date: 1962

Military effort by France during 1954–1962 to maintain its hold on its last, largest, and most important colony in the face of a Muslim insurgency. France regarded the Algerian War as part of the larger Cold War and tried unsuccessfully to convince its North Atlantic Treaty Organization (NATO) partners that maintaining French control over Algeria was in the best interests of the alliance. Unsupported by its allies, France found itself increasingly isolated in diplomatic circles. Ultimately, France experienced a humiliating defeat and a colonial exodus.

For 130 years, Algeria had been at the core of the French Empire. France conquered Algiers in 1830 and expanded the territory. Algeria became the headquarters of the French Foreign Legion (at Sidi-Bel-Abbès) and home to the largest number of European settlers in the Islamic world. In 1960 there were 1 million Europeans (known as colons or pieds-noirs) in Algeria. Unique among French colonies, Algeria became a political component of France, as Algiers, Constantine, and Oran were departments of the French Republic and had representation in the French Chamber of Deputies.

Nonetheless, Algeria was not fully three French departments, as only the European population enjoyed full rights there. The colon and Muslim populations lived separate and unequal lives, with the Europeans controlling the bulk of the wealth. Meanwhile, the French expanded Algeria's frontiers deep into the Sahara.

The Great Depression of the 1930s affected Algeria's Muslims more than any experience since their conquest, as they began to migrate from the countryside into the cities in search of work. Subsequently, the Muslim birthrate climbed dramatically because of easier access to health care facilities.

While the colons sought to preserve their status, French officials vacillated between promoting colon interests and advancing reforms for the Muslims. Pro-Muslim reform efforts ultimately failed because of political pressure from the colons and their representatives in Paris. While French political theorists debated between assimilation and autonomy for Algeria's Muslims, the Muslim majority remained largely resentful of the privileged status of the colons.

Reference Book - Room Use Only

MARK & HELEN OSTERLIN LIBRARY
NORTHWESTERN MICHIGAN COLLEGE
TRAVERSE CITY, MICHIGAN 49686-3061

The first Muslim political organizations appeared in the 1930s, the most important of these being Ahmed Messali Hadj's Mouvement pour le Triomphe des Libertés Démocratiques (MTLD, Movement for the Victory of Democratic Liberties). World War II (1939–1945) brought opportunities for change that increasing numbers of Algerian Muslims desired. Following the Anglo-American landings in North Africa in November 1942, Muslim activists met with American envoy Robert Murphy and Free French general Henri Giraud concerning postwar freedoms but received no firm commitments. As the war in Europe was ending and the Arab League was forming, pent-up Muslim frustrations were vented in the Sétif Uprising of May 8, 1945. Muslim mobs massacred colons before colonial troops restored order, and hundreds of Muslims were killed in a colon reprisal termed a "rat-hunt."

Returning Muslim veterans were shocked by what they regarded as the French government's heavy-handed actions after Sétif, and some (including veteran Ahmed Ben Bella) joined the MTLD. Ben Bella went on to form the MTLD's paramilitary branch, the Organization Speciale, and soon fled to Egypt to enlist the support of President Gamal Abdel Nasser. Proindependence Algerian Muslims were emboldened by the Viet Minh's victory over French forces at Dien Bien Phu in Vietnam in May 1954, and when Algerian Muslim leaders met Ho Chi Minh at the Bandung Conference in April 1955, he assured them that the French could be defeated.

Ben Bella and his compatriots formed the Front de Libération Nationale (FLN, National Liberation Front) on October 10, 1954, and the FLN revolution officially began on the night of October 31–November 1. The FLN organized its manpower into several military districts, or *wilayas*. Its goal was to end French control of Algeria and drive out or eliminate the colon population. Wilaya 4, located near Algiers, was especially important, and the FLN was particularly active in Kabylia and the Aures Mountains. The party's organization was rigidly hierarchical and tolerated no dissent. In form and style, the party resembled Soviet bloc Communist parties, although it claimed to offer a noncommunist and non-Western alternative ideology, articulated by Frantz Fanon.

As France steadily increased the number of its military forces in Algeria to fight the growing insurgency, French officials sought support from NATO partners in the Algerian War, arguing that keeping Algeria French would ensure that NATO's southern flank would be safe from communism. As a part of France, Algeria was included in the original NATO Charter, but this argument fell on deaf ears in Washington.

The Arab League promoted Pan-Arabism and the image of universal Arab and Muslim support for the FLN. The French grant of independence to both Tunisia and Morocco in March 1956 further bolstered Algeria's Muslims. When France, Britain, and Israel invaded Egypt in the Suez Crisis of 1956, both the United States and the Soviet Union condemned the move, and the French, unable to topple

Members of the Algerian National Liberation Front (FLN) pose before their World War II surplus machine guns in the mountains of Algeria on June 6, 1957. The rebel group was formed by Ahmed Ben Bella and other nationalists in 1954 to fight for Algerian independence from France. That goal was realized in 1962, following nearly eight years of warfare. (Bettmann/Corbis)

Nasser, were forced to contend with an FLN supply base that they could neither attack nor eliminate.

On August 20, 1955, the FLN attacked colon civilians in the Philippeville Massacre, and colon reprisals resulted in the deaths of several thousand Muslims. In September, FLN operative Saadi Yacef commenced a terrorist-style bombing campaign against colon civilians in Algiers. Meanwhile, other FLN leaders targeted governmental officials for assassination. The FLN movement faced a setback on October 22, however, when Ben Bella was captured.

Under Socialist premier Guy Mollet, in 1956 the bulk of the French Army was transferred to Algeria, and in December 1956 and January 1957, battle-tested French troops with combat experience in Indochina arrived in Algeria to restore order in the city of Algiers. Among them were General Raoul Salan (commander in chief), paratrooper division commander Brigadier General Jacques Massu, and Colonels Yves Godard and Marcel Bigeard, both of whom were adept at intelligence gathering and infiltration. Massu's men made steady headway, and Saadi Yacef was captured in September 1957. The Battle of Algiers was now won. The 1966 film *The Battle of Algiers,* produced by Gillo Pontecorvo and Saadi Yacef with Algerian support, garnered international acclaim while depicting the French as brutal occupiers and revealing the murders and torture practiced by the French Army. The FLN, on the other hand, routinely murdered captured French soldiers and colon civilians.

Despite victory in Algiers in 1957, French forces were not able to quell the Algerian rebellion or gain the confidence of the colons. Some colons grew fearful that the French government was about to negotiate with the FLN, and in the spring of 1958 groups of colons began to hatch a plan to change the colonial government. Colon veteran Pierre Lagaillarde organized hundreds of commandos and began a revolt on May 13, 1958. Army leaders, believing that they had been sold out by the Paris government in Indochina, were determined that this would not happen in Algeria. Soon, tens of thousands of colons and Muslims arrived outside of the government building in Algiers to protest French government policy. Massu quickly formed a Committee of Public Safety, and Salan assumed leadership of the body. Salan then went before the throngs of protesters.

Although the plotters would have preferred someone more frankly authoritarian, Salan called for the return to power of General Charles de Gaulle. Although de Gaulle had been out of power for more than a decade, on May 19 he announced his willingness to assume authority.

Massu was prepared to bring back de Gaulle by force if necessary, and plans were developed to dispatch paratroopers to metropolitan France from Algeria, but the military option was not required. On June 1, 1958, the French National Assembly named de Gaulle premier, technically the last premier of the Fourth Republic. The colons and the army professionals had managed to change the political leadership of the mother country.

De Gaulle visited Algeria five times between June and December 1958. At Oran on June 4, he said about France's mission in Algeria that "she is here forever." A month later, he proposed a budget allocation of 15 billion francs for Algerian housing, education, and public works, and that October he suggested an even more sweeping proposal, known as the Constantine Plan. The funding for the massive projects, however, was never forthcoming, and true Algerian reform was never realized. It was probably too late in any case for reform to impact the Muslim community.

Algeria's new military commander, General Maurice Challe, arrived in Algeria on December 12, 1958, and launched a series of attacks on FLN positions in rural Kabylia in early 1959. Muslim troops loyal to the French guided special mobile French troops called Commandos de Chasse. An aggressive set of sorties deep in Kabylia made much headway, and Challe calculated that by the end of October, his men had killed half of the FLN operatives there. A second phase of the offensive was to occur in 1960, but by then de Gaulle, who had gradually eliminated options, had decided that Algerian independence was inevitable.

De Gaulle braced his generals for the decision to let go of Algeria in late August 1959 and then addressed the nation on September 19, 1959, declaring his support for Algerian self-determination. Fearing for their future, some Ultras created the

Front Nationale Français and fomented another revolt on January 24, 1960, in the so-called Barricades Week. Mayhem ensued when policemen tried to restore order, and many people were killed or wounded. Challe fled Algiers on January 28, but the next day de Gaulle, wearing his old army uniform, turned the tide via a televised address to the nation. On February 1, army units swore loyalty to the government. The revolt quickly collapsed. Early in 1961, increasingly desperate Ultras formed a terrorist group called the Secret Army Organization (OAS) that targeted colons whom they regarded as traitors.

The Generals' Putsch of April 20–26, 1961, seriously threatened de Gaulle's regime. Challe wanted a revolt limited to Algeria, but Salan and his colleagues (ground forces chief of staff General André Zeller and recently retired inspector general of the air force Edmond Jouhaud) had all prepared for a revolt in France as well. The generals had the support of many frontline officers in addition to almost two divisions of troops. The Foreign Legion arrested the colony's commander in chief, General Fernand Gambiez, and paratroopers near Rambouillet prepared to march on Paris after obtaining armored support. The coup collapsed, however, as police units managed to convince the paratroopers to depart, and army units again swore loyalty to de Gaulle.

On June 10, 1961, de Gaulle held secret meetings with FLN representatives in Paris and then on June 14 made a televised appeal for the FLN's so-called Provisional Government to come to Paris to negotiate an end to the war. Peace talks during June 25–29 failed to lead to resolution, but de Gaulle's mind was already made up. During his visit to Algeria in December, he was greeted by large pro-FLN Muslim rallies and anticolon riots. The United Nations recognized Algeria's independence on December 20, and on January 8, 1962, the French public voted in favor of Algerian independence.

A massive exodus of colons was already under way. Nearly 1 million returned to their ancestral homelands (half of them went to France, while most of the rest went to Spain and Italy). Peace talks resumed in March at Évian, and both sides reached a settlement on May 18, 1962. The formal handover of power occurred on July 4 when the FLN's Provisional Committee took control of Algeria, and in September Ben Bella was elected Algeria's first president.

The Algerian War resulted in some 18,000 French military deaths, 3,000 colon deaths, and about 300,000 Muslim deaths. Some 30,000 colons remained behind. They were ostensibly granted equal rights in the peace treaty but instead faced official discrimination by the FLN government and the loss of much of their property. The FLN remained in power until 1989, practicing a form of socialism until changes in Soviet foreign policy necessitated changes in Algerian internal affairs.

William E. Watson

See also Algiers, Battle of; *Battle of Algiers;* Ben Bella, Ahmed; Bigeard, Marcel; Challe, Maurice; Front de Libération Nationale; Godard, Yves; Ho Chi Minh; Massu, Jacques Émile; Sétif Uprising

Further Reading

Horne, Alistair. *A Savage War of Peace: Algeria, 1954–1962.* New York: Viking, 1977.

Kettle, Michael. *De Gaulle and Algeria, 1940–1960.* London: Quartet, 1993.

Servan-Schreiber, Jean-Jacques. *Lieutenant in Algeria.* Translated by Ronald Matthews. New York: Knopf, 1957.

Talbott, John. *The War without a Name: France in Algeria, 1954–1962.* New York: Knopf, 1980.

Watson, William E. *Tricolor and Crescent: France and the Islamic World.* Westport, CT: Praeger, 2003.

Algiers, Battle of

Start Date: January 1957
End Date: March 1957

Key engagement of the Algerian War (1954–1962), fought for control of the Casbah district of some 100,000 people in the Algerian capital city during January–March 1957. With the guillotining in Algiers in June 1956 of several Front de Libération Nationale (FLN, National Liberation Front) members who had killed Europeans, Saadi Yacef, commander of the FLN Algiers Autonomous Zone, received instructions to "kill any European between the ages of 18 and 54. But no women, no children, no old people." During a three-day span in June, Yacef's roaming squads shot down 49 Europeans. It was the first time in the war that such random acts of terrorism had occurred in Algiers and began what would become a spiral of violence.

Hard-line European supporters of Algérie Française (French Algeria) now decided to take matters into their own hands. On the night of August 10, André Achiary, a former member of the French government's counterintelligence service, planted a bomb in a building in the Casbah that had supposedly housed the FLN. The ensuing blast destroyed much of the neighborhood and claimed 79 lives. No European was ever arrested for the blast, and the FLN was determined to avenge the deaths.

Yacef, who had created a carefully organized network of some 1,400 operatives in addition to bomb factories and hiding places, now received orders to undertake random bombings against Europeans, a first for the capital. On September 30, 1956, 3 female FLN members planted bombs in the Milk-Bar (a popular hangout), a cafeteria, and a travel agency. The latter bomb failed to go off due to a faulty timer, but the other two blasts killed 3 people and wounded more than 50, including a number of children.

With the insurgents emboldened by the French defeat in the Suez invasion, violence now took hold in Algiers. Both Muslim and European populations in the city were in a state of terror. Schools closed in October, and on December 28 Mayor Amédée Froger was assassinated.

On January 7, 1957, French governor-general in Algeria Robert Lacoste called in General Raoul Salan, new French commander in Algeria, and Brigadier General Jacques Massu, commander of the elite 4,600-man 10th Colonial Parachute Division, recently arrived from Suez. Lacoste ordered them to restore order in the capital city, no matter the method.

In addition to his own men, Massu could call on other French military units, totaling perhaps 8,000 men. He also had the city's 1,500-man police force. Massu divided the city into four grids, with one of his regiments assigned to each. Lieutenant Colonel Marcel Bigeard's 3rd Colonial Parachute Regiment had responsibility for the Casbah itself.

The French set up a series of checkpoints. They also made use of identity cards and instituted aggressive patrolling and house-to-house searches. Massu was ably assisted by his chief of staff, Colonel Yves Godard, who soon made himself *the* expert on the Casbah. Lieutenant Colonel Roger Trinquier organized an intelligence-collection system that included paid Muslim informants and employed young French paratroopers disguised as workers to operate in the Casbah and identify FLN members. Trinquier set up a database on the Muslim civilian population. The French also employed harsh interrogation techniques of suspects, with the use of torture that included electric shock.

The army broke a called Muslim general strike at the end of January in only a few days. Yacef was able to carry out more bombings, but the French army ultimately won the battle and took the FLN leadership prisoner, although Yacef was not captured until September 1957. Some 3,000 of 24,000 Muslims arrested during the Battle of Algiers were never seen again. The French side lost an estimated 300 dead and 900 wounded.

The Battle of Algiers had a widespread negative impact for the French military effort in Algeria, however. Although the army embarked on an elaborate cover-up campaign, its use of torture soon became public knowledge and created a firestorm that greatly increased opposition in the metropole to the war.

Spencer C. Tucker

See also Battle of Algiers; Bigeard, Marcel; Godard, Yves; Massu, Jacques Émile; Salan, Raoul Albin-Louis; Trinquier, Roger

Further Reading

Alleg, Henri. *La Question.* Paris: Éditions de Minuit, 1958.

Aussaresses, Paul. *The Battle of the Casbah: Terrorism and Counter-Terrorism in Algeria, 1955–1957.* New York: Enigma Books, 2010.

Horne, Alistair. *A Savage War of Peace: Algeria, 1954–1962.* New York: Viking, 1977.

Talbott, John. *The War without a Name: France in Algeria, 1954–1962.* New York: Knopf, 1980.

Al-Harakat Al-Islamiyya.

See Abu Sayyaf

American Civil War Insurgency and Counterinsurgency

Start Date: 1861
End Date: 1865

The role of guerrillas and unconventional warfare during the American Civil War was much greater than what has been commonly believed. Rather than being a sideshow to the major campaigns of the war, insurgency and counterinsurgency measures actually dominated much of the conflict. Union soldiers in the field, and later their commanders, escalated the brutality of the war by targeting the property of Southern civilians because they allegedly harbored pro-Confederate guerrillas. As the war progressed, Union officers who had firsthand experience dealing with guerrillas in the western theater, including Generals Ulysses S. Grant, Henry W. Halleck, William T. Sherman, and Philip H. Sheridan, employed these tactics to escalate the scope and brutality of the war in the eastern theater. Anti-Confederate insurgents were active as well. Unionists, deserters, and blacks actively opposed Confederate civil authority, and by the last months of the war, many Southern whites had given up any confidence in their new government's ability to protect them.

At the beginning of the conflict, many Southerners, citing the Revolutionary War experience (1775–1783), were attracted to the concept of irregular forces to counter the large invading Union armies. Guerrillas could impede invaders by disrupting lines of advance and logistics in the rear. They would force the Union to disperse its forces in pursuit, therefore making the guerrilla band a force multiplier for the Confederacy.

The Confederate experiment in organizing guerrilla units was authorized by the April 21, 1862, Partisan Ranger Act. A few organizations, such as Colonel John Singleton Mosby's 43rd Virginia Cavalry Battalion, proved to be assets to the Confederacy. However, the high command, including General Robert E. Lee, believed that they were uncontrollable and drained valuable manpower from the regular forces. The Confederate Congress repealed the law on February 17, 1864. The army permitted only two partisan bands to remain in service, Mosby's men and a similar unit led by Captain John Hanson McNeill.

Simply defining irregular warfare in the Civil War is challenging. Some units, including the commands of Generals Nathan Bedford Forrest and John Hunt Morgan, were regularly raised forces that often raided behind Union lines. Although unconventional, these forces were not insurgents. Other units, including Mosby's Rangers, were authorized and enrolled by the Confederate government as partisan forces.

Mosby's unit was well organized and disciplined and operated within the military chain of command. His targets in northern Virginia were always military. He gained fame by appearing behind Union lines, surprising isolated outposts, and capturing Union troops and supplies. At one point he even captured a Union general, who was taken in bed.

Guerrilla fighting continued throughout the war. In addition to border regions, wherever the Union armies advanced in the South, locals armed themselves to defend their homes against invading armies and local Unionists. Such fighting occurred in border areas such as West Virginia, Kentucky, Tennessee, and Missouri and even in Northern states such as Ohio, Iowa, Indiana, Pennsylvania, and Illinois. Border areas not under complete civil and military control of either side saw some of the bloodiest fighting. In addition to western Missouri, pro-Southern men such as Champ Ferguson, living along the border of Tennessee and Kentucky, formed irregular units to fight similar pro-Union men, including "Tinker" Dave Beaty.

Guerrillas did not always follow the normal rules of warfare as practiced by conventional field armies, such as the taking of prisoners. The guerrilla war was personal and local. This fighting continued after the war, and Ferguson was one of the few guerrillas to be executed after the war as a war criminal.

Insurgents went by many titles. Southerners called themselves partisans, scouts, rangers and raiders. Union guerrillas included jayhawkers, Red Legs, and buffaloes. Interestingly, both sides referred to the other side's irregulars as bushwhackers, bandits, murderers, and marauders. The federal government attempted to define enemy insurgents with General Order No. 100, written by famous jurist Francis Lieber and implemented on April 24, 1862. To the Union, guerrillas were

> Men, or squads of men, who commit hostilities, whether by fighting, or inroads for destruction or plunder, or by raids of any kind, without commission, without being part and portion of the organized hostile army, and without sharing continuously in the war, but who do so with intermitting returns to their homes and avocations, or with the occasional assumption of the semblance of peaceful pursuits, divesting themselves of the character or appearance of soldiers—such men, or squads of men, are not public enemies, and, therefore, if captured, are not entitled to the privileges of prisoners of war, but shall be treated summarily as highway robbers or pirates.

The bloody careers of many Union and Confederate insurgents matched that definition exactly.

In occupied areas of the South, federal troops tired of guerrilla raids and began targeting the property of civilians who appeared to have harbored the guerrillas. U.S. forces burned homes and barns, at times driving out entire communities. Captured guerrillas were not treated as prisoners, and many were summarily executed. Missouri, where a guerrilla war had been going on since the Kansas-Nebraska

Act of 1854, is a good example. In response to guerrilla raids, including William Clark Quantrill's attack on Lawrence, Kansas, Union officials began holding civilian communities responsible for harboring irregulars. On August 25, 1863, Union general Thomas Ewing issued General Order No. 11, ordering the Union Army to burn out four counties along the Kansas-Missouri border, displacing as many as 20,000 noncombatants.

Responding to Southern sniping and shelling of Union Mississippi River traffic, the Federals began a series of retaliatory raids that included the burning of many towns and settlements up and down the river. Union Army and naval forces destroyed entire towns, including Donaldsonville, Louisiana; Randolph, Tennessee; and Hopfield, Arkansas. In addition, countless farms and plantations of those who had allegedly harbored guerrillas along the river were destroyed. In February 1864 after the fall of Vicksburg, Major General William T. Sherman launched an offensive targeting the rail junction in Meridian, Mississippi. Along the route to and from their target, Sherman's troops burned towns and property in retaliation for the harboring of guerrillas. By the time of his famous March to the Sea, Sherman and his men had already perfected their own form of punitive war.

The fighting in the East began in a conventional 19th-century manner but by the end of the war incorporated punitive campaigns. In July 1863 when Union colonel John T. Toland attempted to take the western Virginia mining town of Wytheville, his forces came under fire from houses in the town. After Toland was killed in the fighting, Union forces took the town and burned many of its most important dwellings, claiming that they had been fired upon by civilians—including women. In the northern Shenandoah Valley, Union authorities faced resistance from organized and enlisted partisan bands, including the men of Colonel Mosby's command. Union commanders became increasingly exasperated in attempting to control the area of Mosby's operations in Virginia, known as Mosby's Confederacy, and began resorting to collective punishment of the civilian population and execution of prisoners.

Virginians in the Shenandoah Valley felt the full force of the punitive war with the arrival of Lieutenant General Ulysses S. Grant in 1864. Grant sent a series of expeditions into the area that ended with the destruction of much civilian property. Major General David Hunter's forces burned the Virginia Military Institute and destroyed property in Lexington, Virginia. After Hunter was driven from the valley, Major General Philip Sheridan launched a punitive campaign that would lay waste to much of the area. Sheridan burned much of the town of Dayton, Virginia, in reprisal for guerrillas firing at his command. Although Grant had ordered him to destroy supplies and property that could support the Confederate Army, Dayton held little that could do so. Sheridan's intent was clearly vengeful. Later, under orders from Sheridan, Brigadier General Wesley Merritt burned his way through the heart of Mosby's Confederacy, destroying much of Loudoun and Fauquier Counties in clear retaliation for the civilians having supported guerrillas.

Rather than prolonging the war by diverting resources from the Union war effort, the Southern insurgency likely hastened the end of the conflict by convincing Union forces to target civilian property. Much of the complete collapse of Confederate morale during the final months of the war can be attributed to Union counterinsurgency actions.

Thomas D. Mays

See also Mosby, John Singleton

Further Reading

Mays, Thomas D. *Cumberland Blood: Champ Ferguson's Civil War.* Carbondale: Southern Illinois University Press, 2008.

Mountcastle, Clay. *Punitive War: Confederate Guerrillas and Union Reprisals.* Lawrence: University Press of Kansas, 2009.

Sutherland, Daniel. *A Savage Conflict: The Decisive Role of Guerrillas in the American Civil War.* Chapel Hill: University of North Carolina Press, 2009.

American Indian Wars in the West

Start Date: 1866
End Date: 1890

The final act in the nearly 300-year-long conflict between Native Americans, the original inhabitants of what became the United States, and European Americans played out during the second half of the 19th century (1866–1890) in the American West. That vast area of incredibly varied terrain and stark extremes of climate encompassed 2 million square miles between the Mississippi River and the Pacific coast, bounded north and south by the Canadian and Mexican borders. Inhabiting that immense region when significant numbers of European Americans began moving through it in the mid-19th century—and eventually settling and occupying it by 1890—were numerous Native American tribes and cultural groupings with often quite different customs, attitudes, and behavior. Resistance to European American encroachment mounted by many Native American tribes—although by no means all Native American tribes—in the West resulted in the U.S. Army's longest sustained counterinsurgency campaign in American history.

The Indian Wars in the American West did not, as some now claim, constitute genocide as we understand that term today. Genocide is a conscious, deliberately chosen policy of extermination of a targeted population through organized, state-sanctioned mass murder. Rather, the Indian Wars were a tragic clash of two entrenched, incompatible cultures in which neither side was willing to accept compromise on the other's terms. Although the Indians adopted some items and elements of European American culture that made their daily lives easier, they were determined to preserve and pursue their way of life. To European Americans,

Indians were simply in the way of westward expansion. Indian assimilation or removal, not genocidal extermination, was U.S. government Indian policy.

Neither side showed much willingness to understand the other's culture or to pursue interaction within their opposite number's very different cultural framework and worldview. One telling indication of this cultural bias is the European Americans' naive and unrealistic insistence on dealing with the many individual Indian tribes as nations, in which tribal chiefs not only spoke for the entire tribe (typically consisting of various smaller bands that might have only infrequent contact with each other) but were also expected to force tribal members to abide by treaty provisions. European Americans either did not understand the individualistic nature of Indian culture or were unwilling to try to understand it and work within the Indians' frame of reference, since this made dealing with the numerous tribes complicated and confusing. The cultural blindness of both sides was also evident in the way Indians and European Americans retaliated for wrongs against them committed by the other: Indians attacked European Americans who had nothing to do with the act being retaliated for, and European Americans murdered Indians who may not have even been members of the same tribe responsible for the incident that had set the European Americans on a quest for revenge. Both sides could—and did—kill the other's women and children, mutilate their opponents' corpses, and perpetrate massacres in brutal no-quarter combat.

The various western Indian tribes reacted to the aggressive European American encroachment in different ways. Some (Lakotas, Cheyennes, Comanches, and Apaches, for example) fiercely resisted; others (Crows, Tonkawas, and Pawnees, for example) allied themselves with European Americans in wars against other tribes for various reasons. The Indian Wars therefore played out as a series of widely scattered, separate campaigns waged against individual tribes in which Indians were allies as well as opponents.

Since Indian resistance to the increasingly relentless European American pressure depended on how each individual tribe reacted to it, there was no unifying, overall insurgency strategy that united all the tribes for a single goal. Indeed, since warfare was part of the very way of life of many western Indian tribes and was an important means of earning respect and gaining status within a tribe, much of the violence directed against European American settlers and soldiers should be understood as simply the continuation of an eons-old warlike lifestyle with new targets—European Americans replacing other Indians as a tribe's traditional enemy. Yet some Indian resistance clearly constituted insurgency, a sustained series of planned, coordinated operations intended to seize or maintain control of a specific region. One notable example is Red Cloud's War (1866–1868), the successful insurgency campaign waged by the Lakotas for control of the Powder River country of northern Wyoming and southern Montana. In the Fetterman Massacre (December 21, 1866)—a carefully planned and brilliantly executed insurgency campaign featuring constant small-scale harassment attacks and a stunning major victory in a carefully planned ambush in which all 81 soldiers in Captain William J. Fetterman's command were killed—the Lakotas forced the complete evacuation of the region by the U.S. Army garrison, compelling the U.S. government to officially recognize the Lakota victory in the 1868 Fort Laramie Treaty.

At the tactical level, Indians followed their traditional means of fighting, with the most characteristic tactic being the sudden surprise raid or ambush. Much like today's insurgents, the Indians preferred to attack soft targets such as isolated settler farms, small parties of civilians or soldiers caught exposed on the open prairie, or wagons traveling alone. Given the tribes' generally limited number of warriors and low birthrates, keeping Indian casualties minimal was critical, and the tribes generally avoided directly confronting large bodies of opposing U.S. Army troops. Although pitched battles occurred—most famously, the Battle of the Little Big Horn (June 25–26, 1876) in which 1,800–2,000 Indian warriors defeated about 600 men of the U.S. 7th Cavalry—most of the Indian Wars' approximately 1,500 armed clashes were small engagements. If Indians could not win an overpowering, quick victory against a vulnerable opponent, they sensibly broke off the fight, seeming to virtually vanish into the vast western landscape. Such tactics typically meant that finding the Indians was a more challenging, difficult, and resource-intensive task than actually fighting them.

Although European American civilian settlers typically bore the brunt of Native American vengeance attacks and plunder raids, conducting organized combat operations against the warring tribes was the responsibility of the regular U.S. Army—nearly all of which during the 1866–1890 period was stationed throughout America's western frontier. The U.S. frontier army, never numbering more than about 25,000 men, was scattered in small detachments over the area, which covered 2 million square miles. Led by a small and mainly West Point–trained officer corps, the frontier army was manned mostly by soldiers recruited from the bottom tier of American society, and drunkenness, desertion, and psychologically numbing isolation were constant plagues that vexed commanders even more than their infrequent armed clashes with Indians. Frontier army service was typically an onerous duty that the army was compelled to perform, carrying out frequently misguided policies originating in Washington that were formed by politicians and government officials who usually had no idea of the actual situation on the ground in the West.

During the 1866–1890 period, U.S. Army counterinsurgency strategy against the western Indian tribes evolved from a primarily defensive and reactive-oriented strategy to a proactive offensive strategy that owed much to the total-war Civil War experiences of the era's two principal army leaders: U.S. Army commanding general William T. Sherman and Department of the Missouri commander Major General Philip H. Sheridan. Prior to the mid-1870s, the frontier army's efforts mainly were limited to reacting to Indian attacks and taking defensive measures to prevent them. Countless forts with small troop garrisons were established throughout the

West, generally along wagon train, stagecoach, and railway routes, to safeguard travelers and protect the setters in their areas. Cavalry and infantry detachments patrolled their respective sectors and reacted to Indian raids by mounting retaliatory operations to catch and punish the raid's perpetrators. All too often, the raiders easily evaded army pursuit. Treaties with the numerous tribes were eagerly sought in attempts to reduce Indian depredations by confining the tribes to reservations and holding Indian leaders accountable for attacks by their warriors. Frequently, however, the individualistic warriors simply ignored the treaties, and many Indian tribes treated reservations as merely convenient places to spend the winter while reverting to traditional hunting and raiding at will in the summer months.

With a defensive counterinsurgency strategy mostly ineffective, in the mid-1870s Sherman and Sheridan turned to a ruthless total-war offensive-oriented strategy that targeted the keys to Indian survival: mobility and sustenance. During the Civil War, both Sherman (in Georgia and the Carolinas during 1864–1865) and Sheridan (in the Shenandoah Valley in 1864) had successfully broken Confederate resistance through brutal campaigns that devastated huge areas and destroyed the South's resources necessary to continue the war. They applied the same resource-targeting strategy to warring Indian tribes. Since finding Indians had proven the frontier army's most difficult task, expeditions were mounted in winter when tribal bands gathered in large camps and severe weather and shortage of grass for their horses kept warriors inactive. When the camps were found, army surprise attacks focused not on inflicting Indian casualties but instead on eliminating the tribes' huge pony herds (mobility) and destroying the Indians' food, shelter, and camp supplies (sustenance). Deprived of horses, shelter, and food, the Indians had no choice but to enter reservations.

One of the most successful examples of this strategy was the 4th U.S. Cavalry Regiment's September 28, 1874, attack on Comanche and Kiowa tribes sheltering in the remote Palo Duro Canyon in the Texas panhandle. Although only one soldier and three Indians were killed, the operation destroyed the Indians' pony herd, food, camp supplies, and shelter. This victory broke the back of Comanche and Kiowa resistance for good, forcing the Indians to enter the Fort Sill Reservation.

An important contributor to the army's total-war counterinsurgency strategy against the principal Plains Indian tribes (Comanches, Kiowas, Lakotas, and Cheyennes) was the near annihilation of their main means of subsistence, the buffalo. Sheridan enthusiastically encouraged the slaughter of the vast herds by legions of civilian commercial buffalo hunters, and the buffalo was nearly extinct by 1884. The slaughter of the buffalo and the killings of Indian pony herds may seem today to be brutal and unnecessarily ruthless acts, yet the fact that U.S. Army leaders were forced to resort to such extreme measures testifies to the vast scope of and great difficulty in subduing the decades-long insurgency they faced.

Although much fewer in number and occupying a smaller area than the Plains Indians, the Apaches of the Southwest proved to be the most difficult tribe to subdue. Apache resistance continued until Geronimo's final surrender in 1886. The frontier army fought more engagements with Apaches than with any other tribe—nearly 250, more than twice as many as the next-ranking tribe (122 with Comanches)—and Arizona, the Apache homeland, was the scene of more Indian–European American fights (329) than any other state. In the end, it was the frontier army's stubborn perseverance of even following the Apaches into Mexico and the effective use of Apache scouts serving in army units rather than any brilliant counterinsurgency strategy that finally subdued the Apaches.

By December 1890, European Americans had won the western Indian Wars. Tribes across the West had been consigned to a bleak, subsistence-level existence on scattered reservations—typically sited on land that no European American coveted—and active combat operations had ceased with Geronimo's 1886 surrender. Yet a horrific postscript to the Indian Wars occurred on December 29, 1890, that underlined the tragic nature of the conflict. One final burst of violence erupted that bleak winter day on the Lakota Pine Ridge Reservation in South Dakota when an attempt by the 7th U.S. Cavalry Regiment to disarm a band of Lakotas went horribly wrong. Prompted by a series of confused events and misunderstandings, Lakotas and soldiers opened fire. When the shooting stopped, 84 Lakota warriors, 44 women, and 18 children lay dead. The soldiers suffered 64 casualties (25 killed and 39 wounded), representing 7th Cavalry losses during the Indian Wars second only to the regiment's disastrous losses at the Battle of the Little Big Horn (268 killed and 55 wounded).

Indian Wars historian Gregory Michno calculates that there were about 21,000 total casualties in the western Indian Wars, with European Americans (soldiers and civilians) accounting for about 6,600 (31 percent) and Indians accounting for about 15,000 (69 percent). These casualty figures, however, do not include a substantial number of additional Indian deaths from disease, sickness, or displacement-induced starvation.

Jerry D. Morelock

See also Crook, George; Custer, George Armstrong; Geronimo; Miles, Nelson Appleton

Further Reading

Feherenbach, T. R. *Comanches: The History of a People.* New York: Anchor, 2003.

Greene, Jerome A. *Washita: The U.S. Army and the Southern Cheyennes, 1867–1869.* Norman: University of Oklahoma Press, 2004.

Gwynne, S. C. *Empire of the Summer Moon: Quanah Parker and the Rise and Fall of the Comanches, the Most Powerful Indian Tribe in American History.* New York: Scribner, 2011.

Michno, Gregory F. *The Settlers' War: The Struggle for the Texas Frontier in the 1860s.* Caldwell, ID: Caxton, 2011.

Rickey, Don, Jr. *Forty Miles a Day on Beans and Hay: The Enlisted Soldier Fighting the Indian Wars.* Norman: University of Oklahoma Press, 1973.

Utley, Robert M. *Frontier Regulars: The United States Army and the Indian, 1866–1890.* Lincoln, NE: Bison Books, 1984.

Utley, Robert M. *The Last Days of the Sioux Nation.* New Haven, CT: Yale University Press, 2004.

American Revolutionary War

Start Date: 1775
End Date: 1783

The American Revolutionary War (1775–1783) did not begin as an explicit bid for independence but certainly contained many of the hallmarks of a classical insurgency. The American Revolution began as a revolt in response to British government provocations, with supporters demanding redress but not severance of the colonial relationship. However, the Revolution quickly evolved into a multinational struggle for independence from the most powerful military state on earth and included both conventional battles and guerrilla attacks, with regular and irregular forces combining to fight the British. As is true for many successful insurgencies, an external source of supply and an ability to call upon the populace for resources and protection proved invaluable. Ultimately, the insurgency relied on a combined strategy of attrition and exhaustion, frustrating British attempts to quell the rebellion and retain control of its most important colonial possession.

The conflict began in Boston, Massachusetts, and its environs. The imposition of new taxes and attempts to limit the traditional liberties of the colonists provoked substantial unrest, as did a number of heavy-handed responses to rebellious incidents. The lack of direct colonial representation in Parliament exacerbated the problem. In 1770 a mob of protesters approached the Boston Customs House, hurling insults and threatening its lone guard. The guard called for assistance, and a squad of reinforcements quickly arrived. After a few desultory attempts to disperse the crowd, the troops opened fire, killing five protesters and scattering the rest. Radicals successfully portrayed the Boston Massacre, as the incident is known, as a deliberate decision to murder innocent Americans.

In 1773, radicals in Native American guise swarmed aboard East India Tea Company ships in Boston Harbor and threw several tons of tea into the water in protest of the British tax on tea. This led Parliament in January 1774 to pass the Intolerable (Coercive) Acts, among these the closure of the port of Boston until the destroyed tea was paid for, and the Massachusetts Government Act, which placed that colony under direct British rule. The Intolerable Acts galvanized colonial opposition and for many Americans confirmed the oppressive and capricious nature of the British government.

Anticipating further conflict, American radicals began to stockpile weapons, ammunition, and supplies in Concord, a small town 20 miles distant from Boston.

British lieutenant general Thomas Gage, North American commander in chief and now military governor of Massachusetts, sent men to destroy the supplies in a surprise raid on the night of April 18–19, 1775. En route, the men fought a short skirmish with colonial militiamen at Lexington and another at Concord. After destroying some of the stockpiles, the British withdrew but faced an aroused countryside with ambushes and sniping during the entire march back to Boston, eventually losing nearly 300 men killed, wounded, or missing, as opposed to 93 militia casualties.

British attempts to confine the conflict to Massachusetts and later to New England failed. Although Loyalists constituted as much as a third of the population and provided some recruits for the British, the Loyalists never came close to matching the Patriot militia in numbers or motivation. While colonial militia units played a major role in the conflict, particularly in retaining control of the countryside, guarding lines of communication, maintaining close ties with the populace, and supporting American regulars in major campaigns, they could not win the war by themselves. Time and again, the militia proved incapable of facing British regulars in the field.

To win conventional battles, the American Patriots needed a conventional force, and in the summer of 1775 the Continental Congress created the Army of the United Colonies (the Continental Army) and gave its command to George Washington. An exceptionally able leader who learned from his mistakes and was a fine judge of character, General Washington quickly realized that his most important task was to maintain the Continental Army in being. The army could not be risked without the possibility of victory and must fight only on favorable terms.

After forcing the British to evacuate Boston in March 1776, the Continental Army suffered a string of major defeats, beginning with its ejection from New York City in September. These losses demonstrated the British ability, thanks to the Royal Navy, to project power at any point along the populous coast. If the British commanders could force Washington to offer battle, they might destroy his force and open the door to reconquest of the rebellious colonies. Driven from New York and with an expedition into Canada having failed, by the autumn of 1776 the Continental Army had begun to disintegrate under the weight of battlefield failure, sickness, desertion, and the expiration of enlistments. In a desperate attempt to prop up sagging morale and recruitment before the bulk of his enlistments expired, Washington launched two surprise attacks against British outposts in New Jersey, at Trenton on December 26, 1776, and at Princeton on January 3, 1777. The victory at Trenton was especially important, as the Continental Army defeated a garrison of German mercenaries (known collectively as Hessians) whose presence had greatly angered the colonists. These small successes revived the flagging Revolutionary cause. For the rest of the winter of 1776–1777, Patriot forces attacked small British garrisons throughout New Jersey, destroying supplies, eroding British morale, and terrorizing Loyalists, all while avoiding stand-up fights.

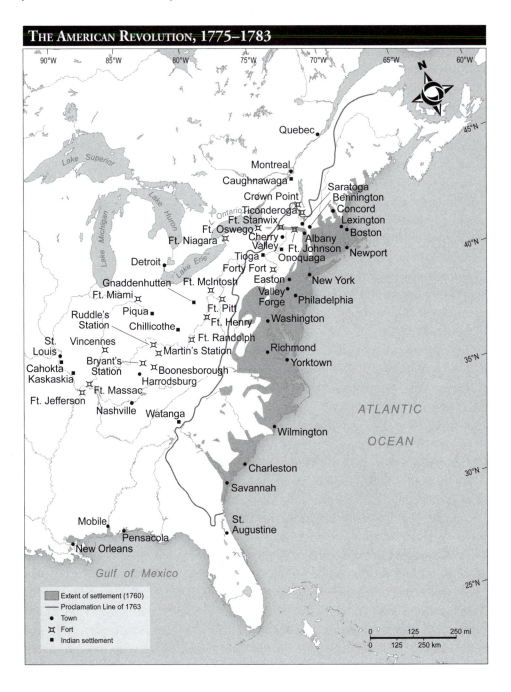

THE AMERICAN REVOLUTION, 1775–1783

90°W   85°W   80°W   75°W   70°W   65°W   60°W

N

Lake Superior

Lake Michigan

Lake Huron

Lake Erie

L. Ontario

Quebec

Montreal

Caughnawaga

Crown Point

Saratoga

Bennington

Ticonderoga

Concord

Lexington

Ft. Stanwix

Ft. Oswego

Boston

Ft. Niagara

Cherry Valley

Albany

Detroit

Tioga

Ft. Johnson

Newport

Onoquaga

Forty Fort

Gnaddenhutten

Ft. McIntosh

Easton

New York

Ft. Miami

Valley Forge

Philadelphia

Ruddle's Station

Piqua

Ft. Pitt

Chillicothe

Ft. Henry

Washington

Ft. Randolph

St. Louis

Vincennes

Martin's Station

Richmond

Cahokta

Bryant's Station

Boonesborough

Yorktown

Kaskaskia

Harrodsburg

Ft. Massac

Ft. Jefferson

Nashville

Watanga

ATLANTIC

OCEAN

Wilmington

Charleston

Savannah

Mobile

St. Augustine

Pensacola

New Orleans

Gulf of Mexico

45°N

40°N

35°N

30°N

25°N

Extent of settlement (1760)

Proclamation Line of 1763

• Town

☒ Fort

■ Indian settlement

0   125   250 mi

0   125   250 km

The two British campaigns in 1777 demonstrated their poor grasp of the war's character. Major General William Howe, who had replaced Thomas Gage as commander of British forces, moved against Philadelphia. Howe hoped thereby to force Washington into defending the colonial capital and to destroy the Continental Army. Washington accepted the challenge, and while he was defeated at the Battle of Brandywine Creek (September 11, 1777), he extracted his force. The British capture of Philadelphia did not end the rebellion, as no American city could be considered vital to the war effort. Simultaneously, Lieutenant General John Burgoyne invaded New York from Canada, planning to move down the Hudson River Valley to cut off New England. His force faced continual harassment as it pushed through the wilderness toward Albany, while Continentals under Major General Horatio Gates assumed defensive positions near Saratoga. Burgoyne detached part of his force in a foraging raid, but it met defeat at Bennington, Vermont (August 16, 1777). The two subsequent battles of Saratoga (Freeman's Farm on September 19 and Bemis Heights on October 7) failed to drive off the Americans. With dwindling supplies and no hope of relief, Burgoyne surrendered on October 17.

Saratoga was one of the turning points of the war. Determined to exact revenge for the British victory over its forces in the Seven Years' War (1756–1783; in America the French and Indian War [1754–1763]), the French government, which had already been sending considerable quantities of covert military aid to the Americans, now decided to openly enter the war. France provided invaluable and substantial land and naval forces to assist the Americans. Eventually Spain and the Kingdom of the Netherlands also entered the war against Britain. Such foreign assistance was vital to the American cause. The French posed a direct invasion threat to Britain, forcing London to retain assets for home defense and to contest the French in other parts of the world, including the West Indies and India.

In 1778 the British shifted their focus to the American South. New British commander Lieutenant General Sir Henry Clinton headed an expeditionary force that captured first Savannah, Georgia, in December 1778 and then, in the greatest defeat for the Continental Army in the war, Charleston, South Carolina, on May 12, 1780. The Charleston victory netted the British some 5,000 prisoners and substantial stocks of arms. Clinton then returned to New York, turning over command in the South to his able subordinate, Lieutenant General Charles Cornwallis.

At Camden on August 16, 1780, Cornwallis decisively defeated what remained of the Continental Army in the South under Gates, its new commander. Cornwallis then dispersed his troops into the countryside in an attempt at pacification. While this reflected a better understanding of how the war might be won, it also created opportunities that partisan bands in the Carolinas soon moved to exploit. Even though Cornwallis had an advantage in troops, resources, and fortified positions, he could not control the countryside and remained entirely dependent upon extensive logistical lines vulnerable to attack. Bands of partisans roamed the territory, launching attacks and then disappearing. Militia leaders such as Francis Marion,

Andrew Pickens, and Thomas Sumter operated in independent commands loosely coordinated by Gates's replacement, Major General Nathanael Greene. Even British tactical victories such as the Battle of Waxhaws (May 29, 1780) could be strategically disadvantageous. There, Lieutenant Colonel Banastre Tarleton failed to heed a Patriot attempt at surrender. Waxhaws became a rallying cry, a recruiting tool, and a justification for offering no quarter. At the Battle of Kings Mountain (October 7, 1780), Patriot militia bands united to trap and destroy a Loyalist unit under British Army major Patrick Ferguson, during which nearly 300 Loyalists and Ferguson were killed.

Cornwallis dispatched Tarleton and his dragoons in an effort to round up a Colonial Army force under Greene's subordinate, Brigadier General Daniel Morgan. On January 17, 1781, Tarleton's troops came on Morgan's combined Continental Army and militia force at Cowpens in South Carolina. Tarleton ordered a charge without first reconnoitering, only to discover that he had led his forces into a trap. Morgan's militia appeared to flee but instead circled around a rise and struck the British flank, while his regulars maintained a steady fire from an elevated position. Tarleton barely escaped the fight, but he lost nearly 90 percent of his command in only an hour of fighting. A military masterpiece, the battle is sometimes called the American Cannae.

Cornwallis found that he could march anywhere and capture any position, but he couldn't catch the re-formed Continentals under Greene, who remained tantalizingly close but out of reach. After chasing Greene through the Carolinas and back into Virginia, Cornwallis moved the bulk of his forces to the small Virginia tobacco port of Yorktown, where he could resupply and if necessary extract his troops by water. The timely arrival of a large French fleet cut off this escape route by winning the Second Battle of the Chesapeake (Virginia Capes, September 5, 1781), and Cornwallis found himself trapped by the arrival from New York of Washington's Continentals and French forces under Lieutenant General Jean-Baptiste de Rochambeau. After a siege of three weeks, Cornwallis surrendered on October 19.

This British defeat, coupled with the lack of progress in other theaters of the war, brought down the British government and induced London to open negotiations for peace at Paris, eventually resulting in an independent United States in 1783 that included territory to the Mississippi River. Canada, however, remained British.

Fundamentally, the British lost the war because they did not grasp the nature of the conflict. They continually sought to fight in a conventional manner against troops who refused to play to British strengths. The British also lost the propaganda war. In addition, the British government did almost nothing to address the underlying causes of the war, assuming that most Americans were loyal to the Crown and that popular support for the rebellion would wane as a consequence of British military victories. Even on the battlefield, British commanders often underestimated the capabilities of Americans, particularly in the latter stages of the war. Of course, much credit must also be given to the American leadership, particularly Washington, who faced the task of fighting a war while attempting to hold together a force that fluctuated wildly in size and was but poorly supplied. Unlike his British counterparts, Washington understood the nature of the conflict. Despite reverses, he kept the Continental Army in the field, prolonging the conflict and increasing its costs to Britain. Washington, whose leadership proved invaluable, created a model followed by many subsequent leaders in wars of national liberation.

Paul Joseph Springer

See also Guerrilla; Marion, Francis; Sumter, Thomas

Further Reading

Hibbert, Christopher. *Redcoats and Rebels: The American Revolution through British Eyes.* New York: Norton, 1990.

Martin, James Kirby. *A Respectable Army: The Military Origins of the Republic, 1763–1789.* Arlington Heights, IL: H. Davidson, 1982.

McCullough, David G. *1776.* New York: Simon and Schuster, 2005.

Shy, John W. *A People Numerous and Armed: Reflections on the Military Struggle for American Independence.* New York: Oxford University Press, 1976.

Ward, Christopher. *The War of the Revolution.* 2 vols. Edited by John Richard Alden. New York: Macmillan, 1952.

Angolan Insurgency

Start Date: 1961
End Date: 1975

The Portuguese first arrived in what is now Angola in Southwestern Africa in the late 15th century, but initial settlements were limited to the Atlantic coast. The Portuguese did not penetrate the interior until the late 19th century, after the Berlin Conference of 1885 officially set Angola's borders. During the centuries of Portuguese colonial settlement, there was near constant warfare with the indigenous tribes.

Although it was possible for Africans to become fully assimilated Portuguese citizens, this process was extremely difficult, and Portuguese colonial policy was both suppressive of native rights and economically exploitative. World War II (1939–1945) brought the winds of change throughout Africa, with the days of colonialism clearly numbered. Like the French and Belgian governments, however, the Portuguese government was determined to hold onto that country's vast colonial empire.

In January 1961 an insurgency began in Angola when members of the military wing of the Marxist Movimento Popular de Libertação de Angola (MPLA, Popular Movement for the Liberation of Angola), led by António Agostinho Neto, attacked Portuguese cotton plantations in the northern part of the country. The MPLA insurgents were trained in Algeria and later in Communist bloc countries. They operated first from the Republic of the Congo, then from Zaire, and then back in the Republic of the Congo. Although the MPLA had 3,000–5,000 fighters, few were actually based in Angola itself.

Soon the MPLA was joined by two other insurgent groups: Holden Roberto's Frente Nacional de Libertação de Angola (FNLA, National Liberation Front of Angola), organized from among the Bakongo tribe of northern Angola, and the União Nacional para a Independência Total de Angola (UNITA, National Union for the Total Independence of Angola), which broke off from the FNLA when Roberto was unwilling to expand his base in the southern part of the country. UNITA was headed by Jonas Savimbi and centered in southern Angola among the Ovimbundu and Chokwe peoples. UNITA was the only insurgent group based in Angola itself but had only several hundred fighters. The FNLA operated largely out of Zaire.

All three insurgent groups were savaged by Portuguese Army forces, particularly after those forces received helicopters. Portuguese control of the air was an immense advantage, especially in the largely open eastern part of the country. The Portuguese also carried out resettlement operations, moving the native peoples into government-controlled *dendandas* (defended villages). The guerrillas struck back with mines, and the MPLA also employed artillery fire and rockets to attack important Portuguese economic targets such as the Gulf Oil operations in the Cabinda enclave, although without great success.

The situation reached a stalemate in 1974, but the economic cost of Portuguese military operations in Angola as well as in Mozambique and Guinea, where it was also fighting insurgencies, was staggering. In April 1974 young, progressive Portuguese Army officers seized power in Lisbon in what became known as the Carnation Revolution. Their new government then agreed to grant colonial independence, and Portuguese troops departed Angola on its independence on November 11, 1975.

The anticommunist FNLA and UNITA had now formed an alliance, supported by a Zairean military intervention, in order to prevent the Marxist MPLA from taking power. The anticommunists were, however, defeated in battle by the timely arrival of Cuban troops airlifted into Luanda by the Soviet Union. Although the MPLA held power with Neto as president, a bloody and protracted civil war followed that pitted the MPLA and Cuban forces supported by the Soviet Union against UNITA and the FLNA, backed by the United States, Zaire, and South Africa. Perhaps half a million Angolans died before it came to an end in 1992. The MPLA, which subsequently abandoned Marxist-Leninism in favor of social democracy, retains power in Angola today.

Spencer C. Tucker

See also Aircraft in Counterinsurgency Operations; Castro Ruz, Fidel Alejandro; Frente Nacional de Libertação de Angola; Movimento Popular de Libertação de Angola; Politicization of Armed Forces; Roberto, Holden Álverto; Savimbi, Jonas Malheiro; União Nacional para a Independência Total de Angola

Further Reading

Klinghoffer, Arthur Jay. *The Angolan War.* Boulder, CO: Westview, 1980.

Marcum, John A. *The Angolan Revolution.* 2 vols. Cambridge, MA: MIT Press, 1969 and 1978.

Annual, Battle of

Event Date: July 22, 1921

Key battle during the Rif Rebellion (1920–1926), also known as the Rif War. Spanish forces came under attack in their zone of Morocco not only from Mulai Ahmed el Raisuni (known as Raisuli), leader of the Rifian Berbers in Morocco and considered by many to be the rightful heir to the throne of Morocco, but also from Rif forces led by able chieftain Muhammad ibn Abd el-Krim al-Khattabi.

Spanish general Fernandes Silvestre moved southwest into the Rif Mountains at the head of about 20,000 men. He failed to carry out adequate reconnaissance or take sufficient security precautions, and on July 22 at Annual in present-day northeastern Morocco, the column encountered the Spanish garrison fleeing from the post at Abaran. In the ensuing confusion, Rif forces under Abd el-Krim fell on both flanks of Silvestre's column, leading to widespread panic and the death of some 12,000 Spanish troops. Several thousand Spaniards were also taken prisoner. The Spaniards also lost some 20,000 rifles, 400 machine guns, and 129 artillery pieces. Silverstre committed suicide. Some 1,000 Rifians perished in the battle.

News of this defeat (referred to by the Spaniards as the Annual Disaster) created a political firestorm in Spain and brought strongman General Miguel Primo de Rivera to power that September. With the support of King Alfonso XIII, Primo de Rivera created a virtual military dictatorship until his resignation in January 1930.

In Morocco, meanwhile, the Rifs overran more than 20 Spanish posts and massacred their garrisons. By the end of 1924, the Spanish were obliged to withdraw to the coastal enclaves of Melilla and Tetuán.

Spencer C. Tucker

See also Abd el-Krim al-Khattabi, Muhammad ibn

Further Reading

Woolman, David S. *Rebels in the Rif: Abd El Krim and the Rif Rebellion.* Palo Alto, CA: Stanford University Press, 1968.

Arab Revolt against Ottoman Rule

Start Date: June 5, 1916
End Date: October 31, 1918

Uprising during World War I (1914–1918) by the Arab peoples of north, central, and western Arabia against Ottoman rule. Since the 16th century, the Ottoman government in Constantinople had controlled the area of present-day Syria, Palestine, and Iraq as well as the western provinces of Saudi Arabia and part of Yemen. Much of the region's population of some 6 million people was nomadic. In 1908 the Young Turks came to power in the Ottoman Empire and promoted Turkish nationalism at the expense of other nationalities, which the Arabs and other peoples resented. The new government also sent troops into Arab lands and introduced conscription, both of which angered the Arabs.

Under the terms of the Ottoman Constitution of 1909, the Arab peoples of the empire sent representatives to the Imperial Parliament in Constantinople, where they openly supported Arab rights. Also, in the Arab lands, newspapers and political organizations—some secret—promoted Arab nationalism. Damascus and Beirut were centers of this activity but were too close geographically to Anatolia to risk overt action. Arab power was in fact diffuse and was largely wielded by local chieftains who had little ability to initiate hostilities against Constantinople on their own.

The center of the Arab nationalist movement was the Hejaz region of central Arabia, which contained the holy cities of Mecca and Medina. The region was connected to Anatolia by the Damascus-Medina (Hejaz) Railway. Sharif of Mecca Hussein ibn Ali ibn Mohammed was nominal head of the Hejaz. His position was strengthened by his senior position in the Muslim religious hierarchy as a direct descendant of the Prophet Muhammad. Hussein saw the railway as an infringement on his control and had long hoped for an independent Arab kingdom under his rule. World War I provided that opportunity.

As early as February 1914, Hussein, through his son Abdullah, had been in communication with British authorities in Cairo. Abdullah met with the British high commissioner in Egypt, Field Marshal Horatio Kitchener, and told him that the Arabs were prepared to rebel in return for British support. The British were skeptical, but the entrance of the Ottoman Empire into the war on the side of the Central Powers changed their attitude. Both Sir Harold Wingate, British governor-general of the Sudan, and Sir Henry McMahon, Kitchener's successor as high commissioner in Egypt, remained in contact with Hussein.

In the spring of 1915, Hussein sent his third son, Emir Faisal, to Damascus to reassure Ottman authorities there of his loyalty and to sound out Arab opinion. Faisal had favored the Turks, but the visit to Damascus and the profound discontent of the Arab population that he discovered there reversed this view.

Hussein entered into active negotiations with McMahon in Cairo. Hussein promised to declare war on the Ottoman Empire and raise an Arab army to assist the British in return for British support for him as king of a postwar Pan-Arab state. The British agreed and soon were providing some rifles and ammunition to the Arabs. Meanwhile, the Turks were endeavoring to stamp out Arab nationalism in Damascus, where they executed a number of Arab nationalist leaders. Many other Arab patriots fled south to Mecca, where they urged Hussein to take up arms. The Turks were well aware of the Arab preparations and from May 1916 blockaded the Hejaz from arms shipments and began a buildup of their forces in Damascus. The actual revolt was initiated by the dispatch of Turkish troops to reinforce their garrison at Medina. Outside Medina on June 5, 1916, Hussein's eldest son Ali and Faisal officially proclaimed the start of the Arab Revolt.

Joined by 30,000 tribesmen, Faisal immediately led an assault on the Ottoman garrison at Medina, but the Turks drove off the attackers. The Arabs did succeed in cutting the railway to the north of the city. To the south, Hussein led an attack on the 1,000-man Turkish garrison at Mecca, taking the city after three days of street fighting. Another Arab attack shortly thereafter against the port city of Jiddah was also successful, supported by the British Royal Navy seaplane carrier *Ben-my-Chree.* Other cities also fell to the Arabs. In September, the 3,000-man garrison at Taif, the last city in the southern Hejaz held by the Turks, surrendered to Arab forces supported by British-supplied artillery.

On November 2, Hussein proclaimed himself "King of the Arab Countries." This created some embarrassment for the British government with the French. Finally, the Allies worked out a compromise by which they addressed Hussein as "King of the Hejaz." Hussein largely left leadership of the revolt to his four sons. A number of Arabs serving in the Ottoman Army (including officers) who were taken prisoner in the fighting helped provide a leadership cadre for the so-called Arab Army. Military strength of its four main forces commanded by Hussein's sons fluctuated greatly, and few of the men involved, who ranged widely in age, were trained.

In October 1916, the Turks managed to drive the Arab Army south of Medina and reopened the railway. The British sent a party of advisers to Hussein. Arabist captain T. E. Lawrence became Faisal's official adviser and successfully urged Faisal to resume the offensive. Rather than meet Turkish power head-on, the two men initiated a series of hit-and-run raids over northern Arabia that took advantage of the support of the local populations and forced the Turks to divert increasing numbers of troops to the region.

In the spring of 1917, Faisal received pledges of Arab support from Syria once military operations reached there. In July 1917 Lawrence led an attack that captured Aqaba, which then became Faisal's chief base, while forces under Abdullah and Ali contained the Turkish garrison at Medina and protected Mecca. Faisal's northern wing of the Arab Army was the revolt's chief military force and acted on the right flank of Lieutenant General Edmund Allenby's British forces in Palestine. In the autumn of 1917, Lawrence, who understood and effectively practiced guerrilla warfare, led a series of successful attacks on Turkish rail traffic. Allenby's calls for diversionary attacks by the Arab Army produced a series of raids that diverted some 23,000 Ottoman troops from participation in the fighting in Palestine. Faisal also cooperated closely with Allenby in the Megiddo Offensive and, with 30,000 men, led the revolt's climactic action, the entrance into Damascus in October 1918.

The Arab Revolt had immense repercussions in the Arab world in terms of fueling Arab nationalism. The revolt helped free the Arab lands from Turkish rule and led to the formation of Arab states. But the victorious Allies thwarted Hussein's ambitions. McMahon's pledge to Hussein preceded by six months the 1916 Sykes-Picot Agreement between the British and French governments, a breach of promises made to the Arabs that in effect set up British and French spheres of influence in the Middle East. Ultimately, much of the territory was awarded as mandates to Great Britain and France under the League of Nations. Faisal received Syria but was deposed and became king of Iraq under British protection. Abdullah became king of the newly created Transjordan. Hussein declared himself caliph of Islam in March 1924 but was forced to abdicate as king of the Hejaz to his son Ali when Abd al-Aziz al-Saud (Ibn Saud) conquered most of the Hejaz.

Spencer C. Tucker

See also Lawrence, Thomas Edward

Further Reading

Fromkin, David. *A Peace to End All Peace: The Fall of the Ottoman Empire and the Creation of the Modern Middle East.* New York: Avon, 1989.

Hourani, Albert. *A History of the Arab Peoples.* Cambridge: Harvard University Press, 1991.

Tauber, Eliezer. *The Arab Movements in World War I.* London: Frank Cass, 1993.

Thomas, Lowell. *With Lawrence in Arabia.* New York: Garden City Publishing, 1924.

Arab Revolt of 1936

Start Date: April 1936
End Date: 1939

In 1936 a general revolt occurred among Arabs in the British mandate of Palestine. Although the uprising was aimed primarily at British interests, attacks against Jews were not uncommon. The revolt was the culmination of growing Arab unrest over Jewish immigration and land purchases in Palestine and economic dislocation resulting from increased urbanization and industrialization and was the most severe of a number of communal disturbances between Jews and Arabs dating from the early 1920s. Despite its failure, the Great Revolt (as it is known by Muslims) marked the dawn of a distinctive Palestinian Arab nationalism.

The unrest was triggered in part by events outside the region. Growing anti-Semitism in Eastern Europe and Nazi control of Germany from 1933 led to an increase in Jewish immigration into Palestine. At the same time, growing land purchases by Zionists brought the expulsion of large numbers of Arab peasants from lands on which they had been tenant farmers. This was part of a deepening economic crisis as Palestinian agricultural exports to Europe and America declined during the worldwide Great Depression (ca. 1930–1940).

The revolt was centered on landless Arabs, often forced into slums around the cities. Its leadership came from the more politically conscious Arab elite dominated by the Husseini family, led by Haj Amin al-Husseini, mufti of Jerusalem, and their rivals, the Nashashibis, represented by Fakhri al-Nashashibi. The revolt's true leadership, however, came from local Arab committees in Jerusalem and other population centers.

Arab horsemen gather in Nablus, near the Palestine border on October 31, 1938. The Arab Revolt of 1938–1939 in Palestine was triggered by displeasure with the British mandate government and policies that permitted an influx of Jewish settlers and land purchases. The revolt marked the beginning of a distinctive Palestinian nationalism. (AP Photo)

Tensions among Arabs, Jews, and British administrators in Palestine had been building for several months prior to the revolt's outbreak in April 1936, thanks not only to economic conditions but also to a surge of Islamic extremism led by Sheikh Izz al-Din al-Qassam, a Syrian-born, Egyptian-educated cleric who had been preaching fundamentalist Islam and calling for a jihad (holy war) against both Britons and Jews. His followers murdered a Jewish policeman near Gilboa, and al-Qassam was killed in a subsequent shootout with British troops on November 20, 1935. His death triggered Arab nationalist demonstrations throughout Palestine. At the same time, discovery by the British of an arms cache in a shipment of cement barrels intended for a Jewish importer fed rumors that the Jews were arming for a war against the Arabs. These developments pushed a tense atmosphere into outright rebellion. The revolt officially began in April 1936 in the hill country around Tulkarm and spread rapidly. The first six months of the revolt claimed the lives of 200 Arabs, 80 Jews, and 28 British soldiers and policemen.

The initial British reaction was restrained. London hoped that the disturbances would blow over without forcing measures that might scar Anglo-Arab relations. Only in September 1936 did British authorities impose martial law. Eventually the government sent 20,000 troops from Britain and Egypt and recruited 2,700 Jewish supernumeraries to deal with the disturbances.

The Jewish Agency for Palestine worked to strengthen the Haganah, its self-defense force, and fortify Jewish settlements, leaving suppression of the revolt to the British. As the uprising continued and attacks on Jewish settlements increased, however, Palestinian Jews resorted to aggressive self-defense, including ambushes of rebel Arab bands and reprisals against neighboring Arab villages suspected of harboring guerrillas. This doctrine of harsh reprisals developed by the Zionist leadership during the revolt became a permanent fixture of Zionist military policy.

In the first months of the revolt, the British succeeded—through the use of night curfews, patrols, searches, and ambushes—in pushing Arab rebels out of the towns. By mid-May 1936, rural Palestine had become the center of gravity of the revolt and would remain so until the revolt's end in 1939. Leadership remained with the local committees. The Arab Higher Committee was increasingly paralyzed by rivalries between the Husseini and Nashashibi clans but did provide money, arms, and rhetorical support.

By the autumn of 1937, some 9,000–10,000 Palestinian fighters, augmented by non-Palestinians brought in and financed by the Arab Higher Committee, were roaming the countryside, often motivated as much by the desire for loot as by nationalist zeal. Internecine violence among rival families resulted in more deaths among the Arabs than from action by the British or Zionists. The rebels' practice of extorting food and other valuables from Arab peasants damaged the rural economy and increasingly alienated the rebels from their base of support. To pacify the countryside, the British shrewdly exploited Arab divisions and employed combined British-Zionist Special Night Squads (the best known of which was commanded by Captain Orde Wingate) to ambush rebel bands, launch retaliatory strikes against Arab villages suspected of harboring guerrillas, and carry out targeted assassinations of rebel leaders.

The Arab Revolt collapsed in 1939 in the face of eroding support in the countryside, the arrest or exile of the senior leaders, lack of cohesion in the revolt's organization and leadership, and mounting British pressure. Nevertheless, the revolt had profound consequences for the mandate and the Arabs and Zionists. The uprising led London to send a commission to Palestine chaired by Lord William Robert Peel in late 1936. The commission's report of July 1937 proposed the partition of Palestine into a Jewish area and a much larger Arab area, the first time that partition had been advanced as a solution. Both sides essentially rejected partition, and the British eventually backed away from it.

Palestinian Jews were shocked by implementation of the British government White Paper of May 1939, which restricted Jewish immigration and land purchases and promised an independent Palestinian Arab state in 10 years if the rights of the Jewish community were protected. From the Jewish perspective, the White Paper represented a surrender to Arab violence and intimidation. The White Paper also closed Palestine to European Jews at a time when anti-Jewish violence in Germany and Eastern Europe was intensifying. Indeed, the measure permanently damaged relations between Britain and the Jews in Palestine.

The worst damage, however, was to Palestinian Arabs. Although the Arab Revolt gained a permanent place in Arab nationalist mythology, the Arabs were left with the consequences of a failed revolt. Most of the political leadership was in prison, exiled, or had left politics. Blood feuds between families that had supported the uprising and those opposed disrupted Palestinian society and paralyzed political life for years.

The Arab Revolt unraveled throughout 1939, with armed violence largely ceasing by the end of the year. Nonetheless, casualties had been high. Some 5,000 Arabs, 400 Jews, and 200 British soldiers and officials died in the uprising.

The overall legacy of the Arab Revolt, then, was the further poisoning of relations between Arabs and Jews and the further alienation of the British from both communities. The revolt also led to the separation of the Arab and Jewish economies, which had previously been somewhat integrated. This burdened Palestinian Arabs with poverty, high unemployment, and homelessness for two succeeding generations. Although divisions among Arabs, Jews, and Britons remained largely dormant during World War II (1939–1945), they resurfaced afterward in an even more violent manner.

Walter F. Bell

See also Wingate, Orde Charles

Further Reading

Gelvin, James L. *The Israel-Palestine Conflict: One Hundred Years of War.* New York: Cambridge University Press, 2005.

Morris, Benny. *Righteous Victims: A History of the Zionist-Arab Conflict, 1881–2001.* New York: Vintage Books, 2001.

Porath, Yehoshua. *The Palestinian National Movement, 1929–1939: From Riot to Rebellion.* London: Cass, 1974.

Stein, Kenneth W. *The Land Question in Palestine, 1917–1939.* Chapel Hill: University of North Carolina Press, 1984.

Swedenburg, Ted. *Memories of Revolt: The 1936–1939 Rebellion and the Palestinian National Past.* Minneapolis: University of Minnesota Press, 1995.

Arafat, Yasser

Birth Date: August 24, 1929
Death Date: November 11, 2004

Palestinian nationalist and leader of the Palestine Liberation Organization (PLO) during 1969–2004. Born Muhammad Abd ar-Ra'uf al-Qudwa al-Husayni on August 24, 1929, in Cairo, Egypt, Yasser Arafat as a teenager in Cairo became involved in smuggling arms to Palestinians who were fighting the British and the Jews. He also fought against the Jews in Gaza in 1948, a struggle that the Arabs lost.

Arafat studied briefly at the University of Texas before completing his engineering degree in 1956 at the University of Faud I in Egypt, where he was also president of the Union of Palestinian Students. In 1952 he had joined the Muslim Brotherhood. After a brief stint in the Egyptian Army during the 1956 Suez Crisis, Arafat moved to Kuwait, where he formed his own contracting company.

In 1958 Arafat founded Al Fatah, an underground insurgent group dedicated to liberating Palestine. In 1964 he left his job, moved to Jordan, and devoted all his energies to organizing raids against Israel. That same year, the PLO was formed. Arafat fought in the 1967 Six-Day War, allegedly escaping from Israel disguised as a woman. Gradually Al Fatah came to dominate the PLO, and in February 1969 Arafat became chairman of the PLO.

After skirmishes with Jordanian authorities, Arafat was forced to relocate the PLO to Lebanon in 1970. During much of the 1970s, he spent considerable time reorienting the PLO's emphasis from Pan-Arabism to Palestinian nationalism. During the Lebanese Civil War that witnessed brutal fighting between Lebanese Muslims and Lebanese Christians, the PLO sided with the Muslims. Arafat moved the PLO to Tunisia in 1982. In the 1980s he regrouped his organization, which had sustained heavy losses during the Lebanon fighting. The PLO received important monetary aid from both Iraq and Saudi Arabia during the 1980s, and in 1988 Palestinians declared the formal State of Palestine. With that, Arafat announced that the PLO would renounce all forms of terrorism and would recognize the State of Israel, a radical departure in the PLO's philosophy.

In 1993 the PLO participated in the Oslo Accords and hammered out a peace deal with Israeli prime minister Yizhak Rabin. The PLO located to the West Bank in 1994, an important first step toward the creation of an autonomous Palestinian state. In 1996 Arafat was elected head of the new Palestinian Authority, which was to provide governance, security, and other services to Palestinians in the West Bank and the Gaza Strip. However, Israeli-Palestinian relations deteriorated rapidly upon the 1996 election of the rightist Israeli prime minister Benjamin Netanyahu.

Despite efforts by U.S. president Bill Clinton to preserve peace between Israel and the PLO in the summer of 2000, negotiations broke down, and radical groups such as Hamas and the Islamic Jihad commenced the Second (al-Aqsa) Intifada. This began four years of violence in Israel and the Occupied Territories. Arafat was increasingly marginalized, and in 2004 U.S. president George W. Bush declared that the PLO leader was ineffective and that negotiating with him was impossible.

After having developed a mysterious illness, Arafat traveled to Paris for medical treatment, where he died on November 11, 2004. The future of the Palestinian cause remains very much in question.

Amy Hackney Blackwell

See also Harakat al-Jihad al-Islami fi Filastin; Harakat al-Muqawama al-Islamiyya; Intifada, Second; Palestine Liberation Organization

Further Reading

Aburish, Said K. *Arafat: From Defender to Dictator.* New York: Bloomsbury, 1998.

Hart, Alan. *Arafat: A Political Biography.* Revised ed. London: Sidgwick and Jackson, 1994.

Rubin, Barry M., and Judith Colp Rubin. *Arafat: A Political Biography.* New York: Oxford University Press, 2003.

Arango, Doroteo.

See Villa, Francisco

Arminius

Birth Date: 17 BCE
Death Date: 21 CE

German military leader and national hero. Arminius (the latinized form of Hermann or Armin) was born in Germany in 17 BCE, the son of Segimer, prince of the Cherusci. Arminius served in the Roman Army during 1–6 CE and was awarded Roman citizenship for his services. Returning to Germany, he found his people chaffing under the rule of Roman governor Publius Quinctilius Varus and secretly took leadership of a revolt of the German tribes against Rome beginning in 6 CE in Dalmatia and Pannonia (comprising the Roman province of Illyricum). In 9 CE Arminius, after apparently having suggested the Roman route of march, then slipped away and led an ambush of Varus and three legions in the Teutoburg Forest (Teutoburger Wald), utterly destroying them. Very few of the 20,000–30,000 men in the three legions escaped alive, and Varus committed suicide.

This disaster caused Roman emperor Augustus to shorten Rome's defensive front and withdraw its legions from the Elbe to the Rhine. Arminius was unable to follow up his victory, however, as there were no plans to conquer the Roman provinces.

In 15 CE, however, Germanicus Caesar led Roman legions against Arminius, in the process taking as prisoner Arminius's wife, Thusnelda. Following an indecisive battle in the Teutoburg Forest in which Germanicus barely escaped the fate of Varus, Arminius was finally defeated in 16 CE. The campaign had been so costly, however, that Germanicus was recalled, and Rome gave up the idea of a frontier on the Elbe.

The Germans then fell to fighting among themselves. Arminius was successful in warfare against Marbo, king of the Marcomanni, but was murdered in 21 CE. Germans later hailed Arminius as a national hero, celebrating his achievement in song and writing. In 1875 the Germans raiscd a large monument to him on Grotenburg Mountain near Detmold, Klopstock, in the Teutoburg Forest.

Spencer C. Tucker

See also Teutoburg Forest, Battle of the

Further Reading

Grant, Michael. *The Army of the Caesars.* New York: Scribner, 1974.

Tacitus. *The Annals of Imperial Rome.* Translated by Michael Grant. London: Penguin, 1974.

Arriaga, Kaúlza de Oliveira de

Birth Date: January 18, 1915
Death Date: February 2, 2004

Portuguese general and politician. Kaúlza de Oliveira de Arriaga was born in Porto, Portugal, on January 18, 1915. He graduated from the University of Porto with a degree in mathematics and engineering and then joined the Portuguese Army in November 1935. After graduation from the Portuguese Military Academy in 1939, he held mostly administrative positions, including an assignment to the Portuguese Institute of Military Studies, where he proposed reforms in conscription and the integration of airborne forces into the Portuguese Air Force. Arriaga was secretary of state for aeronautics during 1955–1962 and chair of the Atomic Energy Board in 1967.

In 1968 Arriaga was promoted to full general, and in 1969 he assumed command of Portuguese ground forces in Mozambique fighting the Frente de Libertação de Moçambique (FRELIMO, Front for the Liberation of Mozambique). The next year he had charge of all Portuguese forces in that colony and proceeded to intensify antiguerrilla military efforts. He directed Operation NÓ GÓRDIO GORDIAN KNOT, a large search-and-destroy undertaking that involved airborne troops in 1970 and was the largest Portuguese military operation of the post–World War II colonial wars in Africa. The operation saw 10,000 troops clearing FRELIMO guerrillas from northern Mozambique. At the same time, the troops resettled native populations in *aldeamentos* (strategic villages) and endeavored to win the hearts-and-minds struggle through construction of hospitals and schools as well as improving the quality of native cattle herds. Arriaga also sought to expand the number of native troops serving with his forces. Known to his troops as the "Pink Panther," Arriaga created around himself something of a personality cult and was noted for the political indoctrination of his own forces. Following allegations in July 1973 that on December 16, 1972, Portuguese troops had massacred between 60 and 400 natives of the village of Wiriyamu believed to be FRELIMO sympathizers, Arriaga was recalled to Portugal.

A staunch conservative and defender of the authoritative Portuguese government and its African empire, Arriaga was angered by criticism of Portuguese colonial policy by fellow general António de Spinola. Retired by Spinola's government after the Carnation Revolution of April 25, 1974, Arriaga was imprisoned that September after Spinola was in turn ousted by more radical Portuguese leaders. Arriaga was held until June 1976. In 1977 he established the right-wing political party Movimento Independente para a Reconstrução Nacional (MIRN, Independent Movement for National Reconstruction) and served as its chairman until its disbandment following the 1980 parliamentary elections. Arriaga died in Lisbon on February 2, 2004.

Spencer C. Tucker

See also Mozambique Insurgency

Further Reading

Arriaga, Kaúlza. *The Portuguese Answer.* London: Stacey, 1973.

Cann, John. *Counterinsurgency in Africa: The Portuguese Way of War, 1961–1974.* Westport CT: Greenwood, 1997.

Maxwell, Kenneth. *The Making of Portuguese Democracy.* Cambridge: Cambridge University Press, 1995.

Aussaresses, Paul

Birth Date: November 7, 1918

French Army general. Born on November 7, 1918, in Saint-Paul Cap-de-Joux, in the Tarn Department, France, Paul Aussaresses was an officer cadet in Algeria in 1941. Joining the Free French forces, he parachuted into German-occupied France in August 1944 to work with the French Resistance in Ariège. Aussaresses continued in the French Army after the war and commanded the 11th Choc Battalion, a commando unit, during 1947–1948. He then fought in the Indochina War (1946–1954) with the 1st Parachute Regiment.

With the beginning of the Algerian War (1954–1962), in 1955 Aussaresses joined the 41st Parachute Demi-Brigade at Philippeville as its intelligence officer. On August 20, 1955, he learned that Front de Libération Nationale (FLN, National Liberation Front) planned to attack the police in Philippeville, employing civilians as human shields. Aussaresses's battalion opened fire, killing 134 FLN members and human shields and wounding many more. Two Frenchmen died, and perhaps 100 were wounded. Aussaresses was to have taken part in the 1956 Anglo-French Suez Operation but was injured in a parachute training exercise beforehand.

In January 1957 French governor-general in Algeria Robert Lacoste invested Brigadier General Jacques Massu with full power to break a general strike proclaimed in Algiers by the FLN, part of the so-called Battle of Algiers that had begun on September 30, 1956. Massu, impressed with what Aussaresses had accomplished at Philippeville, called on him to work in French intelligence operations there. Operating with ruthless efficiency, the French employed torture to root out the FLN and break the general strike. French Army troops also murdered prominent prisoners, including FLN leader Larbi Ben M'Hidi and attorney Ali Boumendjel. Both deaths were claimed by the French government at the time as suicides, but in 1970 Aussaresses acknowledged that they were were murders. The Battle of Algiers, certainly the most dramatic episode of the Algerian War (1954–1962), ended in a French victory in March 1957.

In 1961 Aussaresses became French military attaché in Washington, D.C. He also helped instruct U.S. Army Special Forces at Fort Bragg, North Carolina. Assigned to Brazil in 1971, Aussaresses advised the Latin American government on counterinsurgency techniques. He retired as a brigadier general in 1975.

Aussaresses caused a storm of controversy in 2000 when, in an interview with the influential French newspaper *Le Monde,* he not only acknowledged that torture had been ordered by the highest levels of the French military during the Algerian War but also defended its use. Aussaresses argued that torture is a necessary element of counterinsurgency and counterterrorism when the insurgents and terrorists are themselves employing the most brutal methods against civilians. In the aftermath of his remarks, the government stripped Aussaresses of his rank and the Légion d'Honneur.

Spencer C. Tucker

See also Algerian War; Algiers, Battle of; Massu, Jacques Émile

Further Reading

Aussaresses, Paul. *The Battle of the Casbah: Terrorism and Counter-Terrorism in Algeria, 1955–1957.* New York, Enigma Books, 2001.

Horne, Alistair. *A Savage War of Peace: Algeria, 1954–1962.* London: Macmillan, 1971.

B

Bacon's Rebellion

Start Date: June 1676
End Date: January 1677

A violent uprising in the English colony of Virginia during 1676–1677 led by Nathaniel Bacon, a member of the rural planter class. At one time identified as the first manifestation of revolutionary sentiment in English North America, Bacon's Rebellion is now seen as more the result of a power struggle between colonial leaders.

A number of factors contributed to the revolt, chief among them a declining economy brought on by a sharp drop in the price of tobacco, the result of increasing competition from Maryland and the Carolinas. The economic crisis affected small farmers and planters alike, as many Virginia farmers relied almost exclusively on tobacco cultivation. Meanwhile, the ongoing Anglo-Dutch Wars disrupted trade and increased the price of imported English manufactured goods. A series of natural disasters, including hurricanes, dry spells, and hailstorms, also took a toll, and internal Virginia politics played a key role. In an effort to expand their landholdings, the English colonists increasingly encroached onto Native American lands in the western part of the colony.

In July 1675, apparently in a dispute over nonpayment of trade items, members of the Doeg tribe of Native Americans raided a plantation in the Northern Neck area of Virginia. The colonists then mounted a retaliatory strike against the wrong tribe, the Susquehannocks. This led to a series of native raids along the western frontier.

Virginia governor Sir William Berkeley sought to find a middle ground that would prevent all-out war, but a meeting between the two sides led to the murder of several chiefs. Berkeley's efforts to pursue a moderate course also angered many western colonists, who believed that the government had abandoned them in the face of the native threat.

The leader of the western colonists was the intemperate yet charismatic Nathaniel Bacon, a distant relative of Berkeley and a member of the House of Burgesses since 1675. Bacon opposed Berkeley's conciliatory policies and disregarded a direct order by seizing some members of the Appomattox tribe for allegedly stealing corn, whereupon Berkeley reprimanded him.

Berkeley meanwhile ordered local natives to give up their powder and ammunition, and in March 1676 he called the Long Assembly. This body declared war on hostile Native Americans and took steps to strengthen the Virginia frontier defenses. But such action also necessitated a sharp increase in taxes. The assembly also took charge of trading with the natives, insisting that this be done through a government commission supposedly to see that the natives were not receiving arms and ammunition but also bringing financial gain to close associates of the governor.

Bacon was one of those who had traded with the natives and was adversely affected by the government commission. Angered when Berkeley denied him a militia commission, Bacon secured election as the "general" of a local militia, promising to pay for its operations against the natives himself.

When Bacon and his men drove a number of friendly Pamunkeys from their lands, Berkeley rode to Bacon's headquarters at Henrico with some 300 well-armed men to confront him, whereupon Bacon and 200 followers fled into the forest. Berkeley then declared Bacon a rebel while offering to pardon his followers if they would return to their homes. Although Berkeley promised that Bacon would receive a fair trial, Bacon refused to give himself up and indeed led an attack on friendly Occaneechee natives along the Roanoke River, seizing their stocks of beaver pelts.

With events now seemingly spinning out of control, Berkeley announced that he was ready to forgive Bacon's disobedience and pardon him if he agreed to be sent to England for trial there. The House of Burgesses, however, insisted that Bacon apologize and beg the governor's forgiveness. At the same time, supported by the western landowners who approved of his actions toward the natives, Bacon won election to the House of Burgesses.

In June 1676 Bacon traveled to Jamestown to take part in the new assembly, his only real platform being opposition to Native Americans. On arriving at Jamestown, he was arrested and taken before Berkeley and the Crown Council, where Bacon apologized for his actions. Berkeley then pardoned Bacon and allowed him to take his seat. Neither Berkeley nor the members of the council understood the level of support that Bacon enjoyed in the colony, however.

In the course of debate regarding Native American policies, Bacon stalked out of the meeting and left Jamestown, returning a few days later with some 500 armed followers, who surrounded the assembly. Bacon then confronted Berkeley and demanded at gunpoint to be given charge of all the colony's forces against the natives. Berkeley refused, offering Bacon only his previous militia commission. But with some of Bacon's men threatening to shoot members of the House of Burgesses, Berkeley at length granted Bacon's request that he be made general and commander of the Virginia Militia and to lead it, free of government interference, in a campaign against the natives.

For the next three months Bacon had firm control of Jamestown, and on July 30 he issued his "Declaration of the People," claiming that Berkeley was corrupt and that his native policies had been shaped to bring financial reward to himself and his friends. Bacon also issued a decree requiring an oath in which the swearer would have to agree to obey him in any manner Bacon deemed necessary. Berkeley meanwhile fled to his estate on the Eastern Shore and there again declared Bacon a rebel. Much to Berkeley's dismay, he found that he could attract few armed supporters. Indeed, many Virginians were upset with Berkeley for turning on Bacon in the middle of a campaign against Native Americans.

Bacon meanwhile led some 1,000 colonists against the Native Americans, not to the western part of the colony where the threat actually lay but instead against the Pamunkeys, who had been at peace with the English since 1646. In a monthlong campaign, the colonists drove the Pamunkeys into Dragon Swamp, killing some 60, most of them women and children.

Bacon emerged from the campaign to learn that Berkeley's followers had infiltrated the Virginia Navy, enabling Berkeley to return to Jamestown. Bacon then marched on Jamestown, besieging it. On September 16 the Loyalists briefly sallied from Jamestown and attacked Bacon's siege positions, only to be driven back with a dozen casualties. Berkeley then abandoned Jamestown by ship with his followers for the Eastern Shore.

Bacon now overreached. On September 19 he ordered Jamestown, the oldest permanent English settlement in the New World, burned to the ground, although he did save most of the valuable state records. This deed cost him the support of many Virginians, while he angered others when he admitted to military service both indentured servants and slaves, an action that threatened to overturn the entire social order of the colony.

On October 26, 1676, Bacon died suddenly of "Bloodie Flux," a fever accompanied by virulent dysentery, probably a direct result of the time in the backwoods and swamps. An obscure follower, Joseph Ingram, took control of the insurgents, and the rebellion turned from its chief raison d'être of warfare against hostile Native Americans to mere looting and robbery.

Berkeley's forces gradually grew in strength. Aided by the addition of several larger merchant vessels that they intercepted on arrival from England, they controlled the rivers and mounted an increased number of raids up the James and York against rebel strongholds. Thomas Grantham, acting on Berkeley's authority, negotiate the capitulation of the rebel stronghold of West Point. With the surrender there of some 700 freemen, servants, and slaves in January 1677, Bacon's Rebellion was for all intents and purposes at an end.

In the spring of 1677 at Middle Plantation, the Virginia government entered into a number of peace treaties with the natives in order to try to repair relations. Charles II reacted to news of the rebellion by recalling Berkeley and dispatching 1,000 soldiers, who arrived after the rebellion was over. The first regular English troops stationed in Virginia, they were soon withdrawn.

Jaime Ramón Olivares and Spencer C. Tucker

Further Reading

Washburn, Wilcomb E. *The Governor and the Rebel*. Chapel Hill: University of North Carolina Press, 1957.

Webb, Stephen Sanders. *1676: The End of American Independence*. New York: Knopf, 1984.

Wertenbaker, Thomas Jefferson. *Torchbearer of the Revolution: The Story of Bacon's Rebellion and Its Leader*. Princeton, NJ: Princeton University Press, 1940.

Bar Kokhba Revolt

Start Date: 132 BCE
End Date: 136 BCE

Jewish revolt against the Roman Empire, the third such major revolt and the last war by the Jews against Rome. The revolt is named for its leader, Simeon bar Kosiba, hailed by the influential Rabbi Akiva as the messiah who would restore the state of Israel and given by him the surname Bar Kokhba ("son of a star").

Following the failed Great Jewish Revolt of 70 CE that had ended in the destruction of Jerusalem, the Romans stationed in Judea an entire legion, the X Fretensis. In 130 Emperor Hadrian visited the ruins of the temple at Jerusalem and reportedly promised to rebuild it. Jews were angered when they learned, however, that his intent was to build upon its ruins a temple dedicated to Jupiter instead. Another factor in the revolt seems to have been Hadrian's ban on circumcision, which he viewed as mutilation. In any case, a second legion, the VI Ferrata, was stationed in Judea to secure order, and the next year work was begun on the temple at Aelia Capitolina, Jerusalem's projected new name.

The revolt of 132 took the Romans by surprise. Much better organized than that of 70, the revolt quickly spread across Judea. Its course remains obscure, but the rebels enjoyed initial success, resulting in the establishment of Israeli independence for two and a half years. Bar Kokhba took the title of prince, issued coinage overstruck from Roman pieces, and established the seat of his government at Jerusalem.

Hadrian was determined to crush the revolt and dispatched to Judea up to eight legions. Roman governor Tineius Rufus built roads to encircle the rebel-held area and established numerous strong points. In 133 Hadrian recalled General Sixtus Julius Severus from Britain and sent him to Judea. Severus had learned that frontal attacks on the rebels were costly and unproductive, and he adopted an attrition strategy, made possible by superior numbers. The Romans finally crushed the revolt in the summer of 135. Bar Kokhba and what remained of his army had abandoned Jerusalem and made a last stand at the fortress of Betar, which the Romans took after a siege, slaughtering those who remained, including Bar Kokhba.

Although the Romans reportedly suffered heavy casualties in crushing the revolt (one Roman unit—perhaps an entire legion—was decimated by being given poisoned wine), according to a Roman source the revolt claimed the deaths of 580,000 Jews in battle, while many more died of famine, disease, and the destruction of their habitats. Fifty fortified towns were razed, along with nearly 1,000 villages. Prisoners were sold into slavery.

Hadrian now set out to destroy Judaism. He caused the execution of Hebrew scholars and forbade practice of the Jewish faith. At the site of the former temple, he ordered erected a statue of Jupiter and another of himself. The name "Judea" was replaced with Syria Palaestina (for the enemy of the Jews, the Philistines). Jerusalem became Aelia Capitolina, and Jews were forbidden entrance except on the day of Tisha B'Av. Many scholars date the Jewish Diaspora from the aftermath of the revolt. The center of Judaism shifted to Babylon. Not until the modern era would Judea again be the center of Jewish life.

Spencer C. Tucker

See also Jewish Revolt against Rome

Further Reading

Faulkner, Neil. *Apocalypse: The Great Jewish Revolt against Rome.* Stroud, Gloucestershire, UK: Tempus, 2004.

Grant, Michael. *The Jews in the Roman World.* New York: Scribner, 1973.

Yadin, Yigael. *Bar-Kokhba: The Rediscovery of the Legendary Hero of the Second Jewish Revolt against Rome.* New York: Random House, 1971.

Basmachi Revolt

Start Date: 1916
End Date: 1934

A Muslim insurgency that began against Czarist Russia and continued with the Soviet Union. The Basmachi Revolt occurred in the Turkic region of Central Asia (today's Turkmenistan). The word "Basmachi" comes from the Turkish word *Basmak,* meaning "to plunder or violate. "

There had been a long history of unrest against Russian rule in the region, which saw land taken from the indigenous Turkic population and given to Russian settlers as well as the disruption of the region's typical nomad lifestyle. There was also religious tension between the Russian Orthodox Church and Islam, the religion of the region. Protests, riots, and occasional uprisings were not uncommon, and Pan-Turkish and Pan-Islamist ideologies spread, with opposition centered in the Fergana Valley in Turkestan.

The event that touched off the Basmachi Revolt was the conscription of Muslims into the Russian Army during World War I (1914–1918). At the end of June 1916, manpower shortages led the czarist government to rescind the exemption extended to Muslims from Russian military service, although the Muslim inductees were to be restricted to duty as labor troops, thus freeing others for combat. Compounding Muslim opposition to conscription was a provision in the decree permitting the wealthy to purchase substitutes.

The first demonstration occurred in Khojent on July 4, with protests quickly spreading to other parts of Turkestan. On July 11 in the course of a rally in Tashkent, the Russian police fired on the crowd, killing a number of people. This act initiated the Basmachi Revolt, which soon swept much of Turkestan and grew into calls for independence. The Russian government's response was to declare martial law. Still, widespread unrest continued.

After the Bolsheviks seized power in Russia in November 1917, they dissolved the autonomous Turkestan government at Kokand. In April 1918 they established the Turkestan Autonomous Soviet Socialist Republic (ASSR), with its capital at Tashkent. Many in the region came to view Bolshevism as a threat to their Islamic faith and also to the traditional tribal hierarchy. The Basmachi Revolt was reignited.

At peak strength the rebels probably numbered 20,000 men, but they lacked military training, were poorly armed, and were divided by tribal loyalties. With local Soviet forces unable to contain the insurgency, in December 1919 Mikhail Frunze took command of the Turkestan Red Army. He commenced an aggressive military offensive against the rebels in February 1920, inflicting several major defeats. Simultaneously, he conducted a population-centric campaign that included political, religious, and land reforms in an effort to separate the bulk of the population from the rebels.

Enver Pasha, the former Ottoman Empire minister of defense during World War I, arrived in Tashkent in September 1921. He briefly united the rebels and enjoyed early success. Suffering defeat in the Battle of Kafrun in June 1922, he was forced to retreat and was killed in August while leading a cavalry charge.

Selim Pasha, another militant, fought on until forced to retreat into Afghanistan (1923), while Basmachi general Sher Muhammad Bek was forced to flee into Afghanistan the next year. In October 1924 the Soviet government divided the Turkestan ASSR into the Turkmen Soviet Socialist Republic (SSR, now Turkmenistan), the Uzbek SSR (now Uzbekistan) with the Tajik ASSR (now Tajikistan), the Kara-Kirghiz Autonomous Oblast (now Kyrgyzstan), and the Karakalpak Autonomous Oblast (now Karakalpakstan).

From 1924 until the revolt finally ended in 1934, the Basmachi rebels conducted raids from sanctuaries in Iran, Afghanistan, and China. Soviet forces pursued the insurgents into Afghanistan, forcing the Afghans to take steps to prevent the raids in order to prevent Russian incursions. One such raid in 1929 saw Basmachi forces surround the Soviet garrison in Gharm in the Tajik ASSR. Soviet general Mikhail M. Tukhachevsky responded by airlifting in troops to relieve the garrison in what has been acclaimed as the first airborne assault in history.

By 1929, the Basmachi insurgents had been reduced to a maximum of several thousand. At the same time, the Soviets committed large number of troops, including some Islamic units, and Soviet general Semyon M. Budenny employed both artillery and aircraft against insurgent villages. In June 1931 Basmachi leader Ibrahim Bek was captured and executed. The last major combat occurred in October 1933 in the Karakum Desert when Soviet forces defeated Dzhunaid Khan, the former ruler of Kiva. Although the Basmachi revolt was at an end by 1934, sporadic violence continued thereafter.

Donald A. MacCuish and Spencer C. Tucker

See also Frunze, Mikhail Vasilyevich; Tukhachevsky, Mikhail Nikolayevich

Further Reading

Allworth, Edward, ed. *Central Asia.* 3rd ed. Durham, NC: Duke University Press, 1994.

Caroe, Olaf. *Soviet Empire: The Turks of Central Asia and Stalinism.* 2nd ed. London: Macmillan, 1967.

Olcott, Martha B. "The Basmachi or Freeman's Revolt in Turkestan 1918–24." *Soviet Studies* 33(3) (June 1981): 352–369.

Rywkin, Michael. *Moscow's Muslim Challenge: Soviet Central Asia.* Armonk, NY: M. E. Sharpe, 1990.

Batista y Zaldivar, Fulgencio

Birth Date: January 16, 1901
Death Date: August 6, 1973

Cuban president and dictator whose regime was overthrown in 1959 by insurgents led by Fidel Castro. Born in Banes, Cuba, on January 16, 1901, Fulgencio Batista y Zalvidar joined the army in 1921, eventually becoming a military stenographer. He was a leading figure in the so-called Sergeant's Revolt that deposed the Gerardo Machado dictatorship in 1933. During the short-lived Ramón Grau San Martín government (September 1933–January 1934), Batista was the army chief of staff and military strongman behind the scenes and was ultimately responsible for the collapse of the Grau government.

Batista was then the power behind the throne in a series of puppet governments during 1934–1940. In 1940, however, he was elected president, and his four-year term was noted for its progressive social reforms, links with the Communist Party, and support for the Allied side in World War II (1939–1945). Batista provided the United States with access to naval and air bases and sold to the United States nearly all of Cuba's sugar production.

Batista was succeeded by another democratically elected leader, Grau, whom Batista had helped overthrow in January 1934. The increasing corruption of the Grau government and its successor facilitated Batista's return to power in 1952.

In a widely welcomed move, in March 1952 Batista seized power in a blood-less coup. The new regime suspended the constitution and declared its loyalty to the United States. Batista now backed away from his earlier reformism and consolidated the anticommunist measures introduced by his predecessors. In the mid-1950s, with support from the U.S. Federal Bureau of Investigation, Batista established a repressive anticommunist political police force.

Batista's regime was marked by increasing corruption that alienated virtually all elements of Cuban society. Although in 1953 he easily crushed a revolt led by Fidel Castro, Castro returned to Cuba in December 1956 with a band of followers who established themselves in the Sierra Maestra of eastern Cuba. The unpopularity of Batista's regime, the ineffectiveness of its military, and the withdrawal of U.S. support led to Batista's fall at the end of 1958. On January 1, 1959, he fled Cuba for the Dominican Republic as Castro's forces closed in on Havana. Batista died on August 6, 1973, in Estoril, Portugal.

Barry Carr

See also Castro Ruz, Fidel Alejandro; Cuban Revolution

Further Reading

Gellman, Irving. *Roosevelt and Batista: Good Neighbor Diplomacy in Cuba, 1933–1945.* Albuquerque: University of New Mexico Press, 1973.

Morley, Morris. *Imperial State and Revolution: The United States and Cuba, 1952–1986.* Cambridge: Cambridge University Press, 1987.

Battle of Algiers

Written and directed by Gillo Pontecorvo, the film *The Battle of Algiers* treats the January–March 1957 battle of the same name during the Algerian War (1954–1962). Critically acclaimed and widely influential, the film is regarded as a major source in insurgency and counterinsurgency studies worldwide.

The film was inspired by *Souvenirs de la Bataille de Algiers,* the published campaign account of former Algiers Front de Liberation Nationale (FLN, National Liberation Front) military commander Saadi Yacef, who claimed to have written the book while imprisoned by the French. The Algerian government then com-missioned Italian director Pontecorvo to do the film. Shot in black and white with a newsreel-like documentary effect, it traces the increasing violence between the Muslim FLN insurgents and the pieds-noirs (European colonists who had settled in Algeria beginning in the 19th century), culminating in the introduction of Brigadier General Jacques Massu's 10th Colonial Parachute Division into the city to restore French control. The film details the systematic destruction of the FLN cells in Algiers through assassination and capture of their leaders, made possible by the army's use of murder and torture. The film ends with a coda showing celebrations of Algerian independence, making clear that while France may have won the Battle of Algiers, it lost the war.

First shown in Algeria in 1966, the film was banned in France until 1974, when it was released only in a cut version. The film has received numerous awards, although many French veterans of the Algerian War deplore its bias. *The Battle of Algiers* has been widely shown as a training film for military forces engaged in counterinsurgency operations in such countries as Argentina, Israel, and the United States.

Henri Alleg's book *La Question,* which first revealed the use of torture by the army, inspired a French film on the Battle of Algiers. Released in 1977 and also called *La Question,* the film was directed by Laurent Heynemann.

Spencer C. Tucker

See also Algerian War; Algiers, Battle of; Massu, Jacques Émile

Further Reading

Alleg, Henri. *La Question.* Paris: Éditions de Minuit, 1958.

Aussaresses, Paul. *The Battle of the Casbah: Terrorism and Counter-Terrorism in Algeria, 1955–1957.* New York: Enigma Books, 2010.

Begin, Menachem

Birth Date: August 16, 1913
Death Date: March 9, 1992

Zionist insurgent leader and subsequently prime minister of Israel. Born in Brest-Litovsk, Poland, on August 16, 1913, Menachem Begin attended Warsaw University, where he received a law degree in 1935. An ardent Zionist, Begin became active in the Revisionist Zionist Movement, headed by Ze'ev Jabotinsky, in Eastern Europe and then Palestine. Begin was involved in the East European resistance effort against the German occupation and helped various Zionist groups infiltrate British-controlled Palestine. After the German invasion of the Soviet Union in 1941, he joined the Polish Army, was posted to the Middle East, and wound up in Palestine.

In 1943 Begin assumed command of the militantly Zionist Irgun Tsvai Leumi (National Military Organization), known as Etzel for its contracted Hebrew initials but generally referred to as Irgun. Held by the British to be a terrorist organization, Irgun was known for its harsh retaliatory attacks following violence against the Jewish community and for its advocacy of military action against the British. On November 6, 1944, in Cairo, the terrorist Jewish group Lohamei Herut Israel (Lehi) assassinated British minister resident in the Middle East Walter Edward Guinness, Lord Moyne, allegedly in retaliation for the British 1939 White Paper's restrictions on Jewish immigration into Palestine that supposedly contributed to the deaths of Jews in the Holocaust. Then on July 22, 1946, Irgun bombed the British military, police, and civil headquarters at the King David Hotel in Jerusalem, killing 91 people. Begin and Irgun claimed to have issued three warnings in an attempt to limit casualties.

During the struggle that led to the establishment of Israel in 1948, Begin's militancy was at odds with mainstream Zionists headed by David Ben Gurion. Begin and his partisans established the Herut Party in 1948 to foster the Revisionist Zionist program for a Greater Israel that included territories east of the Jordan River. The Herut Party was later broadened to include other political sentiments opposed to Ben Gurion's so-called Labor Zionism. The party was renamed Likud in 1973.

Part of a National Unity Government in the mid-1960s, the Likud Party won a majority of seats in the Knesset (Israeli parliament) elections of 1977 and formed a government with Begin as prime minister that year. As prime minister, Begin actively promoted immigration to Israel, particularly from the Soviet Union and Ethiopia, and sought to move the Israeli economy away from the central-ized command-style policies of the Labor Party. Begin's six-year tenure as prime minister was marked by a number of important events. In addition to his economic restructuring agenda, he pursued a vigorous foreign policy.

Begin's foreign policy achievements began in 1977, when he participated in the groundbreaking Camp David peace talks with Egyptian president Anwar Sadat, sponsored by U.S. president Jimmy Carter. The talks led ultimately to the 1978 Camp David Accords, followed by a formal Israeli-Egyptian peace treaty, signed in 1979, that ended 30 years of war between the two nations. Begin and Sadat shared the 1978 Nobel Peace Prize for their work toward the Camp David Accords.

Despite his peace overtures, Begin did not hesitate to exercise Israeli military force. In 1981 he ordered an air attack against an Iraqi nuclear power plant near Osirak that destroyed the facility. He also ordered the Israeli military to retaliate against Palestinian terrorist attacks. The latter effort included sending Israeli forces into Lebanon in 1977 and 1982. Begin retired in September 1983 to his home in Yafeh Nof, near Jerusalem, and died in Tel Aviv on March 9, 1992.

Daniel E. Spector

See also Lohamei Herut Israel

Further Reading

Hirschler, Gertrude, and Lester S. Eckman. *Menachem Begin: From Freedom Fighter to Statesman.* New York: Shengold, 1979.

Quandt, William B. *Camp David: Peacemaking and Politics.* Washington, DC: Brookings Institution Press, 1986.

Silver, Eric. *Begin: The Haunted Prophet.* New York: Random House, 1984.

Bell, James Franklin

Birth Date: January 9, 1856
Death Date: January 8, 1919

U.S. Army officer, counterinsurgency tactician, and Medal of Honor recipient. James Franklin Bell was born on a farm near Shelbyville, Kentucky, on January 9, 1856. In 1878 he graduated with honors from the U.S. Military Academy, West Point, and was commissioned a second lieutenant. He served in the 9th and 7th Cavalry Regiments and took part in actions against Native Americans in the Dakota Territory. From 1882 to 1886, Bell trained troops at Fort Buford. From 1886 to 1889, he taught military science and tactics at the Southern Illinois Normal School (now Southern Illinois University), where he also earned a law degree. Promoted to first lieutenant in 1890, he was assigned to South Dakota in 1891 before taking a teaching position at the Cavalry and Light Artillery School at Fort Riley, Kansas. In 1894 Bell was transferred to California and then undertook garrison duty at Fort Apache, Arizona, before becoming judge advocate of the Department of the Columbia in 1898.

With the beginning of war with Spain in April 1898, Bell asked to be sent to Cuba but was instead ordered to the Philippines as a major of volunteers and an engineer officer to fight the Filipino insurrection. In June he became head of military information and was assigned to Manila to gather intelligence. Serving for a time as chief of scouts, in the war against the Filipino insurgents Bell sought to employ tactics that he had learned earlier while fighting Native Americans. In July 1899 he became colonel of the 36th Volunteer Infantry Regiment, fighting the insurgency in various parts of the Philippines. Later he was awarded the Medal of Honor for gallantry in charging a Filipino patrol and forcing its surrender in September 1899 near Porac, Luzon. Bell was appointed a brigadier general of volunteers in December 1899. The next year he became provost marshal of Manila.

In February 1901 Bell was promoted to brigadier general in the regular army while commanding the 1st District of the Department of Luzon and then the 3rd Brigade in Batangas. Here he uprooted some 10,000 Filipinos, resettling them into protective zones to deny their support of the insurgents, and ordered the destruction of crops, livestock, and buildings outside these areas. Although Bell was popular with his commanding officers, his tactics against the insurgents remain highly controversial for their uncompromising harshness, even brutality. He was accused of war crimes and even of planning a war of extermination and was the subject of a U.S. Senate investigation in 1902.

Transferred stateside, Bell became commandant of the Army Service and Staff College at Fort Leavenworth, Kansas, in 1902. He left that post to become chief of staff of the army during 1906–1910. Bell was appointed major general in January 1907. During this time, he oversaw the early development of army aviation and

San Francisco earthquake relief efforts. He also commanded the Army of Cuban Pacification in 1905.

Bell commanded the Department of the Philippines during 1911–1914. He subsequently led the 4th Division in Texas when war seemed possible with Mexico and then the Department of the West and, in 1917, the Department of the East, and in that capacity he was responsible for the first officer training camps. In August 1917 he took command of the 77th Division at Camp Upton. Sent as an observer to the Western Front during World War I (1914–1918) in December 1917, he returned in March 1918 but failed to pass the physical examination required of those being sent overseas and instead resumed command of the Department of the East, which he held until his death in New York City on January 8, 1919.

Gregory Ference

See also Philippine Islands and U.S. Pacification during the Philippine-American War

Further Reading

Gates, John M. *Schoolbooks and Krags: The United States Army in the Philippines, 1898–1902.* Westport, CT: Greenwood, 1973.

May, Glenn A. *Battle for Batanga: A Philippine Province at War.* New Haven, CT: Yale University Press, 1991.

Miller, Stuart Creighton. *"Benevolent Assimilation": The American Conquest of the Philippines, 1899–1903.* New Haven, CT: Yale University Press, 1982.

Ben Bella, Ahmed

Birth Date: December 25, 1916
Death Date: April 11, 2012

Algerian revolutionary leader and first president of Algeria. Ahmed Ben Bella was born in Maghnia in western Algeria on December 25, 1916. Algeria was then under French rule and was considered an integral part of France as three French departments. Nonetheless, the majority Muslim population did not enjoy equal rights with the Europeans.

Ben Bella attended school in Tlemcen but failed his brevet examination and dropped out of school. In 1936 he volunteered for the French Army, one of the few avenues of advancement available to Muslims. He saw combat in the Battle for France in May–June 1940 but was demobilized on the French defeat. He then joined a Moroccan regiment of the Free French forces and fought in the Italian Campaign, winning the Médaille militaire for his actions in the Battle of Monte Cassino. Offered a French Army commission, he declined it on learning of the French repression in Algeria following rioting at Sérif on May 8, 1945.

Returning to Algeria, Ben Bella became a founding member of the Organization Spéciale, formed to fight French colonial rule and predecessor to the Front de

Liberation Nationale (FLN, National Liberation Front). Arrested by the French authorities in 1951, he was sentenced to eight years in prison. Escaping from Blida Prison, he made his way to Tunisia before settling in Egypt, where he became the most important figure in the nine-man Revolutionary Committee of Unity and Action heading the FLN.

Emboldened by the French defeat in the Indochina War (1946–1954) and enjoying the support of Egyptian leader and Arab nationalist Gamal Abdel Nasser, the FLN began a military campaign against French rule in Algeria on the night of October 31–November 1, 1954, with a series of widespread attacks that inflicted little loss but took the French authorities by surprise. The revolt continued to grow, and by 1956 the bulk of the regular French Army had been transferred there.

On October 22, 1956, French authorities, acting with questionable legality, ordered the forcing down of an airliner carrying Ben Bella and took him prisoner. While imprisoned in France, he was elected a vice premier of the rebel Algerian provisional government. He was released upon Algerian independence in 1962.

Regarded by many Algerians as the father of their new nation and enjoying wide support among the Algerian armed forces, Ben Bella was elected president of Algeria on September 20, 1962. After directing fighting against Morocco, he worked to stabilize his new country and carried out land reform. Increasingly attracted to socialism, Ben Bella also proved to be an inept and authoritarian ruler who alienated many of his colleagues and supporters. On June 19, 1965, his close associate and war hero Colonel Houari Boumédiènne seized power in a near-bloodless coup d'état and on July 5 was installed as president. Ben Bella was placed under house arrest until 1980, when he was allowed to go into exile in Switzerland. He was permitted to return to Algeria in 1990 and died in Algiers on April 11, 2012.

Spencer C. Tucker

See also Algerian War; Front de Libération Nationale; Sétif Uprising

Further Reading

Horne, Alistair. *A Savage War of Peace: Algeria, 1954–1962.* New York: Viking, 1977.

Talbott, John. *The War without a Name: France in Algeria, 1954–1962.* New York: Knopf, 1980.

Benevolent Assimilation

Benevolent assimilation refers to the rationale for the annexation of the Philippine Islands by the United States following the Spanish-American War. On December 21, 1898, just 11 days after the signing of the Treaty of Paris that ended the Spanish-American War, U.S. president William McKinley issued a proclamation that formally asserted American control over the islands. In his proclamation, McKinley attempted to assure Filipinos, Americans, and the larger world that the United States would rule the islands with beneficence.

The declaration read in part:

Finally, it should be the earnest wish and paramount aim of the military administration to win the confidence, respect, and affection of the inhabitants of the Philippines by assuring them in every possible way that full measure of individual rights and liberties which is the heritage of free peoples, and by proving to them that the mission of the United States is one of benevolent assimilation substituting the mild sway of justice and right for arbitrary rule.

Just as McKinley had used benevolent assimilation to usher through Congress the annexation of Hawaii on July 7, 1898, he would use it to win the debate to annex the Philippines, Puerto Rico, and Guam. Benevolent assimilation asserted that American control of overseas possessions would be different—and more enlightened—than European-style imperial rule. On the whole, Americans were reluctant to assume the mantle of a colonial power, so the notion of a benevolent colonial lordship enabled McKinley to combat opponents of annexation and sell his idea to the American public. The notion of benevolent assimilation further enabled the president to show the world how different the United States was from its European rivals. U.S. colonial policies were not designed to exploit the lands under its control but instead were designed to bring colonial inhabitants the blessings of liberty. U.S. control would also result in the education of the natives, gradually transforming them into productive citizens who would be steeped in American values.

McKinley sent the proclamation on to Major General Elwell Otis, U.S. commander in the Philippines. Otis in turn sent a doctored version to Filipino nationalist leader Emilio Aguinaldo y Famy, who had established a nationalist government and then proclaimed Philippine independence on June 12, 1898. Among changes that Otis made in the original declaration was the substitution of "free people" for "supremacy of the United States." Aguinaldo, however, soon secured the original version.

In the end, rhetoric notwithstanding, benevolent assimilation was predicated upon traditional U.S. expansionism and American exceptionalism augmented by paternalism, racism, social Darwinism, and the prevailing ideologies of colonialism and imperialism.

Rick Dyson

See also Aguinaldo y Famy, Emilio

Further Reading

Brands, H. W. *Bound to Empire: The United States and the Philippines*. New York: Oxford University Press, 1992.

Kramer, Paul. *The Blood of Government: Race, Empire, the United States, and the Philippines*. Chapel Hill: University of North Carolina Press, 2006.

Miller, Stuart Creighton. *"Benevolent Assimilation": The American Conquest of the Philippines, 1899–1903.* 4th ed. New Haven, CT: Yale University Press, 1982.

Betancourt, Rómulo

Birth Date: February 22, 1908
Death Date: September 28, 1981

Venezuelan politician, provisional president, and president. Born into a modest family in Guatire, Miranda, on February 22, 1908, Rómulo Betancourt became involved in politics while attending the University of Caracas, leading student protests against the dictatorship of Juan Vicente Gómez. Arrested in 1928 but released after several weeks in jail, Betancourt was exiled to Costa Rica until Gómez's death in 1935.

A founder of the Costa Rican Communist Party, Betancourt became an admirer of the New Deal policies of U.S. president Franklin D. Roosevelt after pragmatism and nationalism led Betancourt to renounce dogmatic, Moscow-directed communism. In September 1941 he helped establish Acción Democrática (Democratic Action), a left-wing anticommunist party that came to power in Venezuela's October Revolution of 1945. Appointed provisional president, Betancourt established a new constitution and initiated a program of moderate social reforms. He handed power over to a democratically elected president in 1948, but a coup a few months later led by General Marcos Pérez Jiménez again forced Betancourt into exile. He spent the next decade abroad directing the outlawed Acción Democrática.

After Jiménez was overthrown in 1958, Betancourt returned to Venezuela and was elected president in 1959. His reformist administration passed an agrarian reform law to expropriate large estates, initiated public works programs, and fostered industrial development to reduce dependence on petroleum reserves. Betancourt exercised greater control over foreign-dominated petroleum companies, increased government tax revenue from oil production, and supported the formation of the Organization of Petroleum Exporting Countries (OPEC).

Betancourt adopted a policy of nonrecognition of undemocratic governments. He also praised President John F. Kennedy's Alliance for Progress and supported U.S. efforts to isolate Fidel Castro's Cuba. Beleaguered by forces from both the Left and the Right, Betancourt played a key role in suppressing the 1963–1965 armed insurgency by leftist admirers of the Cuban Revolution known as the Movimiento de Izquierda Revolucionaria (MIR, Movement of the Revolutionary Left), which adopted the foco method of insurgency in which small groups of guerrillas engaged security forces in the hopes that this would result in repressive government measures that would then cause the people to turn against the government and bring the insurgents to power. Betancourt also countered rightist military uprisings led by the Frente de Liberación Nacional (FLN, National Liberation Front), formed of former MIR adherents and disaffected members of the military, and he survived an assassination attempt planned by Dominican dictator Rafael Trujillo.

After his presidential term ended in 1964, Betancourt became the first Venezuelan in history to hold the presidency by a legitimate election and to relinquish the office to a popularly elected successor. He lived for eight years in Switzerland before returning to Venezuela in 1972. Betancourt died in New York City on September 28, 1981.

David M. Carletta

See also Foco Theory; Venezuelan Insurgency

Further Reading

Alexander, Robert J. *Rómulo Betancourt and the Transformation of Venezuela.* New Brunswick, NJ: Transaction, 1982.

Dávila, Luis Ricardo. "Rómulo Betancourt and the Development of Venezuelan Nationalism, 1930–1945." *Bulletin of Latin American Research* 12(1) (January 1993): 49–63.

Schwartzberg, Steven. "Rómulo Betancourt: From a Communist Anti-Imperialist to a Social Democrat with U.S. Support." *Journal of Latin American Studies* 29(3) (October 1997): 613–665.

Bifurcation

Bifurcation means the splitting of a body into two parts. In military terms, bifurcation means the division in outlook within an army between career soldiers and conscripts. Among prominent examples in the 20th century are the French Army during the Algerian War (1954–1962), the Portuguese Army in Africa (1961–1974), and the U.S. Army in Vietnam (1965–1873). French Army conscripts did not serve in Southeast Asian during the Indochina War (1946–1954). When conscripts were dispatched to Algeria in the fighting there, the regulars assumed that they shared their own determination that Algeria remain part of France. They did not. As it worked out, the elite professional units did most of the fighting, and it was they and not the conscripts who supported failed efforts to topple the Fifth Republic when it moved toward Algerian independence.

During the fighting by the Portuguese Army against nationalist movements in Angola, Portuguese Guinea, and Mozambique, a division developed between the regulars and conscripts. The former did most of the fighting, while the latter were restricted to garrison duties and hearts-and-minds activities, such as building roads and schools. Meanwhile, expansion of the army led to the introduction of many young university graduates as officers and their rapid promotion to encourage them to remain in the military. A division developed between them and the older professionals over the efficacy of the wars themselves. The younger officers formed the Movimento das Forças Armadas (MFA, Armed Forces Movement) and were responsible for the Carnation Revolution of April 25, 1974, that toppled the Portuguese government and led to the independence of the nation's overseas territories.

In contrast to the French and Portuguese experiences, draftees did most of the U.S. Army fighting during the Vietnam War and suffered most of its casualties. This helped create major morale problems and led to increased insubordination and drug use as well as a general questioning of the war.

The lesson to be drawn here is that it is far better for a country to combat an insurgency with professional soldiers rather than conscripts.

Spencer C. Tucker

See also Algerian War; Angolan Insurgency; Hearts and Minds; Mozambique Insurgency; Vietnam War

Further Reading

Paret, Peter. *French Revolutionary Warfare from Indochina to Algeria: The Analysis of a Political and Military Doctrine.* New York: Praeger, 1964.

Porch, Douglas. *The Portuguese Armed Forces and the Revolution.* Stanford, CA: Hoover Institution Press, 1977.

Shafer, D. Michael. *Deadly Paradigms: The Failure of U.S. Counterinsurgency Policy.* Princeton, NJ: Princeton University Press, 1988.

Bigeard, Marcel

Birth Date: February 14, 1916
Death Date: June 18, 2010

French Army officer, one of the most decorated soldiers in French history, and a leading figure in French unconventional warfare. Born in Toul, Meurthe-et-Moselle, France, on February 14, 1916, Marcel "Bruno" Bigeard enlisted in the army as a private in 1936. In June 1940 he was captured by the Germans and sent to a prisoner-of-war camp. He escaped and made his way to Africa, where he joined the Free French and was commissioned a second lieutenant. Subsequently, he parachuted into occupied France to lead the Resistance in the Ariège, using the call sign "Bruno," the nickname by which he would be known the rest of his life.

In October 1945, Bigeard was sent to Indochina. Initially assigned to command a colonial infantry battalion, he subsequently volunteered to train Thai auxiliaries for operations against the Viet Minh along the Laotian border. During a second tour, which began in 1948, Bigeard served with the 3rd Colonial Parachute Regiment in the northern Tonkin Highlands.

In mid-1952 Bigeard returned to Indochina as commander of the 6th Colonial Parachute Battalion. During the next two years, he established a name for himself and for his unit because of what he demanded of his men, his unit's operational performance, and his panache and ability to generate publicity.

Bigeard figured prominently in the later stages of the Battle of Dien Bien Phu. He coordinated counterattacks and achieved one of the few French successes in the battle. Promoted to lieutenant colonel for his efforts, Bigeard was a prisoner of war for three months before his repatriation by the Viet Minh.

Within a year Bigeard was sent to Algeria, where he took on command of the 3rd Colonial Parachute Regiment, which he trained using the same grueling regimen of the 6th Colonial Parachute Battalion in Indochina. His regiment registered considerable success, notably during the 1957 Battle of Algiers in which the regiment was responsible for destroying the Front de Libération Nationale (FLN, National Liberation Front) organization in the Casbah and during operations later that year in the Atlas Mountains.

Bigeard's success was largely due to his leading from the front, his iron will and determination to ask no more from his men than he demanded of himself, his intuitive mastery of terrain, and his adoption of several innovative counterinsurgency techniques, to include *quadrillage* (surveillance through use of a grid pattern) and intense interrogation of suspects that sometimes included torture, which was approved by his superiors. Bigeard would later state that under the circumstances, torture had been a "necessary evil." Many of these techniques were later detailed by Roger Trinquier, Bigeard's successor as commander of the 3rd Colonial Parachute Regiment, in his classic work *Modern Warfare.*

Bigeard did not participate in the failed Algerian officers' putsch of 1961. Promoted to brigadier general in 1967, he assumed command of French ground forces in Dakar, Senegal, and then commanded French forces in the Indian Ocean territory. From 1975 to 1976, when he retired from the army as a lieutenant general, he was state secretary in the Ministry of Defense. From 1978 to 1988, Bigeard represented the Meurthe-et-Moselle region in the National Assembly. A prolific author, he wrote more than a dozen books on his experiences. Bigeard died at Toul on June 18, 2010.

George M. Brooke III

See also Algerian War; Algiers, Battle of; Indochina War

Further Reading

Bigeard, Marcel Maurice. *Ma Guerre de l'Algérie* [My Algerian War]. Paris: Hachette, 1995.

Horne, Alistair. *A Savage War of Peace.* New York: Viking Penguin, 1987.

Trinquier, Roger. *Modern Warfare.* New York: Praeger, 1964.

Windrow, Martin. *The Last Valley.* Cambridge, MA: Da Capo, 2004.

Black and Tans and the Auxiliaries

Ex-servicemen recruited to supplement the Royal Irish Constabulary (RIC) and regular army units during the Anglo-Irish War (1919–1921), also known as the

Irish War of Independence. The conflict, largely a guerrilla-style war, pitted the Irish Republican Army (IRA) against the British government and its forces in Ireland.

Until 1918, the RIC had maintained law and order in Ireland, backed up by small garrisons of British Army troops. Michael Collins, a top military leader in the IRA, directed IRA forces to target members of the RIC early in the Anglo-Irish War. Intimidation and, should that not work, assassination were employed to lower the morale of the RIC. This guerrilla-style warfare led to mass resignations from the force. Unwilling to deploy additional army units to Ireland, British authorities searched elsewhere to make up this loss of manpower.

The idea of recruiting demobilized World War I (1914–1918) soldiers to combat the IRA was suggested by Field Marshal Earl French in May 1919, but recruiting did not begin until the end of the year. A further lack of preparation meant that enlistees were issued a combination of surplus khaki and RIC bottle-green uniforms. The mix of trousers and tunics earned them the name "Black and Tans." While the origins of the name are not entirely clear, it seems to have been first given to a famous pack of hounds from a Limerick hunt. Tellingly, those who experienced Black and Tan ruthlessness often referred to the 1919–1921 conflict as simply the Tan War.

In July 1920, recruitment began for what was officially known as the Auxiliary Division of the RIC. Although often thought to be one and the same, the Auxiliaries and Tans were separate forces. Among other things, only former military officers were eligible to serve in Auxiliary companies. Irish claims that the Tans and Auxiliaries were recruited from English prisons were untrue. Many in fact had been decorated for gallantry during World War I; three had been awarded the Victoria Cross. It is probable that some of these men had been psychologically scarred by their experiences in the trenches, which in any case was not the best preparation for combating guerrilla fighters. At the same time, there was often friction with the regular army, which seldom had authority over these self-contained forces.

While the Tans and Auxiliaries were not criminals, they soon earned a fearsome reputation. A policy of unofficial reprisals, followed by officially sanctioned reprisals, linked them to some of the worst incidents of the war, including Bloody Sunday on November 21, 1920, during which 31 people died, among them 14 Irish civilians. After the sack of Cork City on December 11–12, 1920, one Auxiliary admitted that in all his life he had "never experienced such orgies of murder, arson, and looting."

Even though critics pointed out that reprisals were ultimately self-defeating, a truce was not declared until July 1921. In the meantime, public opinion in both Ireland and Britain had turned against the Black and Tans and the Auxiliaries.

In total, about 7,000 Black and Tans and Auxiliary forces served in Ireland. No further recruits were sought for either force after July 1921, and the first Tan and Auxiliary units were withdrawn from Ireland in October 1921. The RIC was disbanded the following year.

C. Kevin Matthews

See also Collins, Michael; Ireland Revolutionary Era; Irish Republican Army

Further Reading

Bennett, Richard. *The Black and Tans.* Boston: Houghton Mifflin, 1960.

Cottrell, Peter. *The Anglo-Irish War: The Troubles, 1913–23.* Oxford, UK: Osprey, 2006.

Hart, Peter. *The IRA at War, 1916–1923.* Oxford: Oxford University Press, 2003.

Hopkinson, Michael. *The Irish War of Independence.* Montreal: McGill-Queen's University Press, 2002.

Black Hawk War

Event Date: 1832

Conflict fought between factions of the Sauk (Sac) and Fox (Mesquakie) people and the United States. The fighting occurred throughout northern Illinois and southern Wisconsin. As with most Native American wars, the root cause of the Black Hawk War was land, particularly disputes that arose from the Treaty of 1804.

The Algonquian-speaking Sauk and Fox tribes had originally lived near the St. Lawrence River, but with the arrival of European settlers, the tribes were slowly forced south and west to territory in Illinois and Wisconsin. During the French and Indian War (1754–1763), many had fought with the British, presuming that the British government would then protect their land from encroachment. This of course did not occur, and the outcome of the American Revolutionary War (1775–1783) ensured American dominance of the area.

Almost immediately after American independence, pressure from settlers on the tribal lands grew. The Northwest Ordinance of 1787 even went so far as to devise a scheme for dividing up the lands without Native American consent. Tensions between the tribes and white settlers steadily increased. Repeated attempts by the U.S. government to negotiate a treaty that called for the Sauks and Foxes to vacate the land were rebuffed.

Pressure mounted for the U.S. government to remove the Sauks and Foxes from their lands between the Appalachian Mountains and the Mississippi River. At the same time, conflict between the Sauks and Foxes and the Osage tribe heightened tensions between the Sauk and Fox tribes and the United States. The Osages had signed a treaty with the U.S. government that frustrated the Sauks and Foxes, who sought war against their longtime enemy. Older members of the tribes, however, sought to alleviate tensions between themselves and the settlers and secure peace with the U.S. government. They reasoned that this would strengthen the tribes in relation to their Native American rivals and would secure American-made goods.

In 1804 a delegation of Sauk and Fox leaders traveled to St. Louis to negotiate for the release of captured warriors, make amends for attacks on white settlers, and secure American goods and arms. Coincidentally, William Henry Harrison, governor of the Indiana Territory, was in St. Louis. The lands occupied by the Sauks and Foxes fell within Harrison's jurisdiction, and he sought to remove the tribes from their land. Little is known about the treaty negotiations except that at the end of the talks, the Sauk and Fox diplomats agreed to vacate all lands east of the Mississippi River for a modest sum of money. They were supposed to move into present-day Iowa.

The 1804 treaty was immediately repudiated by a number of the tribal elders and young leaders, however. They argued that the delegation had not been authorized to cede territory. Most Sauks and Foxes remained on their lands and refused to relocate west of the Mississippi. One of the more vocal opponents of the treaty was young chief Black Hawk.

Following the War of 1812 in which the Sauks and Foxes backed the British, the U.S. government began to press the two tribes to move across the Mississippi to Iowa. Black Hawk refused to leave. However, a growing faction of the tribe under the leadership of Keokuk, a rival of Black Hawk, came to the conclusion that moving across the river was the best thing for the tribe, and in 1829 Keokuk and a significant portion of the tribe did so. Black Hawk and his followers remained near present-day Rock Island, Illinois, vowing to resist any attempts to move them.

Black Hawk mistakenly believed that the British would aid him in his fight with the Americans. In 1831 he and his followers were forced off their land by Illinois militiamen and into Iowa, where they took up residence with Keokuk's band. However, in 1832 Black Hawk led some 400 warriors and their families back into Illinois, hoping to join the Rock River Winnebago tribe and settle in the region. The Illinois Militia and federal troops pursued Black Hawk and his followers across northern Illinois.

The Black Hawk War was short but bloody, and Native American forces scored a stunning victory in the Battle of Stillman's Run (May 14, 1832), routing a contingent of the Illinois Militia. However, the war soon turned against Black Hawk, who was soundly defeated at the mouth of the Bad Axe River in southern Wisconsin on August 2, 1832. As many as 150 Native Americans died in this battle, while some 75 were captured, including Black Hawk, who was imprisoned. A subsequent treaty between the Sauks and Foxes and the United States, signed on September 21, 1832, forced the Sauks and Foxes to cede much of their lands in Iowa.

Rick Dyson

See also American Indian Wars in the West

Further Reading

Black Hawk. *Black Hawk: An Autobiography.* Edited by Donald Jackson. Urbana: University of Illinois Press, 1964.

Jung, Patrick J. *The Black Hawk War of 1832.* Norman: University of Oklahoma Press, 2007.

Trask, Kerry A. *Black Hawk: The Battle for the Heart of America.* New York: Holt, 2006.

Wallace, Anthony F. C. "Prelude to Disaster: The Course of Indian-White Relations Which Led to the Black Hawk War of 1832." *Wisconsin Magazine of History* 65 (1982): 247–288.

Boer War, Second.

See South African War

Bolívar, Simón

Birth Date: July 24, 1783
Death Date: December 17, 1830

South American revolutionary leader, general, and liberator. Born into a wealthy family in Caracas, Venezuela, on July 24, 1783, Simón Bolívar was orphaned at age six and raised by an uncle and educated by tutors. Bolívar traveled to Spain in 1799 to complete his education and there married a young Spanish noblewoman in 1802. The next year he returned with his wife to Venezuela, where she died of yellow fever. Bolívar traveled to Spain in 1804. After visiting France, he returned to Venezuela in 1807.

Napoleon Bonaparte's removal of the Bourbons from the Spanish throne in 1808 brought upheaval to the Spanish colonies in Latin America, and Bolívar joined the Latin American movement seeking independence. Dispatched on a diplomatic mission to Britain by the Venezuelan Junta in 1810, he was unable to secure assistance and returned to Venezuela in March 1811 with Francesco Miranda, who had led an unsuccessful revolution in Venezuela in 1806. Bolívar joined the army of the new republic (declared on July 5, 1811) and commanded the fortress of Porto Cabello. But when Miranda was forced to surrender to the Spanish in July, Bolívar fled to Cartagena de Indias.

South American revolutionary leader Simón Bolívar was the most influential figure in the liberation from Spanish rule of Venezuela, Colombia, Ecuador, Peru, and Bolivia. (Library of Congress)

Securing a military command in New Grenada (now Colombia), Bolívar led an invasion of Venezuela in May 1813 and defeated the Spanish in six hard-fought battles, known as the Campaña Admirable. He entered Mérida on May 23 and was proclaimed El Liberador. Bolívar took Caracas (August 6) and was confirmed as El Liberador.

Civil war soon broke out. Bolívar won a series of battles but was defeated at La Puerta (June 15, 1814) and forced to flee to New Grenada. Gaining control of forces there, he liberated Bogotá only to be defeated by Spanish troops at Santa Maria and forced into exile in Jamaica in 1815. There he requested and received assistance from Haitian leader Alexandre Pétion in return for a promise to free the slaves.

Returning to Venezuela in December 1816, Bolívar fought a series of battles but was again defeated at La Puerta (March 15, 1818). Withdrawing into the Orinoco region, he raised a new force. Joined by several thousand British and Irish volunteers who were veterans of the Napoleonic Wars (1803–1815) and linking up with other revolutionary forces, Bolívar crossed the Andes by the Pisba Pass and caught Spanish forces by surprise, winning the important Battle of Boyacá (June 11, 1819) and taking Bogatá (August 10).

On the creation in September 1821 of Gran Colombia, a federation comprising much of present-day Venezuela, Colombia, Panama, and Ecuador, Bolívar became its president. Victories over the Spanish in the Battle of Carabobo (June 25, 1821) and the Battle of Pichincha (May 24, 1822) consolidated his authority in Venezuela and Ecuador.

In September 1823 Bolívar arrived in Lima to raise a new army. In the Battle of Junín (August 6, 1824) he defeated Royalist forces and then departed to liberate Upper Peru, which was renamed Bolivia by its people. Bolívar wrote the new state's constitution, which provided for a republican form of government with a strong presidency. Bolívar's subsequent efforts to bring about Latin American unity were unsuccessful. Disheartened by the secession of Venezuela from the Gran Colombia in 1829, Bolívar, now in failing health, resigned his presidency on April 27, 1830. Intending to travel to Europe, he died near Santa Marta, Colombia, of tuberculosis on December 17, 1830.

Tenacious, bold, and resourceful, Bolívar was a great motivator of men. He was a staunch republican who favored limited government, property rights, and the rule of law. Not a brilliant tactician as a general, he was more important as an inspirational leader. Credited with having led the fight for the independence of the present nations of Venezuela, Colombia, Ecuador, Panama, and Bolivia, Bolívar was disappointed in his efforts to achieve continental unity. He is today regarded as one of Latin America's greatest heroes.

Spencer C. Tucker

See also San Martín, José Francisco de

Further Reading

Bolívar, Simón. *El Libertador: The Writings of Simón Bolívar.* Edited by David Bushnell. Translated by Frederick H. Fornoff. New York: Oxford University Press, 2003.

Lynch, John. *Simón Bolívar: A Life*. New Haven, CT: Yale University Press, 2006.

Masur, Gerhard. *Simon Bolivar.* Albuquerque: University of New Mexico Press, 1948.

Borneo Insurgency.

See Indonesia-Malaysia Confrontation

Bosnia-Herzegovina

The 18th century saw the continued decline of the Ottoman Empire, regarded by many as "the Sick Man of Europe." The empire suffered military reversals, outbursts of plague, growing hostility for the lack of meaningful progress toward reforms that would benefit the bulk of the population, and revolts, including a peasant rebellion in 1875. Unrest in the Balkans ultimately led to wider war between the Balkan states and the Ottoman Empire that ultimately involved Russia. Before that occurred, in July 1876 Austro-Hungarian ruler Emperor Franz Joseph met with Russian czar Alexander II at Reichstadt and secured a pledge from the czar that if Russia intervened militarily in the Balkans and territorial changes resulted, Austria-Hungary would receive the Ottoman territory of Bosnia-Herzegovina.

Following victory by the Russian and allied Balkan states over the Ottoman Empire in the Russo-Turkish War of 1877–1878, however, Russia imposed a harsh peace on the Ottoman Empire in the Treaty of San Stefano in March 1878 that completely ignored the pledge made to Franz Joseph. Bosnia and Herzegovina were to receive a measure of autonomy in the interests of their Christian subjects, but nothing was said about handing these provinces over to Austria-Hungary.

With most of the rest of Europe opposed to the Treaty of San Stefano that so favored Russian interests and indeed threatened war, Russia agreed to an international conference to discuss the Balkans. The ensuing Congress of Berlin of June–July 1878 undid the Treaty of San Stefano. Among the decisions of the conference were that Austria-Hungary gained the right to occupy and administer but not annex Bosnia and Herzegovina. The Dual Monarchy immediately dispatched troops.

Four imperial divisions of 72,000 troops crossed into Bosnia and Herzegovina on July 31, 1878. Roman Catholics welcomed the occupation, while Muslims deplored it. In Sarajevo, Muslims overthrew the Ottoman authorities, seized munitions, and organized guerrilla resistance. Of 41 Ottoman battalions stationed in Bosnia in the summer of 1878, 30 consisted of Muslim conscripts who were prepared to fight for their homeland against the "Christian occupier." Austro-Hungarian forces found themselves contending with a classic guerrilla campaign of raids and sniping. Although Sarajevo was conquered in house-to-house fighting in August 1878, resistance continued in the countryside. Victory in November 1878 required some 250,000 Austro-Hungarian troops, about a third of the total combat strength of the Dual Monarchy, although there were uprisings after that date.

The Austro-Hungarians did pacify Bosnia. Vienna invested in infrastructure and built more than 600 miles of railroads as well as new roads and bridges. Industrial development also proceeded, in forestry, mining, steelworks, chemical factories, and agribusinesses. As part of this development, the Austrians also built many secular schools that taught modern subjects. Previously, education had been only in religious schools. Attendance initially was voluntary, but after 1909 it was made compulsory. Thanks to this education, however, many Bosnian youths became well versed in the nationalistic, socialistic, and anarchist philosophies sweeping Europe at the time.

Spencer C. Tucker

See also Insurgency

Further Reading

Okey, Robin. *Taming Balkan Nationalism: The Habsburg 'Civilizing' Mission in Bosnia, 1878–1914*. Oxford: Oxford University Press, 2007.

Phillips, Douglas A. *Bosnia and Herzegovina*. Philadelphia: Chelsea House, 2004.

Boudica

Birth Date: ca. 25 CE
Death Date: ca. 60–61 CE

Boudica (alternate spellings Boudicca, Boadicea, and, in Welsh, Buddug) was queen of the Iceni tribe in Britain and leader of an insurgency against the Romans. The absence of native British literature in this period means that knowledge of Boudica and her rebellion against Rome relies entirely on the writings of Roman historians. Boudica was apparently not of the Iceni tribe, although she was of royal descent. Roman sources describe her as highly intelligent, tall, and with long reddish-brown hair that came to her waist. The name "Boudica" is derived from the Celtic and apparently means "victory." The closest English name would probably be Victoria.

Sometime between 43 and 45 CE, Boudica was married to Prasutagus, king of the Icenis, a Celtic tribe located in East Anglia in southern Britain. Emperor Claudius and his Roman army conquered large areas of Britain in 43. Although the Icenis were somewhat isolated geographically, Prasutagus understood the realities of Roman power and thus traveled to Camulodunum (today Colchester in Essex) and agreed to ally with Rome as a client king. Although subject to Roman authority, the Icenis were thus able to maintain their culture. Prasutagus had no male heirs, and his will provided that on his death, the kingdom would go jointly to his daughters and the Roman emperor (Nero). But when Prasutagus died in 60 CE his will was ignored, as Roman law did not permit inheritance in the royal inheritance by females. The kingdom was annexed as if conquered, the royal kinsmen were enslaved, and Boudica was flogged and forced to watch her daughters, then reportedly about 12 years old, being raped.

In 60 or 61 while Roman governor Gaius Suetonius Paulinus was leading a military operation on the island of Anglesey in northern Wales, Boudica led the

Icenis in revolt, it not being unusual in Celtic society for women to occupy positions of power and influence. The indigenous peoples had suffered heavily under Roman rule, and the erection of a temple in Camulodunum (today Colchester) to Emperor Claudius, who had conquered the Celts and destroyed much of their culture, and the Roman attack on the Druid religion caused other tribes, among them the Trinovantes, to join the revolt. The insurgents destroyed Camulodunum, formerly the Trinovante capital, and routed the IX Hispana Legion, sent to relieve Camulodunum, probably at today's village of Great Wratting in Suffolk.

Learning of the revolt, Suetonius proceeded to the Roman commercial settlement of Londinium (London), the rebels' next target. Concluding that he lacked the numbers to defend it, Suetonius evacuated Londinium. The rebels burned it to the ground and killed all those who had not evacuated earlier. The same process occurred at Verulamium (St. Albans). Tens of thousands of people were reported killed in the three Roman settlements.

Suetonius meanwhile regrouped his forces in the West Midlands and, despite being heavily outnumbered, employed superior training and maneuverability, body armor (which the Celts lacked), and discipline to defeat and then massacre the Celts in the critical Battle of Watling Street. According to the Roman historian Tacitus, almost 80,000 Celts fell in the battle. Emperor Nero had been considering withdrawing Roman forces from the island, but Suetonius's victory secured Roman control of the province. Boudica escaped from the battle and returned to her kingdom, where she committed suicide or fell ill and died. Boudica remains an important cultural symbol in the United Kingdom.

Spencer C. Tucker

Further Reading

Collingridge, Vanessa. *Boudica.* London: Ebury, 2004.

Hingley, Richard, and Christina Unwin. *Boudica: Iron Age Warrior Queen.* London: Hambledon Continuum, 2004.

Roesch, Joseph E. *Boudica, Queen of the Iceni.* London: Robert Hale, 2006.

Tacitus, Cornelius. *The Annals of Imperial Rome.* Translated by Michael Grant. London: Penguin, 1989.

Webster, Graham. *Boudica: The British Revolt against Rome, AD 60.* London: Routledge, 2000.

Briggs, Sir Harold Rawdon

Birth Date: July 14, 1894
Death Date: October 27, 1952

British Army general and director of operations during the Malayan Emergency (1948–1960). Born in the United States on July 14, 1894, Harold Rawdon Briggs and his brother Rawdon, also a future British general, were by 1901 living with their widowed mother in Bedford, England. Harold Briggs attended the Bedford School and then the Royal Military College, Sandhurst. He was commissioned in the (British) Indian Army in 1914 and was assigned to the King's Regiment. In 1915 he joined the 31st Punjab Regiment. During World War I (1914–1918), he fought against the Germans in France and the Ottomans in Mesopotamia and Palestine.

In 1923 Briggs transferred to the 10th Baluch Regiment, serving with it in the North West Frontier of India and taking part in the 1930 Waziristan Campaign. Briggs was promoted to major in 1932 and to lieutenant colonel in 1937, when he assumed command of the 2nd Battalion of the 10th Baluch Regiment.

In September 1940 Briggs was promoted to brigadier and given command of the 7th Indian Infantry Brigade, with which he campaigned in East Africa and the Western Desert during 1940–1942, winning two Distinguished Service Orders (DSOs). In May 1942 Briggs assumed command of the 5th Indian Division and fought with it in a number of Western Desert battles. In Autumn 1942 the division was ordered to Persia (present-day Iran) and then in early 1944 to Burma (present-day Myanmar). Briggs was made a commander of the British Empire in May 1945 for his Burma service. In July he received substantive promotion to major general. In May 1946 Briggs was promoted to lieutenant general and made commander in chief, Burma Command. He retired in January 1948 and settled in Cyprus.

In 1950, chief of the Imperial General Staff Field Marshal Sir William Slim, under whom Briggs had served in Burma, recalled Briggs to active duty and appointed him director of operations, Federation of Malaya. Briggs arrived in April. The Malayan Emergency was then in progress, and the fighting was going badly for the British, with the Malayan Communist Party (MCP) seemingly having the upper hand. Briggs drew on his extensive experience in Burma and knowledge of jungle warfare. He understood the need to eliminate the Min Yuen, the political organization of the MCP, as well as the need to defeat the MCP's military organization of the Malayan Races Liberation Army (MRLA). His Briggs Plan was centered on protection of the civilian population, isolating it from the insurgents, and winning its loyalty.

Briggs insisted on close cooperation between the civilian and military authorities and created an elaborate committee structure. He also initiated a resettlement program, moving Chinese squatters, the segment of the population most susceptible to MCP influence, into new villages with schools and medical services, along with plots of land to which they could receive eventual title. Briggs also forced owners of rubber plantations and tin mines to group their workers in supervised camps, and he introduced strict controls on movement through identity cards, restrictions on food supplies out of the new villages, and curfews. Emergency decrees provided for the death sentence in some cases of terrorism. The MRLA was increasingly cut off from the civilian population on which it relied and was forced deeper into the jungles.

The MRLA realized the threat that these measures posed and initiated a series of attacks on the new villages. While there was heavy fighting during 1951–1952,

Briggs had laid the foundation for the ultimate British victory. He did not live to see this. Forced to retire for health reasons in December 1951, he died in Cyprus on October 27, 1952.

Spencer C. Tucker

See also Malayan Emergency; Templer, Sir Gerald Walter Robert

Further Reading

Beckett, Ian F. W. *Encyclopedia of Guerrilla Warfare.* Santa Barbara, CA: ABC-CLIO, 1999.

Short, Anthony. *The Communist Insurrection in Malaya, 1948–1960.* London: Muller, 1975.

Stubbs, Richard. *Hearts and Minds in Guerrilla Warfare: The Malayan Insurgency, 1948–1960.* New York: Oxford University Press, 1989.

Broz, Josip.

See Tito

Brunei Insurgency.

See Indonesia-Malaysia Confrontation

Bugeaud de la Piconnerie, Thomas Robert

Birth Date: October 15, 1784
Death Date: June 10, 1849

Marshal of France. Robert Thomas Bugeaud was born into a noble family in Limoges, France, on October 15, 1784. The youngest of 13 children, he ran away from home and for some years worked as an agricultural laborer. Bugeaud enlisted as a private in the light infantry of the Imperial Guard during the Napoleonic Wars (1803–1815) and fought in the Battle of Austerlitz (December 2, 1805). Commissioned the next year, he took part in the Battle of Jena (October 14, 1806) and the Battle of Eylau (February 8, 1807). Sent to Spain, he was in Madrid during the uprising of December 2, 1808. He won promotion to rank of captain during the Second Siege of Zaragoza (Saragossa) (December 20, 1808–February 20, 1809). In the course of subsequent fighting in the Peninsular Campaign, he was promoted to major and took command of a regiment. With the first restoration of Louis XVIII, Bugeaud sided with the Bourbons and became a colonel, but he rallied to Napoleon during the Hundred Days of 1815 and saw service in the Alps region.

With the overthrow of Napoleon and the second restoration, Bugeaud was dismissed from the army. He settled in the Périgueux region and occupied himself with agricultural pursuits. With the July Revolution in 1830, he returned to military service. An unflagging supporter of new king Louis Philippe, Bugeaud received command of a regiment and in 1831 was commissioned maréchal de camp. Elected to the Chamber of Deputies the same year, he was an outspoken opponent of democracy and helped crush riots in Paris in 1834.

Bugeaud had opposed the French expedition to Algiers in 1830. Initially sent to Algeria in a subordinate capacity, he ultimately played the key role in the French pacification of that vast territory. After a highly successful six-week campaign, which included the defeat of Algerian forces under Emir Abd al-Qadir at Sikkah (July 6, 1836), Bugeraud was promoted to lieutenant general. The next year he signed the generous Armistice of Tafna (June 1, 1837) with Abd al-Qadir. Necessary because of the political and military situation, the armistice nonetheless led to much criticism of Bugeaud in France.

In December 1840, Bugeaud returned to Algeria as its first governor-general. The next year he instituted his system of light, highly mobile flying columns, which proved highly effective against Abd al-Qadir. Bugeaud also employed native troops. Well respected by his men, he was known as "Père Bugeaud" (Father Bugeaud). In 1842 he undertook the construction of a network of roads to help secure the pacification of the country, and in 1843 he was promoted to marshal of France. His victory over Abd al-Qadir's allied Moroccan forces in the Battle of Isly (August 14, 1844) led to him being made a duke, known as Duc d'Isly.

In 1845 following the French defeat at Sidi Brahim (September 22–25), Bugeaud again took the field. He was almost constantly campaigning until his final departure from Algeria in July 1846, brought about over differences with the French government's refusal to adopt his program of military colonization. During Bugeaud's years in Algeria, the number of French settlers increased from 17,000 to 100,000.

During the Revolution of 1848, Bugeaud took command of the army but was unable to prevent the overthrow of Louis Philippe. Approached about being a candidate for the presidency to oppose Louis Napoleon, Bugeaud refused. Following service as commander of the Army of the Alps, established during 1848–1849 in consequence of events in Italy, Bugeaud retired and died in Paris of cholera on June 10, 1849.

One of France's greatest colonial soldiers and administrators, Bugeaud was a model for Joseph Gallieni and Hubert Lyautey. Although conservative in his political views, Bugeaud had considerable sympathy for the Algerian peasants and sought to protect them from the excesses of French colonial administration.

Spencer C. Tucker

See also Abd al-Qadir; Algeria, French Pacification of; Gallieni, Joseph Simon; Lyautey, Louis Hubert

Further Reading

Azan, Paul. *L'armée d'Afrique de 1830 à 1852* [The African Army from 1830 to 1852]. Paris: Plon, 1936.

Azan, Paul. *Bugeaud et l'Algérie: Par l'épée et par la charrue* [Bugeaud and Algeria: By Sword and Plow]. Paris: 1930.

Bugeaud d'Ideville, Count H. *Memoirs of Marshal Bugeaud.* 2 vols. Edited by Charlotte M. Yonge. London: Hurst and Blackett, 1881.

Sullivan, Anthony Thrall. *Thomas-Robert Bugeaud: France and Algeria, 1784–1849; Politics, Power, and the Good Society.* Hamden, CT: Archon Books, 1983.

C

Cabral, Amílcar

Birth Date: September 12, 1924
Death Date: January 30, 1973

Agronomist and leader of the insurgency in Guinea against Portuguese rule. Amílcar Cabral was born to Cape Verde parents in Bafatá, Portuguese Guinea, on September 12, 1924. Following studies in Guinea and Cape Verde, Cabral attended the Instituto Superior de Agronomia in Lisbon, where he also founded student movements dedicated to the independence of Portugal's African colonies.

Returning to Guinea, in 1956 Cabral formed the Partido Africano da Independência de Guiné e Cabo Verde (PAIGC, African Party for the Independence of Guinea and Cape Verde). Following the failure of political efforts to secure independence, he established training camps in the neighboring Republic of Guinea (Guinea-Conakry) and in Senegal, both of which had just received their independence from France, and in January 1963 he initiated a military campaign against Portuguese rule.

Widely regarded as a brilliant revolutionary theorist and tactician, Cabral was certainly the most effective of the insurgent leaders fighting the Portuguese in Africa. Taking advantage of the fact that much of Portuguese Guinea was low-lying or underwater, Cabral adopted some of the revolutionary theories of Mao Zedong (Mao Tse-tung) in China to establish so-called liberated zones. Cabral sought to win the hearts and minds of the people by employing his training as an agronomist to increase crop yields and insisting that his men assist farmers in their fields when not actually fighting the Portuguese. He also set up a trade-and-barter bazaar system to get goods to the local population at lower cost than those available through colonial merchants, and he arranged for local hospitals and triage stations to aid his own forces but also to bring about improved local medical care.

With some 6,000–7,000 men under arms by 1971 and aided by arms from the Soviet Union, Cabral claimed to control some 80 percent of the territory of Portuguese Guinea. He established a government-in-exile in Conakry, Republic of Guinea, and in 1972 began to plan for a popular assembly and a proclamation of independence. Before he could realize these, he was assassinated in Conakry on January 30, 1973, by a rival, Inocêncio Kani, with the possible assistance of Portuguese authorities.

Guinea-Bissau was granted independence on September 10, 1974. Amílcar Cabral's half brother, Luis Cabral, became the new state's first president.

Spencer C. Tucker

See also Guinea Insurgency; Hearts and Minds; Mao Zedong; Partido Africano da Independência de Guiné e Cabo Verde; Spinola, António Sebastião Ribeiro de

Further Reading

Cabral, Amílcar. *Revolution in Guinea: Selected Texts.* New York: Monthly Review Press, 1970.

Cann, John. *Counterinsurgency in Africa: The Portuguese Way of War, 1961–1974.* Westport, CT: Greenwood, 1997.

Chabal, Patrick. *Amílcar Cabral: Revolutionary Leadership and People's War.* New York: Cambridge University Press, 1983.

Caesar, Gaius Julius

Birth Date: July 12 or 13, 100 BCE
Death Date: March 15, 44 BCE

Roman general and political figure. Born in Rome on July 12 or 13, 100 BCE, into a prominent Roman family that was no longer in the ruling circle, Gaius Julius Caesar served as a praetor in Spain in 61. Returning to Rome, in 60 Caesar joined with two others to oppose the ruling faction in the Roman Senate. This First Triumvirate (60–51) consisted of Caesar, popular general Gnaeus Pompeius Magnus (Pompey the Great), and wealthy businessman Marcus Licinius Crassus. The alliance was cemented by Pompey's marriage to Caesar's daughter Julia.

Under the First Triumvirate, Caesar became one of two consuls in 59, followed by a military command for 5 years, later increased to 10 in Illyricum (Yugoslavia) and Gaul on both sides of the Alps (France and northern Italy). Employing innovative attacks and utilizing his cavalry to good advantage, Caesar also relied heavily on Roman military engineering. He quickly subjugated the disunited tribes of northern France and Belgium during 58–57 and then conducted amphibious operations on the Atlantic seaboard in 56. In a memorable engineering feat, Caesar caused a bridge to be built across the Rhine in June 55, then marched into Germany to intimidate the German tribes. Receiving the submission of several tribes, he returned to Gaul, destroying the bridge.

With two legions, Caesar invaded Britain in 55 and spent three weeks there. He returned in 54 with five legions, taking the capital at Wheathampstead and campaigning. He received the submission of the British but effected no conquests.

Caesar returned to Gaul to confront a powerful coalition of tribes that had revolted against Roman rule. He proved himself a master of both rapid offensive movement and siege warfare. The culmination of the campaign was the great siege of Alesia (July–October 52), stronghold of Gallic leader Vercingetorix. Caesar's victory broke Gallic resistance to Roman rule and added a rich and populous territory, indeed one of the largest territorial additions in Roman history. During the conquest of Gaul, Caesar's army had grown from 2 to 13 legions.

Pompey had received the governorship of Spain but exercised it from Rome. In 53 Crassus was killed in a campaign in Mesopotamia, and the Triumvirate ended. In 52 amid increasing civil unrest, Pompey became sole consul. His wife, Caesar's daughter, had died in 54, and Pompey now broke with Caesar.

By 49, Caesar and Pompey and their legions were fighting over control of Rome. The Senate, allied with Pompey, demanded that Caesar give up his command and return to Rome. Caesar proposed a general disarmament, but the Senate demanded that he give us his command or be declared an enemy of the state. On January 19 Caesar crossed the Rubicon River, bringing his legions from Gaul to Italy. He quickly occupied Rome and Italy, and Pompey withdrew with a number of senators to the Balkans. Caesar pursued him there after a rapid expedition to Spain, and in 48 at Pharsalus in northern Greece, Caesar defeated Pompey (subsequently murdered in Egypt) and the Senate forces.

Caesar then campaigned in Egypt and Asia Minor, accompanied by the beautiful 22-year-old Cleopatra, whom he confirmed as queen and who bore Caesar a son, Caesarian. Caesar returned to Rome and then in two rapid campaigns crushed Pompey's sons in North Africa in 46 and Spain in 45.

In 46 Caesar secured appointment by the Senate as dictator for 10 years. Although the formality of elections continued, Caesar in fact held power. What he intended is unclear. In 44 he caused his dictatorship to be extended for life and secured deification. A month in the calendar was renamed July after him. He seems to have wanted the kingship, but the public apparently opposed this step, and he was not to have the time to convince the public otherwise.

Rational and logical, Caesar carried out extensive reforms. He began projects to restore Corinth and Carthage, the destruction of which had marked the end of Mediterranean trade, and believed that this restoration would employ the Roman urban poor. He reformed local government by moving toward decentralization and also reformed the calendar. Caesar made many provincials citizens, including the entire province of Cisalpine Gaul.

Not all Romans approved of Caesar's reforms. Many traditionalists, powerful vested interests, and republicans were upset by his changes and cosmopolitan attitude. Shortly after he extended his dictatorship to life, Caesar was assassinated— stabbed him to death in Rome—on March 15, 44 BCE, by a group of men who had once been his loyal supporters. Believing that they had killed a tyrant and were restoring liberty, they brought anarchy instead.

Although Caesar was not a great military innovator, he was certainly one of history's great captains. He possessed an offensive spirit, a sense of the moment to strike, a perfect comprehension of supply problems, and the ability to make maximum utilization of the forces at his disposal.

Spencer C. Tucker

See also Vercingetorix

Further Reading

Caesar, Julius. *War Commentaries of Caesar.* Translated by Rex Warner. New York: New American Library, 1960.

Gelzer, M. *Caesar: Politician and Statesman.* Cambridge, MA: Harvard University Press, 1985.

Goldsworthy, Adrian. *Caesar: Life of a Colossus.* New Haven, CT: Yale University Press, 2006.

Grant, Michael. *Julius Caesar.* New York: M. Evans, 1992.

Callwell, Sir Charles Edward

Birth Date: 1859
Death Date: May 16, 1928

British Army general and military theorist. Born in 1859, Charles Edward Callwell was educated at Haileybury College (1871–1876) and at the Royal Military Academy, Woolwich (1876–1877). Commissioned into the Royal Field Artillery, in 1878 Callwell was assigned to India. He fought in the Second Anglo-Afghan War (1878–1882) and in South Africa during the First Boer War (1880–1881). Callwell attended the British Army Staff College at Camberley during 1885–1886 and contributed regularly to military journals. In 1887, then a captain, he received the Royal United Service Institution gold medal for his essay on lessons learned from the colonial campaigns in which British forces had been employed since 1865.

Because of his linguistic skills, Callwell was assigned to the intelligence branch of the War Office during 1887–1892. He subsequently expanded his prize essay into his book *Small Wars: Their Principles and Practice of Military History,* published in 1896. He also published *The Effects of Maritime Command on Land Campaigns since Waterloo* (1897) and *Tactics of Today* (1900).

During the Second Boer War (1899–1902), Callwell commanded first an artillery battery and then a flying column operating against Boer commandos. With the end of the war, Callwell returned to the War Office. He continued writing and published *Maritime Operation and Maritime Preponderance* (1905), treating joint army-navy operations, and *The Tactics of Home Defence* (1908).

Callwell retired from the army as a colonel in 1909 and devoted himself to writing but was recalled to service in 1914 during World War I (1914–1918) as a temporary major general to serve at the War Office as director of Military Operations and Intelligence. He held that post until January 1916, when he was relieved because of the failure of the Dardanelles Campaign. He was then part of the British military mission to Russia before serving in the Ministry of Munitions and was knighted in 1917. Callwell died in London on May 16, 1928.

Callwell's military career was distinguished but not spectacular. His major contribution came in his writing, which included histories, biographies, and two volumes of autobiography, but he is remembered today for his works on military theory, especially his book *Small Wars,* which went through three editions and was translated into French. *Small Wars* was comprehensive, almost encyclopedic, in scope. In it, Callwell drew on a wide variety of British, French, and Russian imperial campaigns and rebellions for universal small-war combat lessons. Within the British Empire, these included India, Afghanistan, the Zulus, the Boers in South Africa, the dervishes in the Sudan, and the Maoris in New Zealand.

Callwell warned against an army becoming bogged down in a guerrilla war and stressed the need to bring native forces to battle before they could disperse. Lessons that were applicable in a wide variety of colonial conflicts included the need for effective intelligence collections, the importance of terrain and climate, the need to take the initiative ("boldness and vigor") to keep irregular forces off balance, the vital role of intelligence, the importance of seizing and holding important terrain (most often the high ground), and the final war-winning requirement to "seize what the enemy prizes most." Callwell also warned against a reliance on technological superiority, which he said was not sufficient in itself to secure victory. Superior discipline and tactics were the keys to victory.

Military historian Ian Beckett calls *Small Wars* "the single most original and distinctive contribution by any British soldier to the theory of war." Certainly Callwell's writings heavily influenced U.S. Marine Corps doctrine regarding insurgencies in the period after World War I. Interest in Callwell's work revived in the 1990s because of its relevance to peacekeeping operations and what has become known as asymmetric combat or low-intensity conflict.

Spencer C. Tucker

See also South African War

Further Reading

Beckett, Ian F. W. *Encyclopedia of Guerrilla Warfare.* Santa Barbara, CA: ABC-CLIO, 1999.

Callwell, Charles E. *Small Wars: Their Principles & Practice.* 3rd ed. 1906; reprint, Lincoln: University of Nebraska Press, 1996.

Cambodia, Vietnamese Occupation of

Start Date: 1979
End Date: 1991

The Vietnamese invasion and occupation of Cambodia during 1979–1991 may have been one of the most successful counterinsurgency efforts of the 20th century. During the fighting, which claimed the lives of some 25,000 Vietnamese soldiers, the Vietnamese used many of the same counterinsurgency and nation-building techniques employed by the United States against the Viet Cong during the Vietnam War (1957–1995).

The Cambodian conflict grew out of the 1977–1978 border war between Vietnam and the radical pro-Chinese Khmer Rouge Cambodian regime led by Pol Pot. In December 1978, Vietnam launched a massive invasion of Cambodia. The Cambodian capital of Phnom Penh was captured on January 7, 1979, and by late spring, large-scale Khmer Rouge resistance had been crushed. The remnants of Pol Pot's forces fled across Cambodia's western border to take refuge inside Thailand.

After rebuilding and rearming in Thailand, the Khmer Rouge, supported by China, and two smaller noncommunist resistance groups, backed by the United States and the noncommunist Southeast Asian states, sent guerrilla forces back into the Cambodian interior in an effort to drive the Vietnamese forces, supported by the Soviet Union, from Cambodia and overthrow the new Vietnamese-installed Cambodian government.

The toppling of the genocidal Khmer Rouge regime left Cambodia with no governmental structure, no police forces, and no army. Its economy was in shambles, and its people were starving. The Vietnamese had to build an entirely new governmental structure and a new Cambodian Army.

Vietnam quickly deployed civilian and military advisory teams to Cambodia. These teams, organized down to the province level, set up local governments and trained military units from village militia forces up to division-sized regular army units. Ultimately the Vietnamese military trained five People's Republic of Kampuchea (PRK) army divisions. Civilian Vietnamese advisers counseled and oversaw the activities of the new pro-Vietnamese PRK government. Every Cambodian province had both a civilian advisory team and a Military Specialist Group, which consisted of military advisers, armed propaganda teams who lived and worked with the local Cambodians, and Vietnamese Army security battalions assigned to hunt down and eliminate resistance forces.

The Vietnamese Army maintained a force of 8–10 infantry divisions in Cambodia through most of the 1980s. Most of these were stationed near the Thai-Cambodian border to block the infiltration of resistance forces back into Cambodia and to conduct search-and-destroy operations not very different from those that the United States had carried out in South Vietnam.

The Vietnamese experienced many problems during the course of their nation-building effort in Cambodia. Pen Sovan, the secretary-general of the Vietnamese-backed Kampuchean People's Revolutionary Party, was the first premier. Installed in June 1981, he proved to be too independent and was removed that December and imprisoned, not to be released until January 1992. In 1985 Hun Sen became premier. Ancient enmities between Cambodia and Vietnam caused endless problems. Vietnamese attacks on resistance bases and refugee camps on the Thai border resulted in armed clashes between the Vietnamese and the Thai Army and widespread international condemnation of Vietnam. Vietnamese troops in Cambodia felt forgotten and ignored by their country, morale was often poor, and desertion rates were high.

Faced with flagging Soviet support to Vietnam in the mid to late 1980s, Vietnam decided that it would have to withdraw its troops and force the new Cambodian regime to stand on its own. Vietnam then began to seek a political solution in Cambodia as well as rapprochement with China. Vietnam began to withdraw its advisers and military units and promised that all Vietnamese troops would be out of Cambodia by the end of 1989.

The end game did not go smoothly. Immediately after the Vietnamese withdrawal in September 1989, resistance attacks, especially by Khmer Rouge forces, resulted in the loss of considerable territory. In the autumn of 1989, Vietnam covertly sent military advisory teams and more than a divisional equivalent of combat troops into Cambodia to beat back the worst of the attacks and shore up the PRK government. The last of these Vietnamese military forces were not withdrawn until July 1991, shortly before an international agreement was reached on October 23 that created a United Nations (UN) peacekeeping force and provided for UN-supervised elections. Noncommunist resistance forces quickly collapsed, and with the cessation of Chinese support, Khmer Rouge units gradually disintegrated or were integrated into the PRK Army. More than two decades after the end of the conflict, Hun Sen continues to hold power.

Merle L. Pribbenow

See also Khmer Rouge; Pol Pot; Viet Cong; Vietnam War

Further Reading

Bekaert, Jacques. *Cambodian Diary: A Long Road to Peace, 1987–1993.* Bangkok: White Lotus, 1998.

Bekaert, Jacques. *Cambodian Diary: Tales of a Divided Nation, 1983–1986.* Bangkok: White Lotus, 1997.

Gottesman, Evan. *Cambodia after the Khmer Rouge: Inside the Politics of Nation Building.* New Haven, CT: Yale University Press, 2002.

Nguyen Van Hong. *Cuoc Chien Tranh Bat Buoc* [The Unwanted War]. Ho Chi Minh City, Vietnam: NXB Tre [Youth Publishing House], 2004.

Castro Ruz, Fidel Alejandro

Birth Date: August 13, 1926

Cuban Communist revolutionary insurgent fighter and leader of Cuba during 1959–2008. Fidel Alejandro Castro Ruz was born on August 13, 1926, in the municipality of Mayarí (Oriente Province). His father was a wealthy sugarcane planter of Spanish origin. A student at the University of Havana, Castro earned a law degree there in 1950. Dissatisfied with chronic government corruption, he had joined the new Ortodoxo (Orthodox) Party of Eduardo Chibás and in 1947 participated in actions to overthrow Dominican Republic dictator Rafael Trujillo.

After the 1952 Cuban military coup carried out by Fulgencio Batista, Castro and his Orthodox Party allies initiated a campaign of resistance against the newly installed dictatorship. On July 26, 1953, the youthful rebels attacked the Moncada military barracks in Santiago de Cuba, the country's second-largest city. The assault failed, and Castro was ultimately imprisoned on the island of Pines. His speech at his trial, titled "History Will Absolve Me," was a powerful denunciation of social and economic injustice in Cuba.

In 1955 Castro was released from prison as part of a general amnesty. He went to Mexico, where he and his comrades, who would eventually establish the July 26 Movement, connected with Argentinean physician and revolutionary Ernesto "Che" Guevara de la Serna. In December 1956 Castro, Guevara, and their followers sailed from Mexico in the yacht *Granma* and landed in southeastern Cuba. This marked the beginning of a two-year military and political campaign to overthrow the U.S.-supported Batista regime. In the last days of 1958 Batista fled the island, and Castro entered Havana in triumph in January 1959.

From that point on, Castro steadily increased his influence. In February 1959 he made himself premier, a post he held until 1976, when he also became president, remaining in that position until 2008. He was also first secretary of the Communist Party of Cuba from 1956 to 2006. Increasingly, Castro based his regime on anti-Americanism. During 1959–1962, he moved Cuba radically to the Left. Two agrarian reforms—confrontation with the United States concerning American investments in Cuba and U.S. support for counterrevolutionary movements culminating in the 1961 Bay of Pigs invasion—led to a break in diplomatic relations with the United States.

In December 1961 Castro declared that he was a Marxist-Leninist. Industry and business were nationalized under state ownership. Economic, political, and military ties with the Soviet Union strengthened steadily throughout the 1960s.

Settlement of the October 1962 Cuban Missile Crisis led to Cuban anger over what was seen as a Soviet betrayal of Cuban interests. This initiated a complex period in Cuban-Soviet relations characterized by Castro's suspicion of the Soviet Union's motives tempered by a growing reliance on Soviet economic assistance.

Castro's foreign policy, especially in Latin America, embraced the strategy of armed revolution conducted by guerrilla movements in Guatemala, Venezuela, Peru, Bolivia, Grenada, El Salvador, and Nicaragua. He also assisted revolutionary movements and left-wing governments. This challenged Soviet support for policies of peaceful coexistence with the West. By the end of the 1960s, the failure of the first wave of Castro-inspired guerrilla wars and the collapse of his ambitious plans to industrialize Cuba and produce a record sugar crop of 10 million tons in 1970 led to an accommodation with Soviet economic and strategic goals in the 1970s.

This did not completely erode Castro's commitment to support of Socialist liberation movements, however.

Castro also dispatched Cuban military forces to Angola in November 1975. The Cubans helped to turn the tide there against South Africa's attempt to defeat the left-wing Movimento Popular da Libertação de Angola (MPLA, Popular Movement for the Liberation of Angola) and to seriously weaken the apartheid regime. Nonetheless, the Cuban-supported Sandinista government in Nicaragua was defeated, and civil war in El Salvador was settled by negotiation.

The collapse of communism in Eastern Europe and the dissolution of the Soviet Union itself in 1991 were serious setbacks for Castro both economically, with a sharp falloff in Soviet aid, and diplomatically. In the 1990s, Castro announced a gradual shift away from Soviet-style economic institutions toward a limited tolerance for private economic enterprises. Confounding predictions, the end of the Cold War did not bring about the demise of the Castro regime. Poor health, however, forced Castro to the sidelines. His brother Raúl Castro became president in 2008.

Barry Carr

See also El Salvador Insurgency; Frente Sandinista de Liberación; Guatemala Insurgency; Guevara de la Serna, Ernesto; Movimento Popular de Libertação de Angola; Nicaragua Insurgency; Peru Insurgencies; Venezuelan Insurgency

Further Reading

Castro, Fidel, with Norbeto Fuentes and Anna Kushner. *The Autobiography of Fidel Castro.* New York: Norton, 2010.

Leonard, Thomas M. *Fidel Castro: A Biography.* Westport, CT: Greenwood, 2004.

Szulc, Tad. *Fidel: A Critical Portrait.* New York: William Morrow, 1986.

Challe, Maurice

Birth Date: September 5, 1905
Death Date: January 18, 1979

French Air Force general and commander of French forces in Algeria during 1958–1960. Maurice Challe was born on September 5, 1905, at Pontet in the Vaucluse Department in southeastern France. Challe entered the École Spéciale Militaire de Saint-Cyr in 1923 and was commissioned an air force second lieutenant in 1925. Earning his wings, he was promoted to captain in 1932 and then in 1937–1939 as a commandant d'escadrille (major) attended the École Supérieure de guerre aériemme.

During the May–June 1940 Battle for France, Commandant (lieutenant colonel) Challe flew numerous missions against the Germans in northern France, for which he was awarded the Legion of Honor. Following the French defeat, he took command of a reconnaissance squadron at Avignon.

After the German occupation of the remainder of France at the end of 1942, Challe joined the French Resistance and provided valuable information concerning German Air Force dispositions in France prior to the 1944 Normandy Invasion, for which he was awarded the Distinguished Service Order by the British government. With the liberation of France, he was assigned to a bomber squadron.

Promoted to general of brigade, Challe commanded French air units in Morocco in 1949, and in 1953 he was named director of the École supérieure de guerre aérienne. Promoted to general of division, he became chief of staff of the Air Division of the General Staff in 1955, working with the British to plan the 1956 abortive Anglo-French Suez Invasion. Promoted to général de corps aérien (air force lieutenant general) in 1957 and then général d'armée aérienne (full air force general), in October 1958 he was named second-in-command to General Raoul Salan, commanding French forces in Algeria. That December, Challe succeeded Salan as commander of French forces battling the Front de Libération Nationale (FLN, National Liberation Front) insurgents.

Challe proved to be a highly effective counterinsurgency commander. His Challe Plan included improvements to the Morice Line, the infiltration barriers along the Tunisian and Moroccan borders, and taking the offensive to the FLN. He used the army's Muslim units (Harkis) to provide intelligence on the FLN, then employed highly mobile units of French paratroopers and Foreign Legionnaires of the Réserve Générale to take the fight to the FLN, clearing the latter from their strongholds in the Kabylia, Ouarsernis, and Hodna Mountains. He planned to take on the FLN in the Aurès Mountains in an effort to win the war but grew concerned that President Charles de Gaulle was preparing to give up the fight to retain Algeria. Recalled to the metropole in 1960, Challe expressed his disapproval of the government's plan for Algerian self-determination. Until his voluntary resignation from the service in January 1961, he headed North Atlantic Treaty Organization air forces in Central Europe.

Following de Gaulle's announcement on April 11, 1961, of his intention to hold a plebiscite in Algeria on the issue of independence, Challe agreed to join a plot hatched by a small group of French senior officers to attempt to overthrow the government. With the failure of this April 21–25 putsch, Challe promptly surrendered rather than see French soldiers fighting one another. Tried and convicted by a military tribunal on May 31, 1961, Challe was sentenced to 15 years imprisonment but was freed in 1966 and amnestied by de Gaulle in 1968. Challe then ran a freight business and published his memoirs, *Notre révolte*. He died in Paris on January 18, 1979.

Spencer C. Tucker

See also Algerian War; Front de Libération Nationale; Salan, Raoul Albin-Louis

Further Reading

Challe, Maurice. *Notre révolte* [Our Revolt]. Paris: Presses de la Cité, 1968.

Horne, Alistair. *A Savage War of Peace: Algeria, 1954–1962.* New York: Viking, 1977.

Chechen War, Second

Start Date: 1999
End Date: 2009

The Second Chechen War (1999–2009) was only the most recent in a series of major conflicts between the Russian government and Chechen separatists. Following an accord of August 1996, the First Chechen War (1994–1996) was formally ended by the signing of the Moscow Peace Treaty of May 12, 1997, by president of Russia Boris Yeltsin and former insurgent leader and newly elected president of Chechnya Aslan Maskhadov. The treaty formalized relations between the Russian Federation and the Chechen Republic of Ichkeria. Yeltsin heralded the agreement as ending 400 years of conflict between Russia and Chechnya.

Maskhadov's tenuous hold on Chechnya was, however, undermined by Islamist radicals seeking to unite Chechnya and Dagestan. The Second Chechen War began when the radical Islamic International Peacekeeping Brigade (IIPB) invaded Dagestan from Chechnya on August 7, 1999. Although the ensuing war can be characterized as but one in a long history of northern Caucasus rebellions against Russian rule, it also attracted a number of foreign Islamist radical fighters who saw it as a holy war, or *gazavat*.

At the request of a Dagestani separatist movement known as the Shura of Dagestan, the IIPB had earlier mounted attacks from Chechnya against the Dagestani police. Consisting of Caucasian and international Islamists, the IIPB was led by Wahhabi Salafists Shamil Basayev and Saudi national Ibn al-Khattab. IIPB fighters invaded Dagestan in force on August 7, and by August 10 they had taken several towns and declared the Independent Islamic State of Dagestan.

Many Dagestanis opposed the invaders and joined with the police and Russian military in an effort to oust the religious fanatics. Colonel General Viktor Kazantsev, commander of the Russian North Caucasus Military District, soon mounted a counterattack not only in Dagestan but also in Chechnya, as the Russian government now declared the Moscow Treaty of 1997 null and void. The Russian military response was a strong one and not limited to rebel hideouts in Chechnya. Meanwhile, there were terrorist bombings in Moscow and the kidnapping of Russian government officials by Chechen militants. After a car bomb in Buynaksk killed 62 family members of Russian soldiers, the Russian military responded by attacks on Chechen apartment buildings, most notably in the capital city of Grozny.

Russian forces utilized Dagestani volunteers to repel a second IIPB invasion near Khasavyurt and Karamakhi. Massive air campaign against militant hideouts in Chechnya followed. By mid-September, the IIPB militants had been pushed back into Chechnya, while the Russian Air Force pounded Grozny.

On October 1, the Russians mounted a ground invasion to retake Grozny. Maskhadov, who had opposed the IIPB's invasion of Dagestan, offered to root out warlords in Grozny and Chechnya, but new Russian president Vladimir Putin

Chechen warlord and Islamic separatist Shamil Basayev in the Botlikh region during a raid in Dagestan on August 11, 1999. Chechnya's most feared warlord, Basayev outraged much of the world with savage attacks that targeted hospitals, a theater, and even schoolchildren. He was killed in July 2006. (AP Photo)

rejected the peace offer, declared the Maskhadov government illegitimate, and insisted that the invasion go forward.

The Russians could call on a far superior arsenal of weaponry, to include complete air superiority. Although the Russian military effort was aimed primarily against the militants, the ensuing urban fighting claimed a large number of innocent civilians. Moscow went to great lengths to control media coverage of the conflict, portraying the Russian military as the guarantors of Chechen sovereignty in the face of a militant Islam incongruent with Chechen culture, religion, and history.

The Chechen separatists found themselves limited to guerrilla and terrorist attacks, including suicide bombings, car bombs, convoy ambushes, kidnappings, and assassinations. They also appealed for support from international human rights groups and multinational organizations. The Russians, however, were quite successful in highlighting the illegal nature by international law of many of the Chechnyan rebel tactics.

Russian artillery and air attacks preceding the first phase of the Russian ground attack, aimed at taking the northern third of Chechnya to the Terek River, caused some 300,000 people to flee. There were numerous civilian casualties from Russian tank fire and cluster bombs. Such heavy-handedness was the modus operandi for the Russians, who achieved their first objective on October 5. Maskhadov responded by declaring a *gazavat* against the Russian forces.

In the second phase of their operation to take Grozny, the Russians employed short-range ballistic missiles. Some struck refugee convoys, killing many people. By November 12 the Russians had retaken Gudermes, the second-largest city in Chechnya, and they employed fuel-air explosives in capturing several other cities that had proved difficult to take in the First Chechen War.

By December 4, Russian forces had surrounded Grozny. The insurgents fought back in the villages of Alkhan-Yurt, Argun, Gudermes, and Uruz-Martan, only to meet fierce response by the Russians. The Battle of Grozny, which did not end until February 2, 2000, left the city in ruins. Official Russian figures indicate that at least 1,500 militants and hundreds of Russian soldiers and militiamen died in the fight for Grozny. Although the Russian so-called counterterrorism operation officially ended on February 29, insurgent attacks on Russian civilian and military targets continued. The Russian military countered with indiscriminate heavy-handed attacks that produced civilian casualties. The separatists, to include Basayev and Khattab, soon realized that conventional attacks were beyond their capability and that they would have to go over to terrorism.

President Putin proclaimed Russian political control of Chechnya in May 2000, and in March 2003 he appointed Akhmad Kadyrov to head an interim government. That same month, Chechens were offered a referendum on the new constitution. Its passage was largely discredited by the large number of Chechens electing not to vote. Chechen separatists assassinated Kadyrov in 2004. He was succeeded first by his son, Ramzan Kadyrov, and then by Alu Alkhanov.

The violence continued until 2009. Militant groups increased terrorist techniques after 2003 and employed suicide bombings and improvised explosive devices as well as assassinations of pro-Moscow Chechen officials and attacks against Russian military targets. Many of the attacks occurred outside Chechnya, with the insurgents striking targets in Russia. The Russians responded with air strikes and artillery against suspected insurgent strongholds, but the United Nations Commission on Human Rights, Amnesty International, and other international human rights groups documented numerous abuses of international law by both sides during the insurgency. These included killing prisoners, targeting medical personnel, denying access to independent monitors, and carrying out extrajudicial executions. Basayev has been credited with orchestrating bombings and terrorist attacks that led to the deaths of more than 1,000 people in the first four years of the insurgency.

Chechen extremists targeted Moscow apartment buildings in 1999 and were responsible for the taking of hostages at a Moscow theater in 2002. In one week in 2004, Chechen separatists downed two Russian aircraft, bombed a subway in Moscow, and held the teachers and pupils of a school in Beslan hostage. The insurgents hoped thereby to undermine the Russian government and drive a wedge between it and the people, such as during the Soviet-Afghan War and the First Chechen War.

The Russian response to hostage taking in particular drew strong domestic criticism, as the Russian military was not trained or equipped to deal with such attacks.

This was evident in the use of fatal chemical agents by Russian forces to end the taking of hostages at the Moscow theater. On February 2, 2005, Maskhadov called for a cease-fire. It lasted 20 days. The cease-fire was honored, although Russian forces killed Maskhadov in Tolstoy-Yurt on March 8. Following his death, leaders endorsed by Basayev took over and espoused a more radical Islamist ideology than Chechen nationalists supported. In 2005 also, anti-Russian and Islamist groups from multiple ethnic groups and fronts united under a political and military framework known as the Chechen Front. In 2007, separatist president Doku Umarov declared Chechnya a Caucasus emirate and called for global jihad, in keeping with the Caucasian Front's religious rhetoric. Although a number of Chechen separatists maintained a more nationalist line, Umarov's declaration garnered international attention, especially in the Middle East.

Russian counterinsurgency and counterterrorism efforts were directed toward cutting off external support to the separatists, establishing a pro-Moscow government in Chechnya, and defending against acts of terrorism in Russia that might destroy domestic Russian support. On April 16, 2009, Russian president Dmitry Medvedev formally declared the counterterrorism operation in Chechnya at an end, although Chechen separatists continue to carry out occasional terrorist attacks.

Larissa Mihalisko

See also Chechnya Insurgency

Further Reading

Oliker, Olga. *Russia's Chechen Wars, 1994–2000: Lessons from Urban Combat.* Santa Monica, CA: RAND, 2001.

Schaefer, Robert W. *The Insurgency in Chechnya and the North Caucasus: From Gazavat to Jihad.* Santa Barbara, CA: Praeger Security International, 2011.

Seely, Robert. *Russian-Chechen Conflict, 1800–2000: A Deadly Embrace.* Portland, OR: Frank Cass, 2001.

Chechnya Insurgency

Start Date: 1940
End Date: 1944

The peoples of the northern Caucasus have been in conflict with one another and with their neighbors since at least 1500. The 1940–1944 war in Chechnya was but one manifestation of the long-standing conflict with Chechnya's northern neighbors. Following the 1917 Bolshevik Revolution, Chechens set up a provisional government of sheikhs and eventually declared their independence from Russia under the All-Mountaineer Alliance of the North Caucasus. Despite the declaration and initial optimism, local commanders of the northern Caucasus fought among one another as well as against the Bolshevik and White forces, both of which opposed independence.

Several factions included Bolsheviks, Whites, secular nationalists, and Muslim fighters carrying on the *gazavat* (holy war) in the mountains begun 200 years earlier. As a result of this factionalism, the Bolsheviks were able to subdue the Chechnya-Ingushetia region in May 1921 with the promise of a degree of autonomy and Sharia (Islamic) law. These pledges were later ignored under Soviet leader Joseph Stalin with the introduction of Sovietization, collectivization, and resettlement.

Inspired by early Finnish successes against the Red Army in the Winter War of 1939–1940, on his release from prison Communist Party writer and agitator Hassan Israilov began an insurrection in Chechnya in February 1940. That same year, he convened an assembly that established the Provisional Popular Revolutionary Government of Chechnya-Ingushetia. Garnering support from Galanchozh, Sayasan, Chaberloi, and parts of Shatoysky districts, Israilov recruited forces in preparation for a future fight against the Red Army. He and his brother, Hussein Israilov, put together a force of upwards of 5,000 guerrillas during the summer of 1941. These numbers steadily rose during the next three years as more Chechens supported the cause.

The Red Army periodically bombed suspected insurgent hideouts in the northern Caucasus throughout 1941, but commitments elsewhere prevented them from mounting a ground campaign in this mountainous region. Indeed, the bombing campaign produced heavy civilian casualties and caused more people to take up the fight against the Soviets. What began as a largely Chechen uprising turned into a multiethnic alliance with Ingush, Dagestani, Karachai, Kalmyk, and Balkar supporters. They came together to form the Special Party of Caucasus Brothers in January 1942. In February 1942, insurgent leader Mairbek Sheripov from southwestern Chechnya-Ingushetia allied his forces with Israilov, thus expanding the Chechen-Ingush insurrection into the strategically important areas of Grozny, Gudermes, and Malgobek.

With the German invasion of the Soviet Union in June 1941, Chechen rebels permitted the Germans to rid their lands of Soviet overlordship. Both the Soviet and German armies were keen on securing the industrial centers of Baku and Grozny. A marriage of convenience between the Chechen rebels and Germans initially raised hopes that the Soviets would be ousted, although Israilov and the provisional government insisted that the Germans recognize Caucasian independence. Although they appear to have been partnered against the Soviets, the relationship between the Chechen-Ingush rebels and the Germans was tenuous at best. Israilov's insistence on an independent Caucasian nation as well as his refusal to yield military command and control to the Germans were but two points of friction.

In July 1942 in Operation EDELWEISS, German Special Forces troops were parachuted into Chechnya, met up with Israilov's forces, and seized the Grozny petroleum refinery prior to the retreat of the Red Army. The intent of the operation was to appropriate the oil fields of the northern Caucasus and liberate areas of Soviet control before the arrival of German armored forces. Within 11 days the Germans seized Stavropol, and during the next three weeks they took the important northern Caucasus cities of Novorossiysk, Maikop, Pyatigorsk, and Mozdok. The Chechens helped sap Soviet resources, but they and the Germans were not strong enough to liberate the northern Caucasus, especially as Adolf Hitler drew off German resources to feed the great Battle of Stalingrad. Meanwhile, the Soviets prepared for offensive operations and pounded German and Chechen forces from the air. At the same time, ideological and political differences caused the breakdown of the German-Chechen partnership against the Soviets.

In early 1943, the Red Army had mounted a massive offensive in the northern Caucasus, causing the Germans to depart Chechnya on December 6, 1943. On February 23, 1944, Stalin initiated Operation LENTIL, a vast resettlement program of the Chechen and Ingush populations to Central Asia. This was undertaken both in retribution for the Chechen cooperation with the Germans and as a means of preventing a future insurgency. Soviet records cite 145,000 Chechen and Ingush deportee deaths en route. Many others were killed in their villages, and still more died once they arrived in the harsh conditions of their new settlements. Some estimates place the number deported at more than 2 million. Stalin also redrew the boundaries of the northern Caucasus, dissolving Chechnya and Ingushetia and the smaller state of Grozny. Hassan Israilov eluded Soviet intelligence until December 29, 1944, when he was finally captured and killed.

Larissa Mihalisko

See also Chechen War, Second

Further Reading

Dunlop, John B. *Russia Confronts Chechnya: Roots of a Separatist Conflict.* Cambridge: Cambridge University Press, 1998.

Schaefer, Robert W. *The Insurgency in Chechnya and the North Caucasus: From Gazavat to Jihad.* Santa Barbara, CA: Praeger Security International, 2011.

Seely, Robert. *Russo-Chechen Conflict, 1800–2000: A Deadly Embrace.* New York City: Frank Cass, 2001.

Chieu Hoi Program

Start Date: 1962
End Date: 1973

Amnesty program in the Republic of Vietnam (RVN, South Vietnam) during 1963–1973. The Chieu Hoi Program, also known as the Great National Solidarity Program and the Open Arms Program, was initiated by South Vietnamese president Ngo Dinh Diem in April 1963 to subvert the Communist military effort by convincing primarily members of the Viet Cong (VC, Vietnamese Communists) but also People's Army of Vietnam (PAVN, North Vietnamese Army) troops to desert or rally to South Vietnam.

The basic theme of the program was that both sides were brothers in the same family. Because all wanted to end the war, the best and least costly way to do so was to renounce internecine bloodletting, forsake hatred, and cooperate in rebuilding the nation. The campaign promised clemency, financial aid, free land, job training, and family reunions to those Communists who stopped fighting and agreed to live under South Vietnamese authority. To this end, the government and its allies used family contacts, radio and loudspeaker broadcasts, and propaganda leaflets to convince the Communists to defect.

At first, the Chieu Hoi Program produced an encouraging number of defections. It soon faltered, however, and fell short of the annual goal of 40,000 defectors set for 1964. Beginning in September 1964, the government offered financial rewards to defectors who surrendered with weapons or who volunteered to lead allied forces to guerrilla arms caches or base areas. This campaign uncovered a significant number of Communist arsenals and revived the program, aided in no small part by the arrival of U.S. combat forces in March 1965. During 1965, more than 11,100 VC defected, followed by 20,000 in 1966 and 27,000 more in 1967.

Another reward campaign, the Third Party Inducement Program, was begun in mid-1967 in the IV Corps tactical zone in the Delta region. People who induced a Communist to defect received a financial reward commensurate with the defector's rank and importance. Although most participants during the life of the program were of relatively low rank, evidence suggests that the Communists were hurt in limited ways by Chieu Hoi–induced manpower shortages.

The reward programs of 1964 through 1967 and the increased allied military activities of 1967 and 1968 provided the entire Chieu Hoi Program with a needed boost, and in 1969 the number of defectors shot up from approximately 17,800 the previous year to more than 47,000. It was soon discovered, however, that many participants were not actually Communist defectors but instead were peasants organized by corrupt South Vietnamese officials to surrender in return for a part of the reward. It was estimated in some areas that as many as 30 percent of all defectors were not actually VC but had claimed such to be awarded one year's deferment on conscription. When evidence of corruption became manifest in 1969, the financial reward aspects of the Chieu Hoi Program were terminated, causing a sharp drop in the number of defectors to about 16,400 by mid-1970.

The Chieu Hoi Program was run by the South Vietnamese government's Chieu Hoi Ministry. The ministry controlled a countrywide system of offices at the provincial, district, and village levels. Defectors were initially collected at provincial Chieu Hoi Centers or in Saigon, where they underwent reeducation and rehabilitation. During the early years, participants were well treated and were allowed to correspond with their families and receive visitors. Depending on personal preferences, defectors were given access to vocational training, as the policy of the government was to help them acquire a skill to earn a living when they were eventually released after a period of 45–60 days. Defectors who wanted to return to their home villages were provided with an allowance to do so. The government also constructed more than 42 Chieu Hoi villages, 1 for each province, and provided free housing to defectors who had no place to go.

Depending on their success at reeducation and rehabilitation, defectors were allowed to apply for civil service jobs; enlist in South Vietnamese regular, territorial, or paramilitary forces; or seek jobs in private industry. Of the total number who volunteered for government service as of 1970, 27 percent were employed in some capacity by the South Vietnamese government or armed forces, while another 20 percent were in private industry. The vast majority—more than 50 percent—returned to their villages and lived as farmers on land provided by the government.

Efforts to reintegrate defectors into society through government service had drawbacks. By late 1970 and early 1971, for example, evidence indicated that a concerted Communist effort was under way to use the various elements of the Chieu Hoi Program to infiltrate VC cadres into South Vietnamese territorial and paramilitary forces and pacification programs.

Defectors were employed by U.S. military forces in large numbers, especially in units such as the Kit Carson Scouts, where their knowledge of terrain and Communist tactics proved useful. Many other defectors were utilized for intelligence work against VC infrastructure throughout South Vietnam and came to make up the bulk of the membership of the Provincial Reconnaissance Units that operated as part of the Phoenix Program after 1968. They also participated in long-range reconnaissance operations in Communist-controlled areas, including those north of the 17th Parallel.

From 1963 to 1973, the Chieu Hoi Program produced more than 159,700 Communist defectors, of whom 30,000 were positively identified as members of the VC infrastructure. The program also netted 10,699 individual weapons and 545 crew-served weapons. The most successful year for the Chieu Hoi Program was 1969, when more than 47,000 cadres, VC, and People's Army of Vietnam (PAVN) soldiers defected, primarily because of the setbacks suffered the previous year during the Tet Offensive and from the increasing pressures being placed on the VC infrastructure by South Vietnamese pacification programs.

Clayton D. Laurie

See also Ngo Dinh Diem; Phoenix Program; Vietnam War

Further Reading

Andrade, Dale. *Ashes to Ashes: The Phoenix Program and the Vietnam War.* Lexington, MA: D. C. Heath, 1990.

Dinh Tan Tho. *Pacification.* Washington, DC: U.S. Army Center of Military History, 1980.

Lewy, Guenther. *America in Vietnam.* New York: Oxford University Press, 1978.

Chin Peng

Birth Date: Late October 1924

Malayan insurgent leader. Chin Peng was born in late October 1924 as Ong Boon Hua in the seaside town of Sitiawan, Malaysia. In 1937 he joined the Chinese Anti Enemy Backing Up Society, formed to aid China after the Japanese invasion. That same year he joined the Malayan Communist Party (MCP). He planned to go to China but was persuaded to remain in Malaya to help grow the MCP.

After the Japanese conquered Singapore in February 1942, Chin Peng fled into the jungle to continue the fight against the Japanese. Soon a prominent figure in the MCP, he worked with British agents organizing anti-Japanese guerrilla units. In 1943 he narrowly avoided capture during a Japanese raid and roundup of senior MCP leaders. At the end of the war, Chin Peng was awarded the Order of the British Empire by the Britain government for his efforts against the Japanese. In 1946 he was elected secretary-general of the MCP.

Chin Peng led the MCP insurgent campaign against the British in 1948. Until the autumn of 1951, the MCP insurgents waged a bloody campaign that included targeting women and children. In October 1951 Chin Peng abandoned this approach as counterproductive, substituting a three-point war strategy to cultivate support from the masses by legal means, infiltrate all levels of the government, and continue a less vicious guerrilla campaign. However, his initial approach had so damaged the insurgency that the new strategy was never effective.

In 1960 Chin Peng and the remaining insurgents fled to Thailand, where they hoped to continue his fight. Eventually friends persuaded him to give up his struggle, and in 1989 he signed peace agreements with Britain and Malaysia that brought the insurgency to a close. The agreements permitted Malayan-born MCP members to petition the government to return home. Chin Peng filed numerous unsuccessful petitions; a final appeal was denied in 2008. Chin Peng lives in Bangkok.

Donald A. MacCuish

See also Malayan Emergency

Further Reading

Asprey, Robert B. *War in the Shadows: The Guerrilla in History.* 2 vols. Garden City, NY: Doubleday, 1975.

Jackson, Robert. *The Malayan Emergency & Indonesian Confrontation.* Barnsley, UK: Pen and Sword Books, 2011.

Church, Benjamin

Birth Date: 1639
Death Date: January 17, 1717

New England soldier and frontiersman and the first of the border captains who figured so prominently in the North American colonial wars against Native Americans.

Benjamin Church was born in 1639 at Duxbury in Plymouth Colony. To the dismay of the more conventional English soldiers in the Plymouth and Massachusetts Bay Colonies, Church counseled adopting Native American ways of fighting (the so-called skulking way of war). He also urged use of Native American allies to defeat King Philip (Metacom) and his warriors in King Philip's War (1675–1676). Church practiced what he preached. He taught colonials under his command to move silently through the forests and swamps, to "scatter" as the Native Americans did if attacked, and to "never fire at an Indian if you can reach him with a hatchet."

Ranging through Massachusetts and Rhode Island, Church and his mixed band of Native Americans and handpicked Plymouth soldiers burned enemy villages and crops and took many native prisoners. Finally on August 12, 1676, Church and his rangers tracked the Native American leader King Philip to his camp near Mount Hope, Rhode Island, and killed him when he tried to escape. The dead chief's head was cut off and taken to Plymouth, where it remained atop a pole for some 25 years as a trophy of English victory. For Church's exploits, Plymouth authorities awarded him the sum of 30 shillings.

Church frequently fell out with colonial leaders over treatment of native foes during the war. On more than one occasion, Native Americans he had convinced to surrender or who had been captured were sold into slavery, to his great fury. This was the fate of King Philip's wife and son, taken by Church and his rangers 10 days before they killed the Native American leader.

When King William's War broke out in 1689, Church was commissioned a major and led Plymouth forces in the fight against the French and their Native American allies in Maine, then part of Massachusetts Colony. His troops participated in the Battle of Brackett's Woods, which helped lift the siege of Fort Loyal. Church led other expeditions into Maine and what is today New Brunswick, Canada, in retaliation for French and Native American raids against the eastern borders of New England.

In March 1704 Church, although by now a rotund 65-year-old, was granted a commission as colonel of Massachusetts troops and was ordered to raid into Acadia in retaliation for French and native destruction of the town of Deerfield, Massachusetts, the month before. Fortified by a promise of £100 for each Native American scalp, moving from place to place by whaleboat and taking to snowshoes when necessary, Church's 550 New England volunteers attacked native villages, seized and burned the towns of Les Mines (Grand Pré) and Chignecto, and threatened the French base at Port Royal.

After the Acadia raid, Church retired. He and his son Thomas composed two volumes of his memoirs of King Philip's War and the struggles against the French and Native Americans, largely based on a diary Church had kept. The volumes are noteworthy for Church's insistence on the importance of human agency—his own, primarily—in the victories of the colonists over their enemies. Other contemporary historians of the wars, such as William Hubbard and Cotton Mather, had seen the triumphs as evidence of God's will. Church's memoirs made him a model for other border captains, such as Robert Rogers, to follow. Church died on January 17, 1717, near his farm at Little Compton, Rhode Island.

Bruce Vandervort

See also Skulking Way of War

Further Reading

Church, Benjamin, and Thomas Church. *Entertaining Passages Relating to Philip's War, Which Began in the Month of June 1675.* Boston: B. Green, 1716.

Church, Benjamin, and Thomas Church. *The History of King Philip's War, Commonly Called the Great Indian War, of 1675 and 1676: Also of the French and Indian Wars at the Eastward, in 1689, 1690, 1692, 1696, and 1704.* Exeter, NH: J. and B. Williams, 1829.

Leach, Douglas E. *Arms for Empire: A Military History of the British Colonies in North America, 1607–1763.* New York: Macmillan, 1973.

Civil Operations and Revolutionary Development Support

Umbrella organization for U.S. pacification efforts in the Republic of Vietnam (RVN, South Vietnam) during the Vietnam War (1957–1975). Civil Operations and Revolutionary Development Support (CORDS) organized all civilian agencies involved in the pacification effort in South Vietnam under the military chain of command. Established under the Military Assistance Command, Vietnam (MACV), on May 10, 1967, CORDS was directed by Robert Komer, a MACV civilian deputy commander. Komer, special assistant to President Lyndon B. Johnson, held the rank of ambassador and the military equivalent of three-star general and reported directly to MACV commander General William C. Westmoreland. Upon Komer's departure in November 1968, William E. Colby, who had been the assistant chief of staff for CORDS, took over its direction.

CORDS succeeded the Office of Civil Operations, originally created to assume responsibility over all civilian agencies working in South Vietnam under the jurisdiction of the U.S. embassy in Saigon. CORDS integrated American aid programs targeting the social and economic development of South Vietnam. These were viewed as the basis upon which to build the Vietnamese nation and win the hearts and minds of the Vietnamese people in the face of Communist political and military opposition. CORDS activities were primarily directed toward the 80 percent of the South Vietnamese population in the rural villages and hamlets most vulnerable to the Viet Cong (VC, Vietnamese Communists). In this way, the Communists would be deprived of their traditional population base.

CORDS was organized into six operational divisions: Chieu Hoi, Revolutionary Development, Refugees, Public Safety, Psychological Operations, and New Life Development. The Chieu Hoi (Open Arms) program was designed to induce defections by the VC and People's Army of Vietnam (PAVN, North Vietnamese Army) soldiers through government propaganda campaigns and monetary payments. Returnees were given job training, welfare services, and resettlement assistance and were also integrated into Army of the Republic of Vietnam (ARVN, South Vietnamese Army) military units.

The Revolutionary Development (RD) division was organized into 59-member teams designed to provide security and promote economic development at the village level. RD teams were trained at the National Training Center in Vung Tau and assigned to villages throughout the country. Working through the U.S. Agency for International Development (USAID), the refugee program was designed to resettle millions of displaced villagers across the country, often through the establishment of refugee resettlement centers, and to provide them security.

CORDS integrated all military and civilian personnel into a single chain of command by assigning them to the same missions through the establishment of CORDS advisory teams at the province level. During 1968, for example, there were some 4,000 CORDS personnel in the 12 II Corps provinces. CORDS teams at the province level consisted of State Department, USAID, U.S. Information Agency, and U.S. Public Health Service personnel. In Khanh Hoa Province, for example, Team 35 had 87 military and 23 civilian personnel, including foreign service officers, public health nurses, and rural health and agricultural advisers. Priority projects in 1968 were the resettlement of Montagnard tribesmen and improving the quality and effectiveness of Regional Forces/Popular Forces (RF/PF) units to provide security at the village level.

With the war intensifying and with the increasing vulnerability of civilian aid efforts in the countryside, providing security for what became known as nation building or pacification became a military priority. In September 1969 there were 6,464 U.S. military advisers assigned to CORDS, 5,812 of whom served in the field. Major efforts were made within the U.S. Army in particular (which had 95 percent of CORDS military advisers) to assign qualified military advisers to CORDS advisory teams. Three army civil affairs companies were directly involved in pacification programs under CORDS administration. Major efforts were also made under both Komer and Colby to improve the effectiveness of RF/PF units by increasing both their manpower and their firepower to be equivalent to local VC units. By the end of 1969, RF/PF units numbered 475,000 men. Their effectiveness was a major factor in providing security at the village level in support of pacification efforts.

With the January 1973 Paris Peace Accords and the withdrawal of U.S. armed forces, the rationale for CORDS was removed, and it ceased operations on February 27, 1973. Selected functions were assumed by the office of the special assistant to the ambassador for field operations, a civilian operation headed by George Jacobson, who had been assistant chief of staff of CORDS under Colby.

David M. Berman

See also Chieu Hoi Program; Colby, William Egan; Combined Action Platoons, U.S. Marine Corps; Komer, Robert William; Pacification; Westmoreland, William Childs

Further Reading

Hunt, Richard A. *Pacification: The American Struggle for Vietnam's Hearts and Minds.* Boulder, CO: Westview, 1995.

Wiesner, Louis A. *Victims and Survivors: Displaced Persons and Other War Victims in Viet-Nam, 1954–1975.* Westport, CT: Greenwood, 1988.

Civil War, American, Insurgency and Counterinsurgency.

See American Civil War Insurgency and Counterinsurgency

Civilian Irregular Defense Group

Indigenous self-defense force during the Vietnam War (1957–1975). In 1961 and 1962, U.S. Army Special Forces (Green Berets) on temporary duty established a number of isolated camps in remote areas in the Republic of Vietnam (RVN, South Vietnam). These camps were intended to extend the influence of the South Vietnamese government, provide security for the local population, and isolate the people from Communist influence and intimidation.

The Special Forces recruited volunteers from the local populations and trained them as soldiers. Known as the Civilian Irregular Defense Group (CIDG) and until July 1963 paid by the Central Intelligence Agency (CIA) Combined Studies Division/Group through the Special Forces (in July 1963, the U.S. military took over funding for the program), the CIDG played a significant role in securing sparsely populated highland areas. At peak strength, the CIDG numbered some 45,000 men. U.S. Special Forces first operated around Ban Me Thuot in the Central Highlands with Rhade and Jarai Montagnards. The vast majority of CIDG personnel throughout Vietnam were Montagnard tribesmen, although there were also Cambodians and Vietnamese.

The initial Special Forces approach was to organize the Montagnards, place them under government control, and train them to fight the Communist guerrillas, known as the Viet Cong (VC). Special Forces personnel organized the CIDG into combat units. CIDG units were assigned specific missions: border surveillance and interdiction of Communist infiltration, communications and supply routes, offensive operations against VC units and sanctuaries, identification and destruction of VC infrastructure, and establishment of area security. Another CIDG concept was to organize and train tactical reserve reaction forces to serve as mobile strike force units.

Army of the Republic of Vietnam (ARVN, South Vietnamese Army) Special Forces (Luc Luong Dac Biet) placed officers in each camp to serve as its commander and staff. The Special Forces assumed the CIA mission and served as advisers. Camps were organized into three companies of 132 men each, three reconnaissance platoons, a heavy weapons section with two 105-millimeter howitzers, and a political warfare section. Each camp was authorized a total of 530 men.

Because of their isolated locations, many CIDG camps came under attack or siege. In 1965 People's Army of Vietnam (PAVN, North Vietnamese Army) forces besieged the CIDG camp at Duc Co in the Central Highlands for more than two months. In June 1965 VC units overran the CIDG camp at Dong Xoai but failed to take the town because of fierce CIDG resistance. In March 1966 two PAVN regiments attacked the A Shau CIDG camp, forcing U.S. and ARVN Special Forces to withdraw. Other CIDG camps were abandoned because of insufficient manpower. The CIDG program also experienced problems with fraud and corruption, and in March 1970 U.S. and South Vietnamese military leaders agreed to convert the CIDG camps to ARVN Border Ranger camps. The last two CIDG border camps were officially converted on January 4, 1971.

Hieu Dinh Vu and Harve Saal

See also Special Operations Forces, U.S.; Viet Cong; Vietnam War

Further Reading

Ahern, Thomas L. *Vietnam Declassified: The CIA and Counterinsurgency.* Lexington: University Press of Kentucky, 2009.

Kelly, Francis J. *The Green Berets in Vietnam, 1961–71.* New York: Brassey's, 1991.

Clausewitz, Carl Philipp Gottfried von

Birth Date: June 1, 1780
Death Date: November 16, 1831

Regarded by many as history's most influential military theorist, Carl Philipp Gottfried von Clausewitz was born in Burg bei Magdeburg, Prussia, on June 1, 1780, and entered the Prussian Army at age 12. He campaigned with the Prussian and Austrian force that invaded France in 1792 to begin the Wars of the French Revolution. After Prussia left the war in 1795, Clausewitz spent six years in garrison duties, during which time he bettered his education. In 1801 he entered the Kriegsakademie (War College) in Berlin, studying under Gerhard Johann David von Scharnhorst. On graduation, Clausewitz was appointed an aide to Prince August Ferdinand of Prussia in 1804. Clausewitz witnessed the destruction of Prussia's armies at the hands of Napoleon Bonaparte and the French in 1806. In October, Clausewitz fought in the Prussian defeat in the Battle of Auerstädt and was taken prisoner at Prenzlau later that month.

Following his exchange in 1807, Clausewitz assisted both Scharnhorst and August von Gneisenau in the reform of the Prussian Army during 1807–1811. At the same time, Clausewitz was an instructor to Crown Prince Friedrich Wilhelm. Angered by Prussian king Friedrich Wilhelm III's decision to supply a contingent of troops to Napoleon for the French invasion of Russia, Clausewitz resigned his commission and left Prussia. During the 1812 Campaign, he was first an observer and then a staff officer in the Russian forces. He remained with the Russian army through the 1813 War of German Liberation, rejoining the Prussian Army in 1814. During Napoleon's return to France in the Hundred Days (1815), Clausewitz took part in the Waterloo Campaign as a staff officer in III Corps.

In 1818 Clausewitz was appointed director of the Kriegsakademie. Reflecting on his experiences in the French Revolutionary War (1792–1802) and the Napoleonic Wars (1803–1815), he began work on his seminal book that would be published posthumously in 1832 as *Vom Kriege* (On War). In it Clausewitz sought to discover the fundamental principles of war.

In his writings, Clausewitz acknowledges the existence of people's wars. Inspired by the successes of guerrilla warfare against the French in Spain, Scharnhorst had charged Clausewitz with creating a course examining small wars. Since there was little formal writing on the topic, Clausewitz created case studies from the French Revolutionary War and Hessian forces in America during the American Revolutionary War (1775–1783); however, intellectually he never separated small wars from the construct of conventional conflict and identified this type of warfare as adjunct to "big wars." In his *Bekenntnisdenkschrift* (Confessional Memoir) of 1812, however, Clausewitz proposed guerrilla warfare against France, recommending a "Spanish civil war in Germany," as Prussia was too weak to fight Napoleon's powerful army conventionally. In *Vom Kriege* (On War), Clausewitz devotes an entire chapter to people's war. In it he advances his original perspectives on irregular warfare by recognizing and extolling the value of mobilizing the masses in conjunction with conventional troops as part of the broader spectrum of defensive capabilities. He notes that small-scale attacks against enemy detachments, logistical outposts, and lines of communication, while incapable of decisively defeating an enemy army, could compel an enemy change in policy. Clausewitz, however, offers little analysis on countering a people's war. He posits that small wars waged by a population in its own territory could extend over a considerable period, while states waging counterinsurgencies are more restrained politically and militarily. He acknowledges that attempts would most likely be made by state forces to demoralize the guerrillas through inhumane treatment and executions. Insurgents would most likely retaliate in kind, matching "atrocity with atrocity, violence with violence." Overall, Clausewitz cautioned about a conflict fought by a politically charged populace against a conventional force as likely to have devastating effects on both sides. Since the Prussian Crown opposed arming the population, political pragmatism prevented Clausewitz from commenting on this publically.

Clausewitz was not happy with *Vom Kriege* (On War), but he never had a chance to revise it. In 1830 he was assigned to the Russian border as a major general and chief of staff of Prussian forces cooperating with the Russians to prevent Poles fleeing the Revolution of 1830 from entering Prussia. Clausewitz contracted cholera and died in Breslau, Silesia, on November 16, 1831.

Bradford A. Wineman and Spencer C. Tucker

Further Reading

Clausewitz, Carl von. *On War.* Revised ed. Edited and translated by Michael Howard and Peter Paret. Princeton, NJ: Princeton University Press, 1984.

Strachan, Hew. *Carl von Clausewitz's* On War: *A Biography.* New York: Atlantic Monthly Press, 2007.

Sumida, Jon Tetsuro. *Decoding Clausewitz: A New Approach to On War.* Lawrence: University Press of Kansas, 2008.

Colby, William Egan

Birth Date: January 4, 1920
Death Date: April 27, 1996

Key figure in the U.S. pacification effort in the Republic of Vietnam (RVN, South Vietnam) during the Vietnam War (1957–1975). Born on January 4, 1920, in St. Paul, Minnesota, William Egan Colby graduated from Princeton University in 1940. A U.S. Army officer during World War II (1939–1945), he was assigned to the Office of Strategic Services. Colby's responsibilities included sending agents into German-occupied Europe and assisting resistance forces.

In 1947 Colby earned a law degree from Columbia University, and in 1950 he joined the Central Intelligence Agency (CIA). In 1959 he became CIA station chief in Saigon. During the next three years Colby and other CIA officials experimented with various forms of security and rural development programs. From these endeavors, the Citizens' (later Civilian) Irregular Defense Groups (CIDGs), the Mountain Scout Program, and the Strategic Hamlet Program emerged in 1961.

In 1962 Colby became chief of the CIA's Far East Division, a position he held until 1968. In this post, he stressed pacification as the key to victory in Vietnam. In 1965, CIA analysts established the Hamlet Evaluation System (HES) to measure certain factors in the villages in South Vietnam; these elements contributed to identifying the progress of pacification in the countryside. Despite this, an aggressive pacification strategy did not emerge until 1968.

In 1968 Colby returned to Vietnam with ambassadorial rank, succeeding Robert W. Komer as deputy to the commander, U.S. Military Assistance Command, Vietnam, for Civil Operations and Revolutionary (later changed to Rural) Development Support. While serving in this post, Colby oversaw the accelerated pacification campaign. Initiated in November 1968, the campaign focused on enhanced security and development within South Vietnam's villages and included such components as the Phoenix Program and the People's Self-Defense Force.

From 1969 to 1970, planning for pacification and development shifted from the Americans to the South Vietnamese in accordance with the Richard M. Nixon administration's policy of Vietnamization. Then in 1971, the program shifted to a more self-oriented role for the villages of South Vietnam. A year later Colby returned to Washington, D.C., to become executive director of the CIA and then, from May 1973 until his retirement in November 1976, the director.

Colby assumed leadership of the CIA during the worst crisis in its history. He revealed to Congress the agency's involvement in illegal domestic surveillance programs, plots to kill foreign leaders and overthrow governments, use of humans as guinea pigs in mind-control experiments, and other violations of its charter. Colby held that revealing these actions to Congress helped save the CIA from congressional abolition. This action earned Colby admiration from many in Congress and the public but brought the enmity of many Cold War supporters, who helped bring an end to his tenure as director in 1976.

In retirement, Colby maintained that the United States and South Vietnam might have won the war if only they had fought the CIA's kind of war and countered Communist guerrilla tactics, a theme developed in his 1989 memoir. He claimed that in the early 1970s, Vietnamization was succeeding and pacification was building the base for a South Vietnamese victory, culminating in the defeat of the 1972 Communist offensive with U.S. air and logistical support but no ground assistance. He held that this chance for victory was thrown away when the United States sharply reduced its military and logistical support and then sold out the South Vietnamese government during negotiations in Paris. The final straw came when Congress dramatically cut aid to South Vietnam, making inevitable the 1975 Communist victory.

Colby drowned in a canoeing accident off Rock Park, Maryland, on April 27, 1996.

R. Blake Dunnavent

See also Civil Operations and Revolutionary Development Support; Komer, Robert William; Phoenix Program; Strategic Hamlet Program

Further Reading

Andrade, Dale. *Ashes to Ashes: The Phoenix Program and the Vietnam War.* Lexington, MA: D. C. Heath, 1990.

Colby, William. *Honorable Men: My Life in the CIA.* New York: Simon and Schuster, 1978.

Colby, William, with James McCargar. *Lost Victory: A Firsthand Account of America's Sixteen-Year Involvement in Vietnam.* Chicago: Contemporary Books, 1989.

Collins, Michael

Birth Date: October 16, 1890
Death Date: August 22, 1922

Irish soldier, revolutionary leader, and politician. Born near Clonakilty, County Cork, Ireland, on October 16, 1890, Michael Collins immigrated to London, where he joined the Irish Republican Brotherhood (IRB) and a branch of the pro–home rule Irish Volunteers. A participant in the 1916 Easter Rising in Dublin, Collins later condemned the insurgency's doomed heroics.

While in prison, Collins and other leaders of what soon would be called the Irish Republican Army (IRA) developed their concept of urban guerrilla warfare. Since it could not defeat the British in open battle, the IRA decided to rely on hit-and-run attacks. Collins realized the need to apply these tactics to Ireland's cities as well as in the countryside.

Collins was equally aware that military action alone could not achieve Irish independence. Released from prison in December 1916, he set to work uniting the nonviolent moral-force wing of the nationalist movement, represented by Sinn Féin, with the physical-force wing represented by the IRA. While its members prepared for war, their energies were also directed toward electing Sinn Féin candidates in a series of parliamentary by-elections. Collins was one of a handful of leaders to escape capture when British authorities ordered mass arrests in the wake of the 1918 anticonscription campaign. He was on the run until the end of the Anglo-Irish War (1919–1921).

Elected to the Dáil Éireann (the lower house of the Irish Parliament) in 1918, Collins held a number of government positions, chiefly minister of finance. Although not the IRA's supreme commander, he directed many of its activities, including the infiltration of British intelligence operations. Collins's subordinates decimated the ranks of the Royal Irish Constabulary (RIC) through intimidation and, if that failed, assassination. Mass resignations from the RIC forced British authorities to recruit ex-servicemen to serve in what became known as the Black and Tans. This twilight war climaxed with what became known as Bloody Sunday. On November 21, 1920, the IRA executed 14 British undercover agents on Collins's orders. That afternoon the Black and Tans retaliated, killing 14 spectators at a Gaelic football match and injuring numerous others.

Although the IRA could not win the Anglo-Irish War, these incidents proved that it could not be beaten either. A truce was called in July 1921, followed by peace negotiations that autumn. Collins, along with Arthur Griffith, headed the Irish delegation. The British negotiating team included David Lloyd George, Winston Churchill, Lord Birkenhead, and Austen Chamberlain. On December 6 the two sides signed the Anglo-Irish Treaty. Although the agreement granted Ireland practical independence as a British Dominion, it split the nationalist movement. With President Eamon de Valera leading the opposition, Dáil Éireann ratified the agreement by a mere seven votes.

Collins spent the remaining months of his life trying to head off civil war. His other goal was to enforce the treaty's so-called Ulster clauses in an attempt to reunify Ireland, which had been partitioned in 1920. Collins was killed in an ambush by antitreaty members of the IRA at Béal na Bláth, just a few miles from his birthplace in County Cork, on August 22, 1922.

Collins was a staunch Irish nationalist but a political realist, and his strategy of urban guerrilla warfare helped inspire numerous 20th-century revolutionaries.

C. Kevin Matthews

See also Black and Tans and the Auxiliaries; Ireland Revolutionary Era; Irish Republican Army; Urban Guerrilla Warfare

Further Reading

Coogan, Tim Pat. *Michael Collins: A Biography.* London: Hutchinson, 1990.

Doherty, Gabriel, and Dermot Keogh, eds. *Michael Collins and the Making of the Irish State.* Dublin: Mercier, 1998.

Matthews, Kevin. *Fatal Influence: The Impact of Ireland on British Politics, 1920–1925.* Dublin: University College Dublin Press, 2004.

Colombian Insurgency

Start Date: 1964
End Date: Ongoing

Like so many other Latin American states, the South American country of Colombia experienced periods of dictatorship and civil strife. In 1948 Jorge Gaitan, a reformist and candidate of the Colombian Liberal Party for the presidency, was assassinated in Bogotá. A wave of violence, known as La Violencia, swept the country during 1948–1957 that pitted liberals against conservatives and put Colombia on the brink of civil war. That episode also influenced relations between Colombia and the United States, as leaders in both countries feared Communist inroads. Colombia severed diplomatic relations with the Soviet Union and worked with the United States to contain the threat of communism throughout the hemisphere. Because the Partido Comunista Colombiano (PCC, Colombian Communist Party) was not very powerful in the early 1950s, these efforts were concentrated on Colombian labor movements in which both Communists and Socialists were active. While violence continued for some years, in 1958 the conservatives and liberals came together to create the National Front, a power-sharing arrangement that lasted until 1974 and brought a degree of political stability.

In the 1960s, however, the Cuban Revolution served as the ideological underpinning of a number of Latin American guerrilla movements. In Colombia, revolutionaries followed the foco formula of rural republics favored by Ernesto "Che" Guevara that was centered on rural guerrilla warfare. Assisted by the United States, the Colombian government in 1962 adopted Plan Lazo, a counterinsurgency program that by the end of 1965 had ended the foco threat.

Meanwhile, the surviving guerrilla forces came together in 1964 in two main organizations: the pro-Cuban Ejército de Liberación Nacional (ELN, National Liberation Army), founded by Fabio Vásquez Castaño and others trained in Cuba, and the pro-Soviet Fuerzas Armadas Revolucionarias de Colombia–Ejército del

Pueblo (FARC-EP, Revolutionary Armed Forces of Colombia — People's Army), founded by Manuel Marulanda. Both were Marxist-Leninist in political philosophy. In 1964, they commenced an insurgency against the Colombian government. FARC-EP became the most numerous of the two groups opposing the government, and the ensuing insurgency is usually named for it. In 1967 a third insurgent group formed: the pro-China Ejército Popular de Liberación (EPL, Popular Liberation Army), influenced by the teachings of Mao Zedong.

The insurgent effort greatly benefitted from rural anger over the Colombian government's adoption of a policy of Accelerated Economic Development that involved the introduction of agribusiness in large-scale farming and ranching enterprises, which brought the dispossession by 1969 of some 400,000 Colombian peasants.

During the 1970s, Colombia's policy toward Communist regimes softened. The government reestablished diplomatic relations with both the Soviet Union and Cuba and recognized the new Angolan government and the Sandinista government in Nicaragua. Colombian leaders pursued an independent foreign policy and supported the Non-Aligned Movement.

President Julio Turbay Ayala (1978–1982) shifted Colombian foreign policy in 1981, when he broke diplomatic relations with Cuba and aligned his policy with that of U.S. president Ronald Reagan. This shift occurred chiefly because of alleged Cuban and Nicaraguan support for the Movimiento 19 de Abril (M-19, April 19 Movement), an urban group that emerged in 1970 following a split in the Alianza Nacional Popular (ANAPO, National Popular Alliance), which had failed to win the presidency in the national elections of April 1970. M-19 soon became the second most important Colombian guerrilla movement after FARC.

Belisario Betancourt, Colombian president during 1982–1986, brought Colombia formally into the Non-Aligned Movement and called for Latin American solidarity. Betancourt also became one of the chief opponents of the Reagan administration's Central America policy. Escalation of the conflict there led Betancourt to encourage a peaceful settlement for the embattled region. Together with Mexico, Panama, and Venezuela, Colombia created the Contadora Group in 1983.

Betancourt's active diplomacy in Central America was, however, challenged by domestic realities. Colombian guerrilla violence intensified, as did drug trafficking. The latter led the Betancourt government to seek talks with the EPL and M-19 in 1984, but these collapsed in 1985. M-19 had secured considerable international attention when it seized diplomats at the Dominican embassy in Bogotá in 1980 in what turned out to be a 61-day siege (February 27–April 27). Then in November 1985, M-19 took over the Supreme Court building in the capital, leading to the deaths of 11 justices and more than 100 other people in the ensuing fighting.

The increasing power of the drug cartels and the inability of the government to effectively deal with either the insurgency or drug trafficking led to the formation of right-wing death squads, the so-called *sicarios* ("sacred ones"). The situation also brought improved bilateral relations with the United States, which extended military assistance to Colombia.

In 1987 the insurgents formed a new grouping, known as the Coordinstora Guerrillera Simón Bolívar (CGSB, Simón Bolívar Coordinating Board), named for the early 19th-century leader of Latin American liberation. Nonetheless, in March 1989 M-19, led by Carlos Pizzaro Leongomez, signed a cease-fire agreement with the government. After a follow-on peace agreement a year later, M-19 competed in local, regional, and national elections.

Despite the defection of M-19, the insurgency continued. Most of the members of the EPL demobilized in 1991, forming the Esperanza, Paz y Libertad (Hope, Peace and Liberty) Party, although a small dissident faction continued to operate. Reportedly, FARC killed a number of ex-EPL personnel, choosing to regard them as traitors.

U.S. funding for Colombia increased in 2001, and the government engaged a number of local and international organizations to provide rural assistance, especially to those peasants forced from their villages. U.S. funds also provided resources to investigate killings on both sides and prosecute those responsible as well as to train the Colombian military and police militarily and also in human rights and the rule of law. In 2003 the Colombian government adopted a population-centric approach in which civilians took the lead and that sought to provide security to the rural population while also enhancing social services. As a result, the Colombian military was able to establish a considerable degree of trust and credibility that had previously been lacking.

By 2007, the Colombian government could point to impressive gains in security. The government had control over more of the national territory, some 30,000 illegal paramilitary forces had agreed to demilitarize and demobilize, and there were sharp declines in terrorists attacks, kidnappings, and murders and economic gains in the rural areas. Although the government made some progress in dismantling the big drug cartels, cocaine production did not diminish and indeed accounted for some 90 percent of the world's supply. Latin America's longest-running insurgency also continued, albeit at a far lower level.

Both FARC and the ELN maintained forces and continued military operations. In 2012 the ELN had perhaps 5,000 men under arms and operated chiefly in the eastern Andean foothills. The ELN had few links with the drug cartels and directed its attacks primarily against Colombia's rapidly expanding mining and oil sectors in the Casanare region. FARC developed close links with the drug cartels and was by far the largest of the insurgent groups, with some 8,000 to 10,000 people under arms in 2012. Its stronghold was in southwestern Colombia.

A new round of peace talks occurred in Oslo, Norway, in October 2012 to deal with such issues as victim rights, rural landownership, and drug production and smuggling. However, Colombian president Juan Manuel Santos rejected calls from FARC leader Rodrigo Londono for a cease-fire similar to that a decade earlier, when the rebels had used the cease-fire to greatly enhance their supply of weapons and increase drug trafficking.

Spencer C. Tucker

See also Bolívar, Simón; Cuban Revolution; Foco Theory; Fuerzas Armadas Revolucionarias de Colombia–Ejército del Pueblo; Guevara de la Serna, Ernesto; Mao Zedong

Further Reading

Brittain, James J. *Revolutionary Social Change in Colombia: The Origin and Direction of the FARC-EP.* London: Pluto, 2010.

Bushnell, David. *The Making of Modern Colombia: A Nation in Spite of Itself.* Berkeley: University of California Press, 1993.

Rochlin, James. *Vanguard Revolutionaries in Latin America.* Boulder, CO: Lynne Rienner, 2003.

Combined Action Platoons, U.S. Marine Corps

U.S. Marine Corps pacification initiative. The tactical area of responsibility assigned to the U.S. Marine Corps in Vietnam lay in the northernmost portion of the Republic of Vietnam (RVN, South Vietnam), designated as the I Corps Tactical Zone. More than most U.S. military forces, the marines took countryside pacification seriously. Marine officers realized that they had to gain the confidence of villagers if they were to deny the Viet Cong (VC), the Communist insurgents, local support and bases of operations.

Called at various times by such names as internal defense and development, rural reconstruction, stability operations, revolutionary development, internal security, nation building, and neutralization operations, pacification was not "the other war," as U.S. Military Assistance Command, Vietnam, commander General William C. Westmoreland and many others thought of it. Pacification was the supporter of military combat operations and at least as important. Based on earlier experiences in the Caribbean and in Central America, the III Marine Amphibious Force (MAF) formed combined action platoons (CAPs) in the autumn of 1965 as a means of support for South Vietnam's Revolutionary Development Program.

Administered by the G-5 Civil Affairs section based in Danang, III MAF fielded four battalions of CAPs between October 1967 and July 1970. Each consisted of one marine rifle squad and one navy corpsman plus one platoon of South Vietnamese Regional Force/Popular Force (RF/PF) soldiers. These men were assigned to a particular village, often one that was home to the RF/PF members of the unit, and made it their base of operations for extended periods. Marines got to know villagers as individuals, helped in civic and health projects, and taught locals the arts of booby-trapping, entrapment, ambush, and self-defense.

In 1970 the program changed to combined action groups, using a marine company and an RF/PF battalion. The last such unit was withdrawn in the spring of 1971.

Cecil B. Currey

See also Civil Operations and Revolutionary Development Support

Further Reading

Cincinnatus [Cecil B. Currey]. *Self-Destruction: The Disintegration and Decay of the United States Army during the Vietnam Era.* New York: Norton, 1981.

Corson, William. *The Betrayal.* New York: Norton, 1968.

Peterson, Michael E. *The Combined Action Platoons: The U.S. Marines' Other War in Vietnam.* New York: Praeger, 1989.

Concentration Camps in the Second Boer War

The term "concentration camp" was first employed during the Second Boer War (South African War) of 1899–1902. The British had originally established refugee camps to provide shelter for those whose homes had been destroyed in the fighting. In November 1900, however, General Herbert Kitchener assumed command of British forces in the war, and the function of the camps dramatically changed.

By the end of 1900, the British had 200,000 men (including 140,000 regulars) in Southern Africa. Although the principal Boer armies had been defeated and the capitals of the Transvaal and Orange Free State were occupied, the Boers had then simply gone over to guerrilla warfare. Boer forces, held by the British to be some 10,000 men but actually closer to 20,000, carried out raids into Cape Colony and attacked isolated British troop detachments and lines of communication.

To counter the Boer tactics, Kitchener decided to remove the Boer population from their farms on the Veldt and concentrate them in camps. Those remaining outside the camps would be presumed to be guerrillas. The army would conduct regular sweeps, destroying the guerrillas' means of subsistence and forcing them to conclude peace. Such a policy had been previously employed by the Spaniards in Cuba and by the Americans in the Philippine-American War (1899–1902), but this was the first time it had been applied on such a comprehensive basis. In fact, this uprooting of a large percentage of the Boer population dominated the last phase of the Second Boer War.

Ultimately the British established 45 such camps for the Boers and 64 for black Africans. Kitchener never did visit one of his concentration camps, but he claimed that the people there were "happy." The camps were not to be comfortable, but they were supposed to provide a minimum standard of living, something they clearly failed to do. Meanwhile, British troops systematically destroyed the Boer farms, crops, and livestock.

Little thought had been given by the British to medicine, blankets, or even food, and many of those being held in the camps were soon starving and prey to epidemics. There were also two scales of rations, with the lower one for women and children whose husbands and fathers were still fighting the British.

The camps ultimately held some 150,000 Boers, 28,000 (a figure more than twice the number of soldiers killed in the war) of whom died, most of them children (22,000). The majority of the dead succumbed to epidemics of measles and typhoid that could easily have been prevented.

Press reports on the camps led to a public outcry in Britain. Kitchener then abandoned the concentration camps in favor of an even more inhumane program of leaving the women and children on the devastated Veldt, refusing them admission to the camps. In the summer of 1901 Kitchener went over to a strategy of protected areas, progressively working out from these to clear the countryside of guerrillas and restore civilian life. The British also made use of barbed-wire fences and blockhouses. More successful than these, however, was an improved native intelligence-collection system and raiding tactics adopted from the Boers. The plight of their families, exhausted resources, and fears of an African rising that would leave their families unprotected finally prompted the Boers to conclude peace in the Treaty of Vereeniging of May 1902.

Spencer C. Tucker

See also Pacification; Philippine Islands and U.S. Pacification during the Philippine-American War; *Reconcentrado* System; South African War

Further Reading

Judd, Denis, and Keith Terrance Surridge. *The Boer War.* New York: Palgrave Macmillan, 2003.

Pakenham, Thomas. *The Boer War.* New York: Random House, 1979.

Contras

Paramilitary insurgent force trained and funded by the United States to challenge Nicaragua's leftist Sandinista regime. The 1979 overthrow of the Anastasio Somoza Debayle regime in Nicaragua brought to power a government committed to socialism and openly allied with Cuba. This government, headed by President Daniel Ortega and leaders of the Sandinista Liberation Front, promised radical social and political reforms. Fearing that leftist and Communist regimes would spread revolution across Central America, the administration of President Ronald Reagan created an anti-Sandinista force, known as the Contras. The Central Intelligence Agency (CIA), under authority granted to it by National Security Decision Directive 17 of November 23, 1981, coordinated the establishment of a force of local combatants capable of carrying out attacks in Nicaragua.

The Contra program had three active fronts. Mercenaries, many of whom were displaced soldiers and officers from the national guard of the deposed Somoza dictatorship, trained in Honduras. Their units, organized as the Nicaraguan Democratic Force (Fuerza Democrática Nicaragüense) launched raids into northern Nicaragua beginning in August 1981. Also, Moskito Indians were encouraged to wage their own resistance movement along Nicaragua's Caribbean coast. Inside neighboring Costa Rica, a more heterogeneous collection of opposition groups, ranging from ex-Somoza followers to disaffected Sandinistas, formed the Democratic Revolutionary Alliance (Alianza Revolucionaria Democrática) in 1982 to pressure the new Nicaraguan government from the South.

The Contras helped drain the military resources of the Sandinista government. By 1984, Contra forces numbered more than 10,000 men. Their leaders promised to overthrow the Sandinista government with help from the United States.

The Contras soon became the target of international protest. Comparing their operations to earlier U.S. interventions in Guatemala and Cuba, the Sandinista government and sympathetic supporters in Canada and Europe challenged the U.S. effort both in the United Nations (UN) and in the International Court of Justice. In 1986 the International Court of Justice ruled against the United States and urged it to cease all support. U.S. officials countered that the court had no jurisdiction in the matter, and Washington simply ignored the verdict.

In the United States, revelations of human rights abuses mobilized congressional opposition to the Contras. Congress first banned, under the December 1982 Boland Amendment, any funding from the CIA or the Department of Defense for the Contras. Then in October 1984, Congress voted to forbid support from any government agency for them. Relying on intermediaries, such as Argentine military officers, to provide training and matériel, the Reagan administration sustained the program for five more years.

To circumvent the congressional restrictions, the Reagan administration developed alternative funding sources, including an exchange of military equipment designated for use by the Israeli Army for cash from Iran. Revenue generated by inflating the price of missiles, spare parts, and other matériel provided profits that staff members in the U.S. National Security Agency diverted to the Contra forces. In 1986, Lebanese press sources revealed the scheme. This forced the Reagan administration to form a special commission, led by former senator John Tower, to investigate and report on the matter in December 1986. Congress conducted its own investigation. The Iran-Contra Hearings concluded in March 1988 with indictments of Oliver North and John Poindexter, who had helped organize the prohibited support of the Contras from their positions within the government.

Despite efforts of Central American leaders to broker a regional peace and despite the Contras' lack of support in Nicaragua, the program remained a core component of U.S. policy in Central America throughout much of the 1980s. The Sandinistas' electoral defeat in 1990 ended their control of the Nicaraguan government. With the raison d'être of the Contras gone, UN peacekeeping forces supervised the disarmament of the Contras.

Daniel Lewis

See also Frente Sandinista de Liberación; Nicaraguan Revolution

Further Reading

Dillon, Sam. *Commandos: The CIA and Nicaragua's Contra Rebels.* New York: Henry Holt, 1991.

Pastor, Robert. *Condemned to Repetition: The United States and Nicaragua.* Princeton, NJ: Princeton University Press, 1988.

Cordon Sanitaire

The literal meaning of the French term cordon sanitaire is "sanitary cordon." Originally it meant to cordon off an area to prevent a disease from spreading. During the Cold War, the term was used to describe the containment policy of the Soviet Union advanced by George Kennan.

In counterinsurgencies, a cordon sanitaire consists of a physical barrier to deny insurgents access to certain areas or to separate them from the population. One element of Lieutenant General Sir Harold Briggs's plan to deal with the Communist insurgents in Malaya in 1950 was to relocate Chinese squatters to so-called New Villages, where the government could control those who entered and left. This technique deprived the guerrillas of food, money, intelligence, and other support from the population. The Strategic Hamlet Program of the Vietnam War had the same goal.

During the Rhodesian Bush War, the cordon sanitaire was a border of minefields stretching along the Rhodesian borders with Zambia and Mozambique. During the Angolan Civil War, the South Africans established a 1,000-mile cordon sanitaire of fences, minefields, and free-fire zones along the border between Namibia and Angola.

Donald A. MacCuish

See also Angolan Insurgency; Briggs, Sir Harold Rawdon; Colby, William Egan; Kenya Emergency; Malayan Emergency; Rhodesian Bush War; Selous Scouts; Strategic Hamlet Program

Further Reading

Beckett, Ian F. W. *Modern Insurgencies and Counter-Insurgencies: Guerrillas and Their Opponents since 1750.* London: Routledge, 2001.

Cann, John P. *Counterinsurgency in Africa: The Portuguese Way of War, 1961–1974.* St. Petersburg, FL: Hailer, 2005.

Jackson, Robert. *The Malayan Emergency & Indonesian Confrontation.* Barnsley, UK: Pen and Sword, 2011.

Counterinsurgency Manuals, U.S. Military

Joint Publication 3–24: Counterinsurgency Operations is the capstone U.S. Defense Department document for counterinsurgency (COIN) operations at the strategic and operational levels. The document defines insurgency as an organized movement aimed at the overthrow of a constituted government through the use of subversion and armed conflict. Put simply, to the insurgent, a combination of subversion and violence would bring about the desired political change. Counterinsurgents must develop comprehensive civilian and military efforts operating in concert to address core grievances feeding the insurgency. Civilians should lead the overall COIN effort and coordinate among government, nongovernment, and military organizations to assist the governments of failed, failing, and recovering states. If civilians are unable to take the lead, then the military joint force commander may be tasked with taking the initiative, even though the military instrument is only one element of a comprehensive approach for success.

COIN operations can be difficult to coordinate because security operations (fighting) and addressing core grievances (building) may need to be addressed simultaneously. Offensive and defensive counterguerrilla operations would be aimed at insurgent combatants, while stability operations address the core grievances of insurgency as well as drivers of conflict.

Joint Publication 3–24 identifies the primary objective of any COIN operation as fostering the development of effective governance by a legitimate government.

Field Manual 3–24 and *Marine Corps Warfighting Publication No. 3–33.5: Counterinsurgency* focus on the operational and tactical levels of war. *Field Manual 3–24* states that long-term success in COIN depends on the people taking charge of their own affairs and consenting to the government's rule. Achieving this condition requires the government to eliminate as many causes of the insurgency as feasible. This may include eliminating those extremists whose beliefs prevent them from ever reconciling with the government.

Over time, counterinsurgents aim to enable a country or regime to provide the security and rule of law that allow establishment of social services and growth of economic activity. COIN thus involves the application of national power in the political, military, economic, social, information, and infrastructure fields and disciplines. *Field Manual 3–24* challenges commanders and staffs to identify the root cause or causes of the insurgency, the extent to which the insurgency enjoys internal and external support, the basis (ideology and narrative) on which insurgents appeal to the target population, the insurgents' motivation and depth of commitment, likely insurgent weapons and tactics, and the operational environment in which insurgents seek to initiate and develop their campaign and strategy.

Subsequent chapters in *Field Manual 3–24* focus on unity of effort, intelligence, designing and executing COIN campaigns and operations, and the development of host-nation security forces.

Field Manual No. 3–24.2: Tactics in COIN establishes fundamental principles for tactical counterinsurgency operations at the company, battalion, and brigade levels. *Field Manual 3–24.2* introduces the eight operational variables and the six mission variables that are critical to developing a COIN plan that can defeat the insurgency. The eight interrelated operational variables used to analyze the operational environment are political, military, economic, social, information, infrastructure, physical environment, and time (known as PMESII-PT). The six mission variables that guide an in-depth analysis of the civil considerations include areas, structures, capabilities, organizations, people, and events (known as ASCOPE). *Field Manual 3–24.2* identifies the differing elements and organizations contributing to an insurgency and then provides the requirements for successful COIN operations at the tactical level. This includes discussion of the clear-hold-build operation, which is a full spectrum operation that combines offense (finding and eliminating the insurgent), defense (protecting the local populace), and stability (rebuilding the infrastructure, increasing the legitimacy of the local government, and bringing the rule of law to the area) operations. Subsequent chapters discuss planning, offensive operations, defensive operations, and stability operations, concluding with how-to advice on support to host-nation security forces.

Field Manual No. 3–07: Stability Operations presents overarching doctrinal guidance and direction for conducting stability operations encompassing various military missions, tasks, and activities conducted outside the United States in coordination with other instruments of national power. Stability operations leverage the coercive and constructive capabilities of the military force to establish a safe and secure environment; facilitate reconciliation among local or regional adversaries; establish political, legal, social, and economic institutions; and facilitate the transition of responsibility to a legitimate civil authority. Through stability operations, military forces help to set the conditions that enable the actions of the other instruments of national power to succeed in achieving the broad goals of conflict transformation. Providing security and control stabilizes the area of operations. These efforts provide a foundation for transitioning to civilian control by the host nation.

While stability operations are usually conducted to support a host-nation government, they may also support the efforts of a transitional civil or military authority when no legitimate government exists. *Field Manual 3–07* describes the essential stability tasks, including planning for stability as well as security sector reform.

Field Manual No. 3–07.1: Security Force Assistance is focused on the operational and tactical levels. *Field Manual 3–07.1* provides doctrinal guidance and direction for how U.S. forces contribute to security force assistance (SFA) and focuses on the brigade combat team conducting SFA and advising foreign security forces. Initial chapters provide a framework for SFA and considerations for the brigade combat team operations process, for augmenting the modular brigade for security force assistance, for unit employment, and for sustainment considerations. The remainder of the manual focuses on the adviser, adviser cultural and communication considerations, the adviser working with counterparts, and cross-cultural influencing and communication.

Biff L. Baker

Further Reading

U.S. Department of the Army. *Field Manual No. 3–07: Stability Operations,* Washington, DC: U.S. Army, Training and Doctrine Command, 2008.

U.S. Department of the Army. *Field Manual No. 3–07.1: Security Force Assistance.* Washington, DC: U.S. Army, Training and Doctrine Command, 2009.

U.S. Department of the Army. *Field Manual No. 3–24 and Marine Corps Warfighting Publication No. 3–33.5: Counterinsurgency.* Washington, DC: U.S. Army, Training and Doctrine Command, 2006.

U.S. Department of the Army. *Field Manual No. 3–24.2: Tactics in COIN.* Washington, DC: U.S. Army, Training and Doctrine Command, 2009.

U.S. Department of Defense. *Joint Publication 3–24: Counterinsurgency Operations.* Washington, DC: Headquarters, Department of the Army, 2009.

Crazy Horse

Birth Date: ca. 1840
Death Date: September 5, 1877

Lakota Sioux war chief who fought U.S. forces on the Great Plains. Crazy Horse remains one of the most mysterious figures in American history. Most sources accept that he was born sometime in 1840. His father, who survived him and became one of the major sources of information about him, had also been called Crazy Horse, but when his son reached maturity and wished to take that name, his father took the name Worm. The tribal affiliation of Crazy Horse's mother is also somewhat ambiguous. Most sources identify her as a Brule Sioux, but some contend that she was a Miniconjou Sioux.

As a young warrior, Crazy Horse earned a reputation for skill and fearlessness in battle against the Lakotas's tribal enemies: the Arikarass, Blackfeet, Crows, Pawnees, and Shoshones. After the Lakotas allied themselves with the Cheyennes, Crazy Horse distinguished himself in his first battles against the U.S. military, at Red Buttes and Platte River Bridge Station. He first came fully to the attention of the U.S. military and of the American public during Red Cloud's War (1866–1868). In violation of existing treaties, the U.S. Army had constructed forts along the Bozeman Trail, which provided an eastern route to gold-rich Virginia City, Montana. On December 21, 1866, Crazy Horse led a small number of warriors who lured cavalry and infantry units away from Fort Phil Kearny and into a trap sprung by many more Indians. Outnumbered more than 10 to 1, the 80 soldiers were wiped out in what became known as the Fetterman Massacre for the commander of the doomed unit, Captain William Fetterman. It was to this point the worst defeat suffered by the army during the Plains Indian Wars.

On August 2, 1867, Crazy Horse attempted to repeat the Fetterman Massacre when he led an attack on a woodcutting party sent out from Fort Phil Kearny. But in what became known as the Wagon Box Fight, the soldiers surprised and eventually drove off the Lakotas with the much enhanced firepower provided by their recently issued breech-loading rifles.

Ten years later during what became known as the Sioux War or Great Sioux War (1876–1877), Crazy Horse led about 1,500 Lakota and Cheyenne warriors against Brigadier General George Crook's roughly equal force of cavalry, infantry, and Native American allies in the Battle of the Rosebud on June 17, 1876. Although neither side committed fully enough to the battle to sustain sizable losses, Crook's advance into Sioux territory was temporarily checked, delaying his rendezvous with the 7th Cavalry Regiment under Lieutenant Colonel George A. Custer.

All Native American sources agree that Crazy Horse had a decisive role in the annihilation of Custer's men at the Battle of the Little Big Horn (June 25–26, 1876). Yet nothing is known about Crazy Horse's specific actions during the engagement. Nonetheless, his notoriety following the massacre of Custer and his troopers made Crazy Horse a prime target of the forces sent to subdue the Sioux and Cheyennes.

After his surrender in May 1877, Crazy Horse was held at Camp Robinson, Montana. Rumors of a possible insurrection among the Lakotas led to an order for his arrest. On September 5, 1877, Crazy Horse was bayoneted when resisting arrest and died that night.

Martin Kich

See also American Indian Wars in the West; Crook, George; Custer, George Armstrong

Further Reading

Ambrose, Stephen E. *Crazy Horse and Custer: The Parallel Lives of Two American Warriors.* New York: Anchor Books, 1996.

Matthiesen, Peter. *In the Spirit of Crazy Horse.* New York: Viking, 1991.

McMurtry, Larry. *Crazy Horse.* New York: Lipper/Viking Book, 1999.

Crook, George

Birth Date: September 8, 1828
Death Date: March 21, 1890

U.S. Army officer. George Crook was born near Dayton, Ohio, on September 8, 1828. He graduated from the U.S. Military Academy, West Point, in 1852 and was commissioned a second lieutenant and assigned to the Pacific Northwest. Promoted to first lieutenant in 1856 and to captain in 1861, in September following the outbreak of the American Civil War (1861–1865), Crook entered the volunteer establishment as colonel of the 36th Ohio Infantry Regiment and participated in actions in western Virginia. Wounded in May 1862, he was promoted to brigadier general of volunteers on September 7, 1862. Crook commanded a brigade in the Kanawha Division in the Battle of South Mountain (September 14, 1862) and in the ensuing Battle of Antietam (September 17). In the early months of 1863, he played a prominent role in operations in eastern Tennessee before assuming command of the 2nd Cavalry Division in the Army of the Cumberland in July 1863.

Given command of the Kanawha District in February 1864, Crook led a series of operations to disrupt Confederate communications between eastern Tennessee and Lynchburg, Virginia. During Major General Philip Sheridan's Shenandoah Valley Campaign (August 7, 1864–March 2, 1865), Crook commanded the Department of Western Virginia and the Army of Western Virginia (VIII Corps), and he played a conspicuous role in the succession of Union victories during that campaign. In October 1864 he was promoted to major general and continued to command the Department of Western Virginia from his headquarters in Cumberland, Maryland. On February 21, 1865, Crook and Brigadier General Benjamin Kelley were taken prisoner in a daring raid by Confederate partisans. Exchanged on March 20, Crook subsequently led a cavalry division in the Army of the Potomac as it drove toward Appomattox. Crook was breveted major general in the regular army on March 27, 1865.

After the Civil War, Crook reverted to lieutenant colonel in the regular army and assumed command of the 23rd Infantry Regiment. He spent the next few years fighting Paiute Native Americans in the Idaho Territory. In 1871 in a controversial move, Crook was assigned to command the Department of Arizona while still a lieutenant colonel.

In Arizona, Crook developed three key methods that helped him to become, in the view of many, the nation's premier Indian fighter. There were several reasons for this. First, he employed Native Americans not only as scouts but also to provide insight into the possible courses of action of his foes. Second, he discarded wagons and used only mule trains, giving him greater flexibility and speed. Third, he followed his adversaries wherever they went, even into northern Mexico, until he could bring them to battle. After the notable success of his 1872–1873 campaign, in another controversial move he was promoted directly to brigadier general.

Crook's approach paid off, and by early 1875 the hostile Apaches had been temporarily subdued. Crook then worked to improve the lot of the Apache people and show them that the benefits of peace outweighed those of war.

In March 1875 Crook was named commander of the Department of the Platte, headquartered in Omaha, Nebraska. He participated in the Sioux War of 1876–1877 and commanded one of three converging columns during the army's spring offensive. In the Battle of the Rosebud (June 17, 1876), Crook's men engaged Native Americans under Chief Crazy Horse in a spirited stand-up fight, which was unusual for Native Americans, and were forced to fall back and regroup, rendering Crook unable to support the other columns or to communicate news of his setback. Following the devastating defeat of Lieutenant Colonel George A. Custer's 7th Cavalry at the Little Big Horn, Crook largely directed the army's response, including Colonel Ranald S. Mackenzie's destruction of Cheyenne chief Dull Knife's village.

In 1882 Crook returned to Arizona, where he again employed his innovative approaches, including a heavy reliance on Indian scouts and small expeditions, but his efforts to deal with the Apaches encountered strong opposition from civilian agents and his old roommate and now rival Lieutenant General Philip Sheridan. Crook's opponents were strengthened when Geronimo led a group of Chiricahuas off the San Carlos Agency on May 17, 1885. Crook's forces wore Geronimo down, and the Apache leader finally agreed to surrender. Sheridan rejected Crook's terms, however, and demanded Geronimo's unconditional surrender. Geronimo and some of his men again fled U.S. control. Sheridan blamed Crook and his Apache scouts, and Crook was replaced by Brigadier General Nelson A. Miles.

Crook spent the last years of his life attempting to win the return of Apaches from prison in Florida to Arizona and battling with Miles and Sheridan in print. President Grover Cleveland promoted Crook to major general in April 1888 and assigned him to command the Division of the Missouri. Crook died in Chicago on March 21, 1890, while still on active duty.

Alan K. Lamm

See also American Indian Wars in the West; Custer, George Armstrong; Geronimo

Further Reading

Aleshire, Peter. *The Fox and the Whirlwind: General George Crook and Geronimo; A Paired Biography.* New York: Wiley, 2000.

Crook, George. *General George Crook: His Autobiography.* Edited by Martin F. Schmidt. Norman: University of Oklahoma Press, 1960.

Hutton, Paul A. *Phil Sheridan and His Army.* Lincoln: University of Nebraska Press, 1985.

Hutton, Paul A., ed. *Soldiers West: Biographies from the Military Frontier.* Lincoln: University of Nebraska Press, 1987.

Cuban Revolution

Start Date: 1953
End Date: 1959

The Cuban Revolution began in July 1953 and ended with the overthrow of dictator Fulgencio Batista's regime on January 1, 1959. Initially, the revolution was an urban movement incorporating student groups and other political entities. Batista's coup d'état in 1952 had sparked widespread popular outrage, and Fidel Castro's movement was only one of a number that sprang up in opposition.

Castro launched his insurgency on July 26, 1953, with an assault on the Moncada Barracks at Santiago. The attack was a failure. Castro claimed later that 9 insurgents died in the fighting and that 56 others were killed afterward. Castro and his brother Raúl were among those taken prisoner. Fidel Castro was tried and sentenced to 15 years in prison; Raúl Castro received a sentence of 13 years. Fidel Castro's trial made him a national political figure, however. In the course of his nearly four-hour-long remarks, Castro told the court, "Condemn me, it does not matter. History will absolve me."

In 1955 following his election as president, Batista succumbed to political pressure and released a number of political prisoners, including the Castro brothers, who then left Cuba for Mexico. That June, Fidel Castro met Argentine revolutionary Ernesto "Che" Guevara, who would come to play a large role in the insurgency. In recognition of the Moncada Barracks attack, Castro named his insurgent group the Movimiento 26 de Julio (26th of July Movement).

Following some training, 82 insurgents traveled to Cuba in the yacht *Gramma,* arriving at Playa Las Colcordas on December 2, 1956. After coming ashore, the men began the trek to the Sierra Maestra mountain range of southeastern Cuba. En route, Batista's soldiers killed the majority. No more than 20 insurgents reached the Sierre Maestra, and it was some time before they were able to link up, aided by sympathetic peasants.

Meanwhile, on March 13, 1957, the anticommunist Directorio Revolucionario (DR, Revolutionary Directorate), consisting largely of students, assaulted the

Presidential Palace in Havana, hoping to kill Batista. The attack was a failure. As part of the growing international opposition to the Batista regime, the United States imposed an economic embargo on Cuba and recalled its ambassador.

While Castro's insurgents operated in the rural areas of Cuba, Frank País concentrated on mobilizing urban opposition to the Batista regime. Castro believed that strikes supported by military action would bring down the regime. The growth of the urban insurgency made it difficult for Batista to eradicate the movement, although País was assassinated in 1957. The workers who went on strike in response caused Castro to redouble his efforts against the regime.

Throughout the last half of 1957, Batista's government forced many opponents into exile, leading to a large expatriate community in Miami, Florida. Meanwhile, Castro remained the only opposition leader with an armed force still fighting inside Cuba. At the same time, poorly armed irregulars known as *escopeteros* harassed Batista's soldiers in Oriente Province and assisted Castro by providing intelligence and protecting his supply lines. In February 1958, Castro launched a propaganda effort through the establishment of a clandestine radio station.

Batista made several efforts to co-opt the insurgency. In early 1958 he restored civil liberties. He also encouraged the opposition to participate in what he claimed would be open elections. At the same time, the insurgents were greatly aided by an arms embargo imposed by the United States on the Batista regime in March 1958. This especially crippled the Cuban Air Force, which was unable to secure spare parts. Throughout this period Castro only commanded some 200 men, while the Cuban Army numbered 30,000–40,000. Its numerical advantage was offset by poor training and ineffective leadership.

Castro hoped to be able to topple the regime through a general strike coupled with a military offensive. The nationwide strike began in April 1958 but failed to destabilize the regime, while the insurgents lacked the military strength required for successful large-scale operations. Then in Operation VERANO, Batista sent some 12,000 soldiers into the mountains against the rebels, only to see the latter win a series of small clashes. In one such battle, the Battle of La Plata (July 11–21), Castro's forces defeated a government battalion and took 240 prisoners. But on July 29, Castro's forces were badly mauled in the Battle of Las Mercedes. Castro secured a temporary cease-fire on August 1, and during a week of fruitless negotiations he succeeded in extracting his men from the government trap.

On August 21, 1958, Castro began his own military offensive in Oriente Province, utilizing weapons captured during the government offensive and those smuggled in from abroad by aircraft. On December 31, a combined rebel offensive took Santa Clara, capital of Villa Clara Province. Recognizing the inevitable, Batista departed Cuba on January 1, 1959, leaving General Eulogio Cantillo in charge of the government.

Cienfuegos fell to anticommunist rebel forces cooperating with Castro on January 2. Castro then initiated negotiations to take Santiago de Cuba. The Cuban Army commander there ordered his soldiers not to fight, and on January 2, 1959,

Castro entered Santiago without a shot being fired. At the same time, the Cuban capital of Havana fell to the rebels. Castro himself arrived there in January 8.

Castro established an interim government, with Manuel Urrutia Lleó as president, on January 3. A month later Castro took the office of prime minister, and in December 1976 he also became president. Castro held effective power in Cuba until February 2008.

Gates Brown and Spencer C. Tucker

See also Castro Ruz, Fidel Alejandro; Guevara de la Serna, Ernesto

Further Reading

Farber, Samuel. *The Origins of the Cuban Revolution Reconsidered.* Chapel Hill: University of North Carolina Press, 2006.

Leonard, Thomas M. *Castro and the Cuban Revolution.* Westport, CT: Greenwood, 1999.

Pérez-Stable, Marifeli. *The Cuban Revolution: Origins, Course, and Legacy.* New York: Oxford University Press, 2012

Sweig, Julia. *Inside the Cuban Revolution: Fidel Castro and the Urban Underground.* Cambridge, MA: Harvard University Press, 2004.

Cuban War of Independence

Start Date: February 24, 1895
End Date: August 1898

An insurrection against Spanish colonial rule in Cuba began on February 24, 1895, and lasted until the defeat of Spain by U.S. forces in August 1898 in the Spanish-American War. The Cuban War of Independence was the last of three separate revolts on the island in the last half of the 19th century. The other two were the Ten Years' War of 1868–1878 and the Little War (La Guerra Chiquita) of 1879–1880.

In the 1890s the Cuban Revolutionary Party, led by José Martí y Pérez, was the leading proponent of Cuban independence. Founded in 1892 by Martí, the party sought independence from Spain, removal of legal distinctions based on race, amity with those Spaniards who supported the party and the revolution, and economic and land reforms. However, many planters and a large segment of the middle class wished to remain part of the Spanish Empire while securing increased autonomy from Spanish rule.

The Cuban War of Independence began on February 24, 1895, near Santiago de Cuba in the poorer eastern part of the island. Attempts to spread the uprising across the island faltered when Spanish officials arrested rebel leaders en masse in Havana and Matanzas. For most of the year, the rebellion was largely confined to eastern Cuba. The death of Martí in May 1895 further hampered the rebellion. Spain's appointment of Arsenio Martínez de Campos, the victor in the Ten Years' War, as captain-general offered hope for a quick end to the conflict. Martínez was a conciliatory figure with appeal to those in Cuba seeking autonomy and reform.

Cuban insurgents in the field during the Cuban War of Independence, 1898. (Paine, Ralph D. *Roads of Adventure*, 1922)

Any hope for a quick reconciliation ended when Martínez was unable to confine the uprising to the eastern part of the island or reach any agreement with the autonomists. Spanish conservatives now gave up any pretense of a negotiated end to the conflict and became determined to eradicate the rebellion on the field of battle. The rebels were now fighting both the Spanish colonial authorities and the planters. The planters sided with the colonial regime because of the need to protect their holdings and their status in Cuban society.

While Martí had been the intellectual and political leader of the rebellion, the rebel army was led by Máximo Gómez y Báez and Antonio Maceo Grajales. Gómez, a former Spanish general, developed the strategy of hit-and-run tactics, avoiding pitched battles with the better-equipped and more numerous Spanish colonial troops. He also made war on the lifeblood of the Cuban elite and the colonial regime by attacking and destroying Cuban sugar plantations. In this the rebels received significant support from the peasants and black plantation workers in the countryside. As the war dragged on into 1896, the Cuban Junta—a Cuban exile group in the United States—was able to swing American popular opinion to the rebel side. The junta was also instrumental in funneling arms and money to the rebels. In 1896 the rebels were also able to inflict significant damage to both the Cuban and Spanish economies when they attacked the sugarcane industry in the more prosperous western part of Cuba.

As the rebellion endured, it turned increasingly vicious on both sides. The rebels' invasion of western Cuba led to the appointment in 1896 of General Valeriano Weyler y Nicolau as Cuban governor and leader of the Spanish forces, replacing Martínez. Weyler believed that the way to defeat the rebels was to cut them off from the support of the peasants in the countryside. Toward that end, he introduced the policy of *reconcentrado* (reconcentration), which involved the forced relocation of peasants from their homes and farms into fortified government-run cities and camps. More than 500,000 Cubans were relocated as a result of this policy.

Weyler's policy led to economic, political, and military catastrophe. Not only were the peasants removed from their land, but their crops were burned and their animals were slaughtered. Thousands of relocated peasants also died, for the relocation centers were ill-equipped to feed or shelter their inhabitants. Others died from diseases caused by the close quarters and the abysmal sanitation.

To be fair to Weyler, the destruction of property was not new to the conflict, but his forced and draconian removal of the peasants from their land added a new twist. Weyler's heavy-handed measures swelled the ranks of the rebel army. World public opinion also strongly opposed Weyler's policies. This was especially true in the United States, where attitudes were shaped by the sensationalist yellow press. With international pressure mounting, Weyler was recalled to Spain in October 1897.

The war's destruction increased as the Spanish retreated into the cities and fortified villages and the rebel Cubans increasingly controlled the countryside. This led to a vicious war of attrition as the rebels inflicted more damage on the large planters and the Spanish made war against the peasants. The war dragged on, with neither side able to defeat the other. At the beginning of 1897, the tide slowly turned against the Spaniards as the rebels grew stronger and bolder, while Spanish morale plummeted. It was now apparent to most knowledgeable observers that the Spanish cause was lost and that the Spanish government was desperately looking for a way out of the Cuban morass.

A great shadow loomed large over the Cuban War of Independence, that of the United States. Indeed, segments of the American population had a long-standing interest in Cuba. Before the American Civil War (1861–1865), many Southerners expressed a desire to annex Cuba to help offset Northern power in Congress. While this did not occur, Cuba did attract significant American capital in plantations and sugar-processing plants. Following the Civil War, American investment in the island steadily grew, as did American involvement in Cuban internal affairs. There was also renewed interest in seizing Cuba from Spain and making it part of the United States. This time, the lead was taken by business leaders and proponents of American empire. American investments by the time of Cuban insurrection had grown enormously, and tensions between the United States and Spain increased as the United States became frustrated with Spanish colonial rule and economic restrictions.

Cubans seeking independence from Spain had long had a presence in the United States, and they lobbied hard for American political and popular support for independence. The Cuban Junta succeeded in casting the Cuban revolt in terms of an oppressed American people attempting to gain their freedom from a European power. In order to gain support from the American public, Cuban publicists often compared their struggle to the American Revolutionary War and portrayed the Spanish government as corrupt, brutal, and repressive.

All of this propagandist agitation succeeded, for the U.S. government and the American people strongly supported the rebels. The yellow press played a key role. American newspapers sent reporters to the island, who reported in lurid detail the deprivations of the cruel Spanish colonial overlords. Many of the stories, filed from the safety of Havana, were full of fabrications and lacked any notion of balanced reporting. Once Weyler had instituted his *reconcentrado* system, story upon story appeared detailing the horrid consequences of the policy. Tensions between the United States and Spain, spurred by the rantings of the yellow press, the U.S. desire to protect American commercial interests on the island, and the drumbeat of American imperialists, grew to dangerous proportions by 1898. The explosion and destruction of the U.S. Navy battleship (armored cruiser) *Maine* in Havana Harbor on February 15, 1898, was an ideological breaking point that ultimately led to the Spanish-American War.

The U.S. conquest of the island of Cuba and the defeat of Spain in August 1898 enabled Cuba to gain its independence from Spain. Cuban independence was delayed, however, as the United States established an occupation government in an effort to secure a stable regime that would protect American economic interests. The issue was decided in 1901 via the Platt Amendment, as Cuba was granted its hard-won independence. In 1902 Cuba formally became an independent nation, albeit one under the thumb of its powerful neighbor to the north. Most Cubans soon found out that the formalized Spanish policies that had resulted in inequity and repression were merely replaced by informal political-economic policies that were in large part controlled by Americans.

Rick Dyson

See also Ten Years' War in Cuba

Further Reading

Ferrer, Ada. *Insurgent Cuba: Race, Nation, and Revolution, 1868–1898.* Chapel Hill: University of North Carolina Press, 1999.

Pérez, Louis A., Jr. *Cuba: Between Reform and Revolution.* New York: Oxford University Press USA, 2006.

Pérez, Louis A., Jr. *Cuba between Empires, 1878–1902.* Pittsburgh, PA: University of Pittsburgh Press, 1983.

Tone, John L. *War and Genocide in Cuba, 1895–1898.* Chapel Hill: University of North Carolina Press, 2006.

Cultural Anthropology and Insurgency and Counterinsurgency

The term "anthropology," coined by German philosopher Magnus Hundt in 1501, is the study of humanity. Cultural anthropology is a branch of anthropology that focuses on the study of cultural variation among humans, including the collection of data about the impact of global economic and political processes on local cultural realities. Modern anthropologists use a variety of methods, including participant observation, interviews, and surveys. This fieldwork has the anthropologist spending extended periods of time at the research location.

In an insurgency or counterinsurgency environment, cultural anthropology can provide an analysis of the population's grievances as well as the appropriate response of the government or counterinsurgent forces (both military and civil) to these. There are three factors that must be considered throughout discussions of anthropology and warfare. First, no matter where operations are located in the spectrum of violence, they are about people. Second, hostile, neutral, or friendly populations are the center of gravity in military operations. Third, military forces operate in environments vastly different from that to which they are accustomed.

Beginning with the U.S. Marine Corps' *Small Wars Manual* in 1940, the U.S. military recognized that an appreciation of cultural factors is important to the success of military operations in a foreign theater.

The Department of Defense and the Department of State routinely gather cultural information that will help facilitate the achievement of diplomatic or security and defense goals. Various operational dimensions are involved here; these are physical, economic, social, political, and belief systems.

Physical Dimension

The physical dimension includes water, land, food, shelter, and climate. Throughout history, man has fought over access to and control of water and resources. Thus, many societies have intricate and often unspoken rules that regulate their use.

From a cultural perspective, water and land are more than the physical entity. Many cultural groups believe that certain places hold a symbolic meaning that is significantly greater than the simple physical features of terrain. Water may be used in religious or other rituals that are not readily apparent. Thus, a deploying unit must ask who, locally, has the legitimate ability to determine outsiders' access to land and water. Lack of access may have been one of the points of discontent by the indigenous population against the ruling elite.

Food, shelter, and climate are all part of the physical dimension. Drought and/ or a lack of arable land can have a significant impact on the availability of food. Understanding the climate and the seasons may contribute to a greater understanding of attacks by insurgents or periods of docility required in order to plant or cultivate crops.

Economic Dimension

A governmentally regulated, controlled, and taxed formal economy is a key indicator of a strong state. The presence of a nonregulated informal economy is often a key indicator of a weak state. Some informal economies include human trafficking and prostitution, drug trafficking, and black market bartering of quasi-legal goods and services.

Throughout history, informal economies have existed that are intertwined with the formal economy as interdependent networks of exchange. Such economic interactions have a significant impact on social relationships in every culture. Money secured from uncontrolled and unregulated trade, especially that in illegal drugs, may be used to fund insurgent activities. Bartering (e.g., exchanging guns for drugs) is a major concern for counterinsurgent forces.

Social Dimension

Social structures consist of a set of organized relationships or ties among people. Hence, there are numerous social factors that influence insurgency and counter-insurgency operations. These include age, gender, kinship, class, ethnicity, and religious membership.

Not all cultures define age, or age-appropriate roles, in a similar manner. In some societies, children may start work at age six or seven. Children may also participate in military and insurgent activities, as being a warrior is associated with adulthood.

Cultures also define gender roles differently. Thus, girls may be married by the age of 12 or 13 and may be denied education opportunities. Also, purdah, or gender separation of men and women, stretches from West Africa to Central and South Asia.

Kinship is defined as a relationship between those who share a genealogical origin through biological, cultural, or historical descent. Tribes have a corporate identity (e.g., common ancestor), and individuals have a position and role in the tribal structure according to lineage. Some tribal leaders are selected in part on the basis of birth. Counterinsurgent forces must remember that not all tribes are the same.

Class is a way of stratifying groups of people according to their economic status and power and may include wealth, education, occupation, and inheritance. An insurgency may arise when a privileged elite controls wealth and politics while those at the bottom are poor and marginalized.

Ethnic identity is distinguished by specific behaviors, characteristics, and social symbols that may include language, symbols, unique traditions, rituals, and holidays; clothing or dress unique to the group; a shared sense or memory enshrined in mythical stories or folktales; or attachment to a place or region that holds symbolic meaning.

Religious membership is defined as being part of a group of people who consider themselves united by religious faith.

Political Dimension

Political structures may include bands, tribes, chiefdoms, or states. A band is a small group of people who know each other face-to-face and work closely for survival.

Groups in the initial stages of an insurgency often reflect the characteristics of a band. A tribe is a group based on the internal assumption of kinship, which binds members together in economic, political, and social relationships. Leadership is usually determined by inheritance. The chiefdom is a political structure with a chief who possesses authority. Chiefdoms rely on the support of subordinate chiefs and groups, often through patron-client relationships. Finally, there is the state. A state is a larger political structure with centralized authority and control and defined territorial boundaries. A failed or failing state may be facing an insurgency due to its incapacity to perform functions that the indigenous population has come to expect.

Belief Systems

Belief is a certainty, learned through inherited group experiences and practices, about the substance and meaning of phenomena and human activity. Beliefs may be cultural beliefs and ideals expressed through observable words and actions; historical stories and myths; symbols, rituals, and icons; and taboos governing acceptable or forbidden behaviors. Counterinsurgents may learn much about local beliefs by determining who are the important icons, historical figures, mythical figures, and present-day heroes.

Knowledge of rituals and ceremonies is important because of their sociopolitical context and meaning to those involved. Such knowledge allows counterinsurgents to show respect and understanding toward indigenous people. Counterinsurgents must understand norms, mores, and taboos of the local people. Cultural beliefs are often a reflection of religious beliefs and cultural expectations about how a person ought to behave in a given situation. Violations of local cultural beliefs usually provoke serious repercussions, such as honor killings for infidelity.

Counterinsurgents must distinguish between what people actually do, as in the practice of their religion, and what the formal religious authorities say they should do. Religious interpretations and daily practices are often based on local traditions, beliefs, superstitions, and taboos, all reinforcing existing cultural norms.

A knowledge of cultural anthropology and these operational dimensions (physical, economic, social, political, and belief systems) and the attention paid toward verbal and nonverbal behavior will assist the counterinsurgent in a greater understanding of the local populace. However, since the beginning of the Global War on Terror, some professional organizations such as the American Anthropology Association have opposed employing anthropologists in a military environment.

Biff L. Baker

Further Reading

Salmoni, Barak A., and Paula Holmes-Eber. *Operational Culture for the Warfighter: Principles and Applications*. Quantico, VA: Marine Corps University Press, 2011.

U.S. Department of the Navy. *NAVMC Manual No. 2890: United States Marine Corps Small Wars Manual*. Washington, DC: U.S. Marine Corps, 1940.

Custer, George Armstrong

Birth Date: December 5, 1839
Death Date: June 25, 1876

U.S. Army officer. George Armstrong Custer was born on December 5, 1839, in New Rumley, Ohio, although he spent part of his childhood in Monroe, Michigan. At age 16 he was admitted to the U.S. Military Academy, West Point, where he graduated, last in his class, in 1861.

Despite his mediocre student record, Custer excelled during the American Civil War. He fought in the First Battle of Bull Run (July 21, 1861), and his daring reconnaissance patrols and valor brought him to the attention of Union Army general in chief Major General George B. McClellan. Custer then served as a captain and staff officer for McClellan and Major General Alfred Pleasonton. Custer so impressed his superiors that he was promoted to brigadier general on June 29, 1863, and given command of the 2nd Brigade of the 3rd Cavalry Division at age 23.

With a flamboyant uniform that he himself designed and with his long, flowing, reddish hair, Custer became a national hero. From the Battle of Gettysburg (July 1–3, 1863) through the end of the war, he was renowned for his fearless and often decisive cavalry charges. In October 1864 he took charge of the entire 3rd Cavalry Division and became a close confidant of Major General Philip Sheridan during the Shenandoah Valley Campaign (August 7, 1864–March 2, 1865). Custer also led his men in the Third Battle of Winchester (September 19, 1864), the Battle of Fisher's Hill (September 22, 1864), and the Battle of Five Forks (April 1, 1865), among other battles. By the end of the war, he was a major general and was considered one of the most brilliant cavalry officers in the army.

Following the war, Custer reverted to his permanent rank of lieutenant colonel and was assigned to the 7th Cavalry Regiment. Because his commanding officer was frequently absent, Custer was for all intents and purposes in command. He quickly made a name for himself on the Great Plains. Dressed in fringed buckskin instead of a traditional uniform, he was the embodiment of the dashing Indian fighter. His best-selling book, *My Life on the Plains* (1874), and several popular magazine articles helped to reinforce his reputation as a military genius. Yet the Custer myth did not always square with reality.

Indeed, Custer's first experience fighting Native Americans in 1867 ended in humiliating failure during a campaign against the Cheyennes. Not only did he fail to defeat any Indians, but he was court-martialed and sentenced to a year's suspension from rank and pay for being absent without leave. He rebounded from this setback in 1868 when he surprised Chief Black Kettle's peaceful Cheyenne village in a brutal and strategically questionable attack at the Battle of the Washita (November 27, 1868) that burnished Custer's public reputation.

In 1874 Custer and the 7th Cavalry escorted a large exploratory expedition that located gold in the Black Hills of the Dakota Territory. When the U.S. government's subsequent effort to buy the Black Hills from the Sioux failed, the government essentially appropriated the land and attempted to confine the Sioux and Northern Cheyennes to significantly reduced reservations. In the spring of 1876 thousands of Sioux and Cheyennes departed for hunting grounds in the Powder River and Yellowstone River Valleys, and this gave U.S. officials the justification to send in the military in the Sioux War of 1876–1877. The 7th Cavalry spearheaded Brigadier General Alfred Terry's column, part of a large three-pronged campaign to subdue the Indians.

On June 25, 1876, Custer's scouts located a massive Indian encampment on the Little Big Horn River in southwestern Montana. Perceiving an opportunity, Custer divided his 7th Cavalry into three battalions and, without waiting for the commands of Terry and Colonel John Gibbon to arrive, rashly attacked the encampment. Custer led his battalion of some 225 men in an effort to outflank the Sioux. The other two columns were quickly repulsed, while that led by Custer was surrounded. Outnumbered 10 to 1, it was slaughtered. Custer's Last Stand, as the event became known, stunned Americans and attached to Custer an immortality that he probably did not deserve but that fit with his reputation and public persona.

Andy Johns

See also American Indian Wars in the West

Further Reading

Ambrose, Stephen E. *Crazy Horse and Custer: The Parallel Lives of Two American Warriors.* New York: Doubleday, 1975

Monaghan, Jay. *Custer: The Life of General George Armstrong Custer.* Lincoln: University of Nebraska Press, 1971.

Wert, Jeffrey D. *Custer: The Controversial Life of George Armstrong Custer.* New York: Simon and Schuster, 1996.

Cyprus Insurrection

Start Date: 1955
End Date: 1959

Between April 1, 1955, and March 1959, Greek Cypriots seeking to end British rule on Cyprus and bring about union with Greece fought British forces and won one of the most lopsided insurgent victories of modern times. The British government planned to retain Cyprus as a strategic base to support its interests in the Middle East, while the roughly 80 percent of Cypriots who claimed Greek ethnicity sought independence or preferably union (enosis) with their motherland. As spiritual leader of the Greek Cypriots, Archbishop Makarios III (1913–1977) organized protests against the British occupation in Greece, the United States, and the United Nations.

Colonel Georgios Grivas (1898–1974) directed the insurgency. Born on the island, Grivas had been a Greek Army officer before and during World War II (1939–1945), when he had organized right-wing insurgents during the Axis occupation of Greece. After the war, however, Grivas planned and managed the insurgency in Cyprus. Prior to initiating hostilities, he oversaw the smuggling into and stockpiling of arms on the island. His force was known as the Ethniki Organosis Kyprion Agoniston (EOKA, National Organization of Cypriot Fighters). At maximum strength, EOKA numbered only about 350 full-time insurgents, but twice that number of Greek Cypriots provided intelligence and helped smuggle arms and explosives.

Grivas recruited Greek Cypriot spies in the Cyprus police force, and at the start of the revolt on April 1, 1955, EOKA assassinated three special branch intelligence officers, thereby blinding the occupiers and discouraging other Greek Cypriots from serving in the police force. Grivas insisted that EOKA maintain popular support by taking nothing from the populace. The resulting solid support for EOKA made the insurgents almost invisible and invulnerable.

British officials, especially Field Marshal John Harding, governor-general of the island from 1955 to 1957, unwittingly helped Grivas by heavy-handed tactics that treated the revolt purely as a police matter. Harding attempted to follow the successful model of the Malayan Emergency (1948–1960) by integrating the military, police, and civil servants. Unfortunately for the British, the police force consisted disproportionately of Turkish Cypriots when the revolt began, and Harding expanded that force largely by hiring poorly educated and inadequately trained Turks. They alienated many Greek Cypriots, who accused the new policemen of theft and torture. A board of police officials from Britain recommended disbanding the new police force, but Harding refused and focused purely on repression of the revolt. He not only imposed curfews but also ordered the detention without trial of suspected insurgents and the execution of those people found carrying weapons or materials used in the manufacture of bombs. Several executions angered Greek Cypriots and led to criticism of Harding in Britain and abroad.

Given all this, the British found it difficult to gain cooperation or information from the population. In parallel to EOKA terrorist attacks, Greek Cypriots conducted numerous peaceful protests against British rule, many of which involved schoolchildren. When Harding refused to permit schools to fly the Greek flag, 418 of 499 elementary schools on the island closed, claiming that EOKA would take reprisals about the flag.

Having lost most of their other military bases and influence in the region, the British refused to yield control of Cyprus, which it had administered since 1878. Similarly, Turkey opposed change in the island's government, fearing that such a change might jeopardize the status of Turkish Cypriots. After repeated bombings and failed negotiations with Archbishop Makarios, on March 9, 1956, Harding exiled the cleric to the Seychelles Islands, where he nonetheless provided a propaganda symbol.

In addition to the expanded police force, Britain brought in military reinforcements. By March 1956, the British garrison on the island numbered some 14 battalions of 17,000 men. Counting police, the security forces approached 40,000 men. Even the British theater reserve for the Middle East, the 16th Parachute Brigade, became involved in counterinsurgency actions.

This large force registered some successes. The fact that there were few insurgent attacks near the Kykko Monastery in western Cyprus suggested that EOKA might be using this area as a base or sanctuary, and in May 1956 a reinforced brigade launched Operation PEPPERPOT to sweep this area. The operation enjoyed some success. Although Grivas escaped, the British recovered his diary, which documented Archbishop Makarios's involvement in the insurgency and the violent nature of EOKA plans. EOKA effectiveness was further reduced when the British banned Cypriots of Greek origin from their military bases.

Unfortunately for the British, they lacked both civilian informants and Greek-language skills to collect information. Although British intelligence officers eventually discovered Grivas's system of letter drops that were used to pass orders and information throughout the island and developed extensive information about their opponents, by that point the war had become unwinnable.

Public pressure in Britain forced Harding's resignation in 1957. He was succeeded by diplomat Hugh Foot. The British government decided that as an alternative to controlling the entire island, it would be willing to relinquish the rest of Cyprus in return for control of two military bases.

Hostilities were largely in abeyance while Britain attempted to negotiate a compromise government acceptable to both Greek and Turkish Cypriots. Despite opposition from both Athens and Ankara, following complicated negotiations the two sides reached agreement in Zurich on February 19, 1959. The London and Zurich Agreement led to an independent Cyprus on August 16, 1960, with governmental power sharing between Greek and Turkish Cypriots. The Cyprus Insurgency had claimed the lives of 105 British soldiers, 51 members of the police force, and 238 civilians, along with an estimated 90 EOKA members.

As part of the agreement, London insisted that Grivas go into exile. Meanwhile, Archbishop Makarios returned to Cyprus and, as its president, outmaneuvered all parties and controlled the island until he was overthrown in the course of a renewed Greek revolt against him, headed by Grivas, that prompted a Turkish military invasion in 1974.

Jonathan M. House

See also Ethniki Organosis Kyprion Agoniston; Grivas, Georgios; Harding, John Allan Francis

Further Reading

Corum, James S. *Training Indigenous Forces in Counterinsurgency: A Tale of Two Insurgencies.* Carlisle, PA: Strategic Studies Institute, 2006.

Crawshaw, Nancy. *The Cyprus Revolt: An Account of the Struggle for Union with Greece.* London: Allen and Unwin, 1978.

Dimitrakis, Panagiotis. "British Intelligence and the Cyprus Insurgency, 1955–1959." *International Journal of Intelligence and Counter-Intelligence* 21(2) (Summer 2008): 375–394.

Grivas, George. *The Memoirs of General Grivas.* Edited by Charles Foley. New York: Praeger, 1964.

D

Dang Xuan Khu.

See Truong Chinh

Davydov, Denis Vasilyevich

Birth Date: July 27, 1784
Death Date: May 4, 1839

Russian partisan leader, military theorist, and poet. Born into a military family on July 27, 1784, Denis Vasilyevich Davydov grew up in Moscow, where he was home schooled. An avid student of military history, he opted for a military career, which began in the cavalry in 1801 during the French Revolutionary War (1792–1802). Davydov's satirical poetry led to his dismissal from the Horse Guards and transfer to the Hussars, but he returned to the Horse Guards in 1806 as aide-de-camp to Russian general Prince Petr Bagration.

Davydov distinguished himself in his first combat in January 1807 at Wolsdorf during the War of the Fourth Coalition (1806–1807). He also fought at Eylau and was awarded a golden saber for his performance in the Russian defeat at the Battle of Friedland. Following the conclusion of peace between France and Russia, Davydov fought in the Finnish War of 1808–1809 and in the war with the Ottoman Empire (1806–1812). When Napoleon I's Grand Armée invaded Russia in June 1812, Davydov was a lieutenant colonel commanding a Hussar battalion in Bagration's army.

Prior to the Battle of Borodino (September 7, 1812), Bagration granted Davydov's request to raid French lines of communication westward. Davydov understood the need to have the support of the peasants and for easy identification had his men dress in peasant garb. He enjoyed considerable success and in one raid reportedly captured some 2,000 French soldiers. Davydov insisted on strict discipline and humane treatment of prisoners.

During the 1813 German War of Liberation, Davydov commanded a Hussar regiment. His performance brought promotion to major general. He then took part in the Russian occupation of Paris in 1814.

Following the Napoleonic Wars, Davydov took command of a brigade, but he tired of military service and retired in 1823. Already he had published several military works, including *Essay Towards a Theory of Guerrilla Warfare* (1821). Davydov returned to the army in 1825 to fight in the Russo-Persian War of 1825–1828, then again retired but rejoined the army on the occasion of the Polish Revolt of 1830–1831. For his role in helping to crush the revolt, he received promotion to lieutenant general. Davydov retired for a final time and settled at his wife's estate of Vekhnyaya Maza in central Russia, where he continued to write. He died there on May 4, 1839.

In his poetry, Davydov celebrated the life of the cavalryman. In his *Essay Towards a Theory of Guerrilla Warfare,* he stressed the need for strict discipline, securing the support of the peasantry, and surprise, speed, and mobility by the partisan force. His watchwords were *ubit-da-uiti* ("kill and escape").

Spencer C. Tucker

See also Guerrilla

Further Reading

Davidov, Denis. *In Service of the Tsar against Napoleon: The Memoirs of Denis Davidov, 1806–1814.* Edited and translated by Gregory Troubetzkoy. Westport, CT: Greenhill, 1999.

Laqueur, Walter. *Guerrilla: A Historical and Critical Study.* Boston: Little, Brown, 1976.

Debray, Jules Régis

Birth Date: September 2, 1940

French revolutionary theorist, writer, and presidential adviser. Born in Paris on September 2, 1940, Jules Régis Debray graduated from the École Normale Supérieure in 1965 with a degree in philosophy. In 1961 he visited Cuba and volunteered to teach in a rural education program. Because of a close association with French philosopher Jean-Paul Sartre, Debray was able to secure lengthy interviews with Cuban leader Fidel Castro. These led Debray to become a supporter of revolutionary movements in Latin America.

In 1966 Debray became a professor of philosophy at the University of Havana, and he began to write at length about the foco theory of revolution, based on guerrilla bands. Debray gained international recognition when he went to Bolivia to interview Cuban revolutionary Ernesto "Che" Guevara. Afterward, Debray was arrested by Bolivian authorities, tried, and sentenced to 30 years in prison. He is best known for his book *Revolution in the Revolution?* (1967). Released in 1970, Debray went to Chile and there interviewed Marxist president Salvador Allende Gossens. This led Debray to conclude that radical Socialist reform was possible through democratic, parliamentary systems.

Returning to France, in 1974 Debray joined the Socialist Party headed by François Mitterrand. Debray also served as an adviser to Mitterrand's presidential campaign of the same year. Debray then returned to writing, producing a great many works, including commentaries on revolution as well as fiction and works of philosophy.

On the election of Mitterrand to the presidency in May 1981, Debray became a special assistant in the Office of the President, responsible for advising Mitterrand on policy toward the Third World and especially Latin America. The next year Debray also became adviser to Mitterrand on cultural matters. Debray resigned in 1988 but until the mid-1900s held a succession of French government posts. By the 1990s, however, he had moved considerably to the Right politically. He also presented a critical portrait of Guevera, seemingly rejecting the revolutionary icon that Debray had done so much to help create.

Michael D. Richards

See also Castro Ruz, Fidel Alejandro; Cuban Revolution; Foco Theory; Guevara de la Serna, Ernesto

Further Reading

Debray, Régis. *Revolution in the Revolution? Armed Struggle and Political Struggle in Latin America.* New York: Monthly Review Press, 1967.

Huberman, Leo, and Paul M. Sweeney, eds. *Regis Debray and the Latin American Revolution.* New York: Monthly Review Press, 1968.

Reader, Keith. *Regis Debray: A Critical Introduction.* London: Pluto, 1995.

Decker, Carl von

Birth Date: April 21, 1784
Death Date: June 29, 1844

Prussian Army officer and guerrilla warfare theorist. The son of a Prussian Army general, Carl von Decker was born in Berlin on April 21, 1784. At age 13 he joined a Prussian artillery unit commanded by his father and then fought in the French Revolutionary War (1792–1802) and the Napoleonic Wars (1803–1815). Commissioned a lieutenant in the horse artillery during the War of the Fourth Coalition (1806–1807), Decker distinguished himself in the Battle of Eylau (February 7–8, 1807), for which he was awarded the Pour le Mérite in 1809.

Decker was promoted to major in 1817 and subsequently taught at the War College and at the Artillery and Engineering School. He was promoted to colonel in 1835. Decker died on June 29, 1844.

A prolific author of nearly a dozen books, Decker wrote on a wide range of military subjects, including artillery and cavalry doctrine and the French Revolutionary and Napoleonic Wars, such as Napoleon Bonaparte's Italian Campaign of 1796. Decker also wrote on partisan warfare. *Der Kleine Krieg im Geiste der neueren Kriegsfhrung* (The Small War in the Spirit of the New Conduct of Warfare) was published in Berlin in 1822, while *Algerien und die dortige Kriegführung* (Algeria and Local Warfare), a two-volume work treating French efforts to pacify Algeria that incorrectly predicted French failure, was published in 1844.

Decker believed that partisan warfare was the most appropriate use of irregular tactics. Partisans could be especially useful in attacking enemy lines of communication.

Decker believed that partisans required special qualities, and he stressed the need for mobility and the necessity of good relations with the local population.

Brian J. Tannehill and Spencer C. Tucker

See also Algeria, French Pacification of; Bugeaud de la Piconnerie, Thomas Robert; Davydov, Denis Vasilyevich

Further Reading

Beckett, Ian F. W. *Encyclopedia of Guerilla Warfare.* Santa Barbara, CA: ABC-CLIO, 1999.

Laqueur, Walter. *Guerrilla: A Historical and Critical Study.* Boston: Little, Brown, 1976.

DEFENSIVE SHIELD, **Operation**

Start Date: March 29, 2002
End Date: May 3, 2002

Operation DEFENSIVE SHIELD was a large-scale Israeli offensive military operation launched in the spring of 2002 to degrade the ability of a variety of Palestinian insurgent organizations to attack Israel. The operation occurred during the Palestinian uprising known as the Second (al-Aqsa) Intifada (2000–2005). The Israeli plan called for the deployment of some 20,000 Israel Defense Forces (IDF) personnel into the occupied West Bank of the Jordan River to seize and destroy bomb factories and weapons caches as well as to capture or kill Palestinian militant fighters, leaders, bomb makers, and financiers. It was the largest military operation in the occupied West Bank area since Israel seized the territory from Jordan during the 1967 Arab-Israeli War.

Operation DEFENSIVE SHIELD targeted the six most populous cities in the West Bank: Jenin, Tulkkarm, Qalqiliya, Nablus, Ramallah, and Bethlehem. Some 325,000 civilians lived in these urban areas that were subject to the operation. Although most of the population was sympathetic to insurgent attacks on Israel, only a small portion was actively engaged in supporting terrorist activity.

Operation DEFENSIVE SHIELD began on March 29, 2002, when Israeli military forces moved into the West Bank to seize control of Ramallah. The major objective here was the headquarters of the Palestinian Authority (PA) and its leader, Yasser Arafat. IDF forces quickly penetrated into Arafat's Tegart fort compound and surrounded his offices. Thirty defending Palestinian militants and PA police were killed. Arafat remained in his headquarters under effective house arrest, with all communications cut off, until May.

Two days after the seizure of Ramallah, on April 1 the IDF took control of the border towns of Tulkarm and Qalqiliya. The IDF operations did not encounter serious resistance in either town. In Tulkarm 9 militants were killed, and an IDF air strike destroyed the Tegart fort in the city used by the PA. The next day, IDF forces moved across the border into Bethlehem. That operation, thought to be relatively simple, became an international incident when the IDF surrounded and laid siege to three dozen militants holding more than 200 hostages in the Christian Church of Saint Mary, thought to be the site of the birth of Jesus Christ. During the ensuing 39-day siege, IDF snipers shot and killed 8 militants there, while 2 Israeli border police were wounded in one of several small firefights. The siege was ended diplomatically, with all the hostages released unharmed and 39 militants going abroad.

The major focus of Operation DEFENSIVE SHIELD was the urban centers of Nablus and Jenin, attacked on April 2 and 3. Operations against Jenin began on April 2, with the IDF moving into the city and sealing it off from outside communications and support. In the eight-day battle for the control of the Jenin Refugee Camp, the IDF suffered 23 soldiers killed and 52 wounded. From a casualty point of view, it was the most significant combat action for the IDF since the 1982 invasion of Lebanon. Detailed analysis by non-Israeli investigators determined that the defending Palestinian militants lost 27 fighters killed, hundreds wounded, and more than 200 taken prisoner. Civilians remaining in the city suffered 23 killed and hundreds wounded. More than 100 buildings were completely destroyed, and another 200 were rendered uninhabitable, leaving more 4,000 people homeless.

Operations in Nablus commenced on April 3. Five days later the last militant fighters holding out in the old-city Casbah surrendered. In Nablus, Israeli forces enjoyed considerable success in killing or capturing militants while at the same time minimizing Israeli and civilian casualties and collateral damage. Only eight civilians died in the fighting in Nablus, and despite Israeli employment of bulldozers, tanks, and demolitions, only four buildings were completely destroyed, although hundreds were significantly damaged. The IDF took several hundred prisoners and killed or arrested numerous insurgent leaders.

Operation DEFENSIVE SHIELD claimed Israeli casualties of 30 killed and 127 wounded. Palestinian losses are estimated at some 240 killed and 400 wounded. A total of 4,258 Palestinians were detained. As soon as the IDF withdrew, the militants acquired and trained new recruits, and the intifada continued. Operation DEFENSIVE SHIELD did, however, reduce the ability of Palestinian insurgents to carry out terrorist attacks inside Israel, and Israeli authorities therefore judged the operation a success.

Louis A. DiMarco

See also Intifada, Second; Palestine Liberation Organization

Further Reading

Cordesman, Anthony H. *Arab-Israeli Military Forces in an Era of Asymmetric Wars.* Stanford, CA: Stanford University Press, 2008.

DiMarco, Louis A. *Concrete Hell: Modern Urban Warfare from Stalingrad to Iraq.* Oxford, UK: Osprey, 2012.

Dhofar Rebellion

Start Date: 1962
End Date: 1976

The Dhofar Governorate is the largest in area of the four governorates constituting the Sultanate of Oman, which is located on the southeastern coast of the Arabian Peninsula at the strategically important mouth of the Persian Gulf. Dhofar is in southern Oman and borders Yemen and has a centuries-long tradition of defying its rulers. Geographically remote from the Omani capital city of Muscat, Dhofar features difficult terrain combining desert and forbidding mountain ranges. Its population is culturally distinct from the rest of Omani society, sharing an affinity with the tribal cultures of the Arabian Peninsula's desert interior. This orientation was fundamentally at odds with the more cosmopolitan cultural outlook of Oman's northern communities, the history of which had been shaped by their interactions with the maritime commercial world of the Indian Ocean and the Persian Gulf. A heritage of political autonomy reinforced the geographical and cultural distinctions.

Until 1959 when it was formally united with the Sultanate of Oman, Dhofar's formal status was that of an autonomous region, reflecting a 19th-century arrangement that split temporal power in Oman between the secular sultanate based in Muscat and the religious Islamic imamate based in the tribal communities of Dhofar. Over time, the institution of the imamate became the rallying point for opponents of the successive sultans, generating the momentum for several uprisings against the sultanate throughout the 19th and early 20th centuries.

The tensions between these two centers of power flared up during the reign of Sultan Said bin Talmir (r. 1931–1970). A conservative ruler determined to insulate Oman from Western ideas and institutions, Said presided over a repressive regime that had little tolerance for Dhofar's traditions of autonomy. Said implemented a limited program of internal improvements designed to raise his subjects' standard of living, education, and health, but most of these initiatives benefitted Oman's northern communities, not the Dhofar region. Said's failure to provide a meaningful response to an extended drought that ravaged Dhofar's agriculture- and livestock-based economy in the late 1950s further alienated the region's population from their ruler. This ecological and economic crisis forced hundreds of Dhofaris to seek work in neighboring nations' booming oil industries. While abroad, many were influenced by Arab nationalism and Marxist-inspired notions of national liberation and class struggle, concepts providing Dhofaris with an ideological framework for their resentment of Said's regime.

In 1962 Dhofari opposition groups united under the umbrella of the Dhofar Liberation Front (DLF), an organization whose composition reflected the fragmented character of Said's Dhofari opponents. Although the DLF espoused regional autonomy, modernization, and internal development as its principal goals, it remained essentially conservative, affirming a strong commitment to perpetuating traditional tribal and Islamic religious values. Beginning in 1963, the DLF initiated a series of limited attacks against the sultan's forces, initiating the first phase of the insurgency. But while it enjoyed limited support from Saudi Arabia and Yemen, the DLF never succeeded in gaining the support of a critical mass of the Dhofari population. At the same time, Said's small military establishment, though increasingly benefitting from British-led reorganization and training, lacked the capacity to eradicate the insurgency, which continued inconclusively throughout the mid-1960s.

The insurgency gained a new lease on life in 1967, when the DLF's radical leftist elements seized control of the insurgent movement. Led by Muhammad bin Ahmad al Ghasani, the insurgency's Marxist wing renamed itself the Popular Front for the Liberation of the Occupied Arabian Gulf (PFLOAG). This signaled a fundamental shift in the nature of the insurgency from a tribally oriented struggle for regional autonomy to a mass revolutionary movement that aspired to overthrow the sultanate, replace it with a Marxist state, and transform Oman into a springboard for leftist revolutionary activity throughout the Arabian Peninsula. In keeping with its ideological orientation, the PFLOAG received weapons and training from the newly independent People's Democratic Republic of Yemen (PDRY) as well as from the Soviet Union, China, Iraq, and the Palestine Liberation Organization (PLO).

By 1970, the PFLOAG had grown to a force of approximately 3,000–4,000 active fighters who dominated the interior of Dhofar. Oman's counterinsurgent strategy was heavy-handed and unimaginative, focusing on kinetic methods that stressed search-and-destroy tactics and virtually ignored civic action or political and economic reform.

With the PFLOAG on the threshold of victory and the counterinsurgency efforts in tatters, Said's son Qaboos bin Said al-Said mounted a coup that removed his father from the throne in 1970 and dramatically altered the strategic course of the war. Qaboos radically reoriented the government's strategy by making civic action, modernization, and internal reform integral elements of the counterinsurgency campaign. These initiatives sought to deprive the PFLOAG of popular support among Dhofaris, many of whom were growing disenchanted with the insurgent movement's attempts to eradicate Islam and impose Marxist socioeconomic norms in areas under its control. By targeting the insurgency's root causes, Qaboos's civic action plan drove a wedge between the PFLOAG fighters and the people on whose behalf they claimed to be fighting, seriously undercutting the insurgents' political legitimacy.

In parallel with these initiatives, Qaboos revived the military elements of the counterinsurgency. Using revenues from Oman's nascent oil industry, he expanded and modernized the country's armed forces. New equipment and training, in combination with the assistance of British military advisers, enhanced the effectiveness of the sultan's military. Airpower in the form of helicopters, airlift assets, and light ground-attack aircraft provided the counterinsurgents with mobility and firepower that negated the insurgents' ability to exploit the Dhofar region's rugged terrain. In addition, British Special Air Service (SAS) teams seconded to the Omani military trained former insurgents, known as *firquats,* to assist with the counterinsurgency effort. Intimately familiar with Dhofar's terrain, they provided valuable intelligence and proved highly effective in fighting their former comrades.

At the strategic and policy level, the Dhofar Development Committee, consisting of military commanders and members of Qaboos's government, ensured that military action would function in support of the civic action program. By 1976, the combination of the two elements had completely eradicated the insurgency.

Sebastian H. Lukasik

See also Popular Front for the Liberation of the Occupied Arabian Gulf; Qaboos bin Said al-Said; Special Air Service

Further Reading

Akehurst, John. *We Won a War: The Campaign in Oman, 1965–1975.* Wiltshire, UK: M. Russell, 1982.

Allen, Calvin H., and W. Lynn Rigsbee. *Oman under Qaboos: From Coup to Constitution, 1970–1976.* London: Routledge, 2000.

Gardiner, Ian. *In the Service of the Sultan: A First-Hand Account of the Dhofar Insurgency.* London: Pen and Sword, 2007.

Peterson, John. *Oman's Insurgencies: The Sultanate's Struggles for Supremacy.* London: Saqi, 2007.

Dimokratikós Stratós Elladas

Communist insurgent force during the Greek Civil War (1946–1949). The Ellinikós Laïkós Apeleftherotikós Stratós (ELAS, Greek People's Liberation Army) was the military arm of the left-wing Communist-dominated Ethniko Apeleftherotiko Metopo (EAM, National Liberation Front) that fought the German and Italian forces occupying Greece during World War II (1939–1945). As the war drew to a close in late 1944, ELAS controlled some three-fifths of Greek territory and had some 150,000 men and women under arms. In these circumstances, the EAM sought to establish its authority over all Greece.

Greece was in the British sphere of influence, and British prime minister Winston L. S. Churchill was determined to prevent the Greek Communists from seizing power. Meanwhile, relations between the British-backed Greek monarchy and the EAM/ELAS steadily deteriorated. The British returned monarchist military units to Greece and demanded that ELAS disarm. On December 2, 1944, in Athens, the Greek police opened fire on antigovernment demonstrators, triggering the Battle for Athens. The British brought in reinforcements, and the nationalists secured a victory.

Under the Varkiza Agreement in February 1945, ELAS was to disband in return for a plebiscite and general election. The EAM now splintered as moderates and Socialists abandoned it, and the Kommounistikon Komma Elladós (KKE, Greek Communist Party) membership precipitously declined from more than 400,000 to only 50,000. Meanwhile, the British strengthened the Greek National Guard and allowed government security forces to take action against the Communists.

In the Greek parliamentary elections of March 1946, the rightist candidates won a landslide victory, in part because of a Communist boycott on the claim that the government had not lived up to its promises. The KKE then declared a state of civil war and on December 27, 1946, renamed its reorganized ELAS units the Dimokratikós Strató Elladas (DSE, Democratic Army of Greece), under the leadership of Markos Vaphiadis. Operating primarily in the northern Greek mountains where they could receive assistance from the Communist Yugoslavia, Albania, and Bulgaria, the DSE insurgents boasted a maximum strength of some 25,000 men. The KKE, led by Nikos Zachariadis, committed a major strategic error when in December 1947 it committed the DSE to a conventional military offensive in the hopes of establishing a provisional government in a liberated zone of Greece.

Vaphiadis favored a continuation of guerrilla operations, but he was ousted by Zachariadis, who insisted on a static defense of DSE mountain strongholds. These could not stand against superior Greek Army firepower and resources as well as Greek airpower, thanks in large part to military assistance from the United States that rebuilt the Greek military. Tito's withdrawal of Yugoslav military support to the DSE was also a major blow, as was the Greek government's enforced resettlement of the civilian population in the mountains. All of this spelled an end to the insurgency. The DSE announced a final cease-fire on October 16, 1949, bringing the Greek Civil War to an end.

Spencer C. Tucker

See also Ellinikós Laïkós Apeleftherotikós Stratós; Greek Civil War; Tito

Further Reading

Close, David H. *The Greek Civil War, 1943–1950: Studies of Polarization.* London: Routledge, 1993.

Close, David H. *The Origins of the Greek Civil War.* New York: Longman, 1995.

Gerolymatos, Andre. *Red Acropolis, Black Terror: The Greek Civil War and the Origins of Soviet-American Rivalry.* New York: Basic Books, 2004.

Iatrides, John O. *Greece in the 1940s: A Nation in Crisis.* Hanover, NH: University Press of New England, 1981.

Dirty War.

See Guerra Sucia

Dominican Republic Insurgency and U.S. Intervention

Start Date: 1916
End Date: 1924

In April 1916 General Desiderio Arias, Dominican Republic minister of war, attempted to overthrow President Juan Isidro Jiménerz. This followed a number of years of U.S. mediation of contested presidential elections in the Dominican Republic, and U.S. president Woodrow Wilson now decided to take direct action. American troops were already in Haiti on the island of Hispaniola (shared by the Dominican Republic and Haiti), and beginning on May 5, 1916, the senior U.S. military official there, Rear Admiral William Caperton, landed some of these marines in the Dominican Republic.

Caperton arrived in the Dominican Republic on May 12. Two days later he met with Aris and demanded that he disband his forces. Aris refused to do this but did withdraw from Santo Domingo, and the marines completed their occupation of the city on May 15.

By May 28, there were 11 companies of marines in the Dominican Republic. It was soon obvious that government forces were incapable of crushing the rebellion, and this task was then turned over to the marines, whose strength continued to grow. On June 21 Colonel Joseph H. Pendleton assumed command of the marines, now designated the 2nd Provisional Marine Brigade.

On June 26 the marines advanced in two columns on General Arias's stronghold of Santiago. The major battle of the campaign occurred at Guayacamas on July 3, when Pendleton's column dispersed the rebels at a cost to itself of 1 man killed and 10 wounded; the marines counted 27 rebels dead. On July 5 as the marines approached Santiago, Arias sent word that he was disbanding his forces, and the marines occupied Santiago the next day without opposition.

On November 19 a military government was proclaimed under Rear Admiral Harry S. Knapp. The Dominican economy was restored, and a professional military organization, the Dominican Constabulary Guard, or Guardia Nacionale, was established in April 1917. Nonetheless, most Dominicans resented the loss of their sovereignty and the U.S. occupation.

In the northeastern province of San Francisco de Macorís, governor Juan Perez, an adherent of Arias, refused to order his men to hand over their arms to the Americans. On the night of November 19, 1916, two companies of marines surrounded the fortress at San Francisco, and First Lieutenant Ernest C. Williams led 12 men to rush its entrance, securing it before it could be closed. Eight of his men were wounded, but the fortress was taken. Williams was subsequently awarded the Medal of Honor for this action.

Most of the Dominican opposition was centered in the eastern provinces of El Seibo and San Pedro de Macorís. From 1917 to 1921, U.S. forces battled a strong insurgent movement there, known as the *gavilleros* and led by Vicente Evangelista. Eventually the *gavilleros* succumbed to the marines' superior firepower, airpower (a squadron of six Curtiss Jennies), and often harsh counterinsurgency tactics.

U.S. president Warren G. Harding, who assumed office in March 1921, had campaigned against the U.S. occupations of Haiti and the Dominican Republic. Following lengthy negotiations, in March 1924 Horacio Vásquez Lajara was elected president of the Dominican Republic, and his political party, Partido Alianza, won a majority in both houses of Congress. With his inauguration on July 13, the United States returned control of their government to the Dominicans and withdrew the marines.

Spencer C. Tucker

See also Haitian Insurgency and U.S. Intervention

Further Reading

Pons, Frank Moya. *The Dominican Republic: A National History.* Princeton, NJ: Markus Wiener, 1998.

Rodman, Selden. *Quisqueya; A History of the Dominican Republic.* Seattle: University of Washington Press, 1964.

Dye Marker, Project.

See McNamara Line

E

East Timor

The island of Timor is located at the southeastern edge of the Indonesian archipelago. East Timor became a Portuguese colony in the 16th century, while the western portion of the island was controlled by the Dutch. During World War II (1939–1945), East Timor was occupied first by Australia and then by Japan. After the Japanese surrender in August 1945, the Portuguese returned to East Timor. When the Portuguese government was overthrown in the April 1974 Carnation Revolution, the new military rulers announced their determination to grant independence to Portugal's colonial possessions, including East Timor. This set the stage for a brief power struggle over who would rule a newly independent East Timor.

The local independence movement was badly split, and the pro-Portuguese conservative União Democrática Timorense (UDT, Timorese Democratic Union) staged a coup on August 11, 1975, allegedly to preempt a Communist takeover. The left-leaning Frente Revolucionária Timorense de Libertação e Independêcia (FRETILIN, Revolutionary Front for the Liberation and Independence of East Timor) was ultimately victorious in the ensuing power struggle, however, and soon controlled most of East Timor. Because the Portuguese had left the island, FRETILIN proclaimed independence on November 28, 1975. The new state was not officially recognized by Portugal and Indonesia or by the United Nations (UN), which still regarded Portugal as the administering power.

Fearing a potential Communist regime in the region, in Operation KOMODO Indonesia sent military forces, identified as volunteers, to occupy East Timor on December 7, 1975. U.S. president Gerald Ford and Secretary of State Henry Kissinger had approved this step during their visit to Jakarta, Indonesia, the day before. On August 14, 1976, the Indonesian Army encountered fierce and prolonged FRETILIN resistance, which was finally broken with brute force. By 1979, official Indonesian figures reported 372,921 civilians in refugee camps, while at least 100,000 people of a population of some 680,000 had been killed since the beginning of the invasion and in the ensuing insurgency. The UN Security Council denounced the situation and called upon Indonesia to withdraw its troops but failed to formally condemn the invasion in a December 1975 resolution. While the UN never recognized Indonesian sovereignty, several Arab and Asian states recognized the occupation.

In the years following the invasion, the United States, Canada, Japan, and Australia were among the powers recognizing de facto Indonesian sovereignty. Australia granted de jure recognition in February 1979, when it opened negotiations for the exploration of oil fields off the Timorese coast. Washington regarded Indonesian dictator General Suharto as a bulwark against Soviet influence in Southeast Asia. Furthermore, the Ombai-Wetar Straits off the coast of East Timor permitted undetected submarine passage between the Pacific and Indian Oceans, an important aspect of U.S. Navy strategy.

There was, however, widespread international outrage following severe Indonesian repressions and the killing of some 250 demonstrators by Indonesian soldiers in the so-called Santa Cruz Massacre (Dili Massacre) on November 12, 1991, an event filmed by two American journalists. Still, without strong international support, Timorese insurgents, led by Xanana Gusmao, had little prospect of winning independence, even after its international spokesmen, Jose Ramos-Horta and Bishop Belo, were awarded the Nobel Peace Prize in 1996.

Subsequent to Suharto's resignation in May 1998, his successor B. J. Habibie surprisingly offered to stage a referendum on the future of East Timor. The vote went ahead on August 30, 1999, with 78.5 percent opting for independence. Only hours after the vote had been tallied, however, pro-Indonesian militias embarked on violence and looting. After a UN fact-finding mission concluded that the violence had been orchestrated by the Indonesian Army, international pressure persuaded Habibie to accept a UN peacekeeping force; it arrived on September 20, 1999. East Timor was placed under UN supervision and finally achieved independence on May 20, 2002. Officially the Democratic Republic of Timor-Leste, it consists of the eastern part of Timor, several nearby smaller islands, and an enclave in the northwestern part of Indonesian Timor.

Jan Martin Lemnitzer

Further Reading

Krieger, Heike, ed. *East Timor and the International Community: Basic Documents.* Cambridge: Cambridge University Press, 1997.

Nevins, Joseph. *A Not-So-Distant Horror: Mass Violence in East Timor.* Ithaca, NY: Cornell University Press, 2005.

Taylor, John. *East Timor: The Price of Freedom.* London: Zed, 2000.

Ellinikós Laïkós Apeleftherotikós Stratós

Greek resistance organization during World War II (1939–1945) that sought to seize power in the country at the end of the conflict. The Ellinikós Laïkós Apeleftherotikós Stratós (ELAS, Greek People's Liberation Army) was the military arm of the left-wing Ethniko Apeleftherotiko Metopo (EAM, National Liberation Front). With Greece already occupied by Axis forces, on the German invasion of the Soviet Union in Operation BARBAROSSA on June 22, 1941, the Kommounistikon Komma Elladós (KKE, Greek Communist Party) called for military resistance and formed the EAM with other leftist groups to fight the Axis occupiers.

ELAS commenced military action against the German and Italian forces occupying Greece on June 7, 1942. The major operation of ELAS during the war and one of the largest guerrilla operations of the entire war was undertaken on November 25–26, 1942, in cooperation with agents of the British Special Operations Executive and Greek fighters of the largest noncommunist resistance organization and bitter rival of ELAS, the Ethnikós Dimokratikós Ellinikós Syndesmos (EDES, National Republican Greek League), to blow up the key Gorgopotamos Railroad Bridge, delaying shipment of German supplies to the Afrika Korps for several weeks.

By 1944 the EAM claimed nearly 2 million members, and ELAS had as many as 150,000 men and women under arms. The EAM then controlled perhaps three-fifths of Greek territory. With the outcome of the war now apparent, fighting was already occurring between the EAM and the much smaller EDES. British prime minister Winston L. S. Churchill, fearful of a Communist takeover of Greece, flew to Moscow in October 1944 and struck a deal with Soviet leader Joseph Stalin that granted Great Britain paramount influence in Greece.

Relations between the British-backed Greek monarchy and the EAM deteriorated as the Communists sought to assert control over the country. The British returned monarchist military units to Greece and demanded that ELAS disarm. On December 2, 1944, in Athens, the Greek police fired on antigovernment demonstrators, triggering the Battle for Athens. The British brought in reinforcements, and the battle ended in victory for the nationalists and the disarming of ELAS.

Under the Varkiza Agreement of February 12, 1945, ELAS was to disband in return for a plebiscite and general election. The EAM splintered as moderates and Socialists abandoned it, while KKE membership plummeted from more than 400,000 to only 50,000. Meanwhile, the British strengthened the Greek National Guard and allowed government security forces to take action against the Communists. In the Greek parliamentary elections of March 1946, the rightist candidates won a landslide victory, in part because of a Communist boycott on the claim that the government had not lived up to its promises. The KKE then declared a state of civil war and reorganized ELAS units as the Dimokratikós Strató Elladas (Democratic Army of Greece).

Jonathan M. House and Spencer C. Tucker

See also Dimokratikós Stratós Elladas; Greek Civil War; Tito

Further Reading

Close, David H. *The Greek Civil War, 1943–1950: Studies of Polarization.* London: Routledge, 1993.

Close, David H. *The Origins of the Greek Civil War.* New York: Longman, 1995.

Gerolymatos, Andre. *Red Acropolis, Black Terror: The Greek Civil War and the Origins of Soviet-American Rivalry.* New York: Basic Books, 2004.

Iatrides, John O. *Greece in the 1940s: A Nation in Crisis.* Hanover, NH: University Press of New England, 1981.

El Popé.

See Popé

El Salvador Insurgency

Start Date: 1980
End Date: 1992

The Central American nation of El Salvador saw an insurgency lasting from 1980 to 1992. For much of its modern history, El Salvador was dominated by a small group of wealthy coffee growers and their military allies. Representatives of the so-called fourteen families (the economic elite) monopolized politics through the 1920s and retained considerable power until the 1980s.

In 1932 after the collapse of coffee prices precipitated by the Great Depression, a peasant uprising erupted, supported by the El Salvador Communist Party. The rebellion was led by Augustin Farabundo Martí. The army's repression of the uprising, known as La Matanza (The Slaughter), resulted in 30,000 deaths and inaugurated several decades of harsh military rule. Martí was executed by the army, but his name was preserved in the title of the Frente Farabundo Martí de Liberación Nacional (FMLN, Farabundo Martí National Liberation Front) insurgent organization.

During 1959–1965, modest economic growth increased the size of the Salvadoran middle class, but poverty and high unemployment continued to polarize society. The peasantry was especially oppressed, as there was little land available to them for independent cultivation. In 1972 the military arrested and removed from power popularly elected civilian president José Napoleon Duarte. Army repression quickly radicalized the population, and the first armed-struggle movements began to coalesce by the mid-1970s.

In October 1979, alarmed by signs of growing violence and revolutionary upheaval, army officers carried out a coup against the government of General Humberto Romero. The coup brought to power a series of military-civilian juntas whose reformist officers and civilians were weakened after only a few months in power. By the mid-1980s, political power had fallen to conservative military figures in alliance with the Christian Democrats, with Duarte as president (1984–1989). As the country sank into civil war, the Duarte government implemented wide-ranging social and economic reforms. These focused particularly on land and agrarian reforms. However, Duarte was unable to control the paramilitary terror waged by the armed forces against civilians suspected of sympathizing with the FMLN. Indeed, on March 28, 1980, a right-wing death squad murdered Catholic archbishop Oscar Romero, who had criticized the military's terror tactics and U.S. support for the government.

With the advent of the administration of U.S. president Ronald Reagan in 1981, the civil war in El Salvador became a central piece in what became known as the Second Cold War in the Americas. The U.S. government accused Cuba, the Soviet Union, and the newly installed Sandinista government in Nicaragua of supporting and arming the FMLN insurgents. To counter this, the Reagan administration provided the country with $6 billion in military and economic aid during 1981–1992.

Growing evidence linking the Salvadoran military and government to death squads led to widespread criticism of U.S. policy in El Salvador. The uproar over the army's murder of six Jesuit academics in November 1989, the 1990 electoral defeat of the Sandinistas in Nicaragua, the collapse of the Soviet Union in December 1991, and the sense that a stalemate had been reached in the civil war encouraged moves for a negotiated settlement of the conflict. In April 1990 the United Nations (UN) began to supervise negotiations between the Salvadoran government and the FMLN, and a cease-fire was signed in January 1992.

Under the UN-brokered end to hostilities, the Salvadoran army and police forces were purged of their worst human rights violators, and the FMLN became a legalized political party. Measures to achieve national reconciliation and to reincorporate FMLN guerrilla and army forces into civilian life were only partially successful, however. Unfortunately, it has been difficult to resolve the conflicts created by a legacy of more than 75,000 war-related deaths.

Barry Carr

See also Frente Farabundo Martí para la Liberación Nacional; Frente Sandinista de Liberación; Nicaraguan Revolution

Further Reading

Dunkerley, James. *The Long War: Dictatorship and Revolution in El Salvador.* London: Junction Books, 1982.

North, Lisa. *Bitter Grounds: Roots of Revolt in El Salvador.* Toronto: Between the Lines, 1982.

William Stanley. *The Protection Racket State: Elite Politics, Military Extortion, and Civil War in El Salvador.* Philadelphia: Temple University Press, 1996.

Emmerich, Andreas

Birth Date: 1737
Death Date: 1809

Born near Hannau, in Germany in 1737, Andreas Emmerich was a German mercenary officer who fought with the British Army during the American Revolutionary War (1775–1783), rising to lieutenant colonel. Both Emmerich and fellow Hessian officer Johann von Ewald, who also took part in the war and wrote on tactics based on his experiences, stressed the value of guerrilla warfare. Although Ewald has been the most cited, he called Emmerich "the first partisan of our age."

Emmerich's book *The Partisan in War: Or the Use of a Corps of Light Troops to an Army* was based on his experience in America. It was published in London in 1789 and in Germany in Dresden two years later and offered practical advice for those troops conducting partisan warfare. As with Ewald, Emmerich saw troops engaged in partisan warfare simply as regular forces detached for temporary service and operating on the flanks or in the rear of an opposing force.

Emmerich's advice for partisans included the need for mounted troops to minimize noise when moving about at night. This would included placing straw on bridges to muffle the sound of horses' hooves and loosely playing with a horse's reins to minimize the possibility of the animal neighing. Emmerich recognized that special qualities were necessary in effective partisan leaders, especially the ability to make effective decisions on their own, as they would be operating away from their commanding officers. He noted the importance of changing camp often and warned against the delusion that bad weather would preclude an enemy attack. Emmerich also stressed the importance of intelligence gathering, often using women for this purpose; the need to win the support of the local civilian population by never offending them; and the necessity of treating prisoners well.

After his retirement from the military, in 1809 Emmerich took part in the unsuccessful Marburg Uprising against the French and was executed.

Spencer C. Tucker

See also American Revolutionary War; Ewald, Johann von

Further Reading

Beckett, Ian F. W. *Encyclopedia of Guerrilla Warfare.* Santa Barbara, CA: ABC-CLIO, 1999.

Emmerich, Andreas. *The Partisan in War: Or the Use of a Corps of Light Troops to an Army.* London: Printed by H. Reynell for J. Debrett, 1789.

Laqueur, Walter. *Guerrilla Warfare: A Historical & Critical Study.* New Brunswick, NJ: Transaction, 1998.

Eritrean War for Independence

Start Date: 1962
End Date: 1992

The East African nation of Eritrea was an Italian colony during 1889–1941 and was under British-administered control during 1941–1952. Eritrea became federated with Ethiopia in September 1952 but lost all autonomy in 1962, when it was reduced to province status. Several armed groups ideologically committed to the Communist bloc fought for independence from 1962 until the fall of Addis Ababa and Asmara in 1991. An Eritrean provisional government was then established until 1993, when a referendum granted the country official independence.

Disagreement over the 1945 United Nations provisions for Eritrean sovereignty and a desire for independence resulted in the creation of the Muslim League in 1946. The Muslim League was replaced by the Eritrean Liberation Front (ELF), formed in 1961, and the Eritrean Liberation Movement, a secular movement founded in 1958 by activists in neighboring Sudan.

From the beginning of ELF, Osman Solih Sabbe was a key figure in the organization. He secured financial assistance from states hostile to Ethiopia. To drum up support, ELF emphasized Ethiopia's links to the United States and subsequently to Israel. This strategy resulted in the perceived association of Eritrean nationalism with Islam.

A 1974 coup in Ethiopia overthrew the pro-Western emperor Haile Selassie. Replacing Selassie's government was a nominally Socialist-oriented military junta called the Derg (Committee) chaired by Colonel Mengitsu Haile Mariam. This also meant a change of policy for Sudan, which had supported Ethiopia since the 1972 Addis Ababa Agreement (leading to a period of peace in Sudan).

Following this radical change in regimes, the Tigray People's Liberation Front (TPLF) was established in 1975 in the province of Tigray in northern Ethiopia, while by 1974 the Eritrean People's Liberation Front (EPLF) emerged from disenchanted members of ELF. Disagreements between existing armed groups led to a civil war in 1972–1973 and eventually by 1981 to expulsion of ELF from Eritrea, making the EPLF the dominant military and political force there. Both the TPLF and the EPLF were Marxist in orientation and opposed the Mengitsu regime, but while the EPLF favored independence, the TPLF remained undecided between independence and a role within Ethiopia.

Organizational and leadership differences eventually led to a three-year breach between the two organizations in 1985, when the TPLF began supporting Eritrean opposition movements against the ELPF's perceived hegemony. Disagreements escalated after the creation of the Derg and as the result of Soviet support for Ethiopian military offensives against the Eritrean independence groups, especially during 1977–1979. In this period, the EPLF carried out a strategic withdrawal from central and southern Eritrea into the northern province of Sahel, while the TPLF continued to fight the Ethiopian Army, despite the latter's initial victories.

From the beginning, the TPLF was more sympathetic to an Albanian model of self-reliant communism, whereas the EPLF continued to regard Soviet-style communism with favor. In addition, the TPLF interpreted the independence struggle within a neo–Marxist-Leninist framework, with differences based not on class but rather on ethnicity. The TPLF also favored an ethnic federal system, which the EPLF sought to avoid.

From 1978 onward, the EPLF consolidated its position until in 1980 it drove back Ethiopian forces on all fronts. Finally, in March 1988 the EPLF defeated Ethiopian forces at Afabat. Within a year the Ethiopian Army had evacuated Tigray Province.

Teenage recruits training at an Eritrean People's Liberation Front (EPLF) camp in northern Eritrea, June 18, 1978. (Alex Bowie/Getty Images)

The EPLF conquered the northwestern part of Eritrea and then took the port of Massawa in 1990 and entered Asmara in May 1991. The same year, the Ethiopian People's Revolutionary Democratic Front (EPRDF), an umbrella organization founded in 1989 that gathered all anti-Derg movements, captured the Ethiopian capital of Addis Ababa, imposing its rule and forcing Mengitsu to flee the country.

In May 1991 a conference was held in London to resolve the situation and was chaired by the United States, which held out the promise of aid. The conference was successful and formally ended the war. In July another conference, at Addis Ababa, led to the establishment of an Ethiopian provisional government, and Eritrea was granted the right to hold a referendum on independence, with the EPLF as the provisional government. In 1993, 99.8 percent of the population voted for Eritrean independence, whereupon the EPLF transformed itself into the People's Front for Democracy and Justice and became the sole legal and ruling party of Eritrea.

Abel Polese

Further Reading

Pool, David. *From Guerrillas to Government: The Eritrean People's Liberation Front.* Oxford, UK: James Currey, 2001.

Reid, Richard. "Old Problems in New Conflicts: Some Observations on Eritrea and Its Relations with Tigray, from Liberation Struggle to Inter-State War." *Africa* 73(3) (2003): 369–400.

Tekeste, Negash, and Kjetil Tronvoll. *Brothers at War: Making Sense of the Ethiopian-Eritrean War.* Athens: Ohio University Press, 2001.

Tekle, Amare, ed. *Eritrea and Ethiopia: From Conflict to Cooperation.* Lawrenceville, NJ: Red Sea, 1994.

Erskine, Sir George Watkin Eben James

Birth Date: August 23, 1899
Death Date: August 29, 1965

British Army general who commanded forces in East Africa from June 1953 to May 1956 during the Kenya Emergency. George Watkin Eben James Erskine was born on August 23, 1899. The son of a British Army general, Erskine was commissioned in the King's Royal Rifle Corps and fought on the Western Front during World War I (1914–1918). Following service in India, he returned to Britain in 1937 and was assigned to the Eastern Command.

In 1939 Erskine joined the 1st London Division of the Territorial Army. In 1941 he was assigned to North Africa in command of a battalion of the King's Royal Rifle Corps, then part of the 69th Infantry Brigade. In 1942 Erskine assumed command of the famed 7th Armoured Division, taking part in the march to Tunis. He fought in the Italian Campaign and the Normandy Invasion of 1944. Criticized for what some regarded as excessive caution in the struggle for Normandy, he was removed from his command position and appointed head of the Supreme Headquarters Allied Expeditionary Force. Postwar assignments included in succession command of the 43rd Wessex Division, British forces in Hong Kong, the Territorial Army, British forces in Egypt and the Mediterranean Command, and in 1952 the Eastern Command.

In May 1953 Erskine was appointed to head the East Africa Command. He thus had operational command over British efforts to crush the Mau Mau Uprising in Kenya. Determined to take the offensive, Erskine launched Operation ANVIL in Nairobi in April 1954. This operation broke the back of the Mau Mau political organization. He also initiated aggressive sweeps in the countryside. Erskine understood the necessity of not alienating the non–Mau Mau native population and toward that end insisted on strict discipline. He also formed members of the Kikuyu Home Guard into countergangs or psuedoforces, later renamed Special Force Teams, to seek out the Mau Mau in the forests.

During 1955–1958 Erskine headed the Southern Command, and from 1958 to 1963 he was lieutenant governor and commander in chief of Jersey. Erskine died on August 29, 1965.

Spencer C. Tucker

See also Kenya Emergency; Pseudoforces

Further Reading

Clayton, Anthony. *Counter-Insurgency in Kenya*. Nairobi: Transafrica Publishers, 1976.

Mead, Richard. *Churchill's Lions: A Biographical Guide to the Key British Generals of World War II*. Stroud, UK: Spellmount, 2007.

Ethniki Organosis Kyprion Agoniston

The Ethniki Organosis Kyprion Agoniston (EOKA, National Organization of Cypriot Fighters), organized by retired Greek Army colonel Georgios Grivas, was the Greek Cypriot paramilitary organization that waged the Cyprus Insurgency of 1955–1959 to end British rule of that island and bring about enosis (union) with Greece. The maximum strength of EOKA was only about 350 full-time fighters.

For security purposes, EOKA was divided into small cells. Seven groups of no more than 15 individuals each operated in the Trodos Mountains in central Cyprus, while some 50 cells of 5 to 6 individuals each were stationed in the major cities, including Nicosia. Supporting these were some 750 individuals, including women and children, who provided intelligence and smuggled weapons and bombs used to attack British soldiers and the Cypriot police. A favorite EOKA tactic was the use of bombs, of which 1,782 exploded. Because most were crude homemade types, many more than that number failed to go off.

EOKA's effectiveness was sharply reduced by the British military Operation PEPPERPOT, conducted in the Troddos Mountains, and the British decision to ban all Greek Cypriots from their military bases. Nonetheless, the British were persuaded to yield control of Cyprus in 1959 in return for the retention of two military bases. EOKA ultimately killed 105 British servicemen and 51 members of the Cypriot police. A total of 238 Cypriot civilians also perished in the insurgency, while EOKA lost perhaps 90 of its members.

When Cyprus became independent in August 1960, it was in effect a defeat for EOKA's goal of enosis, as new Cypriot president Archbishop Makarios established his own personal rule. Grivas then returned to the island to established EOKA-B, bent on overthrowing Makarios and bringing about union with Greece. Although Grivas died in early 1974, his followers attempted a coup against Makarios that August, which led to a Turkish military invasion of the island and also the overthrow of the Greek junta in Athens.

Spencer C. Tucker

See also Cyprus Insurrection; Grivas, Georgios

Further Reading

Crawshaw, Nancy. *The Cyprus Revolt: An Account of the Struggle for Union with Greece*. London: Allen and Unwin, 1978.

Dimitrakis, Panagiotis. "British Intelligence and the Cyprus Insurgency, 1955–1959." *International Journal of Intelligence and Counter-Intelligence* 21(2) (Summer 2008): 375–394.

Grivas, George. *The Memoirs of General Grivas.* Edited by Charles Foley. New York and Washington, DC: Praeger, 1964.

Etzel.

See Irgun Tsvai Leumi

Ewald, Johann von

Birth Date: March 20, 1744
Death Date: June 14, 1813

German Army officer who served with British forces in North America during the American Revolutionary War (1775–1783). Born at Kassel in Hesse Kassel on March 20, 1744, Johann von Ewald joined the army in 1760 during the Seven Years' War (1756–1763). Raised to ensign in 1761 for battlefield bravery, he was promoted to second lieutenant in 1766 and to captain in 1774. In the latter year he published a treatise on junior officer leadership, dedicated to King Frederick II of Prussia.

In 1775 Frederick signed an agreement to provide mercenary troops to the British army fighting in North America, and Ewald arrived with his jaeger company at New York City in October 1776. He served with distinction in the New Jersey and Philadelphia campaigns of 1777. Among other engagements, Ewald saw combat in the Battle of Brandywine Creek and the Battle of Germantown. He subsequently took part in the siege and capture of Charleston, South Carolina, in 1780 and in operations in Virginia in 1781, culminating in his capture with the British capitulation at Yorktown. He returned to Kassel in 1784.

In 1785 Ewald published another treatise, *Abhandlung über den kleinen Krieg* (Essay on Partisan Warfare). In 1788 while still a captain, he secured a commission as a lieutenant colonel in the Danish Army. He was promoted to colonel in 1795, to major general in 1782, and to lieutenant general in 1809. Commanding Danish forces in Schleswig-Holstein, Ewald retired from the army in 1813 and died on June 14 in Kiel.

In addition to his treatises on tactics, Ewald kept a journal while he was stationed in North America. Although only three of the four volumes are extant, they have been described as the most important diary by a Hessian during the war. While it was Ewald's work that was frequently cited by Karl von Clausewitz and others, Ewald called fellow Hessian officer Andreas Emmerich, who also fought in America and wrote of his experiences, "the first partisan of our age." Indeed, Ewald's advice regarding partisan warfare closely paralleled that of Emmerich. Ewald noted that many officers lacked practical knowledge of partisan warfare, and he devoted several chapters of his book to surprise attacks and ambush techniques. He advised that neither horses nor dogs be employed in ambushes, as barking or neighing risked giving away the ambush force. Such caution extended even to those soldiers who might have a cold and could sneeze and give away the ambush position. As with Emmerich, Ewald wrote that there was no excuse for a partisan commander to be taken by surprise, and Ewald stressed the absolute necessity of maintaining the good will of the local population. Thus, any marauders should be punished by death or at the very least should receive a severe beating. Ewald believed that British soldiers, no matter how brave, were unsuited for the type of partisan warfare that marked the fighting in America because they did not have the patience for the difficulties in this type of warfare, nor did they possess the arduousness that it required.

Spencer C. Tucker

See also American Revolutionary War; Emmerich, Andreas

Further Reading

Beckett, Ian F. W. *Encyclopedia of Guerrilla Warfare.* Santa Barbara, CA: ABC-CLIO, 1999.

Ewald, Johann. *Diary of the American War: A Hessian Journal.* Translated and edited by Joseph P. Tustin. New Haven, CT: Yale University Press, 1979.

Laqueur, Walter. *Guerrilla Warfare: A Historical & Critical Study.* New Brunswick, NJ: Transaction, 1998.

F

Fall, Bernard B.

Birth Date: November 11, 1926
Death Date: February 21, 1967

War correspondent, author, professor, and Indochina analyst. Born in Vienna, Austria, on November 11, 1926, Bernard B. Fall grew up in France. He served in the French Resistance against the Germans from 1942 and then in the French Army. After discharge in 1946, he was a research analyst at the Nuremberg War Crimes Tribunal. In 1951 he went to the United States as a Fulbright scholar and the following year earned a master's degree at Syracuse University.

In 1953 Fall traveled to Indochina to do research for his doctorate. There he observed firsthand the end of French rule in Indochina and was allowed to accompany French forces in the field. Fall returned to the United States in 1954 and completed his doctorate at Syracuse in 1955. He then began an academic career as an assistant professor at American University; later he went to Howard University. Attaining a full professorship, he remained on the faculty there until his death.

Fall wrote seven books and more than 250 magazine articles about Vietnam and Southeast Asia. His 1961 book *Street without Joy* became a classic account of the Indochina War. In 1966 he also published *Hell in a Very Small Place: The Siege of Dien Bien Phu,* a definitive account of that battle. Both books were widely read by American officers who served in Vietnam.

Fall was deeply critical of both French and U.S. approaches to the war. He admitted that America, with its massive mobility and firepower assets, could not be defeated militarily by the Communists. But the Vietnam War, he maintained, was first and foremost political—a fact that neither the Americans nor the French before them fully understood. Because of this, Fall predicted failure, first for the French and then for the Americans. Because he analyzed all sides of an issue with the same degree of penetrating criticism, his writings were often cited by supporters as well as opponents of the war.

On February 21, 1967, while accompanying a U.S. marine patrol near the coast northwest of Hue, Fall was killed by a Viet Cong mine.

David T. Zabecki

See also Indochina War; Vietnam War

Further Reading

Fall, Bernard B. *Hell in a Very Small Place: The Siege of Dien Bien Phu.* New York: J. B. Lippincott, 1966.

Fall, Bernard B. *Last Reflections on a War.* Garden City, NY: Doubleday, 1967.

Fall, Bernard B. *Street without Joy.* Harrisburg, PA: Stackpole, 1961.

Fall, Dorothy. *Bernard Fall: Memories of a Soldier-Scholar.* Dulles, VA: Potomac Books, 2006.

Fedayeen

Term used to refer to various (usually Arab) groups that have engaged in either armed struggle or guerrilla tactics against civilians and sometimes governments. The term *fedayeen* (or *fidaiyyun*) is the plural Arabic word meaning "one who is ready to sacrifice his life" and has been used to reference Palestinians who waged attacks against Israelis in the 1950s, Iranian guerrillas opposed to Shah Reza Pahlavi's regime in the 1970s, and a force loyal to Iraqi dictator Saddam Hussein during the Iraq War of 2003.

Following the rejection by Arab leaders of the 1947 United Nations partition plan that would have created a Palestinian state in the West Bank and the Gaza Strip and the resulting proclamation of the State of Israel the following year, Palestinian refugees flooded into the areas surrounding the new Jewish state. Anti-Israel activity became prevalent, particularly in West Bank and Gaza Strip areas, where unemployment was high and living conditions were poor. Supported by money and arms from some Arab states, a number of Palestinians mounted attacks against Israeli citizens, and in 1951 the raids became more organized. The perpetrators began operating under the name "Fedayeen." The fighters created bases in Egypt, Jordan, and Lebanon, with the Egyptian intelligence service training and arming many of them. Between 1951 and 1956, Fedayeen guerrillas orchestrated hundreds of raids along the Israeli border, killing an estimated 400 Israelis and injuring 900 others, employing such tactics as ambushing civilian buses and employing suicide bombers.

Despite being largely trained by Egyptians, the Fedayeen operated primarily out of Jordan, which bore the brunt of the retaliation carried out by the Israel Defense Forces (IDF) and Jewish paramilitary groups. Fedayeen attacks and subsequent retaliations were significant factors in the outbreak of hostilities during the 1956 Suez Crisis. The Fedayeen continued their activity after that, launching attacks into Israel from Jordanian territory. The fighters included those associated with the Palestine Liberation Organization (PLO), the Popular Front for the Liberation of Palestine, and various other militant groups.

King Hussein of Jordan was initially supportive of the Fedayeen groups, but by 1970 he deemed their presence detrimental to Jordan and a threat to his own position. Although based in refugee camps, the Fedayeen were able to obtain arms and financial support from other Arab countries and therefore clashed with Jordanian government troops who attempted to disarm them beginning in 1968. The civil war that erupted in 1970 during what has been called Black September saw the eventual defeat and removal of the Fedayeen from Jordanian soil.

The Fedayeen were forced to recognize Jordanian sovereignty via an October 13, 1970, agreement between PLO leader Yasser Arafat and King Hussein. Although PLO members often participated in Fedayeen raids, the PLO denied playing a role in several terrorist attacks. After being ousted from Jordan, the PLO and the Fedayeen moved their headquarters to Lebanon, from where they continued to attack Israel. The term "Fedayeen" is still used by many Palestinian militants who do not recognize Israel's right to exist and who seek the establishment of a Palestinian state in the region.

Fedayeen was also a name taken by a radical Islamic group opposed to the reign of Shah Reza Pahlavi of Iran. Between 1971 and 1983, Iranian Fedayeen carried out numerous attacks, including political assassinations, against those supportive of the shah. This campaign was ultimately successful, and the shah was forced to abdicate and leave Iran as a consequence of the 1978–1979 Iranian Revolution.

Most recently, the term "Fedayeen" was used in reference to those who were loyal to Iraqi leader Saddam Hussein. They were often referred to as the Fedayeen Saddam. Established by Hussein's son Uday in 1995, the group drew international attention only with the Iraq War (2003–2011). Like their Palestinian counterparts, members of the Fedayeen Saddam were mostly young unemployed men and did not constitute part of Iraq's regular army. These irregular soldiers were doggedly loyal to the Iraqi Baathist regime. Prior to the Iraq War, the Saddam Fedayeen engaged in several terror campaigns, killing political dissidents and petty criminal offenders such as prostitutes, of which a number were reportedly beheaded. After the March 2003 U.S.-British invasion, the Fedayeen turned their attention to coalition troops, using rocket-propelled grenades, machine guns, and mortars, some mounted in pickup trucks, to attack U.S. forces. However, the Sunni Fedayeen fighters lacked the support of the majority Shiite population, and U.S. forces were able to defeat most of them by April and eliminate them as a threat. Although an active and aggressive insurgency continued in Iraq thereafter, few adherents of the Fedayeen Saddam were involved in it.

Jessica Britt

See also Arafat, Yasser; Palestine Liberation Organization; Terrorism

Further Reading

O'Neill, Bard E. *Revolutionary Warfare in the Middle East: The Israelis vs. the Fedayeen.* Boulder, CO: Paladin, 1974.

Rubin, Barry M. *Revolution until Victory? The Politics and History of the PLO.* Cambridge, MA: Harvard University Press, 1996.

Fighters for the Freedom of Israel.

See Lohamei Herut Israel

Filipino Scouts.

See Macabebe Scouts

Fire Force, Rhodesian

During the Rhodesian Bush War (1964–1979), beginning in 1972 guerrilla incursions into Rhodesia grew rapidly, especially in the tribal areas. With Rhodesian active military forces severely strained, part of the solution was an increased reliance on reserve forces. Despite their dedication, these proved to be of limited value, and Fire Force was the tactic developed to thwart the increased guerrilla activity.

Fire Force was a joint effort by the Rhodesian Army and the Rhodesian Air Force during 1974–1980. There were four Fire Force staging areas located at forward airfields. Army personnel involved in the Fire Force were drawn from the Rhodesian Light Infantry, Rhodesian African Rifles, Selous Scouts, and Special Air Service. Each contingent was on station for six weeks and sometimes for several months. The air force contribution was typically four Alouette III helicopters, one of which was for command and control.

A typical operation began when an observation post manned by Selous Scouts or other reconnaissance teams called in a mission to the Joint Operations Center. A Fire Force would be launched with each helicopter, except the command and control, carrying a four-man team. The observation post would direct the attacking force to the enemy position by radio while marking its own position. The landing zone would be prepped by either a fix-winged aircraft or one of the helicopters with a gunship capability. The Fire Force teams would then land and attack the enemy. Later in the war Douglas DC-3 aircraft were added, with some of the Fire Force troops being parachuted in to set up blocking positions. Fire Force enjoyed considerable success even though the guerrillas developed countermeasures.

Donald A. MacCuish

See also Aircraft in Counterinsurgency Operations; Frente de Libertação de Moçambique; Pseudoforces; Rhodesian Bush War; Selous Scouts

Further Reading

Cocks, Chris. *Fireforce: One Man's War in the Rhodesian Light Infantry.* 4th ed. Rugby, UK: 30 Degrees South, 2009.

Moorecraft, Paul, and Peter McLaughlin. *The Rhodesian War: A Military History.* Barnsley, UK: Pen and Sword Military, 2008.

Firqat

British pseudoforce raised by the British Special Air Service during the Dhofar campaign in Oman (1970–1975). The term "firqat" is Arabic for "force." Firqat fighters were raised from former insurgents who had deserted from the Popular Front for the Liberation of the Occupied Arab Gulf (PFLOAG). The first firqat was organized around a group of 24 men, led by Salim Mubarak, who deserted from the PGLOAG in September 1970. They had left the PGLOAG because, as a Marxist organization, it opposed Islam and the tribal structure of Dhofar Province in Oman.

By January 1975, more than 1,000 former guerrillas had deserted from the PGLOAG. They made up a majority of the 1,600 men who eventually constituted 21 firqats. A mutiny in Firqat Salahadin in April led to the decision to keep the tribal groups in separate formations.

Although they were often poorly disciplined and not always reliable—three of five firqats deployed during Operation JAGUAR in October 1971 refused to fight during Ramadan—they were nonetheless a highly effective local defense force that inhibited PGLOAG operations in the Jebel Akhdar region of the Al Hajar mountain range in Oman.

Spencer C. Tucker

See also Dhofar Rebellion; Popular Front for the Liberation of the Occupied Arabian Gulf; Pseudoforces; Special Air Service

Further Reading

Beckett, Ian F. W. *Encyclopedia of Guerrilla Warfare.* Santa Barbara, CA: ABC-CLIO, 1999.
Jeapes, Tony. *SAS Secret War.* London: HarperCollins, 1986.

Foco Theory

The term "foco" (Spanish for "focus") was coined by French intellectual Jules Régis Debray to describe a new theory of rural guerrilla warfare devised by Marxist revolutionary Ernesto "Che" Guevara de la Serna. Foco is also known as focalism (Spanish, *foquismo*). Foquistas challenged the orthodox Communist emphasis on parliamentary and legal struggle, advocating instead the establishment of rural peasant-based centers (focos) that would foment revolution. This was based on Guevera's role in the successful revolution in Cuba in 1959, begun in eastern Cuba by fewer than 100 men in 1956.

Debray and Guevera believed that the Cuban model could be transplanted elsewhere in Latin America and indeed throughout the Third World. They saw the guerrillas themselves as a fusion of political and military authority. Whereas Mao Zedong (Mao Tse-tung) had posited a lengthy period of political indoctrination of the peasantry as necessary for success, foquistas downplayed the necessity for political indoctrination and posited more rapid success. Popular support was to be created during the armed struggle itself. Small bands of dedicated guerrillas would be successful wherever there was a minimum of popular discontent with a government. Popular support would sustain the guerrillas, while government authorities, frustrated by their inability to crush the guerrillas, would take action against the population as a whole, thereby increasing revolutionary sentiment.

This theory incorrectly interpreted the circumstances in Cuba, where a weak and widely corrupt government had made possible the Communist victory. Although revolutionary leader Fidel Castro and his followers had overcome the Cuban Army of some 30,000 men, the regime of Fulgencio Batista was corrupt and widely hated by the Cuban people, and the army had failed to fight resolutely to defend it. The foco theory also overemphasized the revolution's urban aspects, ignoring the role played by revolutionary cells in the cities. The particular elements present in Cuba that made possible Castro's victory did not exist elsewhere, and the U.S. government employed military aid and the Alliance for Progress to strengthen Latin American regimes susceptible to revolution. Foco-inspired groups failed in Colombia in 1961, in Ecuador and Guatemala in 1962, and in Peru in 1963 as well as in Bolivia in 1966–1967, where Guevara was captured and executed. These failures led to a shift in emphasis to urban guerrilla warfare in the late 1960s.

Louis A. DiMarco and Spencer C. Tucker

See also Batista y Zaldivar, Fulgencio; Castro Ruz, Fidel Alejandro; Cuban Revolution; Debray, Jules Régis; Guevara de la Serna, Ernesto; Peru Insurgencies

Further Reading

Anderson, Jon Lee. *Che Guevara: A Revolutionary Life.* London: Bantam, 1997.

Debray, Régis. *Revolution in the Revolution? Armed Struggle and Political Struggle in Latin America.* New York: Monthly Review Press, 1967.

Guevara, Che. *Guerrilla Warfare.* Introduction by Max Becker. Omaha: Bison Books, University of Nebraska Press, 1998.

Lowy, Michael. *The Marxism of Che Guevara: Philosophy, Economics and Revolutionary Warfare.* New York: Monthly Review Press, 1974.

Franc-tireur

Term, literally meaning "free shooter," used to describe French irregulars during the Franco-Prussian War (1870–1871). Many franc-tireur units originated as rifle marksmanship clubs. When the Franco-Prussian War began on July 19, 1870, the French government assumed control of these clubs and organized volunteers into other companies, giving them officers and in many instances uniforms. Some of their leaders were simply members of the upper class, but others were army veterans. After the Germans defeated most of the regular French Army, the franc-tireur companies continued to operate in no-man's-land and behind German lines, employing guerrilla tactics.

The Germans vilified the francs-tireurs as murderous criminals, falsely claiming that they masqueraded as civilians. The francs-tireurs employed ambushes, snipers, and sabotage against German logistics lines during the September 19, 1870–January 28, 1871, siege of Paris. They enjoyed success in this, tying down some 120,000 German troops. When captured, francs-tireurs were most often summarily executed. The Germans also employed collective punishment against French communities.

World War I (1914–1918) and World War II (1939–1945) saw a revival of the term "franc-tireur," which became synonymous with partisans and guerrillas.

Jonathan M. House

Further Reading

de Belleval, René. *Journal d'un Capitaine de Francs-Tireurs* [Journal of a Captain on the Francs-Tireurs]. Paris: E. Lachaud, Editeur, 1872.

Howard, Michael. *The Franco-Prussian War: The German Invasion of France, 1870–1871.* New York: Collier Books, 1969.

French Pacification of Algeria.

See Algeria, French Pacification of

Frente de Libertação de Moçambique

The Frente de Libertação de Moçambique (FRELIMO, Front for the Liberation of Mozambique) was the principal nationalist insurgent group fighting the Portuguese in Mozambigue. Formed in September 1962, FRELIMO was led by American-trained anthropologist Dr. Eduardo C. Mondlane. On February 3, 1969, Mondlane was assassinated in Dar es Salaam by a book bomb. Following a leadership struggle, in 1970 Samora Machel, a male nurse, emerged as FRELIMO's leader.

FRELIMO's first military action occurred on September 25, 1964, in the Cabo Delgado region of northern Mozambique, and by the time of Mondlane's assassination, FRELIMO had some 7,000 men under arms. FRELIMO's principal difficulty was that it drew the bulk of its support from the Makonde people of northern Mozambique, who represented only about 3 percent of the total population. In addition, to get to Mokonde territory, FRELIMO fighters would have to traverse lands controlled by the largely Muslim Macua people, enemies of the Makonde. The Yao and Nyanja peoples were also hostile. FRELIMO's military operations consisted principally of the placement of land mines.

In 1968 FRELIMO switched its base of operations to Zambia and commenced operations to the Tete region, where the Portuguese were building the important Cabora Basin Dam. FRELIMO then extended its operations south and east.

By late 1974, however, the Portuguese Army and FRELIMO were largely locked in a military stalemate. Following the April 1974 military coup in Portugal (the Carnation Revolution), the Portuguese government began the process of dismantling its colonial empire. Lisbon commenced negotiations with FRELIMO, leading to independence for Mozambique in June 1975. The conservative Resistência Nacional Moçambicana (RENAMO, Mozambique National Resistance), supported by the Rhodesian intelligence service contested the election results, leading to civil war in 1977. Machel moved against the opposition parties, caused the death of a number of their leaders, and established a single-party Marxist-Leninist state. His domestic economic programs proved to be a disaster, and in foreign affairs he allowed insurgent forces opposing the minority white regimes in Rhodesia (present-day Zimbabwe) and South Africa to train in and operate from Mozambique, leading to confrontation first with Rhodesia and then with South Africa.

Machel died in a suspicious plane crash in October 1986. His successor as president, Joaquim Chissano (in office during 1986–2005), changed the political tenor of the country and ushered in free elections. The Mozambican Civil War was brought to an end by a peace agreement in 1992. As of 2013, however, FRELIMO remains the ruling party of Mozambique, with Armando Guebuza as president. RENAMO is the leading opposition party.

Donald A. MacCuish and Spencer C. Tucker

See also Machel, Samora Moïses; Mondlane, Eduardo; Mozambique Insurgency; Resistência Nacional Moçambicana

Further Reading

Beckett, Ian F. W. *Encyclopedia of Guerrilla Warfare.* Santa Barbara, CA: ABC-CLIO, 1999.

Beckett, Ian F. W. *Modern Insurgencies and Counter-Insurgencies: Guerrillas and Their Opponents since 1750.* London: Routledge, 2001.

Cann, John P. *Counterinsurgency in Africa: The Portuguese Way of War, 1961–1974.* St. Petersburg, FL: Hailer, 2005.

Frente Farabundo Martí para la Liberación Nacional

The Frente Farabundo Martí para la Liberación Nacional (FMLN, Farabundo Martí National Liberation Front) was a coalition of five guerrilla organizations formed in El Salvador in 1980 and one of the principal participants in the civil war there of 1980–1992. The five were the Fuerzas Populares de Liberación Farabundo Martí (FPL, Popular Liberation Forces Farabundo Marti); the Ejército Revolucionario del Pueblo (ERP, People's Revolutionary Army); the Resistencia Nacional (RN, the National Resistance); the Partido Comunista Salvadoreño (PCS, Communist Party of El Salvador), founded by Farabundo Martí in 1930; and the Partido Revolucionario de los Trabajadores Centroamericanos (PRTC, Revolutionary Party of

Central American Workers). All of these groups had carried out petty terrorist activity from 1970 to 1979, including kidnappings, murders, extortion, bombings, and bank robberies.

The FMLN was named for Farabundo Martí, a Communist who had fought with Augusto Sandino against U.S. marines in Nicaragua in the 1920s and was executed following the defeat of a Communist revolt in El Salvador in 1932. Despite the establishment of the coalition in 1980, there was no single leader, and each group maintained its own internal practices and ideological perspectives. The FMLN was allied domestically with the Frente Democrático Revolucionario (FDR, Democratic Revolutionary Front) and internationally with the Cuban and Nicaraguan governments and with social democratic movements in the United States and Europe. The FMLN's stated principles were those of social democracy rather than Marxism. None of the groups extolled political violence for its own sake, with terrorism to be reserved primarily for military targets.

Following the conclusion of a peace agreement and the end of the civil war, the FMLN was recognized as a legal political party on September 1, 1992. The FMLN came to power as a result of the March 2009 election when its presidential candidate Mauricio Funes Cartagena garnered 51 percent of the vote.

Brian J. Tannehill

See also El Salvador Insurgency

Further Reading

Bracamonte, José Angel Moroni, and David Spencer. *Strategy and Tactics of the Salvadoran FMLN guerrillas.* Westport, CT: Praeger, 1995.

McClintock, Cynthia. *Revolutionary Movements in Latin America: El Salvador's FMLN and Peru's Shining Path.* Washington, DC: United States Institute of Peace Press, 1998.

Frente Nacional de Libertação de Angola

Angolan insurgent organization formed by Holden Roberto to fight the Portuguese. The Angolan Insurgency (1961–1975) officially began in January 1961 when António Agostinho Neto's Movimento Popular de Libertação de Angola (MPLA, Popular Movement for the Liberation of Angola) attacked the Portuguese. That March, Roberto led some 4,000–5,000 members of the Bakongo tribe of northern Angola from Kinshasa to attack Portuguese border posts and farms in Angola. In March 1962 Roberto officially established the Frente Nacional de Libertação de Angola (FNLA, National Front for the Liberation of Angola). The FNLA received support from President Mobutu Sese Seko of Zaire (now the Democratic Republic of the Congo) and from Israel.

In 1964 Jonas Savimbi, who had joined Roberto's movement the year before and was the foreign minister in Roberto's self-proclaimed Revolutionary Government of Angola in Exile, broke with Roberto when the latter refused to expand the FNLA base of support beyond the Bakongo tribe of northern Angola. Savimbi founded his own insurgent organization, the União Nacional para a Independência Total de Angola (UNITA, the National Union for the Total Independence of Angola). Thus, there were three groups—the MPLA, the FNLA, and UNITA—fighting the Portuguese in Angola. The FNLA largely operated from bases in Zaire and claimed to have some 10,000 men in 1972.

On the eve of Angolan independence in 1975, the FNLA and UNITA formed an alliance, and Mobuto sent Zairean forces into the country to assist it in a bid to block the leftist MPLA from taking power. This failed thanks to a Soviet airlift of Cuban troops, who defeated the FNLA, UNITA, and Zairean forces.

A Cold War proxy battle ensued between the MPLA on the one side and the FNLA and UNITA on the other. The Marxist MPLA government of Angola enjoyed the support of the Soviet Union and Cuba, while the anticommunist FNLA and UNITA received assistance from the United States, Zaire, and China. In 1991 both UNITA and the FNLA agreed to the Bicesse Accords, which allowed Roberto to return to Angola and run for president, but he received only 2 percent of the vote. The FNLA, although it had won five seats in the new parliament, dissolved.

Spencer C. Tucker

See also Angolan Insurgency; Movimento Popular de Libertação de Angola; Neto, António Agostinho; Roberto, Holden Álverto; Savimbi, Jonas Malheiro; União Nacional para a Independência Total de Angola

Further Reading

Klinghoffer, Arthur Jay. *The Angolan War.* Boulder, CO: Westview, 1980.

Marcum, John A. *The Angolan Revolution.* 2 vols. Cambridge, MA: MIT Press, 1969 and 1978.

Frente Sandinista de Liberación

Nicaraguan revolutionary movement and political party that toppled the dictatorship of Anastasio Somoza Jr. in 1979 and ruled Nicaragua during the 1980s. After 1960, Somoza's restrictions on political opposition coupled with the success of revolutionary movements in Cuba and elsewhere emboldened a group of activists to challenge his hold on power. Led by Carlos Fonseca, Tomás Borge, and Silvio Mayorga, the Frente Sandinista de Liberación Nacional (FSLN, Sandinista National Liberation Front), formed in July 1961, began operations in Nicaragua's largest cities. The Sandinistas took their name from Augusto César Sandino, who had led a nationalist rebellion against the U.S. military occupation of Nicaragua during 1927–1933.

As an urban insurgent force, the FSLN had little impact. The corruption of the Somoza regime, however, helped sustain the FSLN's organizational efforts. Shifting from urban to rural districts, the FSLN survived military defeats and factionalism well into the 1970s. In 1975 the FSLN split into three organizational lines. The first led the effort to mobilize the population for war against the dictatorship. The second focused on organizing workers and the urban underclass. The third, which would form the core of the Sandinistas' political force after 1979, built connections with business groups and other political opposition forces.

Somoza steadily lost popular support during the 1970s. His reactionary policies and vast corruption helped the Sandinistas build their base and expand military operations. In 1974 the FSLN sponsored the formation of the Movimiento Pueblo Unido (United People's Movement), which linked unions, university students, and church-affiliated groups with their struggle. After 1977 the Sandinistas coordinated their military effort with allied groups. Attacks against symbols of the Somoza regime, high-

Jubilant Sandinista insurgents arriving in Managua following the overthrow of Nicaraguan strongman Anastasio Somoza, July 1979. (John Giannini/Sygma/Corbis)

lighted by the occupation of the National Palace and an ensuing prisoner exchange in 1978, demonstrated the FSLN's capabilities while it continued to build popular support.

International pressure and dwindling support from the Jimmy Carter administration in the United States led Somoza to choose exile before defeat, and on July 19, 1979, the Sandinistas occupied Managua and took control of the government. The FSLN plans for Nicaragua included agrarian reform, progressive social reforms, universal medical care, and popular education.

The Carter administration briefly offered humanitarian assistance, but U.S. domestic political pressure from conservatives forced the administration to end the aid in 1980. The staunchly anticommunist Ronald Reagan administration treated the Sandinistas much more harshly. In 1981 the Reagan administration engineered the end of financial support from international lending agencies and authorized the Central Intelligence Agency to coordinate a counterrevolutionary movement in Nicaragua. The next year the Nicaraguan Contra rebels began military operations against the Sandinista government. Although their meager resources were severely strained, the Sandinistas organized a government structure that allowed them to dominate the political process. The FSLN created youth groups and neighborhood committees to expand its base, and corporate bodies coordinated the political life of students, workers, and professionals.

Internationally, the Sandinistas counted on support from Cuba and the Soviet Union. The Sandinista leadership chose to affiliate with the Socialist International rather than the Moscow-dominated Cominform. Placed under a U.S. trade embargo that affected economic relations with its neighbors and harassed by Contra incursions, the Sandinistas came to rely more and more on economic and military aid from their Communist allies.

With Nicaragua increasingly isolated, its economy performed poorly under the Sandinistas. Inflation, shortages, and meager productivity hindered the government's efforts to diversify and expand the economy. Ultimately the flagging economy undermined the Sandinistas' many ambitious social projects. Defense programs interfered with the agrarian reform program and exacerbated prickly government relations with the Misquito Indians in eastern Nicaragua.

In 1984 the U.S. Congress cut off further Contra funding. The Reagan administration skirted the restriction by illegally selling weapons to Iran to generate funds for Contra operations. Revelations in 1986 of these extralegal maneuvers rocked the Reagan administration, but the Contra war continued.

To bring legitimacy to their regime, the Sandinistas organized national elections in 1984. Splits in the opposition forces allowed the Sandinistas to use their organizational strength to great effect. Daniel Ortega won election as president, and the Sandinistas worked to preserve their revolution's achievements, seeking international assistance in their ongoing conflict with the United States. Latin American efforts to negotiate a peace settlement bore no fruit until 1989. Led by Costa Rican president Oscar Arias Sánchez, the 1989 Central American Peace Initiative brought about a final settlement. Under the plan, the Contras would disarm, and the Sandinistas would authorize a national election, scheduled for February 1990.

Opposition forces united behind candidate Violeta Barrios de Chamorro, the widow of a leading opponent of the Somoza dictatorship who had been assassinated in 1978. Poor economic conditions and factionalism among the Sandinistas allowed the United Nicaraguan Opposition movement to capture the presidency and a majority of the seats in the National Congress. The Sandinistas' 1990 electoral defeat left the movement weakened and divided. Out of power, Sandinista leaders recast their movement as a social-democratic political party that competes effectively in local and national elections.

Daniel Lewis

See also Contras; Nicaraguan Revolution

Further Reading

Brentlinger, John. *The Best of What We Are: Reflections on the Nicaraguan Revolution.* Amherst: University of Massachusetts Press, 1995.

Gilbert, Dennis. *Sandinistas: The Party and the Revolution.* New York: Basil Blackwell, 1988.

Front de Libération Nationale

The primary Algerian insurgent movement opposing French colonial rule during the Algerian War (1954–1962) and the predominant political force in Algeria since 1962. French troops landed at Algiers in 1830 and then gradually expanded their holdings to create what would become the modern state of Algeria. The French dominated the economic life of Algeria, and tens of thousands of French, Italian, and Spanish settlers (colons) came to Algeria to engage in agriculture and commerce. Unlike Morocco and Tunisia, Algeria, which was divided into three departments, was considered an integral part of France. The reality was quite different, for the political structure, as with the economy, was rigged in favor of the Europeans. Moderate Arabs who spoke French and admired French institutions found to their dismay that despite repeated promises, France was not willing to extend equal rights to the Muslim population, which came to outnumber the Europeans in Algeria about nine to one.

The failure of the French government to understand the need for meaningful reform led to the Sétif Uprising at the end of World War II (1939–1945) and the growth of radical nationalism. Algerian nationalists formed the Comité Révolutionnaire d'Unité et d'Action (Revolutionary Committee of Unity and Action), which became the Front de Libération Nationale (FLN, National Liberation Front) in July 1954. Its military wing, the Armée de Libération Nationale (ALN, National Liberation Army), commenced guerrilla operations on the night of October 31–November 1, 1954, beginning the Algerian War.

The FLN divided Algeria into six *wilayas* (command zones). Leadership divisions plagued the FLN both in the *wilayas* and among the senior collective leadership, based first in Egypt and later in Tunisia. The FLN's chief base of support was in the city of Algiers. Despite the transfer of the bulk of the French Army to Algeria in 1956, the grant of independence to Morocco and Tunisia that same year greatly complicated the situation for the French, as the FLN used both countries—especially Tunisia—as base areas to resupply its forces in Algeria.

The French consistently defeated the ALN in pitched battle, aided by the so-called 200-mile Morice Line along the Tunisian border as well as the smaller Pedron Line with Morocco. Nonetheless, the insurgency continued as more and more Muslim Algerians became radicalized with the lack of meaningful French reform. Meanwhile, the war's costs and mounting French casualties had their effect in Metropolitan France.

Failure in rural operations prompted the FLN to launch urban warfare in Algiers, culminating in the Battle of Algiers in 1957, won by the French under Brigadier General Jacques Massu thanks to aggressive search and interrogation techniques that included torture and execution of prisoners. Documented reports of atrocities created outrage in France, however.

Reports that the French government was considering peace talks with the FLN led to rioting among the Europeans in Algeria, and the French Army professionals stepped in. A threatened military takeover in May 1958 was averted only by the return to power of General Charles de Gaulle and establishment of the Fifth Republic. De Gaulle pledged to maintain French control over Algeria while attempting reform, including the promise of a vast economic program known as the Constantine Plan. It came too late.

In April 1961 a group of disaffected French generals attempted to topple the de Gaulle government. Having exhausted all other options, de Gaulle finally opened peace talks with the FLN, leading to Algerian independence on July 5, 1962. The fighting had claimed some 158,000 members of the FLN along with 39,000 French and some 35,000 non-FLN Muslims.

Soon after independence, fighting erupted among the rival FLN factions. Eventually Ahmed Ben Bella secured control of the country. In 1965 his continued efforts to outmaneuver rivals provoked a military coup led by Houari Boumediene, who ruled Algeria until his death in 1978. The FLN remained the governing party until Islamists of the Front Islamique du Salut (FIS, Islamic Salvation Front) won the December 1991 elections, with the FLN finishing third behind Berber nationalists. In January 1992, however, the Algerian military seized power, nullified the elections, and began arresting Islamist leaders.

The move sparked an insurgency. FIS members joined other Islamists to form the Armée Islamique du Salut (Islamic Salvation Army). The Groupe Islamique Armé (GIA, Armed Islamic Group), an extremist group formed from Algerian veterans of the anti-Soviet jihad in Afghanistan, also began attacks throughout Algeria. Atrocities committed by the GIA were so horrific that the populace resumed support for the FLN, despite its many shortcomings. Ultimately, the conflict claimed more than 150,000 lives.

The terrorist threat in Algeria has subsided but not entirely disappeared. Abdelaziz Bouteflika, president of Algeria since 1999, granted amnesty to thousands of insurgents, but many reportedly rejoined militant groups, such as Al Qaeda in the Islamic Maghreb. Although the FLN now shares power, many smaller parties are led by former FLN members, with moderate Islamists playing a diminished role.

Chuck Fahrer

See also Algerian War; Algiers, Battle of; Ben Bella, Ahmed; Massu, Jacques Émile; Morice Line

Further Reading

Bennoune, Mahfoud. *The Making of Contemporary Algeria, 1830–1987.* Cambridge: Cambridge University Press, 1988.

Horne, Alistair. *A Savage War of Peace.* New York: Viking, 1978.

Ruedy, John. *Modern Algeria: The Origins and Development of a Nation.* Bloomington: Indiana University Press, 1992.

U.S. State Department. *Background Note: Algeria.* Washington, DC: Bureau of Public Affairs, U.S. State Department, 2007.

Front for the Liberation of Occupied South Yemen

Insurgent organization operating in the Federation of South Arabia (now South Yemen) during the Yemen Emergency of 1963–1967. Led by Abdullah al Asnag, a labor leader in the Aden Trades Union Congress, the Front for the Liberation of South Yemen (FLOSY) sought independence for Yemen from British rule. FLOSY was created in opposition to the other insurgent organization in Aden, the Marxist-oriented National Liberation Front (NLF), and vied with it for leadership of the insurgency and the subsequent governance of Aden with it. Both groups fought the British and the sheikhs of southern Arabia as well as each other.

The NLF had originally enjoyed Egyptian support, but its Marxist ideology led Egyptian president Gamal Abdel Nasser to shift his support to FLOSY. Nasser, however, was forced to withdraw Egyptian military support from FLOSY because of the June 1967 Arab-Israeli War. As a consequence, when the British departed Aden in November 1967, the NLF was able to defeat FLOSY militarily and seize power, proclaiming the People's Republic of Yemen. FLOSY then ceased to exist.

Spencer C. Tucker

See also Aden Emergency; National Liberation Front of Aden

Further Reading

Kostiner, Joseph. *The Struggle for South Yemen.* New York: St. Martin's, 1984.

Naumkin, Vitaly. *Red Wolves of Yemen: The Struggle for Independence.* Cambridge, UK: Oleander, 2004.

Walker, Jonathan. *Aden Insurgency: The Savage War in Yemen, 1962–1967.* Barnsley, South Yorkshire, UK: Pen and Sword Military, 2011.

Frunze, Mikhail Vasilyevich

Birth Date: February 2, 1885
Death Date: October 31, 1925

Russian general and political leader. Born into a military family in Pishpek (Frunze), Moldavia (now Bishkek, Kyrgyzstan), on February 2, 1885, Mikhail Vasilyevich Frunze graduated from the Verryi Academy in 1904 and then studied at the St. Petersburg Polytechnic Institute, where he joined the Bolshevik Party in 1905 and became a professional revolutionary. Frunze was arrested and sentenced to internal exile several times during 1905–1914, the last time to permanent exile in Siberia. He returned illegally during World War I (1914–1918) to become a statistician in the All-Russian Zemstov Union. He then headed the Bolshevik underground organization in Minsk and was elected a delegate to the First Congress of the Soviet of Peasant Deputies in Petrograd (St. Petersburg), where he met Vladimir Lenin in May 1917. Frunze chaired the Soviet of Workers', Peasants', and Soldiers' Deputies in Shuya and then led several thousand workers and soldiers in the Moscow Uprising on October 30, 1917.

When the Russian Civil War (1917–1920) began, Frunze went through several promotions to head the Southern Army Group in March 1919. Following victories over Admiral Aleksandr Kolchak's White forces, Frunze took command of the Eastern Front in July.

Given command of forces against the Basmachi Revolt (1916–1934), Frunze arrived in Turkestan in February 1920. Recognizing the need to address social and economic issues in order to end the unrest, he instituted certain measures such as reopening Muslim courts and schools to undermine support for the insurgents. Although he departed Turkestan in September, his policies remained in place. Frunze then secured control of the Crimea and in November 1920 pushed White forces, commanded by Pyotr Wrangel, out of Russia entirely.

In 1921 Frunze joined the Central Committee and three years later became a candidate member of the Politburo. Frunze was appointed deputy director for military affairs in March 1924, and he became commissar for military and naval affairs, in effect head of the Russian armed forces, in January 1925. An ardent Communist who believed in world revolution and the political indoctrination of the Russian armed forces, as commissar Frunze created a network of military schools and presided over compulsory peacetime military service and the standardization of training. He bequeathed a mass conscript army, preferences for maneuver warfare and tactical initiative, and the concept of unified command of combined arms. A prolific author, he wrote *The Military and Political Education of the Red Army* (1921) and *Lenin and the Red Army* (1925). Frunze died from chloroform poisoning during a routine stomach operation on October 31, 1925. There is some speculation that Soviet dictator Joseph Stalin ordered his death.

A talented field general and a gifted military theorist, Frunze is considered one of the fathers of the Red Army. The Frunze Military Academy is named for him.

Spencer C. Tucker and Donald A. MacCuish

See also Basmachi Revolt

Further Reading

Erickson, John. *The Soviet High Command: A Military-Political History, 1918–1941.* New York: St. Martin's, 1962.

Gareev, Makmut A. *M. V. Frunze, Military Theorist.* Washington, DC: Pergamon-Brassey's, 1987.

Fuerzas Armadas de Liberación Nacional of Puerto Rico

The Fuerzas Armadas de Liberación Nacional (FALN, Armed Forces of National Liberation) was a Marxist-Leninist Puerto Rican insurgent organization that sought independence for Puerto Rico. The U.S. Federal Bureau of Investigation classified the FALN as a terrorist organization. One of many Latin American insurgent groups influenced by the Cuban Revolution (1953–1959), the FALN was formed in the 1960s by Filiberto Ojeda Ríos. The Puerto Rican FALN should not be confused with the Venezuelan insurgent group of the same name.

The FALN's goal was to draw attention to what it termed the "colonial condition" of Puerto Rica, protest the U.S. military presence in Puerto Rico, secure the release of so-called political prisoners, and ultimately achieve independence for the island. The FALN was the predecessor to the Boricua Popular Army.

The FALN undertook a series of bombings in a variety of locations in Puerto Rico but also in the United States, most notably in New York City, which has a large Puerto Rican population. At the time of its dissolution, the FALN claimed responsibility for more than 120 bombings in the United States between 1974 and 1983. Targets included government offices, restaurants (a blast at Fraunces Tavern in New York City killed 4 people and injured more than 50), banking institutions, and corporate headquarters in New York City, Chicago, and Washington, D.C.

In April 1980, U.S. authorities arrested 11 FALN members in Evanston, Illinois. Others were taken later. In August 1999 in a decision that drew considerable criticism, President Bill Clinton offered pardons to 16 convicted FALN members on condition that they renounce violence. In defense of his action, Clinton said that those he had pardoned had not been convicted of any of the bombings or of deaths and injuries to victims.

Spencer C. Tucker

See also Cuban Revolution

Further Reading

Ayala, César J., and Rafael Bernabe. *Puerto Rico in the American Century: A History since 1898.* Chapel Hill: University of North Carolina Press, 2007.

Mickolus, Edward F. *Transnational Terrorism: A Chronology of Events, 1968–1979.* Westport, CT: Greenwood, 1980.

Torres, Andrés, and José E. Velázquez. *The Puerto Rican Movement: Voices from the Diaspora.* 1998.

Fuerzas Armadas de Liberación Nacional of Venezuela

The Fuerzas Armadas de Liberación Nacional (FALN, Armed Force of National Liberation) was the urban insurgent group in Venezuela during 1963–1965. The FALN formed against the government of Rómulo Betancourt, who became president of Venezuela in February 1959 and whose ruling Actión Democrática (Democratic Action) Party largely disenfranchised the Partico Communista de Venezuela (PCV, Venezuela Communist Party).

The Cuban Revolution (1953–1959) had an immense influence on leftist groups throughout Latin America, and Venezuela was no exception. In April 1960, leftist students in Venezuela organized the Movimiento de Izquierda Revolucionaria (MIR, Revolutionary Movement of the Left).

Betancourt took a firm stance against the Cuban government of Fidel Castro, and the Betancourt government's support for the expulsion of Cuba from the Organization of American States led to several bloody uprisings in Venezuela, which were suppressed by the government. Betancourt then moved against the Venezuelan Left, ordering the arrest of members of the PCV and MIR in the Venezuelan Congress.

The militant response was the FALN. Formed in January 1963 by dissident military officers and members of the MIR, the FALN was led by Douglas Bravo. The FALN mounted a series of attacks, mostly in urban centers, with the intention of provoking a repressive response that would rally popular support against the government. FALN operations included the bombing of the U.S. embassy in Caracas, destroying a Sears Roebuck warehouse, and sabotaging oil pipelines. These actions failed in their aim of rallying the urban poor against the government, and an FALN attack on an excursion train in September 1963 allowed Betancourt to introduce emergency legislation. The FALN attack on innocent civilians rallied a majority of Venezuelans behind the government action. Nor did the FALN succeed in disrupting the December 1963 national elections.

The United States also provided extensive aid, including police instructors to assist in training the Venezuelan security services. The insurgency ended in 1965.

Spencer C. Tucker

See also Castro Ruz, Fidel Alejandro; Cuban Revolution; Venezuelan Insurgency

Further Reading

Alexander, Robert. *Rómulo Betancourt and the Transformation of Venezuela.* New Brunswick, NJ: Transaction, 1982.

Ewell, Judith. *Venezuela and the United States.* Athens: University of Georgia Press, 1996.

Kohl, James, and John Litt. *Urban Guerrilla Warfare in Latin America.* Cambridge, MA: MIT Press, 1974.

Levine, Daniel. *Conflict and Political Change in Venezuela.* Princeton, NJ: Princeton University Press, 1973.

Fuerzas Armadas Revolucionarias de Colombia–Ejército del Pueblo

The Cuban Revolution (1953–1959) served as an inspiration and ideological support for a number of Latin American insurgencies. In Colombia, which had undergone a period of near civil war between liberals and conservatives during 1948–1957 in what was known as La Violencia, rural revolutionaries sought to follow the foco formula advocated by Ernesto "Che" Guevara der la Serna. Assisted by the United States, the Colombian government adopted Plan Lazo, a combined military and pacification program that by the end of 1965 had ended the foco threat.

Meanwhile, the surviving guerrilla forces came together in two main organizations: the pro-Cuban Ejército de Liberación Nacional (ELN, National Liberation Army) and the pro-Soviet Fuerzas Armadas Revolucionarias de Colombia–Ejército del Pueblo (FARC-EP, the Revolutionary Armed Forces of Colombia–People's Army), founded by Manuel Marulanda. Both were Marxist-Leninist in political philosophy, and both sought to take advantage of the plight of the rural poor to commence an insurgency in 1964 against the Colombian government. Although other insurgent groups formed later, including the Maoist and pro-China Ejército Popular de Liberación (EPL, Popular Liberation Army) and the urban guerrilla group M-19, FARC-EP (usually identified simply as FARC) was by far the largest and most important of the Colombian insurgent organizations, and the ensuing insurgency often bears its name.

FARC drew its strength from the rural poor and from widespread unrest following implementation of the government's Accelerated Economic Development Program that introduced large-scale farming and ranching enterprises but dispossessed as many as 400,000 peasants. FARC's program was anti-imperialistic and agrarian. FARC strongly opposed what it regarded as the undue influence of the United States in Colombian affairs as well as the exploitation of Colombian natural resources by large foreign corporations. FARC claimed to represent the poor peasants exploited by the landowning bourgeoisie.

FARC funded its operations through kidnappings and ransoms, the mining of gold, and drug trafficking. More than any other Colombian insurgent group, FARC became closely linked to the drug cartels that came to plague Colombia. FARC was also branded a terrorist organization by the United States and other governments.

In the 1980s and 1990s, the Colombian government entered into negotiations with the insurgent groups. Both M-19 and the EPL demobilized and became legitimate political parties. Meanwhile, repeated negotiations with FARC and the ELN broke down, with both sides citing bad faith and violation of cease-fire agreements. Ultimately the two insurgent groups came to control a third of Colombian territory. FARC was especially active in the jungle areas of southeastern Colombia.

In November 1998 in a confidence-building measure, Colombian president Andrés Pastrana entered into a cease-fire agreement with FARC that granted it an area of 16,000 square miles as a safe haven. The area was supposed to have been demilitarized, but following a series of high-profile guerrilla military actions and the kidnapping of several political figures, Pastrana ended the peace talks in February 2002 and ordered the Colombian armed forces to start retaking the FARC controlled zone. Shortly after the end of talks, FARC forces kidnapped Oxygen Green Party presidential candidate Ingrid Betancourt. She was ultimately rescued by Colombian forces in July 2008.

Meanwhile, U.S. funding and military assistance and the Colombian government's adoption in 2003 of a population-centric approach, with civilians taking the lead, led to considerable government success by 2007. FARC's area of control was greatly diminished, and government programs led to improved security for the rural population while providing enhanced social services. The government could point to sharp declines in terrorist attacks, kidnappings, and murders, and there were economic gains in the rural areas. Although the government made some progress in dismantling the big drug cartels, cocaine production did not diminish, with FARC continuing to be heavily involved in cocaine trafficking.

Both FARC and the ELN continued military operations. In 2012 the ELN had perhaps 5,000 people under arms, while FARC had twice that number. In 2012 FARC leader Rodrigo Londono announced that FARC would no longer carry out kidnappings for ransom. FARC also released the last 10 soldiers and police officers held as prisoners, although it has kept silent regarding hundreds of civilians still reportedly held as hostages. Yet another round of peace talks between the government and FARC occurred in October 2012, but tremendous pitfalls remained.

Spencer C. Tucker

See also Bolívar, Simón; Colombian Insurgency; Cuban Revolution; Foco Theory; Guevara de la Serna, Ernesto

Further Reading

Brittain, James J. *Revolutionary Social Change in Colombia: The Origin and Direction of the FARC-EP.* London: Pluto, 2010.

Bushnell, David. *The Making of Modern Colombia: A Nation in Spite of Itself.* Berkeley: University of California Press, 1993.

Rochlin, James Francis. *Vanguard Revolutionaries in Latin America: Peru, Colombia, Mexico.* Boulder, CO: Lynne Rienner, 2003.

Funston, Frederick

Birth Date: September 11, 1865
Death Date: February 19, 1917

Filibuster and U.S. Army officer. Frederick Funston was born in New Carlisle, Ohio, on September 11, 1865, but moved with his family to Kansas when he was 16 years old. He failed to gain entry to the U.S. Military Academy, West Point, and during 1885–1888 attended the University of Kansas but did not earn a degree. From 1888 to 1890, Funston worked as an assistant engineer for the Santa Fe Railroad. He then became a newspaper reporter in Kansas City, Missouri. In 1891 Funston joined an expedition exploring the flora of California's Death Valley. During 1893–1895 he was an employee of the U.S. Department of Agriculture in Alaska.

In 1896, inspired by the Cuban War of Independence (1895–1898), Funston participated in a filibuster expedition transporting arms and supplies to the Cuban rebels. He then joined the Cuban Revolutionary Army as a captain of artillery and saw action in a number of campaigns before contracting malaria and having to return to the United States in 1897.

Funston recovered sufficiently by 1898 to join the U.S. Army when the war with Spain began. Commissioned a colonel of volunteers on May 13, 1898, he commanded the 20th Kansas Volunteer Infantry Regiment and in the late summer was sent to the Philippines. There he participated in Brigadier General Arthur MacArthur's Luzon Campaigns.

When the Philippine-American War began in February 1899, Funston's unit played a major role in the fighting. A publicity seeker, Funston made certain that his daring exploits against Filipino insurgents, many of which he led in person, were reported by American newspaper correspondents. Many of his actions, however, became highly controversial, and his direct participation in cavalry charges and bayonet assaults went against official army regulations.

In April 1899 Funston personally led an assault against a rebel stronghold at Calumpit by swimming across the Bagbag River, crossing the Rio Grande under murderous fire, and engaging in a brief bayonet charge. Although the rebel camp was found to be deserted, Funston's exploits made front-page headlines in the United States and brought him promotion to brigadier general of volunteers that same year.

In March 1901 Funston played a key role in the capture of insurgent leader Emilio Aguinaldo y Famy. Again leading the expedition, Funston and his men disguised themselves as Filipinos. Working with the Philippine Scouts, they gained access to Aguinaldo's camp by pretending to be prisoners. Once inside the stronghold, Funston and his accomplices seized Aguinaldo. This feat brought Funston promotion to brigadier general in the regular army.

Funston's exploits were not without controversy, however. He was repeatedly accused of having engaged in atrocities against Filipinos and approving the looting of Filipino homes and public buildings. The most outlandish allegations included the looting of Roman Catholic churches and the holding of a mock Catholic Mass to amuse his men. Funston managed to avoid any official charges, however, and in one case brought charges against a San Francisco newspaper for libel. By 1902, Funston's controversial actions and anti-Filipino and proexpansionist statements had earned him the enmity of the Theodore Roosevelt administration, which officially reprimanded him. Still, Funston escaped any formal charges, and his popularity in the United States seemed to immunize him from significant trouble.

As commander of the Presidio in San Francisco, Funston took control of the city after the 1906 earthquake, playing an important role in the recovery efforts but also drawing criticism for his order that looters be summarily shot. In 1911 he published his memoirs. During U.S. operations against Mexico in 1914, troops under Funston's command occupied Veracruz. Funston also took part in the hunt for Mexican revolutionary Pancho Villa.

In November 1914, President Woodrow Wilson approved Funston's promotion to major general. Funston was reportedly Wilson's choice to command American forces in France should the United States enter World War I (1914–1918) but died suddenly of a heart attack in San Antonio, Texas, on February 19, 1917.

Paul G. Pierpaoli Jr.

See also Aguinaldo y Famy, Emilio; Cuban War of Independence

Further Reading

Crouch, Thomas W. *A Yankee Guerrillero: Frederick Funston and the Cuban Insurrection, 1896–1897.* Memphis: Memphis State University Press, 1975.

Funston, Frederick. *Memories of Two Wars: Cuban and Philippine Experiences.* New York: Scribner, 1911.

Silbey, David J. *A War of Frontier and Empire: The Philippine-American War, 1899–1902.* New York: Hill and Wang, 2006.

G

Gallieni, Joseph Simon

Birth Date: April 13, 1849
Death Date: May 27, 1916

French Army marshal and colonial soldier and administrator. Born on April 13, 1849, at St. Beat (Haute Gironde), Joseph Simon Gallieni attended the French Military Academy of Saint-Cyr. Commissioned in the French Naval Infantry (marines) in 1870, he distinguished himself in the Franco-Prussian War of 1870–1871.

Gallieni spent most of his military career in the French colonies. He first served in Réunion and Senegal. Promoted to captain in 1878, he directed topographical surveys in Niger. From 1883 to 1886, he was in Martinique. He was then stationed in the Sudan. Returning to France in 1888, Gallieni graduated with distinction from the École de Guerre. Promoted to colonel in 1892, he was assigned to Tonkin in Indochina in the area bordering China. There he instituted highly effective pacification policies centered on strong points to ensure security and win over the local population. This became known as the Oil Slick policy, the gradual spreading of control over the countryside. Gallieni's success in Tonkin earned him a posting in 1896 as military governor of Madagascar, then in revolt against France. General Gallieni suppressed the revolt and during nine years on the island instituted reforms, improving the lot of the people, and carried out public works such as building roads and railroads.

Hailed as a colonial hero, Gallieni returned to France in 1905 to restore his health. Appointed inspector general of colonial troops, he became a member of the Supreme War Council, in which capacity he helped nominate one of his subordinates from Madagascar, General de Division Joseph Joffre, as commander of the French Army. General de Division Gallieni retired from the army in April 1914.

Recalled to active military service in August 1914 with the beginning of World War I (1914–1918), Gallieni assumed the post of military governor of Paris, then threatened by the German advance. He was also designated successor to Joffre should the latter be killed or incapacitated. On September 2 the French government withdrew to Bordeaux, leaving Gallieni in charge of the capital.

Gallieni had temporary command of General de Division Michel Maunoury's Sixth Army. Learning that the German First Army had turned to move southeast of the city, Gallieni knew that the Germans would be vulnerable to a flanking movement from Paris. Employing both the Sixth Army and the Paris garrison, Gallieni orchestrated the blow that initiated the Allied victory of the First Battle of the Marne

(September 5–12), the most decisive battle of the war. Appointed minister of war in October 1915, Gallieni provided effective service in that post until he was obliged to withdraw for health reasons in March 1916. He died at Versailles on May 27, 1916. Gallieni was posthumously named a marshal of France in April 1921.

Gallieni wrote numerous books on his colonial activities. These included *Mission d'exploration du Haut-Niger: Voyage au Soudan français* [Exploring Mission of the Upper Niger: Travel to French Sudan] (1885); *Deux campagnes au Soudan français, 1886–1888* [Two Campaigns in French Sudan, 1886–1888] (1891); *Trois colonnes au Tonkin, 1894–1895* [Three Columns to Tonkin, 1894–1895] (1899); *Madagascar de 1896 à 1905* [Madagascar from 1896 to 1905] (1905); and *Neuf ans à Madagascar* [Nine Years in Madagascar] (1908). An exceptional colonial officer and administrator, Gallieni was not afraid to try innovative approaches.

Philippe Haudrère and Spencer C. Tucker

See also Madagascar Revolt

Further Reading

Gallieni, Joseph. *Memoires du Général Gallieni: Défense de Paris, 23 août–11 septembre 1914*. Paris: Payot, 1920.

Michel, Marc. *Gallieni*. Paris: Fayard, 1989.

Porch, Douglas. *The March to the Marne: The French Army, 1871–1914*. Cambridge: Cambridge University Press, 1981.

Galula, David

Birth Date: January 10, 1919
Death Date: May 11, 1967

French Army officer and important counterinsurgency theorist. David Galula was born into a Jewish family in the North African French protectorate of Tunisia on January 10, 1919. In 1924 his father secured French citizenship for the entire family. Much of Galula's early life was spent in Morocco, and he earned his baccalaureate from the Lycée Lyautey in Casablanca.

Deciding on a military career, Galula entered the French military academy of Saint-Cyr in October 1939. France had already declared war against Germany, and Galula was hastily graduated and commissioned along with the rest of his class in March 1940, but in July France was defeated by Germany. Although he escaped action under the new French Vichy government's First Jewish Statute of October 1940, the Second Jewish Statute of June 1941 brought Galula's expulsion from the army that September, and he returned to North Africa as a civilian.

Following the November 1942 Allied invasion of French North Africa, Galula joined the Free French forces of General Charles de Gaulle, although restoration of Galula's commission was delayed until May 1943. He took part in the June 1944

French invasion of Elba, where he was wounded, and in the Allied landing of southern France that August.

In 1945 Galula was assigned as the assistant to the French military attaché in China and served there until 1948. This afforded Galula his first opportunity to observe revolutionary warfare firsthand. While in China, he learned both Chinese and English. In 1947 while traveling in the Chinese interior, Galula was captured by Communist forces. During several weeks of captivity, he observed how they interacted positively with the peasantry and won the latter's trust and support. Maoist theories of warfare would become the focus of Galula's subsequent writings on counterinsurgency.

Following his service in China, Galula was assigned to the United Nations Special Commission on the Balkans, where he observed the end of the Greek Civil War (1946–1949). After a short staff tour in Paris, he returned to China as French military attaché to Hong Kong during 1951–1956. He closely observed French counterinsurgency efforts during the Indochina War (1946–1954) and also studied American and Filipino pacification efforts during the Hukbalahap Rebellion (1946–1954) in the Philippines.

In 1956 Galula, now a captain, was transferred to Algeria, where he commanded a company of the 45th Bataillon d'Infanterie Coloniale against the growing insurgency against French rule. In Algeria, he put into practice counterinsurgency theories based on his study of the Chinese, Greek, Vietnamese, and Huk insurgencies. During a two-year span, first leading troops in the field and then as a staff officer, Galula achieved significant success.

In 1958 Galula was transferred to metropolitan France and assigned to the National Defense Headquarters in Paris. In 1960 he attended the U.S. Armed Forces Staff College in Norfolk, Virginia, and in 1962 he participated in a RAND Corporation symposium on counterinsurgency. That same year he resigned from the French Army and wrote his first book, *Pacification in Algeria, 1956–1958* (1963), for the RAND Corporation. The book is a detailed account of his personal experience with counterinsurgency in Algeria. Galula then joined the Harvard Center for International Affairs as a research associate. In 1963 he returned to France and worked in the private sector for companies specializing in military radar.

In 1964 Galula published his most important work, the widely heralded *Counterinsurgency Warfare,* a primer on the theory and conduct of counterinsurgency. In it, Galula proposes a detailed strategy for defeating Maoist theories of revolutionary war. Noting Chinese Communist leader Mao Zedong's dictum that revolutionary warfare is 80 percent political action and only 20 percent military, Galula advanced four principles: the aim of revolutionary warfare is to secure the support of the people rather than to secure territory; most of the population will be neutral in an insurgency, and their support can be gained by an active friendly minority; counterinsurgency forces must be able to protect the population so that it may feel free to cooperate with the security forces without fear of retribution; and counterinsurgency efforts will be successful by first defeating armed opponents and then winning the support of the general population before building an infrastructure and establishing a lasting relationship with the population.

Success in counterinsurgency will be accomplished area by area, securing first one area and then a neighboring area. Galula defines victory not in the destruction of insurgent armed forces or their political organizations but instead by securing the permanent isolation of the insurgents from the general population, with this isolation embraced by the people themselves rather than being imposed on them.

To accomplish the goal of defeating an insurgency, Galula outlines the following steps for any given geographical area: concentrating sufficient counterinsurgency forces to drive out most of the armed insurgents; committing sufficient forces to oppose the insurgents' subsequent military riposte, with these forces to be stationed in the places where the people live; cutting ties between the population and the insurgents; rooting out and destroying the local insurgent political organization; establishment, through elections, of new village and town governments; assigning to the newly elected authorities of specific tasks, including the organization of self-defense units; removing incompetent and self-serving leaders and providing full support for those who are effective; organizing the effective leaders into a national political movement; and winning over or defeating the last holdout insurgents.

Galula's writings strongly influenced U.S. Army counterinsurgency doctrine developed by General David H. Petraeus and James N. Mattis and employed by the United States and its coalition partners in Iraq and Afghanistan. Galula died of cancer at Arpajon, France, on May 11, 1967.

Louis A. DiMarco and Spencer C. Tucker

See also Algerian War; Guerre Révolutionnaire; Hukbalahap Rebellion; Indochina War; Mao Zedong; Petraeus, David Howell

Further Reading

Cohen, A. A. *Galula: The Life and Writings of the French Officer Who Defined the Art of Counterinsurgency.* Santa Barbara, CA: Praeger, 2012.

Galula, David. *Counterinsurgency Warfare, Theory and Practice.* Westport, CT: Praeger Security International, 1964.

Marlowe, Ann. *David Galula: His Life and Intellectual Context.* Carlisle, PA: United States Army War College, Strategic Studies Institute, 2010.

Garibaldi, Giuseppe

Birth Date: July 4, 1807
Death Date: June 2, 1882

Italian patriot and insurgent leader in the Italian unification movement, known as Il Risorgimento. Born in Nice on July 4, 1807, Giuseppe Garibaldi became a merchant seaman and then enlisted in the navy of the Kingdom of Sardinia

(Sardinia-Piedmont) in 1833. Embracing the cause of Italian unification, Garibaldi joined Giuseppe Mazzini's Young Italy movement that sought to bring about unification and a democratic government. Involved with Mazzini in a plot to overthrow the Sardinian monarchy, Garibaldi was forced to flee abroad and was sentenced to death in absentia in 1834.

Arriving in South America, Garibaldi became a privateer captain for the Brazilian state of Rio Grande do Sul. Transferring his allegiance to Uruguay in 1843, he raised a unit of expatriate Italians to fight against Argentina during 1843–1847. He won an early battle at Sant-Antonio (1846) but sailed for Europe upon learning of the revolutionary upheavals of 1847–1848 and arrived at Nice in June 1848. Garibaldi wrote to King Charles Albert offering to fight in the Sardinian Army against Austria. Not receiving a reply, Garibaldi joined the fight against the Austrians at Milan and led a small number of patriots out of that city following its surrender on August 9. He then waged a guerrilla campaign lasting several weeks against the occupying Austrians but was forced into Switzerland.

Invited to Rome to lead Republican forces there, Garibaldi arrived in that city on December 12, 1848, and took command of its defenses, repulsing the initial French Army attack on Rome (April 29–30, 1849) and then Neapolitan troops at Palestrina (May 9) and Velletri (May 19) and a second French assault on Rome (June 3). The French reinforced and settled down to a siege of Rome. Realizing that the situation was hopeless, Garibaldi concluded an agreement with French commander Marshal Nicolas Oudinot on June 30 that allowed him and some 4,000 volunteers of his men to march out of the city on July 2. Hoping to join his men to the defenders of the Republic of Venice, Garibaldi marched north, but most of his men were killed, captured, or dispersed by the far more numerous French, Austrian, Spanish, and loyalist Italian pursuing forces.

During 1849–1854, Garibaldi was in exile in America. Reaching agreement with the Sardinian government, he returned there and on the outbreak of war with Austria in March 1859 assumed command of a brigade in the Sardinian Army as a major general. Victorious at Varese (May 26),

Italian patriot Giuseppe Garibaldi dedicated his life to the unification of Italy. An inspirational leader of irregular troops, Garibaldi and his Red Shirts conquered Sicily and southern Italy for the new Kingdom of Italy, which was proclaimed in 1861. (Perry-Castaneda Library)

he liberated considerable territory before the armistice of Villafranca ended hostilities in July. Under the terms of the armistice, Sardina secured Lombardy but not Venetia. Disgusted with the outcome, Garibaldi went to Tuscany to assist the revolutionary government there and plan a march on Rome. Forbidden to embark on the latter course by Sardinian king Victor Emmanuel I, Garibaldi resigned his commission in the Sardinian Army.

In May 1860 Garibaldi sailed with a handful of steamers from Genoa with 1,000 handpicked followers, known as the Red Shirts, to assist a revolt in Sicily. He won a victory at Calatafimi (May 15) and then captured Parma (May 27–30), held by 20,000 men. Crossing over the Straits of Messina to Naples on August 18–19, he entered Naples (September 7) and then waited for the Sardinian Army to march south, agreeing to surrender his conquests to Sardinia and enabling the new Kingdom of Italy to annex the former Kingdom of Naples. Declining all honors, he retired to home on Caprera Island.

In 1861 on the outbreak of the American Civil War, Garibaldi offered his services to the Union side, providing he be placed in command of all the forces. President Abraham Lincoln declined the offer. In 1862 Garibaldi again tried to seize Rome, now garrisoned by the French Army, but was prevented from doing so by troops of the Kingdom of Italy and was wounded and captured in May. In 1866 when Italy allied with Prussia against Austria, Garibaldi again led a small force against the Austrians but was defeated at Bececca (July 21). He again attempted to seize Rome but was defeated at Mentana by a French and Papal force (November 3, 1867).

In early September 1870 on the outbreak of war between France and Prussia, the French troops were recalled from Rome, and Italian troops marched in (September 20). Pope Pius IX shut himself up as the "prisoner in the Vatican." Garibaldi had realized his dream, for Rome now became the capital of a united Italy.

Recruiting 20,000 Italian volunteers, Garibaldi entered the Franco-Prussian War on the side of the French Republic, fighting in the Battle of Belfort (January 15–17, 1871). Elected to the new National Assembly of the French Republic that same year, he soon resigned and returned to Italy, where he was elected to the Italian Parliament in 1874. Garibaldi died on the island of Caprera off Sardinia on June 2, 1882.

A staunch patriot and a brave and capable commander of irregular troops, Garibaldi was probably the best-known revolutionary of the 19th century. A lifelong advocate of democratic government, he was, however, out of his element in regular warfare and the higher levels of government and diplomacy.

Spencer C. Tucker

Further Reading

Hibbert, Christopher. *Garibaldi and His Enemies: The Clash of Arms and Personalities in the Making of Italy.* Boston: Little, Brown, 1966.

Mack Smith, Denis. *Garibaldi.* Englewood Cliffs, NJ: Prentice Hall, 1957.

Martin, George. *The Red Shirt and the Cross of Savoy: The Story of Italy's Risorgimento (1748–1871)*. New York: Dodd, Mead, 1969.

Trevelyan, George M. *Garibaldi and the Thousand*. London: Longmans, Green, 1909.

German Peasants' Revolt

Start Date: 1524
End Date: 1525

The German Peasants' Revolt of 1524–1525 was one of the largest such upheavals in Europe prior to the French Revolution of 1789. The revolt began in the summer of 1524 and reached its height in the summer of 1525, when it may have involved more than 300,000 peasants and had spread over much of present-day southern Germany, Austria, Switzerland, and Alsace.

The leader of the Protestant Reformation in Germany, Martin Luther, while a revolutionary in matters of religion, was fundamentally conservative when it came to social and economic issues. Although Luther's tract *Address to the Christian Nobility of the German Nation* of 1520 called for secular reform, Luther consistently warned his followers against the use of violence to bring about either social or religious change. As the conservative nature of Lutheranism became apparent, more radical leaders came to the fore among the peasants of Germany.

The peasantry was hard-pressed economically, as the nobles ignored the peasants' common law rights and imposed Roman law that favored landholders. Rising inflation and property values meant that nobles were less generous to their charges, with many nobles seeking to maximize their revenues by reviving old rights at peasant expense. When it became clear that the peasants could not rely on the emperor to assist them in redress of grievances against the nobles, radical preachers came to the fore, and the peasants began to form associations to advocate for direct action in relief of economic and social oppression. These associations often included townspeople and members of the lower clergy. Influenced by the followers of Czech religious reformer Jan Hus (1369–1415), the associations embraced egalitarianism and socialism.

The uprising began in Stühlingen in the Black Forest of southwestern Germany in June 1524 when the countess of Lüpfen demanded that the peasants gather strawberries and snail shells for a banquet. As the revolt spread, the peasants refused to pay taxes or perform feudal work. They expressed opposition to the seizure of common lands by the nobles as well as to high taxes, the heavy burdens of labor, and unequal justice. The revolt quickly spread to Swabia and Württemberg and before long included about a third of Germany. The nobles were unable to effectively deal with the revolt, in large part because most of the military forces of the Swabian League were then fighting in Italy. Also, the revolt was not yet marked by great violence because the nobles were still negotiating with its leaders. The demands of the autumn harvest also detracted from its momentum.

Throughout the winter months the insurgents continued to agitate, and in February 1525 the peasants rose up again, this time with better organization and more numbers. Their demands came to be embodied in the Twelve Articles, which appeared at Memmingen in February 1525. These included the right of each community to select its own pastor; acceptance of the tithe on grain but rejection of other imposed tithes; denunciation of serfdom as contrary to Christian teaching; assertion of the right to fish and hunt and to cut wood in common lands; demands for relief from excessive feudal dues, forced labor, and rents; the assertion of common law and demands for impartial justice; rejection of the seizure of common lands without fair compensation; demands for the abolition of the inheritance tax as unfair to widows and orphans; and, finally, willingness to withdraw any of the articles if they were found contrary to the Word of God.

In the Twelve Articles and other such pronouncements, the peasants held that they were acting in accordance with the gospel as espoused by Luther, and they pledged not to use force unless as a last resort. Not all of the peasant demands were as moderate, however, and as the movement spread, these became more radical. One of their leaders, Thomas Müntzer, attempted to set up a theocratic state in Mühlhausen. Other radicals demanded a Communist state with the confiscation of church property and common ownership of all property. Some radical leaders and preachers asserted that before God's kingdom could be established on Earth, all godless people should be killed.

Peasant bands numbered 20,000 or more men. Some were well armed, even having their own artillery. However, the peasants lacked effective leadership, organization, discipline, and the cavalry possessed by the nobles. Most important, there was no broad organization tying them together. When soldiers began to return to Germany following the Battle of Pavia (February 24, 1525), the nobles acted. Because the peasants never came together in one coherent military force or movement, the nobles had little trouble defeating it piecemeal.

Luther condemned the Peasants' Revolt and even penned a virulent pamphlet titled *Against the Murdering Hordes of Peasants* in which he called on the nobles to put the revolt down with the sword. They did so gladly, showing little moderation in crushing the insurgency. Although no accurate casualty figures exist, as many as 100,000 peasants may have perished.

Luther's embrace of the subordination of church to state certainly aided the reception of Lutheranism by many nobles but ended it as a genuinely popular movement in Germany. The threat of a repetition of the revolt also brought a sharp increase in noble power. In addition, Catholic princes chose to regard the victory over the peasants as a divine judgment against Protestantism. They also used the revolt to bolster their argument that religious insubordination was necessarily accompanied by political and social upheaval.

Gates Brown and Spencer C. Tucker

Further Reading

Baylor, Michael. *The German Reformation and the Peasant's War: A Brief History with Documents.* New York: St. Martin's, 2012.

Grimm, Harold J. *The Reformation Era.* New York: Macmillan, 1973.

Scott, Tom. *The German Peasants' War: A History in Documents.* New York: Prometheus, 1994.

Geronimo

Birth Date: June 16, 1829
Death Date: February 26, 1909

Chiricahua Apache war leader and medicine man. Geronimo was born on June 16, 1829, on the upper Gila River near the present-day Arizona–New Mexico border. Named Goyahkla at birth, he was called "Geromino" by the Mexicans. "Geronimo" is Spanish for "Jerome," and Saint Jerome is the Catholic saint of lost causes. Legend has it that Mexican soldiers invoked Saint Jerome when they fought against Geronimo's raiding parties, and the name eventually stuck. Geronimo was born into the Bedonkohe band, which was closely associated with the Chiricahuas. As a youth, he honed his skills as a hunter and marksman and, most importantly, learned survival techniques that would subsequently serve him well.

In 1850 Geronimo joined Mimbres Apache war leader Mangas Coloradas in raiding several Mexican settlements near Janos, Mexico. During Geronimo's absence, a group of Mexicans attacked his family's encampment and killed his mother, wife, and three young children. The event instilled in Geronimo a deep hatred of Mexicans.

After the 1850 expedition, Geronimo continued to develop his skills under Mangas Coloradas. Geronimo engaged in a number of raids against both Mexicans and Americans and is thought to have been a participant in the Battle of Apache Pass in July 1862. He also associated with other notable Apache leaders, such as Victorio, Juh, and Cochise, and lived among the followers of Cochise. Geronimo continued to raid settlements on both sides of the U.S.-Mexican border and earned infamy in the American and Mexican presses.

Geronimo eventually allied himself with Victorio and in 1877 took up residence with his followers at the Ojo Caliente Reservation in New Mexico. Shortly thereafter, the reservation agent had Geronimo arrested and placed in irons. This began a long series of breakouts and arrests. Whether Geronimo broke out of imprisonment or was released is somewhat unclear, but by 1878 he was back in Mexico and allied with the Nednhi Apache war chief Juh, participating in numerous raids conducted by Juh and his followers. Juh's band subsequently took up residence at the San Carlos Reservation in southern Arizona, where Juh and Geronimo were forbidden to leave by U.S. authorities. Nevertheless, in 1881 Geronimo escaped, along with Juh and their followers. They remained in Mexico's Sierra Madre for about a year. In 1882 Geronimo and Juh led a daring raid on the San Carlos Reservation, ostensibly to win the release of Chief Loco, but as many as several hundred Native Americans there decided to follow Geronimo and Juh.

In 1884 after Geronimo had again returned to San Carlos, he voluntarily surrendered to American authorities; however, less than two years later he was again on the run. Geronimo remained at large until March 1886, when he agreed to surrender to Brigadier General George Crook just south of the U.S.-Mexican border. However, Geronimo and his followers halted temporarily in southeastern Arizona, where an unscrupulous liquor salesman from Tombstone clandestinely entered the encampment and provided sufficient liquor to inebriate Geronimo and his followers. The salesman then convinced Geronimo that if he and his followers did not leave the area at once, they would likely be killed by U.S. forces.

Geronimo and his people were then on the run for at least six months. Meanwhile, Geronimo continued to conduct raids. U.S. forces pursued Geronimo and the Apaches tenaciously, however, and by the late summer of 1886 the Native Americans were exhausted, sick, and hungry. In early September 1886, Geronimo sent word that he would surrender. He met personally with Brigadier General Nelson A. Miles in Skeleton Canyon, Arizona, to discuss the terms. On September 4 the Apaches formally surrendered. Geronimo and some of his followers remained at Fort Bowie until September 8, at which time they were placed on a train bound for Florida.

Eventually Geronimo and other Apache leaders were detained at Fort Marion in St. Augustine. Their families, however, were sent to Fort Pickens near Pensacola, some 300 miles distant. This violated the terms of the surrender, which guaranteed that families would not be split. By May 1888, the Apaches were reunited in Mount Vernon, Alabama. Geronimo embraced his new life, cooperating with U.S. officials and missionaries, converting to Christianity, and even becoming a local justice of the peace. In 1892 the Apaches were relocated again, this time to Indian Territory (Oklahoma). Geronimo died at Fort Sill, Oklahoma, on February 26, 1909.

Paul G. Pierpaoli Jr.

See also American Indian Wars in the West; Crook, George; Miles, Nelson Appleton

Further Reading

Debo, Angie. *Geronimo: The Man, His Time, His Place.* Norman: University of Oklahoma Press, 1976.

Skinner, Woodward B. *The Apache Rock Crumbles: The Captivity of Geronimo's People.* Pensacola, FL: Skinner, 1987.

Stockel, H. Henrietta. *Survival of the Spirit: Chiricahua Apaches in Captivity.* Reno: University of Nevada Press, 1993.

Godard, Yves

Birth Date: December 21, 1911
Death Date: March 3, 1975

French Army officer and counterinsurgency practitioner. Yves Godard was born in Saint-Maixent, Sarthe Department, France, on December 21, 1911. He was commissioned in the army upon graduation from the French military academy of Saint-Cyr and served in the Chasseurs Alpins, the elite mountain infantry. In September 1939 when World War II (1939–1945) began, Godard was serving as a ski instructor in Poland, but he quickly returned to France.

In the Battle for France (May–June 1940), Godard was taken prisoner. He was successful on his third escape attempt and joined the French Resistance. With the liberation of France, he returned to the active army and commanded a Chasseurs Alpins battalion.

After World War II, Godard served in the French occupation forces in Austria and on the French General Staff. In 1948 Lieutenant Colonel Godard was assigned to command the 11th Bataillon Parachutiste de Choc, an elite airborne commando unit organized to operate behind enemy lines. He commanded the battalion through its deployment to Indochina, where it took part in the failed attempt to relieve the 1954 siege of Dien Bien Phu. In 1955 Godard was assigned as chief of staff of the 10th Parachute Division, commanded by Brigadier General Jacques Massu, which was deployed to Algeria.

During the Algerian War (1954–1962), Colonel Godard played a leading role in the Battle of Algiers (January–March 1957), having charge of the French intelligence network that identified the members of the Front de Libération Nationale (FLN, National Liberation Front) operating in the city. Massu had been ordered to restore order in any way possible, and Godard oversaw the employment of harsh interrogation techniques including torture, which he defended as necessary against those who would attack women and children. While effective in destroying the FLN Algiers network, the use of torture by the French Army had decidedly negative long-term consequences. When the army's employment of torture became public knowledge, opposition in France to the war significantly increased.

Godard continued to serve in Algeria after the Battle of Algiers, and in the summer of 1959 he was appointed director general of the Algerian Sûreté (Algerian Police). Many professionals in the army became convinced that the French government was on the path toward granting Algerian independence, and they began planning attempts to overthrow the Fourth Republic. Godard was a key figure in these efforts that toppled the Fourth Republic in May 1958 and brought Charles de Gaulle back to power. Godard was also involved in the so-called Barricades Week in January 1960 that was designed to influence the new government's Algerian policy.

Early in 1961, Godard was reassigned to metropolitan France in an attempt to limit his political activities. He returned to Algeria that April and participated in a failed putsch against the Fifth Republic. Godard then deserted the army and helped organize the underground Organisation de l'Armée Secrète (OAS, Secret Army Organization) that carried out terrorist activities in Algeria and in metropolitan France. Tried in absentia for treason, he was found guilty and sentenced to death. Godard eventually settled in Belgium, where he ran a small factory. Although the French government pardoned former OAS members in 1968, Godard refused to return to his native country. He was writing a history of the Algerian War at the time of his death in Lessines, Belgium, on March 3, 1975.

Louis A. DiMarco

See also Algerian War; Algiers, Battle of; *Battle of Algiers;* Front de Libération Nationale; Galula, David; Guerre Révolutionnaire; Massu, Jacques Émile; Organisation de l'Armée Secrète; Salan, Raoul Albin-Louis; Trinquier, Roger

Further Reading

Henissart, Paul. *Wolves in the City: The Death of French Algeria.* New York: Simon and Schuster, 1970.

Horne, Alistair. *A Savage War for Peace: Algeria, 1954–1962.* New York: New York Review of Books, 2006.

Gordon, Charles George

Birth Date: January 28, 1833
Death Date: January 26, 1885

British general. Born at Woolwich, England, on January 28, 1833, the son of a British general, Charles George Gordon entered the Royal Military Academy, Woolwich, at age 15 and was commissioned a 2nd lieutenant in the Royal Engineers in 1852. He fought in the Crimean War (1853–1856) as a lieutenant and attracted attention as an intelligent and capable young officer. Gordon then served on the international commission surveying the Russo-Turkish border in Armenia during 1856–1858. During the Second Opium War (*Arrow* War) of 1859–1860, he volunteered for service in China, where he distinguished himself in the assault on the Dagu (Taku) Forts on August 21, 1859, and the capture of Peking (Beijing) on October 6. Gordon stayed on in China and secured a commission as a general in the Chinese Imperial Army and command of the Ever Victorious Army in April 1863, a mercenary force that won some 30 victories and contributed to the defeat of the great Taiping Rebellion (1850–1864). His extensive service in China and affectation of Chinese attire earned him the nickname "Chinese Gordon."

Returning to Britain, Gordon commanded the Royal Engineers post at Gravesend in 1865 and then served on the Danubian Commission in Romania in 1871. Appointed governor of southern Sudan in late 1873, he took up his post in March 1874. Following a brief time in Britain during December 1876–March 1877,

Gordon became governor of the entire Sudan. During his years in the Sudan, he traveled extensively, built a series of military outposts, and worked to eradicate the slave trade.

Returning to Britain in May 1880, Gordon traveled to China, where he advised the Chinese government not to go to war with Russia. Following a year in Britain, he assumed command of the engineer post in Mauritius during April 1881–April 1882 and then was briefly in the Cape Colony, reorganizing local forces. He spent nearly the entire year of 1883 in Palestine studying the Bible. Gordon then accepted appointment from King Leopold I of Belgium to serve as governor of the Congo in January 1884.

Meanwhile, a prophet arose in the Sudan. Calling himself the Mahdi, he soon raised thousands of followers known as Dervishes. Following the annihilation of Egyptian forces sent against the Madhi, British prime minister William Gladstone decided to evacuate Europeans and Egyptians from the Sudan and charged Gordon with this task, although his orders were somewhat ambiguous.

Deeply religious and more than a little eccentric, Gordon also had a martyr fixation. Reaching Cairo, he ignored his orders and convinced the Egyptian government to pursue a course of reestablishing control of the Sudan. Proceeding up the Nile, he arrived at Khartoum on February 18, 1884. Although 2,000 women and children were successfully evacuated, Gordon dallied, and his force became besieged at Khartoum on March 13, 1884. A furious Gladstone delayed sending out a relief expedition under General Sir Garnet Joseph Wolseley, who also dallied. As Wolseley's men at last moved up the Nile and neared Khartoum, the Dervishes swept over the British defenses and killed Gordon on the steps of the palace on January 26, 1885, placing his severed head before the feet of the Mahdi. The British did not return to the Sudan until 1896, under General Sir Herbert Kitchener.

A remarkable individual and a gifted commander of foreign forces, Gordon was also a superb organizer and an indefatigable administrator.

Spencer C. Tucker

See also Mahdist Uprising in Sudan; Taiping Rebellion

Further Reading

Elton, Godfrey, Baron Elton. *General Gordon.* London: Collins, 1954.

Farwell, Byron. *Eminent Victorian Soldiers: Seekers of Glory.* New York: Norton, 1985.

Trench, Charles Chenevix. *The Road to Khartoum: A Life of General Charles Gordon.* New York: Norton, 1979.

Great Iraqi Revolution.

See Iraq Revolt

Great National Solidarity Program.

See Chieu Hoi Program

Great Revolt.

See Arab Revolt of 1936

Great Rising.

See Peasants' Revolt in England

Great Syrian Revolt

Start Date: 1925
End Date: 1927

As a consequence of the Allied victory in World War I (1914–1918), the Ottoman Empire came to an end, and much of its former territory was taken from it and given as mandates under the League of Nations to France and Britain. France received the mandate over Syria and Lebanon. The Arab Revolt of 1916–1918 had greatly stimulated Arab nationalism, but Faisal ibn al-Husain, who had proclaimed a kingdom of Syria and Iraq, recognized the futility of resistance and ultimately accepted the throne of Iraq (which was a British mandate) instead. This did not lesson Arab nationalism, however.

In October 1919, the French government appointed General Henri Gouraud as high commissioner of the Levant, with authority over Syria and Lebanon. He and the French troops in Syria immediately encountered opposition. During 1920–1921, Alawites and Bedouins revolted, followed in 1921 by an insurrection in the city of Aleppo and in southwestern Syria.

After defeating nationalist forces under Yusuf al-Azmah in the Battle of Maysalun two days earlier, on July 25, 1920, French forces entered Damascus. Gouraud was succeeded in April 1923 by General Maxime Weygand, who sought to follow the assimilationist policies of Marshal Hubert Lyautey in Morocco. Such policies were poorly executed in Syria, however, with French officials tending to follow the traditional French system of centralized rule that failed to recognize local traditions of governance. Minority groups such as the Alawites and the Druze felt their autonomy threatened.

French general Maurice-Paul-Emmanuel Sarrail succeeded Weygand in November 1924. Sarrail tired to introduce secular reforms and create an even more centralized state. A drought, inflation, and rising nationalism—especially in the cities—fed opposition to French rule.

The ensuing Great Syrian Revolt (also known as the Great Druze Revolt) of 1925 actually involved many different groups, including the majority Sunnis but also Druze and Christians. Its immediate cause was the perceived harsh treatment of the Druze in Jabal al-Druze in southwestern Syria by French intelligence officer Captain Gabriel Cabrillet, who ironically had been selected to govern by the Druze Council of Notables. Cabrillet introduced a number of reforms, but he also insisted on full payment of taxes and disarmament of the population. He also employed prisoners and peasants in forced labor. Sarrail then imprisoned without cause Druze emissaries sent to the high commissioner to inform him that Cabrillet's auctions were alienating most of the local population.

Sultan pasha al-Atrash now led a revolt against French rule, with the fighting beginning on July 21, 1925. Many of the Druze now taking up arms against the French had served in the Ottoman Army in World War I or had fought in the Great Arab Revolt of 1916–1918, and Druze infantry and cavalry soon laid siege to the small French garrison at al-Suwayda. On August 2 at al-Mazra, Bedouin and Druze forces attacked a relief column of some 3,000 French troops under General Roger Michaud, commander of the Army of the Levant. The rebels killed some 800 French soldiers and captured 2,000 rifles and a large number of supplies. With this insurgent success, all Syria rose in rebellion.

Initially, French forces in Syria were in no position to deal with the revolt. They numbered only some 14,400 men, along with 6,000 Circassian and Syrian auxiliaries. France was then deeply involved in the Rif War, a major counterinsurgency effort in Morocco, and few reenforcements were immediately available. The French therefore relied heavily on airpower. Sarrail's extensive air campaign included the indiscriminate bombing of Syrian villages, a step that further inflamed the general population. The rebels also learned to disperse their forces.

In the early autumn of 1925, the rebellion spread to urban areas, most importantly Damascus. Here urban nationalists and rural Druze and Bedouins launched a series of attacks, capturing Syrian gendarmes but failing in an effort to kidnap Sarrail. The insurgent effort was handicapped by poor coordination between its urban and rural elements, with the citizenry of Damascus fearful of control by rural elements. In September, General Maurice Gustav Gamelin replaced Michaud. In October, Gamelin launched a massive aerial and artillery bombardment of Damascus in what was one of the first uses of airpower against an urban insurgency. The French also set up barricades to block off and protect the Christian quarter of the city.

The insurgents failed in their urban attacks but carried out a number of raids and sought to cut off the French in Damascus by destroying railroad lines. Public executions of insurgents by the French and their aerial and artillery bombardments brought an international outcry and forced the removal of Sarrail in December 1925 and his replacement as high commissioner with French civilian politician Henry de Jouvenel, who was in turn succeeded by Auguste Henri Ponsot in August 1926.

French efforts to arm the Syrian Christian villages largely failed, with the insurgents seizing the weapons. Some insurgent bands even had artillery and machine guns. Meanwhile, the extensive fighting soon destroyed the rural economy.

By February 1926, Damascus was surrounded by a belt of barbed wire and machine-gun posts. With the Rif War drawing to a close, France was also able to dispatch reinforcements from Africa. Soon the French had 50,000 troops in the country. Gamelin launched combined arms attacks with tanks and aircraft but these proved only marginally effective, and in August he began employing armed auxiliaries of Kurds, Armenians, and Circassians. These units cleared the area around Damascus, although by that time much of the city had been destroyed. The revolt was now purely a rural affair.

Jouvnel's approach also differed from that of Sarrail. Jouvnel offered amnesty to the rebels and convinced some captured nationalist leaders to urge surrender. The remaining insurgents soon fell to quarreling among themselves, and most of the leaders were driven into exile. The Druze were decisively defeated in the spring of 1927, and by June the rebellion was over. At least 6,000 insurgents had been killed, and 100,000 Syrians were rendered homeless.

The French now scaled back their plans and adopted a more realistic approach to rule in Syria. In March 1928 they proclaimed a general amnesty for the rebels, although this excluded some of the insurgent leaders.

William T. Dean III and Spencer C. Tucker

See also Arab Revolt against Ottoman Rule; Lyautey, Louis Hubert; Rif War; Syrian Insurgency

Further Reading

Khoury, Philip. *Syria and the French Mandate: The Politics of Arab Nationalism, 1920–1945.* Princeton, NJ: Princeton Univercity Press, 1987.

Neep, Daniel. *Occupying Syria under the French Mandate: Insurgency, Space and State Formation.* Cambridge: Cambridge University Press, 2012.

Provence, Michael. *The Great Syrian Revolt and the Rise of Arab Nationalism.* Austin: University of Texas Press, 2005.

Greek Civil War

Start Date: March 1946
End Date: August 1949

The Greek Civil War was the first post–World War II example of a politically motivated insurgency. During the Greek Civil War, the Kommounistikon Komma Elladós (KKE, Greek Communist Party) sought to seize power from the anticommunist Greek nationalists. The conflict was rooted in age-old divisions within Greek society, complicated by the Cold War, and indeed was one of the earliest tests of will between East and West in the Cold War. Both sides committed atrocities and tried to settle old scores under the guise of conflicting ideologies. The fighting claimed some 80,000 lives, a total surpassing the number of Greeks killed in World War II (1939–1945).

In the early years of the 20th century, conservative and liberal parties in Greece struggled for power and engaged in a series of bloodless purges that heightened political instability and created much anger and bitterness. This atmosphere provided fertile ground for authoritarianism, and in 1936 General Ioannis Metaxas established a fascist-style dictatorship, further polarizing the country.

Metaxas's death in 1941 and the flight of the Greek government abroad after the German invasion left Greece in virtual chaos. The KKE, persecuted under Metaxas, stepped into the power vacuum by creating the Ethniko Apeleftherotiko Metopo (EAM, National Liberation Front), dedicated to the liberation of Greece. By 1944 the EAM claimed nearly 2 million members, and its military arm, the Ellinikós Laïkós Apeleftherotikós Stratós (ELAS, Greek People's Liberation Army), had as many as 150,000 fighters and controlled three-fifths of the country.

In October 1944 British prime minister Winston Churchill, fearful of a Communist takeover in Greece and the loss of control over the eastern Mediterranean, met with Soviet premier Joseph Stalin in Moscow and struck a deal over influence in the Balkans. Although the Soviets were accorded predominance in most of the Balkans, Great Britain was to be dominant in Greece.

Relations between the British-backed Greek monarchy and the EAM quickly soured as the Communists suppressed dissent and tried to assert control over the country. In retaliation, the British rehabilitated the collaborationist police, returned monarchist military units to Greece, and demanded that ELAS disarm. On December 2, 1944, the police fired on antigovernment demonstrators, triggering the Battle for Athens. The British brought in reinforcements, and the battle ended in victory for the nationalists and in the disarming of ELAS.

Under the Varkiza Agreement of February 1945, ELAS formally agreed to disband in return for a plebiscite and a general election. The EAM splintered as moderates and Socialists abandoned it, while KKE membership plummeted from its peak of more than 400,000 to only 50,000. KKE leader Nikos Zachariades attempted to impose tighter party discipline but was stymied by the strength of the nationalist forces.

In an attempt to maintain order, the British strengthened the Greek National Guard and turned a blind eye as security forces conducted a campaign of repression against the Communists. In the Greek parliamentary elections of March 1946, the rightist candidates won a landslide victory, in part because of a Communist boycott on the claim that government pledges had not been fulfilled. These allegedly rigged elections prompted the KKE to declare a state of civil war.

The start of the Greek Civil War is usually dated from March 31, 1946, and an attack on a Greek Gendarmerie station at Litochoro that killed 12 gendarmes and 2 civilians. On December 27, the KKE designatcd its fighting units as the Dimokratikós Strató Elladas (DSE, Democratic Army of Greece).

DSE insurgents took to the hills, mainly in the mountainous north of the country where they could receive supplies from the Communist governments of Yugoslavia, Albania, and Bulgaria. Under the leadership of Markos Vaphiadis, the DSE, numbering about 25,000 men, won notable gains in the first year of fighting, thanks in part to this Communist support. In 1947 the KKE established the Provisional Democratic Government, known as the Mountain Government, which, however, never was accorded international recognition.

Hard-pressed financially themselves and fearing that the nationalists might indeed lose the war against the DSE, the British appealed to the United States for assistance. Previous British requests for American assistance in Greece had been rebuffed, but by 1947 American attitudes had undergone change. President Harry S. Truman's growing antipathy toward the Soviets with the tightening of their grip over Eastern Europe hardened his stance. On March 12, 1947, Truman addressed a joint session of Congress and enunciated the Truman Doctrine, which committed the United States to come to the aid of any nation threatened by Communist takeover. Truman requested $300 million to support the Greek nationalists and anticommunists in nearby Turkey. The Truman Doctrine proved to be the Greek Civil War's greatest legacy, setting the stage for the Containment Policy.

The KKE did not take the Truman Doctrine seriously and believed that the nationalists would capitulate even with U.S. support. Meanwhile, on British advice, the Greek government had embarked on relocating people from vulnerable areas and also instituting social programs to win their support. By 1948, when its 3rd Division was all but destroyed, it was clear that the DSE was in dire straits. The American-backed nationalist army grew exponentially, with Lieutenant General James Van Fleet heading the U.S. assistance group. In Operation KORONIS (June 16–August 21, 1948), 70,000 Greek Army troops defeated some 12,000 DSE fighters, after which the surviving DSE withdrew into Albania.

In January 1949, KKE leaders foolishly declared that the goal of the Greek Civil War was no longer the restoration of parliamentary democracy, as they had previously stated, but rather the establishment of a proletarian dictatorship. Zachariades also shifted the DSE from a mobile war of attrition, advocated by Vaphiadis, to a campaign to defend territory, a tactical miscalculation that played into the hands of the revitalized nationalist army.

In the spring of 1949, the nationalist army, now numbering some 180,000 men, cleared the Communist rebels out of southern Greece and launched a two-pronged offensive designed to drive them completely out of the country. As the fighting reached its climax, Yugoslavia closed its border and ended arms shipments that had kept the DSE insurgency viable. On August 1, Greek Army commander General Alexander Papagos launched Operation TORCH, a highly effective military campaign against the fixed DSE defenses in the Grammos and Vitsi Mountains

More than 150 Greek guerrillas, captured by government soldiers, are paraded through the streets of Langadia, east of Salonika, on February 12, 1948. (AP Photo)

of northern Greece, forcing most of the remaining DSE fighters to withdraw into Albania at the end of August 1949. Other Communist groups departed thereafter, and the DSE declared a cease-fire on October 16, effectively ending the Greek Civil War and sealing the Greek government's victory.

Vernon L. Pedersen and Spencer C. Tucker

See also Dimokratikós Stratós Elladas; Ellinikós Laïkós Apeleftherotikós Stratós; Tito

Further Reading

Close, David H. *The Greek Civil War, 1943–1950: Studies of Polarization.* London: Routledge, 1993.

Close, David H. *The Origins of the Greek Civil War.* New York: Longman, 1995.

Gerolymatos, Andre. *Red Acropolis, Black Terror: The Greek Civil War and the Origins of Soviet-American Rivalry.* New York: Basic Books, 2004.

Iatrides, John O. *Greece in the 1940s: A Nation in Crisis.* Hanover, NH: University Press of New England, 1981.

Grivas, Georgios

Birth Date: May 23, 1898
Death Date: January 27, 1974

Cypriot insurgent leader and Greek Army general. Born in Trikomo, Cyprus, on May 23, 1898, Georgios Grivas enrolled in the Royal Hellenic Military Academy in Athens in 1916 and participated in the Greco-Turkish War (1919–1922) following World War I (1914–1918). In 1925 he won a scholarship to study at the École de Tir and École d'Infanterie at Versailles, France.

Prior to World War II (1939–1945), Grivas served in various Greek Army units and lectured on tactics at the War School. He fought in the defense of Greece following the 1940 Italian invasion, and during the German occupation he established his own guerrilla group (known as "X"). After the end of the occupation in 1944 the group was disbanded, and Grivas rejoined the regular army and fought in the civil war against the Communists (1946–1949).

Following the government victory in the civil war, Grivas had several meetings with Archbishop Makarios III to advance the cause of the union (enosis) of Cyprus and Greece. In November 1954 Grivas moved back to Cyprus and fomented a violent insurgency against the British occupation of the island. He also took the name Dighenis, a legendary Byzantine hero, and organized the National Organization of Cypriot Fighters (EOKA) with direct military support from Greece.

The EOKA terrorist campaign commenced on April 1, 1955, and reached its climax during Makarios's exile in 1956. Grivas eluded capture on several occasions between December 1955 and May 1956. During the EOKA campaign 504 people died, including 142 Britons and 84 Turks. After the February 8, 1959, Greco-Turkish agreement on Cypriot independence, Grivas ordered a cease-fire. But his dream of enosis had yet to be realized.

Grivas returned to Greece in March 1959, welcomed as a national hero and decorated with the highest honors. Shortly thereafter he formed a political party, the Movement of National Regeneration. In 1964 he returned to Cyprus as commander of the Greek Cypriot National Guard but was recalled to Athens in November 1967. In 1971 he created the armed underground movement EOKA B against the ruling Greek military junta but also against his former ally, Makarios III, who opposed a Greco-Cypriot union. Grivas was forced underground as he waged yet another guerrilla war but died on January 27, 1974, in Limassol, Cyprus. His supporters continued his efforts, staging a coup against Makarios in 1974 that brought not enosis but instead a Turkish invasion and partition of the island.

Lucian N. Leustean

See also Cyprus Insurrection

Further Reading

Dodd, Clement Henry. *The Cyprus Imbroglio.* Huntington, Cambridgeshire, UK: Eothen, 1998.

Gibbons, Harry Scott. *The Genocide Files.* London: Charles Bravos, 1997.

Grivas, Georgios. *The Memoirs of General Grivas.* Edited by Charley Foley. London: Longmans, 1964.

Guatemala Insurgency

Start Date: 1960
End Date: 1996

The Central American nation of Guatemala was one of the first to experience the foco theory of revolutionary rural warfare advanced by Ernesto "Che" Guevara de la Serna and Jules Régis Debray as a consequence of Fidel Castro's insurgency in Cuba during 1953–1959. Although the circumstances that made possible Castro's success were unique to Cuba and could not be duplicated in Guatemala, Guatemala underwent great turmoil in coups, military rule, intervention by the United States, and a protracted and very bloody insurgency between 1960 and 1996.

On October 20, 1944, in what has come to be known as the October Revolution, armed students and workers as well as dissident military officers ousted the dictatorial Jorge Ubico regime. In its place, an interim regime led by Francisco Arana and Jacobo Arbenz held a presidential election in which Juan José Arévalo won 85 percent of the vote and the presidency. The revolution and the subsequent elections marked the beginning of what has been termed the Ten Years of Spring, lasting from 1945 to 1954.

Arévalo democratized the state by granting universal suffrage to all adults except illiterate women. He also arranged for freedom of speech and freedom of the press, and he permitted all political parties to function except the Communist Party. He devoted large amounts of government funding to social programs and also improved labor codes, which angered Guatemala's largest landholder, the American-owned United Fruit Company (UFCO).

Although Arévalo was a staunch antiliberal individualist and anti-Marxist, the U.S. press was quick to label him a Communist. Indeed, Washington demanded that he modify the labor codes and terminate a number of his cabinet members because of their alleged Communist proclivities.

In 1951 after two failed coup attempts, Defense Minister Arbenz was elected president. He proceeded to expropriate nearly 1.5 million acres of land, much of which belonged to the UFCO, and distributed it to roughly 100,000 peasant families. Even though the UFCO received what was arguably fair monetary compensation for the land, the UFCO along with Guatemala's landed oligarchy demanded an immediate reversal of the land reforms.

Early in 1953, the American Central Intelligence Agency (CIA) developed a plan to overthrow Arbenz. The CIA also trained and equipped a mercenary force of mostly Guatemalan exiles. In June 1954 the self-styled Liberacionista Army (Liberation Army), consisting of between 150–200 men, crossed into Guatemala from neighboring Honduras. The army did not press on, however, instead allowing three U.S.-provided planes (flown by U.S. pilots) to menace Guatemala City and other urban centers. Fearing U.S. intervention, Guatemala's military leaders forced Arbenz from power; he went into exile in Mexico.

The army leadership that took power in Guatemala was firmly anticommunist and allowed American personnel to be directly involved in government decision making. In 1956 the military leaders, now in complete control of the government, reversed Arbenz's reforms.

General José Miguel Ramón Ydígoras Fuentes was president from March 1958 to March 1963. A number of leftist junior officers who had been loyal to Arbenz attempted a coup against Ydígoras and the military leadership on November 13, 1960. The coup failed, and the survivors fled to the Izabel Mountains and there formed the Movimento Revolucionara 13 de Noviembre (13 November Revolutionary Movement, or simply MR-13). Receiving aid from Cuba, they attempted to rally the peasants against the government. Although in 1963 the MR-13 joined the Guatemalan Communists and other dissident groups to form the Fuerzas Armadas Rebeldes (FAR, Rebel Armed Forces), the new organization suffered from serious internal divisions.

The military continued to direct the country even in the face of failed coup attempts and escalated guerrilla warfare. The Pentagon directed the Guatemalan counterinsurgency movement during 1966–1968, with some 1,000 U.S. Army Special Forces in the country (28 U.S. servicemen died in Guatemala during this period). Under the guise of antiterrorist campaigns, the military suspended civil rights, carried out mass assassinations and kidnappings, and prevented opposition parties from participating in the political process. These brutal tactics led to Guatemala's increasing international isolation as well as strong internal resistance. At the same time, however, U.S. assistance enabled the inauguration of a significant civic action program that saw the construction of schools, hospitals, and new roads.

The most intense fighting occurred during 1980–1983. Under the leadership of Guatemalan president General Romeo Lucas García (1978–1983), newly formed death squads attempted to quell guerrilla forces in the cities and the countryside. In rural areas, a scorched-earth policy resulted in the destruction of entire villages— sometimes with their inhabitants—and decimated jungles and forests.

By 1982, there were a number of different coup plots in which the CIA was involved. Lucas, realizing that he could not remain in charge, stepped down, and General José Efraín Ríos Montt took over as head of a military junta. He was forced to resign in August 1983, however, because he continued to stall democratic reforms. General Oscar Mejía Victores then assumed power. Supported by the United States, he held the country's first real and free election since 1951.

A civilian, Vinicio Cerezo, was elected president in 1985. Yet during 1983–1989, the military still held the reins of political power and fought against the guerrillas amid constant coup attempts. In January 1996 Álvaro Arzú Irigoyen was elected president, and following negotiations with the insurgent umbrella organization Unidad Revolucionaria Nacional Guatemalteca (Guatemalan National Revolutionary

Unity) that December, he signed a peace accord to end the insurgency. In the 36 years of strife, as many as 200,000 civilians may have perished, and another 100,000 have disappeared.

Jonathan Alex Clapperton and Spencer C. Tucker

See also Castro Ruz, Fidel Alejandro; Debray, Jules Régis; Foco Theory; Guevara de la Serna, Ernesto

Further Reading

Fried, Jonathan L., Marvin E. Gettleman, Deborah T. Levenson, and Nancy Peckenham, eds. *Guatemala in Rebellion: Unfinished History.* New York: Grove, 1983.

Jonas, Susanne. *The Battle for Guatemala: Rebels, Death Squads, and U.S. Power.* Boulder, CO: Westview, 1991.

Schirmer, Jennifer. *The Guatemalan Military Project: A Violence Called Democracy.* Philadelphia: University of Pennsylvania Press, 1998.

Guerra Sucia

Start Date: 1976
End Date: 1977

Guerra Sucia (Dirty War) is the name given to an instance of state-sponsored terrorism: the Argentine government's brutal suppression of an insurgency during 1976–1977. After the Argentine military ousted the government of Maria Estella "Isabella" Perón in March 1976, the new government of General Jorge Videla moved to eliminate any left-wing opposition. Its targets included trade unionists, journalists, students, Marxists, and Perónists.

A number of victims were foreigners. A majority of the disappeared were, however, guerrillas of the Movimiento Peronista Montonero (MPM, Peronist Montonero Movement) and the Communist Ejército Revolucionario del Pueblo (ERP, People's Revolutionary Army), who were waging an insurgency against the government in Buenos Aires and other Argentine cities. A chief government instrument in the war was the Alianza Anticommunista Argentine (AAA, Argentine Anticommunist Alliance) of right-wing death squads, often including off-duty policemen.

In 1982 the Argentine generals badly miscalculated when they sought to boost their flagging popularity by retaking the Malvinas (Falkland) Islands from Britain. The ensuing war ended in an Argentine defeat and overthrow of the junta. The democratic government that came to power in 1983 initiated legal action against many of those involved in the war. Debate concerning the issue of amnesty for those involved in the war has been long-running, and during the presidency of Carlos Menum (1989–1999), the perpetrators could not be prosecuted. At the end of 2006, however, the Argentine Congress declared this legislation illegal, and in 2006 trials commenced for a number of people involved in the war.

Estimates of the number of Argentine citizens killed in the Guerra Sucia range from 9,000 to 30,000, with an Argentine commission setting the figure at some 13,000.

Spencer C. Tucker

Further Reading

Gillespie, Richard. *Soldiers of Perón: Argentina's Montoneros.* New York: Oxford University Press, 1982.

Lewis, Paul H. *Guerrillas and Generals: The "Dirty War" in Argentina.* Westport, CT: Praeger, 2002.

Guerre Révolutionnaire

During 1946–1954, the French had fought a protracted war in Indochina. French Army forces were then almost immediately transferred to Algeria, where an insurgency against French rule had begun in late 1954 and continued until Algerian independence in 1962. By 1956 with the fighting intensifying, the French military began to articulate a counterinsurgency doctrine. Known as guerre révolutionnaire, it was not formally adopted French Army doctrine but instead was a doctrine articulated by influential French officers and disseminated unofficially through association and writings. It was specifically based on the French experience in Indochina and the understanding of theories advanced by Communist leader Mao Zedong (Mao Tse-tung). French experience in resisting the German occupation of World War II (1939–1945) was also an influence.

The crux of guerre révolutionnaire was that the French army had to win the support of the Algerian people. This would be achieved through providing an alternative ideology based on the French concept of democracy with strong Christian overtones. The tactics supporting the doctrine were in general effective and rested on five fundamentals: the isolation of the insurgents from popular support; local security for the population; the execution of effective strike operations against the insurgents; the establishment of French political legitimacy through local, indigenous political and military forces; and a robust intelligence capability.

The French understood that the insurgents must be isolated from popular support. To accomplish this, the French constructed the so-called Morice Line along the border with Tunisia; similar fortifications were also built along the Moroccan border. These static, fence, minefield, and guard tower positions were reinforced by mobile patrols, aerial reconnaissance, and strong mobile reaction forces. While costly to build and maintain, these barriers were quite effective in denying the insurgents in Algeria logistical support as well as in preventing an estimated 35,000 trained fighters in Tunisia and Morocco from moving into Algeria.

Guerre révolutionnaire also addressed the elimination of internal support for the insurgent cells. The French sought to accomplish this through operations mounted to provide security for citizens and facilities. These included passive checkpoints and defenses as well as patrols to locate and intercept insurgents. These activities were accomplished by organizing the country through what was called the *quadrillage* system. This divided the country into quadrants, with each assigned a garrison that provided security within its assigned area through static positions and mobile patrols. These units sought to build a relationship with the local population and ensure that military commanders were intimately familiar with the terrain and the population in their operational area.

Backing up the *quadrillage* system was a mobile strike reserve of elite mechanized, airborne, and Foreign Legion forces. These units could be moved rapidly anywhere in the country to reinforce local security forces. The mobile forces conducted strike operations against key insurgent targets.

The political aspect was a key element of guerre révolutionnaire. Units known as Special Administrative Sections (SAS) were stationed in each quadrant, separate from the garrison security forces. They worked to establish French political legitimacy among the local population and build indigenous democratic institutions. They reformed local government, set up medical services, and trained local officials and police forces. The SAS units also were heavily engaged in the establishment of local educational institutions and made great efforts to inculcate Algerian youths with democratic, Western ideals.

The SAS units also oversaw the training of harka forces. Harkas were loyal indigenous military units charged with providing local security. As they became better trained, they also could conduct offensive operations against the insurgents, relieving regular French Army forces of the local security role. Because of their extensive contact with the local population, SAS units also became important centers for intelligence information.

The French Army recognized the absolute necessity of timely and accurate intelligence and developed an increasingly robust human intelligence (HUMINT) system. This system included local loyal Algerians, turned former Front de Libération Nationale (FLN) members, paid informers, and the aggressive interrogation of prisoners. The system was managed by a combination of SAS, police, and constabulary forces and carefully selected military intelligence officers.

The key to success of the intelligence system was the rapid dissemination of information to strike units. The French sought to strike identified targets within hours of uncovering the information. High-stress interrogation techniques, including torture, were integral to the system.

The French realized that the local population was key to their success, and they therefore undertook detailed and accurate documentation of that population. This included an accurate census and issuance of identification cards, giving the army the ability to track individuals within the wider population.

The French Army implemented its guerre révolutionnaire doctrine and supporting tactics with increasing effectiveness beginning in 1957. The FLN found itself unable to move men and supplies into Algeria from Tunisia and Morocco, while insurgent formations already within Algeria found it harder to operate. Once able to assemble in battalion strength, the insurgents were forced to form into increasingly smaller groups to avoid detection. Whenever the FLN attempted large-scale conventional operations, they were decisively crushed by mobile French reaction units and airpower.

By 1959, the insurgents were restricted to isolated small cells and limited to increasingly less frequent and more ineffective terrorist actions. Many FLN leaders were identified and taken prisoner. Harka units had also become increasingly effective, and the insurgents found it increasingly difficult to hide among the local population. By 1960, the French Army had essentially eliminated the insurgents' ability to conduct effective military operations and had significantly degraded the insurgent organization in Algeria. From a purely military point of view, the French Army had pacified the country.

Despite this success, the French Army had sown the seeds for losing the war. The Muslim population of Algeria was less inclined to accept French rule in 1960 than they had been in 1954. Harsh interrogation techniques and torture served to delegitimize French efforts and garner support for the FLN. The French also failed to realize that the insurgents' primary motivation was not ideological—that is, Communist—but instead was nationalist. The French also failed to understand that their liberal Christian ideology would have only a limited appeal to a predominately Muslim population. Thus, despite military defeat, the FLN secured the support of the bulk of the Algerian population.

By 1960, a significant portion of the population of Metropolitan France had turned against the war. The revelation of the use of torture by the army caused a sensation in France and alienated many French citizens; the heavy economic costs and continued casualties also undermined support. There were also sharp divisions within the army itself, with the professionals favoring an aggressive policy of Algérie Française and the conscripts wanting an end to the war and being willing to let Algeria go. In addition, President Charles de Gaulle's ambitious development scheme for Algeria, the Constantine Plan of October 1959, came too late to succeed. Within a few years de Gaulle had closed out all other options and concluded that Algeria must receive independence.

Algerian independence in 1962 discredited guerre révolutionnaire as an effective counterinsurgency doctrine. However, the fault lay primarily in aspects of its execution and the unique political situation in Algeria rather than in the doctrine itself. Many of its elements influenced U.S. counterinsurgency doctrine during the Vietnam War and the Iraq War.

Louis A. DiMarco

See also Algerian War; Algiers, Battle of; *Battle of Algiers;* Front de Libération Nationale; Galula, David; Godard, Yves; Indochina War; Mao Zedong; Massu, Jacques Émile; *Quadrillage* and *Ratissage;* Salan, Raoul Albin-Louis; Trinquier, Roger

Further Reading

Paret, Peter. *French Revolutionary Warfare from Indochina to Algeria: The Analysis of a Political and Military Doctrine.* London: Pall Mall, 1964.

Shy, John, and Thomas W. Collier. "Revolutionary War." In *Makers of Modern Strategy: From Machiavelli to the Nuclear Age,* edited by Peter Peret, 815–862. Princeton, NJ: Princeton University Press, 1986.

Guerrilla

Historically, the term "guerrilla" referred to the overt military component of a resistance movement or insurgency. Derived from Spanish, the word means "little war" and has been in use since at least the 18th century. An individual member of a guerrilla was a guerrillero. Today, a guerrilla force is a group of irregular, predominantly indigenous personnel organized along military lines to conduct military and paramilitary operations in enemy-held, hostile, or denied territory.

Guerrilla forces are usually at a significant disadvantage in terms of training, equipment, and firepower; however, they have the major advantage of the initiative. Guerrillas only attack when there is a relative state of superiority. They are aided in this by their absolute familiarity with the terrain in which they operate, and they have the advantage of the support of at least some of the indigenous population.

Depending on the operational environment and circumstances, guerrilla forces can range from as few as a handful of men up to 1,000 or more. In the early stages of an insurgency, guerrilla capabilities might be limited to small standoff attacks. If the base of support from the civilian population grows, so does the ability of the guerrillas to challenge government security forces more openly with larger-scale attacks. At some point in an insurgency or resistance movement, guerrillas may achieve a degree of parity with threat forces in certain areas and commence open warfare rather than acting as guerrilla bands. A premature decision regarding this can be disastrous, however, as in the case of the Communist Dimokratikós Strató Elladas (DSE, Democratic Army of Greece) in the Greek Civil War (1946–1949). In well-developed insurgencies, formerly isolated pockets of resistance activity may eventually connect and create liberated territory, possibly even linking with a friendly or sympathetic border state. Base areas are certainly important, as in the case of Yugoslavia, Albania, and Bulgaria to the DSE during the Greek Civil War and in the case of the People's Republic of China to the Viet Minh during the Indochina War (1946–1954).

Certainly one of the most important early studies of guerrilla warfare was Captain Thomas Auguste Le Roy Grandmaison's *La Petite Guerre* (The Small War) of 1756. Grandmaison served in the Flanders Volunteer Corps during the War of Austrian Succession (1740–1748). He urged selection of the fittest men with great endurance for the conduct of guerrilla operations and was a major proponent of utilizing surprise and night attacks to create confusion among enemy forces. American militia officer Robert Rogers carried out highly successful guerrilla operations during the French and Indian War (1754–1763). In 1757 Rogers authored "Rogers' Ranging Rules," detailing his tactical methodologies. These are still taught to U.S. Army Rangers today.

While there were numerous theorists who wrote about guerrilla warfare during the 19th and 20th centuries, the individual who achieved the greatest success as a practitioner was Chinese Communist leader Mao Zedong. His *On Guerrilla Warfare* (1937) includes critical insights such as that guerrilla warfare derives from the masses and is supported by them, guerrilla warfare can neither exist nor flourish if it separates itself from their sympathies and cooperation, and military action is a method used to attain a political goal—it is impossible to separate one from the other.

Mao's initial chapters defend guerrilla operations from detractors and reinforce that guerrilla fighters need to work with the traditional military to defeat invaders. His final chapter borrows maxims from Sun Tzu's *Art of War* to include emphasis on speed, knowing one's enemy, and employment of an indirect approach.

Biff L. Baker and Spencer C. Tucker

See also American Revolutionary War; Dimokratikós Stratós Elladas; Greek Civil War; Indochina War; Mao Zedong; Rogers, Robert

Further Reading

Beckett, Ian F. W. *Encyclopedia of Guerrilla Warfare*. Santa Barbara, CA: ABC-CLIO, 1999.

Boot, Max. *Invisible Armies: An Epic History of Guerrilla Warfare from Ancient Times to the Present*. New York: Liveright, 2013.

Laqueur, Walter. *Guerrilla Warfare: A Historical & Critical Study*. New Brunswick, NJ: Transaction Publishers, 1998.

Mao Tse-tung. *On Guerrilla War*. Translated by Samuel B Griffith. Mineola, NY: Dover, 2005.

U.S. Department of the Army. *Training Circular No. 18-01: Special Forces Unconventional Warfare*. Washington, DC: U.S. Army, Training and Doctrine Command, 2011.

Guevara de la Serna, Ernesto

Birth Date: June 14, 1928
Death Date: October 9, 1967

Argentine Marxist revolutionary and theorist of revolutionary warfare. Born on June 14, 1928, to a middle-class family in Rosario, Argentina, Ernesto "Che" Guevara de la Serna trained as a medical doctor at the University of Buenos Aires. After graduation in 1953 he traveled throughout Latin America, witnessing the early months of the Bolivian National Revolution and the last months of the October

Revolution in Guatemala during the reign of Jacobo Arbenz. America's covert 1954 operation that ousted the leftist Arbenz from power radicalized Guevara, as did his later encounter in Mexico with Cuban revolutionaries, including Fidel Castro. Guevara subsequently joined Castro's expedition to Cuba in December 1956 and fought with Castro's July 26 Movement until it triumphed in January 1959.

Guevara became the first president of the National Bank and then minister of industry in Cuba's early postrevolutionary government, where he espoused unorthodox Marxist economic ideas about the scope and timing of economic transformation. His notion of the New Man and his advocacy of centralized planning and the urgency of abolishing capitalist influences pitted him against more orthodox Marxist and Soviet advisers. Guevara's line won out in the early and mid-1960s, leading to a reliance on moral rather than material incentives and experiments with the abolition of currency. What was sometimes called Sino-Guevarism climaxed in the disastrous Ten-Million-Ton Sugar Harvest Campaign of 1968, after which Cuba's economic policy retreated from Guevarista utopianism.

Guevara left Cuba in 1965, possibly because of disagreement with its political leadership and certainly because of a long-standing commitment to promoting worldwide revolution. In his early years in Cuba, he had been a proponent of the political and military ideas of what became known as foco theory. The foquistas, including the French philosopher Jules Regis Debray, challenged the orthodox Communist emphasis on parliamentary and legal struggle, advocating instead the establishment of rural peasant-based centers (focos) to foment revolutionary commitments.

Guevara traveled to the Congo in 1965 and then to Bolivia in 1966. It is now believed that his project to initiate an insurrection in Bolivia was prompted by a desire to use it as a base for the transformation of neighboring countries rather than making revolution in Bolivia itself, where a major social revolution had begun in 1952. Guevara's overwhelming goal was to provide a diversion that would weaken U.S. resolve and resources that at the time were dedicated to waging war in Vietnam.

The foquistas were aware that postrevolutionary Cuba would increase American efforts to prevent more revolutions by modernizing Latin American militaries and reform projects such as the Alliance for Progress. But they underestimated the speed with which sections of the Bolivian armed forces would be transformed by U.S. aid and training once Guevara had located there.

Guevara's revolutionary expedition was also handicapped by tense relations with the Bolivian Communist Party and its leader, Mario Monje, who was offended by Guevara's insistence on maintaining leadership of the revolutionary focos. There was also little peasant support for the Guevarista force, which was made up of both Bolivian recruits and experienced Cuban revolutionaries. Difficult terrain also complicated the revolutionaries' work, and eventually they split into two groups.

The most controversial issue surrounding the collapse of Guevara's efforts in Bolivia concerns the degree of Cuban support for the guerrillas. Some Guevara biographers have suggested that Soviet and Cuban relations with the revolutionaries were partly shaped by Soviet annoyance at the impact that the new revolutionary front might have on its relations with the United States, but there is no conclusive evidence to support this.

A Bolivian army unit captured Guevara in the Yuro ravine on October 8, 1967, and summarily executed him the next day at La Higuera, Villagrande. One of his hands was removed to facilitate identification by U.S. intelligence. A copy of Guevara's diaries was smuggled to Cuba, where it was published (along with an edition brokered by the U.S. Central Intelligence Agency) as his *Bolivian Diaries*. Guevara's body was uncovered in an unmarked site in Bolivia in 1997 and, together with the remains of a number of other Cuban revolutionaries who died in Bolivia, was removed to Cuba for internment in a monument in Santa Clara City.

Barry Carr

See also Castro Ruz, Fidel Alejandro; Debray, Jules Régis; Foco Theory

Further Reading

Anderson, Jon Lee. *Che Guevara: A Revolutionary Life*. London: Bantam, 1997.

Castañeda, Jorge. *Companero: The Life and Death of Che*. New York: Vintage, 1998.

Lowy, Michael. *The Marxism of Che Guevara: Philosophy, Economics and Revolutionary Warfare*. New York: Monthly Review Press, 1974.

Guillén, Abraham

Birth Date: March 13, 1913
Death Date: August 1, 1993

Spanish author, economist, and educator who developed one of the first theories of urban guerrilla warfare. Abraham Guillén was born in Guadalajara, Spain, on March 13, 1913. He fought in the Spanish Civil War (1936–1939) on the Republican side against the Nationalists (Fascists). After the latter's victory, Guillén was arrested. Condemned to death, he was ordered to be executed, but the sentence was subsequently commuted to 10 years in prison. Guillén escaped in 1945 and fled to France, where he remained for 3 years.

In 1948 Guillén immigrated to Argentina. There he became the editor of the journal *Economia y finanzas* and also wrote under pseudonyms for several newspapers. His book *The Agony of Imperialism,* published in 1957, cost him his job and led to him being banned from journalism in Argentina. In 1960 he was briefly employed as an economic consultant to the Argentine government. The next year he was imprisoned for several months on the charge that he was a member of the Uturuncos guerrilla organization active in northwestern Argentina.

In 1962 Guillén sought political asylum in Uruguay, where he soon made contact with revolutionaries. In 1966 he published *Estrategia de la guerrilla urbana*

(Strategy of the Urban Guerrilla). In this important book, Guillén found himself in agreement with revolutionary Ernesto "Che" Guevara de la Serna on many points but in disagreement with Guevara's espousal of rural guerrilla warfare. Guillén sensed the insurgency potential in Latin America's large cities, teaming with impoverished inhabitants who possessed strong social grievances. He also understood the role that radicalized students might play in an insurgency. Guillén was unable, however, to resolve the problem of how small groups of urban guerrillas operating at night might attract mass support. He welcomed the advent of the Movimiento de Liberación Nacional (National Liberation Movement), popularly known as the Tupamoros, but strongly opposed gratuitous violence.

Guillén wrote for the Montevideo newspaper *Action,* often under a pseudonym. Constantly under investigation by various Latin American police agencies and the U.S. Central Intelligence Agency, he also lived in Peru before returning to Spain, where he taught at the Autonomous University of Madrid, espoused theories of self-management and communal action, and continued to write and publish. Guillén died in Madrid on August 1, 1993.

Spencer C. Tucker

See also Guevara de la Serna, Ernesto; Movimiento de Liberación Nacional

Further Reading

Guillén, Abraham. *Estrategia de la guerrilla urbana* [Urban Guerrilla Strategy]. Montevideo: Manuales del Pueblo, 1966.

Guillén, Abraham. *The Philosophy of the Urban Guerrilla: The Revolutionary Writings of Abraham Guillén.* Edited by D. C. Hughes. New York: Morrow, 1973.

Guinea Insurgency

Start Date: 1961
End Date: 1974

The Portuguese first arrived in Guinea on the west coast of Africa in the mid-15th century. Soon they had set up there a thriving trade in slaves. The Portuguese presence was largely limited to the coastal enclaves of the port of Bissau and Cacheu. Portuguese Guinea was administered as part of the Cape Verde Island colony but in 1879 became a separate Portuguese colony. At the beginning of the 20th century, the Portuguese began a systematic effort to control the interior. This was largely complete by 1915, although some fighting against the animist tribes there continued into 1936.

In 1956 Amílcar Cabral founded the Partido Africano da Independência de Guiné e Cabo Verde (PAIGC, African Party for the Independence of Guinea and Cape Verde). Following the failure of political efforts to secure independence, in January 1963 Cabral initiated a military campaign against Portuguese rule.

Only two Portuguese Army infantry companies were in the colony at the time, but Portugal ultimately committed some 30,000 men to the struggle against some 10,000 insurgents.

The PAIGC adopted guerrilla tactics. In their struggle the insurgents had the significant advantage of bases, training, and weapons in neighboring Senegal and Guinea, both of these countries having recently achieved their independence from France. Certain Communist states also provided weaponry and training. Cabral was a brilliant revolutionary theoretician and practitioner of insurgency. He sought to improve local crop yields and ordered his men to assist farmers in their fields when they themselves were not fighting. He established trade-and-barter bazaars to bring goods to the natives at cheaper cost than those available through colonial merchants, and he set up field hospital and triage stations to aid his men but also to bring improved medical care to the rural population. Cabral established a government-in-exile in Conakry, the capital city of Guinea, but he was assassinated there in January 1973.

The Portuguese meanwhile took advantage of tribal rivalries, and ultimately half of their 30,000-man force consisted of native troops. Nonetheless, the insurgency in Guinea cost the Portuguese disproportionately higher casualties than those in Angola and Mozambique. General Arnaldo Schulz, the military commander in the colony during 1964–1968, initiated a resettlement program, which his successor, General António de Spinola, was able to utilize to full advantage. Spinola restored Portuguese Army morale through frequent visits to the troops and indoctrination programs for his own men. He also adopted the slogan "Guiné Melhor" ("Better Guinea") and began a hearts-and-minds program that won back many refugees. In addition, he took advantage of the arrival of helicopters to withdraw isolated garrisons and restore mobility. The Portuguese did not mount cross-border operations but did support an abortive landing by Republic of Guinea exiles in 1970 and may have been involved in the assassination of Cabral. The military situation was largely stalemated by Spinola's departure in 1973.

Although the Portuguese controlled the coastal areas and principal population centers, the PAIGC controlled wide swaths of the northern and southern regions of the country and claimed to control 80 percent of the country by 1971. At Madina do Boe next to Guinea on September 24, 1973, the PAIGC declared the independence of Guinea-Bissau.

The wars in Guinea, Angola, and Mozambique were a tremendous drain on the Portuguese economy, and in April 1974 a group of progressive young Portuguese military officers, heavily influenced by Spinola, seized power in Lisbon in the so-called Carnation Revolution. The new government opened negotiations with the colonial insurgents. Guinea-Bissau was granted independence on September 10, 1974. Luis Cabral, half brother of the slain Amílcar Cabral, became the new state's first president.

Spencer C. Tucker

See also Angolan Insurgency; Cabral, Amílcar; Hearts and Minds; Mozambique Insurgency; Partido Africano da Independência de Guiné e Cabo Verde; Spinola, António Sebastião Ribeiro de

Further Reading

Beckett, Ian, and John Pimlott, eds. *Armed Forces and Modern Counter-Insurgency.* New York: St. Martin's, 1985.

Cann, John. *Counterinsurgency in Africa: The Portuguese Way of War, 1961–1974.* Westport, CT: Greenwood, 1997.

Guzmán Reynoso, Abimael

Birth Date: December 3, 1934

Leader of Peru's Maoist Sendero Luminoso (Shining Path) guerrilla group. Abimael Guzmán Reynoso was born into a middle-class family at Arequipa, Peru, on December 3, 1934. He earned both a law degree and a doctorate in philosophy from Arequipa's San Agustin National University and then taught philosophy at the University of San Cristóbal de Huamanga in southeastern Peru from 1962 until 1978. Here Guzmán became involved in the plight of the region's Quechua natives. Rejecting the traditional Latin American approach of urban guerrilla warfare, he became attracted to Mao Zedong's theories of peasant revolutionary warfare. The acts of the authoritarian government of Peru reinforced Guzmán's belief in the need for an insurgency and made him intolerant of reformist activity.

Guzmán joined the Communist Party of Peru in the late 1950s but left it in 1964 to join the Maoist Bandera Roja. He spent time during the Chinese Cultural Revolution attending a military academy in China, returning to Peru an as advocate of Zedong's theory of people's war. In 1970 Guzmán was expelled from the Bandera Roja for doctrinal heresy, and the subsequent split in Peru's Communist Party resulted in the formation of Shining Path.

By the late 1970s, Guzmán had organized his student followers into a clandestine and hierarchical structure in preparation for armed struggle. He was arrested in 1979 but after a brief period of detention was released and went underground. In 1980 Shining Path was ready to carry out terrorist activity against anyone associated with or supportive of the so-called bourgeois order. In 1982 the Peruvian government launched a counterinsurgency effort.

Guzmán developed a powerful cult of personality. Known as Chairman Gonzalo, he not only urged people's war against the government and the right wing but also came to believed that any group on the Left that sought to use nonviolent methods to improve the plight of the poor was his enemy. By 1992 Shining Path had created an atmosphere of terror in Peru, with some 32,000 people having perished in the conflict. In April of that year, President Alberto Fujimori assumed dictatorial powers. His enhanced counterinsurgency efforts were rewarded on September 12,

1992, when security forces captured Guzmán, an action that greatly undercut the strength of the revolutionary Maoist group.

In a military trial in October 1992, Guzmán was convicted on terrorism charges and sentenced to life imprisonment without parole. In 2003 his military trial was declared unconstitutional, but a new trial in civilian court in 2006 brought the same result. Guzmán is currently serving his sentence in virtual isolation on San Lorenzo Island, a naval base off the Lima coast.

Spencer C. Tucker

See also Peru Insurgencies; Sendero Luminoso

Further Reading

Gorriti Ellenbogen, Gustavo. *The Shining Path: A History of the Millenarian War in Peru.* Chapel Hill: University of North Carolina Press, 1999.

Palmer, David Scott, ed. *Shining Path of Peru.* New York: St. Martin's, 1992.

Poole, Deborah, and Gerardo Rénique. *Peru: Time of Fear.* New York: Monthly Review Press, 1992.

Taylor, Lewis. *Shining Path: Guerrilla War in Peru's Northern Highlands.* Liverpool: Liverpool University Press, 2006.

Gwynn, Sir Charles William

Birth Date: November 4, 1870
Death Date: November 12, 1962

British Army general and author of a seminal work on counterinsurgency. Charles William Gwynn was born on November 4, 1870, in County Down, Ireland, and was the son of the regius professor of divinity at Trinity College in Dublin. Gwynn studied at Sr. Columbia's College in Dublin and at the Royal Military Academy in Woolwich. Commissioned in the Royal Engineers in 1889, he was a member of the expedition against the Sofas in Sierra Leone, West Africa, during 1893–1894, for which he won the Distinguished Service Order. Following service with the Intelligence Branch of the War Office and after the British retook the Sudan, Gwynn undertook a survey of the Sudanese-Abyssinian border.

During 1911–1914 Gwynn taught at the Royal Military College, Duntroon, Australia. Returning to Britain with the start of World War I (1914–1918), he was posted to the Middle East as a staff officer in the 2nd Australian Division. He ended the war as a brevet colonel and chief of staff of the II ANZAC Corps.

Following the war, Gwynn held various staff assignments. Promoted to major general in 1925, he was commandant of the Staff College, Camberley, during 1926–1930. Gwynn retired in 1931 and was knighted.

In 1934 Gwynn published *Imperial Policing,* a book based on case studies at Camberley. The book became the standard British work on counterinsurgency. Gwynn laid down four core principles: the need for civilian primacy over the military effort, the need for minimum force, the need for firm and timely action in order to make certain that the political situation does not get out of hand, and the need for close coordination of the civilian and military efforts. His basic principles were reflected in the official British Army manual on the subject published in 1934, *Notes on Imperial Policing,* and in subsequent British country insurgency practice.

Gwynn died in Dublin, Ireland, on November 12, 1962.

Spencer C. Tucker

Further Reading

Beckett, Ian F. W. *Encyclopedia of Guerrilla Warfare.* Santa Barbara, CA: ABC-CLIO, 1999.

Beckett, Ian F. W., ed. *The Roots of Counterinsurgency: Armies and Guerrilla Warfare.* New York: Bnaldford, 1988.

Gwynn, Charles. *Imperial Policing.* London: Macmillan, 1934.

Mockaitis, Thomas. *British Counterinsurgency, 1919–1960.* London: Macmillan, 1990.

H

Hai Ba Trung.

See Trung Trac and Trung Nhi

Haitian Insurgency and U.S. Intervention

Start Date: 1915
End Date: 1934

In March 1915 General Vilbrun Guillaume Sam assumed office as president of Haiti. Dr. Rosalvo Bobo then led a revolt against Sam. On July 1, U.S. Navy rear admiral William Caperton arrived at Cap Haitien (Cap-Haïtien) in the armored cruiser *Washington,* ordered there by Secretary of the Navy Josephus Daniels to keep the peace and safeguard U.S. interests. Caperton informed the government forces in Cap Haitien and revolutionary forces outside the city that there must be no fighting there. He also landed marines to maintain communication between the American consulate and the *Washington.*

On July 27 upon learning of an outbreak of fighting near the presidential palace, General Oscar Etienne, governor of Port-au-Prince, ordered the execution of 167 political prisoners being held by the government. News of this sparked an explosion of mob violence in Port-au-Prince. Sam sought sanctuary in the French embassy and Etienne sought sanctuary in the embassy of the Dominican Republic, but mobs invaded both buildings and hacked the two men to pieces.

Shocked by events, worried about regional instability, determined to enforce the Monroe Doctrine and prevent intervention by another power, and concerned about the security of the Panama Canal, U.S. president Woodrow Wilson then ordered marines to Port-au-Prince. On July 28 Caperton landed 330 marines and sailors at Port-au-Prince, and they soon took control of the capital city. Caperton also requested reinforcements, speeded to Haiti in the battleship *Connecticut.* On August 15, U.S. Marine Corps colonel Littleton W. T. Waller reached Haiti in the armored cruiser *Tennessee* with eight companies of the 1st Marine Regiment and the headquarters detachment of the 1st Marine Brigade, of which he assumed command. Waller now commanded some 2,000 men.

Waller then mounted a campaign against the Haitian cacos, the armed bands who in the past had sold their services to various would-be political leaders in the island and thus dominated the Haitian political scene. On the night of October 24–25, a 40-man marine patrol commanded by Major Smedley D. Butler that had just located the caco stronghold of Fort Capois in northern Haiti was ambushed by the bandits. Gunnery Sergeant Dan Daly, who had already won one Medal of Honor during the Boxer Rebellion in China, won a second by making his way through caco lines and then out again, retrieving a machine gun strapped to a horse that had been killed in the attack. Butler launched an attack on the morning of October 25, overrunning the caco position. The marines then destroyed nearby Fort Dipité. By November 8, Butler's men and another marine column led by Captain Chandler Campbell had captured three additional forts, including Capois.

On November 17 Butler led three marine companies, a marine detachment, and a company of sailors from the battleship *Connecticut* to attack and capture Fort Rivière, an old French-built masonry works on high ground near the town of Grande Rivière du Nord. For this action Butler was awarded a second Medal of Honor. The two marines who had preceded him into the fort also received the same award. Fifty cacos were killed. Butler then blew up the fort. This action brought operations against the cacos to a temporary end.

U.S. forces remained in occupation of Haiti and controlled its institutions for the next 19 years. A treaty of November 11, 1915, reluctantly approved by the Haitian legislature, authorized the United States to assume control of the nation's finances and administration and established the Gendarmerie d'Haïti (Haitian Constabulary), later known as the Garde d'Haïti, a step that would be replicated in the Dominican Republic and in Nicaragua. The Gendarmerie d'Haïti was the first Haitian professional military and was the only cohesive Haitian institution.

A rebellion in October 1918 proved to be too much for the Gendarmerie d'Haïti, but marine reinforcements in March 1919 helped crush it, at the cost of perhaps 2,000 Haitian lives. Thereafter, order prevailed.

By 1930, U.S. president Herbert Hoover, concerned about the effects of the occupation, appointed a commission to study the situation and began withdrawing American forces. These continued under President Franklin D. Roosevelt, with the last marines departing in mid-August 1934.

Although the U.S. occupation brought important improvements in infrastructure, including road and bridge construction, disease control, the building of schools, and the establishment of a communications infrastructure, there was no progress in the political sphere. When the marines departed, the Haitian military elite took charge and reverted to the same dictatorial rule that had characterized Haitian government since the colonial period.

Spencer C. Tucker

See also Nicaragua Insurgency

Further Reading

Fatton, Robert. *Haiti's Predatory Republic: The Unending Transition to Democracy.* Boulder, CO: Lynne Rienner, 2002.

McKissick, Patricia C. *History of Haiti.* Maryknoll, NY: Henry Holt, 1998.

Hamas.

See Harakat al-Muqawama al-Islamiyya

Ham Nghi

Birth Date: July 22, 1872
Death Date: January 14, 1943

Seventh emperor of the Nguyen dynasty (1884–1885) and hero of the Vietnamese resistance movement against the French invasion of the late 19th century. Ham Nghi was the ruling name of Ung Lich. Born on July 22, 1872, in Hue, Ham Nghi was placed on the throne at age 12—succeeding his brother, Emperor Kien Phuoc (r. 1883–1884)—by regents Nguyen Van Tuong and Ton That Thuyet, who then effectively controlled the new emperor.

The regents managed to assemble a fair amount of artillery and small arms at the imperial palace. When the French demanded their removal, Thuyet transferred them to a secret location. Believing that French commander General Count Roussel de Coucey intended to crush them, the two regents decided on a desperate surprise attack on the French at their Mang Ca fort near the capital at 1:00 a.m. on July 5, 1885. The French reacted quickly, however, seizing six of the Vietnamese guns, which they then turned against the attackers. The Vietnamese began to disperse before dawn, and Thuyet then forced Ham Nghi to accompany him to the Tan So fortress in Quang Tri Province. Meanwhile, the French seized a considerable number of artillery pieces, small arms, and silver ingots from the imperial palace.

From Tan So, Thuyet forced Ham Nghi to issue an appeal to mandarins, scholars, and the people throughout the country, calling on them to aid him in his fight against the French. Many responded to the appeal, which opened a great anti-French movement known as Phong Trao Can Vuong (Support the King).

Betrayed by a local chief and one of his guards, Ham Nghi was captured by the French on November 1, 1888. Although he had been poorly served by Thuyet, Ham Nghi nonetheless refused to reveal Thuyet's location to the French. Ham Nghi was sent into exile in Algeria that December. There was some discussion about returning him to the throne, but he died in Algiers on January 14, 1943, without seeing his homeland again. His tomb is in Thonac cemetery near Sarlat, Dordogne, France. The Socialist Republic of Vietnam has made efforts to secure the return of the body to Vietnam, where a number of cities have major streets named after Ham Nghi, but the family has thus far refused.

Pham Cao Duong

Further Reading

Chapuis, Oscar. *The Last Emperors of Vietnam: From Tu Duc to Bao Dai.* Westport, CT: Greenwood, 2000.

Le Thanh Khoi. *Le Viet-Nam: Histoire et civilisation.* Paris: Editions de Minuit, 1955.

Harakat al-Jihad al-Islami fi Filastin

Militant nationalist insurgent Palestinian group that was branded a terrorist organization by the United States and other countries. Harakat al-Jihad al-Islami fi Filastin, known as the Islamic Jihad in Palestine but also Palestinian Islamic Jihad (PIJ), was established by Fathi Shiqaqi, Sheikh Abd al-Aziz al-Awda, and others in the Gaza Strip during the 1970s. Several different factions identified with the name "Islamic Jihad," which has caused much confusion over the years.

In the 1970s in Egypt, Shiqaqi, al-Awda, and current director general of the PIJ Ramadan Abdullah Shallah embraced an Islamist vision similar to the Egyptian Muslim Brotherhood but rejected the moderation forced on that organization by the Egyptian government's aim of political participation in tandem with dawa (proselytizing and education). The Palestinian group distinguished itself from secular nationalists and antinationalist Islamists in calling for grassroots organization and armed struggle to liberate Palestine as part of the Islamic solution.

Shiqaqi returned to Palestinian territory, and the PIJ began to express its intent to wage jihad (holy war) against Israel. Israeli sources claim that the PIJ developed the military apparatus known as the Jerusalem Brigades (Saraya al-Quds) by 1985, and this organization carried out attacks against the Israeli military, including Operation GATE OF MOORS at an induction ceremony in 1986. The PIJ also claimed responsibility for the suicide bombing in Beit Led, near Netanya, Israel, on January 22, 1994, that killed 19 Israelis and injured 60.

Shiqaqi spent a year in jail in the early 1980s and then in 1986 was jailed for two more years. He was deported to Lebanon along with al-Awda in April 1988. The PIJ established an office in Damascus, Syria, and began support services in Palestinian refugee camps in Lebanon.

Shallah meanwhile completed a doctorate at the University of Durham, served as the editor of a journal of the World and Islam Studies Enterprise, and taught briefly at the University of South Florida. When Shiqaqi was assassinated by unidentified agents (allegedly the Israeli intelligence service Mossad) in Malta in 1995, Shallah returned to lead the PIJ.

The PIJ emerged prior to Hamas, the largest faction of the Palestine Liberation Organization (PLO). The two organizations were rivals despite the commonality of their nationalist perspectives, but Hamas gained a much larger popular following than the PIJ, whose estimated support is only 4–5 percent of the Palestinian population in the territories. The PIJ has a following among students at the Islamic

University in Gaza and other colleges and was active in the Second (al-Aqsa) Intifada, which began in September 2000.

In Lebanon, the PIJ competes with Fatah, the primary and largest political faction in the PLO. Like Hamas and secular nationalist groups known as the Palestinian National Alliance, the PIJ rejected the 1993 Oslo Accords and demanded full Israeli withdrawal from Palestinian lands. The group has a following among Palestinian refugees.

In June 2003 under significant international pressure, Syria closed PIJ and Hamas offices in Damascus, and Shallah left for Lebanon. Khalid Mishaal went to Qatar, but both Shallal and Mishaal later returned to Syria.

In the Palestinian territories, the PIJ continues to differ from Hamas. Hamas ceased attacks against Israel beginning in 2004 and successfully captured a majority in the Palestinian elections of January 2006. Hamas moderates are also considering the recognition of Israel and a two-state solution. The PIJ, in contrast, called for Palestinians to boycott the 2006 elections and refuse any accommodation with Israel. The PIJ continued to sponsor suicide attacks after 2004 in retaliation for Israel's military offensives and targeted killings of PIJ leaders, including Louay Saadi in October 2005. The PIJ claimed responsibility for two suicide attacks that year.

Israeli authorities continue to highlight Iranian-PIJ links and also assert that the PIJ continues to rely on Syrian support and Iranian funding.

Sherifa Zuhur

See also Harakat al-Muqawama al-Islamiyya; Intifada, Second; Jihad; Palestine Liberation Organization

Further Reading

Abu-Amr, Ziad. *Islamic Fundamentalisms in the West Bank and Gaza: Muslim Brotherhood and Islamic Jihad.* Bloomington: Indiana University Press, 1994.

Knudsen, Are. "Islamism in the Diaspora: Palestinian Refugees in Lebanon." *Journal of Refugee Studies* 18(2) (2005): 216–234.

"The Movement of Islamic Jihad and the Oslo Process: An Interview with Ramadan Abdullah Shallah." *Journal of Palestine Studies* 28 (1999): 61–73.

Harakat al-Muqawama al-Islamiyya

Harakat al-Muqawama al-Islamiyya (Movement of Islamic Resistance), known as Hamas, is an Islamist Palestinian organization formally established in 1987. The word "Hamas" means courage, bravery, or zeal. Hamas combines Islamic fundamentalism with Palestinian nationalism for the goals of the creation of an Islamic way of life and the liberation of Palestine through Islamic resistance. Hamas gained some 30–40 percent support in the Palestinian population within five years of its creation, largely because of the general popular desperation experienced by the Palestinian population during the First Intifada (1987–1993).

Hamas grew out of the Muslim Brotherhood established in Egypt in 1928 and was also able to draw strength from the social work of Sheikh Ahmed Yassin, a physically disabled schoolteacher who had led the Islamic Assembly (al-Mujamma al-Islami), an organization influential in many mosques and at the Islamic University of Gaza.

In December 1987 Abd al-Aziz Rantisi, who was a physician at Islamic University, and former student leaders Salah Shihada and Yahya al-Sinuwwar, who had headed security for the Muslim Brotherhood, formed the first unit of Hamas. Yassin gave his approval, but as a cleric he was not directly connected to the new organization. In February 1988 following a meeting in Amman, the Muslim Brotherhood granted Hamas formal recognition.

The Hamas charter condemns world Zionism. The charter does not condemn the West or non-Muslims but does condemn aggression against the Palestinian people, arguing for a defensive jihad. The charter also calls for fraternal relations with the other Palestinian nationalist groups.

The Izz al-Din al-Qassam Brigades of Hamas carried out major military attacks on Israel. The brigades also developed the Qassam rocket, used to attack Israeli civilian settlements in the Negev Desert. However, much of Hamas's activity during the First Intifada consisted of participation in more broad-based popular demonstrations and locally coordinated efforts at resistance, such as countering Israeli raids and enforcing the opening of businesses.

Hamas greatly expanded by 1993 but decried the autonomy agreement between the Israelis and the Palestine Liberation Organization (PLO) in Jericho and the Gaza Strip as too limited a gain. By the time of the first elections for the Palestinian Authority (PA) Council in 1996, Hamas was caught in a dilemma. It had gained popularity as a resistance organization, but the Taba Accord of September 28, 1995, was meant to end the intifada. The elections would further strengthen the PLO, but if Hamas boycotted the elections and most people voted, Hamas would be more isolated. The Hamas leadership finally rejected participation but without ruling it out in the future. When suicide attacks were launched to protest Israeli violence against Palestinians, Hamas was blamed for inspiring or organizing them, whether or not its operatives or those of the more radical Harakat al-Jihad al-Islami fi Filastin (Islamic Jihad in Palestine) were involved.

Hamas funded an extensive array of social services aimed at ameliorating the Palestinian plight. The organization provides funding for hospitals, schools, mosques, orphanages, food distribution, and aid to the families of Palestinian prisoners. In so doing, Hamas has endeared itself to a large number of Palestinians.

Palestinians living abroad provided money, as did a number of private donors in the wealthy Arab oil states and other states in the West. Iran has been a significant donor. Much aid was directed to renovation of the Palestinian territories and was badly needed, and a great deal of that rebuilding was destroyed in the Israeli campaign in the West Bank in 2002, which in turn was intended to combat the suicide bombings. Over the years, the Israel Defense Force has carried out targeted eliminations of a number of Hamas leaders.

The leadership of Hamas organized very effectively before and since PLO leader Yasser Arafat's 2004 death and has become more popular than the PLO in the West Bank, an unexpected development. A sizable number of Palestinians had already begun to identify with Hamas, mainly because it was able to accomplish what the PAs could not, namely providing for the everyday needs of the people.

Hamas unexpectedly won the Palestinian legislative elections in January 2006. Locals had expected a victory in Gaza but not in the West Bank. Nonetheless, both Israel and the United States (which had supported the holding of an election) steadfastly refused to recognize the Palestinian government under the control of Hamas. The United States cut off $420 million and the European Union (EU) cut off $600 million in aid to the PA's Hamas-led government, which created difficulties for ordinary Palestinians. The loss of this aid halted the delivery of supplies to hospitals and ended other services in addition to stopping the payment of salaries. To prevent total collapse, the United States and the EU promised relief funds, but these were not allowed to go through the PA. The cutoff in funds was designed to discourage Palestinian support for Hamas.

On March 17, 2007, Arafat's successor, Mahmoud Abbas, brokered a Palestinian unity government that included members of both Hamas and Fatah in which Hamas

Supporters of the militant Islamic group Hamas in the West Bank city of Ramallah celebrate their victory in the Palestinian elections of January 26, 2006. Hamas unseated the ruling Fatah party. Hamas now controls the Gaza Strip and has taken a confrontational stance toward Israel, leading to armed clashes and an Israeli economic blockade. (Uriel Sinai/Getty Images)

leader Ismail Haniyeh became prime minister. Yet in May armed clashes between Hamas and Fatah escalated, and on June 14 Hamas seized control of Gaza. Abbas promptly dissolved the Hamas-led unity government and declared a state of emergency. On June 18, having been assured of EU support, Abbas dissolved the National Security Council and swore in an emergency Palestinian government. That same day, the United States ended its 15-month embargo on the PA and resumed aid in an effort to strengthen Abbas's government, now limited to the West Bank. Other governments, including Israel, followed suit. On June 19, 2007, Abbas cut off all ties and dialogue with Hamas, pending the return of Gaza.

By the end of 2007, Hamas had imposed a more religiously conservative regime on Gaza, which was now largely cut off economically from the rest of the world and more than ever was an economic basket case. In the meantime, Israel imposed a blockade against Hamas, which in turn prompted Hamas to begin firing rockets into Israel.

In December 2008 after a five-month cease-fire between Hamas and Israel, Hamas militants again began to fire rockets into Israeli territory. The Israelis retaliated with punishing air strikes late in the month, and on January 3, 2009, Israel sent troops into Gaza. The resulting two-week incursion killed an estimated 1,300 Palestinians (159 of them children) and wounded another 5,400. Reportedly, 22,000 buildings were destroyed or damaged, most of them in Gaza City, with the physical damage alone at $1.9 billion. On January 17, 2009, a shaky cease-fire again took hold.

Israel came under intense criticism from some quarters because of the high civilian casualties during its incursion, also known as the Gaza War, but the Israeli government pointed out that Hamas purposefully used civilians as human shields and melded into the general population in an attempt to escape retribution. The Israeli military action did not weaken Hamas, as Israeli leaders had hoped, and indeed strengthened the prestige of Hamas among West Bank Palestinians at the expense of the more moderate Fatah. There was additional fighting during an eight-day period in November 2012, when Hamas launched (by Israeli count) a total of 21,506 rockets into Israel and the Israelis responded with artillery and air attacks. Hamas continues to govern the Gaza Strip, while Israel maintains its economic blockade.

Harry Raymond Hueston II, Paul G. Pierpaoli Jr., and Sherifa Zuhur

See also Arafat, Yasser; Harakat al-Jihad al-Islami fi Filastin; Intifada, First; Intifada, Second; Jihad; Palestine Liberation Organization; Terrorism

Further Reading

Legrain, Jean-François. "Hamas: Legitimate Heir of Palestinian Nationalism?" In *Political Islam: Revolution, Radicalism, or Reform,* edited by John Esposito, 159–178. Boulder, CO: Lynne Rienner, 1997.

Mishal, Shaul, and Avraham Sela. *The Palestinian Hamas: Vision, Violence, and Coexistence.* New York: Columbia University Press, 2000.

Nusse, Andrea. *Muslim Palestine: The Ideology of Hamas.* London: Routledge, 1999.

Harding, John Allan Francis

Birth Date: February 10, 1896
Death Date: January 20, 1989

British Army field marshal. Allan Francis Harding (he adopted John as his first name in 1921) was born at South Petherton in Somerset, England, on February 10, 1896. Educated at King's College, London, he worked for the Post Office and Civil Service until joining the British Army in May 1914 as a second lieutenant. He fought in the 1915 Gallipoli Campaign and then in the Middle East.

Posted to India in 1921, Harding then served on the staff of the Southern Command and in the War Office. He was promoted to captain in 1923, to major in 1935, and to lieutenant colonel in 1938. During World War II (1939–1945), Harding commanded an infantry battalion and then served in staff positions in the Middle East Command in Egypt. He was promoted to colonel in August 1941. Harding took command of the 7th Armoured Division in September 1942 and fought in the Second Battle of El Alamein the next month, when he was wounded. Returning to Britain in November 1943, he commanded VIII Corps before being posted to Italy in January 1944 as chief of staff to the 15th Army Group. Harding was promoted to substantive major general in July 1944, then took command of XIII Corps in Italy in March 1945.

Promoted to lieutenant general in August 1946, Harding assumed command of British forces in the Mediterranean in November 1946. The next year he took charge of the Southern Command, and in July 1949 he assumed command of British Far East Land Forces during the Malayan Emergency (1948–1960). He was promoted to full general on December 9, 1949, and was made aide-de-camp to the king in October 1950. Harding assumed command of the British Army of the Rhine in August 1951. He was chief of the Imperial General Staff during November 1952–September 1955 and was promoted to field marshal on July 1, 1953.

In October 1953 Harding was appointed governor of the British colony of Cyprus. On April 1, 1955, an armed struggle by Greek nationalist Cypriots of the Ethniki Organosis Kyprion Agoniston (EOKA, National Organization of Cypriot Fighters), led by former Greek Army colonel Georgios Grivas, began a terror campaign against the British and Cypriot police with the aim of securing the end of British rule and uniting the island with Greece. Harding adopted harsh countermeasures, curfews, the banning of the Greek flag in schools (which led to their closure), the detention without trial of suspected insurgents, and the death sentence for those arrested carrying weapons or materials that could be used to manufacture bombs (a favored EOKA tactic).

Several executions led to criticism of Harding in Cyprus, as well as in Britain and abroad. Negotiations with Greek archbishop Makarios III having proven unsuccessful, Harding exiled him to the Seychelles. Growing criticism of Harding's policies led to his recall in October 1957.

Created Baron Harding of Petherton in January 1958, Harding was active in a number of military organizations up to his death at Nether Compton, Dorset, on January 20, 1989.

Spencer C. Tucker

See also Cyprus Insurrection; Ethniki Organosis Kyprion Agoniston; Grivas, Georgios

Further Reading

Corum, James S. *Training Indigenous Forces in Counterinsurgency: A Tale of Two Insurgencies.* Carlisle, PA: Strategic Studies Institute, 2006.

Crawshaw, Nancy. *The Cyprus Revolt: An Account of the Struggle for Union with Greece.* London: Allen and Unwin, 1978.

Heathcote, T. A. *The British Field Marshals, 1736–1997.* Barnsley, South Yorkshire, UK: Pen and Sword Books, 1999.

Hearts and Minds

The term "hearts and minds" refers to the necessity for both insurgents and counterinsurgent forces to win the support of the population if they are to succeed. As Chinese Communist leader Mao Zedong put it, the people are the water through which the guerrillas swim. Insurgents rely on the civilian population for recruits, food, and other logistical support. If these are denied them, the insurgents cannot succeed, and the counterinsurgent forces will triumph.

The phrase "winning hearts and minds" seems to have been coined by General (later field marshal) Sir Gerald Templer, high commissioner in Malaya during the Malayan Emergency (1948–1960). Templer remarked at one point that actual fighting constituted only 25 percent of the counterinsurgency effort, while 75 percent of it was aimed at securing the support of the people. This later may include the building of roads, schools, and hospitals in addition to other programs such as enhancing livestock production and agricultural yields. In Malaya, the British were able to create a significantly improved standard of living for the Chinese squatters—from whom the insurgents drew the bulk of their recruits—and thus end the insurgency.

The hearts-and-minds strategy was utilized effectively by the Americans in the Philippine-American War (1899–1902) and by the British in the aforementioned Malayan Emergency, who also had the advantage of having granted Malaya its independence in 1957. The strategy was less successful during the Vietnam War (1957–1975). Although U.S. Special Forces working in the Central Highlands and in Laos achieved considerable success working with the Montagnard populations and although the U.S. Marine Corps Combined Action Platoons accomplished a good deal, the large Strategic Hamlet Program, backed and paid for by the United States, was marked by widespread graft and corruption by government officials in the Republic of South Vietnam (RVN, South Vietnam). Then too, U.S. commander in South Vietnam, General William C. Westmoreland, was little interested in pacification and saw his task as that of closing with and defeating enemy forces in the field. His efforts were concentrated on large-scale search-and-destroy military operations. Too late, with the Americans seeking to withdraw and having reduced resources, Westmoreland's successor General Creighton Abrams sought to shift over to a more population-centric policy.

In order to win hearts and minds, counterinsurgent forces must be able to demonstrate through their pacification programs tangible benefits for the civilian population. Such programs must also have sufficient duration for an insurgency not to return.

Spencer C. Tucker

See also Abrams, Creighton Williams, Jr.; Combined Action Platoons, U.S. Marine Corps; Malayan Emergency; Philippine Islands and U.S. Pacification during the Philippine-American War; Templer, Sir Gerald Walter Robert; Vietnam War; Westmoreland, William Childs

Further Reading

Carruthers, Susan. *Winning Hearts and Minds: British Governments, the Media, and Colonial Counter-Insurgency, 1944–1960.* New York: Leicester University Press, 1995.

Hunt, Richard A. *Pacification: The American Struggle for Vietnam's Hearts and Minds.* Boulder, CO: Westview, 1995.

Stubbs, Richard. *Hearts and Minds in Guerrilla Warfare: The Malayan Insurgency, 1948–1960.* New York: Oxford University Press, 1989.

Herero Revolt

Start Date: 1904
End Date: 1907

Germany had planted its flag in southwestern Africa in October 1884 and received formal European recognition of its control of German South-West Africa as a consequence of the 1885 Berlin Conference of 1884–1885. German rule was harsh, and treatment of the native peoples was severe. As a consequence, the Herero people revolted. Preparations for the revolt were kept secret and came as a surprise to the white colonists. In January 1904, Herero leader Samuel Maharero ordered the extermination of the German settlers.

The revolt began on January 12, 1904, when several hundred mounted Hereros invaded Okahandja, killed 123 people (most of them Germans), and set fire to its buildings. The fighting spread as the Germans who had escaped Herero attacks on their farms fled to the urban areas for protection. Within a few days, the violence had spread as far as Omarasa, north of the Waterberg escarpment, and a number of German soldiers manning its station had been killed. Maharero granted safe passage for Christian missionaries and a small number of German women and children. They reached Okahandja in early April.

Although German governor Theodor Leutwein was willing to negotiate a settlement, Kaiser Wilhelm II was determined to crush the revolt by force of arms. Troop reinforcements were rushed to the colony, and in May General Lothar von Trotha, a seasoned veteran of African fighting, was appointed to command. On August 11 Trotha crushed organized Herero resistance in the Battle of the Waterberg Plateau. He then ordered his troops to drive the Hereros into the barren Omaheke-Steppe, part of the Kalahari Desert, and then erect guard posts along the border and poison the water holes. On October 2, Tortha ordered that any Hereros inside this area, including women and children, were to be shot on sight even if they were unarmed. Although he later modified this order to the extent that women and children were not to be executed but instead were driven from the territory, the results were nonetheless catastrophic for the Herero people. Their death toll has been variously estimated at from 25,000 to 100,000. Trotha's men also attacked and routed the Nama people. Some 10,000 of them died, and another 9,000 were placed in makeshift camps and employed in forced labor.

Following a wide public outcry, Trotha was relieved of his command, but he remained in the army and was subsequently promoted. The revolt officially ended on March 31, 1907. In 1915 during World War I (1914–1918), the Union of South Africa took control of South-West Africa, formally received as a League of Nations mandate after the war, and ruled South-West Africa until it became independent as Namibia in 1990.

Some historians consider the German actions in South-West Africa to be the first modern example of genocide. In 2004 the German government of Chancellor Gerhard Schröder formally apologized for the atrocities. While rejecting all claims for compensation, Germany did extend financial aid to Namibia.

Spencer C. Tucker

See also Trotha, Lothar von

Further Reading

Drechsler, Horst. *Let Us Die Fighting: The Struggle of the Herero and Nama against German Imperialism, 1884–1915*. London: Zed, 1980.

Kaulich, Udo. *Die Geschichte der ehemaligen Kolonie Deutsch-Südwestafrika (1884–1914): Eine Gesamtdarstellung* [History of the Former German Colony of South-West Africa (1884–1914): A Complete Account]. Frankfurt am Main: P. Lang, 2001.

Speitkamp, Winfried. *Deutsche Kolonialgeschichte* [German Colonial History]. Stuttgart: Reclam, 2005.

Hilsman, Roger

Birth Date: November 23, 1919

U.S. State Department official and influential adviser on Vietnam policy. Born in Waco, Texas, on November 23, 1919, Roger Hilsman graduated from the U.S. Military Academy, West Point, in 1943 and briefly served with Merrill's Marauders in the China-Burma-India theater before being wounded. On recovering, he joined the Office of Strategic Services (OSS) and in August 1945 parachuted into Manchuria to free Japanese prisoners of war, among them his father.

Hilsman left the OSS in 1946 and earned a doctorate in international relations from Yale University in 1951. In 1961 President John F. Kennedy appointed him director of the State Department's Bureau of Intelligence and Research. Charged with analyzing current foreign developments in order to allow for long-term planning, Hilsman was one of the principal architects of early U.S. policy regarding Vietnam.

In January 1962 Hilsman presented the report *A Strategic Concept for South Vietnam.* The report defined the insurgency there as a political struggle and held that the key to victory was policies aimed at the rural Vietnamese, leading to creation of the Strategic Hamlet Program. The report also recommended that the Army of the Republic of Vietnam (ARVN, South Vietnamese Army) adopt counterinsurgency tactics.

In December 1962 Hilsman and Michael Forrestal, head of the National Security Council's Vietnam Coordinating Committee, undertook a fact-finding mission to Vietnam. In July 1963 following attacks on Buddhist dissidents by Ngo Dinh Nhu's police, Hilsman, Forrestal, and W. Averell Harriman recommended that new instructions be relayed to U.S. ambassador Henry Cabot Lodge in Saigon, leading to at least tacit approval by the U.S. government of the military coup that was carried out against Ngo Dinh Diem, president of the Republic of Vietnam (RVN, South Vietnam), and Nhu in November 1963.

Increasingly at odds with President Lyndon B. Johnson and Secretary of State Dean Rusk over U.S. policy regarding Vietnam, Hilsman resigned in February 1964 and joined the political science faculty at Columbia University. In 1967 he wrote *To Move a Nation,* which praised the Kennedy administration's foreign policy and criticized President Johnson's escalation of the war. Hilsman subsequently wrote nearly a dozen books and was associated with the Institute for War and Peace Studies at Columbia.

Robert G. Mangrum

See also Strategic Hamlet Program

Further Reading

Herring, George C. *America's Longest War: The United States and Vietnam, 1950–1975.* New York: McGraw-Hill, 1996.

Karnow, Stanley. *Vietnam: A History.* New York: Penguin, 1984.

Hoche, Louis Lazare

Birth Date: June 24, 1768
Death Date: September 19, 1797

French general, considered one of the most able military commanders in the French Revolutionary War (1792–1802) and a highly successful practitioner of a population-centric counterinsurgency strategy. Louis Lazare Hoche was born at Montreuil on June 24, 1768, into the family of a professional soldier. Hoche had little formal education, and in 1784 at age 16 he joined the French Army as a grenadier. In 1789 he was promoted to corporal. A fervent supporter of the French Revolution of 1789, in August he became a sergeant in the National Guard in Paris.

In April 1792 France went to war with Austria and Prussia, and in May Hoche was promoted to lieutenant. Advanced to captain in June for his role in the defense of Thionville, by the spring of 1793 he was aide-de-camp to General Alexis le Veneur de Tillières, taking part in the Battle of Neerwinden (March 18). For his role in breaking the British siege of the port of Dunkerque, Hoche was promoted to chef de bataillon (major). With the defection to the Austrians of French general Charles François Dumouriez, Hoche came under suspicion of treason. Traveling to Paris to clear his name, he was arrested and imprisoned.

Acquitted following a trial by the Revolutionary Tribunal, Hoche received command of the French garrison at Dunkerque as chef de brigade (colonel). His skillful handling of its defense brought promotion to general of brigade in the autumn of 1793. He had advanced from major to general in only six months.

Taking command of the French Army of the Moselle in November 1793, Hoche initially suffered defeats before winning victories in December that drove the Austrians back across the Rhine. He was then appointed commander of the French Army of Italy. He had hardly taken command at Nice when he was again arrested on suspicion of treason and taken to Paris and imprisoned. Released following the Thermidorian Reaction in July 1794, Hoche was appointed commander of French forces sent to end the Vendée Revolt and crush Chouan insurgents in Brittany. He was promoted to general of division in October 1794.

Hoche had an instinctive feel for counterinsurgency and proved to be a highly effective commander. He reorganized his forces into smaller detachments, assigning each a sector for which they were responsible. He thus helped invent the technique of *quadrillage.* In sharp contrast to the brutal policies of his predecessor, Louis Marie Turreau, Hoche followed an enlightened approach that included the restoration of Catholic worship. He also made extensive use of mobile columns against insurgent villages, which would then be surrounded and the guerrillas arrested. He admonished the locals to pray to God and cultivate their plots. By February 1795, he had pacified most of Brittany.

In July 1795 an English fleet in Quiberon Bay landed a French émigré force of more than 8,000 men, along with substantial numbers of muskets and cannon for the Chouan insurgents. Hoche quickly marched against this force with 9,000 men, defeating the invaders, capturing nearly 6,000, and driving the remainder back to the British ships.

The Directory then ruling France rewarded Hoche by giving him command of the armies of the west, known as the Army of the Ocean. He then hunted down the remaining insurgent bands. Hoche developed an excellent human intelligence system and confiscated grain and cattle in insurgent villages. In February and March 1796 he captured insurgent leaders Jean-Nicolas Stofflet and François de Charette and had them shot. By the summer of 1796, the western rebellion against the French Republic was over.

Hoche then assumed command of a French expeditionary force ordered to Ireland to bring about a revolt there against British rule. The French fleet sailed in December 1796 but fell victim to a storm, and the ships only gradually assembled at Bantry Bay. Hoche's ship was late to arrive, and in the meantime his second-in-command had called off the expedition and returned the ships to France.

Hoche was not blamed for the failure, which was not his fault, and in February 1797 he received command of the French Army of the Sambre and Meuse. Reorganizing his army, he crossed the Rhine and won a series of victories and was poised to take Frankfurt when the Austrians concluded an armistice with General Napoleon Bonaparte at Leoben (April 1797). This was Hoche's last campaign. He took sick and died of consumption at Wetzlar in Hesse on September 19, 1797.

William T. Dean III and Spencer C. Tucker

See also Quadrillage and *Ratissage;* Vendée Revolt

Further Reading

Garnier, Robert. *Hoche.* Paris: Payot, 1986.

Six, Georges. *Dictionnaire biographique des généraux & amiraux Français de la Révolution et de l'Empire (1792–1814)* [Biographical Dictionary of French Generals and Admirals of the Revolution and the Empire (1792–1814)]. Paris: Gaston Saffroy, 2003

Ho Chi Minh

Birth Date: May 19, 1890
Death Date: September 2, 1969

Vietnamese nationalist, leader of insurgencies against the French and Japanese, and prime minister and president of the Democratic Republic of Vietnam (DRV, North Vietnam). Born Nguyen Sinh Cung on May 19, 1890, in Kimlien, Annam (central Vietnam), Ho Chi Minh's father was a Confucian scholar who resigned his position in the bureaucracy to protest French control of Vietnam. When Nguyen was 10, according to Confucian tradition his father gave him the new name of Nguyen Tat Thanh ("Nguyen the Accomplished").

Nguyen received a secondary education at the prestigious National Academy, a French-style lycée in Hue. He attended high school at Hue but left Vietnam in 1911 and lived first in London and then in Paris during World War I (1914–1918), where he became the leader of the Vietnamese community in France. He subsequently changed his name to Nguyen ai Quoc ("Nguyen the Patriot").

Nguyen joined the French Socialist Party and was one of the founders of the French Communist Party when it split from the Socialists in 1920. He then became active in the Comintern and traveled in China and the Soviet Union. In 1925 Nguyen founded the Vietnam Revolutionary Youth League, commonly known as the Thanh Nien, an anticolonial organization that sought the liberation of Vietnam from French control. He was one of the founders of the Indochinese Communist Party in Hong Kong in 1929. In 1940 Nguyen began using the name Ho Chi Minh ("He who enlightens").

During World War II (1939–1945), Ho formed the Viet Nam Doc Lap Dong Minh Hoi (Vietnam Independence League), known as the Viet Minh, a nationalist front organization but dominated by the Communists that fought both the Japanese and the French. In fighting the Japanese, Ho secured assistance from the U.S. Office of Strategic Services.

Taking advantage of the political vacuum in Vietnam following the surrender of Japan, on September 2, 1945, Ho proclaimed the independence of Vietnam as the DRV and became its president in March 1946. Following the failure of diplomatic efforts with France and entrusting the direction of military operations to Vo Nguyen Giap, Ho skillfully led the struggle for independence in the Indochina War against France (1946–1954) and then the long battle against the Republic of Vietnam (RVN, South Vietnam) and the Americans in the 1960s and 1970s.

In 1965 Ho supervised the transition from total battlefield victory to victory through a protracted war strategy, believing that democratic societies had little patience for long and indecisive conflict. Implacable and resolute, Ho measured battlefield success not in Vietnamese lives lost but instead in French and then American casualties. He supposedly remarked that "you can kill 10 of our people for every one I kill of yours, but eventually you will grow tired and go home and I will win." A skillful diplomat, Ho managed to avoid taking sides in the Sino-Soviet dispute and had successfully played one side against the other to secure increased aid, reportedly boasting that "we use Moscow's technology and Beijing's strategy." Ho died in Hanoi on September 2, 1969, and thus did not live to see the final victory of April 1975.

"Uncle Ho" is regarded by Vietnamese as the most important figure in their modern history. Following reunification, the former South Vietnamese capital city of Saigon was renamed in his honor.

Spencer C. Tucker

See also Indochina War; Viet Minh; Vietnam War; Vo Nguyen Giap

Further Reading

Duiker, William J. *Ho Chi Minh: A Life.* New York: Hyperion, 2000.

Ho Chi Minh. *Ho Chi Minh on Revolution: Selected Writings, 1920–1966.* New York: Signet, 1967.

Lacouture, Jean. *Ho Chi Minh: A Political Biography.* Translated by Peter Wiles. New York: Random House, 1968.

Tucker, Spencer C. *Vietnam.* London: UCL Press, 1999.

Ho Chi Minh Trail

A network of roads, paths, and waterways stretching from the Democratic Republic of Vietnam (DRV, North Vietnam) through eastern Laos and Cambodia to the Republic of Vietnam (RVN, South Vietnam) during the Vietnam War (1959–1975). The Ho Chi Minh Trail was the main supply route for troops and matériel from North Vietnam supporting the Communist insurgency in South Vietnam. At its greatest extent, the Ho Chi Minh Trail included some 12,700 miles of paths, trails, roads, and waterways that often traversed extraordinarily difficult terrain. Indeed, the trail represents one of history's great military engineering feats. The U.S. government recognized the importance of this vital logistics link for the Communist forces in South Vietnam and waged a massive air interdiction campaign against the trail in one of the central struggles of the Vietnam War.

On May 19, 1959, Major Vo Ban of the People's Army of Vietnam (PAVN, North Vietnamese Army) received orders to open a supply route to South Vietnam. The Dang Lao Dong Viet Nam Party (Vietnamese Workers' Party, or Communist Party of Vietnam) Central Committee was determined to support the Communist insurgency in South Vietnam, and men and matériel would have to be moved south to support it.

Initially assigned 500 men, Major Ban set to work building the necessary staging areas, depots, and command posts along the ancient system of footpaths and roads that connected North Vietnam and South Vietnam. In August, Ban's Unit 559 (named for the fifth month of 1959) delivered the first supplies—20 boxes of rifles and ammunition—to Viet Cong insurgents in Thua Thien Province. By the end of the year, some 1,800 men had also used the trail to infiltrate South Vietnam.

The need for secrecy led in 1960 to the development of a new route along the western side of the rugged Truong Son Range in Laos. The trail's segments gradually were widened, and bicycles were introduced to transport supplies along the roads. With strengthened frames, each bicycle could handle loads of 220–330

People's Army of Vietnam (PAVN or North Vietnamese Army) troops moving south on the Ho Chi Minh Trail. A network of roads and trails that stretched from North Vietnam through eastern Laos to South Vietnam, the Ho Chi Minh Trail formed the main supply route for troops and equipment supporting Hanoi's war against the Republic of Vietnam. (AFP/Getty Images)

pounds, with occasional loads in excess of 700 pounds. Each bicycle could move 3 or 4 times the load of backpacking porters at 1.5 times the speed of porters on foot.

Hanoi continued to expand the trail during the next two years. Infiltration training centers were established where soldiers underwent physical training and instruction in camouflage techniques. Infiltrators averaged six miles a day along the trail, with the soldiers carrying loads of more than 200 pounds. Civilians also assisted.

By the winter of 1962–1963, the North Vietnamese government had some 5,000 troops and an engineering regiment assigned to the trail. The road complex now stretched for more than 600 miles, nearly all of it well hidden from aerial observation. Engineers widened the roads, and in the summer of 1862 trucks began using portions of the route. Some 100 tons of supplies now moved weekly, transported by trucks, bicycles, elephants, and porters, while some 10,000–20,000 former southerners had made the long journey to South Vietnam since the trail's opening.

In October 1964 following a decision by Hanoi to expand the war in South Vietnam, units of the People's Army of Vietnam (PAVN, North Vietnamese Army) moved down the trail, with the first regiment arriving in South Vietnam's Central Highlands that December. Two additional regiments reached South Vietnam in January and February 1965.

In 1965 the North Vietnamese undertook a massive effort to improve the trail to handle increased traffic. Engineers, assisted by North Korean, Russian, and Chinese advisers, widened footpaths into roads, strengthened bridges, and piled rocks in streams and rivers to create fords. Truck convoys, covering 50 to 75 miles at night, moved increasing amounts of matériel south. Despite the beginning of heavy U.S. air attacks, the number of infiltrators increased from 12,000 in 1964 to 33,000, while truck traffic quadrupled, reaching 300 to 400 tons per week.

Supplies were generally transported at night as trucks moved between stations 6–18 miles apart. The trucks were hidden or camouflaged during daylight hours. Manning each station were 30–60 PAVN soldiers, while PAVN personnel and civilian road repair crews were stationed at vulnerable points, with tools and material to repair or maintain the trail. Refueling facilities were located at every third to fifth station, linked by field telephones. Convoys generally moved between three to seven shelter areas and then returned to their starting points, this in order to familiarize drivers with the run and to familiarize mechanics with particular trucks. This system also lessened the likelihood of a large number of trucks creating bottlenecks and presenting a lucrative target.

By the end of 1966, according to U.S. intelligence estimates, the Ho Chi Minh Trail included some 820 miles of well-hidden fair-weather roads. It was now clear to U.S. planners that a major effort had to be undertaken to cut this essential supply route to South Vietnam.

Such an effort began in 1967. Formally known as Project Practice Nine, Project Dye Marker, and Project Muscle Shoals, it was dubbed the McNamara Line for Secretary of Defense Robert S. McNamara and consisted of a vast system of electronic sensors and aerial mines to identify targets that would prompt air strikes.

Despite what would ultimately amount to more than 3 million tons of bombs dropped on Laos, the infiltration continued. By late 1970, some 70,000 PAVN soldiers defended the trail in Laos. An estimated 8,000 men moved southward each month, along with more than 10,000 tons of war matériel.

In 1971 following an abortive attempt by the Army of the Republic of Vietnam (ARVN, South Vietnamese Army) to cut the trail at Tchepone in Laos (Operation LAM SON 719), the North Vietnamese seized Attopeu and Saravane in southern Laos, widening the trail to the west. The trail now included 14 major relay stations in Laos and 3 in South Vietnam. Each station, with attached transportation and engineering battalions, served as a POL (petroleum-oil-lubricants) storage facility, supply depot, truck park, and workshop. Soviet ZIL trucks, each with a 5–6-ton capacity, traveled by day and night on all-weather roads. Protected by nature and sophisticated antiaircraft defenses, the PAVN thoroughly dominated a vast network of roads, trails, paths, and rivers stretching more than 12,700 miles in length.

Following the Paris Peace Accords, the Ho Chi Minh Trail was extensively improved. By 1973, it had become a two-lane highway that ran from the mountain passes of North Vietnam to the Chu Pong Massif in South Vietnam. By 1974, the trail was a four-lane route from the Central Highlands to Tay Ninh Province, northwest of Saigon. The trail also boasted four oil pipelines. Reportedly from 1965 to 1975, the North Vietnamese government moved nearly 1.8 million tons of supplies south. The North Vietnamese won the battle of supply, a victory that spelled defeat for South Vietnam.

There is a museum in Hanoi devoted exclusively to the Ho Chi Minh Trail and the important role it played in the Communist victory.

William M. Leary

See also McNamara Line; Viet Cong; Vietnam War

Further Reading

Prados, John. *The Blood Road: The Ho Chi Minh Trail and the Vietnam War.* New York: Wiley, 1999.

Staaveren, Jacob Van. *The United States Air Force in Southeast Asia: Interdiction in Southern Laos, 1960–1968.* Washington, DC: Center for Air Force History, 1993.

Stevens, Richard Linn. *The Trail: A History of the Ho Chi Minh Trail and the Role of Nature in the War in Viet Nam.* New York: Garland, 1993.

Tilford, Earl H., Jr. *Crosswinds: The Air Force's Setup in Vietnam.* College Station: Texas A&M University Press, 1994.

Hofer, Andreas

Birth Date: November 22, 1767
Death Date: February 20, 1810

Tyrolean resistance leader during the Napoleonic Wars (1803–1815). Born in the St. Leonhard in Passeier in what was then the Austrian Tyrol (now the Italian province of South Tyrol) on November 22, 1767, Andreas Hofer was an innkeeper by profession. He fought for Austria as a militia captain during the War of the Third Coalition (1803–1806). After the 1806 Treaty of Pressburg (Bratislava) transferred control of the Tyrol from Austria to France's ally Bavaria, Hofer and others organized a rebellion in 1809, with the tacit approval of Austrian emperor Francis I.

Although there were several key rebel leaders, Hofer subsequently became the best known, with his folksy image perfectly capturing the new spirit of Tyrolean nationalism. The rebels assembled a military force and targeted Bavarian authority in any form. Defeating a government force at Sterzing, they then occupied Innsbruck. Franco-Bavarian units tried but failed to recapture it.

French emperor Napoleon I's victory over the Austrians in the Battle of Wagram (July 5–6, 1809) resulted in the sudden withdrawal of Austrian support. Hofer subsequently retreated from Innsbruck and back into the Tyrolean mountains. When Austria signed the Treaty of Schönbrunn (October 14, 1809), the Tyrol was again ceded to the Bavarians. Hofer was granted amnesty but broke his parole four days later. Absent popular support, Hofer's meager force was defeated at Bergisel. He fled, this time with a French bounty on his head. A neighbor revealed Hofer's location, and he was arrested in January 1810, sent to Mantua to face a military trial, and executed there on February 20, 1810.

The Tyrol territory ceased to be a political unit and was divided between Bavaria and the new province of Illyria. Although his rebel career lasted less than a year, Hofer became a martyr and a lasting symbol of resistance against the French and their allies. He remains a national hero in the Tyrol.

Mark M. Hull

See also Tyrolean Revolt

Further Reading

Eyck, F. Gunter. *Loyal Rebels: Andreas Hofer and the Tyrolean Uprising of 1809.* Lanham, MD: University Press of America, 1986.

Harford, Lee S., Jr. "Napoleon and the Subjugation of the Tyrol." In *The Consortium on Revolutionary Europe, 1750–1850: Proceedings, 1989,* edited by Donald Horward and John Horgan, 704–711. Tallahassee: Institute on Napoleon and the French Revolution, Florida State University, 1990.

Hukbalahap Rebellion

Start Date: 1946
End Date: 1954

Philippine insurgency during 1946–1954. Hukbalahap is the acronym for the Tagalog term *Huk*bong *Ba*yan *La*ban sa mga *Hap*on (People's Anti-Japanese Army). Its members were called Huks. Tge Hukbalahap was formed by the Partido

Kommunista ng Pilipinas (PKP, Communist Party of the Philippines) on March 29, 1942, although it had its origins in the Filipino peasant movements of the 1930s.

While ostensibly part of a coalition of Philippine resistance groups organized to fight the Japanese occupiers, the movement also had a strong socioeconomic basis. The Huks gave voice to the grievances of tenant farmers and landless laborers on the sugar plantations of central and southern Luzon. The Huks resented the iniquitous crop sharing, growing indebtedness, and forced labor inherent in the Philippines' exploitative landholding system. By late 1943, the Huks claimed to have 15,000–20,000 active fighters and another 50,000 in reserve. During the war, Huk guerrillas seized many supplies bound for the Japanese, established a training camp to teach Marxist doctrine, and killed many Japanese and Filipino collaborators. The guerrillas also established their own government in many barrios (villages) and towns.

In the immediate postwar period, the situation reverted to the status quo ante for the Hukbalahap. The landed elite who had collaborated with the Japanese now turned to the Americans for support. The Americans, with the advent of the Cold War and their antipathy to communism and sporadic but negative wartime experiences with the Huks, backed the landlords against the Huks. Many Hukbalahap squadrons were disarmed, and their contribution to the war effort was denigrated. Also, local Huk governments were removed from power, while Huk leaders, including Luis Taruc, were imprisoned.

The Huks nonetheless participated in the April 1946 elections that were held prior to Philippine independence on July 4, 1946. They ran under the banner of the Democratic Alliance Party, which had been formed in July 1945 and combined the peasant movement and the urban Left. The Liberal Party emerged victorious. The Democratic Alliance won six seats in Congress representing Central Luzon, but President Manuel Roxas denied the duly elected Communist representatives their seats, including Taruc, on the charge that they had employed terror tactics during the elections.

Finding the constitutional-political channel blocked, the Huks reverted to guerrilla activity. There were many reasons for the popularity of the Hukbalahap among peasants, intellectuals, and nationalists. Discontent had been brewing in the countryside for many decades. The peasants rebelled primarily because of repression by both government officials and the landed elite. They viewed their actions as entirely defensive in nature. Taruc demanded immediate enforcement of the bill of rights and revocation of all criminal charges against the Huks. The Huks also sought agrarian reform, including a more equitable crop-sharing arrangement, and demanded representation in the Philippine Congress.

With the beginning of Huk insurgent operations, President Roxas unveiled his mailed-fist policy in August 1946 by proclaiming his intention to crush the Hukbalahap Rebellion within 60 days. The resultant government strong-arm tactics only fueled peasant anger and bolstered Hukbalahap popularity. The Roxas government also failed to realize the need for a comprehensive counterinsurgency strategy that would include genuine reform to address peasant grievances. In March 1948 as the Hukbalahap Rebellion continued, the Roxas administration outlawed the Hukbalahap.

In 1949, Huks ambushed and murdered Aurora Quezon, chairman of the Philippine Red Cross and the widow of Manuel Quezon, the second president of the Philippines, along with several other members of her party. This act brought widespread international condemnation and led to a change in the formal name of the Hukbalahap organization to the Hukbong Mapagpalaya ng Bayan (HMB, People's Liberation Army).

Huk support was centered in the villages, and the Philippine Army formed special hunter-killer groups known as the Nenita Force, led by Major Napoleon Valeriano, to root them out. The Nenita Force's tactics of intimidation often claimed innocent victims, however, on occasion creating support for the Huks. In July 1950, Valeriano took command of the 7th Battalion Combat Team in Bulacan. It pursued a much more effective comprehensive counterinsurgency strategy that minimized the negative impact of military operations on the rural populations.

In 1950 during the Elpidio Quirino administration, however, the Huks threatened Manila itself and thus the stability of the government. U.S. president Harry S. Truman responded to Quirino's appeal for help by dispatching the Bell Mission (headed by Daniel W. Bell) and extending military aid in the form of equipment and training by a Joint United States Military Advisory Group, along with financial assistance.

A key step in ending the insurgency was the appointment in September 1950 of Ramón Magsaysay as secretary of national defense. Magsaysay was a military hero, acclaimed for his role in fighting the Japanese. One of Magsaysay's lay advisers was U.S. Air Force officer and counterinsurgency expert Edward Lansdale. American assistance allowed the creation of additional Battalion Combat Teams, and Magsaysay's unorthodox methods and experience as a former guerrilla helped check the Hukbalahap Rebellion. He devised a reward system for the identification of Huks and a system for their rehabilitation. Magsaysay understood the need for a hearts-and-minds program and created the Economic Development Corps for new rural facilities and a land program that resettled a number of former Huks on Mindanao. In a single raid conducted in October 1950 in Manila, the entire Communist-Huk politburo was arrested.

In December 1953, Magsaysay became president of the Philippines. His personal charisma and folksy demeanor appealed to rural Filipinos, helping to short-circuit the Huks' popularity. Magsaysay also introduced agricultural reforms to raise productivity, which helped mollify the peasants. Although some agitation continued thereafter, Huk strength had been reduced to some 2,000 by 1954, when the rebellion was for all practical purposes at an end. By that date, 9,695 Huks had been killed and 4,269 had been captured. More important, 15,866 had surrendered. There was a brief Huk revival during 1965–1970 led by Taruc's nephew, but it was easily contained.

Udai Bhanu Singh and Spencer C. Tucker

See also Lansdale, Edward Geary; Magsaysay, Ramón del Fierro

Further Reading

Bautista, Alberto Manuel. "The Hukbalahap Movement in the Philippines, 1942–1952." Unpublished MA thesis, University of California, Berkeley, 1952.

Greenberg, Lawrence M. *The Hukbalahap Insurrection: A Case Study of a Successful Anti-Insurgency Operation in the Philippines, 1946–1955.* Washington, DC: U.S. Army Center of Military History, 1987.

Jones, Gregg R. *Red Revolution: Inside the Philippine Guerrilla Movement.* Boulder, CO, and London: Westview, 1989.

Kerkvliet, Benedict J. *The Huk Rebellion: A Study of Peasant Revolt in the Philippines.* Berkeley and Los Angeles: University of California Press, 1977.

Romulo, Carlos P., and Marvin M. Gray. *The Magsaysay Story.* New York: Pocket Books, 1957.

Valeriano, Napoleon D., and Charles T. R. Bohannan. *Counter-Guerrilla Operations: The Philippine Experience.* New York: Praeger, 1962.

Hungarian Revolution

Start Date: October 23, 1956
End Date: November 4, 1956

The Hungarian Revolution of 1956 was one of the most momentous events of the Cold War. By 1953, the Hungarian economy was in deep crisis. Communist economic policies had proved unsuccessful. The farms produced by land reform were too small for Hungary's economy, and the government had emphasized heavy industry despite a lack of natural resources to sustain it. Indeed, the situation was sufficiently dire that in July 1953 with Soviet blessing, moderate Communist Imre Nagy replaced Mátyás Rákosi as prime minister. Nagy announced major reforms, including administrative changes, an end to or reduction in forced labor, an accommodation with religion, an end to police brutality, curtailment of the power of the secret police, amnesty for political prisoners, an end to the collective farms, and relaxation of economic controls and the pace of industrialization. These would be precisely the demands of 1956. Soviet leader Nikita Khrushchev became concerned about Nagy's reforms, and in April 1955 Nagy was forced to resign. The suspension of his reform program was badly received in Hungary.

Rioting in Poland in June 1956 and Władysław Gomułka's return to power there encouraged the Hungarian reformers. With the situation in Hungary fast deteriorating, Khrushchev ordered Rákosi to resign as party secretary in July 1956, but his Stalinist replacement, Ernõ Gerõ, proved to be just as unpopular. The economy had deteriorated, and a poor harvest and a fuel shortage in the autumn of 1956 added to the already serious situation.

There was also rising discontent among Hungary's intellectuals, who had enjoyed limited freedom in the thaw following the March 1953 death of Joseph Stalin.

The dissidents were not anticommunists; rather, they demanded that the government bring its policies and practices into line with stated Communist ideals.

College and university students were also committed to political change. Students from the Technical University founded a new youth organization and convened an assembly on October 22, 1956, to finalize their main demands, which included the withdrawal of Soviet troops, the appointment of a new government with Nagy as prime minister, political pluralism, new economic policies, and trials for Rákosi and others.

A student-led demonstration on October 23 attracted growing crowds, and the demonstrators moved to Kossuth Square. There in front of the Parliament building, more than 200,000 people listened to a speech by Nagy, who agreed with most of the demands but rejected radical change. Disappointed, the crowd moved on to the building housing the National Radio Network with the plan of announcing their demands on the air. Instead, a speech by Gerõ was broadcast. His remarks enraged the demonstrators, and fighting broke out between them and police defending the National Radio complex. When police tried to disperse the crowd with tear gas and then opened fire, the crowd stormed the radio building and occupied it. On October 24, Hungarian military officers and soldiers joined the demonstrators. The demonstrators toppled a large statue of Stalin, chanting "Russians go home," "Away with Gerõ," and "Long live Nagy."

The night before, the party's Central Committee had voted to bring back Nagy as prime minister, and this decision was announced on October 24, with Nagy delivering a radio speech proclaiming amnesty for the protesters if they stopped the fighting. Also that day, Soviet troops began moving into Budapest and taking up positions in the city.

The demonstration now assumed an anti-Soviet, nationalist character. During the next four days, sporadic fighting occurred between the Soviet troops and groups of students, workers, and former prisoners—the so-called Freedom Fighters. On October 25 in the course of a huge demonstration in front of the Parliament building, Soviet tanks opened fire on the crowd.

Meanwhile, Soviet leaders Anastas I. Mikoyan and Mikhail A. Suslov arrived in Budapest from Moscow and decided to drop Gerõ as secretary-general of the Hungarian Workers' Party (Communist Party). János Kádár, neither a reformer nor a Stalinist, replaced him. Clearly, the Soviet leadership hoped that Nagy and Kádár would be able to control the situation.

Nagy attempted to bring events under control, but the uprising was rapidly spreading throughout Hungary. On October 17 Nagy finalized his new government, which included noncommunist politicians. He then commenced negotiations with the Soviets on a cease-fire agreement.

At first Nagy proposed only limited reforms. His ultimate intention, however, was to implement the political program of his first premiership in 1953. He offered a general amnesty to the demonstrators and promised the withdrawal of

Soviet troops from Hungary. But Nagy soon realized that his 1953 program was not sufficient, and he acceded to most of the popular demands, including the introduction of political pluralism and Hungarian withdrawal from the Warsaw Pact.

On October 28, the new government convened for the first time. The government ordered the dissolution of the secret police. Nagy also announced that Soviet troops would soon withdraw from Budapest, and on October 29, Soviet troops began to leave the city.

A coalition government was founded on October 30, with the Smallholders' Party, the Social Democratic Party, and the National Peasants Party all reconstituted. At the same time, the Hungarian Workers' Party was dissolved. Nagy freed political prisoners, including Cardinal József Mindszenty, who had been sentenced to life imprisonment in 1948. Nagy also announced his intention to permanently abolish the one-party political system.

This was a decisive turning point for Nagy, who now abandoned his moderate reform agenda and became fully committed to the more radical demands of the population. On October 31 he announced that Hungary would begin negotiations to withdraw from the Warsaw Pact, and the next day he declared his intention to leave the Warsaw Pact, proclaimed Hungarian neutrality, and asked the United Nations (UN) to mediate his nation's dispute with the Soviet Union. At the same time, a new Communist party, the Hungarian Socialist Workers' Party, was founded. On the evening of November 1, the secretary-general of the new party, János Kádár, went to the Soviet embassy to begin negotiations with Soviet authorities. He was then secretly flown to Moscow, where he met with Khrushchev.

On November 3 the new government, now a coalition that included the Communists, the Smallholders' Party, the Social Democrats, and the National Peasants' Party, began negotiations for the final withdrawal of Soviet troops. That evening under a pledge of safe conduct, General Pál Maléter, the new minister of defense and one of the heroes of the revolution, visited Soviet Army headquarters to negotiate a Soviet withdrawal and Hungarian departure from the Warsaw Pact. He was not allowed to depart and would be tried and executed in the summer of 1958.

Meanwhile, Khrushchev and the Soviet leadership had become increasingly alarmed about developments in Hungary. While Moscow was willing to make some concessions, a multiparty cabinet and free elections threatened Soviet control of all of Central Europe. Soviet leaders may also have believed, as they charged, that Western agents had been at work stirring up rebellion, while the military leaders demanded action to reverse the humiliation suffered earlier by the withdrawal of Red Army tanks. Nagy's announcement of Hungary's intention to withdraw from the Warsaw Pact was the straw that broke the camel's back and triggered Soviet military intervention.

At dawn on Sunday, November 4, Khrushchev sent 200,000 Soviet troops and 2,000 tanks into Hungary. The Soviets quickly secured Hungary's airfields, highway junctions, and bridges and laid siege to the major cities. Nagy called for resistance, and fighting broke out across Hungary, but the center was Budapest. Unaided from the outside, the fight lasted only a week. Nagy and some of his associates sought and obtained asylum at the Yugoslavian embassy, while Cardinal Mindszenty sought refuge in the U.S. legation, where he remained until 1971.

Kádár immediately denounced Hungary's withdrawal from the Warsaw Pact and, with Soviet military backing, took control of the government. On November 8 he announced the formation of the Revolutionary Worker-Peasant Government and its Fifteen-Point Program. The latter included the protection of the Socialist system from all attacks, an increase in living standards, the streamlining of bureaucracy, the augmentation of agricultural production, a justification for the Red Army's intervention, and the withdrawal of troops from Hungary. The last point was rescinded following pressure from the Warsaw Pact.

Thousands of Hungarians were arrested, and an estimated 200,000 others fled the country, many of them young and well educated, and most of them across the western border into Austria. Nagy, promised safe passage from the Yugoslavian embassy, was arrested by the Soviets and imprisoned. He was subsequently tried and executed in June 1958. Some 70 other people were also executed.

One effect of the failure of the Hungarian Revolution was a loss of faith in the West. Hungarians genuinely believed that they had been promised assistance, and many Hungarians and Western observers held that the United States prolonged the fighting because Hungarian-language broadcasts over Radio Free Europe, then covertly financed by the U.S. government, encouraged Hungarians to believe that either the United States or the UN would send troops to safeguard their proclaimed neutrality. Hungarians had repeatedly asked Western journalists covering the revolution when UN troops would be arriving. President Dwight Eisenhower and Secretary of State John Foster Dulles had talked about "liberating" Eastern Europe and "rolling back communism," but this had been intended largely for domestic U.S. political consumption rather than for the East Europeans. U.S. inactivity over the Hungarian situation, however, indicated tacit acceptance of Soviet domination of their part of the world.

The UN Security Council discussed the Hungarian situation but adjourned the meeting because the Soviets appeared to be withdrawing. Then in a matter of a few hours, the UN was faced with the fait accompli of November 4. At the same time, however, attention was focused on the Anglo-French Suez invasion. This and the split between the United States and its two major allies effectively prevented any concrete action in Hungary. In December 1956 the UN censured the Kádár regime, but this did not in any way change the situation in Hungary.

There was another point worth considering. No matter how the West might have felt about intervening in Hungary, there was no way to get to that country militarily without violating Austrian neutrality. Nonetheless, the West did not come off well.

The effects of the Hungarian Revolution were particularly pronounced in Eastern Europe. Any thought that the people of the region might have had of escaping

Moscow's grip by violent revolution was discouraged by the example of Soviet willingness to use force in defiance of world opinion. Nevertheless, open rebellion by the very groups upon which the Communists were supposedly building their new society was shattering from a propaganda standpoint, as was the crushing of free workers' councils (soviets) that had sprung up in Hungary during the 1956 revolution, nearly four decades after the victory of Russian soviets in the Bolshevik Revolution of 1917. The Soviet military intervention did have a major impact on West European Communist parties. They suffered mass resignations, including some illustrious intellectuals.

The Hungarian Revolution ultimately led to changes in Soviet policy toward Eastern Europe. Moscow allowed some modifications in economic planning within the East European bloc to meet the needs of individual countries, including more attention to consumer goods and agriculture and a slowed pace of industrialization. For the time being, however, an opportunity to begin the liberation of Eastern Europe had led to a heavy-handed reassertion of Soviet mastery.

Anna Boros-McGee and Spencer C. Tucker

Further Reading

Barber, Noel. *Seven Days of Freedom: The Hungarian Uprising, 1956.* New York: Stein and Day, 1974.

Granville, Johanna C. *In the Line of Fire: The Soviet Crackdown on Hungary, 1956–1958.* Pittsburgh, PA: Center for Russian and East European Studies, University of Pittsburgh, 1998.

Litván, György, ed. *The Hungarian Revolution of 1956: Reform, Revolt, and Repression, 1953–1963.* London and New York: Longmans, 1996.

I

Indochina War

Start Date: 1946
End Date: 1954

Fought between the French and Vietnamese nationalists, the Indochina War (1946–1954) was the first phase of what might be called the Second Thirty Years' War, the longest war of the 20th century. The Indochina War began as an insurgency but grew into a full-scale war, although it remained a mosaic of insurgency and conventional warfare throughout.

The French had established themselves in the region in the 1840s, and by 1887 they had formed French Indochina, consisting of Vietnam (Tonkin, Annam, and Cochin China) and the kingdoms of Cambodia and Laos. The cause of the war was the French refusal to recognize the end of the era of colonialism.

In 1941 veteran Vietnamese Communist leader Ho Chi Minh formed the Viet Minh to fight both the Japanese, then in military occupation of Vietnam, and the French. A fusion of Communists and nationalists but dominated by the former, the Viet Minh had by 1944 liberated most of the northern provinces of Vietnam. The defeat of Japan in August 1945 created a power vacuum, as virtually all French troops had been incarcerated in prison camps by the Japanese. At the end of August 1945 in Hanoi, Ho established the provisional government of the Democratic Republic of Vietnam (DRV, North Vietnam), and on September 2, 1945, he proclaimed Vietnamese independence.

Unable to secure support from the Soviet Union or the United States, Ho was forced to deal with France. He and French diplomat Jean Sainteny concluded an agreement in March 1946 to allow 15,000 French troops into North Vietnam, with the understanding that 3,000 would leave each year and that all would be gone by the end of 1951. In return, France recognized North Vietnam as a free state within the French Union. France also promised to abide by the results of a referendum in Cochin China to determine if it would be reunited with Annam and Tonkin.

The Ho-Sainteny Agreement fell apart with the failure of the Fontainebleau Conference in France during the summer of 1946 to resolve outstanding substantive issues and with the decision of new French governor-general of Indochina Admiral Thierry d'Argenlieu to proclaim on his own initiative the independence of a republic of Cochin China. Officials in Paris were not worried. They believed that if there was fighting, the Vietnamese nationalists would, as in the past, be easily crushed. Violence broke out in Hanoi in November 1946, whereupon d'Argenlieu ordered the shelling of the port of Haiphong, and the war was on.

The French motives were primarily political and psychological. Perhaps only with its empire could France be counted as a great power. Colonial advocates also argued that concessions in Indochina would adversely impact other French possessions, including Algeria, Morocco, and Tunisia in North Africa, and that further losses would surely follow.

The North Vietnamese leadership planned for a protracted struggle. Former history teacher Vo Nguyen Giap commanded its military forces, formed in May 1945 as the People's Army of Vietnam (PAVN, North Vietnamese Army). Giap modeled his strategy after that of Chinese Communist leader Mao Zedong. Giap's chief contribution to revolutionary warfare was his recognition of the political and psychological difficulties for a democracy waging a protracted and inconclusive war. He believed that French public opinion would at some point demand an end to the bloodshed. In the populous rice-producing areas, the Viet Minh would employ guerrilla tactics and ambushes. In the less populated mountain and jungle regions, the Viet Minh would engage in large-scale operations.

For eight years the French fought unsuccessfully to defeat the Viet Minh, with a steady succession of French generals directing operations. One French tactical innovation was the use of riverine divisions that consisted of naval and army forces known as the Divisions Navales D'assaut, abbreviated in French as Dinassaut. By 1950, the French fielded six Dinassauts. The French also developed commando formations, the Groupement des Commandos Mixtes Aéroportés (Composite Airborne Commando Groups), later known as the Groupement Mixte d'Intervention (Mixed Intervention Group). Essentially guerrilla formations of about 400 men each, these operated behind enemy lines, sometimes in conjunction with friendly Montagnard tribesmen or Vietnamese. By mid-1954 the French had 15,000 men in such formations, but they placed a heavy strain on the badly stretched French airlift capacity.

Sometimes the French cut deep into Viet Minh–controlled areas, but as soon as the French regrouped to attack elsewhere, the Viet Minh reasserted authority. With their superior firepower, the French held the cities and the majority of the towns, while the Viet Minh managed to dominate most of the countryside, gradually hollowing out French control as the years went by.

French commanders never did have sufficient manpower to carry out effective pacification. The war was also increasingly unpopular in France, and no conscripts were ever sent there, although a quarter of all of France's officers and more than 40 percent of its noncommissioned officers served in Indochina.

With Ho and the Viet Minh registering increasing success, Paris tried to appease nationalist sentiment by setting up a pliable indigenous Vietnamese regime as a competitor to the Viet Minh. In the March 1949 Elysée Agreements, Paris worked out an arrangement with former emperor Bao Dai to create the State of Vietnam (SV). Incorporating Cochin China, Annam, and Tonkin, it was to be an independent entity within the French Union. France never did give the SV genuine

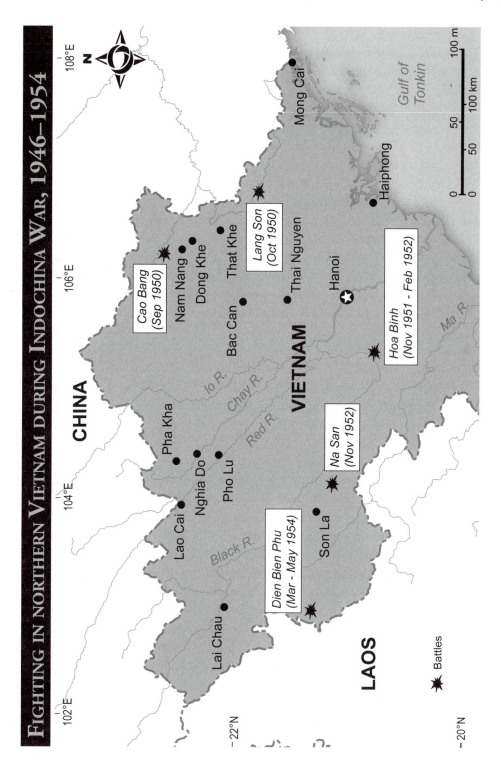

FIGHTING IN NORTHERN VIETNAM DURING INDOCHINA WAR, 1946–1954

independence, however, retaining control of its foreign relations and armed forces. The result was that the SV was never able to attract meaningful nationalist support. There were in effect but two alternatives, the Viet Minh, now labeled by the French as Communists, or the French.

Meanwhile, the military situation continued to deteriorate for the French. PAVN forces achieved their successes with arms inferior in both quantity and quality to those of the French. Disparities in military equipment were offset by the Viet Minh's popular backing.

Until the end of 1949, the United States showed little interest in Indochina apart from urging Paris to take concrete steps toward granting independence. Washington did not press too much on this issue, however, fearful that it might adversely affect France's attitude toward cooperation in the formation of the North Atlantic Treaty Organization (NATO) and the European Defense Community (EDC). France was then virtually the only armed continental West European power left to stand against the Soviet Union. In effect, Washington supported France's Indochina policy in order to ensure French support in containing the Soviet Union in Europe. The United States underwrote the French military effort in Vietnam indirectly. Leaders in Washington expressed confidence based on false assurances from Paris that France was truly granting independence to Vietnam.

The U.S. policy of indirect aid to the French effort in Indochina changed after October 1949 and the Communist victory in China. This and the beginning of the Korean War (1950–1953) shifted U.S. interest to the containment of communism in Asia. Zealous anticommunism now drove U.S. policy and prevented Washington from seeing the nationalist roots of the problem.

With the Communist victory in China, in effect the war was lost for the French. China had a long common frontier with Tonkin, and the Viet Minh could now receive large shipments of modern weapons, including artillery captured by the Chinese Communists from the nationalists. The war now shifted in character, at least in the far north. In 1950 in a series of costly defeats, the French were forced to abandon a string of fortresses in far northern Tonkin. In these battles, the Viet Minh captured French arms sufficient to equip an entire division.

In 1951 an emboldened Giap launched a series of attacks in the Red River Delta area that turned into hard-fought meat-grinder battles during 1951–1952. Giap tried but failed to capture Hanoi and end the war. But as the French concentrated resources in the north, the Viet Minh registered impressive gains in the countryside of central and southern Vietnam.

From June 1950, the United States began major direct military support. This was reinforced by the Communist Chinese decision to enter the Korean War. Paris convinced Washington that the Indochina War was a major element in the worldwide containment of communism.

In January 1950 both the People's Republic of China and the Soviet Union recognized the North Vietnamese government. The next month the United States extended diplomatic recognition to the SV. U.S. military aid to the French in Indochina then grew dramatically, from approximately $150 million in 1950 to more than $1 billion in 1954. Also, by 1954 the United States was paying 80 percent of the cost of the war. The French insisted that all aid to Bao Dai's government be channeled through them, frustrating American hopes of bolstering Bao Dai's independence. Even though a Vietnamese National Army was established in 1951, it remained effectively under French control. Meanwhile, both the Harry S. Truman and Dwight D. Eisenhower administrations assured the American public that actual authority in Vietnam had been transferred to Bao Dai.

By mid-1953, despite substantial aid from the United States, France had lost authority over all but a minor portion of Vietnam. In September, with strong American encouragement, France entered into one final and disastrous effort to achieve a position of strength from which to negotiate with the Viet Minh. Under new commander Lieutenant General Henri Navarre, France now had 517,000 men, 360,000 of whom were Indochinese.

The Battle of Dien Bien Phu (April–May 1954) was the culminating and most dramatic battle of the war. In this remote location in northwestern Tonkin, the French constructed a complex of supporting fortresses. Navarre hoped to entice the Viet Minh to attack this supposedly impregnable position and there destroy them. At best, he expected one or two Viet Minh divisions. Giap accepted the challenge but committed four divisions. The French also mistakenly assumed that the Viet Minh could not get artillery to this remote location, but eventually the Viet Minh outgunned the French. French air assets also proved insufficient. The surrender of Dien Bien Phu on May 7 enabled the French politicians to shift the blame to the army and withdraw France from the war.

Not coincidental to the battle, a conference had already opened in Geneva to discuss Asian problems. The conference now took up the issue of Indochina. The April 26–July 21 Geneva Conference provided for independence for Cambodia, Laos, and North Vietnam. Vietnam was to be temporarily divided at the 17th Parallel, pending national elections in 1956. In the meantime, Viet Minh forces were to withdraw north of that line, and French forces were to withdraw south of the line.

In the war, the French and their allies sustained 172,708 casualties (94,581 dead or missing and 78,127 wounded) and 140,992 French Union casualties (75,867 dead or missing and 65,125 wounded), with the allied Indochina states losing 31,716 (18,714 dead or missing and 13,002 wounded). French dead or missing numbered some 20,000, Legionnaires dead or missing totaled 11,000, African dead or missing were 15,000, and Indochinese dead or missing were 46,000. The war took a particularly heavy toll among the officers, 1,900 of whom died. Viet Minh losses were probably three times those of the French and their allies, and perhaps 150,000 Vietnamese civilians also perished. One major issue was that of prisoners, both soldiers and civilians, held by the Viet Minh in barbarous conditions. Only 10,754 of the 36,979 reported missing during the war returned, and some were not released until years afterward.

The Indochina War had been three wars in one. Begun as a conflict between Vietnamese nationalists and France, it became a civil war between Vietnamese and was also part of the larger Cold War. As it turned out, in 1954 the civil war and the East-West conflict were only suspended. Soon a new war broke out in which the Americans replaced the French.

Spencer C. Tucker

See also Ho Chi Minh; Mao Zedong; Viet Minh; Vietnam War; Vo Nguyen Giap

Further Reading

Dalloz, Jacques. *The War in Indo-China, 1945–54.* Translated by Josephine Bacon. New York: Barnes and Noble, 1990.

Gras, Yves. *Histoire de la guerre d'Indochine* [History of the Indochina War]. Paris: Editions Denoël, 1992.

Tucker, Spencer C. *Vietnam.* Lexington: University Press of Kentucky, 1999.

Indonesia-Malaysia Confrontation

Start Date: 1962
End Date: 1966

The Indonesia-Malaysia Confrontation, also known as the Borneo Insurgency, the Brunei Insurgency, and Konfrontasi, occurred on the island of Borneo (known as Kalimantan in Indonesia) during 1962–1966 and resulted from Indonesian opposition to the creation of Malaysia. Malaya had secured independence from Britain in 1957, and in September 1963 as part of its withdrawal from Southeast Asia, Britain yielded to the Federation of Malaya (now West Malaysia) Singapore as well as Sabah (then North Borneo) and Sarawak (together now known as East Malaysia). The Federation of Malaya was then renamed the Federation of Malaysia. Sabnah, Sarawak, and Brunei are all located in northern Borneo, which is the world's third-largest island. The remaining three-quarters of the landmass of Borneo is part of Indonesia.

The insurgency began with the 1962 Brunei Revolt. Completely surrounded by Sarawak except for an outlet on the sea, Brunei possesses extensive oil reserves, and Sultan Omar Ali Saifuddien III had no interest in joining Malaysia. On December 8, 1962, however, the North Kalimantan National Army (TNKU) of some 4,000 men, which was poorly armed, began an insurrection known as the Brunei Revolt. The TNKU failed in its effort to take the sultan captive, and British troops from Singapore restored order in Brunei Town within little more than one day. By December 16, the British Far Eastern Command announced that all rebel centers had been secured, although mopping-up operations continued into May 1863.

The Indonesian government now reversed its policy toward Malaysia. On January 20, 1963, Foreign Minister Subandrio announced that Indonesia would pursue Konfrontasi, or confrontation with Malaysia, and on July 27, President Sukarno all but declared war when he stated his intention to "crush Malaysia." Among possible motives were Sukarno's failure to secure Dutch New Guinea (later Irian Jaya/West Papua), concerns that an expansion of Malaysian territory would increase British influence in the region, and domestic political pressures.

Sukarno broke off diplomatic relations and withdrew Indonesia from the United Nations. He also sought to take advantage of the fact that both Sabah and Sarawak were ethnically, religiously, and politically diverse and that there was some internal opposition there to being joined with Malaysia.

Some of the members of TNKU managed to reach Indonesian territory following the Brunei Revolt, and they were joined by as many as several thousand Chinese Communists from Sarawak who feared British reprisals. Recruits from the dissident elements of the East Malaysia population were then trained by the Indonesian Army. The insurgents were formed into the North Kalimantan People's Army and the Sarawak People's Guerrilla Forces, known to the British as the Clandestine Communist Organisation.

All-out war appeared a real possibility, but Britain stood fast behind Malaysia and dispatched forces under Major General William C. Walker. Australia and New Zealand also rendered assistance. The Borneo terrain posed a considerable challenge to British counterinsurgency efforts, and there were few roads. Both sides relied heavily on light infantry, and Walker used helicopters to considerable advantage.

The long border with Indonesia prevented Walker from halting infiltration into Malaysian territory. He insisted on close cooperation among the various security forces, the establishment of strong points and joint headquarters, protection of British base areas, control of the jungle, rigorous intelligence collection, and speed and mobility in field forces. Walker also established a permanent military presence in contested areas and developed a comprehensive program to win the loyalty of the natives to include Special Air Service (SAS) and police advising village leaders in addition to the extension of medical and agricultural assistance in rural areas. All of these made it difficult for the Indonesian insurgents to operate in Malaysian territory.

Increased Indonesian military efforts in 1965 led to Operation CLARET, in which Walker sent SAS units in secret cross-border raids into Indonesian Kalimantan. In 1965, Indonesia carried out several military operations in West Malaysia, although with negligible results. By August 1966 during Suharto's rise to power (he would assume the presidency in 1967 and hold it until 1998), a peace agreement was arranged whereby Indonesia accepted the existence of West Malaysia.

Casualties in the insurgency were relatively light. British Commonwealth military casualties were 114 killed and 181 wounded, with the largest number of casualties among the Gurkha units. Indonesian casualties were estimated at 590 killed, 222 wounded, and 771 captured, while civilian casualties were 36 killed and 53 wounded.

Spencer C. Tucker

See also Special Air Service; Walker, Sir Walter Colyear

Further Reading

Easter, D. *Britain and the Confrontation with Indonesia, 1960–1966.* London: I. B. Tauris, 2004.

Fowler, Will. *Britain's Secret War: The Indonesian Confrontation 1962–66.* New York: Osprey, 2006.

Mackie, J. A. C. *Konfrontasi: The Indonesia-Malaysia Dispute, 1963–1966.* Kuala Lumpur: Oxford University Press for the Australian Institute of International Affairs, 1974.

Insurgency

An insurgency is an organized movement aimed at the overthrow of a constituted government through the use of subversion and armed conflict. Insurgencies are organized and generally protracted politico-military struggles designed to weaken the control and legitimacy of an established government, occupying power, or other political authority while increasing insurgent control. Insurgencies grow out of unrest, a sense of relative deprivation, and discontent with the incumbent government. Normally, if the government responds to the needs of the population, then an insurgency cannot take hold. Political power is the central issue in an insurgency, with each side endeavoring to secure popular support for its governance or authority.

Insurgency is typically a form of internal war, one that occurs primarily within one state, not between states, and contains at least some elements of civil war. Successful insurgencies may culminate in a coup d'état that overthrows the existing government, reallocates power within a single state, or breaks away from state control to form an autonomous entity or ungoverned space that the insurgents can control. Power may be seized through revolution, a war of national liberation, or widespread civil war. An insurgency might also be mounted by a legitimate government-in-exile as well as by factions competing for that role, when indigenous elements seek to expel or overthrow what they perceive to be a foreign or occupation government.

Involvement of outside powers should be anticipated in insurgencies. This was evident during the Cold War, when the Soviet Union and the United States supported a wide number of regimes and/or the insurgents opposing them. Often this made for strange bedfellows. Thus, the Soviets supported the Democratic Republic of Afghanistan, while the United States aided the Islamic fundamentalist mujahideen (freedom fighters, holy warriors). Outside involvement does not change the fact that the long-term objective for all parties remains acceptance of the legitimacy of one's claim to political power by the people of the affected state or region.

Insurgents may initially employ nonviolent political mobilization and work stoppages (strikes) but then resort to conventional military operations when conditions appear right. Terrorism and guerrilla tactics are among the most common initial approaches, while insurgencies often culminate in open warfare, especially with logistical support from outside powers.

Insurgency is commonly used by the weak against the strong. Insurgents typically hold the strategic initiative by initiating the conflict. The existing government normally has an initial advantage in resources, but this may be counterbalanced by the requirement to protect a widely spread population and critical resources. Insurgents succeed by sowing chaos anywhere; the government fails unless it maintains a degree of order everywhere. The latter requires a high ratio of security forces to the protected population.

Insurgents hold a distinct advantage in their immediate area of operations. They speak the language, move easily within the society, and are likely to understand the population's wants and needs. They know such critical factors about the population as the organization and leadership of the local society, the relationships and tensions, the prevalent values and motivations, and the means of communication.

The information environment is a critical dimension of insurgencies. Activities such as bombings and suicide attacks create fear and uncertainty and are executed to attract media coverage and inflate perceptions of insurgent capabilities. Subsequent strategic communications are designed to undermine the government's legitimacy, such as identifying government shortcomings. Victory is achieved when the populace consents to the insurgent's legitimacy and ceases supporting the government.

Insurgencies have vulnerabilities that can be exploited. First, insurgencies begin from a position of weakness and use violence to pursue political aims; hence, an insurgency must initially adopt a covert approach for its planning and activities. However, excessive secrecy can limit freedom of action, reduce or distort information about goals and ideals, and restrict communication within the insurgency.

To mobilize their base of support, insurgent groups use a combination of persuasion or propaganda and coercion or intimidation. Insurgents seek to persuade people to support their position. Propaganda will often seek to highlight abuses by the government and point out governmental affiliation with external foreign support.

A base of operations far from the major centers of activity may be secure but risks being too far from the populace in which the insurgents must operate; conversely, a base too near centers of government risks opening the insurgency to observation and infiltration. Most insurgent movements rely heavily on freedom of movement across porous borders. So, the movement of fighters and their external sources of support are vulnerable to attack.

All insurgencies require funding. Criminal organizations, such as drug cartels or gangs, are possible funding sources, but such practices may not be ideologically consistent with the movement's core beliefs and may attract undue attention from government authorities. Funding from outside donors often comes with a political price that affects the overall aim of an insurgency and weakens its popular appeal.

Decisions taken by insurgent leaders can cause some followers to question the cause or challenge their leaders, and factions may form to vie for power. Counterinsurgency forces may then exploit these rifts. Many insurgencies have failed to capitalize on their initial opportunities; if insurgents lose momentum, counterinsurgents can regain the strategic initiative. Nothing is more demoralizing to insurgents than realizing that people inside their movement or trusted supporters among the public are deserting or providing information to government authorities.

The history of insurgency shows how adaptive insurgencies can be. Between 1945 and 1999, there were roughly 122 civil wars that resulted in the deaths of five times the number of state-on-state violence in the same period. Numerous states were prey to insurgencies as a consequence of the decolonization that followed World War II (1939–1945). This state weakness resulted in Communist insurgencies in Southeast Asia and Latin America, Islamic extremism in the Middle East and North Africa, and ethnic nationalism in a great many states.

The 20th century spawned a number of different types of insurgencies, including that advocated by Mao Zedong, the foco approach of Jules Régis Debray and Ernesto "Che" Guevara, and urban insurgency. Interconnectedness and information technology are new aspects of this contemporary wave of insurgencies. Employing the Internet, insurgents can link with sympathetic groups throughout a state, a region, or the entire world. Insurgents often join loose coalitions with common objectives, but groups may have different motivations and no central controlling body. While the communications and technology used for soliciting funds and disseminating propaganda is relatively new, the exploitation of grievances is not.

Although insurgencies take many forms, most share some common elements. An insurgent organization normally consists of five elements: leaders, combatants, the political cadre, auxiliaries, and the mass base.

The movement leaders provide strategic direction to the insurgency. They are the ideologues and planners. Leadership is exercised through force of personality and the power of revolutionary ideas, but in some insurgencies, leaders hold their positions through religious, clan, or tribal authority. Combatants, sometimes called foot soldiers, provide security and do the actual fighting. They support the insurgency's broader political agenda and maintain local control. Combatants protect training camps and networks that facilitate the flow of money, instructions, and foreign and local fighters.

The political cadre is actively engaged in the struggle to accomplish insurgent goals. Members of the political cadre implement guidance provided by the movement leaders. Movements based on religious extremism usually include religious advisers among their cadre. The cadre addresses grievances in local areas and attributes the solutions that they provide to the insurgency. In time, the cadre may seek to replace the bureaucracy and assume its functions in a counterstate.

Auxiliaries are sympathizers who do not participate in combat operations but who provide important support. They run safe houses, store weapons and supplies, act as couriers, provide intelligence and give early warning of counterinsurgent movements, provide funding, furnish forged or stolen documents, and facilitate access to potential supporters.

The mass base consists of the followers of the insurgent movement, that is, the supporting populace. Mass base members are often recruited and indoctrinated by the cadres. However, in many politically charged situations or identity-focused insurgencies, such active pursuit is not necessary. Mass base members may continue in their normal positions in society but clandestinely support the insurgent movement. They may subsequently pursue full-time positions within the insurgency. Insurgent approaches include but are not limited to conspiratorial, military-focused, urban, protracted popular war, identity-focused, composite, and coalition foci.

A conspiratorial approach involves a few leaders and a militant cadre or activist party seizing control of government structures or exploiting a revolutionary situation. The military-focused approach aims to create revolutionary possibilities or to seize power primarily by the application of military force. The Guevera-type focoists believe that a small group of guerrillas operating in a rural environment where grievances exist can eventually gather sufficient support to achieve their aims. In contrast, some secessionist insurgencies reply on major conventional forces to try to secure independence.

The urban approach has been utilized by such organizations as the Irish Republican Army, certain Latin American groups, and some Islamic extremist groups in Iraq. The focus of the urban approach is on the incitement of violence, intimidation of the population, and killing government and opposition leaders to weaken the government and create government overreaction or repression. Some urban insurgencies assume a cellular structure recruited along lines of close association—family, religious affiliation, political party, or social group.

No approach makes better use of asymmetry than the protracted popular war. Mao successfully utilized this approach in China. His theory of protracted war outlines a three-phased politico-military approach. The first phase is the strategic defensive, when the government has a stronger correlation of forces and insurgents must concentrate on survival and building support. The second phase is the strategic stalemate, when force correlations approach equilibrium and guerrilla warfare becomes the most important activity. The third and final phase is the strategic counteroffensive, when insurgents have superior strength and their military forces move to conventional operations to destroy the government's military capability.

The identity-focused insurgency approach mobilizes support based on the common identity of religious affiliation, clan, tribe, or ethnic group. Insurgents may also apply a composite approach that includes tactics drawn from any or all of the other approaches.

To overthrow a constituted government, insurgents must have a popular cause (or causes). By selecting an assortment of causes and tailoring them for various groups within the society, insurgents increase their base of sympathetic and complicit support. A carefully chosen cause is a formidable asset, providing a fledgling movement with a long-term base of support. The ideal cause attracts the most people while alienating the fewest and is one that counterinsurgents cannot co-opt.

Biff L. Baker

See also Debray, Jules Régis; Foco Theory; Guevara de la Serna, Ernesto; Mao Zedong

Further Reading

Fearon, James D., and David D. Laitin. "Ethnicity, Insurgency, and Civil War." *American Political Science Review* 97(1) (2003): 75–90.

U.S. Department of the Army. *Field Manual No. 3-24 and Marine Corps Warfighting Publication No. 3-33.5: Counterinsurgency.* Washington, DC: U.S. Army, Training and Doctrine Command, 2006.

U.S. Department of Defense. *Joint Publication 3-24: Counterinsurgency Operations.* Washington, DC: Department of Defense Joint Staff, 2009.

Internal Macedonian Revolutionary Organization

A prominent precursor of modern insurgency organizations in both its organization and objectives, the Internal Macedonian Revolutionary Organization (IMRO; in Macedonian, Vatreshna Makedonska Revolyutsionna Organizatsiya) was established in 1893 with the goal of securing Macedonian independence from the Ottoman Empire. Commencing in 1896, the IMRO undertook guerrilla operations and within a few years had secured a degree of control in much of the Macedonian countryside, including tax collection.

These early gains were lost in 1903, however, when the IMRO mounted an ill-advised general revolt against Ottoman rule. This so-called Ilinden-Preobrazhenie Uprising involved as many as 15,000 IMRO irregulars and 40,000 Ottoman troops. The revolt ended in failure, with the Ottomans laying waste to some 100 villages. What remained of the IMRO then went over to small guerrilla operations, mounted largely from bases in Bulgaria.

The movement fragmented after World War I (1914–1918) and resorted largely to terrorist activities, including the assassinations of Bulgarian prime minister Aleksandar Stamboliyski in 1923 and King Alexander I of Yugoslavia during a visit to France in 1934. The latter deed brought Bulgarian Army destruction of the IMRO base at Petrich in southwestern Bulgaria, largely ending IMRO influence.

Spencer C. Tucker

Further Reading

Perry, Duncan. *The Politics of Terror: The Macedonian Liberation Movements, 1893–1903.* Durham, NC: Duke University Press, 1988

Intifada, First

Start Date: 1987
End Date: 1993

A spontaneous protest movement by Palestinians against Israeli rule and an effort to establish a Palestinian homeland through a series of demonstrations, improvised attacks, and riots. The First Intifada (the Arab term *intifada* means "the act of shaking off") began in December 1987 and ended in 1993 with the signing of the Oslo Accords and the creation of the Palestinian Authority (PA).

The founding of Israel in 1948 created a situation in which Palestinians and citizens of the new Israeli state occupied the same land but under Israeli control. This basic reality would remain the most contentious issue in the region for decades to come and also led to an emerging Palestinian national consciousness that called for the destruction of Israel. The anti-Israeli sentiment was generally shared by other Arab nations and the Arab world at large. Years of active discontent among Palestinians and the Arab populations near or inside Israel led to the establishment of either de jure or de facto draconian civil and criminal enforcement practices in Israel against Palestinians. These included alleged torture, summary executions, mass detentions, and the destruction of property and homes.

Already badly strained relations were pushed to the limit on October 1, 1987, when Israeli soldiers ambushed and killed seven Palestinian men from Gaza who were alleged to have been members of the Palestinian terrorist organization Islamic Jihad. Days later, an Israeli settler shot a Palestinian schoolgirl in the back. With violence against Israelis by Palestinians also on the increase, a wider conflict may have been inevitable.

The tension mounted as the year drew to a close. On December 4, an Israeli salesman was found murdered in Gaza. On December 6, an Israel Defense Forces (IDF) truck struck a van, killing its four Palestinian occupants. That same day, sustained and heavy violence involving several hundred Palestinians occurred in the Jabalya refugee camp, where the four Palestinians who died in the traffic accident had lived. The unrest spread quickly and eventually involved other refugee camps. By the end of December, violence was occurring in Jerusalem. The Israelis reacted with a heavy hand, which did nothing but fan the flames of Palestinian outrage. On December 22, 1987, the United Nations (UN) Security Council officially denounced the Israeli reaction to the unrest, which had taken the lives of scores of Palestinians.

The escalating spiral of violence resulted in the First Intifada, a series of Palestinian protests, demonstrations, and ad hoc attacks whose manifestations ranged from youths throwing rocks at Israeli troops to demonstrations by women's organizations. Along with general strikes and boycotts, these caused such disruption to the Israeli state that the government responded with military force. The violence escalated. While the Palestinians had initially relied on rocks, they were soon hurling Molotov cocktails and grenades. In the meantime, Israeli defense minister Yitzhak Rabin exhorted the IDF to "break the bones" of demonstrators. Rabin's tactics brought more international condemnation and strained ties with he United States. Moshe Arens, who succeeded Rabin in 1990, seemed better able to understand both the root of the uprising and the best ways of subduing it. Indeed, the number of Palestinians and Israelis killed declined during the period 1990–1993. However, the intifada itself seemed to be running out of steam after 1990, and violence among Palestinians themselves was on the increase.

In the early 1990s, the Palestine Liberation Organization (PLO) officially abandoned the goal of destroying Israel. Despite continued violence on the part of the Harakat al-Muqawama al-Islamiyya (Movement of Islamic Resistance), known as Hamas, on September 13, 1993, Rabin, now prime minister, and PLO chairman Yasser Arafat signed the historic Oslo Accords in Washington, D.C. The accords, which brought both Rabin and Arafat the Nobel Peace Prize, called for a five-year transition period during which the Gaza Strip and the West Bank would be jointly controlled by Israel and the PA, with power eventually to be turned over to the Palestinian people.

The First Intifada caused both civil destruction and humanitarian suffering but also produced gains for the Palestinian people. First, the intifada solidified and brought into focus a clear national consciousness for the Palestinian people and made statehood a clear national objective. Second, the intifada cast Israeli policy toward Palestine in a negative light internationally, especially with the killing of Palestinian children, and thus rekindled public and political dialogue on the Arab-Israeli conflict across other Middle Eastern states as well as Europe and the United States. Third, the intifada helped to bring the PLO out of its Tunisian exile. Finally, the intifada cost Israel hundreds of millions of dollars in lost imports and tourism.

At the time the Oslo Accords were signed in September 1993, the six-year-long First Intifada resulted in the deaths of some 1,160 Palestinians, of which 241 were children. On the Israeli side, 160 died, 5 of whom were children. Clearly, the IDF's inexperience in widespread riot control had contributed to the high death toll, for in the first 13 months of the intifada alone, more than 330 Palestinians were killed. Indeed, the policies and performance of the IDF split Israeli public opinion and also invited international scrutiny.

In 2000, a new wave of violent Palestinian protest broke out and would eventually become known as the Second (al-Aqsa) Intifada.

Paul G. Pierpaoli Jr.

See also Arafat, Yasser; Intifada, Second; Palestine Liberation Organization

Further Reading

Peretz, Don. *Intifada: The Palestinian Uprising.* Boulder, CO: Westview, 1990.

Said, W. Edward. *Intifada: The Palestinian Uprising against Israeli Occupation.* Boston: South End Press, 1989.

Schiff, Ze'Ev, and Ehud Ya'Ari. *Intifada: The Palestinian Uprising—Israel's Third Front.* New York: Simon and Schuster, 1990.

Intifada, Second

Start Date: 2000
End Date: 2005

A popular Palestinian uprising and period of enhanced Israeli-Palestinian hostilities during 2000–2005. The Second Intifada followed the collapse that summer of the

Camp David peace talks to resolve the Palestinian issue. The Second Intifada is also known as the al-Aqsa Intifada because it began at the al-Aqsa Mosque in the Old City of Jerusalem.

On September 28, 2000, Israeli Likud Party leader Ariel Sharon, accompanied by a party delegation and 1,500 police and security forces, entered the Haram al-Sharif complex, the area of Jerusalem's Old City, also called the Temple Mount, where the al-Aqsa mosque and the Dome of the Rock are located. The enclave is one of Islam's three most holy sites and is sacred to Jews as well. Sharon claimed that he was investigating Israeli complaints that Muslims were damaging archaeological remains below the surface of the Temple Mount. By agreement, at the time this area was supervised by Palestinian rather than Israeli security.

Palestinians held that Sharon's action demonstrated Israeli contempt for limited Palestinian sovereignty and for Muslims in general. Soon riots and demonstrations erupted. Israeli troops launched attacks in Gaza, and on September 30, television footage showed the shooting of an unarmed 12-year-old boy, Muhammad Durrah, hiding behind his father as Israeli forces attacked. Muslim protests now grew more violent and involved Israeli Arabs as well as Palestinians. Stores and banks were burned in Arab communities.

Thousands of Israelis also attacked Arabs, destroying Arab property in Tel Aviv and Nazareth over the Jewish holiday of Yom Kippur. On October 12, two Israeli reservists were lynched by a mob at the Ramallah police station, further inflaming Israeli public opinion. In retaliation, Israel launched a series of air strikes against Palestinians.

On October 17, Israeli and Palestinian officials signed the Sharm el-Sheikh agreement to end the violence, but it continued nevertheless. Sharon's election as prime minister in February 2001 heightened Israel's hard-line tactics toward the Palestinians, such as the use of U.S.-supplied F-16 aircraft for the first time. Both Palestinians and Israelis admitted that the high hopes of the Oslo period were over. Some Palestinians characterized their response as the warranted resistance of an embittered population who had received no positive assurances of sovereignty from years of negotiations. Others began or encouraged suicide attacks, as in the June 1, 2001, attack on Israelis waiting to enter a Tel Aviv discotheque and another attack on a Jerusalem restaurant on August 9, 2001. While various Palestinian organizations laid claim to some of the attacks, the degree of organizational control over the bombers and issues such as payments to families of the martyrs remain in dispute.

The attacks in public places terrified Israelis. Those in modest economic circumstances had to use public transportation, but most malls, movie theaters, stores, and children's centers hired security guards. Israeli authorities soon began a heightened campaign of targeted assassinations of Palestinian leaders. Some political figures began to call for complete segregation, or separation, of Arabs and Israelis, even within the Green Line (the 1967 border). This would be enforced by a security wall and even population transfers, which would involve evicting Arab villagers and urban residents from Israel in some areas and forcing them to move to the West Bank.

A virulent campaign against Palestine Liberation Organization (PLO) chairman and president of the Palestinian Authority (PA) Yasser Arafat began in Israel with American assent, complicating the negotiations between the two sides. Israelis charged Arafat with corruption and with supporting the intifada. Some Israelis argued that he had actually planned the intifada. In May 2001, however, when the Israel Defense Forces (IDF) captured the ship *Santorini* filled with weapons purchased by Ahmed Jibril, head of the Popular Front for the Liberation of Palestine's General Command (a PLO faction that did not accept the Oslo Accords) and with the January 2002 capture of the *Karine-A,* a vessel carrying weapons allegedly from Iran, the Israeli anti-Arafat campaign increased.

The regional response to the intifada consisted of cautious condemnation by Egypt and Jordan, which had concluded peace agreements with Israel, and calls of outrage from other more hard-line states such as Syria. In February 2002 Crown Prince Abdullah of Saudi Arabia called for Arabs to fully normalize relations with Israel in return for that country's withdrawal from the Occupied Territories. This plan was formally endorsed at an Arab League Summit in Beirut in March, although Israeli authorities prohibited Arafat from attending the summit. Israeli authorities never acknowledged the proposal.

Instead, in response to a suicide bomber's attack on the Netanya Hotel on March 28, 2002, in which 30 Israeli civilians died, the Israeli military began a major military assault on the West Bank. The PA headquarters was targeted, and international negotiations became necessary when militants took refuge in the Church of the Nativity in Bethlehem. Investigation of charges of a massacre in an IDF assault on Jenin revealed a smaller death count of 55.

The Israeli military response to the intifada did not convince Palestinians to relinquish their aims of sovereignty and seemed to spark more suicide attacks rather than discouraging them. In March 2003 Mahmoud Abbas became the first Palestinian prime minister of the PA because the United States refused to recognize or deal with Arafat. On April 30, 2003, the European Union, the United States, Russia, and the United Nations announced the so-called Road Map for Peace plan that was to culminate in an independent Palestinian state.

The plan did not unfold as designed, however, and in response to an Israeli air strike intended to kill Abd al-Aziz al-Rantissi, the leader of Hamas, militants launched a bus bombing in Jerusalem. At the end of the June 2003 Palestinian militants agreed to a truce, which lasted for seven weeks (longer on the part of certain groups). There was no formal declaration that the intifada had ceased, and additional Israeli assassinations of Palestinian leaders continued, as did suicide attacks. Nevertheless, since 2004 Hamas has respected the cease-fire, and the issues of Israeli withdrawal from Gaza, Arafat's November 2004 death, Palestinian elections, and the Israeli response to their outcome took the spotlight in late 2004 and 2005.

Casualty numbers for the Second Intifada are disputed. Approximately 1,000 Israelis died and 6,700 more were wounded by September 2004. The Israelis reported that by 2003, 2,124 Palestinians had been killed, but a U.S. source reported that by 2005, 4,099 Palestinians had been killed and 30,527 were wounded. Israel's tourism sector also suffered considerably at a time when inflation and unemployment were already problematic.

One outcome of the Second Intifada in the global context of the September 11, 2001, terror attacks on the United States was that Israeli officials have tended to brand all Palestinian resistance, indeed all activity on behalf of Palestinians, as terrorism. The intifada also served to strengthen the ranks of those Israelis who call for separation, rather than integration, of Israelis with Arabs. There was thus widespread support for the construction of the security barrier known as the Israeli Security Fence, which effectively cuts thousands of Palestinians off from their daily routes to work or school.

The Second Intifada dismayed Israeli peace activists and discouraged independent efforts by Israelis and Palestinians to engage in meaningful dialogue. The intifada also had deleterious effects on Palestinians who had hoped for normalcy in the West Bank, particularly since 85 percent of those in Gaza and 58 percent in the West Bank lived in poverty. This was abetted by the IDF's destruction of housing units, although only 10 percent of the individuals involved were in fact implicated in violence or illegal activity.

Another outcome of the Second Intifada was its highlighting of intra-Palestinian conflict, including between the Tunis PLO elements of the PA and the younger leaders who emerged within the Occupied Territories, between Fatah and Hamas, and between Fatah and the al-Aqsa Martyrs Brigades. The conflict also resulted in discord in the Arab world.

Sherifa Zuhur

See also Arafat, Yasser; Harakat al-Jihad al-Islami fi Filastin; Intifada, First; Palestine Liberation Organization

Further Reading

Baroud, Ramzy, et al. *The Second Palestinian Intifada: A Chronicle of a People Struggle.* London: Pluto, 2006.

Bucaille, Laetitia. *Growing Up Palestinian and the Intifada Generation.* Translated by Anthony Roberts. Princeton, NJ: Princeton University Press, 2004.

Iraq Insurgency

Start Date: 2003
End Date: 2011

On March 19, 2003, in Operation IRAQI FREEDOM (OIF), an international coalition led by the United States invaded Iraq to topple the regime of Iraqi president Saddam

Hussein. Some 200,000 U.S. and allied troops, supported by air and naval forces, overwhelmed the Iraqi defenders, and major combat operations were declared at an end on May 1. An Iraqi insurgency then occurred, at first targeting coalition forces and then spiraling into sectarian violence between Sunni, Shia, and Kurdish populations inflamed by the terrorist organization Al Qaeda in Iraq. U.S. forces formally withdrew from Iraq in December 2011, but Al Qaeda in Iraq is still extant.

The March 2003 invasion was accompanied by the dissolution of Iraqi institutions and society, all of which had been tightly controlled by Hussein. Massive looting, the loss of public services, the lack of humanitarian assistance or planning for Phase IV postconflict operations, the mistaken U.S. policy of removing from all influence Hussein's Baath Party, and the opposition to the coalition invasion by the minority Sunni population, many of whom were loyal to Saddam, all initially fueled the opposition and laid the foundation for the insurgency from 2003 until 2006. Former Baathists and the Fedayeen Saddam ("Saddam's Men of Sacrifice"), paramilitary fighters loyal to Hussein, sparked the initial insurgency under the group al-Awda ("The Return"), personally led by Hussein until his capture by U.S. forces in Operation IRON HAMMER on December 13, 2003.

Iraqi Sunnis in particular were the most virulent in opposition to the occupiers, and many former members of the army, which the United States mistakenly disbanded, turned to guerrilla warfare. A favored tactic was the employment of more powerful improvised explosive devices (IEDs) in the form of roadside bombs targeting coalition patrols. Although guerrilla attacks in the early days of the war were not particularly sophisticated, they heightened tensions between Iraqis and coalition forces. The latter's reaction to the attacks, including detentions and destruction of some structures and crops to reduce cover for ambushes as well as the employment of artillery fire that inflicted civilian casualties in response to IED attacks, garnered further support for the insurgents.

Beginning in late 2003, foreign fighters and those supported by Iran and Syria more aggressively infiltrated the Sunni, Baathist, and Fedayeen resistance groups. Additionally, at this stage Al Qaeda elements and Islamists merged with the indigenous insurgency, as was shown in the introduction of suicide bombings. Attacks against a hotel housing United Nations officials, the employment of car bombs against personnel of the International Red Cross, and other such international targets indicated an enemy willing to conduct terrorist-style attacks, as opposed to waging strictly guerrilla warfare. Known as the Ramadan Offensive, this stage was led by Abu Musab al-Zarqawi, the leader of Tawhid wal-Jihad.

By the spring of 2004, fighting in the Sunni areas of the cities of Tikrit, Ramadi, and Fallujah was paralleled by a distinct and separate insurgency in the majority Shia areas such as Najaf and Basra as well as predominantly Shia neighborhoods in Baghdad. This was in part fueled by discontent over the occupation and growing sectarian violence fomented by elements of the embryonic Al Qaeda in Iraq organization. The principal leader of the Shia insurgency was Muqtada al-Sadr,

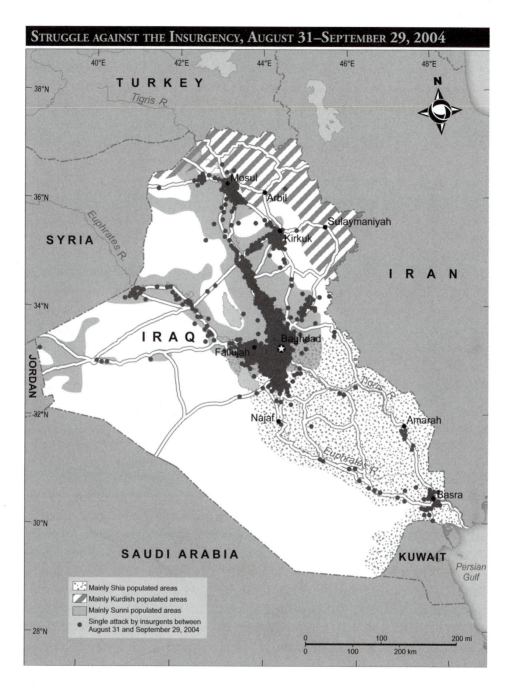

STRUGGLE AGAINST THE INSURGENCY, AUGUST 31–SEPTEMBER 29, 2004

Mainly Shia populated areas
Mainly Kurdish populated areas
Mainly Sunni populated areas
Single attack by insurgents between
August 31 and September 29, 2004

who established the Shia militia known as the Mahdi Army. Additionally, al-Sadr's camp fought a rival Shia and political group vying for power. Only after the deaths of several thousand Mahdi militiamen and civilians did al-Sadr negotiate settlements with the provisional Iraqi government in June 2004 and in 2005.

Meanwhile, the Sunni insurgency intensified, forcing Operation VIGILANT RESOLVE (First Battle of Fallujah), a U.S. Marine Corps–led operation in April 2004 to clear the entire Sunni-dominated city of Fallujah. The insurgents massed more than 2,000 fighters, divided in small-size units and employing urban guerrilla tactics. At the same time, other insurgents attacked coalition positions in Ramadi. Operation VIGILANT RESOLVE lasted from April 4 to May 1 and cleared most of Fallujah, but the city remained a sanctuary for Sunni insurgents as well as Abu Musab al-Zarqawi's fighters. The insurgents also established safe havens in the Sunni-predominant cities of Baquba, Samarra, and Ramadi.

The transfer of power from the Coalition Provisional Authority to the Iraqis in 2004 did not end the insurgency. Al-Sadr's Mahdi Army reengaged coalition forces in the Shiite holy city of Najaf, and a prolonged battle over the holy shrine of Imam Ali lasted several weeks. Only after several coalition operations and negotiations between the Iraqi interim government and Mahdi leadership was another truce arranged in Sadr City. Critically, in October 2004 Zarqawi's militia pledged allegiance to Al Qaeda leader Osama bin Laden and declared itself Al Qaeda in Iraq. It became the deadliest element of the Iraqi Sunni insurgency, tapping into international Al Qaeda networks to secure fighters, weapons, and financial support.

Coalition forces responded to violence in key Sunni areas by multibattalion operations in such locations as Samarra, Fallujah, and Babil. Operation PHANTOM FURY (Second Battle of Fallujah), which took place during November 7–December 23, 2004, pitted some 5,000 U.S., 2,000 Iraqi, and 850 British troops against 5,000–10,000 insurgents. Coalition forces telegraphed their intentions in advance, encouraging civilians to flee in anticipation of the battle, which allowed the coalition to employ air strikes and artillery fire prior to the ground penetration of the city. The insurgents employed guerrilla-style tactics as well as IEDs placed on corpses and in homes. Snipers, mortars, car bombs, and individual suicide bombers were also commonly employed, claiming U.S. casualties of 95 killed and 560 wounded, Iraqi Army losses of 8 killed and 43 wounded, and British casualties of 4 killed and 10 wounded. Some 1,200–1,500 insurgents were killed, and 1,500 were captured. Eight hundred civilians also died.

The Iraqi elections of 2005 brought Kurdish and Shiite control of the Iraqi government, but the Sunnis, many of whom had boycotted the election, felt further disenfranchised. The insurgency took a particularly nasty turn by actively targeting civilians in roadside bombings, suicide bombings, and indirect-fire attacks, directly correlating with the rise of Al Qaeda in Iraq. Sectarian violence heightened, with the majority of the insurgents drawn from Sunni areas of the country and with the Iraqi government dominated by Shia and Kurds. Even with the death of Zarqawi in 2006, violence soared, and there was an influx of foreign fighters from Egypt, Syria, and other Arab states. Attacks, such as the bombing by Al Qaeda in Iraq against the holy Shia al-Askari Mosque, fueled the sectarian divide and resulted in thousands of Sunni and Shia civilian deaths.

Meanwhile, Al Qaeda in Iraq had taken control of the Sunni insurgency in Anbar Province in western Iraq, pushing aside tribal leaders and former Baathists and eventually causing a rift between the extremist Salafi fighters and Iraqi Sunnis. The accompanying civilian violence and aggressiveness of the Al Qaeda and foreign insurgents backfired, however, bringing the Sunni Awakening movement in 2006.

Led by influential Anbar Province tribal leaders and supported by Lieutenant General David H. Petreaus, commander of the Multinational Force–Iraq, the Awakening movement turned the tide against Al Qaeda in Iraq and is credited with ending the insurgency in many Sunni areas.

Despite a reduction in violence since 2008, increased participation of all Iraqi sects in the national government, and the formal departure of U.S. forces in December 2011, hostilities continue. Some elements of Al Qaeda in Iraq remain active, and concerns abound regarding the demonstrated Shia determination to control the government at the expense of Sunnis and Kurds, Iranian influence, Muqtada al-Sadr's Mahdi Army, the Sons of Iraq, and Shia and other militias.

Larissa Mihalisko

See also Petraeus, David Howell

Further Reading

Gordon, Michael R., and Bernard E. Trainor. *The Endgame: The Inside Story of the Struggle for Iraq, from George W. Bush to Barack Obama.* New York: Pantheon, 2012.

Hashim, Ahmed. *Insurgency and Counter-Insurgency in Iraq.* Ithaca, NY: Cornell University Press, 2006.

Kilcullen, David. *The Accidental Guerrilla: Fighting Small Wars in the Midst of a Big One.* New York: Oxford University Press, 2009.

Montgomery, Gary W., and Timothy S. McWilliams. *Al Anbar Awakening: Iraqi Perspectives,* Vol. 2. Quantico, VA: Marine Corps University Press, 2009.

Iraq Revolt

Start Date: July 1920
End Date: October 1920

In accordance with agreements between Britain and France during World War I (1914–1918), confirmed by the Paris Peace Conference of 1919, Britain secured control of Iraq as a League of Nations mandate. This was in sharp variance with the British pledge of support for Arab independence made during the Arab Revolt of 1916–1918 against the Ottoman Empire.

Dissatisfaction with the state of affairs led to peaceful protests against British rule in Baghdad in May 1920. British commissioner Sir Arnold Wilson dismissed the Iraqi demands. The revolt officially began in July with an armed clash in Mosul in northern Iraq and then spread southward. Subsequently known to Iraqis as the Great Iraqi Revolution, it was led by Arab nationalists who sought full independence and Arab rule. Sunni and Shia Muslims made common cause against the British.

The British dispatched reinforcements from both India and Persia (present-day Iran) that ultimately reached more than 29,000 men in four divisions. The British were also able to exploit tribal divisions, as some tribes opposed the revolt. The troops finally put down the rebellion after some three months, thanks in large part to the dispatch to Iraq of Royal Air Force bombers. The Iraq Revolt claimed Arab casualties of as many as 9,000 dead. British losses were some 400 dead, 600 missing, and as many as 1,800 wounded.

Because crushing the revolt was costly in both manpower and economically, the British sought an arrangement that would assure them control at the least cost to British taxpayers. The British then replaced the military regime with a provisional Arab government, which was indirectly controlled by the British. In August 1921 the British proclaimed Faisal, the former king of Syria who had been expelled by the French, as the king of Iraq. The new Iraqi government, however, consisted chiefly of Sunnis, with Shia Muslims largely unrepresented.

Spencer C. Tucker

See also Aircraft in Counterinsurgency Operations; Arab Revolt against Ottoman Rule

Further Reading

Jeffrey, Keith. *The British Army and the Crisis of Empire, 1918–1922.* Manchester, UK: Manchester University Press, 1984

Ireland Revolutionary Era

Start Date: 1912
End Date: 1923

Great Britain reconquered Ireland at the end of the 16th century and in the early 17th century, in the Act of Union (1800), Ireland was joined with Great Britain to constitute the United Kingdom of Great Britain and Ireland. Centuries of British rule that included actions against the Catholic Church, absentee British landlords, and the great Irish Potato Famine (1845–1852) all fueled demands by many Irish for home rule. Unionists—mostly Protestant Englishmen and Scots who had settled in northern Ireland in the so-called Plantation of Ulster—opposed this, seeing in it a step toward independence. The ensuing sectarian violence would last for much of the 20th century.

Irish prisoners move along a Dublin quay under British guard during the bloody, and ultimately unsuccessful, Irish Easter Rising (Easter Rebellion) of April 24–29, 1916. (Library of Congress)

The period from roughly 1912 to 1923 might be called the Irish Revolutionary Era for its widespread political, ethnic, and sectarian strife. The era saw three distinct constituent conflicts: the Easter Rising (1916), the Irish War for Independence (1919–1921), and the Irish Civil War (1922–1923).

The Irish National Volunteers formed in November 1913 to support the passage of a home rule bill for Ireland and in response to threats from northern militants opposed to it. Republicans within the 100,000-man organization broke away in September 1914 when the Irish National Volunteers decided to support the United Kingdom in World War I (1914–1918). The new group, under the leadership of Eóin MacNeill, became the Irish Volunteers, while the original group was known as the National Volunteers. At their height, the Irish Volunteers numbered some 14,000 men. Unconcerned with numbers, they began a revolt against British rule without majority support of the populace.

The Easter Rising

The ensuing Easter Rising (April 24–29, 1916) was planned and executed by the Irish Republican Brotherhood (IRB), employing the Irish Volunteers and a Socialist group called the Irish Citizen Army (ICA). The IRB had infiltrated the Irish Volunteers at every level and steered that group to the uprising.

The IRB plan was to use the annual Easter parade of the Irish Volunteers in Dublin as cover. Just days before, chief of staff of the Irish Volunteers MacNeill, not an IRB member, learned of the plan and called a halt to it. This precipitated a series of orders and counterorders by MacNeill and his deputy (and IRB leader) Padraig Pearse, with the result that few Irish Volunteers arrived, even after the attack was delayed until Easter Monday.

Pearse decided to go through with the action despite learning that a German ship carrying arms for the rebels had been seized and that nominal leader Sir Roger Casement had been taken prisoner. Remarkably, the rebellion still caught the British authorities by surprise.

The uprising began when the Irish Volunteers and the ICA seized strategic points throughout Dublin, including the General Post Office, which served as their headquarters, on Monday, April 24. However, they failed to take Dublin Castle (seat of the Irish administration), Trinity College, and the train terminals, which were also key locations.

Several days passed before the British Army could gather sufficient forces to conduct a robust counterattack. Although suffering heavy casualties, the British systematically reduced the rebel strong points, with the primary surrender occurring on April 29. Although the uprising was over, it had lasting impact.

The army's immediate response was to try 161 participants, sentencing 66 to death. Fifteen were shot before British prime minister Herbert Asquith ordered a halt. Additionally, some 3,000 men were interned in camps and prisons in Britain.

Any initial goodwill for the British action faded rapidly when the army treated Dublin as an occupied enemy city. There was also outrage over what appeared to be secret executions after seemingly dubious trials. Public support soon shifted to the rebels. The prisoners were released by 1917. They then took over the republican Sinn Féin party. Working to get their candidates elected to Parliament, they secured more than 70 percent of the Irish seats in December 1918.

The Irish War for Independence

The Irish War for Independence (1919–1921) began in January 1919 with a lethal ambush by Irish Volunteers of a cartload of explosives bound for the quarry at Soloheadbeg, County Tipperary, that killed two policemen. That same day, the newly elected Sinn Féin members of the British Parliament formed in Dublin the Dáil Éireann (Assembly of Ireland) and declared independence from the United Kingdom. This new struggle was considerably different from that of its predecessors. The struggle became a slow and methodical fight for control of the Irish people as much as for territory.

In 1919 the Irish Volunteers began attacking the Royal Irish Constabulary (RIC), the national police of Ireland. With the British cabinet reluctant to employ military force, the job of restoring peace fell to the police. The newly reconstituted Irish Volunteers under Michael Collins and Richard Mulcahy targeted the RIC as the symbol of British authority in Ireland and in order to secure arms.

The Irish Volunteers applied social and economic pressures against the police and their families, which sometimes turned violent. In republican areas, the campaign worked well; in Unionist areas, it failed. The effort was sufficiently effective, however, that by the end of 1919, the RIC had lost almost 20 percent of its numbers through resignation and retirement. Furthermore, the recruiting pool shrank. When the RIC began to close its outlying stations to concentrate police power in the larger towns, London finally authorized recruitment of World War I veterans from Britain into the force. They became known as the Black and Tans, after their polyglot uniforms. Sent directly into the existing force with little training, they began to arrive in March 1920. Their numbers proved to be insufficient, however. The British government then recruited, beginning in the summer of 1920, another police group, known as the Auxiliary Division of the RIC (ADRIC). The ADRIC soon earned a reputation for brutality and atrocity.

With army support, in the autumn of 1920 the reinforced police struck out into the countryside they had abandoned months before. This put many Irish Volunteer leaders on the run but also forced them into the role of full-time insurgents. Although fighting was sporadic, the Irish Volunteers struck back in November and December 1920. The year ended with increasing casualties on both sides and no end in sight.

The new year brought little change except that the British Army received a mandate to engage in combat operations against the Irish Volunteers, now called the Irish Republican Army (IRA), but this had little effect beyond an increase in violence. Both sides were preparing for increased fighting when in July 1921, the politicians declared a truce. Negotiations followed during the next five months, with the Anglo-Irish Treaty formally ending the war on December 6, 1921.

The new treaty partitioned Ireland. Southern Ireland became independent, while the six northern and primarily Protestant counties were formed into the state of Northern Ireland; it continued as part of the United Kingdom.

The Irish Civil War

The treaty was not a month old when hard-line republicans began to agitate against it in the Dáil Éireann ratification debates, which raged for weeks before it was finally approved by a margin of only seven votes in January 1922. This caused a split in the republican camp, with the antitreaty republican side maintaining that those who had voted for it were traitors because the treaty did not allow a republic and kept Ireland within the British Commonwealth. As the Free Staters formed a government, the IRA prepared to fight. Both sides took provocative actions, but neither seemed eager to fight their former comrades. In February 1922 a large group of IRA members seized the Four Courts complex, the seat of the judiciary, in Dublin and began to fortify it. Leaders on both sides then agreed to allow the people of Ireland to decide through the results of the June 1922 general elections. An overwhelming 73 percent of the vote went to protreaty candidates, whereupon the IRA rejected the result. The Irish Civil War (1922–1923) began within days.

By July 1922, the Free State National Army had retaken the Four Courts and imprisoned hundreds of IRA men. In August, Griffith died of natural causes, and the IRA assassinated Michael Collins, who had participated in the treaty negotiations. The fighting escalated for several months before the antitreaty IRA began losing popular support and finally gave up in the spring of 1923. The bitterness lasted for decades.

The Irish Revolutionary Era was rife with violence but never really reached the intensity of other insurgencies and revolutions, being restricted largely to acts of intimidation, ambushes, and assassinations. It was, however, the first modern insurgency of the 20th century and served as a model to some. A number of ADRIC members subsequently joined the British police in Palestine.

William H. Kautt

See also Black and Tans and the Auxiliaries; Collins, Michael; Irish Republican Army; Royal Irish Constabulary

Further Reading

Hopkinson, Michael A. *The Irish War of Independence.* Ithaca, NY: McGill-Queen's University Press, 2002.

Kautt, W. H. *Ambushes & Armour: The Irish Rebellion, 1919–1921.* Dublin: Irish Academic Press, 2010.

McGarry, Fearghal. *The Rising: Ireland, Easter 1916.* Oxford: Oxford University Press, 2010.

Stewart, A. T. Q. *The Ulster Crisis: Resistance to Home Rule, 1912–14.* London: Faber and Faber, 1967.

Townshend, Charles. *Britain's Civil Wars: Counterinsurgency in the Twentieth Century.* London: Faber and Faber, 1986.

Townshend, Charles. *The British Campaign in Ireland, 1919–1921: The Development of Political and Military Policies.* Oxford: Oxford University Press, 1975.

Irgun Tsvai Leumi

The Irgun Tsvai Leumi (National Military Organization) was a right-wing paramilitary Zionist underground insurgent movement in Palestine during 1931–1948. Later it was better known as Etzel, for its contracted Hebrew initials. Irgun was known for launching immediate and harsh retaliatory attacks on persons or organizations initiating violence against the Jewish community in Palestine and for its advocacy of military action against the British, who controlled Palestine under a League of Nations mandate until May 1948. The British categorized Irgun as a terrorist organization.

Even as the British slowly shifted their support to Palestine's Arab population in the 1930s, the leadership of the Jewish Agency for Palestine, in particular David Ben-Gurion, continued to work closely with the British to promote the interests of the Jewish population. Haganah, the Jewish self-defense organization, supported this position through its military strategy of havlaga, or self-restraint. Some Haganah members rejected this approach, however, given Britain's pro-Arab bias. A minority, led by Avraham Tehomi, left Haganah in 1931 and formed Irgun.

Irgun was based on premises formulated by Ze'ev Jabotinsky, who had led the Jewish Legion that had fought with the British against the Ottoman Turks in Palestine during World War I (1914–1918). Jabotinsky held that swift retaliatory action would forestall Arab attacks on the Jewish community. By 1936, Irgun was largely controlled by Jabotinsky's extremist nationalist Revisionist Zionists (Revisionist Party), which had seceded from the World Zionist Organization and advocated creation by force of a Jewish homeland spanning both banks of the Jordan River.

When Arab attacks during the Arab Revolt of 1936–1939 killed a number of Jews, Irgun launched retaliatory attacks against Arabs, utilizing car bombs in areas of high Arab congregation. These endured until the beginning of World War II (1939–1945) and killed as many as 250 Arab civilians. Irgun, which considered the British mandatory government to be illegal under international law, also directed acts of terrorism and assassination against the British. When the British White Paper of 1939 openly shifted British support away from the Jews to the Arabs by severely restricting Jewish immigration, settlement, and land purchases in Palestine, Irgun focused on attacking British military installations and interests. Its rationale for these attacks was that the new and more severe British restrictions on Jewish immigration from Europe were contributing to Nazi Germany's genocide against Jews (the Holocaust).

During 1941–1943, Irgun suspended its attacks on British interests and supported the Allies against Germany and its Arab allies in the Middle East. However, a small group known as Lohamei Herut Israel (Fighters for the Freedom of Israel), also known as Lehi or the Stern Gang, for its leader Avraham Stern, separated from Irgun in 1941 and continued to attack the British in Palestine. Led by Menachem Begin during 1943–1948, Lehi declared war against the British in February 1944 and resumed attacks on Arab villages and British interests.

On November 6, 1944, in Cairo, Lehi assassinated Walter Edward Guinness, Lord Moyne, the British minister resident in the Middle East. The murder was allegedly in retaliation for the 1939 White Paper's restrictions on Jewish immigration that were allegedly contributing to the deaths of Jews in the Holocaust. At that point, the more moderate Haganah and the Jewish Agency for Palestine launched Operation SEZON (HUNTING SEASON), a campaign against Irgun and Lehi. The British ultimately arrested and jailed about 1,000 Irgun and Lehi members.

Irgun, Lehi, and Haganah allied during October 1944–July 1945 as the Jewish Resistance Movement to fight against British restrictions on Jewish immigration. This alliance ended in August 1945 after Irgun bombed the British military, police, and civil headquarters at the King David Hotel in Jerusalem, killing 91 people on July 22, 1946. Begin and Irgun claimed to have issued three warnings in an attempt to limit casualties. Nevertheless, the British arrested, tried, convicted, and hanged several members of Irgun. When Irgun responded by hanging two British sergeants, the executions stopped, although British arrests of Irgun members continued. On May 5, 1947, Haganah and Irgun combined forces to breach the wall of the supposedly secure British prison at Akko (Acre), freeing 251 prisoners.

In anticipation of and following the partition of Palestine in 1947, from July 1947 to June 1948 Irgun and Haganah increasingly coordinated their forces. Irgun's greatest victory and largest operation was the capture of the Arab city of Jaffa. On May 28, 1948, the provisional government of the newly declared State of Israel transformed Haganah into its national military, the Israel Defense Forces (IDF), and outlawed all other armed forces. In September 1948 the military activities of Irgun were folded into the IDF. Begin meanwhile adapted what remained of the movement into a political party that was the precursor of the Herut (Freedom) Party, which merged in 1965 with the Liberal Party to form the Gahal Party. The Gahal Party served as the foundation for today's Likud Party.

Richard M. Edwards

See also Arab Revolt of 1936; Lohamei Herut Israel; Stern, Avraham

Further Reading

Begin, Menachem. *The Revolt.* Los Angeles: Nash, 1972.

Bell, J. Bowyer. *Terror Out of Zion: Irgun Zvai Leumi, Lehi and the Palestine Underground, 1929–1949.* New York: St. Martin's, 1979.

Ben Ami, Yitshaq. *Years of Wrath, Days of Glory: Memoirs from the Irgun.* New York: R. Speller, 1982.

Levine, David. *The Birth of the Irgun Zvai Leumi: The Jewish Resistance Movement.* Jerusalem: Gefen, 1996.

Irish Republican Army

Irish paramilitary organization, the aim of which was to force home rule and national unity, that is often linked with Sinn Féin. The Irish Republican Army (IRA) descended from the Irish Volunteers, a militia group founded by Irish nationalists in November 1913 during the Home Rule Crisis of 1912–1914. In 1914 the home rule nationalists and the republicans split the Irish Volunteers over the issue of the recruitment of Irishmen for the British Army. The republicans wanted total separation from the United Kingdom.

A small group of Irish Volunteer leaders, who were members of the secretive and radical Irish Republican Brotherhood, organized the 1916 Easter Rebellion (Easter Rising). It failed, but Britain's heavy-handed reaction and in 1918 its plans to introduce conscription in Ireland propelled Sinn Féin to the fore of nationalist groups and helped it win the majority of the Irish seats of Parliament in the December 1918 general election.

In 1919 Sinn Féin claimed to be Ireland's legitimate government, while the IRA openly challenged British security forces. By 1921, the two war-weary sides began negotiations. The Anglo-Irish Treaty of that year granted dominion status to an Irish Free State that would govern Ireland except for six of the eight Ulster counties. Die-hard republicans, however, led by Sinn Féin leader Eamon De Valera, rejected the treaty as a surrender of republican principles and declared themselves Ireland's only legitimate government. In the consequent Irish Civil War (1922–1923) this antitreaty IRA was defeated.

The IRA's fortunes then began a precipitous decline. De Valera abandoned Sinn Féin in 1926 to form Fianna Fáil (Soldiers of Destiny), a political party dedicated to advancing republicanism through conventional political arrangements. In 1932 Fianna Fáil formed a government under De Valera; he rewarded republicans who accepted his constitutionalism and punished those who did not. De Valera banned the IRA in 1936, and two years later the moribund Sinn Féin ceded its political authority to the IRA leadership. Responding to IRA actions in 1939, governments in Dublin, Belfast, and London adopted strong security measures that by 1945 had pushed the IRA to the verge of extinction.

During the next decade strong leadership revived the IRA, but the offensive launched in Northern Ireland in 1956, the so-called Border Campaign, ended ignominiously in 1962. Afterward, a coterie of IRA leaders steeped in revolutionary Marxist theory and attracted to political rather than military action took control of the organization and ousted many of those responsible for the Border Campaign.

The outbreak of sectarian violence in Northern Ireland during the summer of 1969 created another breach in Irish republicanism, yet the IRA's leadership chose to continue in their political direction. In response, those favoring the IRA's traditional military approach—the majority of the IRA, as it turned out—formed the Provisional IRA and the Provisional Sinn Féin in December 1969. The Provos, as they came to be called, almost immediately came to dominate republicanism; for their part, the official IRA dumped its arms in 1972 and faded into relative obscurity by the decade's end. After the split, the term "IRA" actually referred to the Provos.

The Provisional IRA launched a far-reaching campaign of violence, hoping to force a British withdrawal from Northern Ireland, although a lack of modern weapons and a strong British response hampered this effort. Consequently, the IRA adopted the long war strategy in the mid-1970s; thereafter, the Troubles, as the conflict in Ireland and Britain was known, settled into a dispiriting pattern of terrorism, failed negotiations, military operations, and reprisals that led to 3,211 deaths by February 1997.

In the early 1980s the IRA adopted a bullet-and-ballot strategy, thrusting Sinn Féin into conventional politics in Ireland and Northern Ireland while continuing its military operations. This shift eventually caused another split in the republican movement, with the Continuity IRA and the Republican Sinn Féin breaking away in 1986.

By the early 1990s, the IRA–Sinn Féin leadership acknowledged that a military victory was unattainable. Encouraged by Sinn Féin's political successes on both sides of the border, the leadership announced a formal cessation of military operations in 1994. In February 1997 the IRA broke the cease-fire but resumed it after only five months. The 1998 Belfast Agreement guaranteed Sinn Féin a place in Northern Ireland's government and provided for numerous governmental reforms. In 2005 the IRA formally announced the end of its campaign and, under international supervision, destroyed much of its weaponry.

Scott E. Belliveau

See also Collins, Michael; Ireland Revolutionary Era

Further Reading

English, Richard. *Armed Struggle: The History of the IRA*. Oxford: Oxford University Press, 2003.

Kautt, W. H. *Ambushes & Armour: The Irish Rebellion*. Dublin: Irish Academic Press, 2010.

Moloney, Ed. *A Secret History of the IRA*. New York: Norton, 2002.

O'Brien, Brendan. *The Long War: The IRA and Sinn Fein*. 2nd ed. Syracuse, NY: Syracuse University Press, 1999.

Islamic Movement.

See Abu Sayyaf

J

Jacquerie

Start Date: June 1358
End Date: August 1358

Peasant revolt centered in the Oise River Valley north of Paris in 1358. Known in French history as the Jacquerie, it was a reaction to the heavy taxes levied to pay for the Hundred Years' War (1337–1453) against England and especially the ransom of nobles following the English victory in the Battle of Poitiers (September 13, 1356) as well as the pillaging of the countryside by the free companies (discharged mercenary troops) known as Routiers. French King John II had been taken prisoner in the Battle of Poitiers along with many nobles, and central authority had broken down, with the States General largely powerless as the Routiers raped and pillaged. Many peasants blamed the nobility for the disastrous state of affairs in the French countryside.

The revolt began at the village of St. Leu near the Oise River and was centered in the Oise Valley north of Paris. The peasants were led by Guillaume Cale, but the revolt was hardly organized. Its name comes from the noble term for the peasants as "Jacques" or "Jacques Bonhomme," for the padded surplice they wore known as a *jacque.*

The near collapse of authority made the revolt possible. The uprising saw acts of great ferocity on both sides, with the peasants explaining that they were simply carrying out what they had seen others do. Some of the peasants also apparently believed that they might actually be able to do away with the nobility entirely.

The revolt was suppressed by the nobles, led by Charles the Bad of Navarre. The principal battle occurred near Mello on June 10, 1358. Cale had foolishly agreed to talks with the nobles, who then claimed that the laws of chivalry did not apply to one of low birth. The nobles seized and tortured him to death and then decapitated his body. The now leaderless peasant army, which the chronicler Jean Froissart puts at 20,000 men, was then ridden down and destroyed by the mounted knights.

A reign of terror followed that summer in the Beauvais region, with nobles executing large numbers of peasants. Up to 20,000 peasants may have perished, while only a few hundred nobles were victims. An amnesty was declared on August 10, 1358, after which heavy fines were levied on the peasants in the regions that had supported the uprising.

The word *jacquerie* was widely used thereafter both by the French and English to describe a peasant uprising.

Spencer C. Tucker

Further Reading

Bury, J. B. *The Cambridge Medieval History: Decline of Empire and Papacy,* Vol. 7. New York: Macmillan, 1932.

Froissart, Jean. *Chronicles.* London: Penguin, 1978.

Tuchman, Barbara. *A Distant Mirror.* New York: Knopf, 1978.

Jaunissement

French term used to describe the Vietnamization during the 1946–1954 Indochina War. The Elysée Agreements between the French government and the State of Vietnam in March 8, 1949, had called for the creation of the Vietnamese National Army. Paris lauded this as proof that Vietnam was independent, and the agreement helped convince Washington that the war in Indochina had been transformed into a civil war between Vietnamese democrats and Vietnamese Communists rather than a colonial conflict. Proof that the new State of Vietnam was not independent is evident in the fact that the Vietnamese National Army was completely controlled and officered by the French.

The French attitude was shown by French commander in chief in Indochina General Marcel Carpentier when he told U.S. major general Graves B. Erskine that Vietnamese troops would not make good soldiers and were not to be trusted on their own. Erskine said that he replied, "General Carpentier, who in hell are you fighting but Vietnamese?" The French also insisted that all U.S. military support be channeled only to the French. Carpentier said that if this was not done, he would resign within 24 hours.

Carpentier's successor, General Jean de Lattre de Tassigny, pushed *jaunissement,* the creation of wholly Vietnamese units commanded by Vietnamese officers. At the same time, however, he was adamant that France retain overall authority and that the United States channel all aid through the French authorities in Indochina. Perhaps it was already too late. Hopes of the French attracting nationalists to their cause had already been lost, as most Vietnamese nationalists rallied to the Viet Minh.

Spencer C. Tucker

See also Indochina War; Lattre de Tassigny, Jean Joseph Marie Gabriel de

Further Reading

Hammer, Ellen J. *The Struggle for Indochina.* Stanford, CA: Stanford University Press, 1954.

Spector, Ronald H. *Advice and Support: The Early Years, 1941–1960; The U.S. Army in Vietnam.* Washington, DC: U.S. Army Center of Military History, 1983.

Jewish Revolt against Rome

Start Date: 66 CE
End Date: 70 CE

Modern Israel occupies a small land area, slightly less than the state of New Jersey. In ancient times the region of present-day Israel was poor, bereft of natural resources, barely able to provide for itself, and hardly able to resist Roman power. Despite its small area, it was important because it formed a highway between the larger empires of the Assyrians, Babylonians, Persians, and Egyptians and finally the Greeks and Romans.

The unique contribution of the Jews to the West was their development of an exclusive monotheism, the belief in a single all-powerful god, Jehovah, who watched over his chosen people but also demanded a high standard of ethical conduct on pain of severe punishment. No people in history were to fight more tenaciously for their liberty against greater odds. The belief of Jews in their uniqueness in addition to their intolerance of other religions, however, created in the ancient world a sense of separation and widespread animosity against them.

In 63 CE, Roman consul Pompey Magnus (Pompey the Great) annexed Syria and then laid siege to and took Jerusalem. Maladroit decrees by inept Roman administrators produced riots and uprisings that brought savage reprisals. Many Jews became convinced that a reckoning was inevitable. These determined Jews came to be known as Zealots.

Matters came to a head in May 66 CE under Roman procurator Gessius Florus. His tactless decisions led to rioting, and the Zealots seized control of Jerusalem and slaughtered the Roman garrison, despite a promise of amnesty. Gessius soon lost control of all Judea and appealed to the governor of Syria, legate Cestius Gallus at Antioch, who had four legions available.

Cestius took three months to assemble an expeditionary force. It was centered on some 10,800 legionnaires, with 2,000 cavalry and 5,000 auxiliary infantry. Rome's allies, King Antiochus IV of Commagene and King Sohamemus of Emesa, furnished perhaps another 32,000 men. Some 2,000 Greek militiamen of Syria also joined, eager to participate in any action against Jews.

In October 66 CE Cestius easily subdued Galilee, unleashing a terror campaign of widespread destruction in the expectation that this would both remove any threat to his rear area and intimidate the Jewish population en route to Jerusalem. Part of his force took and razed the seaport of Joppa, slaying perhaps 8,000 people there. Other Roman columns secured other potential rebel strongholds.

After his coastal columns rejoined the main force at Caesarea, Cestius moved against Jerusalem. He expected to conclude the campaign in a few weeks before the heavy autumnal rains could make quagmires of the roads. Indeed, thus far Jewish resistance was sporadic and apparently disorganized.

Believing that his terror campaign had worked, on his approach to Jerusalem through the Beth-Horon Gorge (named for two villages 10 and 12 miles northwest of Jerusalem) Cestius failed to follow standard procedure and make an adequate reconnaissance. As a result, the Jews were able to ambush and attack the head of his column before their adversaries could deploy from march formation. According to Jewish sources, the Romans suffered some 500 dead, while the Jews sustained suffered 22 dead.

Cestius recovered, however. Resuming the advance, he set up camp on Mt. Scopus, less than a mile from Jerusalem. The Zealots refused, however, to treat with his emissaries, and after several days of waiting, on October 15 Cestius sent his men into Jerusalem. The Jews fell back to the inner-city wall. The Romans burned the suburb of Betheza, expecting that this would bring submission. It did not.

The Romans then launched full-scale attacks but failed to penetrate the Jewish defenses. After a week, Cestius suddenly withdrew. Jewish resistance that was stiffer than expected in addition to the approach of winter and shortages of supplies and mules for transport were the factors in his decision.

Cestius decided to move back to the coast through the Beth-Horon Gorge. Again he failed to post pickets on the hills, allowing the Jews to attack him in the narrow defile. Other Jewish forces moved to block the Roman escape. This running engagement, known as the Battle of Beth-Horon, turned into a rout. Cestius and the bulk of his force escaped but at the cost of nearly 6,000 men killed and the loss of all of their baggage and much equipment.

The battle had serious consequences. One immediate effect was the massacre of Jews in Damascus. The Battle of Beth-Horon also meant that the Jewish Revolt would not immediately be put down. Jews hitherto reluctant to commit themselves now joined the Zealots, many seeing the victory as a sign of divine favor. By November, the Jews had set up an independent secessionist government in Jerusalem.

The Romans could not allow this. Emperor Nero appointed Titus Flavius Vespasianus (Vespasian) as commander of an expeditionary force to bring Judea to heel. Vespasian moved south from Antioch with two legions, while his son Titus came up from Egypt with another legion. The invasion began in 69 CE, and following some delays, in 70 CE the Romans took Jerusalem without great difficulty, thanks to internal Jewish divisions. The sack of the city was terrible. The Jewish historian Josephus reported that 1.1 million people had died in the siege, and the Romans burned the Temple. Some isolated Jewish fortresses managed to hold out for another several years, but the Jewish state was no more. The Romans renamed it Syria Palestina. It was not until 1948 that there would again be a Jewish nation-state.

Spencer C. Tucker

Further Reading

Grant, Michael. *The Jews in the Roman World.* New York: Scribner, 1973.

Jones, A. H. M. *The Herods of Judea.* Oxford, UK: Clarendon, 1967.

Lendon, J. E. "Roman Siege of Jerusalem." *MHQ: The Quarterly Journal of Military History* 17(4) (Summer 2005): 6–15.

Lendon, J. E. *Soldiers and Ghosts: A History of Battle in Classical Antiquity.* New Haven, CT: Yale University Press, 2005.

Jihad

The term "jihad" is often translated as "holy war." It means "striving" or "to exert the utmost effort" and refers both to a religious duty to spread and defend Islam by waging war (lesser jihad) and an inward spiritual struggle to attain perfect faith (greater jihad). Although interpretations differ, the broad spectrum of modern Islam emphasizes the inner spiritual jihad.

Definitions of the term "jihad" have also been determined by historical circumstances. Indian reformer Sayyid Ahmad Khan (1817–1898) argued for a more limited interpretation of jihad whereby believers could perform charitable acts in place of armed struggle and was only incumbent if Muslims could not practice their faith. The reform movement of Muhammad ibn abd al-Wahhab (1703–1792) in Arabia, in contrast, reasserted the incumbency of jihad as armed struggle for all believers. As the Qur'an contains verses that promote mercy and urge peacemaking but also those (referred to as the Sword Verses) that more ardently require jihad of believers, there is a scriptural basis for both sides of this argument.

Some scholars differentiate the fulfilling of jihad by the heart, the tongue, or the sword as a means of discouraging Muslims from seeing armed struggle as a commandment, but such teachings have by and large been contradicted by the revival of activist jihad, first in response to colonialism and then again in the 20th century.

The broad spectrum of Islam considers foreign military intervention, foreign occupation, economic oppression, non-Islamic cultural realignment, colonialism, and the oppression of a domestic government, either secular or Islamic, of an Islamic people or country to be a sufficient reason, if not a Qur'anic mandate, to participate in a defensive jihad. The more militant and fundamental end of the Islamic spectrum asserts that a social, economic, and military defensive jihad is justifiable and necessary. However, a widespread discussion of jihad is ongoing in the Muslim world today in response to the rise of militancy, and there is a concerted effort to separate the concepts of jihad and martyrdom from each other when they are the rallying call of irresponsible extremists such as Osama bin Laden and his ilk.

Notable defensive jihads in the more recent history of Islam include the resistance of the Afghan (1979) and Chechnya (1940–1944, 1994–1996, and 1999–2009) mujahideen against their respective Soviet and Russian occupations and the Algerian War (1954–1962) against France.

Richard M. Edwards and Sherifa Zuhur

See also Algerian War; Chechen War, Second; Chechnya Insurgency; Mujahideen in the Soviet-Afghan War; Soviet-Afghan War

Further Reading

Bostrom, Andrew G., ed. *The Legacy of Jihad: Islamic Holy War and the Fate of Non-Muslims.* Amherst, NY: Prometheus, 2005.

Delong-Bas, Natana. *Wahhabi Islam: From Revival and Reform to Global Jihad.* Oxford: Oxford University Press, 2004.

Esposito, John L. *Unholy War: Terror in the Name of Islam.* New York: Oxford University Press, 2002.

Kepel, Gilles. *Jihad: The Trail of Political Islam.* Cambridge, MA: Belknap, 2003.

Judas Maccabeus

Birth Date: ca. 190 BCE
Death Date: 161 BCE

Leader of a revolt by the Jews against Rome. Judas Maccabeus (Judah Maccabee) was born around 190 BCE, one of five sons of Mattathias the Hasmonean, a Jewish priest from the village of Mod'lin in Judea. In 168 BCE Seleucid ruler Antiochus IV arrived in Jerusalem following a military defeat in Egypt. Opposed to Judaism, he desecrated the Temple and ordered Jews to honor a Greek god. These actions led to a confrontation in Mod'lin when Mattathias refused to make sacrifice to a Greek god and he and his sons Judas, Eleazar, Simon, John, and Jonathan slew a Seleucid general and some soldiers.

This event triggered the protracted Maccabean Revolt (168–142 BCE). When Mattathias died in 166, Judas assumed leadership of the revolt, which came to be named for him. The surname Maccabeus (Maccabee) given to Judas may mean "hammer," for his leadership in battle, although other scholars claim that it means "the one designated by Yahweh (God)."

A natural leader and military commander of considerable ability, Judas Maccabeus at first avoided major engagements with the well-armed Seleucids and employed guerrilla tactics to defeat a succession of their generals sent to Judea. In 167 BCE at the Ascent of Lebonah, he wiped out an entire Selucid unit. In 166 BCE he defeated a small Seleucid force under Apollonius, governor of Samaria, at Nahal el-Haramiah. Apollonius was among the dead. This victory led many Jews to join the cause.

Shortly thereafter in 166 BCE, Judas defeated a larger Seleucid force under Seron near Beth-Horon. Judas was then victorious at Emmaus, defeating Seleucid generals Micanor and Gorgias. Judas's defeat of the Seleucids at Beth Zur

(Bethsura) near Hebron in 164 BCE allowed him to take much of Jerusalem, including the Temple, although some Seleucids continued to hold out in the Acra, a fortified compound in Jerusalem. Continuing the siege of the Acra, Judas expanded his control over the whole of Judea.

With Antioches campaigning to the east, Seleucid regent Lysias invaded Judea and defeated Judas at Beth Zachariah (162 BCE) but then was forced to return to Syria to suppress a revolt there. That same year, however, Bacchides, commander of Seleucid forces in Judea, defeated Judas at Jerusalem and drove him from the city.

Judas rallied, and in 161 BCE he defeated Syrian general Nicanor at Adasa, with Nicanor among those killed. That same year, however, Judas was defeated and slain by a far more numerous Seleucid force, said to number 20,000 men, under Bacchides in the Battle of Elasa.

The Jewish revolt against the Seleucids continued under Jonathan, who enjoyed considerable success with the guerrilla tactics first employed by his brother. Establishing his headquarters at Jerusalem in 152, Jonathan was recognized as the de facto ruler of Judea until 143 BCE, when he was captured in an ambush at Ptolemais (Acre, Akko) and killed by dissident Jews.

Judas is widely praised in the First Book of Maccabees and is acclaimed by Jews as one of the greatest military leaders in their history. The Festival of Lights, or Hanukkah (Chanukah), in the month of December commemorates the cleansing and rededication of the Temple following the removal of its pagan statuary by Judas in 164 BCE.

Spencer C. Tucker

See also Maccabean Revolt

Further Reading

Robinson, Theodore H., and W. O. E. Oesterley. *A History of Israel.* Oxford, UK: Clarendon, 1932.

Schäfer, Peter. *The History of the Jews in the Greco-Roman World.* New York: Routledge, 2003.

K

Kabila, Laurent Désiré

Birth Date: November 27, 1939
Death Date: January 18, 2001

Longtime opponent of president of Zaire Mobutu Sese Seko, who overthrew Mobutu to become president of the renamed Democratic Republic of the Congo. Laurent Désiré Kabila was born on November 27, 1939, in Baudoinville, Katanga Province, in the Belgian Congo. A member of the Luba tribe, he subsequently studied political philosophy in France. He also studied at the University of Belgrade in Serbia and at the University of Dar es Salaam in Tanzania.

In 1960 Kabila supported Patrice Lamumba, the leftist prime minister of the newly independent Congo, and fought in the Lamumba loyalist forces against the secessionist Moise Tshombe in Katanga. When Mobutu seized power in the Congo from Lamumba in 1961, Kabila supported Lamumbist prosper Mwamba Ilunga. In 1964 Kabila organized the Simba ("Lion") insurgent movement. His forces captured Stanleyville (present-day Kisangani) but were ousted by Belgian forces.

In 1965 Kabila set up operations in neighboring Tanzania, across Lake Tanganyika. That same year, Ernesto "Che" Guevera arrived with some 100 men, hoping to bring about a Communist victory. Guevera thought that Kabila had potential as a guerrilla leader but accused him of "lack of seriousness," and the efforts met failure. Kabila then engaged in gold and timber smuggling and also operated a bar.

In 1967 Kabila and a small number of followers of his People's Revolutionary Party (PRP) established with Chinese assistance a small Marxist enclave state in South Kivu Province. The PRP existed until 1988, when Kabila, now quite wealthy, simply disappeared. Widely rumored to be dead, he was in fact establishing useful contacts with the future leaders of Uganda, Tanzania, and Rwanda.

Kabila returned to Zaire in October 1996. The ethnic struggle in Rwanda had spilled over into Zaire (the former Congo), and the ailing Mobutu's popularity had plummeted. Kabila initiated the First Congo War, leading ethnic Tutsis from South Kiva against the Hutus. Aided by the leaders of Rwanda, Kabila captured Kinshasa on May 20, 1997, and Mobutu fled abroad. Zaire now became the Democratic Republic of the Congo. Critics charged that Kabila's rule differed little from that of Mobutu. Indeed, it was marked by authoritarianism, corruption, human rights abuses, and efforts at self-aggrandizement.

By 1998, Kabila's former allies in Uganda and Rwanda turned against him in what became the Second Congo War. Kabila meanwhile secured the support of Angola, Namibia, and Zimbabwe. A peace accord in 1999 removed most of the foreign troops.

Kabila was shot in Kinshasa by one of his bodyguards on January 16, 2001, in a failed coup attempt. Flown to Zimbabwe for medical treatment, he died there two days later. His son Joseph then became president.

Spencer C. Tucker

Further Reading

Ngolet, François. *Crisis in the Congo: The Rise and Fall of Laurent Kabila.* New York: Palgrave Macmillan, 2011.

Young, Crawford, and Thomas Turner. *The Rise and Decline of the Zairean State.* Madison: University of Wisconsin Press, 1986.

Karen Insurgency

Start Date: 1949
End Date: 1955

The Japanese invasion of Burma (now Myanmar) in 1942 served to exacerbate already existing tensions between the majority Burmese and the minority hill tribes, including the Karens. Some 2 million Karens inhabited the area east of the Sittang River. During the war, the British Special Operation Executive recruited a number of Karens for service against the Burma Independence Army, led by Aung San, that collaborated with the Japanese.

Late in World War II (1939–1945), Aung San switched sides, and in January 1947 his Anti-Fascist People's Freedom League (AFPFL) negotiated independence for Burma with the British. Independence was granted in January 1948. A number of Karens then held leading positions in the army and the government, and their political party, the Karen National Union (KNU), attempted to reach accommodation with the Burmese ethnic majority.

Aung San had hoped that Burma would become a republic with a pluralistic society that would accommodate its diverse ethnic minorities. He was assassinated in July 1947, however. His successor and Burma's first prime minister, U Nu, followed a different course, seeking a syntheses of Buddhism and socialism that alienated many non-Burmese minorities.

While U Nu opened negotiations with the Karens on regional autonomy, at the same time he raised and armed irregular political militias known as the Sitwundan. Commanded by Major General Ne Win, these militias, which went under the guise of auxiliary police, were a law unto themselves, and the KNU established the Karen National Defence Organization (KNDO) to protect the Karen communities. In January 1949, some of the Sitwundan units went on a rampage and killed a number of Karens. That same month, Burmese Army chief of staff General Smith Dun, a Karen, was removed from his post and imprisoned. Ne Win replaced him.

As a consequence of these actions, in 1949 Karen militants, led by Mahn Ba Zan, declared Karen independence. Other minorities also rose in revolt, assisted by defections of Karen military units that had helped put down an earlier Communist rebellion. The Karens initially fielded some 10,000 men. Karen and Katchin units seized Toungoo, Meiktila, Maymyo, and Mandalay. They also advanced on and almost captured the capital of Rangoon (now Yangon). The major battle occurred at Insein, nine miles from the capital, where they held out in a 112-day siege lasting into late May.

The rebels were handicapped, however, by disunity and a lack of firepower. Government control of the air and the rivers was a major factor in the outcome, and that spring their troops retook the locations lost earlier. The KNDO still controlled much of the Irrawaddy Delta, but the threat to the government was pretty much over by 1950. In 1953 and 1955, government troops mounted major operations into Karen-controlled areas. The Karens had been granted autonomy in 1952, and most formally accepted this in 1964, although Mahn Ba Zan did not accept the government terms until May 1980.

Some fighting continued, however. In 1958, General Ne Win and two other senior military officers seized power and established a military dictatorship. (In 1989 the generals renamed the country Myanmar.) Some 20 minority groups joined in an insurgency against the dictatorship. With 20,000 men under arms in the 1980s, the Karen National Liberation Army (KNLA) was the largest of the insurgent groups. By 2006, however, the KNLA had shrunk to only some 4,000 men. The central government's army meanwhile grew to 400,000 men and launched a number of offensives into Karen territory. The KNU continued to seek resolution of the conflict through negotiations. During 1994 and 1995, dissenters from the Buddhist minority in the KNLA formed the Democratic Karen Buddhist Army (DKBA) and defected to the junta side. Decades of war have uprooted as many as 200,000 Karens from their homes and forced 160,000 to seek refuge across the border in Thailand, leading to charges of ethnic cleansing by the Myanmar government.

Spencer C. Tucker

See also Special Operations Executive

Further Reading

Falla, Jonathan. *True Love and Bartholomew: Rebels of the Burmese Border.* Cambridge: Cambridge University Press, 1991.

Smith, Martin. *Burma: Insurgency and the Politics of Ethnicity.* London: Zed, 1991.

Kashmir Insurgency

Start Date: 1987
End Date: Ongoing

The former princely Indian state of Kashmir covers some 86,000 square miles of South Asia. Muslims conquered Kashmir in the 14th century and forcibly converted its mostly Hindu and Buddhist population to Islam. The British sowed the seeds of the subsequent agitation over control of Kashmir by placing a Hindu prince on its throne in 1846.

The dispute over the future of Kashmir began in 1947 with the partition of the Empire of India and the creation of independent India and Pakistan. India is primarily Hindu, while Pakistan is mainly Muslim. Under the terms of the 1947 Indian Independence Bill, Kashmir was to determine which of the two nations it would join. Because of Kashmir's Muslim majority, Pakistanis believed that it should be part of Pakistan.

Kashmir, however, was ruled by Maharaja Hari Singh, a Hindu, and his decision to join Kashmir to India, accepted by the Indian Parliament on October 26, 1947, precipitated conflict with Pakistan. This event sparked an uprising in Kashmir by its predominantly Muslim population and Pakistani tribesmen, the Azad Kashmiri, who marched on the provincial capital of Srinigar. The Indian government responded by airlifting troops into Kashmir, and heavy fighting followed.

In November 1947, Pakistani troops crossed the border into Kashmir and fought an undeclared war with Indian forces through December. Direct negotiations between India and Pakistan concerning Kashmir having failed, the dispute was referred to the United Nations (UN). On January 20, 1948, the UN Security Council set up a commission to resolve the dispute. Sporadic fighting continued, however, including a Pathan uprising in Kashmir on February 8, 1948, that was put down by Indian forces. UN mediation finally brought about a cease-fire on January 1, 1949. India, however, rejected the UN arbitration arrangement, and the continuing Kashmir dispute rendered close relations between India and Pakistan impossible.

Under the January 1949 agreement, UN observers monitored the cease-fire line. Pakistan was left in control of the northern region, known as Azad (free) Kashmir. India maintained control of the remainder, including Jammu, amounting to nearly two-thirds of the state. The vote to decide Kashmir's future called for by the UN never occurred, however. Negotiations took place intermittently between India and Pakistan over Kashmir but with no tangible result. On August 20, 1953, Sheikh Mohammed Abdullah, the prime minister of Kashmir, and Jawaharlal Nehru, the prime minister of India, reached agreement on a plebiscite, but India then withdrew its pledge and imprisoned Abdullah. On January 26, 1957, India officially annexed Kashmir. Pakistan protested this action, and the UN refused to recognize it.

The dispute continued and was a principal cause of war between India and Pakistan in 1965 that saw large tank battles but ended in a stalemate. In the UN-brokered cease-fire of September 22, both sides agreed to withdraw to the lines held on August 5.

On January 10, 1966, India and Pakistan agreed to the Tashkent Declaration, which reestablished the former cease-fire line. Hostilities between India and Pakistan began anew in 1971, this time over the succession of East Pakistan (later Bangladesh) from West Pakistan. Although the war was not fought over Kashmir, fighting did occur along the cease-fire line. The war ended on July 3, 1972, with the Simla Agreement, signed by Pakistani president Zulfiqar Ali Bhutto and Indian prime minister Indira Gandhi. The agreement defined a new Line of Control (LOC) in Kashmir, the same basic line as before with only minor deviations. The LOC is roughly 460 miles long and runs over extremely rugged terrain from Jammu in the southwest through the Himalayas in the northeast. Again, this line was monitored by UN observers. The agreement also called for Pakistan and India to refrain from the use of force in Kashmir.

India currently controls 53,665 square miles of Kashmir, while Pakistan administers nearly 32,358 square miles. The line between the two is monitored by the understaffed UN Military Observer Group in India and Pakistan. Violations mainly consist of small-arms fire and artillery.

Widespread allegations of rigged voting in the 1987 elections held in the Indian-controlled areas of Jammu and Kashmir led a number of those who had been defeated to commence an insurgency against Indian rule. The Pakistan Inter-Services Intelligence Agency was actively involved in the recruitment, training, and arming of these insurgents. India responded with a buildup of its forces. No accurate count of casualties in the insurgency exists, but Indian security forces are said to have suffered some 7,000 killed as opposed to 20,000 insurgents. Estimates of civilian casualties range from 29,000 to as many as 100,000 dead.

Although the insurgency continues, Pakistani government support began to end in 2004 following two attempts by terrorist groups linked to Kashmir to assassinate Pakistani president General Pervez Musharraf. Musharraf's successor, Asif Ali Zardari, has continued the official Pakistani hands-off policy and has labeled the Kashmir insurgents as "terrorists." The Inter-Services Intelligence Agency's role cannot be determined, however.

With upwards of half a million troops in Kashmir (the Indian government refuses to give precise figures), Indian arrests of a number of insurgent leaders, and splits within the insurgent movement (some groups seek union with Pakistan, while others want Kashmiri independence), the situation is now generally calm with only an occasional violent action. Nonetheless, allegations of human rights abuses and the Indian government's curtailment of civil liberties continue to garner support for the insurgents.

Melissa Hebert and Spencer C. Tucker

Further Reading

Bose, Sumantra. *Kashmir: Roots of Conflict, Paths to Peace.* Cambridge, MA: Harvard University Press, 2003.

Ganguly, Sumit. *The Origins of War in South Asia: The Indo-Pakistani Wars since 1947.* Boulder, CO: Westview, 1994.

Margolis, Eric S. *War at the Top of the World: The Struggle for Afghanistan, Kashmir, and Tibet.* New York: Routledge, 2002.

Kenya Emergency

Start Date: 1952
End Date: 1960

The 1885 Berlin Conference recognized the east-central African region of Kenya as being within the British sphere of influence, and Kenya officially became a British protectorate in 1895. Kenya was home to small and scattered tribal groups, among the most important being the Kikuyu, Kamba, Luo, and Masai tribes. Distinct tribal identities persisted.

The British established white-owned plantations on former African tribal lands, although only 7 percent of Kenya's land was arable. In the early 20th century, British authorities provided land for white settlers in Kenya's White Highlands region. The natives, meanwhile, were restricted to the largely unusable holdings. By 1950 in the White Highlands, some 3,000 white settlers farmed an average of 3,460 acres each, while 1.3 million Africans in native landholdings possessed on average only 23.7 acres each.

In the 1920s the economic difficulties of African Kenyans led to the formation of nationalist organizations, and in 1929 Kikuyu leader Jomo Kenyatta traveled to London on behalf of the Kikuyu Central Association in an effort to open negotiations with the British government for independence. World War II (1939–1945) military service enhanced the political awareness of many Kenyans, and in 1944 African Kenyans received the limited right to political participation. Economic hardship for many Africans was exacerbated, however, by the arrival after the war of new white settlers.

Soon after the war, guerrilla groups formed that were bent on expelling the whites and eliminating all vestiges of colonial rule. The most significant of these was the Mau Mau, the members of which took an oath to forcefully expel British occupiers and eliminate Africans who cooperated with or benefitted from colonialism. The principal issue was land. Indeed, Mau Mau members frequently referred to their organization as the Kenya Land Freedom Army.

Although the British government declared the Mau Mau illegal in 1950, it continued to grow. On October 19, 1952, the British colonial government declared a state of emergency and arrested Kenyatta, Achieng Oneko, and other nationalists, although no evidence linked them to the Mau Mau.

The Mau Mau were mostly Kikuyu and the ethnically related Meru and Embu. Few had firearms, and most of their savage attacks were made with axes and machetes. Outnumbered and outgunned, the Mau Mau waged a vicious guerrilla war from the shelter of the forests of Mount Kenya and the Aberdare Mountains, slowly gathering support from other tribes. From prison, Kikuyu leader Jomo Kenyatta wrote letters that advanced Kenyan nationalism and evoked world sympathy.

In March 1953, Mau Mau fighters launched their first military offensive, massacring residents of the loyalist village of Lari. The British then sought to apply lessons learned in the Malayan Emergency (1948–1960). In June 1953 General Sir George Erskine became commander in chief in Kenya. He instituted close coordination by the various security agencies, and special emergency measures were enacted, including an expanded death penalty. The only real Mau Mau organization was in Nairobi, and Erskine attacked it in Operation ANVIL (April 24–May 9, 1954), arresting 16,500 men during large-scale raids in that city.

Sporadic fighting continued after ANVIL, but the raids reduced the number of Mau Mau to some 5,000, and most of their activities were in the Aberdare Forest at the foot of Mount Kenya. Royal Air Force bombing of the forests proved ineffective, and small-unit operations became the norm. Pseudoforces, directed by Ian Henderson, proved particularly effective, and the 25,000-man Kikuyu Home Guard protected Kikuyu villages from early 1953 to January 1955.

Erskine was cognizant of the reasons for the rebellion and instituted hearts-and-minds programs, including public works and agricultural development projects. Influential white settlers opposed concessions to the Africans, however. The white Kenya Police Reserve was also guilty of a number of atrocities.

Some 79,000 Africans were detained by 1956, often in harsh conditions. Among the detainees were leaders of the Kenya African Union, the organization that replaced the Kikuyu Central Association. British-led forces captured Mau Mau leader Dedan Kimathi in October 1956; he was executed in February 1957. With more Mau Mau surrendering and the movement in disarray, the British prevailed.

The rebellion claimed 32 white settlers dead. The security forces sustained some 600 dead, while 2,000 Africans loyal to the government were killed by the Mau Mau. The Mau Mau lost 11,500 killed in action. Another 1,086 were executed, while perhaps 400 Mau Mau prisoners died in captivity, most from disease.

Although the rebellion failed, it led to African access to farmlands and attempts to create an African middle class. Direct elections to the Legislative Council began in 1957. The British lifted the state of emergency on January 12, 1960, and held a conference with African leaders concerning the country's future. One agreement guaranteed that the Africans would have a voice in their government.

The Kenyan African Union became the Kenyan African National Union under Jomo Kenyatta, who had been released from prison in 1961. In a contest with the minority Kenya African Democratic Union, which represented a coalition of small tribes who feared domination by the larger tribes, the Kenyan African National Union won elections in 1963, the same year that Kenya became an independent state, with Kenyatta as its president.

John H. Barnhill and Spencer C. Tucker

See also Hearts and Minds; Mau Mau; Pseudoforces

Further Reading

Branch, Daniel. *Defeating Mau Mau, Creating Kenya: Counterinsurgency, Civil War, and Decolonization.* New York: Cambridge University Press, 2009.

Clayton, Anthony. *Counter-Insurgency in Kenya.* Nairobi, Kenya: Transafrica Publishers, 1976.

Currey, James. *Mau Mau & Nationhood.* Athens: Ohio University Press, 2003.

Pateman, Robert. *Kenya.* New York: Benchmark, 2004.

Khmer Rouge

Cambodian insurgent group. The Khmer Rouge (French for "Red Khmer") held power in Cambodia between 1975 and 1979, during which time millions of Cambodians were herded into slave labor camps, hundreds of thousands were executed, and there were many more deaths from starvation, exhaustion, and disease. After being driven out of Phnom Penh by Vietnamese forces in early 1979, the Khmer Rouge waged a guerrilla resistance that was still active in large areas of the country more than 15 years later, despite an agreement sponsored by the United Nations that was supposed to bring peace to Cambodia after more than two decades of war.

The Khmer Rouge dates from the early 1960s, when a small group of Communist revolutionaries launched an insurgency against Cambodian ruler Prince Norodom Sihanouk. Among the Khmer Rouge leaders was Saloth Sar, better known as Pol Pot.

The uprising remained small during the 1960s as the war in neighboring Vietnam exploded. Khmer Rouge insurgents received no help from the Vietnamese Communists, who had reached an accommodation with Sihanouk that allowed them to resupply and rest their troops on Cambodian territory and, in return, refrained from aiding Sihanouk's enemies.

To Saloth Sar and his colleagues, this branded the Vietnamese as enemies of their own struggle, even though both groups were Communist. Making a virtue of their isolation, the Khmer Rouge nurtured an increasingly extreme and violent vision of a pure revolution that would succeed through sheer ideological zeal and utter indifference to sacrifice and suffering.

After Sihanouk's overthrow by rightist general Lon Nol in March 1970, the Khmer Rouge and the Vietnamese Communists became partners, though mistrustful ones; both were also now allied with Sihanouk, whose injured pride and thirst for revenge led him to join forces with his former enemies. Beside the Khmer Rouge,

A skull resting on the muzzle of his American M-16 rifle, a Khmer Rouge soldier waits with his comrades for word to depart Dei Kraham, some 12 miles south of Phnom Penh, during an operation along Highway 2, on September 5, 1973. (Bettmann/Corbis)

there appeared a Vietnamese-sponsored Cambodian resistance force led mainly by Cambodians who had fought with the Viet Minh against the French and who had lived in Vietnam since the 1950s.

Old antagonisms were submerged for several years, but early in 1973 the Khmer Rouge moved to seize full control of the insurgency. Hundreds of Vietnamese-trained cadres were executed, as were leaders associated with Sihanouk, even while the prince himself, living in China, remained the figurehead leader of the revolutionaries' exile government.

Outside Cambodia, almost nothing was known of the Khmer Rouge. The insurgents were hardly less shadowy to the Cambodians themselves, who commonly referred to them only as the *peap prey* ("forest army"). But behind their veil of secrecy, as the Khmer Rouge consolidated its power and fought against Lon Nol's regime, these fanatical revolutionaries nursed their hatred of the Vietnamese and their fantasies of a revolution so sweeping that it would seek to obliterate every trace of Cambodia's past.

On April 17, 1975, the Khmer Rouge seized control of Phnom Penh. It was for them the first day of Year Zero—the beginning of the total transformation of Cambodian society. Within hours, the new rulers ordered the entire population of the Cambodian capital into the countryside, at once and with no exceptions. An estimated 2 million–3 million people were marched out of Phnom Penh, and 600,000–750,000 more were marched out from other towns and cities—altogether, about half of the country's entire population.

In the countryside, former city dwellers were put to work in slave labor camps, while the new regime, identifying itself only as Angka Loeu ("Organization on High"), embarked on a murderous purge of its former enemies and everyone else considered to represent the old society. Soldiers and civil servants of the former government were killed, as were teachers, Buddhist priests and monks, intellectuals, and professionals.

The party's frenzied search for enemies led inexorably to fantasies of traitors in its own ranks. Hundreds of high-ranking leaders and thousands of their followers were killed, usually after gruesome torture. At Tuol Sleng, a Phnom Penh school converted into an interrogation center, a grisly archive documented approximately 20,000 executions there alone.

Meanwhile, the Khmer Rouge was also engaged in increasingly violent clashes with its former allies, the Vietnamese. Finally, on Christmas Day 1978, 100,000 Vietnamese troops invaded Cambodia, capturing Phnom Penh two weeks later. The Vietnamese installed a new government headed by a former Khmer Rouge commander, Heng Samrin, but they were unable to quell continued resistance from Khmer Rouge soldiers who had regrouped in the countryside. Vietnamese forces withdrew only in 1989 after intense international pressure. Two years later the Khmer Rouge and two smaller rebel factions signed a peace agreement with the Phnom Penh regime, now led by Hun Sen, but the Khmer Rouge never disarmed, despite the pact, nor did it take part in the May 1993 election for a new government. For several years, Khmer Rouge guerrillas harassed government forces in widespread areas of the country.

Beginning in 1996, however, the movement began to splinter. In August 1996 Ieng Sary, Pol Pot's former brother-in-law and one of his closest collaborators while the Khmer Rouge was in power, defected to the government, bringing with him about 4,000 guerrillas who had been operating in western Cambodia. In return, Sary secured a royal amnesty from Sihanouk, despite the fact that Sary had been under a death sentence since 1979 for the bloodshed committed by the Khmer Rouge regime.

In June 1997 there was a last spasm of bloodletting as Pol Pot and his supporters sought to block a cease-fire agreement with Prince Ranariddh. On Pol Pot's orders, longtime Khmer Rouge defense minister Son Sen was executed, along with about a dozen of his family members. Nearly all of Pol Pot's comrades now turned against him and took him prisoner. He was tried several weeks later, not for the hundreds of thousands of murders carried out under his rule but instead for plotting against his fellow executioners. Found guilty, he was sentenced only to in-house detainment. In April 1998, some of Pol Pot's Khmer Rouge followers reportedly agreed to turn him over for trial in an international war crime tribunal. The very same day, the news was leaked to the press that Pol Pot was found dead. No autopsy was performed, and many believe that he either committed suicide or had been poisoned.

Instead of being peacefully reabsorbed into Cambodian life, however, the Khmer Rouge and its new leaders again engaged in armed resistance against the pursuing government army. By 1999, most of the Khmer Rouge leaders, including Ta Mok and Khieu Samphan, had surrendered, and the Khmer Rouge all but dissolved, leaving only nightmares in its wake.

Cambodia has now largely recovered from the Khmer Rouge era. The nation has a very young population, with three-quarters of them too young to remember the Khmer Rouge's time in power. There have been some trials of former Khmer Rouge officials, and in 2009 the Cambodian Ministry of Education began requiring instruction in the schools regarding Khmer Rouge atrocities.

Arnold R. Isaacs

See also Cambodia, Vietnamese Occupation of; Pol Pot

Further Reading

Becker, Elizabeth. *When the War Was Over.* New York: Simon and Schuster, 1986.

Chanda, Nayan. *Brother Enemy.* New York: Harcourt Brace Jovanovich, 1986.

Deac, Wilfred P. *Road to the Killing Fields: The Cambodian War of 1970–1975.* College Station: Texas A&M University Press, 1997.

Ponchaud, François. *Cambodia Year Zero.* Translated by Nancy Amphoux. New York: Holt, Rinehart and Winston, 1978.

Kitchener, Horatio Herbert

Birth Date: June 14, 1850
Death Date: June 5, 1916

British Army field marshal and secretary of state for war. Born to English parents near Listowel in County Kerry, Ireland, on June 14, 1850, Horatio Herbert Kitchener was educated at the Royal Military Academy, Woolwich, and was commissioned in the engineers in 1871. Involved in survey work in Palestine, Anatolia, and Cyprus during 1874–1882, he was then appointed to Cairo as second-in-command of a cavalry regiment and participated with distinction in the unsuccessful effort to relieve British general Charles Gordon at Khartoum during 1883–1884.

Kitchener then served in Zanzibar, the Sudan, and Egypt. Appointed commander of the Egyptian Army in 1892, he organized it into an effective fighting force and in 1896 invaded the Sudan, where he defeated Gordon's killer, the Mahdi, at the Battle of Omdurman (September 2, 1898). Kitchener then proceeded farther up the Nile to Fashoda, where he skillfully conducted negotiations with a French force there while demanding its removal, which he secured on November 3.

Kitchener was governor of the Sudan during 1898–1899 before arriving in South Africa in January 1900 as chief of staff to Field Marshal Sir Frederick Roberts in the South African War (Second Boer War, 1899–1902). Kitchener's skillful planning was a key factor in the British advance to Johannesburg and Pretoria. He succeeded Roberts as commander in November 1900. To deprive the guerrillas of civilian support, Kitchener relocated much of the Boer population, resettling it in what came to be known as concentration camps as well as a network of blockhouses and wired fences. He also harried the Boer fighters in the field, leading them to end the war in the Treaty of Vereeniging on May 31, 1902.

Kitchener returned to Britain a hero and was made a viscount. He commanded the Indian Army during 1902–1909 and fought an internecine political battle with the viceroy, Lord Curzon, forcing the latter's resignation. Promoted to field marshal in September 1909, Kitchener became viceroy of Egypt and the Sudan during 1911–1914.

Kitchener was on leave in Britain at the start of World War I (1914–1918). Prime Minister Hubert Asquith, aware of the perceived Liberal weakness on martial matters, offered Kitchener, then probably Britain's most famous soldier, the post of secretary of state for war in July 1914. Kitchener accepted and immediately announced to a shocked cabinet that the war would last years rather than months and would require a military that was millions of men strong. The cabinet raised no objection to Kitchener's call to enlarge the army by 500,000 men, and the men of Britain eagerly signed up for these new armies. Kitchener issued a call for an additional 500,000 men at the end of August 1914. He struggled with the inadequate military recruiting and training system, but the situation was made worse by his refusal to delegate authority and his disdain of teamwork. A shortage of munitions, the Shells Scandal in May 1915, became a major political issue in Britain.

Although relieved of virtually all his posts at the end of 1915, Kitchener remained in the cabinet as a figurehead. He did not live to see the employment of the forces he had so painstakingly assembled. Sent on a mission to Russia, Kitchener died en route when his ship, the British cruiser *Hampshire,* struck a mine in the North Sea near the Orkney Islands and sank on June 5, 1916.

David J. Silbey

See also Concentration Camps in the Second Boer War; South African War

Further Reading

Cassar, George. *Kitchener: Architect of Victory.* London: W. Kimber, 1977.

Royle, Trevor. *The Kitchener Enigma.* London: M. Joseph, 1985.

Simkins, Peter. *Kitchener's Armies: The Raising of the New Armies.* Manchester, UK: Manchester University Press, 1988.

Kitson, Sir Frank

Birth Date: 1926

British Army general and counterinsurgency author. Born in 1926, Frank Kitson was commissioned in the Rifle Brigade (Prince Consort's Own) in 1946. Kitson saw service in Kenya in 1953–1955 during the Kenya Emergency (1952–1960). He was promoted to captain in 1953 and was awarded the Military Cross for his work in the creation of pseudoforces. Recruited from former Mau Mau, they helped guide security forces in military operations.

Kitson served in Malaya in 1957 during the latter part of the Malayan Emergency (1948–1960) and took part in the defeat of insurgents in Oman during 1957–1959. He served in Cyprus in United Nations peacekeeping operations during 1962–1964. Promoted to lieutenant colonel in 1964 and to colonel in 1969, he served in Aden (present-day Yemen) during 1965–1966 and in Northern Ireland during the height of the Troubles in 1970–1972. He was commandant of the Infantry School during 1972–1974.

Kitson commanded the 2nd Division beginning in 1976 and was commandant of the Staff College at Camberley during 1978–1980. Promoted to lieutenant general in 1980, in 1982 he took command of British land forces as a full general and was aide-de-camp general to the queen during 1983–1985. He retired in 1985.

Kitson wrote a number of books treating low-intensity warfare. *Gangs and Counter-Gangs* (1960) treats his service in Kenya and his role in the formation of the pseudoforces. *Low-Intensity Operations* (1971) was written when he was a Ministry of Defence fellow at Oxford University during 1960–1970. In it he makes clear that there can be no purely military or political solution to insurgencies and that these must operate in concert. His third book, *Bunch of Five* (1977), details British operations in Kenya, Malaya, Cyprus, and Aden and notes the importance of military-political coordination in setting the stage for a political solution and the role played by intelligence. His fourth book, *Warfare as a Whole* (1987), written in retirement, shows how insurgencies fit into the larger picture of warfare.

Noting that most conflicts since World War II (1939–1945) have been low-intensity in nature, Kitson stressed the need for the British Army to devote more attention to training for counterinsurgency warfare. While for the most part his solutions reflected those of Sir Robert Thompson, Kitson differed from Thompson in intelligence collection. Pointing out that the police were usually the first targets in an insurgency, Kitson stressed the need for the military to take control of intelligence operations from the onset. Coming during the Troubles in Northern Ireland, this suggestion caused some unease in political circles.

Donald A. MacCuish and Spencer C. Tucker

See also Aden Emergency; Cyprus Insurrection; Fire Force, Rhodesian; Kenya Emergency; Malayan Emergency; Mau Mau; Northern Ireland Insurgency; Pseudoforces; Rhodesian Bush War; Selous Scouts

Further Reading

Kitson, Sir Frank. *Bunch of Five*. London: Faber and Faber, 1977.

Kitson, Sir Frank. *Gangs and Counter-Gangs*. London: Barrie and Rockliff, 1960.

Kitson, Sir Frank. *Low Intensity Operations: Subversion Insurgency and Peacekeeping*. London: Faber, 1971.

Kitson, Sir Frank. *Warfare as a Whole*. London: Faber and Faber, 1987.

Komer, Robert William

Birth Date: February 23, 1922
Death Date: April 9, 2000

Key U.S. official in the pacification program during the Vietnam War. Born on February 23, 1922, in Chicago, Illinois, Robert William Komer graduated from Harvard in 1942. Following army service in World War II (1939–1945), he earned an MBA at Harvard in 1947. Komer worked for the Central Intelligence Agency (CIA) as an analyst during 1947–1960 and then worked with the National Security Council (NSC) as a senior staff member in 1961–1965.

As a deputy special assistant to the president for national security affairs (1965–1966) and special assistant (1966–1967), Komer became increasingly involved with the pacification program in the Republic of Vietnam (RVN, South Vietnam). In February 1966 President Lyndon Johnson appointed him Washington coordinator for pacification activities.

Komer's office became useful to young U.S. Army officers trying to overcome institutional resistance to results of the 1966 report on the conduct of the war titled *A Program for the Pacification and Long-Term Development of South Vietnam* (*PROVN*). *PROVN* had concluded that the attrition strategy and search-and-destroy tactics being employed by U.S. commander in South Vietnam General William Westmoreland were not working and could not work. The key to success, the report held, was concentration on population security and pacification. Komer was sympathetic to that viewpoint and helped advance such ideas.

Reporting on a June 1966 trip to Vietnam, Komer informed President Johnson that the pacification effort was lagging and that unless this was rectified, victory could not be ensured. Komer proposed that responsibility for pacification be assigned to the U.S. military in South Vietnam but under a civilian deputy. He had in effect written his own job description, although it took Secretary of Defense Robert McNamara's backing for the proposal to be approved. In March 1967 the decision was announced to put the Civil Operations and Revolutionary Development Support (CORDS) program under Westmoreland, with Komer as his deputy. Komer's official title was deputy to the commander, U.S. Military Assistance Command, Vietnam (MAC), for civil operations and revolutionary development support. He had the personal rank of ambassador and held the post until October 1968.

Able and abrasive, Komer earned the nickname "Blowtorch Bob." But he maintained that it was necessary to prod people aggressively if anything was going to be accomplished. He also took pride in his own incorrigible optimism. Westmoreland was relieved to turn over the pacification program to Komer while Westmoreland continued to conduct the military war that he saw as his primary responsibility.

Komer's overall influence on the pacification program remains uncertain. He built up the South Vietnamese territorial forces and pulled together disparate elements of the American advisory effort at the province level. Yet it was only after the Communists suffered disastrous losses during the 1968 Tet Offensive, after General Creighton Abrams assumed command of MACV and William Colby took over as deputy for CORDS, and after President Nguyen Van Thieu personally launched and pushed the Accelerated Pacification Campaign in November 1968 that pacification really began to show results.

Komer served briefly as ambassador to Turkey (1968–1969) and then moved to the RAND Corporation (1969–1977). He was a Pentagon official working on North Atlantic Treaty Organization (NATO) affairs (1977–1979) and then was undersecretary of defense for policy (1979–1981). Komer died of a stroke in Arlington, Virginia, on April 9, 2000.

Lewis Sorley

See also Abrams, Creighton Williams, Jr.; Civil Operations and Revolutionary Development Support; Colby, William Egan; Program for the Pacification and Long-Term Development of South Vietnam; Westmoreland, William Childs

Further Reading

Clarke, Jeffrey J. *Advice and Support: The Final Years, 1965–1973.* Washington, DC: U.S. Army Center of Military History, 1988.

Komer, Robert W. *Bureaucracy at War: U.S. Performance in the Vietnam Conflict.* Boulder, CO: Westview, 1986.

Scoville, Thomas W. *Reorganizing for Pacification Support.* Washington, DC: U.S. Army Center of Military History, 1982.

Konfrontasi.

See Indonesia-Malaysia Confrontation

Krulak, Victor H.

Birth Date: January 7, 1913
Death Date: December 29, 2008

U.S. Marine Corps general. Born in Denver, Colorado, on January 7, 1913, Victor H. ("Brute") Krulak graduated from the U.S. Naval Academy, Annapolis, in 1934. His fellow midshipmen nicknamed him "Brute" in an ironical reference to his diminutive size of 5 feet 4 inches tall and 120 pounds. Krulak's early service included sea duty, a tour at the Naval Academy, and assignments with the 6th Marines, the 4th Marines, and the Fleet Marine Force.

In March 1943 during World War II (1939–1945), Krulak, now a lieutenant colonel, assumed command in the Pacific theater of a parachute battalion of the I Marine Amphibious Corps at New Caledonia. That October he commanded the diversionary landing on Choiseul to cover the Bougainville invasion. Krulak assisted in the planning and execution of the Okinawa Campaign, and at the end of the war he helped negotiate the surrender of Japanese forces in the Tsingato, China, area.

During the Korean War (1950–1953), Colonel Krulak was chief of staff of the 1st Marine Division. In June 1956 he was promoted to brigadier general and named assistant division commander, 3rd Marine Division, on Okinawa. In November 1959 he was promoted to major general, and in December he assumed command of the U.S. Marine Corps Recruit Depot at San Diego.

In February 1962 Krulak became special assistant for the Counterinsurgency Activities Organization of the Joint Chiefs of Staff. During the next two years, much of his time was spent gathering information regarding the developing conflict in the Republic of Vietnam (RVN, South Vietnam). After a fact-finding mission to Vietnam, Krulak held that the war was winnable if the John F. Kennedy administration firmly supported the Ngo Dinh Diem government. Krulak's findings contradicted those of State Department official Joseph Mendenhall, who accompanied Krulak to Vietnam. In March 1964 Lieutenant General Krulak assumed command of the Fleet Marine Force, Pacific, and served in that post until he retired from active duty in May 1968.

While he was commander of the Fleet Marine Force, Pacific, Krulak disagreed with General William C. Westmoreland, commander of the Military Assistance Command, Vietnam (MACV), on several key points. Krulak strongly opposed Westmoreland's search-and-destroy strategy, believing that an attrition strategy favored the Communists. Krulak believed that guerrillas constituted the main threat. His three-cornered strategy included protecting the South Vietnamese people from the guerrillas; concentrating airpower on rail lines, power, fuel, and heavy industry in the Democratic Republic of Vietnam (DRV, North Vietnam); and placing maximum effort in pacification. Krulak believed that the Americans were far more efficient than the South Vietnamese government at civic action. The Vietnamese people were the key to victory, and if the Communists could be denied access to the bulk of them, the war could be won. Thus, the first order of business had to be to protect the civilian population. Krulak constantly pointed out to his superiors that the manpower necessary to protect the villages was sapped by the requirements of a war of attrition.

Krulak retired from the U.S. Marine Corps in June 1968 and settled in San Diego, where he became a manager and writer for Copley newspapers. In 1984 he published his memoirs, *First to Fight.* Krulak died in San Diego on December 29, 2008.

Will E. Fahey Jr.

See also Combined Action Platoons, U.S. Marine Corps; Ngo Dinh Diem; Vietnam War; Westmoreland, William Childs

Further Reading

Coram, Robert. *The Life of Victor Krulak, U.S. Marine.* New York: Little, Brown, 2010.

Krulak, Victor H. *First to Fight: An Inside view of the U.S. Marine Corps.* Annapolis, MD: Naval Institute Press, 1984.

Zaffiri, Samuel. *Westmoreland: A Biography of General William C. Westmoreland.* New York: William Morrow, 1994.

Kurdistan Workers' Party

The Kurdish people, or Kurds, live in West Asia in the mountainous region known as Kurdistan that encompasses southeastern Turkey, eastern Syria, northern Iraq, and western Iran. Kurdistan includes the oil fields around Kirkuk and is rich in other natural resources. Most Kurds are Sunni Muslims, while a minority are Shiites.

The largest number of Kurds—some 15 million—live in Turkey, while there are an estimated 7 million in Iran, 6 million in Iraq, and 2 million in Syria. With at least 30 million people, Kurds constitute the world's largest ethnic group without a state, something they have long sought. This appeared to be on the verge of realization following World War I (1914–1918) and the breakup of the Ottoman Empire. The Treaty of Sèvres between the victorious Allies and Turkey in 1920 promised the Kurds autonomy leading to statehood following a plebiscite, but a second treaty with Turkey, the Treaty of Lausanne of 1923, recognized Turkish sovereignty over northern Kurdistan, while the remainder of the Kurdish territory fell in Iran and the new states of Iraq and Syria. World War II (1939–1945) did not change the situation, and militant Kurds have continued calls for an independent Kurdish state.

During 1961–1963, there was an uprising of Kurds in northern Iraq following Iraqi government refusal to grant them autonomy. Northern Iraq saw another Kurdish rebellion during 1974–1975. Abetted by Iran, the rebellion collapsed when Iran resolved its border dispute with Iraq in March 1975. In late 1979 a Kurdish revolt also occurred in Iran during the Iranian Revolution of that year. In 1988 in what can only be described as a massacre, Iraqi leader Saddam Hussein ordered the Iraqi Army and the Iraqi Air Force into the Kurdish north of the country. Employing both conventional attacks and chemical warfare, the Iraqi military destroyed some 2,000 villages and killed upwards of 180,000 Kurds. The Iraqi Army crushed other Kurdish revolts, following the Persian Gulf War in 1991 and then in 1995.

Since 1984, Turkey, with half of the world's Kurdish population representing some 20 percent of its own population, has experienced a Kurdish insurgency, led by the Partiya Karkerên Kurdistan (PKK, Kurdistan Workers' Party). Initially consisting largely of students and led by Abdullah Öcalan, the PKK was established on November 27, 1978, in the village of Fis, near Lice, Turkey. In addition to Kurdish nationalism, the PKK initially espoused a Marxist ideology.

Almost immediately after its formation, the PKK was locked in combat with right-wing parties in Turkey and with those Kurdish leaders it accused of collaboration with the Turkish government. Since 1984, the PKK has been waging an armed struggle against the Turkish state to secure an autonomous Kurdistan and greater cultural and political rights for Turkish Kurds. This began with attacks and bombings against Turkish government institutions and military installations, and not exclusively in Turkey.

In the mid-1990s the PKK initiated a series of suicide bombings, a majority of which were carried out by women. In March 1995, the Turkish Army carried out Operation STEEL CURTAIN, sending 35,000 troops into the Kurdish zone of northern Iraq in an effort to trap several thousand guerrillas and halt PKK cross-border raids. In the late 1990s, Turkey increased pressure on the PKK when an undeclared war between Turkey and Syria ended open Syrian support. In February 1999, Turkish commandos seized PKK leader Öcalan in Kenya. He was brought before a Turkish court, and his death sentence was subsequently commuted to life imprisonment as part of negotiations for Turkish membership in the European Union. That same month, the Turkish Army again invaded northern Iraq to wipe out PKK bases there.

Meanwhile, the Turkish government sought to allay international criticism by somewhat relaxing legislation directed against the Kurds, including bans on broadcasting and publishing in the Kurdish language. At the same time, the PKK found itself blacklisted in a number of states. Both the United States and the European Union have characterized the PKK as a terrorist organization.

A low-level insurgency continued and involved PKK ambushes of Turkish military patrols and retaliatory Turkish military responses. Kurdish hopes for at least autonomy received a boost from the Iraq War (2003–2011), when the Kurds in northern Iraq all but established their own state. The war also led to tensions between the Turkish government and the United States and coalition forces, with Ankara accusing Washington of failing to wipe out PKK bases in northern Iraq, from which it claimed raids had been launched into Turkey.

The Turkish Army has set the numbers of killed through 1984 at 6,482 Turkish military personnel, 32,000 PKK troops, and 5,560 civilians. It also claimed 14,000 PKK troops taken prisoner. The PKK claims that the Turkish armed forces have destroyed some 8,000 Kurdish communities and displaced 3 million–4 million people. With the large Turkish army unable to crush the insurgency, and with it a considerable drain on Turkish state finances, in January 2013, Turkish Prime Minister Recep Tayyip Erdogan decided to enter into talks with the PKK. A cease-fire agreement was reached in early May, in which the PKK agreed to withdraw its fighters into northern Iraq in return for democratic concessions in a new Turkish constitution.

Spencer C. Tucker

Further Reading

Natali, Denise. *The Kurds and the State.* Syracuse, NY: Syracuse University Press, 2005.

Tahiri, Hussein. *The Structure of Kurdish Society and the Struggle for a Kurdish State.* Costa Mesa, CA: Mazda, 2007.

L

Lansdale, Edward Geary

Birth Date: February 6, 1908
Death Date: February 23, 1987

U.S. intelligence operative and the father of the modern U.S. counterinsurgency doctrine. Born in Detroit, Michigan, on February 6, 1908, Edward Geary Lansdale grew up in Michigan and California. In 1931 with only a few credit hours short of graduation, he dropped out of the University of California, Los Angeles (UCLA), where he was a journalism student. Working in New York City during the next four years, in 1935 he moved to Los Angeles, where he began work as an advertising agent. In 1937 he moved to San Francisco.

Following the December 1941 Japanese attack on Pearl Harbor, Lansdale entered the U.S. Office of Strategic Services (OSS). In 1943 the U.S. Army reinstated his UCLA Reserve Officers' Training Corps (ROTC) commission and assigned him to military intelligence. At the end of the war in the Pacific, Lansdale was a major stationed in Manila.

In 1947 Lansdale transferred to the newly established U.S. Air Force. He returned to the Philippines in 1951, this time on loan to a new governmental intelligence and covert action group, the Office of Policy Coordination (OPC), successor to the OSS and forerunner to the Central Intelligence Agency (CIA). His responsibilities were to revitalize the Philippine Army in its struggle with a Communist-inspired rebellion and to assist that country's new secretary of defense, Ramón Magsaysay, in becoming president in upcoming national elections. Assisted by considerable OPC funds, Lansdale succeeded on both counts.

Lieutenant Colonel Lansdale's next assignment, now under CIA authority, took him to the newly divided Vietnam in June 1954. As chief of the covert-action Saigon Military Mission (SMM), he was tasked with weakening the Democratic Republic of Vietnam (DRV, North Vietnam) through any means available while strengthening the southern State of Vietnam as a separate and noncommunist nation. Within weeks Lansdale became a principal adviser to Ngo Dinh Diem, who was simultaneously the State of Vietnam premier, defense minister, and commander of the military. Diem accepted many of Lansdale's ideas, including urging northerners to move south (ultimately some 1.25 million did so), bribing sect leaders to merge their private armies into Diem's or face battle with him, instituting service organizations and a government bureaucracy, planning reforms, and in October 1955 offering himself and a new constitution as an alternative to Bao Dai.

A lopsided, manipulated vote for Diem occurred. While Lansdale worked with Diem in the Republic of Vietnam (RVN, South Vietnam), part of his SMM team labored in North Vietnam, with largely mixed and insignificant results, to carry out sabotage and to effect a psychological warfare campaign against the Communist government there.

Lansdale became a close personal friend of Diem and was one of the very few men, outside of his own family, to whom Diem listened. Their unofficial relationship bypassed normal channels of diplomatic relations, causing many diplomatic, military, CIA, and civilian leaders in the U.S. government to view Lansdale with distrust. Yet Lansdale's record of success in the Philippines, his early accomplishments in Vietnam, and his own network of friends and contacts in high places prevented his enemies from dismissing him or his ideas.

With his influence lessened by Diem's growing reliance on his brother, Ngo Dinh Nhu, Lansdale returned to the United States in early 1957 and served both the Dwight D. Eisenhower and John F. Kennedy administrations as deputy director of the Office of Special Operations, Office of the Secretary of Defense. Lansdale was also a member of the U.S. Intelligence Board (USIB), helping to formulate national covert intelligence policy. On occasional visits to Vietnam, he maintained his friendship with Diem. Lansdale's views often conflicted with the findings of others who were ready to give up on Diem.

In the declining days of the Eisenhower administration, Lansdale, now a brigadier general, worked with the Operations Coordinating Board of the USIB that oversaw CIA efforts to overthrow Fidel Castro in Cuba. Lansdale argued against such actions.

In 1961 and 1963 as assistant to the secretary of defense for special operations, Lansdale served as executive officer for the president's Special Group, Augmented (SGA), charged with freeing Cuba from Castro, a plan known as Operation MONGOOSE. Lansdale regarded with dismay the CIA-sponsored invasion of the Bay of Pigs, Cuba, by Cuban exiles in April 1961, considering it ill-timed and ill-planned. After several intelligence forays to Central and South American countries, Lansdale retired from the U.S. Air Force in October 1963 as a major general.

President Lyndon B. Johnson recalled Lansdale to government service between 1965 and 1968, sending him to Vietnam with ministerial rank to work on pacification problems. Lansdale's influence was less than in previous years, and his authority was not clearly defined. He accomplished little, and those years were for Lansdale a time of great frustration. He published his memoirs in 1972. Lansdale's career was both extolled and lambasted in two major novels: Eugene Burdick and William Lederer's *The Ugly American* (1958) and Graham Greene's *The Quiet American* (1955). Plagued by ill health in retirement, Lansdale died in McLean, Virginia, on February 23, 1987.

Cecil B. Currey

See also Castro Ruz, Fidel Alejandro; Hukbalahap Rebellion; Magsaysay, Ramón del Fierro; Ngo Dinh Diem; Pacification; Vietnam War

Further Reading

Currey, Cecil B. *Edward Lansdale: The Unquiet American.* Boston: Houghton Mifflin, 1988.

Lansdale, Edward Geary. *In the Midst of Wars: An American's Mission to Southeast Asia.* New York: Harper and Row, 1972.

Lattre de Tassigny, Jean Joseph Marie Gabriel de

Birth Date: February 2, 1889
Death Date: January 11, 1952

French general and high commissioner and commander of French forces in Indochina (1950–1951). Born at Mouilleron-en-Pareds in the Vendée on February 2, 1889, Jean Joseph Marie Gabriel de Lattre de Tassigny graduated in 1910 from the French Military Academy of Saint-Cyr. Wounded six times during World War I (1914–1918), he rose to command an infantry battalion and received eight citations for bravery.

Following the war, de Lattre fought in Morocco and was seriously wounded in the 1925 Rif campaign. He headed the École Supérieure de Guerre (War College) in 1935. He also served as General Maxime Weygand's chief of cabinet and then as chief of staff of Fifth Army. On the eve of World War II (1939–1945), de Lattre commanded an infantry regiment.

During the 1940 German invasion of France, de Lattre commanded the 14th Infantry Division, which had an excellent combat record. Following the armistice, he worked at retraining what remained of the French Army. In September 1941, the Vichy government reassigned him to command French forces in Tunisia. In fighting between British-Free French and German forces in Libya, de Lattre positioned his forces to cut off a German retreat, and in January 1942 he was reassigned to command an infantry division in metropolitan France.

After the November 1942 Allied landings in North Africa, de Lattre deployed his troops to prevent German units, who occupied Vichy France, from quickly reaching the Mediterranean coast, enabling many anti-German French to escape by sea. This led to his arrest and trial by the Vichy government on charges of "attempting a putsch," for which he was sentenced to 10 years in prison. In September 1943 de Lattre escaped from Riom Prison and made his way to England. After several months in a hospital, he joined General Charles de Gaulle's Free French government in Algiers.

De Lattre commanded Free French forces in the June 1944 invasion of Elba. In August he commanded the French First Army in southern France; it and the U.S. Seventh Army made up the Allied 6th Army Group. De Lattre's army was highly

French General Jean de Lattre de Tassigny was arguably France's greatest soldier when he assumed command of French forces in Indochina in 1950. A tough, no-nonsense commander, he well understood the appeal of nationalism and sought to create wholly Vietnamese units commanded by Vietnamese officers. This photograph was taken on September 24, 1951, during his visit to Washington, D.C., to solicit additional American assistance. Consumed by cancer, de Lattre left Vietnam in December 1951 and died in Paris the next month. (National Archives and Records Administration)

successful and by the end of the war had fought its way to the Austrian border. Later de Lattre served on the Allied Control Commission for Germany. In 1945 he was appointed inspector general of the French Army, taking charge of its retraining and modernization. From 1948 to 1950, he was commander of West European land forces.

In December 1950 in a gesture of determination, the French government sent de Lattre, its greatest living soldier, to Indochina, appointing him high commissioner as well as commander of French forces there. De Lattre had both panache and great personal magnetism. Known within the army as "le roi Jean" (King John) for his insistence on military ceremony, he was a tough no-nonsense commander who promised little except that his men would know they had been commanded. De Lattre canceled the planned departure of French women and children from Hanoi because of the effect this would have on morale. "As long as the women and children are here," he said, "the men won't dare go." His blunt approach, including open admiration for his opponents' skill, injected a new spirit among the French forces.

De Lattre concentrated his efforts in the north, specifically the fortification of the Red River Delta with construction of his famous *ceinture* ("belt"), known as the De Lattre Line. Ultimately 51 million cubic yards of concrete went into 900 forts and 2,200 pillboxes, many of which survive today as mute testimony to a failed policy. The Viet Minh simply ignored these fortified positions, which tied down 20 French infantry battalions.

Although the French government agreed to send reinforcements, they were not as numerous as de Lattre wanted. He hoped to make up the shortfall with the Vietnamese National Army (VNA), but in January 1951 the VNA had only 30,000 regulars (65,000 men overall) in 11 infantry battalions and 9 national guard regiments. Using U.S. funds, de Lattre planned to create 11 new battalions. He would do this by *jaunissement* ("yellowing" or "vietnamizing"), creating wholly Vietnamese units commanded by Vietnamese officers. Unfortunately for France, this policy came too late in the war to succeed.

Viet Minh commander Vo Nguyen Giap played into de Lattre's hands by initiating Operation HOANG HOA THAM, which sought conventional battle with French forces. Defeat of the Viet Minh in a series of battles in the first half of 1951 enabled de Lattre to make a forceful appeal for additional U.S. military assistance, a plea that he delivered in the course of a much-publicized September 1951 trip to Washington. The United States increased economic aid to the French but was unwilling to offer any direct military assistance.

Ignoring warnings from his Chinese advisers, Giap now shifted his attention to the Thai Highlands. The resulting December 1951–February 1952 fighting at Hoa Binh initiated by de Lattre became an inconclusive battle of attrition, with high casualties for both sides.

In December 1951, de Lattre left Indochina. Already consumed by cancer, he entered a Paris clinic that same month and died on January 11, 1952. His last audible word was "Bernard," the name of his only son, a French Army lieutenant who had been killed in combat in Indochina the previous May.

Spencer C. Tucker

See also Indochina War; *Jaunissement;* Viet Minh; Vo Nguyen Giap

Further Reading

Clayton, Anthony. *Three Marshals Who Saved France: Leadership after Trauma.* London: Brassey's, 1992.

Fall, Bernard. *The Two Viet Nams.* Revised ed. New York: Praeger, 1964.

Vo Nguyen Giap and Huu Mai. *Duong Toi Dien Bien Phu* [The Road to Dien Bien Phu]. Hanoi: People's Army Publishing House, 2001.

Lawrence, Thomas Edward

Birth Date: August 15, 1888
Death Date: May 19, 1935

British Army officer, archaeologist, and writer who became widely known as "Lawrence of Arabia" for his exploits in the Middle East. Born on August 15, 1888, at Tremadoc, Caernarvonshire, Wales, Thomas Edward Lawrence was the second of five illegitimate sons of Sir Thomas Chapman. Lawrence was about 10 years old when he learned of this, and some believe that it left a permanent imprint on his personality. After earning a history degree at Jesus College, Oxford, in 1910, Lawrence traveled to the Middle East in the five years prior to World War I (1914–1918) to prepare material for his graduate thesis on the architecture of Crusader castles.

An expedition that he accompanied to the Sinai in 1914, ostensibly to explore the area, was in reality designed to gain information for the War Office on military dispositions on the Ottoman frontier east of Suez.

On the outbreak of World War I in 1914, Lawrence failed to meet the height requirement of 5'5" for the army and was posted to the Geographical Section of the War Office. Sent to Cairo, he was attached to the military intelligence staff specializing in Arab affairs. In October 1916 he accompanied a mission to the Hejaz, where Hussein ibn Ali, sharif of Mecca, had proclaimed a revolt against the Ottoman Empire. The following month as a captain, Lawrence was ordered to become a political and liaison officer to Hussein's son, Faisal, commanding an Arab force southwest of Medina.

Lawrence was instrumental in acquiring considerable material assistance from the British army in Cairo for the Arab cause. Recognizing that the key to Ottoman control lay in the Damascus-Medina Railway, along which they could send reinforcements to crush the Arab Revolt, Lawrence accompanied Faisal and his army in a series of attacks on the railway, earning the name "Emir Dynamite" from the admiring Bedouins.

On July 6, 1917, Lawrence led a force of Huwaitat tribesmen in the capture of the port of Aqaba, at the northernmost tip of the Red Sea. Aqaba became the base for Faisal's army. From there, Lawrence attempted to coordinate Arab movements with the campaign of British lieutenant general Sir Edmund Allenby, who was advancing from Jerusalem in southern Palestine. This action brought Lawrence promotion to major.

In November 1917 Lawrence was captured at Dara by the Turks while conducting a reconnaissance of the area in Arab dress. He underwent a short period of humiliating torture but escaped and was present at the Battle of Tafila (January 24–25, 1918). Lawrence, for all his flamboyant poses and his adoption of Arab dress, was never a leader of Arab forces; command always remained firmly in the hands of Emir Faisal. Lawrence was, however, an inspirational force behind the Arab Revolt, a superb tactician, and a highly influential theoretician of guerrilla warfare. During the last two years of the war, Lawrence's advice and influence effectively bound the Arab nations to the Allied cause, thereby tying down about 25,000 Turkish troops who would otherwise have opposed the British Army. For his war service, Lawrence was awarded the Distinguished Service Order and was promoted to lieutenant colonel. Subsequently he was present at the capture of Damascus on October 1, 1918, returning to England the following month, where he was demobilized.

Lawrence then witnessed the defeat of his aspirations for the Arabs when their seemingly incurable factionalism rendered them incapable of becoming a nation. He lobbied in vain against the detachment of Syria and Lebanon from the rest of the Arab countries as a French mandate. He also worked on his war memoir. In 1921 Lawrence was wooed back to the Middle East as adviser on Arab affairs to Colonial Minister Winston Churchill. However, after the Cairo political settlements regarding the Middle East, Lawrence rejected offers of further positions and left the government in protest.

In August 1922 Lawrence enlisted (under the name John Hume Ross) in the Royal Air Force but was discharged six months later when his identity was disclosed by a London newspaper. He then enlisted as T. E. Shaw in the Royal Tank Corps and transferred to the Royal Air Force in 1925, remaining with that service until he was discharged in February 1935. Lawrence died at Bovington Camp Hospital on May 19, 1935, following a motorcycle accident.

Lawrence became an almost mythic figure in his own lifetime. His reputation was to an extent self-generated through his own highly successful literary accounts, including his war memoir *The Seven Pillars of Wisdom* (1922) and lecture tours, assisted by his postwar research fellowship at Oxford University.

James H. Willbanks

See also Arab Revolt against Ottoman Rule

Further Reading

Lawrence, Thomas E. *Revolt in the Desert.* Herefordshire, UK: Wordsworth Editions, 1997.

Lawrence, Thomas E. *Seven Pillars of Wisdom: A Triumph.* Garden City, NY: Doubleday, Doran, 1935.

Korda, Michael. *Hero: The Life and Legend of Lawrence of Arabia.* New York: Harper, 2010.

Wilson, Jeremy. *Lawrence of Arabia: The Authorized Biography of T. E. Lawrence.* New York: Atheneum, 1990.

Le Duan

Birth Date: April 7, 1907
Death Date: July 10, 1986

Secretary-general of the Communist Party of Vietnam and de facto leader of the Democratic Republic of Vietnam (DRV, North Vietnam) during 1969–1986. Born Le Van Nhuan on April 7, 1907, in Quang Tri Province, Annam, French Indochina, Le Duan early on developed a commitment to revolutionary politics. During the 1920s, he worked as a clerk for French Railways in Hanoi and cultivated his Marxist interests. He joined the Vietnam Revolutionary Youth League and in 1930 became a charter member of the Indochinese Communist Party (ICP). In 1939 he was elected a member of the Communist Party Central Committee. An ardent opponent of French rule, Le Duan was twice imprisoned (1931–1936 and 1940–1945) on charges of political subversion.

After World War II (1939–1945), Le Duan became a trusted lieutenant of North Vietnamese president Ho Chi Minh and a key figure in the Viet Minh challenge to

French rule. A capable strategist and tactician, Le Duan directed Viet Minh efforts in Cochin China during 1946–1952 and then worked in the party headquarters. He was elected to membership in the Communist Party Politburo in 1951.

Although the 1954 Viet Minh victory at Dien Bien Phu brought an end to French rule in Vietnam, the brokered agreement at the 1954 Geneva Conference left the country divided. Le Duan, who clung to the nationalist ideal of a united, independent Vietnam, openly opposed the agreement. He nonetheless worked with Ho to secure Communist control in the North.

In 1954 Le Duan was sent back to southern Vietnam, where he again served as secretary of the Dang Lao Dong Viet Nam (Vietnam Workers' Party, or the Communist Party of Vietnam) Central Committee for the Southern Region until 1957. In 1956 he wrote the "Tenets of the Revolution in South Vietnam," which became the foundation of the Communist struggle in South Vietnam. In 1957 Le Duan was recalled to North Vietnam, where he was entrusted with the leadership of the party following the removal of Truong Chinh as secretary-general as the result of the disastrous Land Reform Program in North Vietnam. In 1959 Le Duan was elected party first secretary, a position he held for the next decade. He was also a member of the Lao Dong Politburo as well as the Central Committee and Secretariat.

In 1958 Le Duan secretly revisited the Republic of Vietnam (RVN, South Vietnam) to assess the situation there. He returned with recommendations for a dramatic escalation in the insurgency. He warned that Hanoi-supported Viet Cong (VC) guerrillas operating against the U.S.-backed government of Ngo Dinh Diem faced total destruction unless the effort was prosecuted vigorously. During the course of the next three years, largely under Le Duan's direction, the VC launched a sweeping program of assassinations and urban terrorism while stepping up more conventional forms of military confrontation.

Le Duan continued to play an important role in Hanoi's prosecution of the war. A consistent advocate of the offensive, he supported the infusion of People's Army of Vietnam (PAVN, North Vietnamese Army) forces to South Vietnam as well as stronger support for the VC. In 1965 with the escalation of U.S. involvement in the war, he advocated the move to conventional warfare, joining other North Vietnamese leaders in shunning Chinese advice to de-escalate. He maintained that only through conventional offensive warfare, as practiced against the French, could Vietnam expel the "foreign invaders." Le Duan reportedly had frequent clashes with North Vietnamese defense minister General Vo Nguyen Giap and other party leaders over war strategy and political ideology, culminating in a dispute over the plan for the 1968 Tet Offensive during the summer of 1967. At the same time, Le Duan also presided over what was called the Anti-Party Affair, a purge of senior party and military figures, including a number of General Giap's closest supporters.

With Ho's death in September 1969, Le Duan became the undisputed leader of the party and the North Vietnamese government. He continued to press the war and maintained a hard line during cease-fire negotiations with the United States, viewing a continued division of Vietnam as unacceptable. Under the leadership of Le Duan, Vo Nguyen Giap, and Prime Minister Pham Van Dong, Communist forces cemented their victory over South Vietnam with the capture of Saigon in April 1975.

As the leader of a united Vietnam, Le Duan faced the mammoth task of rebuilding a country ravaged by 35 years of almost continuous war. Reconciling opposing ideologies, restoring the economy, and feeding the people of Vietnam all posed major obstacles, and he dealt with these to varying degrees of success. A devoted Marxist, he maintained close ties with the Soviet Union, a relationship that he solidified with the signing of the Friendship Treaty in 1978. Le Duan died in Hanoi on July 10, 1986.

David Coffey

See also Ho Chi Minh; Indochina War; Viet Minh; Vietnam War; Vo Nguyen Giap

Further Reading

Duiker, William J. *The Communist Road to Power in Vietnam.* Boulder, CO: Westview, 1981.

Military History Institute of Vietnam. *Victory in Vietnam: The Official History of the People's Army of Vietnam, 1954–1975.* Lawrence: University Press of Kansas, 2002.

Lehi.

See Lohamei Herut Israel

Lettow-Vorbeck, Paul Emil von

Birth Date: March 20, 1870
Death Date: March 9, 1964

German Army general and unrivaled leader of guerrilla forces. Born on March 20, 1870, at Saarlouis in the Saarland, Germany, Paul Emil von Lettow-Vorbeck was the son of a Prussian Army general. Lettow-Vorbeck joined the Cadet Corps at Potsdam in 1881 and the 2nd Foot Guards Regiment at Koblenz in 1888. He became a lieutenant of artillery upon graduation from the Kriegsakademie in 1899. After brief service on the General Staff in Berlin, Lettow-Vorbeck was promoted to first lieutenant in 1895. He commanded a company in the German expeditionary force sent to China during the Boxer Uprising (Boxer Rebellion) of 1900–1901 and was promoted to captain in 1901.

Lettow-Vorbeck was in Africa during the Herero Rebellion (1904–1907) in present-day Namibia, where he was wounded during an ambush in 1906. He was promoted to major in 1907 and assigned as an adjutant to XI Corps at Kassel.

In 1909 he took command of the 2nd Seebataillon (marines) at Wilhelmshaven. He was promoted to lieutenant colonel in 1913.

Lettow-Vorbeck soon became an expert in irregular warfare. In October 1913 he was appointed commander of the Kaiserlichte Schutztruppe (imperial garrison troops) in German East Africa, and in April 1914 he was named commander of all German East African colonial forces and promoted to colonel. Lettow-Vorbeck anticipated a general European war and understood that in such circumstances, his forces would be isolated from supplies and reinforcement. He diligently trained his small regular German force and native Askari auxiliaries for mobile offensive operations that required living off the land.

In August 1914 when World War I (1914–1918) began, Lettow-Vorbeck seized the initiative and attacked British rail lines in Kenya. He then successfully defended the port of Tanga against a British amphibious attack (November 3–5) and inflicted heavy losses on the attackers. Lettow-Vorbeck's objective became to tie down as many Allied troops as possible. Although his total command never exceeded more than 3,000 German and 11,000 Askari troops, he was able to divert more than 300,000 Allied troops from use on other fronts. When the German cruiser *Königsberg* was destroyed, he absorbed its crew into his forces and salvaged its guns for land use. Lettow-Vorbeck's greatest asset was his Askaris. He treated them with respect, which they repaid with devotion in combat.

By 1916, Lettow-Vorbeck faced General Jan Christian Smuts, who mounted an offensive against East Africa. As Allied numbers increased, Lettow-Vorbeck resorted to ambushes such as at Mahiwa (October 17–18, 1917), where he inflicted 1,500 casualties on an enemy force 4 times his own number and suffered about 100 casualties. He then left East Africa and shifted his operations to Mozambique and Rhodesia. Lettow-Vorbeck learned about the armistice on November 13, 1918, and surrendered his undefeated force to the Allies at Abercorn on November 25, 1918.

Lettow-Vorbeck returned to Germany a hero and was promoted to general major. He subsequently became involved in right-wing politics to oppose the left-wing Spartacists and served in the Reichstag during 1929–1930, where he opposed the National Socialists of Adolf Hitler. Lettow-Vorbeck died, impoverished, in Hamburg on March 9, 1964.

Steven J. Rauch

See also Herero Revolt

Further Reading

Hoyt, Edwin P. *Guerilla: Colonel von Lettow-Vorbeck and Germany's East African Empire*. New York: Macmillan, 1981.

Lettow-Vorbeck, Paul von. *My Reminiscences of East Africa*. London: Hurst and Blackett, 1920.

Miller, Charles. *Battle for the Bundu: The First World War in East Africa*. New York: Macmillan, 1974.

Le Van Nhuan.

See Le Duan

Liberation Tigers of Tamil Eelam

Sri Lankan insurgent organization. The island of Sri Lanka (Ceylon until 1972) is 75 percent Buddhist Sinhalese, with Hindu Tamil people forming the largest minority of some 20 percent. The Tamils live in northern and eastern Sri Lanka and are related to the Tamils of India. Following the independence of Ceylon in 1948, the Sinhalese majority trumpeted Sinhalese nationalism. Thus, Sinhalese replaced English as the official language of Ceylon in 1956, and Ceylon was renamed Sri Lanka in 1972.

As a result of this ethnic pressure, violence increased, as did Tamil demands for autonomy. Velupillai Prabhakaran founded the Tamil New Tigers youth group in 1972, and in 1976 it became the Liberation Tigers of Tamil Eelam (LTTE). The LTTE demanded independence for the Tamil regions and was aided by supporters in the southern Indian state of Tamil Nadu. LTTE guerrillas were effectively organized and well armed.

The LTTE gained infamy for its innovative techniques now widely employed by insurgent groups worldwide, the most notable of which was suicide bombing. The LTTE fought for decades for the creation of an autonomous Tamil homeland. Toward that end, it allied itself in 1985 with the Eelam Revolutionary Organization of Students, the Eelam People's Revolutionary Liberation Front, and the Tamil Eelam Liberation Organization. However, by 1986, the LTTE had turned against its new antigovernment partners and had assumed control of most of Sri Lanka's northern area, especially the strategically located Jaffna peninsula, where the LTTE ruled the region as a de facto government.

The withdrawal of Indian troops from Sri Lanka in March 1990 solidified the LTTE's power, but in 1993 the Colombo government mounted a successful campaign to oust the rebels from their Jaffna stronghold. The start of the campaign was spurred by an ambush of government troops in which hundreds of soldiers were killed.

The LTTE was long regarded as the primary obstacle to peace between the Tamils and the Sinhalese Buddhist government because of its terrorist activities, hard-line position, and intolerance of dissent. The LTTE was blamed for the 1991 assassination by suicide bombing of former Indian prime minister Rajiv Gandhi, the May 1993 assassination of Sri Lankan president Ranasinghe Premadasa, and the December 1999 attack on Chandrika Bandaranaike Kumaratunga, elected president of Sri Lanka just days later. The LTTE killed scores of politicians, journalists, and others who opposed it.

The LTTE also established its own navy and air force and for a time appeared to pose a real military threat to Sri Lanka's government. However, after the World Trade Center and Pentagon attacks of September 11, 2001, the United States classified the LTTE as an international terrorist group, and funding for its cause began to dry up when foreign governments cracked down on its overseas support.

In 2005 new Sinhalese president Mahinda Rajapakse unleashed the military to destroy the LTTE. In early 2008, Sri Lanka's army intensified its offensive against the LTTE in the northeast, despite the plight of Tamil civilians caught up in the fighting. In May 2009, Sri Lankan troops cornered the remnants of the LTTE on a tiny sliver of land in the northeast, killing or capturing the LTTE combatants and ending both the insurgency and the LTTE, with the military displaying what it claimed was the body of LTTE leader Prabhakaran.

Spencer C. Tucker

See also Sri Lankan Civil War

Further Reading

Bose, Sumantra. *States, Nations, Sovereignty: Sri Lanka, India and the Tamil Eelam Movement.* Thousand Oaks, CA: Sage Publications, in association with the Book Review Literary Trust, New Delhi, 1994.

Hashim, Ahmed S. *When Counterinsurgency Wins: Sri Lanka's Defeat of the Tamil Tigers.* Philadelphia: University of Pennsylvania Press, 2012.

Libyan Civil War

Start Date: February 17, 2011
End Date: October 23, 2011

The Libyan Civil War (also known as the Libyan Revolution and the Libyan Insurgency) was but one uprising during the 2011 tumultuous Arab Spring. Moammar Gaddafi had ruled Libya for 42 years and was the focal point of popular unrest, which was strongest in the eastern region of Libya but also manifest in parts of the western and southern provinces. Opponents protested decades of authoritarianism, corruption, and repression that had produced economic and political dysfunction. Libyans tired of the Gaddafi regime sought to ride the Arab Spring to oust the long-ruling dictator and replace him with a transitional government.

The situation in Libya had been tense since the ousting of Tunisian leader Ben Ali in January, and Libyans abroad who made up the preponderance of organized opposition to the Gaddafi regime began mobilizing prior to the beginning of peaceful demonstrations in Benghazi in eastern Libya on February 15, 2011, protesting the arrest of a human rights lawyer. Two days later the demonstrations escalated, and Libyan security forces opened fire on the crowds. During several days, some 150 people were killed. Protesters overwhelmed the Libyan security forces, which withdrew from Benghazi on February 18. Violence also erupted in al-Bayda, Derna, and Tobruk, and Libyan rebels advanced across the country in makeshift caravans with incredible speed. Gaddafi made clear that he would not yield political power and would rather bring on a civil war.

Libyan insurgents celebrate the capture of Muammar Gaddafi's Bab al-Azizya compound in Tripoli on August 23, 2011. (Florent Marcie/AFP/Getty Images)

The opposition in Libya was far more organized than in some other Arab Spring nations. This proved critical in establishing a transitional political movement as well as garnering international support. The opposition leaders formed the Interim Transitional National Council (TNC) on March 5, 2011. It was originally made up of 31 members representing regions of the country as well as the many clans. Local councils from throughout the country selected representatives and charged them with removing Gaddafi and installing democratic rule. The first TNC chairman was Mustafa Mohammad Abdul Jalil, while Mahmoud Jibril chaired the TNC's Executive Board. The TNC also set up a military committee, led by Omar al-Hariri, although Abdul Fatah Younis Al-Obeidi had actual charge of ground operations.

In the first few days of revolt, Libyan minister of the interior Abdul Fatah Younis Al-Obeidi defected, bolstering rebel support. On February 20, protests reached Tripoli, the nation's capital and Gaddafi stronghold. By late February, Gaddafi had lost control of Cyrenaica, Misrata, Zawiyah, and the Berber areas. Fighting in eastern Libya was intense in February and March, with rebels securing Benghazi and advancing to Brega, site of a major oil and gas refinery. Gaddafi loyalists counterattacked and drove the rebels out of Brega and back to the town of Ajdabiya, a strategic access point to Benghazi. On March 15, Gaddafi mounted a drive on Ajdabiya that ousted the rebels and carried on toward Benghazi.

Meanwhile, the Battle of Misrata raged from February 18 until May 15, as Gaddafi forces laid siege to this city that had been taken by rebels and that in their possession threatened his hold on Tripoli. The rebels quickly organized the Misrata Street and Military Councils, charged with overseeing rebel defenses and continuing public services. Although not as well financed as the TNC, the Military Council led by General Ramadan Zarmuh was able to stave off a loyalist onslaught that ultimately reached more than 10,000 men and saw considerable widespread shelling of the city. Misrata was saved thanks to a sealift of rebel weapons, supplies, and manpower from Benghazi.

During the fighting in Cyrenaica, fears abounded that Gaddafi would wreak havoc on Benghazi, resulting in the deaths of countless innocent civilians in what was Libya's second-largest city. Libyan opposition leaders called for international intervention. To avoid the anticipated massacre, the United Nations Security Council passed Resolution 1973 calling for a no-fly zone over Libya and permission for member states to take all necessary measures to protect civilians there. The resolution did not authorize foreign ground troops.

The French took the lead, and subsequently their warplanes disrupted Gaddafi's advance on March 19, driving the loyalists back to Ajdabiya. The North Atlantic Treaty Organization (NATO) reached agreement on intervention and air strikes, but its aircraft kept the loyalists from massing the forces needed to take Misrata or Benghazi.

Such international intervention, led by the United States, Great Britain, and France, drastically altered the conflict. The air campaign, dubbed Operation ODYSSEY DAWN, ran during March 19–31 and was led by head of the U.S. Africa Command General Carter F. Ham. ODYSSEY DAWN enforced the no-fly zone, destroyed Gaddafi's air force and Libyan air defenses, and mounted air strikes on loyalist armor, artillery, and command-and-control centers. A subsequent NATO operation, UNIFIED PROTECTOR, enforced the arms embargo and assumed command of all NATO operations in Libya.

Even with international intervention, the conflict dragged on for months before resolution. The battle for Misrata continued, with Gaddafi seeking to exploit tribal antagonisms to his advantage. He also sought to use his naval forces against the port, with the result that NATO carried out an attack on the Libyan Navy on May 20.

The three-month battle for Misrata ended in an insurgent victory on May 15. The battle had claimed more than 1,500 rebel and civilian dead. Meanwhile, Gaddafi forces employed tanks and artillery against rebel towns in the Nafusa Mountains. This went on for a span of some four months, with rebel forces here in dire straits until several key victories reopened supply lines and NATO air strikes deflected the loyalists.

Another major battle erupted in late February in the port city of Zawiyah, only 30 miles west of Tripoli. More important than its proximity to the capital were its oil refinery and port facilities. Rebel forces under the command of Colonel Hussein Darbouk were unable to hold the city against Gaddafi's onslaught, and Zawiyah remained under loyalist control until August. When the rebels retook Zawiyah, this prompted a drive from the Nafusa Mountains into Tripoli on August 20.

The Tripoli campaign involved rebel elements from the Nafusa Mountains and Misrata as well as from Tripoli itself. The fighting was block by block, with the last government stronghold falling on August 28. Gaddafi, who had vowed to fight to the end in Tripoli, had already departed for his home of Sirte, which was the objective of a rebel attack in mid-October. Gaddafi was captured while attempting to escape from Sirte on October 20 and was executed. Also killed were his son Mutassim Gaddafi and army chief General Abu Bakr Younis.

On October 23 the TNC declared victory and set elections for 18 months in the future. The NATO mission ended a week later, on October 31.

Numerous challenges remained, including disarming the insurgents, rebuilding the economy and the military, constructing institutions capable of governing the country, and maintaining political unity in a nation sharply divided along tribal and ethnic lines.

Larissa Mihalisko

See also Aircraft in Counterinsurgency Operations

Further Reading

Pargeter, Alison. *Libya: The Rise and Fall of Qaddafi.* New Haven, CT: Yale University Press, 2012.

St. John, Ronald B. *Libya: From Colony to Revolution.* Oxford, UK: Oneworld, 2012.

Vandewalle, Dirk J. *A History of Modern Libya.* Cambridge: Cambridge University Press, 2012.

Lohamei Herut Israel

Radical armed Zionist insurgent organization active in Palestine during the 1940s. The last years of the British mandate over Palestine were ones of great instability and even intense conflict. Lohamei Herut Israel (Fighters for the Freedom of Israel), also known as Lehi or the Stern Gang, contributed to the volatility of the situation by launching attacks against British authorities and the Arab population in Palestine.

Founded in September 1940 and never numbering more than a few hundred fighters, Lehi was a splinter group of the Irgun Tsvai Leumi (National Military Organization), an intensely nationalist Jewish organization. Lehi rejected cooperation or compromise with the mandate government and demanded an immediate end to British rule.

Zionism and the Jewish drive for statehood in Palestine gave rise to a number of armed groups that sought to speed the reestablishment of an independent Israel. Avraham Stern (aka Yair), a radical Irgun member who denounced any plans to limit the borders of a Jewish Palestine, formed Lehi in response to a commitment by other Jewish militias to suspend attacks against the British after the outbreak of World War II (1939–1945). Stern failed to understand that a defeat of

Nazi Germany would necessarily strengthen Jewish interests and instead approved efforts in 1940 to approach Britain's foes and offer them an alliance.

Such ties never materialized, but Lehi's leadership was hardly dissuaded by the setback and initiated an independent terror campaign against the British. The first significant attack in this offensive came in December 1940 with the bombing of the immigration offices in Haifa, a symbolic strike against British-imposed restrictions on the flow of Jews into Palestine. In response, the British condemned Lehi and dismissed it as a criminal organization that had to be neutralized. However, even Stern's death at the hands of the British security forces failed to curtail the threat posed by the organization.

Under new leaders, the most prominent of whom was Yitzhak "Michael" Shamir, a future Israeli prime minister, Lehi continued its attacks, including the infamous killing of Lord Moyne, the British minister resident in Cairo, on November 6, 1944. The murder shocked the British and prompted the Jewish community in Palestine to crack down on the terrorists carrying out such attacks.

At the conclusion of World War II, a broad alliance and unified command emerged among Jewish armed groups in the mandate. Intent on driving out the British and speeding the establishment of an independent Israel, the militias, known collectively as the Hebrew Resistance Movement, renewed their joint operations against the British security forces and Arab interests. Lehi fighters played a prominent role in this campaign, including participation in some of the most heinous terrorist acts committed during the last years of the mandate.

On January 4, 1948, Lehi operatives detonated a truck bomb outside the Arab National Committee offices at the city hall in Jaffa, killing 26 people and wounding scores more. Members of Lehi also joined the April 9, 1948, attack on the Arab village of Dayr Yasin near Jerusalem, in which Jewish fighters massacred more than 100 people and underscored their determination to drive Arabs out of lands claimed for the State of Israel.

An attack of perhaps even greater significance was the assassination in Jerusalem of Count Folke Bernadotte, a Swedish nobleman and the United Nations mediator, on September 17, 1948. Carried out by fighters from Hazit HaMoledet (Homeland Front), a subgroup of Lehi, the attack revealed the level of radicalism that existed in the region, at least among a minority of activists, within the Zionist movement.

In the wake of the Bernadotte murder, the new Israeli government took steps to dismantle Lehi and imprison its leaders. Natan Yellin-Mor, one of the organization's most prominent figures, was soon convicted of involvement in the Bernadotte plot. However, within a year the authorities released Yellin-Mor and allowed him to occupy a seat in the Knesset. Many of Lehi's former members also found a home in the Israel Defense Force.

Jonas Kauffeldt

See also Irgun Tsvai Leumi; Stern, Avraham

Further Reading

Heller, Joseph. *The Stern Gang: Ideology, Politics, and Terror, 1940–1949.* London: Frank Cass, 1995.

Marton, Kati. *A Death in Jerusalem.* New York: Arcade, 1996.

Morris, Benny. *Righteous Victims: A History of the Zionist-Arab Conflict, 1881–1999.* New York: Knopf, 1999.

Long March

Start Date: October 1934
End Date: October 1935

The so-called Long March of October 1934–October 1935 was the most celebrated event of the Chinese Civil War (1927–1949). As a consequence of Fifth Bandit Extermination Campaign against the Communists, carried out by Guomindang (GMD, Nationalist) leader Jiang Jieshi (Chiang Kai-shek), some 300,000 GMD troops surrounded the Communist stronghold of Ruijin (Juichin) in remote Jiangxi (Kiangsi) Province and gradually tightened the noose on its outnumbered defenders. Facing certain annihilation, the Communist leadership, headed by Mao Zedong (Mao Tse-tung), voted to attempt a breakout.

In October 1934 following a diversionary attack by some 130,000 Communist troops, 86,000 other troops, 11,000 political cadres, and many thousands of civilian porters broke free of the Nationalist encirclement and began what became known as the Long March. The other Communist forces remained behind to fight a delaying action and then dispersed as best they could.

The escaping Communists easily made it through the first Nationalist strong points, but they then encountered reinforced Nationalist troops at the Xiang (Hsiang) River in Hunan Province. Here during November 30–December 1, 1934, the Communists lost 40,000 troops and virtually all of their porters. Those Communists who remained had to fight their way across some of the most difficult terrain of western China before proceeding north. The trek lasted 370 days, and during it the Communists were under nearly constant Nationalist attack from the ground and air before reaching the remote northwestern province of Shaanxi (Shensi) and safety. With deaths en route, those left behind as underground cadres, and desertions but adding those who joined en route, about 100,000 people reached Shaanxi.

Although the Communists later embellished the history of the Long March to near-legendary proportions and claimed a distance traveled of up to 8,000 miles (recent scholarship posits 3,700 miles), it was nonetheless an extraordinary feat. As a consequence, Mao and his supporters emerged as the leaders of the Chinese Communist Party.

Spencer C. Tucker

See also Mao Zedong

Further Reading

Jocelyn, Ed, and Andrew McEwen. *The Long March.* London: Constable and Robinson, 2006.

Salisbury, Harrison Evans. *The Long March: The Untold Story.* New York: Harper and Row, 1985.

Shuyun Sun. *The Long March: The True History of Communist China's Founding Myth.* New York: Doubleday, 2008.

Lord's Resistance Army

The Lord's Resistance Army (LRA) is an insurgent group that has wreaked widespread havoc in northern Uganda, South Sudan, the Democratic Republic of the Congo, and the Central African Republic. The LRA initially formed among the Acholi people of Uganda, who believed that they had been marginalized by the central government in favor of other Ugandan ethic groups. The LRA was established and led by Joseph Kony, a self-proclaimed spokesperson of God and spirit medium. Kony claimed to want to establish a theocratic state based on the Ten Commandments and local Acholi tradition, but his army has been guilty of outrageous crimes, including murders, rapes, the sexual enslavement of women and children, and forcing young boys into the army's ranks. Estimates of the size of the LRA vary widely from 500 to as many as 3,000 soldiers, with perhaps 1,500 women and children. Its soldiers have traditionally operated as independent brigades of 15–20 men each.

Counterinsurgency campaigns by the Ugandan military and the decision by the Sudanese government to cut off its support for the LRA led Kony to enter into negotiations in 2006. The International Criminal Court also increased the pressure by issuing arrest warrants against Kony and four of his lieutenants for war crimes and crimes against humanity. The peace talks dragged on without result, however, and were broken off altogether in late 2008.

The failure of the peace talks led to Operation LIGHTNING THUNDER in December 2008, a joint offensive against an LRA camp in the northeastern Democratic Republic of the Congo. The operation involved the militaries of Uganda, the Democratic Republic of the Congo, and South Sudan. Some U.S. military advisers provided logistics, communications, and intelligence support. Although 200–400 LRA fighters were killed, the mission was largely a failure. The LRA leadership learned in advance of the bombing raid that was to proceed the ground attack, and bad weather led to the substitution of jet aircraft for helicopters, reducing accuracy. Poor coordination also saw the ground forces arriving a week later. In the weeks that followed during December 2008–January 2009, the LRA took revenge. LRA fighters killed as many as 1,000 villagers—men, women, and children—in the eastern Congo, most of them hacked to death.

In the autumn of 2011, U.S. president Barack Obama dispatched some 100 U.S. Special Forces personnel to join in the hunt for Kony, said by some to be dead, and his LRA. The LRA insurgency continues to the present in what is certainly one of Africa's longest-running conflicts. To date, LRA forces have killed some 3,000 people, abducted another 3,500, and displaced perhaps 465,000.

Spencer C. Tucker

Further Reading

Allen, Tim, and Koen Vlassenroot. *The Lord's Resistance Army: Myth and Reality.* London: Zed, 2010.

Green, Matthew. *The Wizard of the Nile: The Hunt for Africa's Most Wanted.* Northampton, MA: Olive Branch, 2008.

Singer, Peter W. *Children at War.* Berkeley: University of California Press, 2006.

Lyautey, Louis Hubert

Birth Date: November 17, 1854
Death Date: July 27, 1934

French Army marshal, minister of war, and one of France's greatest colonial soldiers. Born on November 17, 1854, in Nancy, Louis Hubert Lyautey entered the French Military Academy of Saint-Cyr in 1873. Routine assignments in the cavalry followed, including a tour in Algeria. In France, Lyautey met writers such as Jose Maria de Heredia, Henri de Régnier, and Marcel Proust and became concerned about the social cleavage in the army between officers and enlisted men. Lyautey urged that officers take an interest in the social and spiritual welfare of their men. These views, published anonymously in 1891 in an article titled "Du rôle social de l'officier dans le service militaire universel" (On the Social Role of the Officer in Universal Military Service) in *La Revue des Deux Mondes,* apparently angered his superiors and led to his assignment to Tonkin, which proved a turning point in his military career.

In Indochina, Lyautey became chief of staff to Colonel Joseph Gallieni, then commanding French forces in upper Tonkin. Lyautey fully embraced Gallieni's theories regarding the oil slick method of pacification, which included not only military action but also social action and improvements in the quality of life to win the hearts and minds of the people. In 1897 when Gallieni became military governor of Madagascar, Lyautey followed him and took charge of pacifying first the northwestern part of the island and then the southern part. Lyautey was promoted to colonel in 1900, the same year that he published another important article, "Du rôle colonial de l'armée" (On the Colonial Role of the Army) in *La Revue des Deux Mondes,* in which he summarized pacification policies.

Assigned to France in 1902, Lyautey was sent to southern Algeria. In 1904 he carried out an independent action along the Moroccan border that embarrassed

French foreign minister Théophile Delcassé. Continuing to press for French military intervention in Morocco, in 1906 Lyautey took charge of the Oran division as a general. In 1907 he implemented the French military occupation of Oujda on the Moroccan border, without the consent of French premier Georges Clemenceau. Following a tour of duty in France, in 1912 Lyautey was named resident-general of Morocco, with wide civil and military powers. He then gradually imposed French authority on the country.

Despite the depletion of his forces with World War I (1914–1918), Lyautey continued to press French pacification of the Moroccan interior, including the construction of roads, railroads, bridges, and schools. When Premier Aristide Briand reorganized his cabinet in December 1916, he appointed Lyautey as minister of war. But Lyautey arrived in France to discover that he had not been consulted on the appointment of new French commander in chief General Robert Nivelle. Unsupported in his criticism of Nivelle's plans for a great spring offensive, Lyautey resigned on March 14 and by the end of May had returned to his post in Morocco.

Promoted to marshal of France in 1921, Lyautey continued to control French affairs in Morocco until French Army commander Marshal Henri Philippe Pétain replaced him in 1925, following a widespread rebellion led by Abd el-Krim and known as the Rif War. A member of the French Academy since 1921, Lyautey died in Thorey (Lorraine) on July 27, 1934.

Philippe Haudrère and Spencer C. Tucker

See also Abd el-Krim al-Khattabi, Muhammad ibn; Gallieni, Joseph Simon; Rif War

Further Reading

Charrette, Hervé de. *Lyautey.* Paris: Perrin, 1997.

Hoisington, William A. *Lyautey and the French Conquest of Morocco.* New York, St. Martin's, 1995.

Lyautey, Louis. *Lyautey l'Africain: Textes et letters du Maréchal Lyautey* [Lyautey Africanus: Texts and Letters of Marshal Lyautey]. 4 vols. Edited by Pierre Lyautey. Paris: Plon, 1953–1957.

Maurois, André. *Lyautey.* New York: D. Appleton, 1931.

M

Macabebe Scouts

Filipinos from the town of Macabebein Pampanga Province on the island of Luzon who served with the United States military during the Philippine-American War (Philippine Insurrection, 1899–1902). Residents of Macabebe (Maccabebe) were longtime foes of the Tagalogs and had a history of providing military service to Spain. As loyal Spanish mercenaries and fierce warriors, the Macabebes had manned outposts, engaged in foreign campaigns, and suppressed domestic disorder. When Francisco Maniago rebelled in Pampanga in 1660, the Macabebes helped quell the uprising. They also assisted Spanish authorities in putting down the revolutions of 1896 and 1898, compelling a Spanish pledge to remove them to the safety of the Caroline Islands if the revolt prevailed.

Once Spain ceded the Philippine Islands to the United States as a consequence of the Spanish-American War (1898), the Macabebes were essentially abandoned and sought to protect themselves from Tagolog reprisal. Consequently, the Macabebes tendered their services to the U.S. military upon the beginning of the Philippine-American War in February 1899.

With War Department approval, Lieutenant Matthew A. Batson recruited the first company of Macabebes in the spring of 1899. The company was formally established that September and deployed in the Mindanao River (Rio Grande) region. The unit was armed with Krag carbines and, traveling in bancas (outrigger canoes), at once demonstrated its effectiveness by curtailing raids on U.S. military communications.

Other Macabebe troops were established, and soon the U.S. Army VIII Corps could rely on the services of a battalion of five companies designated Batson's Macabebe Scouts. It is estimated that as many as 5,000 Macabebe Scouts served with U.S. forces.

Fiercely loyal to the United States, the Macabebes quickly won the trust and admiration of American officers. They were of great assistance in recognizing insurgents posing as friendly natives in crowds. However, the Macabebes were often cruel and inhumane toward their adversaries and were accused of committing atrocities. Batson stood by the Macabebes, claiming that the accusations of cruelty were simply insurgent propaganda. Yet the Macabebes did use torture to obtain intelligence, and by 1900 both American troops and their mercenaries turned to, among other excesses, the so-called water cure (force-feeding a suspect with water).

In early October 1899, two companies of Batson's Macabebe Scouts were in the vanguard of Brigadier General Samuel B. M. Young's drive to San Isidro in Nueva Ecija Province, and in March 1900 Colonel Frederick Funston led a combined troop of Macabebes and Americans against an enemy base at Fort Rizal in southern Nueva Ecija. To the southwest, Brigadier General Frederick D. Grant employed Lieutenant Colonel William E. Wilder's Macabebes to sweep southward through the Rio Grande Delta to Manila Bay in Bulacan Province. The Macabebes used bancas in the swamps, routing guerrillas who fled to villages, where they were identified and captured. On March 30 the Macabebes reportedly murdered 130 natives, and there were allegations of rape and arson. Yet American officers on the scene continued to defend the Macabebes. On March 23, 1901, Macabebe Scouts were part of a detail led by now-Brigadier General Funston that captured Filipino leader Emilio Aguinaldo y Famy at Palanan in northern Luzon.

Following the Philippine-American War, the Macabebes were folded into the Philippine Constabulary.

Rodney J. Ross

See also Aguinaldo y Famy, Emilio; Funston, Frederick; Philippine Constabulary; Philippine Islands and U.S. Pacification during the Philippine-American War; Philippine Scouts

Further Reading

Gates, John Morgan. *Schoolbooks and Krags: The United States Army in the Philippines, 1898–1902.* Westport, CT: Greenwood, 1973.

Linn, Brian McAllister. *The Philippine War, 1899–1902.* Lawrence: University Press of Kansas, 2000.

Miller, Stuart C. *"Benevolent Assimilation": The American Conquest of the Philippines, 1899–1903.* New Haven, CT: Yale University Press, 1982.

MacArthur, Arthur, Jr.

Birth Date: June 2, 1845
Death Date: September 5, 1912

U.S. Army general who commanded American forces during the Philippine-American War (Philippine Insurrection, 1899–1902). Arthur MacArthur Jr. was born in Chicopee Falls, Massachusetts, on June 2, 1845. At an early age he moved to Milwaukee, Wisconsin, and was educated in local schools. With the start of the American Civil War (1861–1865), MacArthur secured a commission as a first lieutenant in a Wisconsin volunteer regiment and soon distinguished himself in fighting. He was breveted captain following his performance in the Battle of Perryville in October 1862 and also fought effectively at Stone's River (December–January 1863), Chickamauga (September 1863), and Kennesaw Mountain (June 1864). MacArthur was severely wounded at the Battle of

Franklin (November 1984). He received brevet promotions for gallantry and by the end of the war, not yet 20 years old, was a colonel commanding the 24th Wisconsin. In 1890 he was belatedly awarded the Medal of Honor for his actions in the Union assault on Missionary Ridge (November 1863).

With the end of the war, MacArthur joined the regular army as a second lieutenant and was immediately promoted to first lieutenant. He made captain in July 1866. Over the next 20 years, he served in various posts across the United States. In 1886 he was posted to the Infantry and Cavalry School at Fort Leavenworth, Kansas, and in July 1889 he was promoted to major and assigned to the Adjutant General's Department.

MacArthur was promoted to lieutenant colonel in May 1898, and that same month shortly after the U.S. declaration of war on Spain, he was appointed brigadier general of volunteers and assigned to the U.S. expeditionary force sent to the Philippines. MacArthur commanded the 1st Brigade of the 2nd Division in Major General Wesley Merritt's VIII Corps. MacArthur led his brigade in the Battle of Manila on August 13, 1898. Cited for gallantry, he became the provost marshal general and civil governor of Manila.

Promoted to major general of volunteers, MacArthur then commanded the 2nd Division, the chief field force opposing Filipino insurgents led by Emilio Aguinaldo y Famy in the Philippine-American War. MacArthur's forces pacified all of Luzon. Promoted to regular army brigadier general in January 1900, MacArthur succeeded Major General Elwell S. Otis as commanding general, Division of the Philippines, and military governor of the Philippine Islands. MacArthur was promoted to major general in the regular army that July. In ending the war, he combined a mixture of vigorous military action and civic action, including advances for the Filipinos in education, health care, and legal reform.

MacArthur was, however, slow to hand over control to the civilian administrators sent by Washington, headed by Willian H. Taft. MacArthur and Taft clashed repeatedly, and before the year was out, President Theodore Roosevelt replaced MacArthur with a more pliable military governor.

Returning to the United States, MacArthur commanded in turn the Department of Colorado, the Department of Lakes, and the Department of the East. In 1905 he went to Manchuria as a military observer for the last stage of the Russo-Japanese War (1904–1905) and then for a few months was the U.S. military attaché in Tokyo. He toured Asia during November 1905–August 1906. On his return to the United States, he commanded the Department of the Pacific and was promoted to lieutenant general as the senior officer in the army (September 1906). When Taft (then secretary of war), who still bore a grudge against his old nemesis, named a more junior officer chief of staff, MacArthur returned to Milwaukee to await orders. When none were forthcoming, he retired in July 1909. MacArthur died in Milwaukee on September 5, 1912. His son, Douglas MacArthur, was later chief of staff of the army and rose to the rank of general of the army.

Wesley Moody, Paul G. Pierpaoli Jr., and Spencer C. Tucker

See also Aguinaldo y Famy, Emilio; Philippine Islands and U.S. Pacification during the Philippine-American War

Further Reading

Linn, Brian McAllister. *The Philippine War, 1899–1902*. Lawrence: University Press of Kansas, 2000.

Young, Kenneth Ray. *The General's General: The Life and Times of Arthur MacArthur*. San Francisco: Westview, 1994.

Maccabean Revolt

Start Date: ca. 168 BCE
End Date: ca. 142 BCE

The Maccabean Revolt was the uprising of Judea against rule by the Seleucid Empire but was also in part a civil war between urban hellenized Jews and those in the countryside who believed strictly in the Torah. Dates vary widely, from the earliest starting date of 168 BCE and the latest ending date of 142 BCE.

Following his unsuccessful effort to conquer Egypt, in 168 BCE Seleucid ruler of Syria Antiochus IV arrived in Jerusalem and there desecrated the temple by entering its precincts and ordering a pig sacrificed on the altar. He also ordered all residents of Judea to honor a Greek god (which one is unclear). In 167 BCE at the village of Modi'in northwest of Jerusalem, Seleucid general Apelles ordered Mattathias from the priestly family of Hasmonaeus to offer sacrifice to the Greek gods. Mattathias refused, and he and his five sons then killed a Jew who had stepped forward to do so and also slew Apelles and some Seleucid soldiers. Mattathias and his five sons then fled and proceeded to rouse the countryside in revolt.

Nationalism and religion were driving forces in the insurgency. Support for the Hasmonean dynasty's cause came chiefly from the lower classes. Preservation of Judaism and Jewish culture proved to be stronger than class, however, as many moderately hellenized upper-class Jews supported the revolt. Only a minority of upper-class hellenized Jews remained loyal to the Seleucids.

The rebels carried out guerrilla operations against Seleucid patrols and conducted raids in villages to destroy pagan idols, raising the spirits of religious Jews and depressing those of apostate Jews. Following the death of Mattathias, his son Judas Maccabeus became leader of the revolt, giving his name to it. Successfully employing guerrilla tactics in the mountain environment, he won a victory at the Ascent of Lebonah (167 BCE), wiping out an entire Selucid unit, followed by victories at Beth-Horon (166 BCE), Emmaus (166 BCE), and Beth Zur (Bethsura, 164 BCE).

The Maccabee victory at Beth Zur near Hebron gave Judas control of Jerusalem. In December 164 BCE he took most of the city, including the Temple, although some Seleucids continued to hold out in the Acra, a fortified compound in

Jerusalem. The Festival of Lights, or Hanukkah (Chanukah), in the month of December commemorates the cleansing and rededication of the Temple. Judas then continued his siege of the Acra while at the same time expanding his control over the whole of Judea.

With Antioches campaigning to the east, Seleucid regent Lysias invaded Judea and defeated Judas at Beth Zachariah (162 BCE) but then was forced to return to Syria to suppress a revolt there. That same year, however, Bacchides, commander of Seleucid forces in Judea, defeated Judas at Jerusalem, driving him from the city.

Judas rallied, however, and in 161 BCE defeated Syrian general Nicanor at Adasa, with Nicanor among those killed. That same year, however, Judas was defeated and slain by Seleucid forces under Bacchides in the Battle of Elasa.

The Jewish revolt continued under Judas's brother Jonathan, who enjoyed considerable success with the guerrilla tactics first employed by Judas. Establishing his headquarters at Jerusalem in 152, Jonathan was recognized as the de facto ruler of Judea.

In 143 BCE, however, Jonathan was captured in an ambush at Ptolemais (Acre, Akko) and killed by dissident Jews who supported another for the throne. His brother Simon succeeded him and in 142 BCE was recognized by a gathering of priests as high priest and army commander. Simon was also recognized as king of Judea by the Seleucids. Nonetheless, Judea saw considerable turmoil as the Seleucids and other outside powers frequently intervened. The disorder ended when Roman consul Gnaeus Pompeius Magnus (Pompey the Great) captured Jerusalem in 63 BCE and Rome assumed control of Judea.

Spencer C. Tucker

See also Judas Maccabeus

Further Reading

Derfler, Steven Lee. *The Hasmonean Revolt: Rebellion of Revolution?* Lewiston, NY: E. Mellen, 1990.

Harrington, Daniel J. *The Maccabean Revolt: Anatomy of a Biblical Revolution.* Wilmington, DE: Michael Glazier, 1988.

Learsi, Rufus. *Israel: A History of the Jewish People.* Westport, CT: Greenwood, 1972.

Oesterley, W. O. E. *A History of Israel.* Oxford, UK: Clarendon, 1939.

Machel, Samora Moïses

Birth Date: September 29, 1933
Death Date: October 19, 1986

Insurgent leader and first president of Mozambique. Samora Moïses Machel was born on September 29, 1933, in Madragoa, Gaza Province, Mozambique. His father was a successful farmer. Machel received his primary education in a mission school and attended a Catholic secondary school in Zonguene but did not graduate. In 1954 he began studies in the capital city of Lourenço Marques (present-day Maputo) to become a nurse and then worked in a hospital until he left his wife and four children to join Mozambique insurgents based in Tanzania.

Machel joined the Frente de Libertação de Moçambique (FRELIMO, Mozambique Liberation Front) in 1962. A committed Marxist from his observations of the treatment of the poor in Mozambique, he was one of the first members of FRELIMO to receive military training in Algeria, and in September 1964 he led the first group of insurgents from Tanzania into Mozambique. Machel became the FRELIMO defense minister in 1966 and its military commander in chief by 1969. After the death of FRELIMO founder Eduardo Mondlane in February 1969 from a bomb hidden in a book there was a leadership struggle, from which Machel emerged victorious in 1970.

Following the Carnation Revolution in April 1974, the new Portuguese government agreed to grant independence to its African possessions, including Mozambique. Although unelected, Machel became the first president of an independent Mozambique on June 15, 1975. He immediately moved against all opposition groups and caused the execution of some of their leaders, a number of whom were burned alive by Machel's soldiers in June 1977. Machel's domestic economic and financial policies were an unmitigated disaster. His land reform policy of gathering the peasants into agricultural communes proved to be a complete failure. In foreign affairs, he allowed guerrillas fighting the minority white regimes in Rhodesia (present-day Zimbabwe) and South Africa to train in and operate from Mozambique. These regimes retaliated by supporting the Resistência Nacional Moçambicana (RENAMO, Mozambique National Resistance), which enjoyed widespread support in Mozambique with the goal of removing Machel from power. This forced Machel to conclude an agreement with South Africa in 1984 whereby he dropped his support for the African National Congress and South Africa agreed to end its aid to RENAMO. Machel was also forced to abandon some of his Marxist economic policies.

Machel died in the crash of a Soviet airliner at Mbuzini, in the Lebombo Mountains of South Africa, on October 19, 1986, while returning from a meeting with the leaders of other so-called frontline states in the midst of a new confrontation with South Africa.

Spencer C. Tucker

See also Frente de Libertação de Moçambique; Mondlane, Eduardo; Mozambique Insurgency

Further Reading

Henriksen, Thomas H. *Revolution and Counterrevolution: Mozambique's War of Independence, 1964–1974*. Westport, CT: Greenwood, 1983.

Munslow, Barry, ed. *Samora Machel, an African Revolutionary: Selected Speeches and Writings*. London: Zed, 1985.

Madagascar Revolt

Start Date: March 29, 1947
End Date: November 1948

Madagascar, the world's fourth largest island and today the Republic of Madagascar, is located in the Indian Ocean off the southeast coast of Africa. As part of the colonization of Africa by the European powers in the late 19th century, French forces invaded the island in 1883 in the First Franco-Hova War. The pretext was confiscation of property belonging to French citizens. Madagascar was forced to cede Antsiranana (Diego Suarez) on the northern coast to France and pay an indemnity.

During the 1885 Berlin Conference on African affairs, the British agreed to a French protectorate over Madagascar in return for control of Zanzibar, and on June 13, 1885, a French squadron began the Second Franco-Hova War by bombarding both Mahajanga (Majunga) and Tamatave. French troops then came ashore and marched to and took the capital of Antananarivo. Only 20 French troops were killed in the fighting, although another 6,000 died of malaria and other diseases before the end of the war. The Madagascar government then agreed to a treaty yielding significant powers to the French but leaving the native monarchy in place. Madagascar became a French protectorate.

In June 1894 Queen Ranavalona III resisted French demands that would amount to complete French control. On December 12, 1894, a French squadron again bombarded Tamatave, and in February 1895 the French sent ashore at Majunga a 15,000-man expeditionary force under General Jacques C. R. A. Duchesne. The French moved slowly inland, taking the capital of Tananarive on September 30, but then had to contend with a major insurrection against their rule.

France officially annexed Madagascar on August 6, 1896, and General Joseph Simon Gallieni established a military government. The 103-year-old Merina monarchy was abolished, with the queen and the royal family exiled to Algeria. Gallieni then commenced a pacification campaign that only ended in 1905.

France retained firm control of Madagascar until after World War II (1939–1945). Some 34,000 Malagasy citizens had fought for France in the conflict, which greatly impacted them as well as colonialism in general. Certainly Malagasy nationalists were emboldened by the defeat of France and its occupation by the Germans in the war. Madagascar was initially controlled by the Vichy French government, but in 1942 the British had invaded and occupied the island. French prestige was in tatters when in January 1943 the British handed Madagascar over to the Free French.

In 1946 Malagasy nationalists established the Mouvement démocratique de la rénovation malgache (MDRM, Democratic Movement for Malagasy Renewal) with the objective of securing Madagascan independence. Encouraged by colonial upheavals elsewhere, on March 29, 1947, the Madagascar Revolt (Malagasy Uprising) broke out in eastern Madagascar, but it is by no means certain that the MDRM leadership was involved. Soon the insurgents controlled a third of the island.

French authorities, strongly supported by the government of Socialist premier Paul Ramadier in Paris, acted swiftly and with force. Early in the rebellion, French forces on several occasions committed atrocities, such as at Moramanga on May 6, 1947, when between 124 and 160 mostly unarmed MDRM activists were machine-gunned to death. At Mananjary also, hundreds of Malagasy were slain, including a number of women.

With the arrival of five North African regiments at the end of July, the French took the offensive. By late 1948, when the rebellion had been crushed, there were some 30,000 French troops on the island. The French employed with success the *tache d'huile* (oil slick) method of General Gallieni and also utilized several former German Junkers Ju-52 aircraft as bombers to attack rebel strongholds. Tsiazombazaha, the last of these, fell in November. Although French authorities at the time put the casualty total at 8,000–10,000 Madagascans killed, the death toll was probably on the order of 30,000–40,000.

During July–October 1948, the French held a large public proceeding for 77 MDRM officials, although the MDRM continued to insist that it had nothing to do with the revolt. A half dozen people were condemned to death, although these sentences were later commuted to life imprisonment. The French also outlawed the MDRM. Subsequent military and civilian trials convicted 5,765 Madagascan citizens, with 173 death sentences handed down, although only 24 of these individuals were actually executed.

With the establishment of the French Fifth Republic and a new constitutional framework for the French overseas empire, the Malagasy Republic was established on October 14, 1958, as an autonomous state of the new French Community. Full independence was granted on June 26, 1960.

Spencer C. Tucker

See also Gallieni, Joseph Simon; *Tache d'Huile*

Further Reading

Brown, Mervyn. *Madagascar Rediscovered: A History from Early Times to Independence.* Hamden, CT: Archon Books, 1979.

Cole, Jennifer. *Forget Colonialism? Sacrifice and the Art of Memory in Madagascar.* Berkeley: University of California Press, 2001.

Duval, Jean Eugène. *La Révolte des sagaies: Madagascar, 1947* [The Spears Revolt: Madagascar, 1947]. Paris: Harmattan, 2002.

Tronchon, Jacques. *L'Insurrection malgache de 1947: Essai d'interprétation historique* [The Malagasay Uprising of 1947: Historical Interpretation Study]. Fianarantsoa: Éditions Ambozontany Fianarantsoa, 1986.

Madium Affair

Event Date: September 1948

A Communist uprising during the Indonesian War for Independence (1945–1949). Compounding problems for the government of the Republic of Indonesia, the forces of which were then fighting the Dutch, was a threat from the political Left posed by the revitalized Partai Komunis Indonesia (PKI, Communist Party of Indonesia). The PKI was led by Musso, leader of the party from an unsuccessful revolt in 1926, and Tan Malaka. Musso called for Indonesia to ally with the Soviet Union, and clashes between the republic's armed forces and the PKI occurred in Surakarta in September 1948. The Communists then withdrew to Madiun in East Java and there on September 18 issued a call for the overthrow of the Indonesian government and the establishment of a Communist republic.

Troops of the Silwangi Division of the Republic of Indonesia's army crushed the so-called Madiun Affair on September 30. Thousands of Communists were killed, and a reported 36,000 were imprisoned. Musso was killed on October 31, allegedly while trying to escape from prison. Tan Malaka was captured and executed in February 1949.

The Madiun Affair had important international implications in that the U.S. government now came to view the Indonesian republicans as staunch anticommunists, leading to U.S. pressure on the Dutch government to grant Indonesia full independence.

Spencer C. Tucker

Further Reading

Friend, Theodore. *Indonesian Destinies.* Cambridge, MA: Belknap Press of Harvard University, 2003.

Vickers, Adrian. *A History of Modern Indonesia.* New York: Cambridge University Press, 2005.

Magsaysay, Ramón del Fierro

Birth Date: August 31, 1907
Death Date: March 17, 1957

Filipino politician, secretary of national defense, and president of the Philippines. Born the son of a schoolteacher on August 31, 1907, in Iba town, Zambales Province, Ramón del Fierro Magsaysay in 1927 enrolled at the College of Liberal Arts at the University of the Philippines and went on to earn a bachelor of science degree in commerce from Jose Rizal College in 1932. After graduation, Magsaysay joined a bus company in Manila as a mechanic and rose to be the company's manager.

Magsaysay fought against the Japanese following their invasion of the Philippines beginning in December 1941 and became a captain in the Philippine Army's 31st Division. In April 1942 he joined a group of U.S. Army officers who continued guerrilla warfare against the Japanese and became known as the Zambales Guerrillas. The Japanese military listed Magsaysay as Japan's "Enemy Number One." Magsaysay led his followers in liberating Zambales Province ahead of the arrival of American forces on January 29, 1945, and he became the military governor of Zambales the next month. Intelligent and a dynamic speaker and debater, Magsaysay was elected to the Philippine Congress from Zambales Province on the Liberal Party ticket in April 1946 and was reelected in 1949.

In 1950 President Elpidio Quirino appointed Magsaysay secretary of national defense. Magsaysay played a leading role in the defeat of the Communist Hukbalahap (Huk) guerrilla insurgency. His forces captured its entire politburo within a month of assuming office. Magsaysay's frequent and unannounced visits to units helped improve army morale due to the removal of inefficient and corrupt commanders. In combating the insurgency, Magsaysay worked closely with U.S. Army colonel Edward Lansdale. Magsaysay clearly understood the political nature of the insurgency.

A man of principle and conviction, Magsaysay fought corruption in politics. He made enemies in the ruling Liberal Party when his troops helped prevent voter fraud in the 1951 elections. He resigned his cabinet post in 1953 after Quirino removed the police from his authority. Switching to the Nacionalista Party, Magsaysay won the 1953 presidential elections against Quirino.

In foreign policy, President Magsaysay's staunch anticommunism won him American support and ultimately led to the formation of the 1954 South East Asia Treaty Organization (SEATO), with Manila as its headquarters. On the home front, Magsaysay embarked on major land reform initiatives and presided over the end of the Huk Rebellion in 1954. He also began governmental restructuring. Magsaysay's career was abruptly ended when he was killed in a plane crash near Cebu in the Philippines on March 17, 1957.

Udai Bhanu Singh

See also Hukbalahap Rebellion; Lansdale, Edward Geary

Further Reading

Abueva, Josc Veloso. *Ramon Magsaysay: A Political Biography.* Manila: Solidardad Publishing House, 1971.

Corpuz, Onofre D. *The Philippines.* New York: Prentice Hall, 1965.

Romulo, Carlos P., and Marvin M. Gray. *The Magsaysay Story.* New York: Pocket Books, 1957.

Mahdist Uprising in Sudan

Start Date: 1881
End Date: 1898

In 1882 the British, concerned about the security of the Suez Canal, took control of Egypt. They soon found themselves drawn into difficulties to the south in the

Sudan along the upper Nile, where Egypt claimed authority. Muhammad Ahmad bin Abd Allah had in 1881 proclaimed himself Mahdi (Prophet) and proceeded to mount an insurgency against Egyptian rule. In so doing, he took advantage of widespread Sudanese resentment against Egyptian control and of messianic beliefs popular among various Sudanese religious sects and also capitalized on the puritanical forms of Islam that had emerged in reaction to the military and economic dominance of the European powers in the region.

In the autumn of 1883, the Egyptian government ordered forces into the Sudan to put down the uprising. Some 8,500 Egyptian troops, commanded by British former Indian Army officer Colonel William Hicks (Hicks Pasha), marched into the desert, only to be annihilated at El Obeid by the Sudanese forces on November 3. This victory swelled the ranks of the Mahdi's army, and the Sudan was soon in widespread revolt. The Mahdi's lieutenant, Osman Digna, took the Red Sea ports and destroyed another Anglo-Egyptian force at El Reb on February 4, 1884.

The Egyptian government then sought London's assistance, but British prime minister William Gladstone decided that the Sudan should be evacuated of Europeans and Egyptians. He sent General Charles "Chinese" Gordon, who had won acclaim commanding Chinese forces that had helped put down the Taiping Rebellion. Gordon had once been governor of the Sudan for the Egyptians and had helped suppress the slave trade there. A deeply religious man with a martyr complex, Gordon on his own initiative defied his orders and decided to regain control of the Sudan. He proceeded up the Nile to Khartoum, at the confluence of the White and Blue Nile Rivers. Dallying there, his force was besieged beginning on March 12, 1884.

Despite mounting public pressure in Britain for action to relieve Gordon, a furious Gladstone dragged his feet. Not until too late, in October 1884, did General Sir Garnet Wolseley set out with a relief expedition. Wolseley took an inordinately long time in his preparations and advance, and before the expedition reached Khartoum, the Dervishes stormed the city on January 26, 1885; massacred the entire garrison; and presented the Mahdi with Gordon's severed head. Wolseley arrived two days later but was ordered to withdraw. The Mahdi died in June 1885, but his successor, Abdallahi ibn Muhammad, completed the conquest of the Sudan.

Concerned about increasing French interest in the headwaters of the Nile, the British government finally sent forces from Egypt to reconquer the Sudan. Major General Sir Horatio Kitchener, sirdar (commander in chief) of the Egyptian Army, assumed personal command. Moving up the Nile with a considerable force of gunboats and building a railroad as he proceeded, Kitchener encountered strong opposition from the Dervishes but captured Dongola on September 21, 1896, and Abu Hamed on August 7, 1897. He then defeated the Dervishes in the Battle of the Atbara River on April 8, 1898. The remaining Dervish forces under Abdallahi and Osman Digna concentrated at Omdurman, on the west bank of the Nile across from Khartoum, and on September 2 Abdallahi and some 35,000–50,000 Sudanese tribesmen attacked the British lines. The British employed magazine rifles and Maxim guns to kill perhaps 10,000 Dervishes and wound as many more, with 5,000 taken prisoner. The cost to the British side was 48 dead and 434 wounded.

For all practical purposes, the Battle of Omdurman gave Britain control of the Sudan and made Kitchener a British national hero. Kitchener then dislodged the French from Fashoda, farther up the Nile, leading to an understanding in 1899 that established the watershed of the Nile and Congo Rivers as the dividing point between British and French territory and paved the way for the Entente Cordiale of April 1904.

Spencer C. Tucker

See also Gordon, Charles George; Kitchener, Horatio Herbert; Taiping Rebellion; Wolseley, Garnet Joseph

Further Reading

Lewis, David Levering. *The Race for Fashoda: European Colonialism and African Resistance in the Scramble for Africa.* New York: Weidenfeld and Nicolson, 1987.

Nicoll, Fergus. *The Sword of the Prophet: The Mahdi of Sudan and the Death of General Gordon.* Thrupp, Stroud, Gloucestershire, UK: Sutton, 2004.

Voll, John Obert. "The Sudanese Mahdi: Frontier Fundamentalist." *International Journal of Middle East Studies* 10 (1979): 145–166.

Maji Maji Rebellion

Start Date: 1905
End Date: 1907

Tribal insurgency in German East Africa. Since the establishment of this German colony in 1885, there had been several clashes between Europeans and indigenous peoples (most seriously during the Wahehe Rebellion of 1891–1898), largely the result of famines, economic, political, and religious differences. In 1905 an influential shaman named Kinjikitile Ngale, claiming to be the conduit for a snake spirit called Hongo, promised the destruction of the Europeans and protection from their bullets through magic water (*maji*). Ngale's prophecy spread rapidly, but there was little coordination among the 20 or more tribal groups that joined the rebellion. In July 1905, rebels attacked small German outposts, destroyed crops, and killed European colonists.

With only a small Schutztruppe (Colonial Defense Force) of some 2,400 men, including German officers and noncommissioned officers commanding the main force of native Askaris, governor of German East Africa Graf von Götzen requested reinforcements. These arrived in October. Although vastly outnumbered and suffering occasional setbacks, the German security force managed to pacify one region at a time in a series of campaigns in remote and inhospitable terrain. While the rebels had a distinct advantage in numbers, the Schuztruppe possessed modern rifles and machine guns. The mix of technology and determination was lethal. At Mahenge in September 1905, 1 German officer and 60 Askaris successfully held a defensive position against thousands of Maji Maji warriors.

During nearly two years of fighting, 15 Schutztruppe troops and 389 Askaris were killed, compared to a minimum of tens of thousands of Maji Maji rebels. The Germans also destroyed crops and confiscated livestock, thereby cutting off the rebels from their support system. German administrative reforms also helped, and the colony achieved a level of peace by the beginning of World War I (1914–1918). Indeed, German colonel Paul von Lettow-Vorbeck carried on resistance to the Allies in East Africa for four years, with considerable assistance from the same tribal groups that had once fought the Schutztruppe.

The Maji Maji Rebellion is a polarizing subject in a postcolonial world, viewed either as an example of nationalism and resistance to foreign oppression or as a successful pacification campaign against a highly dangerous insurgency.

Mark M. Hull

See also Lettow-Vorbeck, Paul Emil von

Further Reading

Becker, Felicitas, and Jigal Beez. *Der Maji-Maji-Krieg in Deutsch-Ostafrika, 1905–1907* [The Maji Maji War in German East Africa, 1905–1907]. Berlin: Ch. Links Verlag, 2005.

Nigmann, Ernst. *Geschichte der kaiserlichen Schutztruppe für Deutsche-Ostafrika* [History of the Imperial Schutztruppe for German East Africa]. Berlin: Ernst Mittler u. Sohn, 1911.

Speitkamp, Winfried. *Deutsche Kolonialgeschichte* [German Colonial History]. Stuttgart: Reclam, 2005.

Makhno, Nestor Ivanovich

Birth Date: November 8, 1888
Death Date: July 6, 1934

Ukrainian anarchist and insurgent leader. Born into an impoverished peasant family in Huliaipole Governorate (Zaporizhia Oblast, Ukraine), on November 8, 1888, Nestor Ivanovich Makhno was only 10 months old when his father died. Makhno had little formal schooling and was employed first as a shepherd and farmhand. He then worked as a painter and in an iron foundry.

Swept up in politics by the Russian Revolution of 1905, in 1906 Makhno became an anarchist. He was arrested several times by the czarist police and in 1910 was condemned to death, but the sentence was commuted to life imprisonment, and he was released with the Russian Revolution of March 1917. Makhno then organized the Peasants' Union, which confiscated large estates and distributed the land among the peasants.

Following the Russian withdrawal from World War I (1914–1918) following the Bolshevik Revolution of November 1917 and the Treaty of Brest Litovsk of March 1918, Makhno organized the Revolutionary Insurgency Army of Ukraine, which at peak strength numbered some 25,000 men. Makhno and his men fought all those attempting to assert control over southern Ukraine, including German and Austro-Hungarian occupying forces that supported the Hetmanate republic of Pavlo Skoropadsky.

During the 1918–1920 Russian Civil War, Makhno battled not only Ukranian nationalists (the army of Symon Petlura) but also Russian Bolshevik forces and White forces loyal to the czar. Makhno, who was known to his followers as "Batko" ("Father"), demonstrated a considerable understanding of insurgency and enjoyed wide support from the peasantry but could be as being as ruthless as the Bolsheviks in eliminating those who opposed him. In tactical innovations, he is credited with introducing the tachanka, a horse-drawn platform mounting a heavy machine gun.

Makhno's political program included rejection of all political parties, all forms of dictatorship (to include the Bolshevik "temporary" party dictatorship), and any central state. Workers were to be organized through free local workers' cooperatives. Although most of his followers were Ukranian peasants, Makhno considered himself an anarchist and not a Ukranian nationalist.

During 1919–1920, the Bolsheviks arranged a temporary accommodation with Makhno so that they might concentrate their resources on the Whites, but by November 1920 the White threat had diminished to the point that the Bolsheviks could turn against Makhno and destroy his forces. Makhno escaped Ukraine into Romania in August 1921 and finally made his way to Paris, where he wrote a three-volume memoir. In poverty, Makhno died there of tuberculosis on July 6, 1934.

Spencer C. Tucker

Further Reading

Arshinov, Peter. *History of the Makhnovist Movement (1918–1921).* 1923; reprint, Detroit: Black and Red, 1975.

Beckett, Ian F. W. *Encyclopedia of Guerrilla Warfare.* Santa Barbara, CA: ABC-CLIO, 1999.

Malet, Michael. *Nestor Makhno in the Russian Civil War.* London: Macmillan, 1982.

Malabar Revolt.

See Moplah Rebellion

Malagasy Uprising.

See Madagascar Revolt

Malayan Emergency

Start Date: 1948
End Date: 1960

Twelve-year insurgency that began on June 18, 1948. The conflict was an indigenous attempt by the Malayan Communist Party (MCP) to overthrow British colonial rule. Expected to last no more than a few months, the insurgency continued until July 31, 1960, three years after Malaya had gained its independence. The Malayan Emergency was Britain's longest colonial conflict and turned out to be far more costly in human and material terms than had been foreseen.

The war's immediate catalyst was the murder of three rubber plantation managers in Perak, Malaya, on June 16, 1948. Two days later, British high commissioner Sir Edward Gent declared a state of emergency. The MCP guerrillas in the mobile corps committed the murders in response to a call three months earlier by the party for an armed insurrection against British rule. The conflict was given the misnomer "emergency" for economic reasons, as London insurance companies would only cover property losses to Malayan rubber and tin estates during rioting or commotion in an emergency but not in an armed insurrection or civil war.

The Malayan Emergency was rooted primary in postwar economic and political dislocations. The Chinese, who made up the vast majority of the insurgents, feared domination by Malays and Indians. Despite the importance of local factors, the insurgency was bound up in the Cold War paradigm of Communist containment. The inaugural conference of the Cominform (Communist Information Bureau) in September 1947 and the Calcutta conference of the Indian Communist Party in February 1948, which adopted Andrei Zhdanov's two-camps thesis, were presumed to be linked to the armed rebellions against colonial rule in Burma (present-day Myanmar), Indonesia, Malaya, and the Philippines.

Britain coveted its role in Southeast Asia, as Britain relied on the region for both economic and strategic reasons. Britain's massive military commitment to defeat the insurgency, which saw the deployment of nearly 50,000 British troops by October 1950 at a time of severe postwar fiscal austerity, had a significant economic dimension. After the Japanese defeat in 1945, the British were determined to retain control of Malaya. Sales of rubber exceeded in total value all other domestic exports from Great Britain to the United States, and interruption of that supply would inflict significant damage to the British economy. When the insurgency commenced, Britain was struggling to maintain the value of its currency; this made earnings from the Sterling Area, of which Malaya was the linchpin, all the more vital. Crushing the insurgency would ensure the maintenance of British economic interests there.

But the insurrection was not easy to quell. Initially, the British response was fitful, uncertain, and inept. Not until 1950 did the British initiate a more systematic and coordinated approach to the crisis when Lieutenant General Sir Harold

MALAYAN INSURGENCY, 1948–1960

100°E · 102°E · 104°E

N

6°N

Kangar

THAILAND

Alor Setar

Kota Bharu

Georgetown

Kuala
Trengganu

Ipoh

MALAYA

4°N

Strait of

Jerantut

Malacca

Kuantan

Bentong

Kuala
Selangor

Temerloh

Kuala
Lumpur

Port Klang

Seremban

Endau

Gemas

Mersing

2°N

Melaka

South

China

Sea

Johor Bahru

INDONESIA

SINGAPORE

Guerrilla activity mainly
suppressed by:

1955

1955 to 1958

1959 and later

0°

0 · 50 · 100 mi
0 · 50 · 100 km

Briggs took charge of operations. Britain's new program, in which the insurgents were detached from their supply sources and their support bases, provided a key breakthrough in the rebellion. Through a major relocation process, which prefigured the American policy of strategic hamlets in South Vietnam, more than half a million Chinese squatters living near guerrilla areas were moved into 450 so-called New Villages. The villages hampered MCP operations and increased their vulnerability to the military operations of British-controlled security forces.

This population control, initiated by Briggs, was harsh but effective. It was prosecuted even more vigorously by General Sir Gerald Templer, who was appointed high commissioner with full powers over the military, police, and civilian authorities in early 1952. Templer also fought the counterinsurgency on other fronts. He developed an efficient, synchronized, and expanded intelligence apparatus; invented and implemented the concept of hearts and minds; enlarged the intelligence budget so that informers could be paid; and coordinated the use of sophisticated black propaganda and psychological operations by MI6 personnel.

Aerial warfare was refined as well. Safe-conduct passes accompanied by promises of monetary rewards were air-dropped to encourage or accelerate defections. Aerial drops of millions of strategic leaflets, such as handwritten letters and photographs from surrendered guerrillas, were used in conjunction with voice aircraft to personalize propaganda. British aircraft also dropped thousand-pound bombs, chemical defoliants, and napalm on MCP jungle camps.

By 1954 when Templer departed, these measures had transformed the conflict. The insurgents had been forced back into the jungle, where they struggled to sustain themselves. In 1955 the MCP offered in vain to negotiate a settlement, and in 1957 upon Malaya's independence, the insurgency lost its motive as a war of colonial liberation. In 1958 after mass defections the MCP demobilized, and by 1960 the movement was limited to a small nucleus hiding on the Malay-Thai border, from which it conducted hit-and-run raids along the northern Malayan Peninsula for the next 25 years. A final peace settlement was signed on December 2, 1989.

The Malayan Emergency cast a long shadow over the new nation. The event's mythology has come to dominate the modern history of Malaya and became a benchmark of the Cold War in Southeast Asia. For Americans embarking on military involvement in Vietnam and wishing to apply successful British strategies, the Malayan Emergency became the quintessential counterinsurgency primer.

Phillip Deery

See also Briggs, Sir Harold Rawdon; Strategic Hamlet Program; Templer, Sir Gerald Walter Robert

Further Reading

Harper, T. N. *The End of Empire and the Making of Malaya.* Cambridge: Cambridge University Press, 1999.

Peng, Chin. *Alias Chin Peng: My Side of History.* Singapore: Media Masters, 2003.

Ramakrishna, Kumar. *Emergency Propaganda: The Winning of Malayan Hearts and Minds, 1948–1958.* London: Curzon, 2002.

Mao Zedong

Birth Date: December 26, 1893
Death Date: September 9, 1976

Chinese political and military leader and founder of the Chinese Communist Party (CCP) in 1921 and of the People's Republic of China (PRC) in 1949. Born on December 26, 1893, into a prosperous peasant family in Shaoshan, Hunan Province in central China, Mao Zedong (Mao Tse-tung) graduated from the Fourth Teacher's Training School in Changsha, Hunan. He read extensively in both Chinese and Western literature, philosophy, politics, and economics, including Marxist theory. As with many other contemporary young Chinese intellectuals, Mao embraced revolutionary thinking, and in July 1921 he attended a meeting in Shanghai, where the CCP was founded.

Mao became a labor organizer, and following Soviet instructions, in the mid-1920s he and other Chinese Communists cooperated with President Sun Yixian's (Sun Yat-sen) Guomindang (GMD, Nationalist) Party. Mao held several posts in the GMD and in 1925 was appointed secretary of its propaganda department. After Sun's death that year, Jiang Jieshi (Chiang Kai-shek), head of the Huangpu (Whampoa) Military Academy in Guangzhou, Guangdong, cofounded by Communists and nationalists two years earlier, won control of the GMD.

In 1926 Jiang began to eliminate rival political groups, purging the Communists from GMD positions and launching the 1926–1927 Northern Expedition against assorted warlords. In 1927 he turned against such Communists as had escaped his purge and proceeded to establish a base in Jiangxi Province, suppressing several Communist insurrections that year including the Autumn Harvest Uprising of peasants and guerrillas led by Mao. Joined by renegade GMD army officers Zhu De and Lin Biao, who took their troops to join him, Mao founded the Jiangxi Soviet Republic, a Communist redoubt in the province's southeast, and Mao became chairman in October 1931.

Drawing on Chinese military writing, including Sun Tzu's *Art of War,* Mao rejected orthodox Marxist teachings that the urban proletariat must be the driving force of revolution. With China having a relatively small urban proletariat, Mao sought to tap into widespread peasant discontent to bring about the Communist revolution. He elaborated theories of peasant warfare and guerrilla tactics to win control of China.

Mao also established a program for a protracted three-phase struggle. The first was the prerevolutionary phase, when the Communists would remain on the defensive although not passive. They would establish an infrastructure and convince the peasants of the correctness of the Communist cause. Limited intimidation could be employed if necessary, but Mao stressed the necessity to win the goodwill of the peasants. The peasantry was the sea in which the guerrillas must swim.

The second phase was that of strategic stalemate. In it, the Communists would be in a position of approximate equal strength with their opponents, enabling the Communists to embark on guerrilla warfare. Bases would also be established, and the training of regular troop units would begin. In the third and final phase, the Communist side would be in position to launch a conventional military offensive and win the war.

By 1933, the Communists counted some 200,000 people. They launched several uprisings in major Chinese cities, a threat to the authority of Jiang, who took Beijing in 1928, unifying all China south of the Great Wall, and from October headed a new GMD government. From 1930 onward, Jiang mounted annual campaigns against the Communist soviet, the eradication of which apparently ranked higher in his priorities than opposing the 1932 establishment by Japan of a puppet government in China's northeastern region of Manchuria.

In 1934 GMD forces encircled the Jiangxi soviet. Mao and Zhu broke out, leading more than 100,000

Mao Zedong (old spelling Mao Tse-tung), a master of guerrilla tactics, led the Communists in the civil war against the Nationalists in China and was the leader of the People's Republic of China from 1949 to 1976. Although remembered as one of the great Chinese leaders who made China a major player on the world stage, Mao's policies resulted in the deaths of an estimated 40–70 million Chinese. (The Illustrated London News Picture Library)

followers on an epic Long March of 6,000 miles to Yan'an in northern Shaanxi, during which heavy fighting and harsh conditions reduced their numbers to 7,000 and Mao was forced to abandon two of his own children. In 1935 he was elected CCP chairman. That same year Jiang ordered troops under Zhang Xueliang, a prominent northern Manchurian warlord who had pledged allegiance to him, to attack the Communists. However, they rejected the orders and urged all Chinese to join forces against the Japanese. In the December 1936 Xi'an Incident in Shaanxi, Zhang kidnapped Jiang and forced him to form a united anti-Japanese front with the Communists.

In July 1937 the Battle of the Lugouqiao Marco Polo Bridge sparked full-scale war between Chinese and Japanese troops, and in 1938 GMD forces retreated to Chongqing in the southwestern province of Sichuan. The Chinese Communists were greatly strengthened by the Japanese invasion, which prevented GMD forces from concentrating on them. From their Yan'an base the Communists now effectively controlled northwestern China, and the GMD controlled southwestern China.

Mao's Red Army, rechristened the Eighth Route Army, participated in fighting against Japanese troops, and Communist guerrilla forces operated in Henan, Zhejiang, and Shandong Provinces. Mao still anticipated winning eventual Communist control of China and meanwhile consolidated his authority within his own party, which in 1945 adopted a constitution that accepted his teachings as its official ideology.

By early 1941, the Communist-nationalist front had largely broken down after nationalist units defeated the Communist New Fourth Army near the Changjiang (Yangtze) Valley. From then until 1945, Communists concentrated their energies on establishing guerrilla bases and peasant support behind Japanese lines, efforts to harass the enemy that also helped to ensure them of ultimate postwar control of these areas. When the war ended in August 1945, incoming Soviet troops facilitated Chinese Communist moves to take control of much of Manchuria. In early 1946, GMD and Communist forces resumed fighting each other, and American attempts in late 1945 and all of 1946 to negotiate a truce foundered on both sides' rooted antagonism. Civil war continued until January 1949, and the following October Mao proclaimed the new PRC, which the United States only recognized in January 1979.

Until his death, Mao remained China's supreme leader, dominating the country's politics. He was responsible for several controversial policies, including the November 1950 decision to attack American forces during the Korean War (1950–1953), the economically disastrous Great Leap Forward of 1958–1962, and the Great Proletarian Cultural Revolution of 1966, a socially divisive campaign designed to induce a state of permanent revolution in China. His policies claimed the deaths through starvation or execution of between 40 million and 70 million Chinese.

On September 9, 1976, Mao died in Beijing, an event presaged by a major earthquake the previous July in Tangshan, Hebei Province, which to many Chinese symbolized the passing of one of the most forceful characters in Chinese history.

Priscilla Roberts and Spencer C. Tucker

See also Long March

Further Reading

Feigon, Lee. *Mao: A Reinterpretation.* Chicago: Ivan R. Dee, 2002.

Short, Philip. *Mao: A Life.* New York: Henry Holt, 2000.

Snow, Edgar. *Red Star over China.* New York: Random House, 1938.

Terrill, Ross. *Mao: A Biography.* Stanford, CA: Stanford University Press, 1999.

Mappila Rebellion.

See Moplah Rebellion

Marighella, Carlos

Birth Date: December 5, 1911
Death Date: November 4, 1969

Brazilian revolutionary and urban warfare theorist. Carlos Marighella, born on December 5, 1911, in Salvador, Bahia, Brazil, of Brazilian, Sudanese, and Italian descent, joined the Partido Comunista Brasileiro (PCB, Brazilian Communist Party) in 1934. He was arrested, imprisoned, and allegedly tortured in 1932, 1936, and 1939. Elected to the Brazilian Chamber of Deputies in 1946, he lost office two years later when the PCB was banned.

Marighella visited the People's Republic of China during 1953–1954 to study Maoist theory. Returning to Brazil, he was arrested following the military coup of April 1964 and imprisoned for more than a year. He quit the PCB in 1965 because the leadership did not believe that Brazil was ready for revolution and formed his urban guerrilla group, originally the Ala Marighella (Marighella Wing) and renamed the Ação Libertadora Nacional (ALN, National Liberation Action) in 1967. After he had carried out a number of terrorist actions, the Brazilian police ambushed and killed Marighella in São Paulo, Brazil, on November 4, 1969.

Marighella is best known for his advocacy of urban insurgency, what he called urban guerrilla warfare. Although not his first work, his *Minimanual of the Urban Guerrilla* of 1969 explained his basic tenets of revolutionary warfare in an urban environment. Marighella did not seek direct combat with government forces but instead sought to employ assassination and kidnapping to remove police chiefs and military officers. The goal was to tie down the security forces and sap their morale while demonstrating to the people the government's vulnerability. He also believed that such actions would provoke a governmental overreaction, eventually alienating the people and causing them to support the insurgency.

There are problems with Marighella's ideas. First, there was no reason why the people would not blame the terrorists rather than the government. In Brazil, the military coup of 1964 was not as unpopular as Marighella and his apologists claimed. In part this was because of robust economic growth; even with societal and political problems, Brazilians were not ready for revolution.

Marighella's ideas were also devoid of morality. He expressed no concern for the suffering of the people while the urban guerrillas were fighting in their name. Marighella arrogantly believed that his vision was what the people desired. This incorrect assumption ultimately caused the ALN's downfall.

Probably the most important criticism is that as much as Marighella promoted the urban guerrilla, urban operations were only meant to lead directly to the rising of the countryside, the true center of gravity. Margihella profoundly misread the political climate of Brazil and its demography, with a larger urban population than rural population.

The less well-known Spanish terror theorist Abraham Guillén (1913–1993) in fact deserves to be called the father of urban guerrilla warfare. Guillén's book *Estrategia de la guerrilla urbana* (Strategy of the Urban Guerrilla) was published in 1966, three years earlier than Marighella's *Minimanual.*

Marighella was a profound failure as a guerrilla and revolutionary. His concepts were essentially too simplistic to be viable. Yet his fame spread through his writings, especially the *Minimanual,* and he presaged modern terrorism by arguing for the skillful use of propaganda, specifically the manipulation of the news media, and systematic attacks against such targets as transportation infrastructure, food storage and production, water, and fuel.

William H. Kautt

See also Guillén, Abraham; Urban Guerrilla Warfare

Further Reading

Joes, Anthony James. *Urban Guerrilla Warfare.* Lexington: University of Kentucky Press, 2007.

Marighella, Carlos. *Minimanual of the Urban Guerrilla: Terror and Urban Guerrillas; A Study of Tactics and Documents.* Edited by Jay Mallin. Coral Gables, FL: University of Miami Press, 1982.

Marion, Francis

Birth Date: ca. 1732
Death Date: February 27, 1795

Continental Army officer and guerrilla leader during the American Revolutionary War. Francis Marion was born around 1732 in Berkeley County, South Carolina, to parents of French Huguenot descent. Short, slightly built, and beset by deformed ankles and knees, he went on a voyage to the West Indies in 1747, only to have the ship capsize. Marion survived after floating at sea for seven days in a dinghy. He subsequently took up farming.

Marion's first brush with military service came in 1759 when his militia company was ambushed by Cherokee Indians and nearly destroyed. Marion, however, stood his ground and was highly commended by his superiors. He fought the Cherokees again in 1761, gaining a reputation as a competent military leader.

When the American Revolutionary War erupted in 1775, Marion attended the provincial congress as a delegate and secured appointment as a captain of the 2nd South Carolina Regiment. Promoted to major, he served with distinction during the June 28, 1776, repulse of British ships off Charleston, reputedly firing the last cannon at the departing British squadron. That autumn when his regiment became part of the Continental Army, he was appointed its lieutenant colonel, fighting under General Benjamin Lincoln during the failed siege of Savannah in October 1779. Sidelined by a broken ankle, Marion was not present at Charleston when Lincoln surrendered that city to Lieutenant General Sir Henry Clinton in January 1780.

Marion then joined forces with Major General Horatio Gates, the new Continental Army commander in the South. Marion survived the August 1780 defeat at the Battle of Camden that eliminated organized resistance in the Carolinas. It now fell to him and to a handful of Patriots to keep alive the independence struggle in the South.

For several months Marion retreated into the interior, lived off the land, and assaulted British and Loyalist detachments whenever possible. His first action occurred on August 20, 1780, when he successfully attacked a mixed British and Loyalist force at night, freeing 147 Patriot prisoners who had been taken at Camden. Thereafter, his guerrillas struck repeatedly and effectively at isolated garrisons and lines of communication, prompting British lieutenant general Charles Cornwallis to dispatch the dreaded Colonel Banastre Tarleton in pursuit. Having at one point fruitlessly chased Marion's forces for seven hours through swamps, the redoubtable Tarleton declared that "As for this damned old fox, the Devil himself could not catch him." From that point on, Marion was known as the "Swamp Fox."

Marion's mastery of irregular warfare and rapid mobility baffled his British opponents and kept the American Revolution alive in the South. Unlike his contemporary, Thomas Sumter, Marion was a disciplinarian who dressed modestly, abstained from drinking, and forbade his troops from plundering their Loyalist neighbors. He was promoted to brigadier general in 1781 and operated closely with the forces of new Continental Army commander in the South Major General Nathanael Greene against British outposts. Marion's force, which had grown to brigade strength, received additional support in the form of Colonel Henry Lee's legion, with the two men cooperating in reducing a number of British and Loyalist strongholds. Furthermore, he received command of the eastern portion of the state, while Sumter commanded in the western part.

A high point in Marion's military career occurred during the Battle of Eutaw Springs (September 1781), when prompt action by his men spared Greene a costly defeat. By year's end the British could no longer control the countryside, and they withdrew the bulk of their forces into Charleston. On August 29, 1782, Marion fought his final battle at Fair Lawn, where he ambushed 200 British dragoons sent to attack him. But throughout the bitter internecine struggle between neighbors, Marion strictly forbade the torture of Loyalist prisoners or the destruction of their property. He fought humanely and magnanimously, thereby converting several of his erstwhile enemies to the Patriot cause.

After the war, Marion turned to politics and was elected to the South Carolina Senate in 1782. At age 54 he married his wealthy cousin and settled into the life of a gentleman farmer. While in office, he sought to improve public education, a sore point with him since he was barely literate, and he urged the peaceful assimilation of former Tories into American society. Marion died on his estate in Berkeley County on February 27, 1795.

John C. Fredriksen

See also American Revolutionary War; Sumter, Thomas

Further Reading

James, William Dobein. *A Sketch of the Life of Brig. Gen. Francis Marion and a History of His Brigade.* Charleston, SC: Gould and Riley, 1821.

Pancake, John S. *This Destructive War: The British Campaign in the Carolinas, 1780–1782.* University: University of Alabama Press, 1985.

Weems, Mason L. *The Life of Gen. Francis Marion: A Celebrated Partisan Officer in the Revolutionary War, against the British and Tories in South Carolina and Georgia.* Philadelphia: Mathew Carey, 1809.

Martí, Agustin Farabundo

Birth Date: May 5, 1893
Death Date: February 1, 1932

Salvdoran revolutionary leader credited with founding the Communist Party of El Salvador. Born on May 5, 1893, in the Department of La Libertad, El Salvador, Agustin Farabundo Martí grew up among the rural poor. As a young man, he attended the Communist International in Mexico and recruited members throughout Central America. In 1928, outraged at the U.S. military intervention in Nicaragua, he joined Augusto Cesar Sandino's forces fighting the American marines. Sandino, who was not a Communist, broke with Martí in 1930, however.

Martí returned to El Salvador in 1930 during a depression in the market for coffee. In 1931 Arturo Araujo won the first democratic elections of El Salvador's history, but on December 2, 1931, General Maximiliano Hernández Martínez seized power. This coup provoked an uprising among the nation's peasants, and Martí became one of its leaders. The revolt began on January 22, 1932, in the town of Juayua. Martínez's forces crushed the rebellion, killing some 25,000 peasants in what became known as La Matanza (The Massacre).

Martí was among those captured and was executed on February 1, 1932. The Frente Farabundo Martí para la Liberación Nacional (FMLN, Farabundo Martí National Liberation Front) insurgent group, formed in El Salvador in 1980, was named for him.

Brian J. Tannehill

See also El Salvador Insurgency; Frente Farabundo Martí para la Liberación Nacional; Sandino, Augusto César

Further Reading

Brienza, Hernan. *Farabundo Marti.* Buenos Aires: Capital Intelectual, 2007.

Gómez, Jorge Arias. *Farabundo Martí, La biografía clásica.* New York: Ocean Sur, 2010.

Massu, Jacques Émile

Birth Date: May 5, 1908
Death Date: October 26, 2002

French Army general who played an important role in counterinsurgency operations in the Algerian War (1954–1962). Born on May 5, 1908, in Châlons-sur-Marne, France, Jacques Émile Massu graduated from the French Military Academy of Saint-Cyr in 1928 and embarked on a series of assignments in France's African colonies. During World War II (1939–1945) as a battalion commander in the Free French Forces, Massu fought in North Africa and in the 1944 campaign in France, participating in the liberation of Paris.

Following World War II, Massu fought in the Indochina War (1946–1954). He was then transferred to Algeria, where fighting began in late 1954. Promoted to brigadier general in June 1955, Massu commanded the elite 10th Parachute Division in the 1956 Suez Invasion.

In January 1957, French governor-general in Algeria Robert Lacoste invested Massu with full power to break a general strike proclaimed in Algiers by the rebel Front de Libération Nationale (FLN, National Liberation Front), part of the so-called Battle of Algiers (January–March 1957). Massu and his men operated with ruthless efficiency, including the use of torture, to break the general strike and destroy the FLN terrorist cells and organization in Algiers. The Battle of Algiers, certainly the most dramatic episode of the Algerian War, ended in March 1957.

Fearful that the government in Paris was about to grant Algeria its independence, Massu took a leading role in the May 1958 coup in Algiers by rightist European settlers and army officers that resulted in the return to power of General Charles de Gaulle. Following Massu's remarks to a journalist in December 1959 that the army had perhaps erred in bringing de Gaulle back to power, de Gaulle called Massu to France. De Gaulle soon forgave Massu, assigning him command of the French Army garrison at Metz. Massu refused to lend his support to army uprisings against de Gaulle in Algeria in January 1960 and April 1961. Massu retired from the army in July 1969 as a full general.

As with many French veterans of the Algerian War, Massu spent the remainder of his life trying to come to terms with the tactics employed by the French Army in the conflict. In the 1970s, he was one of his own fiercest defenders, writing a book challenging events depicted in the influential 1966 film *The Battle of Algiers*. But in 2001 he struck a more conciliatory tone, raising doubts over the effectiveness of torture in military operations and encouraging increased openness on the consequences of France's Algerian occupation. Massu died in Loiret, France, on October 26, 2002.

John Spykerman and Spencer C. Tucker

See also Algerian War; *Battle of Algiers;* Indochina War

Further Reading

Alexander, Martin S., Martin Evans, and John F. V. Keiger. *The Algerian War and the French Army, 1954–62: Experiences, Images, Testimonies.* New York: Palgrave MacMillan, 2002.

Aussaresses, Paul. *The Battle of the Casbah: Terrorism and Counter-Terrorism in Algeria, 1955–1957.* Translated by Robert L. Miller. New York: Enigma Books, 2002.

Massu, Jacques. *Le Soldat méconnu* [The Unknown Soldier]. Paris: Mame, 1993.

Massu, Jacques. *La Vrai Bataille d'Alger* [The Real Battle of Algiers]. Paris: Presses Pocket, 1974.

Mau Mau

Militant indigenous movement that sought to end British colonial rule in Kenya during the late 1940s and 1950s. The Mau Mau emerged in the late 1940s as a response to the British colonial government's policy to restrict access by the Kenyan population to fertile land in Africa. Members of the Kikuyu tribe particularly suffered under this arrangement, and many of them rejected constitutional politics as a means to redress their grievances.

In the aftermath of World War II (1939–1945), Kikuyu peasants and tenant farmers who had traditionally been denied access to land by white settlers grew increasingly restive. During the war years, moreover, unemployment had increased dramatically in the area around the colony's capital of Nairobi and added to the growing frustration among members of ethnic groups such as the Kikuyus, Embus, and Merus. In the minds of many Africans, the Kikuyu-dominated Kenya African Union (KAU), a political party that fought for an end to colonial rule, had not adequately dealt with these problems. As a result, militant members of the KAU in the Nairobi River Valley and the Central Province began to advocate a more radical plan of action, which sought land for the dispossessed, Kikuyu unity and self-help, and an end to colonial rule, by violence if necessary.

When British authorities first learned of this movement in 1948, they dubbed the militants "Mau Mau." The origins of the term are unclear. In fact, the term "Mau Mau" has no meaning in any Kenyan language. Many militants referred to their movement as *ithaka na wiathi* ("land and moral responsibility" or "freedom through land"). Some members referred to their organization as the Kenya Land Freedom Army.

While the Kenyan colonial government considered Mau Mau a monolithic movement, the Mau Mau lacked unified leadership and consisted of numerous separate groups. The term "Mau Mau" stuck and came to signify savagery and cultism for colonial authorities and white settlers. In particular, the movement's central initiation ritual, the so-called oathing, worried the British, for it required members to pledge their lives to the Mau Mau cause.

Although the Mau Mau was officially declared illegal in 1950, it continued to grow. The Mau Mau movement intimidated or killed white settlers and those Africans who refused to take the oath. Indeed, Africans were its principal victims.

The assassination of Kikuyu chief Waruhiu on October 7, 1952, led Kenyan governor Sir Evelyn Baring to declare a state of emergency and marked the beginning of a four-year armed struggle involving Mau Mau guerrillas, Kenyan loyalists, and British colonial troops. British efforts to suppress the movement also included the arrest of KAU president Jomo Kenyatta, other nationalist leaders, and thousands of Mau Mau supporters. By early 1953, almost 18,000 Africans had been sent to trial for alleged activities in the militant movement. Despite these repressive measures, the Mau Mau continued its activities.

The capture of guerrilla leader Dedan Kimathi in late October 1956 (he was executed in February 1957) marked the end of major combat operations against the Mau Mau. Although Kenyan militants had been defeated militarily, fear of new uprisings compelled British authorities to initiate political reforms during 1957–1958. Kenya gained its independence in 1963.

Simon Wendt

See also Kenya Emergency

Further Reading

Furedi, Frank. *The Mau Mau War in Perspective.* Athens, OH: Ohio University Press, 1989.

Maloba, Wunyabari O. *Mau Mau and Kenya: An Analysis of a Peasant Revolt.* Bloomington: Indiana University Press, 1998.

Odhiambo, E. S. Atieno, and John Lonsdale, eds. *Mau Mau & Nationhood: Arms, Authority and Narration.* Athens: Ohio University Press, 2003.

McCuen, John Joachim

Birth Date: March 30, 1926
Death Date: July 18, 2010

U.S. Army officer and counterinsurgency theorist. Born in Washington, D.C., on March 30, 1926, John Joachim McCuen graduated from the U.S. Military Academy, West Point, in 1948 and later earned a master of international affairs degree from the School of International Affairs at Columbia University. During much of his military career, McCuen was assigned to the Federal Republic of Germany, where he commanded an armored cavalry troop.

Among McCuen's other postings were those to Thailand as a military adviser (1957–1958) and to the Republic of Vietnam (RVN, South Vietnam) as a staff member of the National Defense College (1968–1969) during the Vietnam War. He was a member of the faculty of the Army War College in Carlisle, Pennsylvania, during 1969–1972 before serving in Indonesia (1972–1974). Returning to the United States, McCuen was assigned to the Army Training and Doctrine Command in 1974. He retired from the army as a colonel in 1976.

An expert on counterinsurgency warfare, McCuen was the author of a highly regarded book, *The Art of Counter-Revolutionary War: The Strategy of Counter-Insurgency* (1966). For many years the book was on the list of required reading for army officers. McCuen also wrote extensively on Mao Zedong's theories of warfare and on French counterinsurgency. In *The Art of Counter-Revolutionary War,* McCuen identified four phases in Mao's military theory: subversion, terrorism, guerrilla warfare, and mobile warfare. McCuen then proposed his own countermeasures appropriate to each. He advanced five strategic principles: preservation of oneself and annihilation of the enemy, establishment of strategic bases, mobilization of the masses, acquisition of external support, and unification of the counterinsurgency effort.

Upon retirement from the army, McCuen worked for General Dynamics as its chief of M-1 Abrams tank training and later as manager of the company's field operations. While in his 80s, he lectured at the U.S. Army Command and General Staff College, Fort Levenworth, Kansas, on counterinsurgency tactics to officers who would serve in Afghanistan. McCuen died on July 18, 2010, in Birmingham, Michigan.

Spencer C. Tucker

See also Mao Zedong

Further Reading

Beckett, Ian F. W. *Encyclopedia of Guerrilla Warfare.* Santa Barbara, CA: ABC-CLIO, 1999.

McCuen, John J. *The Art of Counter-Revolutionary War: The Strategy of Counter-Insurgency.* Harrisburg, PA: Stackpole, 1966.

McNamara Line

The McNamara Line (also known as Project Practice Nine, Project Dye Marker, and Project Muscle Shoals) was the unofficial name for a series of electronically monitored anti-infiltration barriers to halt infiltration of People's Army of Vietnam (PAVN, North Vietnamese Army) forces and supplies from the Democratic Republic of Vietnam (DRV, North Vietnam) south into the Republic of Vietnam (RVN, South Vietnam) during the Vietnam War (1959–1975). The project was named for U.S. secretary of defense Robert McNamara, who announced it on September 7, 1967.

Extensive U.S. bombing of North Vietnam and the introduction of U.S. ground troops into South Vietnam in 1965 had not prevented North Vietnam from supporting the Communist insurgency in South Vietnam. Most of the supplies and men moved south through Laos and then into South Vietnam along the so-called Ho Chi Minh Trail. The employment of small ground units in Operation LEAPING LENA in 1964, Operation PRAIRIE FIRE in 1965, and Operation SHINING BRASS in 1966 had proved ineffective. The U.S. Air Force had first attacked the trail in 1964 as part of its Operation BARREL ROLL. Although air attacks increased in 1965 with the systematic bombing of North Vietnam (Operation ROLLING THUNDER), attacks against the trail remained secondary to the air war against North Vietnam. In any event, the bombing did not slow the rate of infiltration.

In 1966, Harvard professor Roger Fisher proposed construction of high-technology barriers on the Ho Chi Minh Trail and across the five-mile-wide supposedly Demilitarized Zone (DMZ), established in 1954 and separating North and South Vietnam. McNamara gave the proposal to the Jason Division, a group of scientists of the Institute for Defense Analyses. The scientists recommended an antipersonnel barrier, staffed by troops, across the southern side of the DMZ from the South China Sea to Laos and an antivehicular barrier, primarily an aerial operation, in the Laotian panhandle to interdict traffic along the Ho Chi Minh Trail.

Certain features were common to both barriers, including the employment of small mines. These included tiny Button bomblets that made a noise when stepped on, alerting acoustic sensors, the signals of which would be picked up by crewmen in monitoring aircraft who could then call in attack aircraft. Larger camouflaged Gravel mines could inflict serious leg and foot wounds when stepped on.

Requirements for both barriers included 300 million Button bomblets, 240 million larger Gravel mines, 120,000 Sadeye cluster bombs, 19,200 acoustic sensors, 68 patrol planes, and 50 aircraft to drop the mines. The estimated total cost for these components was $800 million per year.

The Barrier in Vietnam

The modified DMZ barrier consisted of a stretch of cleared ground 650 to 1,100 yards wide containing barbed wire, minefields, sensors, and watchtowers backed by a series of manned strong points. Behind these were fire support bases (FSBs), capable of providing an interlocking pattern of artillery fire. The barrier began at the coast of South Vietnam below the DMZ and ran westward for about 18.5 miles. From this point to the Laotian border, the barrier would be less comprehensive. Infiltration routes would be marked and blocked by minefields and barbed-wire obstacles, supported by FSBs and reaction forces capable of seeking out and destroying PAVN infiltrators.

Construction of the barrier began in the summer of 1967. The U.S. forces involved quickly encountered difficulties in the form of PAVN offensive operations culminating in the siege of the U.S. base at Khe Sanh and the Tet Offensive of

January 1968 that forced deployment of resources elsewhere. Much of the DMZ barrier was also within range of PAVN artillery situated just north of the DMZ, and the entire area saw frequent PAVN probes. U.S. military forces were also never of sufficient strength to adequately maintain the barrier while also fighting in I Corps. Had an effective barrier been constructed here earlier, PAVN forces would undoubtedly have been sent around it and down the Ho Chi Minh Trail.

The Antivehicular Barrier in Laos

Unlike the antipersonnel DMZ barrier, the antivehicular barrier across the Laotian panhandle was a thorough implementation of the Jason plan. The Ho Chi Minh Trail was a series of trails, roads, and waterways that began in North Vietnam and entered Laos through various mountain passes. Continuing south through the Laotian panhandle, the trail penetrated South Vietnam in Military Regions I and II. Other branches of the trail continued south into Cambodia and then entered South Vietnam in Military Region III.

Supplies moved down the trail by human porters, animals, bicycles, and truck. In an effort to destroy the trucks, the United States deployed aircraft gunships equipped with night-viewing devices. Sensors included a cathode-ray tube that reacted to ignition systems found in vehicles. Some attacking aircraft employed rapid-fire cannon capable of firing up to 6,000 rounds per minute. The aircraft also made use of computers to maximize bombing accuracy and employed laser-guided bombs.

In addition to devices locating targets from the air, a variety of ground sensors were deployed by air. Some detected motion or sound; others were sensitive to metallic objects or to chemicals emanating from mammals. The Infiltration Surveillance Center was the command center of the antivehicular operation, code-named IGLOO WHITE. Computer-generated data would be fed to the aircraft. This interdiction system had all-weather capability and did not require ground forces.

Operation IGLOO WHITE was in operation from 1968 until the end of 1972. Altogether, the United States dropped more than 3 million tons of bombs on Laos during the Vietnam War in what has been described as the largest aerial interdiction campaign ever undertaken. Mountainsides were bombed to create landslides blocking key passes, cumulus clouds were seeded with silver iodide in an effort to extend the rainy season, and chemicals were used to defoliate the jungle. None of these tactics proved effective. The Ho Chi Minh Trail was simply too vast a network to be destroyed.

The U.S. Air Force claimed the destruction of some 35,500 trucks during 1968–1971, but official Vietnamese figures after the war list approximately 6,700 trucks destroyed in that time period. The U.S. Air Force also estimated that only 20 percent of the supplies entering the trail system in 1971 made it to their destination, while Vietnamese records indicate losses of only 13.7 percent that year. U.S. bombing operations began shutting down in December 1972. The last U.S. bombing raid on the Ho Chi Minh Trail was a strike by Boeing B-52 Stratofortress aircraft in April 1973.

It is estimated that between 1966 and 1971, the Ho Chi Minh Trail was used to infiltrate some 630,000 troops, 100,000 tons of food, 400,000 weapons, and 50,000 tons of ammunition into South Vietnam. By 1972, the trail contained paved roads capable of handling armored vehicles and a petroleum pipeline.

Peter W. Brush

See also Ho Chi Minh Trail; Vietnam War

Further Reading

Dickson, Paul. *The Electronic Battlefield.* Bloomington: Indiana University Press, 1976.

Littauer, Raphael, and Norman Uphoff, eds. *The Air War in Indochina.* Boston: Beacon, 1971.

Nguyen Viet Phuong. *Van Tai Quan Su Chien Luoc Tren Duong Ho Chi Minh Trong Khang Chien Chong My* [Strategic Military Transportation on the Ho Chi Minh Trail during the Resistance War against the Americans]. Hanoi: General Department of Rear Services, 1988.

Mexican-American War and Guerrilla Warfare

Start Date: 1846
End Date: 1848

During the Mexican-American War (1846–1848), Mexico relied on guerrilla warfare for four reasons. First, the cavalry arm of the Mexican Army traditionally had been the best branch of that service, and mounted troops were well suited to the high level of mobility required of guerrillas. Second, a substantial percentage of the fighting during Mexico's War of Independence (1810–1821) and during the interwar years (1821–1846) had been waged by guerrillas, so Mexicans had much experience in irregular warfare. Third, the destruction of much of the Mexican Army in fixed battles with the Americans left the nation with little alternative than to turn to this method of warfare. Finally, American lines of supply and communication, necessarily attenuated by operations deep in the Mexican heartland, were tempting targets for interdiction.

During the Mexican-American War, two major guerrilla forces operated against American forces. In northern Mexico, General José de Urrea led Mexican cavalry units in repeated attacks on U.S. major general Zachary Taylor's supply lines running between the port of Camargo and Taylor's base at Monterrey. Urrea's efforts forced the Americans to include substantial escorts with each convoy.

Urrea showed little mercy in his campaign and is best remembered for the Ramos Massacre in February 1847, during which his forces executed 50 American teamsters after having defeated the forces escorting them. Although he controlled a considerable amount of territory, Urrea never possessed the strength to attack Taylor's main forces at Monterrey.

In central Mexico, the primary focus of guerrilla activity was Major General Winfield Scott's supply route running from the port of Veracruz west to Mexico City. Here, volunteer guerrilla bands authorized by substitute president Pedro María Anaya in April 1847 continually harassed U.S. supply convoys. From June of that year until the signing of the Treaty of Guadalupe Hidalgo on February 2, 1848, each U.S. convoy required a minimum escort of 1,200 men, which cost the U.S. Army substantial forces that might otherwise have been utilized in direct combat roles. In October 1847, Scott assigned additional forces to counterguerrilla duties. This included garrisons of 750 men each at Perote, Puente Nacional, Río Frío, and San Juan de Ulúa as well as a 2,200-man force at Puebla. When those numbers are added to those of the escort forces, the U.S. troops in central Mexico assigned to counterguerrilla duties amounted to almost a quarter of Scott's entire force. In spite of such efforts and the subsequent U.S. decision to form a mounted counterguerrilla unit consisting of both regular dragoons and Texas Rangers, the route remained a dangerous one throughout the war.

In both northern and central Mexico, Mexican guerrilla force commanders never attempted to fully involve the main body of the civilian population in their activities. Previous efforts to do so during both Mexico's War of Independence and in subsequent conflicts had demonstrated that armed civilians soon used their newly acquired weapons and training to turn against the existing socioeconomic order. Furthermore, the emergence of armed groups of indigenous peasants who resisted the Mexican state in their efforts to protect both their autonomy and their lands forced Mexican authorities to abandon any hopes for a protracted struggle against the U.S. Army and to refocus their military efforts on crushing the guerrillas.

Irving W. Levinson

See also Taylor, Zachary

Further Reading

Johannsen, Robert W. *To the Halls of the Montezumas: The Mexican War in the American Imagination.* Oxford: Oxford University Press, 1985.

Levinson, Irving W. *Wars within Wars: Mexican Guerillas, Mexican Elites, and the United States of American, 1846–1848.* Fort Worth: Texas Christian University Press, 2005.

Mexican Expedition

Start Date: 1916
End Date: 1917

The U.S. military incursion into northern Mexico during 1916–1917 was an attempt to capture or kill Mexican insurgent leader Francisco "Pancho" Villa and his followers. Villa had been attacking American interests in Mexico in hopes of undermining ties between the U.S. government and Venustiano Carranza—at last recognized by Washington as the legitimate president of Mexico. In January 1916, Villa caused the murder of 16 American mining engineers, and on March 9 he led some 600 men across the border to attack and put to the torch the town of Columbus, New Mexico. Eighteen U.S. citizens died in the raid.

U.S. president Woodrow Wilson mobilized the National Guard along the Mexican border. He also appointed Brigadier General John J. Pershing to lead a 6,000-man column into northern Mexico to find Villa and bring him to justice. The American soldiers crossed the border on March 14, 1916, and ultimately drove some 500 miles into northern Mexico.

Wilson had expected Carranza and Mexican Army forces to remain neutral as Pershing's men hunted down Villa, but Carranza could ill afford to appear to acquiesce in the presence of U.S. troops on Mexican soil. He announced that Villa was no longer a threat and in a bitter, insulting note demanded the withdrawal of the U.S. troops. Wilson refused.

The first major clash, and the expedition's most important victory, occurred on March 29 at San Geronimo Ranch, near Guerrero between 370 men of the U.S. 7th Cavalry Regiment and a large number of Villaistas. Seventy-five of Villa's men were killed or wounded, and Villa was forced to withdraw into the mountains. Only five of the Americans were hurt, none fatally. It was the closest the Americans would come to capturing Villa.

There were clashes with the Mexican Army (Carrancistas), and on June 18 in the Battle of Carrizal, 11 U.S. soldiers were killed and 24 were taken prisoner. Wilson threatened full-scale war and delivered an ultimatum to Carranza, demanding the release of the soldiers. Carranza yielded, and within days the soldiers were freed. Villa, however, was still at large and soon captured a number of towns previously held by Carranza's forces.

By early 1917 war with Germany loomed, and Wilson was obliged to negotiate a settlement with Carranza and order the withdrawal of the U.S. troops. The last troops quit Mexico on February 7, 1917. The expedition claimed 8 U.S. dead; 171 Villaistas were also killed, along with 24 Carrancistas. Villa was never captured.

The so-called Punitive Expedition helped create additional problems with Mexico later, especially after Carranza nationalized church and oil lands. But militarily at least, the intervention was worth the price in terms of the training it provided for the regular U.S. Army. The intervention also provided a field test for new equipment and weapons and showed the superiority of motor transport and the important role of aircraft in reconnaissance.

Spencer C. Tucker

See also Pershing, John Joseph; Villa, Francisco

Further Reading

De Quesada, Alejandro. *The Hunt for Pancho Villa: The Columbus Raid and Pershing's Punitive Expedition, 1916–17.* New York: Osprey, 2012.

Mason, Herbert Molloy. *The Great Pursuit: General John J. Pershing's Punitive Expedition across the Rio Grande to Destroy the Mexican Bandit Pancho Villa.* New York: Random House, 1970.

Smythe, Donald. *Guerrilla Warrior: The Early Life of John J. Pershing.* New York: Scribner, 1973.

Miles, Nelson Appleton

Birth Date: August 8, 1839
Death Date: May 15, 1925

U.S. Army officer. Nelson Appleton Miles was born near Westminster, Massachusetts, on August 8, 1839. After attending public school, Miles moved to Boston in 1856, where he became a store clerk. Interested in the military, he received some instruction from a retired French colonel.

On the outbreak of the American Civil War (1861–1865), Miles recruited some 100 men for a Massachusetts regiment and was commissioned a first lieutenant of volunteers. At first considered too young for battlefield command, he initially served in a staff position during the 1862 Peninsula Campaign. He soon demonstrated a natural capacity for battlefield leadership and began a meteoric advance in rank. Following the Battle of Seven Pines (Fair Oaks) (May 31–June 1, 1862), he was promoted to lieutenant colonel in a New York infantry regiment. He then fought in the Seven Days' Campaign (June 25–July 1) and in the bloody Battle of Antietam (September 17). Promoted to colonel, he was wounded in the First Battle of Fredericksburg (December 13) and again in the Battle of Chancellorsville (May 4–6, 1863), for which he was belatedly (1892) awarded the Medal of Honor. He commanded a brigade in the 1864 Overland Campaign and saw combat in the Battle of the Wilderness (May 5–7) and the Battle of Spotsylvania Court House (May 7–19), after which he was promoted to brigadier general of volunteers. Miles commanded a division in the Siege of Petersburg (June 15, 1864–April 3, 1865) and also briefly commanded (at age 26) a corps. He suffered his fourth wound of the war in the Battle of Reams Station (August 25, 1864). Following the war, in October 1865 Miles was advanced to major general of volunteers and assumed command of II Corps.

In the reorganization of the army in 1866, Miles became colonel of the 40th Infantry Regiment, an African American unit. In 1869 he took command of the 5th Infantry Regiment and saw extensive service in the American West and became renowned as one of the army's finest commanders in the ensuing Indian Wars. He was conspicuously active in the Red River War (1874–1875). In 1876 and 1877 he played prominent roles in the Great Sioux War and the Nez Perce War, personally accepting the surrenders of Sioux war chief Crazy Horse and Nez Perce chief Joseph.

Promoted to brigadier general in the regular army in December 1880, from 1880 to 1885 Miles commanded the Department of the Columbia, and from 1885 to 1886 he had charge of the Department of the Missouri. In 1886 he took command of the Department of Arizona. There he discontinued the wise practice of his predecessor, Brigadier General George Crook, of employing Apaches as scouts, choosing instead to rely mostly on U.S. troops. Following several months of failure, Miles reintroduced Crook's practice and oversaw the final surrender of Geronimo and the Chiricahua Apaches in September 1886. Miles then engaged in a public dispute with Crook concerning the subsequent exile of the Apaches, including the loyal scouts, to Florida.

In 1888 Miles assumed command of the Division of the Pacific. Promoted to major general in April 1890, he directed the suppression of the Sioux

U.S. Army major general Nelson A. Miles distinguished himself in the American Civil War and is regarded as one of the finest commanders in the fighting against Native Americans in the West. Miles served as commanding general of the army during the Spanish-American War. (Library of Congress)

Ghost Dance uprising in the Dakota Territory but was angered by the bloodshed at Wounded Knee on December 29, 1890. Miles wanted to court-martial Colonel James W. Forsyth, who commanded during that action. Although Miles relieved Forsyth from command, the War Department soon reinstated him.

In 1894 Miles was called upon to employ troops in suppressing the Pullman Strike and then commanded the Department of the East. On October 5, 1895, he succeeded Lieutenant General John M. Schofield as commanding general of the army. Miles opposed the Spanish-American War (1898), believing that diplomacy could resolve the differences between Spain and the United States. When the war began, he favored using regulars in Cuba rather than volunteer forces, which he believed should remain in the United States and maintain its defenses against a possible Spanish attack. He also opposed an invasion of Cuba until the Spanish naval squadron had been destroyed but convinced President William McKinley to shift the main American land assault from Havana to Santiago de Cuba. Once Santiago was secured, Miles received approval to proceed with his own invasion of Puerto Rico, an assignment that he had sought early on. He conducted a highly successful campaign in Puerto Rico that was cut short by the armistice of August 12.

After the war Miles was the central figure in the notorious Embalmed Beef Scandal, alleging that the Commissary Department had issued spoiled beef to the troops. He was subsequently reprimanded by the Dodge Commission for making charges that were proven to be substantially unfounded. In June 1900 Miles was promoted to lieutenant general. He opposed Secretary of War Elihu Root's plan to create a General Staff and do away with the position of commanding general of the army, substituting for it the new position of chief of staff.

Miles retired from the army in 1903. Combative, vain, and ambitious, Miles was, along with Ranald Mackenzie, one of the finest field commanders during the Indian Wars in the West, amassing a record second to none. Despite Miles's leadership qualities in battle, he displayed little political sense and did not fit well in the new 20th-century army. In retirement he wrote articles and several books, including a two-volume memoir. Miles died in Washington, D.C., on May 15, 1925.

Jerry Keenan and Spencer C. Tucker

See also Crazy Horse; Crook, George; Geronimo

Further Reading

DeMontravel, Peter R. *A Hero to His Fighting Men: Nelson A. Miles, 1839–1925.* Kent, OH: Kent State University Press, 1998.

Johnson, Virginia. *The Unregimented General: A Biography of Nelson A. Miles.* Boston: Houghton Mifflin, 1962.

Wooster, Robert. *Nelson A. Miles and the Twilight of the Frontier Army.* Lincoln: University of Nebraska Press, 1993.

Mitchell, Colin Campbell

Birth Date: November 17, 1925
Death Date: July 20, 1996

British Army officer who became an iconic figure during the Aden Emergency (1963–1967). Colin Campbell Mitchell was born of Scottish parents on November 17, 1925, in Purley, England, a suburb of London; his father had served as a captain in the Argyll and Sutherland Highlanders in World War I (1914–1918). Mitchell was educated at the Whitgift School in Croydon. Enlisting in the Home Guard at age 14, he joined the British Army in 1943 and was assigned to the Argyll and Sutherland Highlanders. Mitchell was commissioned in 1944 and saw combat in Italy in World War II (1939–1945), where he was lightly wounded at Monte Cassino.

Remaining in the British Army, Mitchell saw service in Palestine, in the Korean War (1950–1953), in the Kenya Emergency (1952–1960), in Cypress, and in Borneo during the confrontation between Indonesia and Malaysia (1962–1966). He also served in Africa with the King's African Rifles. Mitchell was promoted to lieutenant in 1947, to captain in 1952, and to major in 1959. He was breveted lieutenant colonel in 1964 and received that substantive rank in 1966.

Assigned to command the 1st Battalion of the Argyll and Sutherland Highlanders in January 1967, Mitchell was ordered to Aden. There he revealed both a flair for self-promotion and, to the irritation of other British units, a determination that his unit receive the most favorable publicity. Mitchell also found himself at odds with British commander in Aden Major General Philip Tower.

With eruption of the 1967 Arab-Israeli War, Egyptian president Gamal Abdel Nasser charged that the British had aided the Israelis. This led to a mutiny in the South Arabian Federation Army and police, resulting in the deaths of 23 British servicemen and insurgent control of Aden's old Crater District. Two weeks later on July 5 in a classic military operation of its type, known as STIRLING CASTLE, Mitchell's 1st Battalion of the Argyll and Sutherland Highlanders Regiment reoccupied the district, with bagpipes blaring and without a single British casualty (one local resident was killed). Dubbed "Mad Mitch" for what became known as the Last Battle of the British Empire, Mitchell was lionized in the British press. The Argylls then remained in the district until just a few days before the British withdrawal from Aden at the end of November 1967.

Tower's antipathy led to Mitchell being denied the Distinguished Service Order and retiring from the army in 1968. Mitchell's battalion was also disbanded as a consequence of British defense cuts. Mitchell wrote his memoirs, became a leading figure in the subsequent "Save the Argylls" campaign (the Conservatives restored the battalion in 1972), and was elected as a member of the British Parliament in 1970. He refused to stand for reelection in 1974. Following the failure of a business venture, he became a military consultant. From 1989 he headed the Halo Trust, a nonprofit organization undertaking the removal of land mines from former war zones. Mitchell died on July 20, 1996.

Spencer C. Tucker

See also Aden Emergency

Further Reading

Mitchell, Colin. *Having Been a Soldier.* London: Hamilton, 1969.

Naumkin, Vitaly. *Red Wolves of Yemen: The Struggle for Independence.* Cambridge, UK: Oleander, 2004.

Walker, Jonathan. *Aden Insurgency: The Savage War in Yemen, 1962–1967.* Barnsley, South Yorkshire, UK: Pen and Sword Military, 2011.

Mondlane, Eduardo

Birth Date: June 20, 1920
Death Date: February 3, 1969

Founder of the Frente de Libertação de Moçambique (FRELIMO, Mozambique Liberation Front) that led the insurgency against Portuguese rule in Mozambique. Born in Manjacaze, Gaza Province, in Portuguese Mozambique on June 20, 1920,

Eduardo Mondlane was 1 of 16 sons of a chief of the Bantu-speaking Tsonga tribe. Educated at Presbyterian missionary schools in Mozambique and in the Transvaal, South Africa, Mondlane was awarded a scholarship to Witwatersrand University but left within a year with the rise of apartheid. In 1950 he entered the University of Lisbon but secured a scholarship from Oberlin College, Ohio, in the United States, earning a degree in anthropology and sociology there in 1953. He then earned a doctorate in sociology at Northwestern University.

Following a year's study at Harvard University, in 1957 Mondlane joined the United Nations (UN) as a researcher in the Trusteeship Department but resigned within a year to undertake political activities not permitted in the UN position. He joined the faculty of Syracuse University as an assistant professor of anthropology and helped develop its East African studies program.

In 1962 Mondlane resigned from Syracuse and moved to Tanzania. At Dar es Salaam there that September he was elected the president of FRELIMO, formed of four organizations working for the independence of Mozambique. Enjoying support from a number of African states and the Soviet Union, in 1964 FRELIMO commenced military operations against Portugal in Mozambique.

Throughout, FRELIMO was subject to considerable internal divisions, and Mondlane was assassinated in Dar es Salaam by a parcel bomb on February 3, 1969. Some have attributed the deed to the Portuguese intelligence services. Mondlane's successor, Samora Machel, aligned FRELIMO more closely with the Soviet Union.

Spencer C. Tucker

See also Frente de Libertação de Moçambique; Machel, Samora Moïses; Mozambique Insurgency

Further Reading

Mondlane, Eduardo. *The Struggle for Mozambique.* Baltimore: Penguin, 1969.
Newitt, Maryland. *Portugal in Africa: The Last 100 Years.* London: Longman, 1981.

Moplah Rebellion

Start Date: August 1921
End Date: February 1922

The Moplah Rebellion (also known as the Mappila Rebellion and Malabar Revolt) was an Islamic revolt in the heavily Muslim Malabar region of southwestern India. The rebellion began in August 1921 and ended in February 1922. Malabar had long been restive, and a number of disturbances had occurred there from 1836. The situation was exacerbated by the alignment of the Ottoman Empire against Britain in World War I (1914–1918) and the call of the Ottoman sultan (the spiritual leader of Islam) for jihad (holy war) against the British.

In 1920, Muslims in Malabar formed the Kudiyan Sangham. Led by Ali Musaliar, the Kudiyan Sangham protested the exploitation of landless farmers and laborers by mostly upper-caste Hindu landlords who had secured land and eviction rights from the British. Particularly hated was the practice of landlords evicting tenants at will simply to secure higher rents. The revolt began following the arrest by the police of a number of the movement's leaders on August 16, 1921. Rumors that British troops had destroyed the Mamparam mosque led to wide-scale rioting throughout the region against both wealthy Hindus and the British.

Although British army troops soon gained the upper hand in the population centers, a number of the rebels embarked on guerrilla operations, forcing the British to deploy additional military units and initiate aggressive patrolling. The revolt came to an end in February 1922. Ali Musalier was among a dozen leaders tried and sentenced to death. He was hanged at the Ximbatore jail on February 21, 1922. Thousands were also imprisoned. In the revolt, more than 1,000 Malabar Muslims were killed, and more than 14,000 were arrested. In the so-called Wagon Tragedy, 64 of the latter suffocated to death in sealed railway cars in which they had been packed for transportation to Coimbatore.

Spencer C. Tucker

See also Jihad

Further Reading

Panicker, K. N. *Against Lord and State: Religion and Peasant Uprisings in Malabar.* New York: Oxford University Press, 1989.

Wood, Conrad. *The Moplah Rebellion and Its Genesis.* New Delhi: People's Publishing House, 1987.

Morice Line

Physical barrier erected by the French Army during the Algerian War (1954–1962) and completed in September 1957 to prevent the infiltration of men and supplies by the Algerian Front de Libération Nationale (FLN, National Liberation Front) from Tunisia. The line was named after French minister of defense André Morice. It ran for some 200 miles from the Mediterranean Sea in the north into the Sahara in the south. The line was centered on an 8-foot tall 5,000-volt electric fence that ran its entire length. Supporting this was a 50-yard-wide killing zone on each side of the fence rigged with antipersonnel mines. The line was also covered by previously ranged 105-millimeter howitzers. A patrolled track paralleled the fence on its Algerian side. The Morice Line was bolstered by electronic sensors that provided warning of any attempt to pierce the barrier. Searchlights operated at night.

Although manning the line required a large number of French soldiers, the line did significantly reduce infiltration by the FLN from Tunisia. By April 1958, the

French estimated that they had defeated 80 percent of FLN infiltration attempts. This contributed greatly to the isolation of those FLN units within Algeria who were reliant on support from Tunisia.

The French subsequently constructed a less extensive barrier, known as the Pedron Line, along the Algerian border with Morocco.

Spencer C. Tucker

See also Algerian War; Front de Libération Nationale

Further Reading

Hogg, Ian A. *The History of Fortification.* Chicago: St. Martin's, 1981.

Horne, Alistair. *A Savage War of Peace: Algeria, 1954–1962.* New York: Viking, 1977.

Moro Islamic Liberation Front

Sunni Muslim insurgent group in the southern Philippines. In 1969 Nur Misuari established the Moro National Liberation Front (MNLF) with the goal of securing independence for Bangasamoro Land (the Bangasamoro Nation or Mindanao Nation), the territory of Sulu, Mindanao, and Palawan (also known as the Southern Philippines). The MNLF claimed to be egalitarian and to respect all religions.

Moro resentment over the so-called Homestead Program, in which the government took advantage of the lack of land titles to distribute large tracts of land in the southern Philippines to Filipinos from other parts of the country, led to fighting, and the Philippine government dispatched troops. In 1976 the Tripoli Agreement, brokered by Libyan leader Muammar Gaddafi, between MNLF leader Nur Misurai and the Philippine government granted semiautonomy to the affected regions.

The Tripoli Agreement, however, created a split in the MNLF in 1977, with Hashim Salamat leading a breakaway group of the more radical members. Initially known as the New Leadership, it set up headquarters first in Cairo, Egypt, and then in Lahore, Pakistan. In 1984 the New Leadership took the name Moro Islamic Liberation Front (MILF). Gaddafi became a strong supporter.

In January 1987, meanwhile, the MNLF formally agreed to the Philippine government offer of semiautonomy, leading to the establishment of the Autonomous Region of Muslim Minanao. The MILF rejected the agreement, however, and continued its insurgency. In July 1997, however, the government and the MILF agreed to a general cessation of hostilities, but the government nullified the agreement in 2000, and the MILF responded by proclaiming a jihad (holy war) against the government and its supporters.

The MILF denies any association with terrorist organizations such as Jemaah Islamiyah and Al Qaeda, although Jamaah Islamiyah has allowed the MILF to use training camps in areas that the Jamaah Islamiyah controls and the MILF admits having sent some 600 of its members to be trained at Al Qaeda camps in Afghanistan. Despite repeated cease-fires, the insurgency continued, with the MILF insisting on a Muslim substate similar to the state structure in the United States. This substate would not have authority over national defense, foreign affairs, currency, and the like but would be permitted internal security forces.

On October 15, 2012, in Manila following protracted negotiations in Kuala Lumpur, Malaysia, Philippine president Benigno Aquino signed an agreement with MILF leaders to end the nearly 40-year-long insurgency that had claimed more than 120,000 lives. The deal set in motion the creation by the end of Aquino's term in 2016 of a new Bangsamoro autonomous region that would allow more local control, including that of security and local taxes, and permit economic development of that resource-rich region.

Spencer C. Tucker

See also Jihad; Moro National Liberation Front; Moros

Further Reading

Banlaoi, Rommel. *Philippine Security in the Age of Terror.* New York: Taylor and Francis, 2010.

Moro National Liberation Front

Established in 1969 by Nur Misuari, the Moro National Liberation Front (MNLF) seeks independence for Bangasamoro Land (the Bangasamoro Nation or Mindanao Nation), the territory of Sulu, Mindanao, and Palawan also known as the southern Philippines. The MNLF claims to be an egalitarian political organization that respects basic human rights and all religions; indeed, its leadership includes Christians and representatives of other religions as well as Muslims. The MNLF also contends that the Bangasamoro Nation had been independent for "hundreds of years" when it was "illegally annexed" by the government of the Philippines in 1935.

Tensions between Christian and Muslim Filipinos increased in the wake of World War II (1939–1945), when there was considerable resentment among Moros regarding a large influx of Christians into the southern Philippines from other parts of the Philippines. They were attracted by the Homestead Program in which the Philippine government took advantage of the lack of land titles to distribute large tracts of land for farming. Tensions led to fighting and assassinations, and the Philippine government dispatched troops.

The MNLF traced its origins to the so-called Judidah Massacre of March 18, 1968, when 14–68 Filipino Muslim military trainees were killed by Philippine Army troops on Corregidor. This triggered widespread outrage in the Muslim southern Philippines. Dr. Nur Masuari, a University of the Philippines professor, then led the effort to create the MNLF.

Officially established in 1969, the MNLF declared itself a political party the next year. Following recruitment and training efforts, the MNLF launched an insurgency against the government of Philippine president Ferdinand Marcos. Seven years of warfare produced thousands of deaths on both sides and led to the relocation of many more Filipinos.

In 1976, Libyan leader Muammar Gaddafi brokered the so-called Tripoli Agreement between Nur Misurai and the Philippine government. The agreement granted semiautonomy to the affected regions. Not all members of the MNLF accepted the Tripoli Agreement, however, and a more militant Sunni Muslim group broke away in 1984 taking the name of Moro Islamic Liberation Front (MILF). Another extremist group, Abu Sayyaf, separated in 1991.

In January 1987, meanwhile, the MNLF formally agreed to the offer by the new Philippine government of Corazon Aquino of semiautonomy, leading to the establishment of the Autonomous Region of Muslim Mindanao in 1989. In 1993 Aquino's successor, Fidel Ramos, concluded a Joint Cease-Fire Agreement with the MNLA. Both the MILF and Abu Sayyaf rejected the agreement, however, and continued their insurgencies. Despite the Philippine government's pledge to make Minadano the focus of social development and poverty alleviation programs, there remain real doubts over this given the government's lack of resources, economic mismanagement, endemic corruption, and record in human rights abuses.

Spencer C. Tucker

See also Abu Sayyaf; Jihad; Moro Islamic Liberation Front; Moros

Further Reading

Banlaoi, Rommel. *Philippine Security in the Age of Terror.* New York: Taylor and Francis, 2010.

Moros

Native Muslims of the Philippines. The term "Moros" is Spanish for "Moors," referencing the North African Muslims who conquered Spain in 711 CE. Most reside in the southern Philippines in an area called Bangsamoro on the island of Mindanao. They also live in the long archipelago of small islands to the south and west of Mindanao. There were, however, Muslim enclaves and influences as far away as Manila.

The Spanish called all Muslims they encountered during the Age of Exploration Moros, but only in the Philippines did the name take hold. The group that became known as the Moros is believed to have come to the Philippines as part of the Great Polynesian Migration in about 100 CE. By the late 15th century when the Moros had been converted to Islam by merchants from India, the Moros already had a reputation as fierce warriors and pirates.

Islam had arrived in the Philippines only 60 years before the Spanish. The Spanish conquered and Christianized the northern islands, while the southern islands of Mindanao and Sulu became Muslim strongholds. For more than 300 years, the Spanish battled the Moros for complete control of the archipelago. The Moros traditionally allied themselves with Spain's enemies, the British and the Dutch, when the European powers were at war with one another. The Moros also constantly preyed on Spanish merchant ships.

During the Spanish-American War (1898) and the Philippine-American War (1898–1902), the Moros remained neutral. Indeed, rule by a Christian-dominated Republic of the Philippines was as distasteful to the Moros as being governed by the United States. It was not until the Christian Filipinos had been conquered that the Moros and U.S. Army forces began to clash. Although the United States acquired the Philippine archipelago from Spain under terms of the Treaty of Paris of December 10, 1898, the northern Philippine islands had been in revolt against Spanish rule since 1896, and it required nearly three years (1899–1902) for U.S. forces to defeat the Filipino independence movement in what was commonly called the Philippine Insurrection and is today known as the Philippine-American War.

The southern Philippine islands of Sulu and Mindanao had never been completely conquered by Spain, despite more than 400 years of sporadic warfare. The U.S. Army spent 11 more years (1902–1913) fighting on the southern islands against the Moros with only limited success.

When U.S. Army forces occupied Sulu and Mindanao, they were not content merely to establish coastal enclaves as the Spaniards had done but instead sought to Americanize the entire islands. This meant bringing an end to slavery, blood feuds, and the piracy that had been a way of life for the Moros for centuries. On August 20, 1899, Brigadier General John Bates signed a treaty with the sultan of Sulu ostensibly giving the United States control over the islands, ending slavery and piracy, and guaranteeing the sultan certain rights, including an annual stipend.

The Bates Treaty did not have much practical effect, however, as the sultan had little control over Sulu and Mindanao. Real power lay in the dozens of tribal datus (chiefs), who strongly resisted U.S. control over their territories and mounted isolated attacks against American troops and all other foreigners. Although the Moros had rifles taken from the Spanish and the Americans, their principal weapon was a short sword known as the kris.

The Moros proved to be masters at guerrilla warfare, attacking at night and ambushing stragglers and small patrols. Using the jungle to their advantage, they could often be within stabbing distance with the kris before their enemies could return fire. The Moros often charged into gunfire, continuing to rush their enemies despite being hit by bullets. One consequence of the Moro Campaigns was the U.S. Army decision to change its official side arm from the .38 revolver to the semiautomatic .45 because the .38 round did not have the power to stop a charging Moro warrior. Although the Moros were masters of jungle warfare, when attacked

Iman Ibbah and his Moro followers, ca. 1930s. Various Muslim Moro groups in the southern Philippines have mounted insurgencies against the central Philippine government. The Moros are shown with their *bolos*, the large knives with which they went into battle and which also served peaceful uses in the jungle. (Bettmann/Corbis)

they retired to their cottas, small castle-like structures with thick, high walls that dotted the landscape and were almost impenetrable without artillery.

In 1903 Captain John J. Pershing led several expeditions in the Lake Lanao area of Mindanao. In August 1903 Major General Leonard Wood became the civilian governor of the Moro islands. He immediately launched a campaign into the interior in an attempt to capture Datu Ali, the leader of the resistance on Mindanao. In this operation, Wood employed not only the U.S. Army but also the Philippine Constabulary of native Filipinos. During the ensuing months more than 130 cottas were destroyed, and hundreds of Moro warriors were slain.

During March 5–7, 1906, the largest battle of the Moro Campaigns occurred on the extinct volcano of Bud Dajo on Jolo Island, where 1,000 Moros fiercely resisted 800 American soldiers and Filipino Constabulary troops. The Moros were defeated, but the sometimes hand-to-hand fighting claimed more than 700 Moros dead along with 21 Americans and Filipinos killed.

The next several years were relatively quiet, with only sporadic violence. Most Moros had begun to realize that the United States had no intention of trying to convert them to Christianity as the Spanish had attempted to do. This removed a major incentive for Moro resistance. Civic action programs, including the construction of schools, hospitals, and roads, also played a role.

The last major engagement of the Moro Campaigns occurred on the island of Jolo during June 11–15, 1913, when recently promoted Brigadier General Pershing led U.S. Army forces in the Battle of Bud Bagsak. Some 500 Moros were killed along with 15 Americans. The battle broke the last significant resistance to American rule in the southern Philippines.

There was some negative reaction in the United States to the Moro Campaigns, chiefly because of the high casualties inflicted on the Moros in comparison to the number taken prisoner. But Moros usually chose to fight to the death rather than surrender. The Moro Campaigns of 1902–1913 claimed some 130 American soldiers killed in combat, while more than 500 others died of various diseases.

During World War II (1939–1945), the Moros resisted Japanese occupation. After Filipino independence in 1946, the Moros became alarmed over an influx of non-Moro Filipinos into the region. The Philippine government had taken advantage of the lack of land titles to distribute land to settlers from the other Philippine islands. There were also fears of the spread of Catholicism in this Islamic region. In 1969 Nur Misuari established the Moro National Liberation Front (MNLF), which sought independence for Bangsamoro Land (Bangsamoro Nation, or Mindanao Nation) and began an insurgency to achieve that end. In September 1972 the Philippine government of Ferdinand Marcos declared martial law.

In 1976, Libyan leader Muammar Gaddafi brokered the so-called Tripoli Agreement between Nur Misurai and the Philippine government. The agreement granted semiautonomy to the affected regions. Not all members of the MNLF accepted the Tripoli Agreement, however. Some of the more militant Sunni Muslims broke away. Taking the name the Moro Islamic Liberation Front (MILF), they continued the insurgency. Another even more extremist group, Abu Sayyaf, separated in 1991.

In January 1987, meanwhile, the MNLF formally agreed to the offer by the new Philippine government of Corazon Aquino of semiautonomy, leading to the establishment of the Autonomous Region of Muslim Mindanao in 1989. In 1993 Aquino's successor, Fidel Ramos, concluded a Joint Cease-Fire Agreement with the MNLA. Both the MILF and Abu Sayyaf rejected the agreement and continued their attacks on the government and its supporters. Philippine government pledges to improve conditions in the Moro region have yet to be realized. With reports that Abu Sayyaf has received aid from the Al Qaeda terrorist organization and its affiliates, the United States has made the insurgency part of Operation ENDURING FREEDOM in the Global War on Terror and dispatched Central Intelligence Agency agents to help hunt down Abu Sayyaf leaders and also dispatched several hundred U.S. Army Special Forces personnel to assist the Philippine armed forces in counterinsurgency training.

On October 15, 2012, in Manila following protracted negotiations in Kuala Lumpur, Malaysia, Philippine president Benigno Aqino signed an agreement with the MILF to end its nearly 40-year-long insurgency that has reportedly claimed more than 120,000 lives. The deal sets in motion the creation by the time Aquino leaves office in 2016 of a Bangsamoro autonomous region that will allow the region control of security, permit local taxes, and permit economic development of that region, reportedly containing rich deposits of oil and natural gas.

Wesley Moody and Spencer C. Tucker

See also Abu Sayyaf; Moro Islamic Liberation Front; Moro National Liberation Front

Further Reading

Birtle, Andrew J. *U.S. Army Counterinsurgency and Contingency Operations Doctrine, 1860–1941*. Washington, DC: Center of Military History, U.S. Army, 2003.

Hurley, Vic. *Swish of the Kris: The Story of the Moros*. New York: Dutton, 1936.

Rabasa, Angel. *Political Islam in Southeast Asia: Moderates, Radicals, and Terrorists*. New York: Oxford University Press, 2003.

Mosby, John Singleton

Birth Date: December 6, 1833
Death Date: May 30, 1916

Confederate Army officer during the American Civil War (1861–1865) and probably the best known and most successful guerrilla leader of that conflict. John Singleton Mosby was born on December 6, 1833, at McLaurrine Place, Cumberland County, Virginia. In 1840 his family moved to Charlottesville, Virginia. Mosby entered the University of Virginia in 1849, but in March 1850 he shot a fellow student and was sentenced to a year in jail, ending his formal schooling.

While in prison Mosby studied law and then joined a law firm in Albemarle County upon his release. He was practicing law in Bristol, Virginia, when the Civil War began. Mosby immediately joined the Confederate cavalry as a private and fought in the First Battle of Bull Run (July 21, 1961), bringing him to the attention of Brigadier General J. E. B. Stuart, who promoted Mosby to first lieutenant and requested that he join Stuart's cavalry scouts. Mosby played a prominent role in the Confederate cavalry's movement around Major General George B. McClellan's Union forces (the so-called Ride around McClellan) in the Seven Days' Campaign near Richmond (June 25–July 1, 1862). Mosby was captured by Union cavalry soon thereafter and imprisoned in Washington, D.C., but he was released shortly afterward in a prisoner exchange.

In January 1863 General Stuart authorized Mosby to organize a group of partisan rangers for guerrilla action in northern Virginia, and Mosby subsequently received promotion to captain and to major that March. In what was certainly Mosby's most daring and famous exploit, he and 29 of his men raided the Fairfax County Court House, Virginia, on March 9, 1863, capturing 3 high-ranking Union officers, including Brigadier General Edwin H. Stoughton. Mosby's command, commonly known as Mosby's Rangers, was officially designated the 43rd Virginia Cavalry Battalion in June 1863.

On August 13, 1864, Mosby's Rangers successfully ambushed a large Union wagon train at Berryville, Virginia. Early on October 14, 1864, Mosby carried out what became known as the Greenback Raid near Harpers Ferry, West Virginia, in which a Union train on the Baltimore & Ohio Railroad was purposefully derailed. Mosby and his rangers made off with $173,000 sent to pay Union soldiers. Mosby was promoted to lieutenant colonel in January 1864 and to colonel on December 7.

Mosby, now known as the "Gray Ghost," caused widespread disruption to the Union lines of communication. In all, he staged more than 100 separate attacks on Union troops, supply lines, and depots. The destructive results of these activities led to Union Army commander Lieutenant General Ulysses S. Grant's order to summarily execute any captured partisans attached to Mosby's unit. By Mosby's own account, his outfit may have kept as many as 30,000 Union soldiers from reaching the front lines. When some of Mosby's men were executed in Front Royal, Virginia, under the orders of Brigadier General George Custer, Mosby wrote to Grant protesting the treatment of his men, and Grant stayed further executions.

Mosby never had more than 800 or so men under his command and was wounded seven times in the course of the war. Upon the surrender of Confederate forces at Appomattox on April 9, 1865, Mosby disbanded his command. He then returned to the practice of law in Warrenton, Virginia, and embarked on a political career in the Republican Party, eventually working as a campaign manager for General Grant. Mosby was the U.S. consul in Hong Kong from 1878 to 1885, but his highest political assignment came in 1904 when he was appointed assistant attorney general of the United States, a post he held until 1910. Mosby died in Washington, D.C., on May 30, 1916.

Ralph Martin Baker and Paul G. Pierpaoli Jr.

See also American Civil War Insurgency and Counterinsurgency

Further Reading

Jones, Virgil C. *Gray Ghosts and Rebel Raiders.* Charlottesville, VA: Howell, 1998.

Siepel, Kevin H. *Rebel: The Life and Times of John Singleton Mosby.* Cambridge, MA: Da Capo, 1997.

Movimento Popular de Libertação de Angola

Angolan insurgent group and ruling political party of Angola. In 1956 the small underground Partido Comunista de Angola (PCA, Angolan Communist Party) merged with the Partido da Luta Unida dos Africanos de Angola (PLUA, Party of the United Struggle for Africans in Angola) to form the Movimento Popular de Libertação de Angola (MPLA, Popular Movement for the Liberation of Angola).

Viriato de Cruz, president of the PCA, became its secretary-general, and António Agostinho Neto was the president. By 1963, Neto was the undisputed MPLA leader. Most of the MPLA leadership was drawn from the native elite, educated by Christian missionaries, while the bulk of members came from the Mbundu tribe inhabiting the area around the capital city of Luanda. The MPLA was Marxist in orientation.

The armed wing of the MPLA was the Forças Armadas Populares de Libertação de Angola (FAPLA, Armed Forces for the Liberation of Abgola). An initial force of 350 insurgents received training in Algeria, and subsequent recruits were trained in Soviet-bloc countries. In January 1961 Neto initiated the Angolan Insurgency (1961–1975) with attacks on Portuguese cotton plantations in northern Angola. MPLA guerrillas operated first from the neighboring Republic of the Congo, then from Zaire (present-day Democratic Republic of the Congo), and then back to the Republic of the Congo. Although the MPLA numbered some 3,000–5,000 men under arms, only a small number of MPLA guerrillas actually operated inside Angola, and they suffered numerous reverses at the hands of the Portuguese Army.

Following the April 1974 Carnation Revolution in Portugal, the new Portuguese government agreed to grant its colonies independence. Holden Roberto's Frente Nacional de Libertação de Angola (FNLA, National Liberation Front of Angola) and the third Angolan insurgent group, the União Nacional para a Independência Total de Angola (UNITA, National Union for the Total Independence of Angola), headed by Jonas Savimbi, then formed an alliance against the MPLA. Supported by Zairean military forces, they attempted to prevent the Marxist MPLA from taking power but were defeated by the timely arrival of Cuban troops airlifted into Luanda by the Soviet Union.

Although Angola received independence on November 11, 1975, with Neto as president and the FNLA as the country's armed forces, a bloody and protracted civil war followed that pitted the MPLA and Cuban forces supported by the Soviet Union against UNITA and the FLNA, backed by the United States, Zaire, and South Africa. Although Marxist-Leninism was the declared official MPLA doctrine and the words "Partido do Trabalho" (Labor Party) were added to the party name, in practice Neto favored a Socialist, not Communist, model for Angola.

In 1977 the MPLA violently suppressed an attempted coup by the Organização dos Communistas de Angola (OCA, Communist Organization of Angola), with some 18,000 OCA supporters killed (some sources claim that up to 70,000 died) during a two-year span. Neto died in Moscow in September 1979. Meanwhile, the bloody civil war continued. With the end of the Cold War in 1990, the MPLA abandoned its Marxist-Leninist ideology and subsequently adopted social democracy as its official ideology. The civil war with UNITA continued until 2002 and the death of Savimbi. The MPLA, which has been accused of widespread human rights abuses, remains in power in 2013.

Spencer C. Tucker

See also Angolan Insurgency; Castro Ruz, Fidel Alejandro; Frente Nacional de Libertação de Angola; Movimento Popular de Libertação de Angola; Roberto, Holden Álverto; Savimbi, Jonas Malheiro; União Nacional para a Independência Total de Angola

Further Reading

Klinghoffer, Arthur Jay. *The Angolan War.* Boulder, CO: Westview, 1980.

Marcum, John A. *The Angolan Revolution.* 2 vols. Cambridge, MA: MIT Press, 1969 and 1978.

Movimiento de Liberación Nacional

Popularly known as the Tupamaros, the Movimiento de Liberación Nacional (MLN, National Liberation Movement) was an urban insurgent group operating in Uruguay in the decade between 1963 and 1973. The movement was founded by young middle-class radicals, led by Raul Sendic. The name "Tupamaros" was derived from Túpac Amaru II, an 18th-century Inca leader who was executed by the Spanish in 1781. The movement was founded in 1962, and the height of the Tupamaro armed struggle came between 1968 and 1972, a time of increasing financial hard times because of a decline in price for the country's main export of wool in addition to corruption and growing military control of the government.

The Tupamaros sought to cultivate a Robin Hood image, seizing quantities of food and then distributing it to the poor living around Montevideo. Their first armed clashes with the police occurred in 1966, and Uruguay declared a state of emergency in 1968. The Tupamaros employed robbery, kidnapping, assassination, and the theft of private company records to prove government corruption. They hoped to provoke an extreme government reaction, which would then result in a popular revolution.

In April 1972 new Uruguayan president Juan María Bordaberry declared a state of internal war, which allowed him to bring in the military. Within six months the insurgency had been largely extinguished, but then the military seized power in 1973. The last known Tupamaro clash with the police was in 1974.

As military rule moved toward its end in 1984, many Tupamaros returned to Uruguay, and Tupamaro political prisoners were freed in March the following year. The MLN was rejected in its bid to join the Broad Front, a group of leftist political parties, but was accepted into the front before the 1989 elections.

The Tupamaros were originally influenced by the ideas of Mao Zedong and Fidel Castro and remain a radical Socialist group. The Tupamaros also once held that the social revolution should begin in the countryside, although this notion changed early when the movement became urban. More recently, the MLN was one of the main opponents of the general amnesty granted to the military for crimes committed during military rule.

Spencer C. Tucker

See also Castro Ruz, Fidel Alejandro; Mao Zedong

Further Reading

Alexander, Robert J., ed. *Political Parties of the Americas, 1980s to 1990s: Canada, Latin America, and the West Indies.* Westport, CT: Greenwood, 1982.

Beckett, Ian, and John Pimlott, eds. *Armed Forces and Modern Counterinsurgency.* New York: St. Martin's, 1985.

Porzecanski, A. C. *Uruguay's Tupamaros: The Urban Guerrilla.* New York: Praeger, 1973.

Mozambique Insurgency

Start Date: 1964
End Date: 1975

Located in Southeast Africa on the Indian Ocean and a part of the Portuguese overseas empire since the late 1490s, Mozambique developed an indigenous independence movement after World War II (1939–1945). Dissatisfied with the exploitative nature of the colonial regime and inspired by the tide of decolonization evident in the rest of Africa, black Mozambicans' aspirations met with a repressive response from Portuguese authorities, who imprisoned or exiled the most strident advocates of independence. In 1962, nationalist groups coalesced into the Frente de Libertação de Moçambique (FRELIMO, Front for the Liberation of Mozambique), initially led by American-trained anthropologist Dr. Eduardo C. Mondlane and headquartered in newly independent Tanzania, a country whose leftist leadership provided sanctuary and material support for liberation movements throughout sub-Saharan Africa. Attempts to negotiate with Portugal produced no tangible results, and in 1964 FRELIMO initiated a guerrilla war against the colonial authorities.

Operating from bases in their Tanzanian sanctuary, lightly armed FRELIMO fighters conducted cross-border raids that targeted Portuguese military and police posts in northern Mozambique, planted land mines on roads, and ambushed Portuguese security force detachments. Local conditions complicated the Portuguese military response. The insurgents enjoyed considerable though by no means unanimous support among the local population, while the small size of the guerrilla detachments (10–15 fighters) made detection difficult. The insurgents' tendency to intensify their attacks during the monsoon season also minimized the effectiveness of the limited Portuguese air assets in the region. By 1967, FRELIMO's ranks included 8,000 fighters, who began to make excursions into the central parts of the country.

At the same time, FRELIMO's ideological stance continued to shift to the Left, a pattern reflected in an internal power struggle following the assassination of Mondlane that elevated Samora Machel, an avowed Marxist, to leadership.

Machel forged closer links with the Soviet Union, China, and Algeria, which provided FRELIMO with training and weapons, including heavy machine guns and artillery. Under Machel's guidance, FRELIMO broadened its range of activities, supplementing its guerrilla campaign in the countryside with terrorism, subversion, and sabotage in urban areas. Machel also implemented a ruthless campaign of repression against internal dissidents and defectors as well as against those Mozambican communities that displayed reluctance to join the insurgent movement.

Portuguese efforts to combat FRELIMO intensified in 1969, when General Kaúlza de Oliveira de Arriaga assumed command in Mozambique. Influenced by the American counterinsurgency experience in Vietnam, Arriaga favored a heavy-handed search-and-destroy approach epitomized by Operation NÓ GÓRDIO (GORDIAN KNOT) in the summer of 1970. Intended to destroy FRELIMO's bases in the northern Cabo Delgado Province, Gordian Knot combined ground, air, and riverine naval assets and involved some 35,000 personnel.

The largest conventional operation undertaken by the Portuguese military during the colonial struggles of the 1960s and 1970s, Operation NÓ GÓRDIO proved tactically and operationally successful, but its strategic and political implications were more ambivalent. The operation showcased the effectiveness of the combination of special forces, heliborne assaults, and close air support in eliminating guerrilla units and supply bases in difficult terrain. In spite of Portuguese claims of success, backed up by more than 600 guerrillas killed, some 1,800 captured, and more than 200 bases and camps destroyed, the operation was not the knockout blow that Arriaga had hoped. The operation diverted troops and matériel from other parts of Mozambique, a situation that FRELIMO readily exploited by stepping up its activities in locales that had been deprived of their garrisons.

Nevertheless, the guerrillas had been dealt a severe setback that bought the Portuguese a narrow window of time that they sought to exploit by initiating a civic action program designed to win the hearts and minds of black Mozambicans. This too proved controversial. Its centerpiece was the Aldeamentos (Resettlement Villages) Program, an effort that resembled the American Strategic Hamlet initiative in Vietnam. Intended to separate the insurgents from their rural base of support, the program made sense as a counterinsurgency measure but was not widely popular with the Mozambicans who were subjected to it. In consequence, the program was frequently perceived as not much more than a forcible measure that did little to endear Portuguese security forces to the rural population.

Construction of the Cahora Bassa Dam was equally beset by controversy. A high-profile project intended to showcase Portugal's commitment to improving Mozambique infrastructure, the dam absorbed a disproportionate share of scare resources, necessitated the forced resettlement of local inhabitants, and interrupted the cyclical floods of the Zambezi River that local farmers depended on for fertilizing their fields.

In spite of the tactical and operational success of Operation NÓ GÓRDIO, the protracted war was becoming deeply unpopular in Portugal itself. FRELIMO, though crippled, remained a formidable opponent, intensifying its urban terrorism campaign and launching a major operation in the Tete Province in late 1972. The difficulty of combating FRELIMO had profound effects on the military effectiveness of the Portuguese conscripts, who suffered from increasingly poor morale occasioned by the low quality of their weapons and equipment, mounting casualties, and the difficulties inherent in fighting an elusive and resourceful enemy. By 1974, nearly half of the 50,000 Portuguese troops in Mozambique were locally recruited Africans organized into Flechas ("Arrows") units, special forces who played an increasingly vital role in antiguerrilla operations.

Although able to hold their own against FRELIMO in the field, Portuguese security forces could do nothing to address the growing concern in Portugal about the human and material costs of the Mozambique War as well as the counterinsurgency campaigns that Portugal was simultaneously conducting in Angola and Guinea. Domestic dissatisfaction with the protracted colonial conflicts ultimately led in April 1974 to the peaceful military coup known as the Carnation Revolution. Engineered by a group of left-leaning army officers who overthrew the conservative regime of Marcello Caetano, the revolution paved the way for a cease-fire between Portugal and FRELIMO culminating in a negotiated settlement that granted independence to Mozambique in June 1975.

Sebastian H. Lukasik

See also Arriaga, Kaúlza de Oliveira de; Frente de Libertação de Moçambique; Hearts and Minds; Machel, Samora Moïses; Mondlane, Eduardo; Strategic Hamlet Program; Vietnam War

Further Reading

Cabrita, João M. *Mozambique: The Tortuous Road to Democracy.* New York: Palgrave, 2000.

Cann, John P. *Brown Waters of Africa: Portuguese Riverine Warfare, 1961–1974.* St. Petersburg, FL: Hailer, 2007.

Cann, John P. *Counterinsurgency in Africa: The Portuguese Way of War, 1961–1974.* Westport, CT: Greenwood, 1997.

Henriksen, Thomas H. *Revolution and Counterrevolution: Mozambique's War of Independence, 1964–1974.* Westport, CT: Greenwood, 1983.

Mugabe, Robert Gabriel

Birth Date: February 21, 1924

African nationalist, insurgent leader, prime minister, and then president of Zimbabwe since 1987. Born on February 21, 1924, at Kutama Mission in the Zvimba District of Southern Rhodesia (present-day Zimbabwe), Robert Mugabe earned a BA degree from Fort Hare University in South Africa in 1951. He pursued additional studies in education and worked as a teacher in Ghana during 1958–1960.

Mugabe returned to Southern Rhodesia in 1960 as a Marxist and joined Joshua Nkomo's National Democratic Party (NDP). In December 1961 the NDP was banned, and Mugabe became secretary-general of its successor, the Zimbabwean African People's Union (ZAPU), located in Tanzania. Deepening personal and ideological differences with ZAPU led Mugabe to leave the party in 1963; he then became secretary-general of the newly formed Zimbabwean African National Union (ZANU). Mugabe returned to Rhodesia in 1964 and was imprisoned until 1974, when he was released by Prime Minister Ian Smith's white minority government.

Mozambique's independence in 1975 provided ZANU with a secure base of operations, and Mugabe soon developed a close relationship with Mozambican president Samora Machel. From 1976 Mugabe was recognized as the head of the Zimbabwean African National Liberation Army (ZANLA), and he emerged as a leading contender for the top leadership position within an ever fragmenting nationalist movement. Mugabe followed the military precepts of Mao Zedong (Mao Tse-tung). Supported by the People's Republic of China, ZANU became the leading guerrilla force in Zimbabwe. The escalating war gave rise to sustained regional and international attempts to secure a negotiated settlement between the Smith regime and the two main nationalist groups, ZANU and the Zambia-based ZAPU.

During the September 1979 Lancaster House talks, which led to the end of white rule in Rhodesia, Mugabe was persuaded to accept the terms of a political settlement. Unable to resolve long-standing differences with Nkomo, ZANU ran as an independent party (ZANU-PF) in the February 1980 elections. On April 18, 1980, Zimbabwe was declared independent, with Mugabe as prime minister.

In late 1987, the position of prime minister was substituted for that of executive president, which combined the posts of head of state and head of government. Mugabe thus gained more power. His attempts to introduce land reform brought disaster. Farm productivity plummeted, resulting in widespread food shortages. Mugabe remains in power, resisting all calls for reform. His regime has grown steadily more repressive and corrupt, drawing the ire of Zimbabweans and condemnation from regional and world leaders alike.

Peter C. J. Vale

See also Nkomo, Joshua; Rhodesian Bush War; Zimbabwe African National Union; Zimbabwe African People's Union

Further Reading

Compagnon, Daniel. *A Predictable Tragedy: Robert Mugabe and the Collapse of Zimbabwe*. Philadelphia: University of Pennsylvania Press, 2011.

Hill, Geoff. *Battle for Zimbabwe: The Final Countdown*. Cape Town: Zebra, 2003.

Meredith, Martin. *Our Votes, Our Guns: Robert Mugabe and the Tragedy of Zimbabwe.* New York: PublicAffairs, 2003.

Smith, David. *Mugabe.* London: Sphere, 1981.

Mujahideen in the Soviet-Afghan War

Afghan resistance fighters who fought against the Soviet-backed Kabul government and Soviet troops during the Soviet-Afghan War (1980–1989). These fighters were collectively known as the mujahideen (for "struggles" or "people performing jihad"). They were an alliance of seven Sunni political factions and eight Shiite organizations as well as Muslim volunteers from various North African and Middle Eastern countries. Initially trained and funded by Pakistan's intelligence service (the Inter-Services Intelligence) and then later by the United States, the United Kingdom, Saudi Arabia, Iran, the People's Republic of China, and other Sunni Muslim nations, the mujahideen fought the Soviet Union to a bloody stalemate, forcing it to withdraw its troops from Afghanistan in 1989.

The Soviet invasion of Afghanistan on December 27, 1979, and subsequent intervention in Afghan domestic politics in support of the People's Democratic Party of Afghanistan (PDPA) had the unintended consequence of galvanizing a disparate Islamic opposition into a grassroots resistance movement. Indeed, the Soviet invasion triggered a backlash among Afghans that crossed kinship, tribal, ethnic, and geographic lines. The invasion gave the conflict an ideological dimension by linking the Islamic insurgency with the goal of national liberation when mullahs issued declarations of jihad against the Soviet invaders. Islam and nationalism became interwoven as an Islamist ideology replaced tribal affiliations.

At the onset of the Soviet-Afghan War, the mujahideen were divided along regional, ethnic, tribal, and sectarian lines. Mobilization was linked to allegiances of the tribal lashkar (fighting force), as the mujahideen were loosely organized tribal militias under the command of traditional leaders at the local level. Membership was fluid, fluctuating by the season and family commitments, with no coordinated central command structure. Mujahideen commanders owed their position to social standing, education, leadership ability, and commitment to Islam.

With seven major Sunni mujahideen factions based in neighboring Peshawar, Pakistan came to dominate the political and military landscape. These were the Islamic Unity for the Liberation of Afghanistan, the Hezb-i-Islami Afghanistan, Jamiat-i-Islami, the Hezb-i-Islami, the Harakat-i-Inquilabi Islami, the Mahaz-ye Nijate Milli Afghanistan, and the Jabhe-ye Nijate Milli Afghanistan. In addition to the Sunni mujahideen factions, there were eight Shiite mujahideen organizations as well. The main Shiite organizations were Shura, Nasser, Harlat-e-Islami, the Revolutionary Guards, and Hezbollah. The other organizations were either splinter factions or groups that joined larger movements. In March 1980, the

Sunni mujahideen factions created an umbrella organization, known as the Islamic Alliance for the Liberation of Afghanistan, to lobby for international recognition and support.

In the early days of the occupation, the Soviets waged classic large-scale armored warfare in Afghanistan. The mujahideen responded with traditional mass tribal charges. Disorganized, having limited military equipment and training, and facing overwhelming military superiority, the mujahideen were easily defeated in early skirmishes with the Soviet Army in 1980 and 1981. As desertions and defections of Afghan Army units began to increase, however, the mujahideen military capacity increased.

By 1982, the mujahideen began to counter Soviet offensives with a change in tactics and increased firepower. Unable to pacify the countryside, Soviet troops deployed in strategic areas, occupying cities and garrison towns and along supply routes. This allowed the mujahideen to roam freely throughout the countryside, launching raids and ambushes at will. Lacking sufficient numbers of troops to pursue them, the Soviets attempted to deprive the mujahideen of their base support by depopulating the countryside. Villages, crops, and irrigation systems were destroyed, while fields and pastures were mined. Undeterred by the loss of their support, the mujahideen continued to sabotage power lines, pipelines, and government installations and also knocked out bridges, assaulted supply convoys, disrupted the power supply and industrial production, and attacked Soviet military bases throughout 1982 and 1983.

As the war broadened, the mujahideen appealed for arms and ammunition to counter the overwhelming Soviet military superiority. In 1983 the United States, the United Kingdom, Saudi Arabia, and the People's Republic of China became major contributors to the mujahideen cause. Money and weapons were funneled through Pakistan for distribution to the various Sunni mujahideen factions. This enabled the mujahideen to counter Soviet military superiority with increased firepower.

The year 1985 proved decisive. The mujahideen withstood the massive deployment of Soviet forces designed to impose a favorable outcome within a Moscow-set time frame, and the Sunni mujahideen factions formed the Seven Party Mujahideen Alliance to coordinate their military operations against the Soviet Army. By late 1985 the mujahideen had closed in on Kabul, conducting operations against the Moscow-backed Kabul government.

In the spring of 1986, a combined Soviet-Afghan force captured a major mujahideen base in Zhawar, Pakistan, inflicting heavy losses. It was also at about this time that the mujahideen acquired antiaircraft missiles as well as ground-to-ground rockets (the U.S. Stinger and the British Blowpipe), which altered the course of the war. The mujahideen were now able to take down Soviet helicopters, especially the heavily armored Mi-24 Hind attack helicopter, and airplanes. By the time Soviet leader Mikhail Gorbachev decided to withdraw Soviet forces from Afghanistan in the spring of 1989, the mujahideen were content to allow them an orderly retreat as they themselves readied to attack Kabul and replace the Soviet-backed government. Many historians today credit the mujahideen, at least in part, for the fall of the Soviet Union in 1991.

Keith A. Leitich

See also Jihad; Soviet-Afghan War

Further Reading

Bradsher, Henry St. Amant. *Afghan Communism and Soviet Intervention.* Oxford: Oxford University Press, 1999.

Kakar, M. Hasan. *Afghanistan: The Soviet Invasion and the Afghan Response, 1979–1982.* Berkeley: University of California Press, 1995.

Kaplan, Robert D. *Soldiers of God: With Islamic Warriors in Afghanistan and Pakistan.* Boston: Houghton Mifflin, 1990.

Muscle Shoals, Project.

See McNamara Line

N

Namibia Insurgency.

See South-West Africa Insurgency

Nasution, Abdul Haris

Birth Date: December 3, 1918
Death Date: September 5, 2000

Indonesian Army general, chief of staff, and military theorist. Abdul Haris Nasution was born on December 3, 1918, in the village of Hutapungkut in the Tapanuli region, North Sumatra, in what was then the Netherlands East Indies. In 1935 he went to Bandung to study to become a teacher and there also became a nationalist. In 1937 he returned to Sumatra to take up teaching in Bengkulu, where he met Indonesian nationalist leader Sukarno.

In 1940 the German Army occupied the Netherlands, and the colonial authorities in the Netherlands East Indies created an officer reserve corps to include native Indonesians. Nasution volunteered, and after following training at the Dutch military academy in Bandung, in 1941 he became an officer in the Royal Netherlands East Indies Army. In 1942 the Japanese conquered the Netherlands East Indies, and Nasution, fearful of being arrested by the Japanese, went into hiding in Bandung. He subsequently acted as a messenger in the militia set up by the Japanese but was not actually a member of it.

In August 1945 with the end of World War II (1939–1945), Sukarno proclaimed the independence of the Netherlands East Indies as Indonesia. The Dutch, initially assisted by the British, embarked on a military campaign to reestablish their control. Nasution joined the fledgling Indonesian Army, then known as the People's Security Army, and was appointed regional commander of forces in West Java. Following an agreement between the Indonesian and Dutch governments in January 1948 that ceded West Java to Dutch control, Nasution, while only a colonel, became deputy commander of the People's Security Army and carried out a guerrilla war.

The Dutch recognized Indonesian independence in December 1949, and in 1950 Nasution became the chief of staff of the new Armed Forces of the Republic of Indonesia. In 1952, however, he was removed from the post after he led an army protest against civilian influence in military affairs. It was at this time that Nasution wrote the *Fundamentals of Guerrilla Warfare* (1953).

In October 1955 Nasution was reappointed to his former position of army chief of staff. In 1957 Sukarno, disenchanted with popular democracy and acting with the support of the army, proclaimed a state of emergency. In 1959 Nasution became minister of defense.

Following increasing and long-standing tensions between Sukarno and the Indonesian Communist Party, early on October 1, 1965, the party attempted a coup d'état. Although six generals were murdered, Nasution managed to escape, and he and General Suharto then took charge of putting down the revolt, which ultimately claimed as many as 500,000 lives. At the same time, the army ended the military confrontation with Malaysia in the Indonesia-Malaysia Confrontation (1962–1966), also known as the Borneo/Brunei Insurgency.

Sukarno remained president until he was forced from office in 1967 and succeeded by Suharto. Nasution, meanwhile, was chairman of the People's Consultative Congress during 1966–1972. Suharto viewed Nasution as a rival and gradually stripped him of his posts and position, forcing him to retire from the army in 1971. Nasution then became an opponent of the Suharto New Order regime, although the two men reconciled in the late 1990s. Nasution died in Jakarta on September 5, 2000.

Nasution's *Fundamentals of Guerrilla Warfare* is an important and much-studied book. It is based on Nasution's experiences in guerrilla warfare during the Indonesian War of Independence. While the book was written independently from Mao Zedong's theories of people's war, Nasution's thinking bears a striking resemblance to that of the Chinese leader and also shares the conviction that the goal of guerrilla warfare should be the creation of a conventional military force.

Spencer C. Tucker

See also Indonesia-Malaysia Confrontation; Mao Zedong

Further Reading

Nasution, Abdul Haris. *Fundamentals of Guerrilla Warfare.* New York: Praeger, 1965.

Penders, C. L. M., and Ulf Sundhaussen. *Abdul Haris Nasution: A Political Biography.* New York: University of Queensland Press, 1985.

National Liberation Front of Aden

Insurgent organization established in the Federation of South Arabia that sought independence from Britain. A day after Aden joined the British-backed Federation of South Arabia in January 1963, the Yemeni monarchy was overthrown, and civil war began. Inspired by the Pan-Arabism and socialism of Egyptian president Gamal Abdel Nasser, in June 1963 the National Liberation Front (NLF) was established in Aden. Led by Qahtan Muhammads al-Shabi, the NLF enjoyed the support of the Egyptian government. Opposing it were conservative monarchist forces backed by Britain and Saudi Arabia. With the NLF increasingly Marxist in orientation, Nasser shifted Egyptian support from it to a rival insurgent group, the Front for the Liberation of South Yemen (FLOSY).

Following the December 10, 1963, grenade attack on the British high commissioner that killed 1 person and injured 50, the British declared a state of emergency in Aden and sent more substantial military resources there. In February 1967, however, the Labour government of Prime Minister Harold Wilson announced that Britain would quit Aden. This brought fighting between the NLF and FLOSY and heavy casualties for both sides.

The withdrawal of Egyptian military support for FLOSY—a consequence of the June 1967 Arab-Israeli War—greatly aided the NLF. By late November, Britain had removed all its forces from Aden and South Arabia. On November 30 the federation came to an end without any agreement of governance, but the NLF, having secured the support of the Yemni Federal Army, won the brief civil war with FLOSY and proclaimed the establishment of the People's Republic of South Yemen. Al-Shaabi was president until June 1969, when hard-line Marxists within the NLF ousted him and took control. In 1978 the NLF changed its name to the Yemen Socialist Party and made it the only legal political party in the country.

Spencer C. Tucker

See also Front for the Liberation of Occupied South Yemen; Mitchell, Colin Campbell

Further Reading

Kostiner, Joseph. *The Struggle for South Yemen.* New York: St. Martin's, 1984.

Naumkin, Vitaly. *Red Wolves of Yemen: The Struggle for Independence.* Cambridge, UK: Oleander, 2004.

Walker, Jonathan. *Aden Insurgency: The Savage War in Yemen, 1962–1967.* Barnsley, South Yorkshire, UK: Pen and Sword Military, 2011.

National Military Organization.

See Irgun Tsvai Leumi

Navia-Osorio y Vigil, Álvaro de

Birth Date: 1684
Death Date: 1732

Spanish diplomat, general, and military theorist. Don Alvaro Navia-Osorio y Vigil, third Marques of Santa Cruz de Marcenado, was born in Santa Maria de Vega in Asturia, Spain, in 1684. He fought in the War of the Spanish Succession (1701–1714), in Sicily in 1718, and then in North Africa. At the time of his death in battle in North Africa in 1732, he was governor of the Spanish possession of Oran in present-day Algeria.

Between 1724 and 1730, Navia-Osorio wrote seven volumes of *Military Reflections,* published in Turin (1724–1727) and Paris (1730). One volume deals specifically with what are today called insurgencies and counterinsurgencies. Indeed, Navia-Osorio was probably the earliest author to give systematic attention to these subjects. Among his observations in conducting a counterinsurgency is the need to win the hearts and minds of the people. Thus, he cautioned against trying to change the cultural and traditional ways of a conquered people. Navia-Osorio also recommended that amnesty be granted as soon as order had been restored.

Spencer C. Tucker

See also Hearts and Minds

Further Reading

Heuser, Beatrice. *The Strategy Makers: Thoughts on War and Society from Machiavelli to Clausewitz.* Santa Monica, CA: Greenwood/Praeger, 2010.

Santa Cruz de Marcenado, Álvaro Navia Ossorio Marqués de. *Reflexiones Militares.* Madrid: Ministerio de Defensa, Secretaría General Técnica, 2004.

Nepal Insurgency

Start Date: 1996
End Date: 2006

In the 1990s, a sizable majority of the population of the landlocked Himalayan Kingdom of Nepal lived in poverty, and there were widespread demands for democratic change. On April 6, 1990, in the course of prodemocracy demonstrations in the capital city of Katmandu, police and troops killed 63 people. Two days later King Birendra Bir Bikram Shah Deva yielded to political pressure and ended a 29-year ban on political parties, and on April 19 Krishna Prasad Bhattarai became prime minister as head of an independent ministry.

With a lack of substantive change, however, beginning on February 13, 1996, the Communist Party of Nepal (Maoist) launched an insurgency with a series of attacks across the country. Targets included private and multinational corporations and government buildings. The insurgents sought to rid Nepal of the monarchy and replace the parliament and civilian government with a "People's Republic of Nepal" modeled after the People's Republic of China.

At first the monarchy chose to regard this as a matter for the police only and refused to utilize the Royal Nepal Army in the fighting. The Nepalese government was initially unable to control the mounting violence, but international aid, especially from the West, helped turn the tide. In January 2001 the government created the Armed Police Force, the single goal of which was to defeat the insurgency and force the Maoists and their allies to reach a compromise. Peace talks begun in August 2001 collapsed in November when the Maoists withdrew and launched a series of devastating attacks on police and army posts throughout Nepal, killing 186 army and police personnel for only 21 Maoists dead.

On November 26 Prime Minister Sher Bahadur Deuba declared a national state of emergency and unleashed the army against the Maoists. Then following a U.S. State Department declaration of the Maoists as a terrorist organization, in 2002 the U.S. Congress approved $12 million for training and weapons for the Royal Nepal Army. Large battles that May marked a turning point in the struggle against the Maoists.

On November 21, 2006, a 12-point peace accord was finally concluded, ending the 10-year-long insurgency. Under its terms, the Maoists were permitted to participate in the government, and their arms were to be placed under United Nations supervision. The fighting had claimed the lives of at least 13,000 people and displaced as may as 100,000–150,000 others.

The ensuing elections for the constituent assembly on May 28, 2008, overwhelmingly favored the abolishment of the monarchy and the establishment of a federal multiparty representative state, the Democratic Republic of Nepal.

Spencer C. Tucker

Further Reading

Hutt, Michael. *Himalayan People's War: Nepal's Maoist Rebellion.* London: Hurst, 2004.

Karki, Arjun, and David Seddon, eds. *The People's War in Nepal: Left Perspectives.* New Delhi: Adroit, 2003.

Thapa, Deepak, with Bandita Sijapati. *A Kingdom under Siege: Nepal's Maoist Insurgency, 1996–2003.* Kathmandu: Printhouse, 2003.

Neto, António Agostinho

Birth Date: September 17, 1922
Death Date: September 10, 1979

Angolan insurgent leader and the first president of an independent Angola. Born the son of a Methodist minister on September 17, 1922, in Ícolo de Bengo, Bengo Province, Angola, António Agostinho Neto studied medicine at the Universities of Coimbra and Lisbon in Portugal. Arrested in 1951 for his Angolan separatist activities, he was imprisoned by the Portuguese government. Released in 1958, he completed his medical studies and returned to Angola in 1959. In 1956 the Partido Comunista de Angola (Angolan Communist Party) had merged with the Partido da Luta Unida dos Africanos de Angola (Party of the United Struggle for Africans in

Angola) to form the Movimento Popular de Libertação de Angola (MPLA, Popular Movement for the Liberation of Angola), with Neto as president.

On June 8, 1960, Neto was again arrested by the Portuguese. His political supporters and patients marched to demand his release, and Portuguese soldiers opened fire on them, killing 30 and wounding 200 in what became known as the Massacre of Icolo e Bongo. Neto was exiled to Cape Verde and then sent to Lisbon, where he was imprisoned. Following international protests, the Portuguese government of António de Oliveira Salazar released Neto from prison and placed him under house arrest. Neto escaped and made his way to Zaire (present-day Democratic Republic of the Congo).

In January 1961 the MPLA launched a guerrilla war against Portugal in Angola, and the next year Neto traveled to the United States to request aid from the U.S. government but was turned down by the John F. Kennedy administration, which chose to support the anticommunist Frente Nacional de Libertação de Angola (FNLA, National Liberation Front of Angola), headed by Holden Roberto, which was also fighting the Portuguese. Neto then met with and secured the support of Cuban leader Fidel Castro.

Following the April 1974 Carnation Revolution in Portugal, the new Portuguese government agreed to grant its colonies independence. The FNLA and the third Angolan insurgent movement, the União Nacional para a Independência Total de Angola (UNITA, National Union for the Total Independence of Angola), headed by Jonas Savimbi, then joined forces. Supported by military forces from Zaire, they attempted to keep the Marxist MPLA from taking power but were defeated by Cuban troops airlifted into Luanda by the Soviet Union.

Although Angola received independence on November 11, 1975, with Neto as president, a bloody and protracted civil war followed that pitted the MPLA and Cuban forces, supported by the Soviet Union, against UNITA and the FLNA, supported by the United States, Zaire, and South Africa. Although Marxist-Leninism was the official MPLA doctrine, in practice Neto tended to favor a Socialist, not Communist, model for Angola. In 1977 he violently suppressed an attempted coup by the Organização dos Communistas de Angola (OCA, Communist Organization of Angola), with some 18,000 OCA supporters killed during a two-year span. President Neto died in Moscow on September 10, 1979, while undergoing cancer surgery. His birthday is celebrated as National Heroes Day, a public holiday in Angola.

Spencer C. Tucker

See also Angolan Insurgency; Castro Ruz, Fidel Alejandro; Frente Nacional de Libertação de Angola; Movimento Popular de Libertação de Angola; Roberto, Holden Álverto; Savimbi, Jonas Malheiro; União Nacional para a Independência Total de Angola

Further Reading

Klinghoffer, Arthur Jay. *The Angolan War.* Boulder, CO: Westview, 1980.

Marcum, John A. *The Angolan Revolution.* 2 vols. Cambridge, MA: MIT Press, 1969 and 1978.

Ngo Dinh Diem

Birth Date: January 3, 1901
Death Date: November 2, 1963

President of the Republic of Vietnam (RVN, South Vietnam) during 1955–1963. Ngo Dinh Diem was born in Quang Binh Province on January 3, 1901, the son of a prominent official in the imperial court at Hue. Diem attended his father's private school and French Catholic schools in Hue and then graduated near the top of his class from the School of Law and Public Administration in Hanoi.

Assigned to the bureaucracy in Annam, at age 25 Diem became a provincial governor. A popular figure, he sought to carry out land reform and ensure justice for the peasants. In 1929 he uncovered a Communist-led uprising and crushed it, becoming an ardent anticommunist.

In 1933 young emperor Bao Dai appointed Diem interior minister and chief of the new Commission for Administrative Reforms. Discovering that he had no power, Diem resigned after only three months, whereupon the French authorities stripped him of his rank and threatened to arrest him. For the next decade, Diem lived in seclusion in Hue but met regularly with Vietnamese nationalists.

In September 1945 Diem was kidnapped by agents of the Viet Minh, the nationalist front dominated by the Communists that had been fighting both the Japanese and the French. Held in a village near the Chinese border, he contracted malaria. When he recovered, he discovered that the Viet Minh had killed one of his brothers. After six months Diem was taken to Hanoi, where he met Viet Minh leader Ho Chi Minh, who asked Diem to join the Communists. Diem refused even though he expected that this would cost him his life. Instead, Ho released him. Later the Communists sentenced Diem to death in absentia. During the next four years, Diem traveled Vietnam trying to gain political support. Meanwhile, in 1946 the Indochina War began, pitting the Viet Minh against the French.

An attempt on his life in 1950 convinced Diem to go abroad. In Rome, he had an audience with Pope Pius XII. During 1951–1953, Diem spent two years at Maryknoll seminaries in New Jersey and New York as a novice, performing menial jobs and meditating. He also met prominent individuals such as Cardinal Francis Spellman and U.S. senator John F. Kennedy. Diem declared that he opposed both the French and Communists and represented the only real nationalist course in Vietnam.

In May 1953 Diem, frustrated by the Dwight D. Eisenhower administration's support of the French, went to a Benedictine monastery in Belgium but regularly traveled to Paris, gathering supporters in the large community of Vietnamese exiles in France.

In 1954 the Geneva Conference settled the Indochina War, restoring Indochina as three nations—Cambodia, Laos, and Vietnam. Vietnam was temporarily divided

Republic of Vietnam president Ngo Dinh Diem. A staunch Vietnamese nationalist who sought to quell the Viet Cong (Communist) insurgency, Diem nonetheless resisted undertaking genuine reform measures. This led to a falling out with the Kennedy administration and the latter's tacit support for a coup that overthrew Diem, resulting in his death on November 2, 1963. (Library of Congress)

at the 17th Parallel, with national elections that would reunify the country set for 1956. At this time, Vietnamese emperor Bao Dai was in France. Believing that the U.S. government backed Diem, on June 18, 1954, Bao Dai appointed Diem prime minister. With growing American support, Diem returned to Saigon on June 26 and then on July 7 officially formed his new government, supposedly for all of Vietnam.

Fearing that the Communists would overrun this fledgling Asian domino, the Eisenhower administration extended aid. Unfortunately, Diem's power base was largely limited to minority Catholics, rich and powerful Vietnamese, and foreigners. Washington dispatched counterinsurgency expert Colonel Edward Lansdale to advise Diem.

In early 1955 Diem moved to consolidate power. Employing loyal army formations, he defeated his opponents, including the criminal element known as the Binh Xuyen in Saigon. Diem also moved against the political cadres of the Viet Minh, who were allowed in southern Vietnam by the Geneva Convention. In 1955 Diem ignored an effort by Bao Dai (still in France) to remove him from office; instead, Diem called an election for the people to choose between them. He would have won any honest election but ignored appeals of U.S. officials for such, with the announced vote 98.2 percent in his favor. On October 26, 1955, Diem proclaimed the Republic of Vietnam (RVN, South Vietnam), with himself as president. Washington extended official recognition.

Nonetheless, the situation in South Vietnam deteriorated. Diem refused to hold the elections that were to take place in 1956 under the Geneva settlement, using the excuse that his government had not been a party to the agreements. The Eisenhower administration supported Diem in this stance. The Vietnamese Communists then resumed guerrilla activities.

The U.S. government extended massive aid (some $1.8 billion in U.S. aid during 1955–1960), but the vast bulk of this remained in the cities, and much of it was siphoned off in corruption. Little was done to win the support of the peasantry through land reform and rural improvements. Diem also isolated himself in Saigon, choosing to rely only on his extensive family for advice and also making loyalty to him, rather than ability, the test for political and military appointments.

In 1961 when John F. Kennedy became president, he reexamined U.S. policy in Vietnam and demanded that Diem institute domestic reforms. But seeing no alternative to Diem, Kennedy also increased the U.S. military footprint in Vietnam and agreed to an increase in the size of the Army of the Republic of Vietnam (ARVN, South Vietnamese Army) from 170,000 to 270,000 men. ARVN forces as a rule did not perform well, and by October 1963, U.S. forces in Vietnam had increased to nearly 17,000 men.

Despite pleas from Lansdale, Diem's oppression of the Buddhist majority and his political opponents, many of whom were assassinated or imprisoned, grew. Diem's family and friends (mostly Catholics) held all the senior government positions. The government's Agroville and Strategic Hamlet Programs that forcibly resettled whole villages into armed compounds supposedly to protect them from the Viet Cong were awash in corruption and soon alienated the majority of peasants from the regime.

In the summer of 1963, Buddhist protests and rallies became more frequent and intense, with monks publicly burning themselves to death. New U.S. ambassador Henry Cabot Lodge reported in late August 1963 that an influential faction of South Vietnamese generals wanted to overthrow Diem. In retaliation for Diem's actions against the Buddhists, the Kennedy administration suspended some economic aid and also gave the green light to the generals. The coup began on November 1, 1963. The next morning, Diem and his brother Ngo Dinh Nhu surrendered. Although the generals had guaranteed them safe passage out of the country, both men were promptly executed.

Unfortunately for South Vietnam, Washington never did find a viable alternative to Diem. No subsequent leader of the Republic of Vietnam had his air of legitimacy. As a result, U.S. leaders, who had seen Diem as an alternative to Ho Chi Minh and an agent to stop the spread of communism, soon found themselves taking direct control of the war in Vietnam.

William Head

See also Hilsman, Roger; Ho Chi Minh; Indochina War; Lansdale, Edward Geary; Strategic Hamlet Program; Viet Minh; Vietnam War

Further Reading

Jacobs, Seth. *Cold War Mandarin: Ngo Dinh Diem and the Origins of America's War in Vietnam, 1950–1963*. New York: Rowman and Littlefield, 2006.

Warner, Denis. *The Last Confucian*. London: Angus and Robertson, 1964.

Nguyen Sinh Cung.

See Ho Chi Minh

Nicaragua Insurgency

Start Date: 1927
End Date: 1933

In Nicaragua, Conservatives and Liberals had been at loggerheads for decades. The U.S. government, desiring a stable government for American business, had sent marines there during 1912–1925. In 1926 Liberal Party leader Juan Bautists Sacasa returned from exile in Mexico and, with assistance from the Mexican government, established a rival government on Nicaragua's east coast. Civil strife commenced in the so-called Constitutional War between Liberal rebels, led by General José María Moncada, and government forces under Conservative Party leader and Nicaraguan president Adolfo Díaz. U.S. president Calvin Coolidge, worried about a Communist- or Mexican-style revolution in Nicaragua, responded positively to Díaz's request for military assistance, and the marines returned. Ultimately there were 4,000 marines in Nicaragua.

On May 4, 1927, U.S. special envoy Henry L. Stimson persuaded Moncada to accept the U.S.-brokered Peace of Tipitapa, whereby the Liberals and Conservatives agreed to U.S. supervised elections in 1928 and also agreed to give up their arms in return for the creation of a nonpartisan national guard known as the Guardia Nacionale (National Guard), to be trained by the marines. The Liberals agreed under a not-so-veiled threat that if they did not disarm, the marines would force their compliance.

All Liberal officers agreed to the Peace of Tipitapa except for Augusto C. Sandino. He and his followers withdrew into the mountains and commenced guerrilla operations against the marines and the Guardia Nacionale. Numerous small engagements followed. One of the largest occurred very early on July 16, 1927, when Sandino led some 800 rebels in an attack on Ocotal, the capital of Nueva Segovia Province in Nicaragua, that was defended by 37 marines and 47 Guardia Nacionale personnel. The defenders held off the attackers until daylight, when they were saved by the arrival of five De Havilland DH-4 aircraft of Marine Observation Squadron 1. In the first dive-bombing combat attack in history, the DH-4s drove off the attackers. Some 300 Sandinistas and 1 marine were killed.

After the Battle of Ocotal, for the most part Sandino avoided pitched battles, choosing to concentrate on hit-and-run attacks against the Guardia Nacionale and the marines in the interior. A series of small engagements followed in which the DH-4s proved invaluable. On January 14, 1928, the DH-4s bombed and strafed Sandino's El Chipote base, which the marines then occupied.

In November 1928, 1,500 marines supervised the national elections in which General Moncada, the Liberal candidate, was elected president. Although the marines were able to protect the government and the cities and towns in the western part of Nicaragua and also supervise the elections of 1928, 1930, and 1932 and train the Guardia Nacionale, the marines could not completely subdue the insurgents or protect lives and property in the Nicaraguan interior.

Under growing pressure from other Latin American countries and the U.S. public and Congress, President Herbert Hoover decided to withdraw the marines, the last of whom departed Nicaragua on January 3, 1933. In February 1934 Sandino, who laid down his arms and retired to an agricultural commune in return for amnesty, was treacherously taken by the Guardia Nacionale and killed following a meeting at the presidential palace. This deed was carried out on the orders of Guardia Nacionale commander Anastasio Somoza García.

One consequence of the U.S. intervention was the dictatorship of Somoza, who seized power and ruled Nicaragua from 1936 until his assassination in 1956. His sons then ruled the country until 1976.

Spencer C. Tucker

See also Aircraft in Counterinsurgency Operations; Puller, Lewis Burwell; Sandino, Augusto César

Further Reading

Macaulay, Neill, *The Sandino Affair.* Chicago: Quadrangle, 1967.

Nolan, David. *The Ideology of the Sandinistas and the Nicaraguan Revolution.* Coral Gables, FL: University of Miami Institute of Interamerican Studies, 1984.

Sandino, Augusto César. *Sandino: The Testimony of a Nicaraguan Patriot.* Edited by Sergio Ramirez. Princeton, NJ: Princeton University Press, 1990.

Nicaraguan Revolution

Start Date: 1961
End Date: 1990

In 1936 in Nicaragua, Anastasio Somoza García, commander of the U.S.-trained Guardia Nacionale (National Guard), seized power. He ruled this Central American nation until his assassination in 1956, having transformed the country into a family estate. His two sons, Luis Somoza Debayle and Anastasio Somoza Debayle ("Tachito"), continued their father's personal dictatorship. Ruthless dictators who used the Cold War to their advantage, the Somozas presented themselves as the last anticommunist bulwark in Latin America while ruling Nicaragua by torturing and killing their political opponents. The Somozas controlled not only Nicaragua's politics and the army but also the entirety of the economy.

By the mid-1970s, Anastasio Somoza's control began to erode. An earthquake destroyed Managua in 1972, killing more than 10,000 people and leaving many more homeless. Somoza profited immensely from the international aid and the control of government contracts for reconstruction. Such corruption strengthened the opposition, the Sandinista Front, a radical leftist organization inspired by the Cuban Revolution (1953–1959) and named for Nicaraguan nationalist hero Augusto César Sandino, who had fought the government and U.S. marines during 1927–1933. In July 1961 the Sandinista Front had formed the Frente Sandinista de Liberación (FSLN, Sandinista National Liberation Front).

When Jimmy Carter became president of the United States, human rights became a central focus of Latin American policy. Somoza felt betrayed by an American president who placed human rights above anticommunist loyalties. Nonetheless, the Carter administration began to pressure Somoza to implement reforms.

On January 10, 1978, the leader of Nicaragua's moderate opposition, Pedro Joaquin Chamorro, was assassinated. Somoza was widely blamed, catalyzing a united front against the dictatorship. Afraid that a reformist solution might neutralize their insurrection, the radical Sandinistas had accelerated their armed struggle in 1977 and created a national front. The Sandinista opposition found receptive friends not only in Cuba but also in Costa Rica, Venezuela, and Panama, which recognized a state of belligerency in Nicaragua. Indeed, the Organization of American States (OAS) passed a resolution declaring Somoza "the fundamental cause" of the Nicaraguan crisis.

On May 28, 1979, the opposition proclaimed a provisional government in San Jose, centered on a democratic program of political pluralism and a mixed economy. Some members of the opposition were social democrats, others were Marxists, and a significant group consisted of Fidel Castro's sympathizers. During the first half of 1979, the Sandinista leftists launched a formidable offensive with massive military aid from Cuba, Venezuela, Panama, and Costa Rica. The different Sandinista factions suspended ideological differences and focused on the overthrow of Somoza. On July 19, 1979, the insurrectionists triumphed, and Somoza fled to the United States. A Nicaraguan provisional government was inaugurated with massive popular support and international approval. More than 45,000 Nicaraguans had died in the fighting, and the country had suffered immense economic losses.

Carter sought to avoid a confrontation of the kind that pushed Castro into the Soviet bloc. In September 1979 Carter met with Daniel Ortega, Sergio Ramirez, and Alfonso Robelo, leaders of the new government. The Carter administration announced that it would not support the ex-Somoza guardsmen who were organizing against the government while also pointing out that human rights were a major U.S. concern. The Nicaraguan officials expressed support for the policy and committed to not aiding civil conflicts in Guatemala and El Salvador.

The end of détente by 1980 influenced both Washington and Managua. In Nicaragua, the moderate members of the Junta—Alfonso Robelo and Violeta

Barrios de Chamorro—resigned when the Sandinistas packed the Council of State with their own supporters. In the United States, meanwhile, new U.S. president Ronald Reagan defined Nicaragua as a test case to stop Marxist subversion. His presidential campaign platform had called for terminating all economic aid to Nicaragua and for supporting anti-Sandinista forces.

Whereas Carter had tried to keep Nicaragua out of the East-West conflict, the Reagan administration transformed Central America into a Cold War battleground. In 1981 the Reagan administration engineered the end of financial support from international lending agencies and authorized the Central Intelligence Agency to organize covert antigovernment actions and support the group of some 15,000 Somoza loyalists, led by Colonel Enrique Bermudez, who were already battling against the Sandinista government.

In 1982 with nearly $20 million from the United States, the Contra rebels commenced military operations against the Sandinista government. Launching small-scale raids from Honduras and Costa Rica, the Contras created an ongoing military challenge that sapped Sandinista resources. Yet the Reagan administration faced two main obstacles in its unilateralist policy toward Nicaragua. Domestically, the U.S. Congress was reluctant to engage in a war, and it reduced and then, under the Boland Amendment of 1984, banned military aid to the anti-Sandinista forces (Contras). In 1984 the International Court of Justice ruled that American actions in Nicaragua violated international laws, but this had no effect on U.S. policy.

In Nicaragua, a significant sector of the opposition did not support the radicalization of the revolution or the Contras. Indeed, the internal moderate opposition was critical of Reagan's support of the Contras and finally articulated an alternative to both extremes. Meanwhile, a poorly performing economy eroded Sandinista popular support.

Ultimately the Contra insurgency cost more than 30,000 lives and had important ramifications for El Salvador and Guatemala. In addition, in 1986 reports confirmed that Reagan administration officials had diverted profits from arm sales to Iran to provide illegal support to the Contras, in what became the major scandal known as the Iran-Contra Affair.

Alarmed by Reagan's interventionist policy and the deterioration of Nicaraguan democracy under the Sandinistas, Mexico, Venezuela, Colombia, and Panama created the Contadora Grouping in January to search for a Latin American solution. The Contadora Grouping received strong support from Argentina, Brazil, Uruguay, and Peru and from the Democratic Party majority in the U.S. Congress.

In February 1989, another summit of Central American presidents held in El Salvador led the Sandinista government to agree to hold elections in early 1990. The internationally supervised elections of February 25, 1990, brought a sweeping victory by a coalition of 14 opposition parties and a democratic transition process under the moderate leadership of Violeta Barrios de Chamorro.

Arturo Lopez-Levy

See also Castro Ruz, Fidel Alejandro; Contras; Frente Sandinista de Liberación

Further Reading

Brinkley, Douglas. *The Unfinished Presidency: Jimmy Carter's Journey beyond the White House.* New York: Viking, 1998.

Diederich, Bernard. *Somoza and the Legacy of U.S. Involvement in Central America.* New York: E. P. Dutton, 1981.

Grossman, Karl. *Nicaragua: America's New Vietnam?* New York: Permanent Press, 1984.

Walker, Thomas W., ed. *Revolution and Counter-Revolution in Nicaragua.* Boulder, CO: Westview, 1991.

Nkomo, Joshua

Birth Date: June 19, 1917
Death Date: July 1, 1999

Zimbabwean nationalist leader and politician. Born in Matabeleland (a province of Southern Rhodesia, then a British colony) on June 19, 1917, Joshua Nkomo trained as a social worker and entered national politics in 1952, going on to lead a succession of nationalist movements, of which the Zimbabwe African People's Union (ZAPU) was the most important. Nkomo's imprisonment during 1964–1974, imposed by Rhodesia's white minority government of Prime Minister Ian Smith, came to symbolize for the international community the struggle for majority rule in Rhodesia, much as that of Nelson Mandela had in South Africa.

In 1976 under pressure from the leaders of the Frontline States, Nkomo joined his archrival Robert Mugabe to form the Patriotic Front (PF). From bases in Mozambique and Tanzania, PF military formations waged a guerrilla war against the Smith regime during the late 1970s.

Notwithstanding his Soviet sympathies, Nkomo was essential to the success of the negotiations that led to the September 1979 Lancaster House Agreement and majority rule, although he was entirely overshadowed by Mugabe. When black majority rule in Zimbabwe was finally realized in 1980, Nkomo lost the national election to Mugabe's Zimbabwe African National Union (ZANU) but was appointed to a cabinet-level post in Mugabe's government. Nkomo was dismissed in 1982, allegedly for plotting to overthrow the government. He won election to parliament in 1983, and in 1988 after the union of ZAPU and ZANU, he was given a largely ceremonial government position, which he held until his death on July 1, 1999, in Harare, Zimbabwe.

Peter C. J. Vale

See also Mugabe, Robert Gabriel; Rhodesian Bush War; Zimbabwe African National Union; Zimbabwe African People's Union

Further Reading

Matatu, Godwin. "Mugabe Cracks the Whip." *Africa* 160 (1984): 45–46.

Nkomo, Joshua. *Nkomo: The Story of My Life.* London: Methuen, 1984.

Northern Ireland Insurgency

Start Date: 1968
End Date: 1998

A part of the United Kingdom, Northern Ireland underwent a period of insurgency known as the Troubles from the late 1960s until 1998. Northern Ireland, also known as Ulster, consists of six counties and is located in the northern part of the island. The counties include Antrim, Armagh, Down, Fermanagh, Londonderry, and Tyrone. More than 60 percent of the inhabitants are Protestant, with a majority being Presbyterian. Throughout much of the 20th century, Northern Ireland witnessed violence between its Protestant and Catholic populations, especially after 1968, when the Irish Republican Army (IRA), a militant group of Catholics advocating a union with the Republic of Ireland, launched a terror campaign in Ulster.

The conflict between Catholics and Protestants in Ireland stretches back centuries. In the early 17th century the British conquered Ireland, and in 1609 they began sending mainly Scottish Protestants to settle in Ulster. Known as planters, they were given land confiscated from the native Irish in what was known as the Plantation of Ulster. This and other Protestant immigration to Northern Ireland led to conflict with the native Catholics and two bloody ethnoreligious conflicts, the Irish Confederate Wars (1641–1653) and the Williamite War (1689–1691), both of which resulted in Protestant victories. British Protestant political dominance in Ireland was ensured by the passage of laws that curtailed the rights of all those who did not conform to the state church, the Anglican Church of Ireland.

For the next three centuries, Catholics in Ireland agitated for independence. In the 20th century, the British began the process of allowing home rule for southern Ireland. When after World War I (1914–1918) the British partitioned Ireland in 1920 under the Government of Ireland Act, six of the nine Ulster counties in the northeastern section were formed into a separate political entity, with a Parliament at Stormont. During 1921–1939 Northern Ireland struggled economically, and unresolved tensions between Catholics and Protestants continued.

Northern Ireland was important to the Allies during World War II (1939–1945), especially as the southern Irish Free State, under the leadership of Prime Minister Eamon de Valera, announced that it would remain neutral, denying the Royal Navy the right to use its ports. In Ulster, however, the British and the Americans established bases. German bombings of Belfast killed more than 1,000 people and destroyed considerable property.

When the Irish Free State declared itself a republic in 1949, the British responded by passing the Ireland Act, stipulating that Northern Ireland would only leave the United Kingdom by "consent." This act also guaranteed the Irish in Ulster the social benefits enjoyed in England, Scotland, and Wales. The majority of Northern Ireland's population was Unionist, wishing to remain part of the United Kingdom. The opponents, the Republicans, desired to see Ireland united under one government. This political division was abetted by the Protestant-Catholic feud and economic tensions, for Protestants tended to be better off economically.

Tensions between the two sides continued, but in the two decades following World War II, there was little violence. During the same period, Northern Ireland experienced unrest because of a stagnant economy and persistently high unemployment. Problems also arose with London regarding the cost of social legislation and fears that the British government might agree to Ireland's unification (in which the majority Protestants of Ulster would be subsumed by a largely Catholic Ireland) if the Irish Republic agreed to join the North Atlantic Treaty Organization (NATO).

During the 1960s, civil rights groups, in particular the Northern Ireland Civil Rights Associations (NICRA), began to demonstrate in Northern Ireland for equal rights for Roman Catholics. Discrimination against Catholics was widespread, and many professions were closed to them. Modeling their effort after the American civil rights movement, these protesters adopted nonviolent means to achieve their goal of equality for all.

British prime minister Harold Wilson's Labour government (1964–1970, 1974–1976) favored improvements for the Catholic population of Ulster, which put pressure on the government at Stormont to enact measures to alleviate the discrimination and poverty confronting many Catholics. Northern Ireland prime minister Terence O'Neill (1963–1969) introduced several measures to aid the Catholic population. These, however, proved insufficient to satisfy Catholics and went too far for many Protestants. Soon Catholics and Protestants were fighting one another, especially in Londonderry and in the streets of Belfast, Northern Ireland's capital. The bloodshed reached its zenith in 1969, and the Ulster government requested that the British send troops to augment its police forces.

In 1969 Catholic extremists formed the Provisional IRA. Pledged to uniting Ireland by force, the Provisional IRA waged a terror campaign in Ulster. Militant Protestants fought back, especially the Ulster Volunteer Force and the Ulster Defense Association.

During 1969–1972 violence in Northern Ireland escalated, culminating in an event that became known as Bloody Sunday. On January 30, 1972, members of NICRA planned to march in the city of Derry to protest the arrest of hundreds of Republicans who were being held without trial. However, authorities banned the march. When the protesters defied the ban, British paratroopers opened fire on the crowd, killing 13 and wounding 14.

The British government responded to the massacre by closing down the Northern Ireland government and assuming control of Ulster. In 1973 the Provisional IRA began launching terrorist attacks in England. In the ensuing violence during the next 20 years, thousands of people were killed and tens of thousands were wounded. The British maintained a military presence in Northern Ireland during the 1970s and 1980s and found strong support from the United States, particularly during the

Ronald Reagan administration (1981–1989), which supported the British hard-line stance against the IRA. The ongoing violence claimed 3,526 lives.

In the 1990s, peace talks between the warring parties yielded some results, and in 1998 the IRA issued a declaration renouncing violence. On April 10, 1998, all parties signed the Good Friday of Belfast Agreement, establishing the Northern Ireland Assembly and creating a number of institutions between Northern Ireland and the Republic of Ireland and between the Republic of Ireland and the United Kingdom, opening up the possibility for a peaceful solution to the sectarian problems of Ulster.

Justin P. Coffey

See also Black and Tans and the Auxiliaries; Collins, Michael; Ireland Revolutionary Era; Irish Republican Army

Further Reading

Coogan, Timothy Patrick. *The IRA: A History.* Niwot, CO: Roberts Rinehart, 1993.

Dixon, Paul. *Northern Ireland: The Politics of War and Peace.* New York: Palgrave, 2001.

Foster, R. F. *Modern Ireland, 1600–1972.* London: Penguin, 1988.

Hughes, Michael. *Ireland Divided: The Roots of the Modern Ireland Problem.* New York: St. Martin's, 1994.

O

Office of Strategic Services

The Office of Strategic Services (OSS) was a U.S. foreign intelligence agency and forerunner of the Central Intelligence Agency (CIA). The OSS was created in June 1942 and disbanded on October 1, 1945. President Franklin D. Roosevelt established the agency at the urging of Colonel William J. Donovan, a prominent lawyer and former U.S. assistant attorney general who served in the army during World War I (1914–1918), winning the Medal of Honor, and then took an interest in intelligence matters. At the beginning of World War II (1939–1945), Donovan, who had close connections with like-minded British intelligence operatives and with Roosevelt, persuaded the president that the United States needed a centralized civilian-run intelligence agency that would report directly to the White House.

In July 1941 before the United States entered the war, Roosevelt established for this purpose the Office of Coordinator of Information, headed by Donovan. A few months after the Japanese attack on Pearl Harbor, this agency morphed into the OSS, which was to report directly to the newly created Joint Chiefs of Staff. The OSS grew to include some 13,000 operatives during the war.

The OSS undertook a wide variety of activities. In the United States, Donovan recruited academics for research and analysis functions. The OSS also mounted numerous covert activities, operating in both the European and Pacific theater of war. Ultimately the OSS employed several thousand personnel. It had particularly close links with British intelligence services, which Donovan regarded as providing a desirable model for a potential U.S. agency. OSS European operations were based in London and infiltrated Axis-occupied territory, aiding resistance groups and providing the U.S. military with firsthand intelligence. Partisan units raised by the OSS in Europe were the real forerunners of the U.S. Special Forces.

In the Asian theater of war, OSS agents worked closely with nationalist forces in China and Indochina, and as the war drew to a close, they reported favorably though unavailingly to Washington on both the Chinese Communist movement led by Mao Zedong (Mao Tse-tung) and its Vietnamese counterpart, headed by Ho Chi Minh. On occasion, relations were strained between the OSS and the British Special Operations Executive (SOE), such as in Indochina, where the OSS supported Ho and the SOE backed the French.

Despite its successes, the OSS attracted fierce criticism from the American military, particularly General Douglas MacArthur, commander of U.S. forces in the Southwest Pacific; military espionage operatives; and other rival intelligence agencies, such as the Federal Bureau of Investigation. Donovan's forthright style did little to allay such tensions. Immediately after the war ended, in September 1945 President Harry S. Truman disbanded the OSS, ignoring Donovan's forceful pleas to establish a centralized U.S. intelligence agency. Within a few months, however, rising Cold War tensions led Truman to reverse this decision. The OSS was the de facto precursor of the CIA, established by presidential executive order in 1946 and, more formally, by act of Congress in 1947. Many CIA operatives, including several influential directors, such as William E. Colby, began their intelligence careers as OSS agents. The CIA's subsequent heavy reliance on covert operations was another legacy that can be traced directly to its World War II OSS heritage.

Priscilla Roberts

See also Colby, William Egan; Ho Chi Minh; Mao Zedong; Special Operations Executive

Further Reading

Baak, Aaron. *From OSS to Green Berets: The Birth of Special Forces.* Novato, CA: Presidio, 1986.

Dear, Ian. *Sabotage and Subversion: The SOE and OSS at War.* London: Cassell, 1999.

Smith, Richard Harris. *OSS: The Secret History of America's First Central Intelligence Agency.* Berkeley: University of California Press, 1972.

Yu, Maochun. *OSS in China: Prelude to the Cold War.* New Haven, CT: Yale University Press, 1997.

Oil Slick Policy.

See Tache d'Huile

Okamura Yasuji

Birth Date: May 5, 1884
Death Date: September 2, 1966

Japanese Army general who commanded his nation's forces in China during World War II (1939–1945). Born in Tokyo on May 5, 1884, Okamura Yasuji graduated from the Japanese Military Academy in 1904 and the Army War College in 1913. He served on the Army General Staff during 1914–1917, 1923–1925, and 1928. Promoted to major in 1919, he was resident officer in Europe during 1921–1922 and then was stationed in Shanghai during 1925–1927. Promoted to colonel, he commanded a regiment. As vice chief of staff of the Guandong (Kwantung) Army, Okamura helped plan the Japanese takeover of Manchuria in 1931–1932. Promoted to major general and appointed deputy commanding general of the Shanghai Expeditionary Army in February 1932, Okamura was sent to break the boycott of Japanese goods following the takeover of Manchuria.

Okamura was military attaché to the puppet Japanese state of Manzhouguo (Manchukuo) during 1933–1934. He was then chief of the Intelligence Division of the Army General Staff during 1935–1936. Promoted to lieutenant general in 1936, Okamura commanded the 2nd Division in Manchuria during 1936–1938. He played an important role in the Sino-Japanese War (1937–1945) as commander of Eleventh Army in China during 1938–1940. He was well informed regarding Chinese affairs, especially the Guomindang (GMD, Nationalist) government of Jiang Jieshi (Chiang Kai-shek), and was reluctant to escalate the war. Okamura's forces fought the Chinese Communists who had launched their so-called Campaign of a Hundred Regiments against the Japanese in August 1940.

Promoted to full general in 1941, in July Okamura was appointed to command the North China Area Army. He carried out the Japanese Sankō Sakusen ("Three Alls") policy of "Kill All, Burn All, Take All" that was designed to pacify northern China. Initiated in 1940 by Major General Tanaka Ryūkich, the policy was carried out full-scale in 1942 by Okamura, with the full support of Imperial General Headquarters and perhaps even Emperor Hirohito. Northern China was divided into pacified, semipacified, and unpacified areas, and the program included the burning of villages, the confiscation of grain, and having the Chinese peasants construct collective hamlets. The program also included the construction of containment walls, moats, watchtowers, and roads and targeted for death "enemies pretending to be local people" and all males between 15 and 60 "whom we suspect to be enemies." Although no precise figures are available, this policy may have resulted in the death of some 1.7 million Chinese. Japanese resources were now stretched too thin to bring success, however. The Japanese were now fighting both the Chinese Communists and Nationalists and were also waging a wider Pacific war from December 1941.

In 1944 Okamura became commander of the Japanese Expeditionary Army in China and launched Operation ICHI-GO, a major offensive in central and southeastern China from mid-April 1944 to February 1945. Employing 410,000 troops, the Japanese made major territorial gains and realized their goals of eliminating U.S. air bases in China for the strategic bombing of Japan and opening land communications from northern China to French Indochina. Okamura halted the advance because he feared that the Soviet Union would enter the war against Japan.

Although Okamura and his 1 million Japanese soldiers in China were never defeated by the Chinese, he surrendered unconditionally in Nanjing (Nanking) on September 9, 1945. After the war, Okamura was brought to trial by the Nationalist government of China. He had developed close ties with members of the government, so it came as no surprise when he was found innocent. He then worked with the Nationalist government during 1946–1948. The Chinese Communists tried to capture him, but Okamura escaped to Japan. In February 1950 he arranged to send his former staff officers, known as the Pai Tuan (White Company) to Taiwan to assist the Nationalist government there. Okamura died in Tokyo on September 2, 1966.

Ken Kotani and Spencer C. Tucker

Further Reading

Coble, Parks M. *Facing Japan: Chinese Politics and Japanese Imperialism, 1937–1941.* Cambridge, MA: Harvard University Council on East Asia Studies, 1991.

Li, Lincoln. *The Japanese Army in North China, 1937–1941: Problems of Political and Economic Control.* New York: Oxford University Press, 1975.

Lindsay, Michael. *The Unknown War: North China, 1937–1945.* London: Bergström and Boyle Books, 1975.

Morley, James W., ed. *The China Quagmire: Japan's Expansion on the Asian Continent, 1933–1941; Selected Translations from Taiheiyō sensō e no michi, kaisen gaikō shi.* New York: Columbia University Press, 1983.

Wilson, Dick. *When Tigers Fight: The Story of the Sino-Japanese War, 1937–1945.* New York: Viking, 1982.

Open Arms Program.

See Chieu Hoi Program

Organisation de l'Armée Secrète

The Organisation de l'Armée Secrète (OAS, Secret Army Organization) was established during the Algerian War (1954–1962) with the goal of preventing Algerian independence. In May 1958, angered by news that the French government was considering talks with the Algerian rebel Front de Libération Nationale (FLN, National Liberation Front), professional officers within the French military had seized on angry demonstrations by Algerian colons to threaten military action against France itself and to secure the end of the Fourth Republic and the return to power of General Charles de Gaulle and the creation of what became the Fifth Republic.

Although vowing that Algeria would remain French, de Gaulle had announced in September 1959 his intention to hold a plebiscite on the issue in Algeria. This led to the formation of the OAS in Spain that same month. Its most prominent figure and overall commander was General Raoul Salan, who led a failed coup in Algiers in April 1961 and then fled to Spain. Colonel Yves Godard, one of the architects of the French Army victory in the 1957 Battle of Algiers, was its chief of staff.

Members of the OAS were determined that the French Army would not again be sold out by the politicians, as they believed had been the case in the Indochina War (1946–1954). The army's motto was "*L'Algérie est française et le restera*" ("Algeria is French and will remain so").

The OAS sought to create instability in Algeria, and its members inflicted considerable bloodshed through the liberal use of plastic explosives. Led by former

French Foreign Legion lieutenant Roger Degueldre, OAS death squads assassinated opponents. Although Salan opposed this step, the OAS subsequently carried the violence to France itself and attempted to assassinate de Gaulle.

Salan was arrested in April 1962 and was subsequently brought to trial and imprisoned. Others were also taken. Although the OAS continued the violence for several more months, Algeria was granted independence in July 1962. This did not deter OAS operative and former French Air Force lieutenant colonel Jean-Marie Bastien-Thiry, who almost succeeded in another assassination of de Gaulle on August 22. 1962. Captured, tried, and sentenced to death, Bastien-Thiry was executed in March 1963. He remains the last person to die by firing squad in France.

Spencer C. Tucker

See also Algerian War; Algiers, Battle of; Front de Libération Nationale; Godard, Yves; Salan, Raoul Albin-Louis

Further Reading

Henissart, Paul. *Wolves in the City: The Death of French Algeria.* New York: Simon and Schuster, 1970.

P

Pacification

The word "pacification" refers to the restoration of peace. This might be accomplished by means of a peace treaty or an agreement, such as the Pacification of Ghent of 1576. Pacification is the end goal of counterinsurgency operations. In the case of an insurgency, pacification usually involves a combination of military, political, and socioeconomic measures that remove the causes of an insurgency and restore peace, what the British refer to as the successful winning of hearts and minds. The Philippine-American War (1899–1902) is a classic example of a successful pacification effort in which the United States combined robust military action with political initiatives and economic steps—to include the construction of roads, schools, and hospitals—in order to improve the lives of the indigenous people and cause them to rally to U.S. rule.

Spencer C. Tucker

See also Hearts and Minds

Further Reading

Beckett, Ian F. W. *Encyclopedia of Guerrilla Warfare.* Santa Barbara, CA: ABC-CLIO, 1999.

Paiva Couceiro, Henrique Mitchell de

Birth Date: December 30, 1861
Death Date: February 11, 1944

Portuguese Army officer and colonial administrator. Born in Lisbon on December 30, 1861, Henrique Mitchell de Paiva Couceiro enlisted in the Royal Lancers Cavalry Regiment in 1879. The next year de Paiva transferred to the 1st Artillery Regiment, and during 1881–1884 he studied artillery at the Escola Politécnica de Lisboa. Commissioned a second lieutenant, he served with several artillery regiments and with the horse artillery.

Promoted to captain in 1889, de Paiva volunteered for service in Portuguese Africa. Assuming command of a cavalry squadron in Angola, he headed an exploration to the interior, which earned him acclaim. Returning to Portugal in 1891, he served briefly with the Spanish Foreign Legion fighting in the Rif Mountains of Morocco. In 1894 he was appointed aide-de-camp to governor of

Mozambique António Enes. In 1895 de Paiva led an expedition into the Magul region.

De Paiva's principal contribution to advancing Portugal's imperialist ventures came in Angola, where he served as governor-general during 1907–1909. He personally commanded military campaigns (chiefly against the Cuamato people) and helped solidify Portuguese control by public works projects, the construction of railroads to the interior, and the diversification of the economy, which was heavily dependent on the production of rubber and coffee, and by seeking to institute a more efficient colonial administration.

Returning to Portugal in 1909, de Paiva was one of the few prominent officers to fight on the side of the monarchy when it was overthrown in October 1910 and a republican government was established. He resigned from the army in 1911. Exiled to Spain, he led monarchial raids into Portugal from Galicia in 1911 and 1912, for which he was sentenced in absentia to imprisonment and then exile. He also led a failed monarchist coup in 1919. Returning to Portugal in 1924 after an amnesty decree, de Paiva was exiled for six months following his public protest of the neglect of the country's colonies by the Estado Novo dictatorship of António de Oliveira Salazar. This did not halt de Paiva's criticism of government policies, and he was arrested in 1937 and again exiled, this time to the Canary Islands. Permitted to return to Portugal by Salazar in 1939, de Paiva died in Lisbon on February 11, 1944, continuing to the last to defend Portuguese imperial ambitions ("Empire we are, Empire we must remain"). De Paiva wrote a number of books on Portuguese colonization in Africa.

Spencer C. Tucker

See also Angolan Insurgency

Further Reading

Newitt, Marilyn. *Portugal in Africa: The Last Hundred Years.* London: Longman, 1981.

Paiva Conceiro, Henrique. *Angola: Dois anos de Governo Junho 1907–Junho 1909, História e comentários* [Angola: Two Years of Government, June 1907–June 1909, History and Commentary]. Lisbon: Tipografia Portuguesa, 1948.

Pimenta, Alfreda. *Paiva Couceiro.* Lisbon: Edição do Autor, 1944.

Valente, Vasco Pulido. *Um herói português: Henrique Paiva Couceiro (1861–1944)* [A Portuguese Hero: Henrique Paiva Couceiro (1861–1944)]. Lisbon: Aletheia Editores, 2006.

Palestine Liberation Organization

The Palestine Liberation Organization (PLO) is the political and military organization founded in 1964 to unite various Palestinian organizations and to work for the creation of an independent Palestinian state. Numerous factions and organizations fall under the PLO's umbrella. In addition to Fatah (al-Fatah), the largest of these groups, the PLO has included the Popular Front for the

Liberation of Palestine (PFLP), the Democratic Front for the Liberation of Palestine (DFLP), the Palestinian People's Party, the Palestine Liberation Front (PLF), the Arab Liberation Front, As-Sa'iqa (Syrian Baathist), the Palestine Democratic Union, the Palestinian Popular Front Struggle, and the Palestinian Arab Front. Two groups no longer associated with the PLO are the Popular Front for the Liberation of Palestine–General Command (PFLP-GC) and Fatah Uprising (Abu Masa group). The PLO also includes student and professional organizations and trade unions.

The PLO is secular in organization and has called for an independent Palestinian state in which Muslims, Christians, and Jews can live together with full citizenship rights. Also, the PLO has deliberately eschewed embracing any one political philosophy so as to be as inclusive as possible. The PLO has substantial financial assets. In 1993 these were said to be $8 billion to $10 billion, with an average yearly income of $1.5 billion to $2 billion.

The PLO was founded in 1964 by the Arab League and Egypt. Its first president was Ahmed Al-Shukairy (Ahmad Shukeiri). Its stated purpose was the liberation of Palestine. Throughout its existence, the PLO has often employed violence.

The defeat of the Egyptian, Syrian, and Jordanian Armies in the 1967 Arab-Israeli War enhanced the role of Palestinian militias and led to increased guerrilla operations against Israel. On March 21, 1968, the Israel Defense Forces (IDF) crossed into Jordan to attack Yasser Arafat's Fatah militia at Karameh. Fatah stood and fought and, aided by the Jordanian Army, drove off the Israelis. Although Fatah suffered many more casualties, the Israelis suffered 28 dead and 90 wounded. His prestige tremendously enhanced by this battle, Arafat took control of the PLO in 1969 and remained its chairman until 2004. He also headed the PLO's military branch, the Palestinian Revolutionary Forces.

Arafat refused to acknowledge the existence of Israel and insisted on the continuation of the insurgency against the Jewish state. The Fedayeen—groups that insisted on armed struggle against Israel—enjoyed great influence within the PLO. These included the PFLP, the DFLP, and the PLF.

After the 1967 War the PLO was based in Jordan, but its continued attacks on Israel and refusal to abide by an agreement with the Jordanian government led King Hussein in September 1970 to order in the Jordanian Army. Following its defeat in what has been called Black September, the PLO agreed to leave Jordan. Relocating to Beirut, the PLO soon established a firm presence in the Palestinian refugee camps in Lebanon and began launching attacks from Lebanon into northern Israel.

In 1974 an Arab Summit recognized the PLO as the sole representative of the Palestinian people. That same year Arafat appeared before the United Nations (UN) General Assembly, and the UN granted the PLO observer status. Meanwhile, the PFLP and the PFLP-GC left the PLO in protest of the latter's attempt to negotiate with Israel. The PLO became a full member of the Arab League in 1976.

In 1975, civil war erupted in Lebanon between Muslims (supported by the PLO) and the Maronite Christians. The PLO took control of the southern part of the country and western Beirut, and the Christians dominated the remainder. Cross-border attacks into Israel continued, and in June 1982 Israel mounted a full-scale invasion of Lebanon and indeed began shelling Beirut itself. Following several cease-fire agreements and with much of Lebanon in ruins, the PLO agreed to relocate yet again, to Tunis.

Arafat spent most of the 1980s rebuilding the PLO. IDF aircraft bombed the PLO headquarters in Tunis in 1985, killing 73 people. In December 1987 Arafat approved the First Intifada (Uprising). In the 1980s the PLO also increased its activities among Palestinian refugees and was active in the establishment of businesses, social service agencies, and educational programs.

On November 15, 1988, the PLO officially declared the formation of the State of Palestine, claiming all Palestine as defined by the former British mandate, while King Hussein of Jordan yielded to the PLO all territorial claims to the West Bank. That December, Arafat spoke before the UN, promising to end terrorism and to recognize Israel in exchange for the Israeli withdrawal from the Occupied Territories, according to UN Security Council Resolution 242. This was a dramatic change from the PLO's previous position of insisting on the destruction of Israel. The Palestinian National Congress (PNC) elected Arafat president of the new Palestinian state on April 2, 1989.

Arafat and the Israelis commenced peace negotiations at the Madrid Conference in 1991. Although the talks were temporarily set back when Arafat and the PLO supported Iraq in the Persian Gulf War (1991), during the next two years the two parties held a number of secret discussions. These led to the 1993 Oslo Accords in which Israel agreed to Palestinian self-rule in the Gaza Strip and the West Bank and Arafat officially recognized the existence of the State of Israel. Despite the condemnation of many Palestinian nationalists, the peace process appeared to be progressing apace. Israeli troops withdrew from the Gaza Strip and Jericho in May 1994.

In 1994 the PLO established the Negotiations Affairs Department (NAD) in Gaza to implement the Interim Agreement. Mahmoud Abbas, then secretary-general of the PLO Executive Committee, headed the NAD until April 2003, when the Palestinian Legislative Council chose him as the first prime minister of the Palestinian Authority.

In 1996 the PNC agreed to remove from the PLO charter all language calling for armed violence aimed at destroying Israel, and Arafat sent U.S. president Bill Clinton a letter listing language to be removed, although the PLO has dragged its feet on this. The organization claimed that it was waiting for the establishment of the Palestinian state, when it would replace the charter with a constitution. Arafat was elected leader of the new Palestinian Authority in January 1996. The peace process began unraveling later that year, however, after hard-liner Benjamin Netanyahu became prime minister of Israel. Netanyahu condemned the PLO as a terrorist organization responsible for numerous suicide bombings against Israeli citizens. The accord collapsed completely in 2000 after Arafat and Israeli prime minister Ehud Barak failed to come to an agreement at a Camp David meeting facilitated by Clinton. Suicide bombings then increased, although these attacks were almost all launched by the Islamist groups Hamas and Islamic Jihad of Palestine, and Arafat and the PLO took no responsibility for them. But whether right or wrong, many Israelis continue to believe that Arafat clandestinely supported terrorism.

Arafat died on November 11, 2004, and was succeeded by the moderate Abbas, who also headed Fatah. In December 2004 Abbas called for an end to the violence associated with the Second (al-Aqsa) Intifada that began in September 2000. In January 2005 Abbas was elected president of the Palestinian Authority, but he struggled to keep the PLO together and keep Fatah from losing its political and financial clout. In the January 2006 Palestinian Authority parliamentary elections, Abbas and Fatah were dealt a serious blow when the radical Hamas captured a majority of seats. Fighting between Fatah and Hamas erupted beginning in February 2007, and in June Hamas seized control of Gaza, a situation that continues to the present. Despite this serious setback for the PLO, it is today recognized by the UN and more than 100 countries as the "sole legitimate representative of the Palestinian people."

Amy Hackney Blackwell and Spencer C. Tucker

See also Arafat, Yasser; Harakat al-Muqawama al-Islamiyya; Intifada, First; Intifada, Second; Terrorism

Further Reading

Kushner, Arlene. *Disclosed: Inside the Palestinian Authority and the PLO*. Philadelphia: Pavilion, 2004.

Rubin, Barry. *Revolution until Victory? The Politics and History of the PLO*. Cambridge, MA: Harvard University Press, 2003.

Palmach

Jewish fighting force numbering at its height a few thousand soldiers. The Palmach (the Hebrew abbreviation of Plugot Ma'hats, or "strike force") was created jointly by the British and the Jewish Haganah (Hebrew for "defense") on May 15, 1941. The Haganah was the Jewish underground self-defense and military organization formed in 1920 and precursor of the Israel Defense Forces (IDF). Haganah leaders realized the need for a permanently mobilized military organization to defend Jewish settlements that from time to came under harassment from Arab bands. More important to the British, if Axis forces ever entered British Mandatory Palestine, the Palmach would fight them as well.

The new elite Palmach was originally commanded by Yitzchak Sadeh. Consisting of 9 assault teams, it was trained and equipped by the British and dispersed throughout Palestine (3 teams in northern Galilee, 2 in central Galilee, 2 in southern Galilee, and 1 in Jerusalem). The Palmach eventually grew to 12 assault teams that initiated scouting and sabotage missions as well as preemptive strikes into Syria and Lebanon. Some of the Palmach's more notable members were Yigal Allon, Moshe Dayan, Yitzhak Rabin, Chaim Bar-Lev, Uzi Narkiss, and Ezer Weizman.

The Palmach was officially disbanded after the British victory in the Battle of El-Alamein in the summer of 1942 and the threat to the British position from Syria and Lebanon abated. The Haganah then converted the Palmach into an underground commando force and in August 1942 initially assigned it protection of the Yishuv (Jewish settlements) in Palestine. Yitzhak Tabenkin, head of the kibbutzim union, conceived of a plan that assigned Palmach platoons to various kibbutzim. These were to provide the Palmachniks (Palmach members) with food, shelter, and other needs. In return, the Palmach protected the kibbutz to which they were assigned, worked in the agricultural enterprises of the kibbutz, and participated in Zionist education. This combination of training, protection, education, and work was called Ach'shara Meguyeset (Drafted/Recruited Training). Each Palmachnik was to train 8 days a month, stand guard 14 days a month, and rest 7 days a month. However, members were always on call in case of an attack.

The role of the Palmach was not limited to the protection of the Yishuv. By 1943, the Palmach had organized itself into six regular companies and a like number of special units. The Ha-Machlaka Ha-Germanit (German Department) operated against the Nazi infrastructure in the Middle East and the Balkans. The Ha-Machlaka Ha-Aravit (Arab Department, known also as the Arab Platoon because members often dressed in Arabic attire) operated against Arab militias. After the formation of Israel, they formed the basis of the Border Police and IDF infiltration units. The Pal-Yam was the sea force of the Palmach and focused on facilitating the illegal entry of Jewish refugees from Europe in violation of the British White Paper of 1939 that limited Jewish immigration to Palestine. The Palmach's Sabotage Units eventually formed the nucleus of the IDF Engineering Corps. The Palmach Air Force consisted of British-trained Jewish pilots, who, however, had no planes until 1948, when they commenced observation and scouting operations. Additionally, Zionist youth movement participants aged 18–20 were formed into Nahal (Hebrew acronym for *noar halutzi lohem,* meaning "fighting pioneer youth"), or nucleus groups. They were trained by Palmachniks and eventually formed the basis of the Nahal settlements, created as strategic strongholds in case of war.

Palmachniks received basic training in physical fitness, small arms, topography, squad operations, and Krav Maga (Hebrew meaning "contact combat"), a martial art developed in Czechoslovakia in the 1930s. Most Palmachniks also received additional training in one or more of the following combat specialties: sabotage and explosives, reconnaissance, sniping, light and medium machine gunnery, and mortars. Group and platoon training also included live-fire drills using artillery, machine guns, and mortars. Palmach officer training emphasized the development of independent and innovative field commanders who took initiative and led by example.

When it was clear following World War II (1939–1945) that the British were unwilling to create a Jewish state or allow the immigration of large numbers of Jewish refugees into Palestine, the Palmach attacked British infrastructure such as bridges, railways, radar stations, and police stations during 1945 and 1946. These attacks stopped when the British arrested en masse many of the Palmach and Haganah leadership on June 19, 1946, a date known in Israeli history as the Black Sabbath.

Palmach units assumed responsibility for protecting the Jewish settlements from Arab militias when the 1948 Israeli-Arab War erupted following the partition of Palestine and the formation of the State of Israel. These Palmach units persevered until the Haganah relieved them. The Palmach was then formed into two units of the newly created IDF, the Negev Brigade and the Yiftah Brigade. These units stopped the Egyptian army in the Negev and then seized the Gaza Strip and Sharem al-Sheikh.

Many Palmachniks entered Israeli politics, including Yitzchak Rabin, Moshe Dayan, Chaim Bar-Lev, Mordechai Gur, Mati Peled, Yair Tsaban, Shulamit Aloni, Rehavam Zeevi, and Rafael Eitan. Indeed, Palmachniks dominated the IDF command structure for many years and helped shape its distinctive ethos.

Richard M. Edwards

Further Reading

Bar-On, Mordechai, ed. *A Never-ending Conflict: A Guide to Israeli Military History.* Westport, CT: Praeger, 2004.

Creveld, Martin Van. *The Sword and the Olive: A Critical History of the Israeli Defense Force.* New York: PublicAffairs, 1998.

Goldstein, Yaacov N., and Dan Shomron. *From Fighters to Soldiers: How the Israeli Defense Forces Began.* Brighton, UK: Sussex Academic, 1998.

Partido Africano da Independência de Guiné e Cabo Verde

Guinea nationalist movement that led the military effort to achieve independence from Portugal. Amílcar Cabral, born in Guinea and trained as an agronomist in Portugal, founded the Partido Africano da Independência de Guiné e Cabo Verde (PAIGC, African Party for the Independence of Guinea and Cape Verde) in 1956. After the failure of political efforts to secure independence, Cabral resorted to force. He established training camps in the neighboring Republic of Guinea (Guinea-Conakry) and Senegal, both of which had received their independence from France, and in January 1963 initiated military action against the Portuguese in Guinea.

In 1971 with some 6,000–7,000 men under arms, the PAIGC claimed to control some 80 percent of Guinea, although in truth Portuguese forces under the able leadership of General António de Silva were able to bring about a stalemate. Cabral established a government-in-exile in Conakry, capital of the Republic of Guinea, and in 1972 began to plan for a popular assembly and the proclamation of independence. Before he could realize this, internal rivalries within the PAIGC led on January 30, 1973, to Cabral's assassination in Conakry by Inocêncio Kani, with the possible assistance of Portuguese authorities.

Following the Carnation Revolution in Portugal in April 1974, Guinea was granted independence as Guinea-Bissau on September 10, 1974. Amílcar Cabral's half brother, Luis Cabral, became the new state's first president. The Cape Verde Islands decided to become a separate state in July 1975.

Spencer C. Tucker

See also Cabral, Amílcar; Guinea Insurgency; Spinola, António Sebastião Ribeiro de

Further Reading

Cabral, Amílcar. *Revolution in Guinea: Selected Texts.* New York: Monthly Review Press, 1970.

Cann, John. *Counterinsurgency in Africa: The Portuguese Way of War, 1961–1974.* Westport, CT: Greenwood, 1997.

Chabal, Patrick. *Amílcar Cabral: Revolutionary Leadership and People's War.* New York: Cambridge University Press, 1983.

Newitt, Maryland. *Portugal in Africa: The Last 100 Years.* London: Longman, 1981.

Pathet Lao

Front group for Communist forces in Laos. The name "Pathet Lao" means "Land of the Lao" and was applied for the first time to the clandestine resistance government formed by Prince Souphanouvong in August 1950 to fight against the French. The early history of the Pathet Lao paralleled in almost every respect that of the front group formed in Vietnam by Ho Chi Minh in 1941, the Viet Minh (Viet Nam Doc Lap Dong Minh Hoi, Vietnam Independence League), which was also controlled by a small core of Communist leaders.

Just as the Viet Minh front was formed in a secure base area over the border in China, the Pathet Lao front was established at a meeting inside the border in the Democratic Republic of Vietnam (DRV, North Vietnam). Although the Pathet Lao's program was designed to appeal to noncommunist nationalists with its slogan of "Peace, independence, neutrality and prosperity," the Pathet Lao never achieved the same degree of popularity among the Laotians as the Viet Minh did in Vietnam, probably because they were so evidently dependent on the Vietnamese Communists.

Nevertheless, the Pathet Lao, with aid and support from the North Vietnamese government, waged a long civil war and ultimately managed to seize control of the Laotian government in 1975. In December 1975 the group did away with the 600-year-old monarchy and proclaimed the Lao People's Democratic Republic (LPDR). All other political entities were banned, and thousands of former government officials and other noncommunists were sent to so-called seminar camps—a euphemism for internment camps where many perished. Also in December 1975, the Lao People's Revolutionary Party (LPRP) was formed. The LPRP was the Communist political front for the Pathet Lao.

Since the mid-1970s, Laos has been governed exclusively by the LDRP, which has exercised almost complete control over Laotian affairs. Beginning in the 1980s in an attempt to overcome lagging economic performance and grinding poverty, the party enacted limited reforms designed to modernize the Laotian economy. As late as the late 1990s, the LPRP had only about 70,000 members in a nation with more than 6 million people. Laos remains an orthodox Socialist nation today, with an economy heavily dependent upon its Socialist neighbors of the Socialist Republic of Vietnam and the People's Republic of China.

Arthur J. Dommen and Paul G. Pierpaoli Jr.

See also Viet Minh

Further Reading

Zasloff, Joseph J., and MacAlister Brown. *Apprentice Revolutionaries: The Communist Movement in Laos, 1930–1985.* Stanford, CA: Hoover Institution Press, 1986.

Zasloff, Joseph J., and Leonard Unger, eds. *Laos: Beyond the Revolution.* London: MacMillan, 1991.

Peasants' Revolt in England

Event Date: 1381

One of a number of popular insurrections in medieval Europe, the Peasants' Revolt of 1381, also known as Way Tyler's Rebellion and the Great Rising, was perhaps the most extensive popular uprising in English history.

The Black Death that had ravaged England during 1348–1350 had sharply reduced the labor force and increased the bargaining power of the survivors. Many peasants demanded and received their freedom. King Edward III (r. 1327–1377) attempted to reverse this trend in 1351 with the Statute of Labourers, but it was only partially successful. Indeed, attempts to enforce the new law led to unrest and contributed to the ensuing revolt.

Richard II was only 10 years old on his accession as king in 1377, and his uncle, John of Gaunt, Duke of Lancaster, served as regent. The revolt was triggered when the duke, acting for Richard II, attempted to enforce a poll tax levied in 1377. The tax was not assessed fairly, however; it also particularly negatively impacted married women, leading a number to take part in the subsequent revolt.

The revolt began on May 30, 1381, when a royal official attempted to collect the tax in the villages of Fobbing and Brentwood in Essex. Led by Jack Straw and Wat Tyler, Essex and Kent were soon in full insurrection. Lollard priest John Ball attacked the nobles when he preached a sermon containing the famous question "When Adam dealt and Eve span, who was then the gentleman?"

The revolt spread with astonishing speed. Peasant mobs burned manors and with them the medieval records of tenures, rights to game parks, etc. Straw and Tyler then led a march of as many as 100,000 people on London. On June 14, representatives of the mob met with young Richard II and presented him a list of demands that included the dismissal of unpopular ministers and an effective end to serfdom.

The rebels sacked and burned John of Gaunt's palace, the Savoy, along with many other residents of the rich. One group of rebels seized the Tower of London and executed those who had taken refuge there, including Simon of Sudbury, the lord chancellor and archbishop of Canterbury who had authored the poll tax.

Tyler was murdered at Smithfield on June 15 during the course of fresh talks with the king, supposedly on drawing his sword during an argument. The rebel army could see Tyler being surrounded by courtiers and might have moved had not Richard seized control of the situation by riding forward and shouting "You shall have no captain save me!" Richard was able to mollify the peasants with the false claim that Tyler was fine and in fact had been knighted, that he had ridden on ahead, and that the peasants should join him at St. John's Fields. Tyler also assured the mob that its demands would all be met.

Richard meanwhile assembled a force of nobles and loyal militia and took vengeance. The leaders of the revolt, including Ball, were hunted down and killed. Parliament quickly annulled the promised royal reforms and attempted to restore villeinage. The latter proved impossible, however. Thus, the Peasants' Revolt did have the positive effect of marking the beginning of the end of serfdom in England and also increased an awareness in the English upper classes of the necessity for at least modest reform in the existing feudal system.

Spencer C. Tucker

Further Reading

Dunn, Alastair. *The Great Rising of 1381: The Peasant's Revolt and England's Failed Revolution*. Charleston, SC: Tempus, 2002.

Lindsay, Philip, and Reginald Groves. *The Peasants' Revolt, 1381*. Westport, CT: Greenwood, 1974.

Oman, Charles. *The Great Revolt of 1381*. 1906; reprint, Oxford, UK: Clarendon, 1969.

Peninsular War

Start Date: 1808
End Date: 1814

The Peninsular War (1808–1814) was an armed struggle between France and the allied governments of Portugal, Spain, and Great Britain. The war can also be dated from November 1807, when French emperor Napoleon I, having secured permission from France's ally Spain, commenced an invasion of Portugal. This was prompted by Napoleon's desire to expand the Continental System—his effort to close European ports to British goods in order to ruin British overseas trade.

Napoleon's decision to intervene militarily in Iberia was possibly the most disastrous of his career. A classic example of strategic overreach, it resulted in a drain of 300,000 French casualties in five years of fighting in what Napoleon himself referred to as "the Spanish ulcer." The intervention brought one of the first "national" wars and produced extensive guerrilla warfare (the word "guerrilla" comes from the Spanish word *guerra* and is the diminutive, meaning "small war," and is believed to have entered the English language in 1808).

French general Jean Andoche Junot set out from Salamanca in November 1807 and captured the Portuguese capital of Lisbon on December 1. Then in March 1808 on the pretext of guarding the coasts of Spain against the British, Napoleon sent 100,000 French troops into that country under Marshal Joachim Murat. Spanish king Charles IV abdicated in favor of his son Ferdinand VII, but Napoleon summoned both men to Bayonne in May and got each of them to renounce the throne.

On May 2, 1808, in perhaps the most important event of the war, a savage uprising known as Dos de Mayo (Second of May) occurred in Madrid against French rule. The French crushed it with great savagery. Indeed, Napoleon welcomed the insurrection as a means of securing Spanish submission to his authority. As a sign of the planned permanence of his move, Napoleon dispatched his elder brother Joseph to Spain as king (from June 6, 1808), whereupon Murat took Joseph's former place as king of Naples.

On July 19, 1808, Europe was stunned when a Spanish force of some 30,000 regulars and militia defeated a French army of 20,000 at Bailén. This first defeat of a Napoleonic army sent shock waves across Europe, invigorating opposition to French rule in other countries, especially Austria. The defeat was also a tremendous boost to the Spanish resistance and to British hopes for it.

Nationalism was certainly a central factor, but motivations for the Spanish resistance to the French varied from region to region. As many as 30,000 guerrillas operated against the invaders and their French-imposed government. Actual guerrilla field forces varied considerably in size, with the largest probably the 7,000 men under Francisco Espoz y Mina in Navarre. The British provided arms and assistance to the insurgents in both Spain and Portugal and also decided to send an expeditionary force to Portugal, soon commanded by Sir Arthur Wellesley (later the duke of Wellington). The expeditionary force soon defeated the French there and began operations in Spain. There the guerrillas greatly aided the regular allied forces, who attacked isolated French detachments, struck French supply lines, and provided invaluable intelligence. But it is also true that the guerrillas would have been defeated by the French had it not been for British logistical support. Although the guerrillas certainly played a major role, it was the regular military formations of Great Britain, Portugal, and Spain, in cooperation with the Royal Navy, that ultimately defeated the French and drove them back across the Pyrenees and then invaded France itself during the winter of 1813–1814.

Spencer C. Tucker

See also Guerrilla

Further Reading

Esdaile, Charles J. *The Spanish Army in the Peninsular War.* Manchester, UK: Manchester University Press, 1988.

Gates, David. *The Spanish Ulcer: A History of the Peninsular War.* New York: Norton, 1986.

Haythornthwaite, Philip J. *The Peninsular War.* London: Brassey's, 2004.

Pershing, John Joseph

Birth Date: September 13, 1860
Death Date: July 15, 1948

U.S. Army general and highly successful counterinsurgency leader. Born in Laclede, Missouri, on September 13, 1860, John Joseph Pershing worked odd jobs and taught school to support his family until receiving an appointment to the U.S. Military Academy, West Point, in 1882. Commissioned a second lieutenant upon graduation in 1886, he joined the 6th Cavalry Regiment in New Mexico and saw limited action in the final subjugation of the Apache Indians.

In 1891 Pershing became professor of military science at the University of Nebraska, where he also studied law. He completed a law degree in 1893 and, frustrated by the lack of military advancement, toyed with the idea of a legal career. In 1895, however, he returned to the field with the 10th Cavalry, an African American unit. He joined the staff of commanding general Nelson A. Miles in Washington in 1896 and then was an instructor of tactics at West Point in 1897. Cadets unhappy with Pershing's dark demeanor and rigid style labeled him "Black Jack," a derogatory reference to his 10th Cavalry posting.

During the Spanish-American War (1898), Pershing rejoined the 10th Cavalry for the invasion of Cuba, distinguishing himself in the Battle of Las Guásimas (June 24). He was awarded the Silver Star for his role in the fight for San Juan Heights (July 1). Contracting malaria, he returned to the United States to recover.

Promoted to major of U.S. Volunteers in August, he was assigned to the office of the assistant secretary of war, where he had oversight of the War Department's new Bureau of Insular Affairs, charged with administering the Philippines and Puerto Rico. Pershing supported the decision to acquire the Philippines and firmly believed in a U.S. civilizing mission there.

In September 1899 Pershing was assigned to the Philippines. There he campaigned successfully against the Moros in the Lake Lanao region in central Mindanao in 1901–1902, attracting recognition for his ability to win their friendship and trust. Appointed commander of Camp Vicars on Mindanao in June 1902, he put into practice his policy of resorting to force with the Moros only as a last recourse. As recognition of the high esteem in which he was held, the Moros gave him the title of datu (chief).

Pershing returned to the United

One of the most important military leaders in U.S. history, General of the Armies of the United States John J. Pershing commanded the American Expeditionary Forces in France during 1917–1918. Earlier Pershing distinguished himself in counterinsurgency operations against Moro forces in the Philippines and had led the Punitive Expedition into Mexico during 1916–1917. (Library of Congress)

States for General Staff service and to attend the Army War College in 1903. As military attaché to Japan during 1905–1906, he was an official observer of the Russo-Japanese War (1904–1905). Impressed with Pershing, President Theodore Roosevelt nominated him for direct promotion from captain to brigadier general in September 1906, vaulting him ahead of 862 more senior officers.

Pershing spent most of the next eight years in the Philippines, where he continued to display effective leadership as military commander of Moro Province and crushed the last major Moro uprising at Bud Bagsak in January 1912. Returning to the United States, he commanded briefly at the Presidio, San Francisco, before moving to Fort Bliss near El Paso, Texas, in 1914 to confront problems associated with the Mexican Revolution. His wife Frances Warren Pershing and their three daughters, who remained at the Presidio, died in a house fire there in 1915.

Following the raid by Mexican revolutionary leader Francisco "Pancho" Villa on the small border town of Columbus, New Mexico, on March 9, 1916, President Woodrow Wilson named Pershing to command an expeditionary force of 10,000 men into Mexico with orders to capture or kill Villa and his followers while avoiding conflict with Mexico. The expedition lasted 10 months, cut deep into northern Mexico, and threatened all-out war. Although Villa escaped, Pershing tested new technologies, including machine guns, aircraft, motorized transport, and radios.

Following the U.S. declaration of war on Germany on April 6, 1917, Wilson named Pershing, only recently promoted to major general, to command the American Expeditionary Forces in France. Pershing, promoted to full general in October 1917, stubbornly refused to have his forces broken up in smaller units as fillers for British and French forces. However, during the crisis occasioned by Germany's 1918 Spring Offensives, Pershing offered individual U.S. divisions to the Allied command, and the Americans quickly proved their worth.

Pershing directed American forces in the subsequent Aisne-Marne (July 25–August 2, 1918), St. Mihiel Salient (September 12–17), and Meuse-Argonne (September 26–November 11) offensives. He opposed the armistice of November 11, 1918, preferring to fight until Germany surrendered, but was overruled.

After overseeing the demobilization of American forces, Pershing returned to the United States a hero in 1919. Congress confirmed his status as a four-star general with the rank title of general of the armies that September. Pershing served as army chief of staff during 1921–1924 and then retired. In 1923 he became chairman of the American Battle Monuments Commission. He continued serving in that capacity until 1948.

Pershing received the Pulitzer Prize for his memoir, *My Experiences in the World War* (1931). He died in Washington, D.C., on July 15, 1948. Pershing was one of the most significant leaders in American military history.

David Coffey

See also Mexican Expedition; Moros; Philippine Islands and U.S. Pacification during the Philippine-American War; Villa, Francisco

Further Reading

Smith, Gene. *Until the Last Trumpet Sounds: The Life of General of the Armies John J. Pershing.* New York: Wiley, 1999.

Smythe, Donald. *Guerrilla Warrior: The Early Life of John J. Pershing.* New York: Scribner, 1973.

Vandiver, Frank E. *Black Jack: The Life and Times of John J. Pershing.* 2 vols. College Station: Texas A&M University Press, 1977.

Peru Insurgencies

Start Date: 1982
End Date: Ongoing

The South American nation of Peru experienced a major insurgency in the 1980s. As with other Latin American governments, Peru experienced periods of military dictatorship. The Peruvian government distanced itself from Fidel Castro's new government that was established in Cuba in 1959, but the Castro revolution soon influenced much of Latin America, and Peru was no exception. Indeed, the early 1960s witnessed the emergence of revolutionary foco-style groups with pro-Castro sympathies. Hugo Blanco Galdos led the Quechua *campesino* ("peasant") uprising in the Cuzco region. He was captured during the uprising, and the movement was easily put down.

Such movements, however, tilled the ground for future guerrilla movements by Sendero Luminoso (Shining Path), led by Abimeal Guzmán, and by the Movimiento Revolucionsario Tupac Amarú (MRTA, Tupac Amarú Revolutionary Movement), named for the Indian leader executed by the Spaniards in 1780. The latter was the precursor of the Movimiento de Izquierda Revolucionario (Left Revolutionary Movement). Whereas Shining Path was a peasant-based rural insurgency that followed the teachings of Chinese Communist leader Mao Zedong, the MRTA was an urban insurgent movement.

Shining Path commenced terrorist attacks in 1982, and the MRTA followed suit in 1984. The Peruvian government launched a counterinsurgency effort in 1982, placing 19 provinces under a state of emergency. Guerrilla warfare continued.

During the 1980s, popularly elected president Belaunde Terry continued a non-aligned foreign policy, although his sympathy for the Sandinistas in Nicaragua put him at odds with the Ronald Reagan administration in the United States. Belaunde offered military support to Argentina in the 1982 Falklands (Malvinas) War while at the same time presenting a peace proposal to both Argentina and Great Britain, which the British rejected.

Domestically, Belaunde's neoliberal market-oriented economic policies did not gain the support of the population but instead contributed to significant social discontent. The growing presence of Shining Path and the MRTA presented another obstacle for Belaunde's regime, which was accused of committing human rights abuses against civilians during 1983–1985. Although Shining Path was responsible for many casualties among peasants, government forces were responsible for many more.

Peru's diplomacy was nonetheless vital in Central American conflicts. In 1985 Peru, Argentina, Brazil, and Uruguay created the Contadora Support Group in an effort to negotiate a peace agreement for Central America. Despite its active diplomacy toward Central America, President Alan García's government of 1985–1990 was unsuccessful in bringing economic improvement to the country. Peru's economy was in chaos.

In 1990 Alberto Fujimori, a Peruvian of Japanese extraction, and his Cambio 90 (Change 90) Party unexpectedly won the national elections. With the insurgencies continuing in addition to growing inflation and a burgeoning drug trade, Fujimori's answer was a coup against his own presidency in April 1992, whereby he dismissed Congress and assumed dictatorial powers. Fujimori received a boost when Guzmán was captured that September. Then in 1964, Shining Path fragmented when Guzmán negotiated peace terms with the government from his prison cell. Although Fukimori handily won the 1995 elections, he was embarrassed in December 1995 when MRTA seized the Japanese ambassador's residence in Lima, took 500 people there hostage, and demanded the release of prisoners. After a prolonged siege, Peruvian troops stormed the residence. Fujimori was forced to resign following the controversial 2000 elections. Insurgent activities in Peru continue at a low level, having claimed some 27,000 lives since 1982.

Carina Solmirano and Spencer C. Tucker

See also Castro Ruz, Fidel Alejandro; Cuban Revolution; Frente Sandinista de Liberación; Mao Zedong; Sendero Luminoso

Further Reading

McClintock, Cynthia, and Fabian Vallas. *The United States and Peru: Cooperation at a Cost.* New York: Routledge, 2003.

Rochlin, James Francis. *Vanguard Revolutionaries in Latin America: Peru, Colombia, Mexico.* Boulder, CO: Lynne Rienner, 2003.

Petraeus, David Howell

Birth Date: November 7, 1952

U.S. Army general. Born on November 7, 1952, in Cornwall-on-Hudson, New York, David Howell Petraeus graduated from the U.S. Military Academy, West Point, in 1974. Commissioned a second lieutenant of infantry, he graduated from Ranger School and served as a platoon leader in the 509th Airborne Infantry Regiment in Italy. He then held a series of junior officer positions in the 24th Infantry Division (Mechanized).

From 1982 to 1995 Petraeus held command and staff positions, with alternating assignments for professional military and civilian academic education. He graduated from the Army Command and General Staff College in 1983 and then attended Princeton University's Woodrow Wilson School of Public Affairs, earning a master's degree in public administration in 1985 and a doctorate in international relations in 1987. His doctoral dissertation dealt with the U.S. Army in Vietnam and the lessons learned there.

Petraeus returned to West Point to teach international relations and then was a military fellow at Georgetown University's School of Foreign Service. In 1995 he was assigned as the chief operations officer of the United Nations mission during Operation UPHOLD DEMOCRACY in Haiti.

Petraeus's command assignments included the 3rd Battalion, 187th Infantry Regiment, 101st Airborne Division, during 1991–1993 and the 1st Brigade, 82nd Airborne Division, from 1995 to 1997. He was promoted to brigadier general in 1999.

Petraeus's first combat assignment, now as a major general, came as commander of the 101st Airborne Division (Air Assault) in Operation IRAQI FREEDOM in March 2003. The division engaged in the Battles of Karbala and Najar as well as in the feint at Hilla. Petraeus later oversaw the administration and rebuilding of the Mosul and Niveveh Provinces. Subsequently he commanded the Multinational Security Transition Command–Iraq and the North Atlantic Treaty Organization (NATO) Training Mission–Iraq during June 2004– September 2005. Petraeus's next assignment was as commanding general of Fort Leavenworth, Kansas, and the U.S. Army Combined Arms Center, where he exercised direct responsibility for the doctrinal changes to prepare the army for its continued efforts in Afghanistan and Iraq. He also coauthored *Field Manual 3–24: Counterinsurgency.*

On February 10, 2007, now a lieutenant general, Petreus assumed command of the Multinational Force–Iraq. His appointment was the keystone in President George W. Bush's troop surge strategy in Iraq designed to bring an end to the mounting violence there. Petraeus was promoted to full general in December 2007.

Petreaus made security of the Iraqi population, especially in Baghdad, and working with Iraqi forces the focus of the military effort. This included maintaining a permanent military presence in the most threatened population areas, enhancing the capacity of local Iraqi security forces, buttressing Iraqi governmental authority, fostering employment, and improving living conditions for Iraqi citizens.

By the spring of 2008, defying high odds and most critics of the war, the surge strategy appeared to have worked, and Petraeus could point to a significant reduction in sectarian and insurgency-based violence. Also, the Iraqis themselves seemed increasingly willing and able to assume security and policing tasks. As a result, U.S. and coalition troop withdrawals accelerated throughout 2008, and violence in Iraq hit four-year lows.

Petraeus was largely hailed in the United States for his efforts at undermining the Iraqi insurgency, and because of this President Bush tapped him to command the U.S. Central Command (CENTCOM). Petraeus took command in October 1, 2008. As the head of CENTCOM (October 2008–June 2010), he became responsible for U.S. military operations in 20 nations, from Egypt to Pakistan, as well as the ongoing conflicts in Afghanistan and Iraq.

In June 2010 when President Barack Obama removed General Stanley A. McChrystal as commander of U.S. and NATO forces in Afghanistan, the president tapped Petraeus as McChrystal's successor. Petraeus held that post until July 2011. He retired from the U.S. Army in August and assumed the position of director of the U.S. Central Intelligence Agency in September. On November 8, 2012, Petreaus, who had been married for 37 years, submitted his letter of resignation with the admission that he had engaged in an extramarital affair.

Marcel A. Derosier

See also Afghanistan Insurgency; Iraq Insurgency

Further Reading

Cloud, David, and Greg Jaffe. *The Fourth Star: Four Generals and the Epic Struggle for the Future of the United States Army.* New York: Random House, 2009.

Gericke, Bradley. *David Petreaus: A Biography.* Santa Barbara, CA: Greenwood, 2010.

Kaplan, Fred. *The Insurgents: David Petraeus and the Plot to Change the American Way of War.* New York: Simon and Schuster, 2013.

Robinson, Linda. *Tell Me How This Ends: General David Petraeus and the Search for a Way Out of Iraq.* New York: PublicAffairs, 2008.

Philippeville Massacre

Event Date: August 20, 1955

Watershed event during the Algerian War (1954–1962). The insurgent Front de Libération Nationale (FLN, National Liberation Front) originally operated primarily in the rural areas of Algeria, attacking only French military and government targets. This changed in 1955, when the FLN moved into the towns and cities and began attacking the pieds-noirs (colons), the French, and other European civilians who had settled in Algeria.

Youssef Zighout, leader of the FLN's Wikaya 2 that covered the North Constantine Region, and his right-hand man, Lakhdar Ben Tobbal, decided in June 1955 on a dramatic escalation of the insurgency. Zighout called for a massive uprising of Muslim Algerians against the French: "For them, no pity, no quarter!" The targeted area was to be around the port city of Philippeville (now Skikda) in northeastern Algeria. Here on August 20 members of the FLN and their supporters massacred 123 people, 71 of them Europeans, including old women and babies. This was carried out often in the most barbarous and horrific manner, which helps explain the French reaction.

The French Army moved swiftly. The government subsequently announced that 1,273 "insurgents" had been killed. Some estimates, however, place the tally of those slain by the French military, police, and pied-noir gangs as high as 12,000.

What became known as the Philippeville Massacre by the FLN shocked French governor-general Jacques Soustelle, who had arrived in Algeria only in January and had initiated a reform program (the Soustelle Plan) designed to improve the situation of the Muslims. Soustelle now reversed field and instituted repressive measures. These and the initial French reprisals, however, had the net effect of causing many more Algerian Muslims to rally to the FLN.

Spencer C. Tucker

See also Algerian War; Front de Libération Nationale

Further Reading

Horne, Alistair. *A Savage War of Peace.* New York: Viking, 1978.

Philippine Constabulary

Paramilitary police organization formed by the United States on August 8, 1901, to assist in counterinsurgency efforts during the Philippine-American War (1899–1902). The Philippine Constabulary was part of the civil government and was a distinct entity from the U.S. Army and the Philippine Scouts. With a cadre of American officer personnel, the constabulary recruited and trained Filipinos to secure critical local-area knowledge. Recruits were Filipino males ages 18–25 who were in sound health and were conversant in both Spanish and English. Tasked with taking over the security mission from conventional military units, the constabulary garrisoned population centers to protect them from rebel and bandit raids and hunt down the raiders. The constabulary was also capable of operating as a military unit and occasionally joined U.S. Army and Philippine Scout units in actions against rebel strongholds.

After the successful capture of Filipino insurgent leader General Emilio Aguinaldo y Famy in March 1901, hostilities continued with the surviving guerrilla elements. William Howard Taft, the new U.S. governor-general of the islands, decided that a strong police force consisting of Filipinos would eventually remove the need for U.S. Army involvement in pacification efforts. The constabulary was officially authorized with passage of the second Philippine Commission's Organic Act No. 175 on July 18, 1901.

The Philippine Constabulary was officially born as the Insular Constabulary on August 8, 1901, with the appointment of 70 handpicked officers to begin recruiting and training. The majority of the constabulary officers were U.S. Army volunteers, with two Filipinos commissioned as third lieutenants, a revolutionary step at the time. The first chief of the constabulary was Henry T. Allen, a captain in the regular U.S. Army then serving as a lieutenant colonel of a volunteer cavalry battalion. Allen was elevated to brigadier general of volunteers and served until his retirement in 1907.

The Philippine Constabulary adopted the tactics, rank structure, and command style of the U.S. Army. The first group of officers attended an expedited training course to familiarize themselves with police procedures and Filipino society. Upon completion of the training course, teams consisting of 1 captain and 3 or 4 lieutenants were dispatched to areas with civil unrest to recruit local Filipinos who would conduct police duties in coordination with army pacification efforts. Each Philippine province was to receive a force of 150 constables, although this number was rarely achieved.

There was no standardized method for recruitment and training of the Filipino enlistees, especially in provinces far from Manila. Common practice consisted of an officer being issued a supply of guns and uniforms and a cash advance and then being assigned to a specific locality. On-the-job training was usually deemed suitable for preparing the new recruits. Often, as the only representative of the government for miles around, a constable would be called to take on additional duties, such as those of health officer, construction supervisor, school principal, and public works manager.

The Philippine Constabulary focused its efforts on three regions: Luzon, the Visayan islands of Leyte and Samar, and the Moro Provinces. The constabulary's first major challenge was pacification of central Luzon, where many of Aguinaldo's followers still waged a guerrilla war and raided local villages. Raiding provided the rebels with valuable food, weapons, money, and fame that aided in recruiting new rebels but it also proved to be a source of dissatisfaction among the local population. The constabulary thus developed a strategy of garrisoning villages to protect the population, conducting manhunts, gathering intelligence from disaffected locals, and assaulting neighboring rebel hideouts. Resistance rarely developed above the level of common banditry, however, and the rebels were often indistinguishable from criminal gangs or bandits, known as *ladrones*. One estimate holds that in 1901 alone, the constabulary captured or killed at least 3,000 bandits.

Although there were others on Luzon, Macario Sakay was perhaps the greatest insurgent threat there because of his ability to organize the disparate rebel leaders of central Luzon and the southern Tagalogs under his command. He was able to organize larger raiding parties that allowed him to attack and defeat Philippine Constabulary and Philippine Scout garrisons, securing rifles and new followers. His raiding led to a suspension of habeas corpus and passage of a tougher anti-banditry law. A force of 785 constables with more than 2,000 army troops and Philippine Scouts was organized to track down Sakay. Constabulary garrisons were established in every village, linked by telegraph lines, and rural residents were concentrated in controlled camps. Over time Sakay's followers were gradually captured, and he himself finally surrendered in July 1906. Pockets of resistance continued on the island but never proved to be a threat to the government's administration and had virtually ended by 1914.

Efforts to pacify the Visayan islands of Leyte and Samar were referred to as the Pulajan Campaign, named after the local Muslim group. The resistance there was a combination of political resistance and religious motivations built on a localized form of Islam. The Philippine Constabulary arrived on Leyte in August 1901 to find a relatively calm, stable situation. The majority of the constables moved on to Samar in response to the September 28, 1901, Balangiga Massacre, which presented a more pressing security concern. Rebel leader Jorge Capile took advantage of their departure and organized forces to push back the fledgling constabulary garrisons. The authorities found it necessary to bring in more than 200 constables under Colonel Wallace Taylor to pursue Capile until his surrender in June 1902.

An even bigger threat appeared in spiritual leader Papa (Pope) Faustion Ablena, who used his claims of mystical powers to inspire resistance among the Muslim populations of Leyte and Samar. He sold amulets that would supposedly provide immunity from bullets for the true believer. Ablena's raiding of towns for supplies developed the same level of animosity among local populations as on Luzon. However, he consistently evaded capture and always had a willing supply of recruits to replace losses inflicted by the Philippine Constabulary. By July 1904, constabulary units from neighboring islands were moved to Leyte with a U.S. Army and Philippine Scout contingent to capture Ablena.

On Samar, unlike on Leyte, there were many spiritual leaders, or papas, but the greatest was Papa Pablo. The level of violence on Samar was so great—despite Philippine Constabulary, U.S. Army, U.S. Marine Corps, and Philippine Scout efforts—that Colonel Taylor's constables were transferred from Leyte to Samar after they had defeated Capile, although there were still operational needs on Leyte. At the height of the violence, rebels were able to destroy entire patrols and garrisons.

In November 1905, Philippine Constabulary temporary chief Brigadier General Henry Tureman Allen took personal command of the Pulajan Campaign, bringing with him 1,800 constables. The resulting pressure and food control policies allowed the constabulary to reduce rebel forces until Pablo was captured in November 1906 and Ablena was captured in June 1907. The Pulajan Campaign was officially ended in 1907, although pockets of resistance continued to spring up until 1917.

The Philippine Constabulary's greatest challenge was on the islands that make up the southern Philippines, known as the Moro Provinces. Ethnically different from the rest of the islands and Muslim by faith, the area had been ruled by the Spanish in name only. Piracy, rebellion, and internal wars were a culturally accepted norm. Real power belonged to a collection of sultans and local tribal datus (chiefs), none of whom was able to achieve the popularity of Aguinaldo or Ablena. The army had been successful in establishing harmonious relations with the larger port cities and installing garrisons there. Extending authority inland had proved much more difficult, however. The constabulary arrived on the island in 1903 and began to recruit from the local populace, a controversial move because of the locals' apparent hatred of foreign control. They proved to be fierce in battle, and many rebel Moro units were simply annihilated, as they refused to retreat.

The Philippine Constabulary developed a divide-and-conquer strategy that pitted rival datus against each other, making itself a necessary intermediary. Datus who resisted built forts, known as cottas, in remote areas. The constabulary and other security forces engaged in innumerable pitched battles in an effort to eliminate these strongholds. In the battles, the defenders often fought to the death.

The Philippine Constabulary's first major battle took place on the island of Sulu. When regional governor Major General Leonard Wood learned of a datu building a major cotta on Mount Bud Dajo, he ordered a combined army-constabulary force to destroy the outpost. The resulting Battle of Bud Dajo of March 5–8, 1906, ended with only 6 of the estimated 800–1,000 Moro fighters surviving.

By 1909 authorities believed that peace had been established in the south, a notion that was shattered in 1910. A new group of individuals known as Jurametados, who violently opposed the presence of Christians in Moro lands, emerged. The Jurametados believed that the more Christians they killed, the greater the rewards in heaven. Many Jurametados operated singly outside of the control of any group and engaged in suicidal attacks against U.S. forces. As a result, the regional governor at the time, Brigadier General John Pershing, issued a disarmament order on September 8, 1911, that many Moros resisted. The Philippine Constabulary found itself in a new round of cotta reductions and pitched battles. Despite a campaign of civil improvement and the recruitment of Muslims into the government and security forces, resistance in the Moro areas continued until the handover of rule to the Commonwealth of the Philippines in 1946. Some Moro violence continues to this day.

From the start of the Philippine Constabulary, Filipinos filled out the enlisted ranks. Some rose to junior-level officer ranks based on their accomplishments in battle. With U.S. involvement in World War I (1914–1918), Filipino officers began to assume senior positions, replacing American officers deployed to France in the summer of 1917. That same year, the Insular Constabulary was officially renamed the Philippine Constabulary, and command was turned over to a Filipino, Brigadier General Rafael Crame. The Philippine Constabulary continued to operate until World War II (1939–1945), at which time it was folded into the Philippine Army.

James E. Shircliffe Jr.

See also Moros; Pershing, John Joseph; Philippine Islands and U.S. Pacification during the Philippine-American War; Philippine Scouts

Further Reading

Hurley, Vic. *Jungle Control: The Story of the Philippine Constabulary.* New York: E. P. Dutton, 1938.

Linn, Brian McAllister. *The Philippine War, 1899–1902.* Lawrence: University Press of Kansas, 2000.

San Gabriel, Reynaldo P. *The Constabulary Story.* Quezon City, Philippines: Bustamante, 1978.

Philippine Islands and U.S. Pacification during the Philippine-American War

Start Date: 1899
End Date: 1902

Filipino nationalists fought to free the Philippines from U.S. rule during February 1899–July 1902. This conflict, known at the time as the Philippine Insurrection and today as the Philippine-American War, occurred after U.S. military forces had defeated Spanish forces and occupied Manila. The war began with an incident at the San Juan Bridge in Manila on February 4, 1899, and ended when the major Filipino forces were defeated or had surrendered by April 1902. The U.S. Army officially declared the insurrection at an end on July 4, 1902, although small-scale hostilities continued into 1913.

The fighting came as something of a surprise to the United States. Initially, the Filipino nationalists engaged U.S. forces in conventional warfare. This was a failure, as by February 1900 the U.S. Army had won several important victories and destroyed most of the Filipino conventional military capability. Insurgent leader and president of the Philippine Republic Emilio Aguinaldo y Famy then changed strategy and went over to guerrilla warfare, hoping to create sufficient American casualties so as to influence the 1900 U.S. presidential election. He hoped that American opposition to the war would bring the election of Democratic anti-imperialist candidate William Jennings Bryan.

The American response to the guerrilla strategy was slow to evolve but grew to include not only robust military action but also a sophisticated pacification program. General Order No. 100 specifically gave field commanders guidance on authorized actions against guerrillas, civilians supporting guerrillas, and the civil population at large. The order was actually a reissue of one issued in 1863 that was used to define the army's legally permissible actions during the American Civil War.

Twenty-six of the 30 American generals who served in the Philippines were veterans of the various Indian campaigns, as were numerous junior officers, and they were able to apply lessons learned there. The American pacification effort was a two-pronged program, which at its peak involved some 69,000 troops. One part of this was the so-called chastisement component, the effort to destroy the insurgency by force. The other major approach was that of attraction. It was an effort to win the support of the Filipino people by demonstrating the benefits of American rule.

The chastisement policy was brutal but effective. U.S. commanding general and military governor in the Philippines Major General Arthur MacArthur began implementing the policy after the 1900 American elections and the reelection of President William McKinley. The policy involved a range of tactics and techniques that systematically reduced the military capabilities of the insurgents. These included offensive operations against the insurgents, population control by separating the insurgents from their support base, and attacks on the insurgent leadership.

Most offensive operations against the insurgents were local efforts conducted on a relatively small scale. These, called hikes by the American troops, were largely ineffective in locating and destroying insurgent bands. Although not showing significant results in combat, they gave the Americans the initiative in the war and forced the insurgents to concentrate on evasion and survival rather than on offensive operations. The army also mounted large-scale offensive operations designed to destroy or capture major insurgent groups and their supporters. Such operations often included the destruction of crops to deny these to the insurgents.

The Philippine archipelago includes more than 7,000 islands, compounding the difficulty of pacification. The U.S. Navy played a key role in helping to control travel, trade, and communication between the islands. The navy operated more than two dozen seagoing gunboats to interdict traffic between the islands, while the army maintained a dozen shallow-draft river steamers to support operations ashore. U.S. control of waterborne travel in the islands helped fragment and isolate the insurgents.

American commanders quickly recognized the importance of securing the support of the local civilian population. The insurgents secured support through appeals to nationalism as well as coercion, and they established their own system of taxation by a shadow government. The U.S. Army broke down this relationship through a variety of techniques. One was the relocation of the population, concentrating the rural population in towns and villages where small army detachments assisted by loyal Filipinos could monitor them closely. The army was largely successful in avoiding forcible relocations. This so-called reconcentration was accomplished through various incentives, including building town markets and overseeing food distribution in the towns. This combined with destroying crops and isolated residences had the effect of forcing the population to concentrate without orders. Once the population was concentrated, restrictions on travel and curfews kept it controlled. The concentration of the population resulted in large numbers of civilian deaths, however. At least 11,000 people perished in the concentration areas from disease, malnutrition, poor sanitation, and other health problems.

Another more direct means of separating the population from the insurgency was through strong retaliatory action. This included burning homes in the areas where telegraph wires had been cut, destroying homes and crops in areas where ambushes occurred, widespread arrests of suspected insurgents and their family members, deportations, and fines. In the most extreme cases, army commands executed individuals held responsible for the murder of Americans or friendly Filipinos. Although not officially condoned, individual soldiers and units also employed torture to extract information from captured or detained individuals who were suspected of being or supporting insurgents.

During the war, American operations became increasingly effective because of improved intelligence. American officers realized very early in the campaign that effective intelligence was absolutely essential. Toward this end, the army developed a multilayered intelligence capability that included paid informants, spies, translators, and native scouts and guides. As part of the intelligence effort, the Americans systematically documented noncombatants, carrying out a national census and issuing identity cards.

Another technique that proved effective in the pacification effort was the use of indigenous Filipino forces. Soon after arriving, the Americans began organizing loyal Filipinos to support the counterinsurgency. These forces took the form of the Philippine military units (the Philippine Scouts and Macabebe Scouts) and police units (the Philippine Constabulary).

American officers trained and led both of these units. The Americans carefully screened members of the indigenous forces to ensure their loyalty. Indigenous forces had the advantage of knowing the terrain, culture, and language and of being acclimatized to the tropical conditions. They also undermined the morale of the insurgents and their supporters because they served as a visible sign that part of the population was supporting the Americans. Both the Philippine Scouts and Philippine Constabulary proved invaluable in the American victory in the war.

Effective intelligence and able indigenous forces greatly increased the U.S. Army's counterinsurgency capability and greatly aided the effort of neutralizing the insurgent leadership. In March 1901, U.S. and Philippine Scout forces captured Aguinaldo. Subsequently, Aguinaldo declared his loyalty to the United States, inducing many other insurgents, including senior leaders, to surrender.

While the bulk of the army was involved in the operations that were designed to destroy insurgents and provide security, the army also waged a very effective attraction campaign. This campaign to win Filipino loyalty by demonstrating the benefits of American rule had at its foundation public education. The army built thousands of schools and detailed soldiers to function as teachers when required. As American civil administration became operational, thousands of civilian American teachers were brought to the Philippines to run the schools and train Filipino teachers. At the same time, a vigorous economic infrastructure program was begun with the construction of roads and bridges and the laying of telegraph lines. The Americans also sought to improve the overall health and welfare of the population through inoculation programs, instruction in proper sanitary practices, and the enforcement of hygiene regulations. Finally, the army assisted in the development of a civil administration, based on a democratic model, that provided for a civilian judiciary, the election of local officials, and the transition of administration from the army to a civilian governor.

For the first 18 months of the war, the attraction aspects of policy were the main focus. Commanders and the American civil leadership alike understood that the long-term relationship between the Philippines and the United States could not be fundamentally based on coercion. However, commanders also realized that an attraction policy by itself could not be successful as long as an intelligent and ruthless enemy remained free to intimidate the population. In reality, the two aspects of the pacification program—chastisement and attraction—reinforced each other and ultimately brought unchallenged U.S. control of the islands.

Louis A. DiMarco

See also Aguinaldo y Famy, Emilio; Benevolent Assimilation; Macabebe Scouts; MacArthur, Arthur, Jr.; Philippine Constabulary; Philippine Scouts

Further Reading

Birtle, Andrew J. *U.S. Army Counterinsurgency and Contingency Operations Doctrine, 1860–1941.* Washington, DC: Center of Military History, U.S. Army, 2003.

Gates, John M. *Schoolbooks and Krags: The United States Army in the Philippines, 1898–1902.* Westport, CT: Greenwood, 1973.

Linn, Brian McAllister. *The Philippine War, 1899–1902.* Lawrence: University Press of Kansas, 2000.

Miller, Stuart Creighton. *"Benevolent Assimilation": The American Conquest of the Philippines, 1899–1903*. New Haven, CT: Yale University Press, 1982.

Philippine Scouts

Auxiliary military force of native Filipinos established to support the U.S. Army during the Philippine-American War (1899–1902). The Philippine Scouts assisted American troops in the often forbidding terrain of the Philippines and acted as interpreters for a native population that spoke a myriad of dialects.

As a consequence of the Treaty of Paris ending the Spanish-American War, the United States acquired possession of the Philippine Islands, a 7,000-island territory of 10 million people. Following a short conventional conflict with American forces that began in February 1899, a Filipino guerrilla army, known as the Army of Liberation and led by Emilio Aguinaldo y Famy, took to the rural areas and began an insurgency aimed at gaining independence. Among other U.S. military responses to the insurgency was the formation of the Philippine Scouts, a native auxiliary force that would serve alongside U.S. troops in the Philippines for almost 50 years.

The U.S. Army in the Philippines was far from an ideal force to prosecute a conflict that had evolved into a guerrilla war. The approximately 25,000 U.S. troops present in the summer of 1899 were a combination of state volunteer organizations and a growing number of newly recruited regular army personnel. Aside from inexperience, the troops were challenged by the hostile terrain and disease-ridden tropical environment in which they had to operate. The tactical situation dictated that small units, capable of rapid movement and supplied with effective intelligence, would be required to prosecute the counterinsurgency.

In considering this strategy, the U.S. Army could draw upon its experience of the prior 30 years in the struggle against the American Indians of the Great Plains and the Southwest, during which the army had routinely employed Indian scouts operating with regular army units with significant success. These scouts brought a unique knowledge of the environment and the enemy and, when coupled with disciplined troop formations, were formidable fighting organizations.

In the Philippines, the mission of the scouts was to conduct reconnaissance in advance of main American units, warn of contact with the insurgents, and fix enemy forces to facilitate their defeat by main forces. American soldiers had initially performed these missions, but while they served heroically in an extremely difficult assignment, they were seriously hindered by their ignorance of the terrain, the population, and the language. In light of this, initiatives were begun to recruit indigenous forces to serve in the scout mission.

In the recruitment of native scouts, historical and tribal considerations loomed large. Much of the support for the insurrection came from the Tagalogs, the dominant

Filipinos of central Luzon. As a result, the vast majority of scouts were recruited from other tribes—the Ilocanos, Visayans, and most notably the Macabebes, a group that had a history of working with the former Spanish colonial government because of their strong hatred for the Tagalogs. This not only motivated the Macabees but made them prone to committing atrocities.

In the late summer of 1899, Lieutenant M. A. Batson brought the first group of Macabebe volunteers into a U.S. camp. The initial American military reaction was not enthusiastic. Neither Major General Elwell Stephen Otis, military governor of the Philippines and commander of U.S. forces, nor Brigadier General Arthur MacArthur, commander of the army's 2nd Division on Luzon, believed that they could be sufficiently trusted to be armed.

But the Macabebes, in a series of closely supervised local operations against the guerrillas, gradually gained the confidence of the U.S. Army leadership and were hired as civilian employees and issued rifles. This first unit of scouts began training in September 1899. A subsequent successful engagement of Philippine guerrillas precipitated the authorization of several more companies, and by the end of 1899, a complete battalion, dubbed Batson's Macabebe Scouts, was in operation.

The first large-scale use of the Philippine Scouts occurred during the Northern Luzon Campaign of October 1899. Aguinaldo's Army of Liberation was still operating in units of significant size in this area, and Otis feared that the rebels would retreat to the mountains and begin a guerrilla war. Accordingly, the Northern Luzon Campaign plan envisioned a quick three-pronged encirclement of Aguinaldo and his fighters. This two-month campaign did not achieve its overall strategic purpose, as Aguinaldo escaped, and armed resistance continued. The failure was attributed to extremely wet weather, which hampered mobility and logistics, and questionable tactical decisions on the part of American commanders. The Philippine Scouts, however, acquitted themselves admirably in a series of engagements and grueling marches. They also earned the trust and respect of all levels of American leadership. The scouts went on to play a significant role in most subsequent military campaigns in the Philippines.

As 1900 began, the Philippine insurrection had assumed the character of a guerrilla war. Aguinaldo had formally declared as much in November 1899, but given his status as a man on the run and the huge geographic area of the country, the insurrection was in reality a large number of localized conflicts. Local American commanders received considerable leeway in the prosecution of a conflict that was an attempt to both win over the people of the Philippines and subdue many diverse groups of guerrillas. Throughout 1900, the Philippine Scouts steadily expanded in number and came to be a significant factor in achieving the latter goal.

By January 1901, 1,400 Philippine Scouts were in service alongside American troops. Two factors led to a trebling in the size of that force within six months.

First, American commanders continued to lessen their reflexive distrust of armed native auxiliaries. Second, the looming departure of many U.S. volunteer troops whose tours were up presented U.S. leadership with potential personnel shortages. Accordingly, authority to enlist scouts was delegated to a lower level, and by mid-1901 some 5,500 scouts were serving with the army. Various units of these scouts, usually named after their American commanding officers or the tribes from which they were drawn, fought on a number of different islands. Among the most famous units were the Macabebe, Ilocanos, and Cagayan Scouts.

The highly fluid nature of guerrilla warfare, characterized by small units led by junior officers operating far from central authority and often amid the civilian population, unfortunately produced many incidents of atrocities against civilians and abuse of prisoners. Naturally, the Philippine Scouts were implicated in a number of these incidents, most notably on the island of Panay, where in November 1900 Philippine Scouts were responsible for the burning of some 5,000 houses in the town of Igbaris and the torture of its mayor. The single most famous feat of arms performed was undoubtedly the capture of Aguinaldo in March 1901, in which the Macabebe Scouts played a major role.

Thanks to a combination of effective civil affairs efforts aimed at the Filipino people, the destruction of much of the guerrillas' infrastructure by improved American intelligence and tactics (facilitated by the Philippine Scouts), and harsh military retribution on some islands, by mid-1901 many guerrilla leaders had begun to surrender, and the United States declared the Philippine-American War at an end on July 4, 1902. The record of the Philippine Scouts, while not without its blemishes, was on the whole outstanding. They proved themselves to be hardy, canny, and extremely dedicated fighters with a warrior spirit that allowed them to withstand not only savage combat but also the daunting conditions in which they operated.

The Philippine Scouts continued to serve effectively throughout the remainder of U.S. rule in the Philippines. After fighting heroically against the Japanese in World War II (1939–1945), the scouts were disbanded in 1950 in the wake of Philippine independence.

Robert M. Brown

See also Aguinaldo y Famy, Emilio; Macabebe Scouts; MacArthur, Arthur, Jr.; Philippine Islands and U.S. Pacification during the Philippine-American War

Further Reading

Birtle, Andrew J. *U.S. Army Counterinsurgency and Contingency Operations Doctrine, 1860–1941.* Washington, DC: Center of Military History, U.S. Army, 2003.

Gates, John M. *Schoolbooks and Krags: The United States Army in the Philippines, 1898–1902.* Westport, CT: Greenwood, 1973.

Linn, Brian McAllister. *The Philippine War, 1899–1902.* Lawrence: University Press of Kansas, 2000.

Phoenix Program

Start Date: 1968
End Date: 1972

Program to identify and eliminate the Viet Cong (VC, Vietnamese Communists) infrastructure (VCI) in the Republic of Vietnam (RVN, South Vietnam). The VCI represented the political and administrative arm of the Communist insurgency in South Vietnam and logistically supported VC operations, recruited new members, and directed terrorist activities against allied forces.

Initially the South Vietnamese intelligence apparatus and elimination forces proved inadequate at gathering intelligence. In May 1967 Robert Komer, whom President Lyndon Johnson chose to oversee pacification efforts in South Vietnam, arrived in Vietnam to head the U.S. Civil Operations and Revolutionary Development Support (CORDS). This organization combined U.S. and Vietnamese civilian and military intelligence and pacification programs and was placed within the Military Assistance Command, Vietnam (MACV), chain of command.

Supervised by CORDS and financially supported by and directed by the U.S. Central Intelligence Agency (CIA), a new program, Intelligence Coordination and Exploitation (ICEX), began building district intelligence and operations coordinating centers (DIOCCs) to collect, disseminate, and forward information to field units. Additional centers were also built at the province level.

In early 1968, questions were raised as to whether the CIA had violated South Vietnamese sovereignty. To justify the legality of ICEX, William Colby, chief of the CIA's Far East Division, sought and obtained a decree signed by President Nguyen Van Thieu formally establishing Phuong Hoang (Phoenix Program), a name chosen because of its symbolic meaning, to assume ICEX operations. ICEX became the deadliest weapon against the VCI. American and South Vietnamese personnel began collecting and analyzing data while concurrently arresting and neutralizing (killing) targeted individuals.

The DIOCCs circulated to every district and province in South Vietnam blacklists of known VCI operatives so that Phoenix forces could arrest and interrogate these individuals. The blacklists consisted of four rankings from A to D, with A being the most wanted. District and province intelligence centers distributed these lists to Phoenix field forces, which would then apprehend or neutralize the individuals. These included Vietnamese units such as the National Police, the National Police Field Force, Provincial Reconnaissance Units, and U.S. Navy Sea Air Land teams (SEALs). If not killed by these units, the targeted individual was transported to a provincial interrogation center (PIC). Intelligence gathered by PIC personnel, consisting of CIA advisers and their Vietnamese counterparts, was then sent for analysis by DIOCC and CORDS officials.

With the advent of Vietnamization and the withdrawal of American personnel, the Phoenix Program suffered. Also, public pressure generated by news reports led to congressional interest in the program. Reporters described Phoenix as nothing more than an assassination program. This culminated in it being one of the programs to come under congressional investigation, and in 1971 Colby, then deputy to the MACV commander for CORDS (and future CIA director), testified before a House committee regarding the Phoenix Program. Another factor in the program's demise was the People's Army of Vietnam (PAVN, North Vietnamese Army) invasion of South Vietnam in the spring of 1972 that forced the South Vietnamese government to focus on conventional rather than unconventional warfare. Thus, in the spring of 1972 the National Police assumed responsibility for Phoenix, and by December 1972 the United States had ended its role in the program.

Despite negative media reports, top-ranking CIA officials as well as leaders of the VC and the Democratic Republic of Vietnam (DRV, North Vietnam) agree that the Phoenix Program was a success. From 1968 to 1972, captured VC numbered around 34,000. Of these, 22,000 rallied to the South Vietnamese government. VC killed numbered some 26,000.

Proof of the Phoenix Program's success could be seen in Quang Tri Province during the 1972 Spring (Easter) Offensive. For the first time there were front lines, behind which civilians and troops could move freely at night. Most bridges in rear areas did not have to be guarded as in the past. And when Communist forces took northern Quang Tri Province, they were unable to find trustworthy sympathizers at the village level.

R. Blake Dunnavent

See also Civil Operations and Revolutionary Development Support; Colby, William Egan; Komer, Robert William; Pacification

Further Reading

Andradé, Dale. *Ashes to Ashes: The Phoenix Program and the Vietnam War.* Lanham, MD: Lexington Books, 1990.

Colby, William, with James McCargar. *Lost Victory: A Firsthand Account of America's Sixteen-Year Involvement in Vietnam.* Chicago: Contemporary Books, 1989.

DeForest, Orrin, and David Chanoff. *Slow Burn: The Rise and Bitter Fall of American Intelligence in Vietnam.* New York: Simon and Schuster, 1990.

Herrington, Stuart A. *Silence Was a Weapon: The Vietnam War in the Villages; A Personal Perspective.* Novato, CA: Presidio, 1982.

Police Role in Counterinsurgency

Police forces include civil and paramilitary police forces that are not part of the conventional armed forces of a particular country. Police can play an important role in counterinsurgency. With capabilities not replicated in the general armed forces, police have historically been decisive in the success of counterinsurgency operations.

Police have three major functions: maintaining order, enforcing laws, and service. The first two of these are directly related to a counterinsurgency strategy. Police may play their most important role during the insurgency's formative phase as the insurgent leaders organize, build the capacity for violence, and create a political base. In this phase, the police are well placed for broad indicator monitoring (to include weapon and electronic component sales), human and electronic surveillance, and to serve as undercover agents and paid informants. The number of insurgents is relatively small, and their military capability is limited, with the insurgents not yet having the capability of challenging the government directly. The insurgents seek to use violence (including terrorism) and the threat of violence to increase political support and reduce the capability of rivals. The numbers of the police and their tactical capabilities may be sufficient to control the growth of the insurgency if they are effectively employed.

Examples of police forces effectively controlling budding insurgent movements can be seen in the German Federal Police suppressing the Red Army Faction (Baader-Meinhof) movement and the Italian Carabinieri combating the Red Brigades. Both were radical movements that sought to employ violence to establish a political base and advocated the overthrow of the existing government. Although both committed numerous criminal and terrorist acts, neither group was able to challenge government control thanks to effective police work. During this phase of the insurgency, which could extend over a number of years, police forces should be the lead government agency charged with identifying, combating, and destroying an insurgency.

If the police forces are unaware, unavailable, or for some other reason incapable of containing the insurgent movement while it is forming, the insurgents will begin to operate in accordance with the next phase of Maoist revolutionary war strategy, the strategic stalemate. During this phase, the insurgents challenge the institutions and forces of the government directly through the use of guerrilla warfare and terrorism. Police intelligence is vital in identifying and infiltrating the aggressive insurgent forces. Furthermore, the police will be fully engaged in protecting both the government and the civilian population from insurgent attack. The police will likely find themselves under attack by the insurgents. It is critically important that the police be able to survive direct attacks by the insurgents, fight back against them, and simultaneously continue to conduct their law enforcement missions and maintain public order.

As soon as insurgent leaders believe that they have the capability, it is likely that they will order attacks on the police. These serve several purposes, including weakening the police capability, demonstrating the ineffectiveness of the government, and establishing the authority and capability of the insurgents as an alternative to the government. In the Anglo-Irish War of 1919–1921, the Irish Republican Army effectively eliminated the ability of the Royal Irish Constabulary, the government's police force, to control much of rural Ireland as a prelude to a general revolt against British rule.

Police forces must be able to withstand these attacks and continue their mission. If necessary, the government must reinforce police elements under attack with additional police or military forces. As long as the police forces of the counterinsurgency are capable of performing their core missions of maintaining order and enforcing laws, they should remain the lead agency fighting the insurgency. However, if the insurgents are able to erode police capability to the extent that the police cannot continue their core functions, then they should cede the lead role to the military.

During the third, or strategic offensive, period of a Maoist insurgency, police also have an important role to play in support of military operations. As the military forces clear an area of insurgents, the police must be immediately available to fill in and establish law and order and maintain public order. The Iraqi National Police played such a role in the insurgency that followed the Iraq War (2003–2011). As U.S., coalition, and Iraqi Army troops cleared areas of Iraq of insurgents, the Iraqi National Police established police stations and government control. This allowed the limited military forces to move to another area and begin operations there. The police presence frees military forces for subsequent operations, allows the normal process of governance to proceed, and signifies a return to the peaceful conduct of social and economic activity.

Police operations are a valuable metric of success or failure in a counterinsurgency. The ability of the police to continue to conduct normal police operations is a strong indicator of a weak insurgency. The absence of police, the inability of the police to conduct normal police operations, or the replacement or reinforcement of the police by military forces are all indicators of a strong insurgency. The return of police operations after disruption and the replacement of military forces by police are both indicators of counterinsurgency success.

In addition to their general role in counterinsurgency strategy, police forces bring unique tactical capabilities to counterinsurgency. Local police forces have detailed knowledge of local population characteristics, the terrain, and cultural, ethnic, and political issues that directly relate to the counterinsurgency mission. During American counterinsurgency operations in the Philippines, the indigenous police force, the Philippine Constabulary, played an important role in identifying and isolating insurgents from the general population. Police intelligence files, documenting many years of operations at a local level, are extremely important in counterinsurgency operations. During the Algerian War (1954–1962), the French military made extensive use of existing French police intelligence on the population to aid their counterinsurgency effort and win the 1957 Battle of Algiers. Police intelligence-gathering capabilities, including networks of sources and informers as well as covert operatives, are important. This was a key capability that the Royal Ulster Constabulary contributed to the British government's operations against the Irish Republican Army in Northern Ireland during 1969–1998. Police investigative and forensic capabilities are not typically found in the armed forces. For example, during American operations in Iraq, the Federal Bureau of Investigation played an important role in analyzing improvised explosive device designs. These types of police capabilities are vital to analyzing and finding insurgents in the early days of an insurgency and also play a role when several different insurgent organizations may be operating simultaneously in the same area.

The police are vital in the success of counterinsurgency operations. They must therefore be fully integrated into any national counterinsurgency strategy. Their unique capabilities are necessary to the success of counterinsurgency tactics, and they have been decisive in the success of counterinsurgency operations. Most important, the police have a cultural and political legitimacy that military forces, particularly foreign military forces, do not have among the indigenous population, which is the center of gravity of counterinsurgency strategy.

Louis A. DiMarco

See also Algerian War; Algiers, Battle of; Black and Tans and the Auxiliaries; Irish Republican Army; Mao Zedong; Philippine Constabulary; Philippine Islands and U.S. Pacification during the Philippine-American War; Royal Irish Constabulary; Urban Guerrilla Warfare

Further Reading

Anderson, David. *Policing and Decolonization: Nationalism, Politics, and the Police, 1917–1965.* Edited by David Killingray. New York: Manchester University Press, 1992.

Leeson, D. M. *The Black and Tans: British Police and Auxiliaries in the Irish War of Independence, 1920–1921.* New York: Oxford University Press, 2011.

Politicization of Armed Forces

As with conventional wars, counterinsurgencies can have profound impact on the armed forces involved. An unsuccessful counterinsurgency may lead to the politicization of the armed forces and an attempt by them to seize power. The two most prominent examples of this in the second half of the 20th century are undoubtedly France and Portugal.

In the case of France, French forces had fought a long eight-year insurgency in Indochina during 1946–1954. The fighting was never popular in France, and no draftees were ever sent to Indochina. Instead, the war was waged on the French side by the professional soldiers and officers, assisted by colonial troops. Embittered French Army professionals came to believe that the government had never invested sufficient men and resources to win the war. Then, following defeat in the 1954 Battle of Dien Bien Phu, the politicians shifted the blame onto the military and extracted France from the war in the Geneva Accords that summer.

The French professional army was then almost immediately transferred to Algeria to fight the insurgency begun by the Front de Libération Nationale (FLN, National Liberation Front) in late 1954. The army was determined that it would not be sold out again. The professional soldiers came to see the insurgents as the tools of international communism and became convinced that they, not the politicians in France, understood the true threat facing France and the West.

When it appeared that the leaders of the Fourth Republic were about to give up the fight and enter into negotiations to grant Algeria independence, the professional officers staged a putsch in May 1958. With the bulk of the army now in Algeria, their threat to invade the metropole had to be taken seriously and led to Charles de Gaulle returning to power as the last premier of the Fourth Republic and ultimately to a new constitution for the Fifth Republic with de Gaulle as president.

Although de Gaulle asserted that Algeria would remain French, he gradually ruled out other options and determined that independence was the only viable option. This led in 1961 to an attempted repeat of 1958 led by General Raoul Salan, which in any case did not involve the conscripts and was supported only by a minority of the professionals. De Gaulle was able to crush the revolt. Some of the diehards then formed the Organisation de l'Armée Secrète (OAS, Secret Army Organization). Its leaders sought to create instability in Algeria, and the OAS inflicted considerable bloodshed as its death squads assassinated opponents. The OAS subsequently carried the violence to France itself and attempted to assassinate de Gaulle. De Gaulle escaped death, however, and stood firm. Algeria secured independence in 1962.

Ironically, it was the reverse in Portugal, where the army seized power to end the colonial wars. In the 1960s, Portugal faced pressing problems but could not deal with these because it was spending half of its annual budget trying to retain its overseas empire. Fighting began in Angola in 1961, in Guinea in 1963, and in Mozambique in 1964. Ultimately, the Portuguese committed 140,000 troops to the struggle.

In 1968 a disabling stroke forced longtime Portuguese strongman António de Oliveira Salazar to yield power. His successor, Marcelo Caetano, introduced some domestic reforms, but the colonial wars continued, and on the morning of April 25, 1974, in Lisbon, a group of young army officers with no clear political program overthrew the conservative-authoritarian regime. The coup was called the Revolução dos Cravos (Carnation Revolution) because of the prevalence of red carnations worn by the populace, who convinced the forces not to resist. The revolution marked the end of the longest-lived authoritarian regime in Western Europe.

Those responsible for the revolution had fought in the colonies. Poorly compensated, they had also been forced to fight with inferior equipment against guerrillas who were often armed with modern Soviet weapons. Such factors led the disgruntled officers to form the Movimento das Forces Armadas (MFA, Armed Forces Movement). Its political views were shaped by contact with disgruntled Portuguese university students forced to serve in the army and by captured African guerrilla leaders. The MFA came to believe in the need for a thorough change in Portuguese society and leadership. Surprisingly, this was a revolution against the colonial wars, for the MFA was convinced that the army could not win these and indeed would be blamed for the defeats.

The Carnation Revolution brought to power General António de Spinola, the recently dismissed deputy chief of staff who had openly proposed a political democratization of Portugal and an end to the costly colonial wars. His book *Portugal and the Future* (1974), published without military authorization, provided the theoretical justification for the revolution, although Spinola did not participate in it. The revolution was also unusual in that only five people died in it, two of them accidentally. Certainly, the revolutionaries enjoyed overwhelming national support in Portugal.

The new Portuguese leaders immediately moved to divest the nation of its overseas empire. By the end of 1975, Portugal had granted independence to its African colonies as well as to Portuguese Timor in the Indonesian Archipelago.

Spencer C. Tucker

See also Algerian War; Angolan Insurgency; East Timor; Guinea Insurgency; Indochina War; Mozambique Insurgency; Organisation de l'Armée Secrète; Salan, Raoul Albin-Louis

Further Reading

Martin, Michel L. *Warriors to Managers: The French Miulitary Establishment since 1945*. Chapel Hill: University of North Carolina Press, 1981.

Porch, Douglas. *The Portuguese Armed Forces and the Revolution*. Stanford, CA: Hoover Institution Press, 1977.

Pol Pot

Birth Date: May 25, 1928
Death Date: April 15, 1998

Cambodian Communist revolutionary leader who gained international infamy as the architect of genocidal policies against his own people. Pol Pot was born Saloth Sar of ethnic Khmer parents in the village of Prek Sbau near the provincial capital of Kompong Thom on May 25, 1928. Although Sar attempted to conceal his background and claimed to have been a poor peasant, his father had been a prosperous farmer and landowner, and the family had connections with the Laotian royal family.

In the mid-1930s Sar and an older brother went to live in Phnom Penh. Sar spent several months at a Buddhist monastery, where he became literate in the Khmer language. During 1942–1947 he attended the College Norodom Sihanouk. He then studied carpentry at the École Technique. In 1949 he continued his education at the École Française de Radio-Electricité in Paris, where he joined the French Communist Party, probably in 1952.

Returning to Cambodia in 1953, Sar joined the anti-French Vietnamese-dominated underground movement and the secret Communist Party. During the next decade he taught history and geography in a private school and emerged as a well-known left-wing journalist. In 1960 he was elected a member of the Central Committee of the party, and in 1963 he became secretary-general; he was reelected to that post in 1971 and 1976. Distrusting Prince Norodom Sihanouk's 1963 invitation to join a new government, Sar—now known as Brother Secretary or Brother Number One—fled into the jungles and organized the Khmer Rouge (Red Khmer), a Communist guerrilla army, and commenced an insurgency against the Cambodian government.

In March 1970 General Lon Nol seized power in Cambodia. After visiting the Democratic Republic of Vietnam (DRV, North Vietnam) and the People's Republic of China in 1969 and 1970, Sar became military commander of the Cambodian Communist component of the National Front, the Sihanouk-led government-in-exile that sought to overthrow Lon Nol's regime, which was supported by the United States.

The ensuing five-year insurgency provided Sar the opportunity to increase his military power but also the chance to devote attention to political matters and organizational development. These contributed greatly to the Khmer Rouge military victory and the seizure of Phnom Penh on April 16, 1975.

From 1976 to 1978, Sar, now going by Pol Pot, was the prime minister of Democratic Kampuchea (the new name of Cambodia). He envisioned an agricultural utopia populated by the new Cambodian collectivist man. Declaring the Year Zero, the Khmer Rouge emptied the city of Phnom Penh and turned the country into one vast concentration camp, with the population serving as rural forced labor. Khmer Rouge actions obliterated the middle class, with its intellectuals and professionals. As many as 2 million Cambodians died, some 25 percent of the population.

One source quotes Pol Pot in 1977 as saying that "although a million lives have been wasted, our party does not feel sorry." In December 1978 following border fighting between Khmer Rouge forces and troops of the Socialist Republic of Vietnam (SRV), the People's Army of Vietnam (PAVN, North Vietnamese Army) invaded Cambodia and defeated the Khmer Rouge. The SRV then established the People's Republic of Kampuchea.

In 1979 Pol Pot received sanctuary in Thailand, and the Khmer Rouge used that country as the base for a new insurgency, first against the Vietnamese-installed government in Phnom Penh and later to attempt to sabotage a peace plan and an election brokered by the United Nations.

In September 1985 the Khmer Rouge faction of the Kampuchean coalition government announced that Pol Pot was relinquishing command of the rebel army then battling the Vietnamese. Pol Pot's subsequent location, exact role in the Khmer Rouge, and even whether he remained alive were the subjects of much speculation. Then in late July 1997 he at last surfaced, the centerpiece in a show trial in western Cambodia by the Khmer Rouge leadership. Found guilty, he was sentenced to life under house arrest. His trial was probably the result of the murder the month before of another Khmer Rouge leader and his family on Pol Pot's orders. Fearing for their own lives, the remaining leaders arrested Pol Pot and held him. Pol Pot spent his last months in a small wooden shack near the Thai border in the Dangrek Mountains region. He died in his sleep on April 15, 1998, reportedly of a heart attack. However, no autopsy was conducted, and he may have been murdered.

Paul S. Daum and Joseph Ratner

See also Cambodia, Vietnamese Occupation of; Khmer Rouge

Further Reading

Chandler, David P. *Brother Number One: A Political Biography of Pol Pot.* Boulder, CO: Westview, 1992.

Short, Philip. *Pol Pot: Anatomy of a Nightmare.* New York: Holt, 2004.

Pontiac's Rebellion

Start Date: 1763
End Date: 1766

Native American insurgency that followed the French and Indian War (1754–1763). Pontiac's Rebellion, also known as Pontiac's War and Pontiac's Uprising, was named for the principal native leader, Ottawa chief Pontiac (also known as Obwandiyng).

The conflict sprang from the defeat of the French. Most Native Americans had allied themselves with the French against the English in the French and Indian War. Indeed, the alliance between the French and natives had been both long-standing and warm as well as beneficial to both sides. Many Frenchmen lived among the natives and married native women. French policies toward the natives were also far more benign than were those of the English.

The reason for the benevolent attitude of the government of New France toward the natives is obvious. Vastly outnumbered by the English colonists, the European settlers of New France desperately needed Native American support in times of war. That the arrangement worked can be seen in the fact that most Native Americans had fought with the French against the English. It was therefore most disquieting to Native Americans of the Great Lakes and Ohio Valley regions to have their long-standing friends depart and be replaced by their enemies. As early as 1761, the Senecas of New York had circulated a wampum belt calling for the formation of a confederation to continue the armed struggle against the British. Although the appeal elicited little response, it was indicative of the widespread native discontent.

The formation of Native American policy fell to Major General Jeffery Amherst, British commander in chief in North America. Amherst thought little of the natives and did not understand the need for policies that would allay their fears and win their friendship. Although George Croghan and Sir William Johnson, two men with wide knowledge of native affairs, sought to dissuade him, Amherst raised the price of trade goods and ended the long-standing French practice of native gift giving. These decisions outraged and deeply offended many native peoples and made armed conflict virtually inevitable. By the spring of 1763, natives from western New York to the Illinois River were preparing for war.

Two Native Americans had a decided influence on subsequent events. The first was the Delaware mystic Neolin, known as the Delaware Prophet. In part influenced by Christianity, Neolin preached a nativist religion that called on his people to reform their habits and also break off relations with the Europeans and return to the ways of their forefathers. Neolin had an immense influence on the native peoples of the Great Lakes region.

The second individual was Ottawa leader Pontiac. Having decided that the time had come to oust the British from the region, he called for a meeting of Native American leaders, and in April 1763 the Great Lakes nations sent representatives to a place near Detroit on the Ecorse River.

For about a month, the natives discussed the course of action to be followed. Pontiac assured them that the time for action was at hand. For practical reasons, Pontiac told the emissaries that Neolin's teachings regarding Europeans did not include the French, who were to be left alone. It was the British and the few natives allied with them who were to be attacked and annihilated. After the native representatives had reached an agreement to go to war, they returned to their villages to build support there. Each native group was assigned certain military objectives to fulfill.

The British military presence was concentrated at Fort Detroit in the Great Lakes area and at Fort Pitt in the Ohio Valley. Another dozen smaller posts were scattered throughout the region. Pontiac himself took responsibility for the reduction of Detroit, while in semicoordinated attacks, warriors of various nations were to attack the other frontier outposts.

On May 7, Pontiac and a large party of warriors entered Fort Detroit. He had arranged with the commander of the post, Major Henry Gladwin, to hold a ceremonial dance there with the plan that once the dance was begun, the natives, who would carry concealed weapons, would fall upon the unsuspecting English. Perhaps forewarned, Gladwin had his men fully armed, and Pontiac called off the attack.

Pontiac then allowed his followers to open hostilities by mounting attacks on those settlers remaining outside the fort. When Gladwin refused a call to surrender the fort, Pontiac initiated what would become the longest North American native siege of a fortified position.

While the siege of Detroit went forward, the natives enjoyed success elsewhere. On May 16 warriors secured Fort Sandusky, on May 27 they captured Fort Miami (near present-day Fort Wayne, Indiana), and on June 2 in the last surprise attacks on English garrisons, they took Fort Michilimackinac in the far north.

In a two-week span, the natives had taken eight British forts. These included Fort St. Joseph (Niles, Michigan), Fort Ouiatenon (Lafayette, Indiana), Fort Venango

(Franklin, Pennsylvania), Fort Le Boeuf (Waterford, Pennsylvania), and Fort Presque Isle (Erie, Pennsylvania), all of which had been held by fewer than 30 men each. The British abandoned Fort Burd and Fort Edward Augustus. Forts Pitt, Ligonier, and Bedford were all attacked but held out, as did Fort Detroit.

On May 28, a British force of 96 men in 10 bateaux under Lieutenant Abraham Cuyler put in to Point Pelee on the western end of Lake Erie on their way from Niagara to Detroit with supplies, only to come under surprise native attack. Cuyler and only a handful of his men survived, escaping in two bateaux.

Attacks after mid-June 1763 confronted a now-alert British military. Various Native Americans, including but not limited to the Senecas, Mingos, Shawnees, Delawares, and Wyandots, assaulted the string of forts leading to Detroit and the roads that supplied it.

Depiction of the surrender of Native Americans in November 1764 during Pontiac's Rebellion (1763–1766). The Indians are shown relinquishing their British captives to British Colonel Henry Bouquet. The war ended only in July 1766 when Pontiac agreed to the Treaty of Oswego. (Library of Congress)

Detroit was the key, but victory there eluded the natives. Pontiac led a coalition of Ojibwas, Potawatomis, Wyandots, and Ottawas in a loose siege. Although the natives could block access to the fort by land, they could not do so on the water, and the schooner *Huron* and the sloop *Michigan* were able to reach Detroit and resupply it. Pontiac ordered fire rafts floated down the Detroit River into the anchored ships, but the ships were moved in time to avoid destruction. A native attempt to board the ships and take them by storm was discovered and beaten back. In November, a frustrated Pontiac ended the siege and withdrew his forces to the Maumee River.

The British were not idle. Soon reinforcements were on their way to the Northwest. Able British colonel Henry Bouquet led 400 men from Fort Niagara to relieve Fort Pitt, which had been under considerable native pressure. Its commander, Simeon Ecuyer, refused to yield to Delaware demands for surrender and reportedly sent smallpox-infected clothing among the natives that led to an epidemic.

About 30 miles from Fort Pitt, Bouquet's relief column came under heavy attack by a large force of Delawares, Wyandots, Mingos, and Shawnees. In the Battle of Bushy Run (August 5–6, 1763), Bouquet's men drove off the attackers and marched on to Fort Pitt, relieving it.

The Battle of Bushy Run was the turning point in the struggle. Although sporadic warfare continued into 1766, isolated native groups began to conclude peace with the British. Pontiac himself eventually recognized the hopelessness of his position and made peace in August 1765. A formal peace was concluded in July 1766.

Sarah E. Miller and Spencer C. Tucker

Further Reading

Dowd, Gregory Evans. *War under Heaven: Pontiac, the Indian Nations and the British Empire.* Baltimore: Johns Hopkins University Press, 2002.

Nester, William R. *Haughty Conquerors: Amherst and the Great Indian Uprising of 1763.* Westport, CT: Praeger, 2000.

Peckham, Howard H. *Pontiac and the Indian Uprising.* Princeton, NJ: Princeton University Press, 1947.

Popé

Birth Date: Unknown
Death Date: 1688

Spiritual leader from San Juan Pueblo, near present-day Santa Fe, New Mexico, and leader of one of the most effective Native American revolts in North American history. There are no detailed written or oral accounts of Popé's birth or early life. He first appears in the historical record in the early 17th century, when Spanish colonists strove to gain control over the northern provinces of New Spain.

The repressive policies of the Spaniards toward the Pueblo peoples drove Popé (El Popé) into the path of rebellion. Worst of all for Popé was the effort by Franciscan friars to eradicate Pueblo religious icons and ceremonies. Popé preached the maintenance of traditional religious practices and railed against all things Spanish and Christian.

As Popé's message spread throughout the Pueblo settlements, in 1675 Governor Juan Francisco Treviño ordered the arrest of native spiritual leaders and medicine men in the province of New Mexico. Popé and 46 other medicine men were taken by force to the capital in Santa Fe and charged with witchcraft. Four were condemned to death, although 1 committed suicide before the sentence could be carried out. The remainder were whipped and imprisoned.

These Spanish actions led to the threat of revolt by the Rio Grande Pueblos, prompting a worried Treviño to release his captives. Later in 1675, Popé returned first to San Juan Pueblo and then fled to Taos Pueblo after having been implicated in the stoning death of his son-in-law and the governor of the pueblo, whom Popé suspected was spying for the Spanish. At Taos, Popé devised plans for a widespread revolt, successfully overcoming obstacles created by distance and language barriers to unify at least 24 pueblos in a coordinated revolt against the Spanish in early August 1680.

The Pueblo Revolt began on August 10, 1680. Approximately 8,000 of Popé's followers killed nearly 400 Spanish colonists and 21 of the 33 Franciscan friars in the region. Those Spaniards who were not killed or wounded initially fled southward toward El Paso del Norte and Mexico.

Following his successful revolt, Popé ordered the destruction of the remaining vestiges of Spanish culture, including objects associated with Christianity. He likewise banned the use of the Spanish language and Spanish surnames and annulled marriages consecrated by the Catholic Church, insisting on a return to traditional cultural practices.

Exulting in his victory, Popé chose to remain in Santa Fe and reside in the former governor's palace. He soon became overbearing, demanding tribute payments from all the pueblos and punishing those that refused to comply. As Popé's authoritarianism increased his support eroded, and the alliance collapsed as villages returned to their familiar practice of autonomy. When Popé died sometime in 1688, probably in Santa Fe, the stage was set for the Spanish to reconquer New Mexico.

Alan C. Downs

See also Pueblo Revolt

Further Reading

Beninato, Stephanie. "Popé, Pose-yema, and Naranjo: A New Look at the Leadership in the Pueblo Revolt of 1680." *New Mexico Historical Review* 65 (October 1990): 417–435.

Josephy, Alvin M., Jr. *The Patriot Chiefs: A Chronicle of American Indian Resistance.* New York: Penguin, 1989.

Knaut, Andrew L. *The Pueblo Revolt of 1680: Conquest and Resistance in Seventeenth-Century New Mexico.* Norman: University of Oklahoma Press, 1995.

Popular Front for the Liberation of the Occupied Arabian Gulf

Insurgent group in Oman that opposed the rule of reactionary Oman Said bin Taimur, sultan of Oman from 1932 to 1970. Initially known as the Dhofar Liberation Front (DLF) and led by Mussalim bin Nufl, the group enjoyed the support of Ghalib bin Ali, the exiled imam (religious leader) of Oman who claimed power himself. British forces had assisted the sultan in crushing the imam's revolt in Jebel Akhdar in 1955, but Saudi Arabia, which had its own claims on part of Oman, supported him, as did Egyptian leader Gamal Abdel Nasser, who regarded British interference in the region as a threat to Arab nationalism.

Thus, in June 1957 the exiled Ghalib bin Ali led a new revolt against the sultan. Following major fighting near Nizwa on July 15, 1957, Said requested British military assistance. This aid, mostly in the form of air support, enabled him to crush the revolt by mid-August. An effort by Arab states in the United Nations to censure the British for their intervention failed to win approval. In 1958, meanwhile, Said sold the port city and district of Gwadar on the Arabian Sea in coastal Balochistan to Pakistan.

In 1962 the DLF began a sabotage campaign and then in June 1965 led a revolt in the Omani province of Dhofar. Britain's decision to withdraw from Aden in 1967 led to the creation of the Marxist People's Republic of South Yemen, which was quick to support the revolt in Dhofar. At a DLF Congress in August 1968, however, the nationalist leadership led by Mussalim was ousted by hard-line Marxists, and the DLF became the Popular Front for the Liberation of the Occupied Arabian Gulf (PFLOAG), which in 1971 became the Popular Front for the Liberation of Oman and the Arabian Gulf.

The PFLOAG secured arms from China and the Soviet Union, and some of its members received military training in the Democratic People's Republic of Korea (DPRK, North Korea). The PFLOAG then made steady gains in western Dhofar, but on July 23, 1970, Said was overthrown by his progressive-minded son, Qaboos bin Said al-Said. Qaboos pledged to apply his country's considerable oil wealth for the benefit of his people and called on the British for support. They responded with the Special Air Service. The resultant comprehensive counterinsurgency program included a hearts-and-minds component and amnesty for the rebels. At the same time, government forces and the British worked to cut rebel resupply. Aircraft proved to be a major asset, as did aid from Iran.

From a peak of some 2,000 active fighters and 3,000 militia in 1968, the PFLOAG declined to about 800 activists and 1,000 militia by 1974. In August 1974 the PFLOAG divided into the Popular Front for the Liberation of Oman (PFLO) and the Popular Front for the Liberation of Bahrain (PFLOB). Omani government forces made steady gains, and the insurgency was declared at an end in January 1976, although isolated incidents continued into 1983.

Spencer C. Tucker

See also Dhofar Rebellion; Hearts and Minds; Special Air Service

Further Reading

Beckett, Ian F. W. *Encyclopedia of Guerrilla Warfare.* Santa Barbara, CA: ABC-CLIO, 1999.

Halliday, Fred. *Revolution and Foreign Policy: The Case of South Yemen, 1967–1987.* Cambridge: Cambridge University Press, 1990.

Practice Nine, Project.

See McNamara Line

Program for the Pacification and Long-Term Development of South Vietnam

U.S. pacification program during the Vietnam War (1955–1975). In March 1966, the Army Staff in Washington, D.C., produced a report titled *A Program for the*

Pacification and Long-Term Development of South Vietnam (PROVN). The study originated nearly a year before as the result of a meeting between U.S. Army chief of staff General Harold K. Johnson and Vietnam specialist Bernard Fall in April 1965. To his chagrin, Johnson discovered that many of the facts given him by his staff about Vietnam were incorrect.

Already concerned about the worsening situation in Southeast Asia—the United States had just begun sending ground combat troops into Vietnam—Johnson returned from the meeting determined not only to learn the facts but also to formulate proposals for winning the conflict in Vietnam. In June he formed a small team of talented midlevel officers and assigned them the task of developing new courses of action in South Vietnam that would help accomplish U.S. aims and objectives. Assembling in July, the team produced the *PROVN* report the following spring.

The study indicted the U.S. government for failing to create a unified and well-coordinated program for eliminating the insurgency in the Republic of Vietnam (RVN, South Vietnam). *PROVN* argued that pacification—establishing control over and winning the support of the population—was the essence of the problem and that all actions ultimately had to serve it. The report criticized certain aspects of the way in which the war was being fought, urged that military operations focus on securing the population from guerrilla intimidation, and pressed the United States to play a more direct role in overseeing internal affairs in South Vietnam. Finally, *PROVN* called for the United States to overhaul its administrative machinery in South Vietnam by placing all of its pacification efforts under a single manager.

Little of what *PROVN* had to say was new. Most of the shortcomings it identified, the principles it formulated, and the solutions it proposed could be found in prior reports, national policy statements, and U.S. Army doctrine as written in field manuals, taught in army schools and implemented by commander of U.S. forces in Vietnam General William C. Westmoreland.

Recognizing the threat posed by the enemy's powerful combat units, *PROVN* embraced Westmoreland's strategy of attrition and his decision to focus most of the U.S. Army's energies against Communist main force units. The report likewise relegated primary responsibility for pacification and population security to the South Vietnamese. Shortcomings notwithstanding, the report concluded that "few changes in U.S. doctrine are needed."

PROVN's most radical suggestions pertained to political and diplomatic rather than strictly military matters. First, the authors suggested that the United States move beyond persuasion to employ coercion or unilateral action to compel the South Vietnamese government to take actions that U.S. advisers had long sought but that the Vietnamese had resisted. Second, the report recommended that the United States aim not just to reform but also to revolutionize Vietnamese sociopolitical life. This recommendation was tempered by disagreement among the authors as to the degree to which the United States should meddle in Vietnamese internal affairs. Finally, the report joined Westmoreland and many other commentators in criticizing the disjointed manner in which the U.S. and South Vietnamese governments were managing the war. With regard to the United States, the report suggested that all civil and military programs related to pacification be placed under a single civilian official responsible to the ambassador.

Despite having reservations about some of the specifics, Westmoreland argued that these details "should not detract from the overall value of PROVN." Rather, he informed the Joint Chiefs of Staff that the study offered an "excellent overall approach" to defeat the Communist insurgency, and he recommended that the Defense Department forward the document to the White House's National Security Council, where the many policy and interagency questions could be hammered out.

In the end, the U.S. government undertook few of *PROVN*'s specific actions. The fact that the report did not become the blueprint that its authors had hoped should not obscure its significance. The report accurately cataloged the many problems that had bedeviled the war effort and provided additional grist for those who already believed that the U.S. government needed to better integrate the political and military aspects of its activities in Vietnam. *PROVN* was thus part of the general movement—long supported by the U.S. military but generally opposed by the civilian bureaucracies—toward achieving such an integration. Eventually in 1967 President Lyndon B. Johnson dictated the integration not by following the report's recommendation but instead by placing the execution of most civil programs involved with pacification under military control in the guise of the office of Civil Operations and Revolutionary Development (CORDS). Thereafter coordination improved, and both General Creighton W. Abrams, who succeeded Westmoreland as military commander in Vietnam, and Robert W. Komer, the first head of CORDS, expressed their gratitude for the study and implemented some of its ideas.

PROVN's emphasis on a holistic approach to counterinsurgency mirrored U.S. Army doctrine and the policies that the U.S. government had long espoused. The close integration of military operations—both large and small—and political actions was indeed of vital importance, as it is in most counterinsurgency situations. The primary obstacles to achieving greater integration stemmed not from difficulties in conceptualization but instead from bureaucratic parochialism and the political and military realities on the ground. Over time, coordination of the politico-military effort became smoother and the pacification situation improved, thanks in large part to the battlefield defeats suffered by Communist main force units in 1968 and 1969. The sociopolitical revolution that *PROVN*'s authors espoused, on the other hand, never occurred. Whether victory could have been achieved had such a revolution taken place is doubtful. As important as was pacification, *PROVN*'s belief that the outcome of the war would be determined in the villages of South Vietnam and in the hearts of their inhabitants proved to be incorrect. In Vietnam, large-scale military operations were responsible for both laying the groundwork that made progress in pacification possible (as *PROVN* admitted) and determining the final outcome in 1975. As *PROVN* had recognized, the allies' first task was to eliminate the enemy's main force threat. The ultimate failure to achieve this goal, thanks largely to the presence of external sanctuaries, and the triumph of North Vietnam's will over that of America's, ultimately doomed South Vietnam.

Andrew J. Birtle

See also Abrams, Creighton Williams, Jr.; Civil Operations and Revolutionary Development Support; Fall, Bernard B.; Komer, Robert William; Westmoreland, William Childs

Further Reading

Birtle, Andrew J. "PROVN, Westmoreland, and the Historians: A Reappraisal." *Journal of Military History* 72 (October 2008): 1213–1247.

Cosmas, Graham A. *MACV: The Joint Command in the Years of Escalation, 1962–1967.* Washington, DC: U.S. Army Center of Military History, 2006.

Propaganda

Methods used by governments or organized groups to influence public opinion, attitudes, and actions in order to benefit the sponsor. The word "propaganda" was coined by the Catholic Church in 1622 with the establishment in that year of the Sacra Congregatio Christiano Nomini Propagando (Congregation for Propagation of the Faith), charged with the spread of Christianity and the regulation of ecclesiastical affairs in non-Catholic countries. Although the term "propaganda" carries a negative connotation today largely because of propaganda efforts such as those of the National Socialists in Germany in World War II (1939–1945), the term certainly can have a positive connotation as well. Propaganda may include printed matter, advertisements, radio, television, and the Internet.

Propaganda is extremely important to insurgent groups and to governments mounting counterinsurgency efforts in order to win the hearts and minds of the civilian population. Insurgents employ propaganda to spread their ideological message and garner support while diminishing that of the government. To much the same ends, governments use propaganda to illustrate their determination to prevail and also to secure international support.

Propaganda employed by insurgents might take the form of oaths and rituals, as with the Mau Mau in the Kenya Emergency (1952–1960); leaflets; and the extortion of money, often through kidnappings as in the case of many Latin American insurgencies, that is then used to buy food for the poor. Brazilian Carlos Marighella, a principal theorist of urban guerrilla warfare, described his methods as "armed propaganda." Terror tactics, including the targeting of specific individuals, might also be considered a form of propaganda, designed to influence wider public opinion.

Governments have relied extensively on leaflets to distribute their propaganda. They have also used coverage of specific programs that benefit the targeted civilian population, as in the case of government land grants during the Huk Insurgency (1946–1954).

Biff L. Baker and Spencer C. Tucker

See also Hearts and Minds; Marighella, Carlos

Further Reading

Benigni, U. *The Catholic Encyclopedia.* New York: Robert Appleton, 1911.

Carruthers, Susan. *Winning Hearts and Minds.* Leicester, UK: Leicester University Press, 1998.

Lennon, Alexander T. *The Battle for Hearts and Minds: Using Soft Power to undermine Terrorist Networks.* Cambridge, MA: MIT Press, 2003.

Pseudoforces

Psuedoforces are military units made up of former insurgents who have been turned to work with counterinsurgency forces against their former colleagues. This is possible because insurgent rank and filers are generally not as committed as their ideologically bound leaders. Pseudoforces are a tremendous advantage in counterinsurgency operations. They can identify certain of the insurgents, are well familiar with the operational terrain and the villagers, and understand what motivates the insurgents and their supporters. They are of immense importance.

Pseudoforces have played a role in virtually every insurgency since World War II (1939–1945). The British employed some surrendered enemy personnel (SEPs) during the Malayan Emergency (1948–1960), but it was primarily British Army captain Frank Kitson, who served in Kenya during 1953–1955 in the Kenya Emergency (1952–1960), who was responsible for the creation of pseudoforces. In his subsequent book, *Gangs and Counter-Gangs* (1960), Kitson used the term "gangs" to describe the Mau Mau insurgents of the Kikuyu tribe, whom he fought during the Kenya Emergency. Part of the counterinsurgency solution was to create and train countergangs. Members of these countergangs were inserted in small teams. Their primary advantage was that they were indistinguishable from the Mau Mau.

In the Chieu Hoi program during the Vietnam War, the government of the Republic of Vietnam (RVN, South Vietnam) and the United States encouraged Viet Cong (Vietnamese Communists) insurgents to surrender and subsequently turned a number of them to fight on the RVN side during the Vietnam War. During the Dhofar campaigns in Oman (1970–1975), the British made extensive use of pseudoforces, employing some 1,600 in 21 different units based on tribal affiliations. The Portuguese also made extensive use of pseudoforces during the insurgencies in their African territories. Notable among these were the Flechas ("Arrows") in Angola.

When the Portuguese pulled out of Mozambique in 1974, Mozambique became a sanctuary for the Zimbabwe African National Union (ZANU) and its military arm, the Zimbabwe African National Liberation Army (ZANLA). At this point the British Special Air Service and the Selous Scouts changed their tactics from hit-and-run raids into the sanctuaries to tactics that also employed pseudoforces. The pseudoforces in Rhodesia proved to be a highly important addition to the Selous Scouts. Typically, the pseudoforces in Rhodesia dressed as if they were ZANLA regulars and employed local vehicles. This enabled them to penetrate insurgent safe areas in Mozambique with relative impunity.

Donald A. MacCuish and Spencer C. Tucker

See also Angolan Insurgency; Chieu Hoi Program; Dhofar Rebellion; Kenya Emergency; Kitson, Sir Frank; Malayan Emergency; Mau Mau; Mozambique Insurgency; Rhodesian Bush War; Selous Scouts; Zimbabwe African National Union

Further Reading

Baxter, Peter. *Selous Scouts: Rhodesian Counter-Insurgency: Specialists.* Solihull, West Midlands, UK: Helion, 2011.

Beckett, Ian F. W. *Encyclopedia of Guerrilla Warfare.* Santa Barbara, CA: ABC-CLIO, 1999.

Beckett, Ian F. W. *Modern Insurgencies and Counter-Insurgencies: Guerrillas and Their Opponents since 1750.* London: Routledge, 2001.

Kitson, Sir Frank. *Gangs and Counter-Gangs.* London: Barrie and Rockliff, 1960.

Moorecraft, Paul, and Peter McLaughlin. *The Rhodesian War: A Military History.* Barnsley, UK: Pen and Sword Military, 2008.

Pueblo Revolt

Start Date: August 10, 1680
End Date: August 21, 1680

The Spanish conquest of New Mexico began with Francisco Vásquez de Coronado's 1540–1542 quest for the mythical Seven Golden Cities of Cíbola. Intermittent Spanish forays into New Mexico occurred thereafter, although permanent European settlements were not begun until Don Juan de Oñate y Salazar formally established New Mexico in 1598. Franciscan missionaries, eager to convert the sedentary horticulturalists they called Indios de los pueblos (village Indians), soon took up residence in the scattered pueblos.

Relations between the Spanish and the Pueblos took a turn for the worse in 1675, when Governor Juan Francisco Treviño imprisoned 47 Native Americans whom he termed "sorcerers." These men were shamans who were perpetuating their sacred ceremonies. Three of the detainees were executed. Another committed suicide before angry Pueblo warriors forced the zealous governor to release those remaining.

Nearly a century of colonial encroachments, smallpox outbreaks, prolonged drought, forced conversions, demands for tribute, and the suppression of traditional practices led most Pueblos to desire an end to Spanish rule. Popé, a Tewa shaman from San Juan, made this wish reality after experiencing a powerful vision that had followed his 1675 detention.

The Pueblos' plot to drive out the Spanish unfolded on August 9, 1680, when runners carried knotted yucca cords and instructions to two dozen villages as far south as Isleta in New Mexico, a distance of some 400 miles. Tribal leaders receiving the cords were instructed to untie one knot each day until none remained. After the last knot was untied, the warriors would attack the Spanish.

Governor Don Antonio de Otermín learned of the planned uprising from informants. The rebellion was to begin during the night of the new moon and would coincide with the arrival of the triennial Spanish supply caravan dispatched from Mexico City. The governor then ordered the torture of Nicolás Catua and Pedro Omtua, captured runners from Tesuque, for further details. Confident that the uprising would not commence until August 13, 1680, Otermín adopted a strategy of watchful waiting.

After learning that the Spaniards had captured the two Pueblo runners, however, the natives attacked unsuspecting Spanish outposts on August 10, 1680. Otermín responded by dispatching soldiers to subdue the warriors. He also ordered all Spanish colonists to gather within the safe confines of Santa Fe's defenses.

Spanish settlements in northern New Mexico as far west as the Hopi mesas in present-day Arizona felt the fury of war. The uprising claimed the lives of 19 Franciscan friars and 2 assistants. In all, some 380 Spaniards, including women and children, perished. Alonso García, New Mexico's lieutenant governor residing in Ro Abajo, learned of events on August 11. Receiving false reports that all Spanish settlements had been destroyed in the attack and that no colonists had survived, García organized the withdrawal of all remaining Spaniards in the region to El Paso del Norte (present-day Juárez) instead of marching north to the settlers' relief.

Governor Otermín, waiting at Santa Fe for reinforcements that never arrived, prepared for a long siege. Nearly 500 Pueblo warriors attacked the capital of New Mexico on August 15, 1680. Within two days, more than 2,500 Pueblos had joined the fight. Otermín, severely wounded in a desperate counterattack, abandoned Santa Fe on August 21 after the attackers cut off the city's water supply. The Spaniards then withdrew down the Rio Grande Valley.

After the Spanish had departed, Popé and other leaders of the rebellion launched a purification campaign, destroying Catholic churches, statues, and relics. All Pueblos who had received the sacraments were ordered to cleanse themselves by scrubbing their bodies with yucca fibers while bathing in the Rio Grande. Pueblo traditionalists constructed kivas (partially subterranean ceremonial chambers) to replace those destroyed earlier by the Spaniards.

Otermín attempted to reclaim New Mexico for Spain in November 1681, but Pueblo warriors repelled his invading forces. Spain's interest in New Mexico waned until French explorers visited the lower Mississippi River Delta. Eager to secure the Southwest lest it fall to France, Spanish officials dispatched soldiers there in 1688 and 1689. Although unsuccessful, these expeditions revealed fissures in Pueblo civilization. Officials also learned that Ute, Apache, and Navajo raids, combined with drought and famine, had created severe hardship for the Pueblos.

On August 10, 1692, the 12th anniversary of the Pueblo Revolt, Governor Diego José de Vargas vowed to retake New Mexico, and on September 13 a force of 40 Spanish soldiers, 50 Mexican natives, and 2 missionaries reached Santa Fe. Vargas, anxious to assure the defenders that he meant them no harm, pardoned the Pueblo leaders for their past transgressions. Amazingly, the governor eventually entered the city without having to fire a shot. Vargas also visited the outlying pueblos to assure villagers of his desire for peace.

Despite the governor's efforts, violence returned to the region in 1693, when hostile Pueblos recaptured Santa Fe. A furious Vargas retook the city on December 29, 1693, after cutting off the defenders' water supply. The governor's reconquest of New Mexico ended in December 1696, when Vargas secured a lasting peace.

Although the Spanish colonizers and missionaries returned, they had learned an important lesson. After 1696, the villages were allowed to govern themselves, and the missionaries tolerated residents' traditional practices. Thus, the Pueblo Revolt of 1680 had succeeded in ensuring the perpetuation of cherished tribal languages, dances, and ceremonies.

Jon L. Brudvig

See also Popé

Further Reading

Bowden, Henry Warner. "Spanish Missions, Cultural Conflict, and the Pueblo Revolt of 1680." *Church History* 44 (June 1975): 217–228.

Knaut, Andrew L. *The Pueblo Revolt of 1680: Conquest and Resistance in Seventeenth-Century New Mexico.* Norman: University of Oklahoma Press, 1995.

Roberts, David. *The Pueblo Revolt: The Secret Rebellion That Drove the Spanish Out of the Southwest.* New York: Simon and Schuster, 2004.

Pugachev's Rebellion

Start Date: September 17, 1773
End Date: September 15, 1774

Pugachev's Rebellion, the largest popular rebellion in Russian history, was named for its leader, Yemelyan (Emelyan) Ivanovich Pugachev, and resulted from growing tension between the Russian government of Czarina Catherine II (Catherine the Great) and the Yaik Cossacks, who lived in southeastern Russia along the Yalik River in the plain between the southern Ural Mountains and the Caspian Sea. The Yaliks resented the steady expansion of the Russian state eastward and the resulting loss of independence. By 1773, Cossack resentment needed only a spark to explode. This came at an unfortunate time for the Russian government, as Russia was then at war with the Ottoman Empire.

Pugachev provided the spark. A Don Cossack by birth and a deserter from the Russian Army, Pugachev claimed to be Czar Paul III, who had been deposed and murdered a decade earlier. Although he bore little physical resemblance to the dead czar, Pugachev was a charismatic leader who promised the Yaliks reforms and a special place in the Russian state if they would assist him in "regaining" the throne.

On September 17, 1773, Pugachev began the rebellion by leading an attack on and taking the Cossack capital of Yait'sk. Soon he had recruited a large peasant army. The revolt quickly spread to many other non-Russian peoples who had their own grievances against the Russian state and also included peasants who had been forced to work in the Ural iron and copper industry and serfs who saw in the revolt a chance to gain their freedom.

The poorly armed and utterly undisciplined peasants proved to be no match for the Russian Army, however. The end of Russia's war with the Ottoman Empire in July 1774 enabled Catherine to turn her army under General Aleksandr Suvorov against the rebels, then marching on Moscow. Russian troops defeated the rebels at Ufa and Tatishchevo (March 1774), Kazan (July), and Tsaritsyn (August). In the latter battle, some 1,000 Russian troops under Colonel Ivan Ivanovich Mikhelson cornered 12,000 rebels and crushed them.

Pugachev escaped capture, but his followers began to desert, and on September 15, 1774, his own Cossacks delivered him up when he attempted to flee to the Urals. Admitting that he was in fact not the czar, Pugachev was placed in chains in a metal cage and sent to Moscow in a wheeled cart. Tried there and found guilty of treason, he was publically executed on January 10, 1775. In an effort to erase memory of the rebellion, Catherine's government renamed the Yalik Cossacks, the Yalik River, and Yait'sk (respectively, the Ural Cossacks, the Ural River, and Uralsk).

Pugachev's Rebellion had unfortunate consequences for Russia. Wary of yet another peasant uprising, Catherine and her successors embarked on a conservative path and put aside planned reforms, especially efforts to abolish serfdom, a step that they now feared might bring another rebellion.

Spencer C. Tucker

Further Reading

Alexander, John. *Emperor of the Cossacks: Pugachev and the Frontier Jacquerie of 1773–1775.* Lawrence: University Press of Kansas, 1973.

Avrich, P. *Russian Rebels, 1600–1800: Four Great Rebellions Which Shook the Russian State in the Seventeenth and Eighteenth Centuries.* New York: Norton, 1976.

Bodger, Alan. *The Kazakhs and the Pugachev Uprising in Russia, 1773–1775.* Bloomington, IN: Research Institute for Inner Asian Studies, 1988.

Puller, Lewis Burwell

Birth Date: June 26, 1898
Death Date: October 11, 1971

Iconic U.S. Marine Corps general. Born on June 26, 1898, in West Point, Virginia, Lewis Burwell "Chesty" Puller enrolled in the Virginia Military Institute in 1917 but, impatient to participate in World War I (1914–1918), left school to enlist in the U.S. Marine Corps in August 1918. Disappointed not to see World War I service, Puller attended officer candidate school and was commissioned in the reserves in June 1919. Caught in the corps reduction after the war, he was placed on the inactive list but promptly reenlisted as a corporal.

From 1919 to 1924, Puller served in the Haitian gendarmerie as acting first lieutenant. In 1924 on his return to the United States, he was commissioned a second lieutenant. In Nicaragua as a marine first lieutenant and Guardia Nacionale captain during the insurgency of 1927–1934, Puller demonstrated the rapid marching, aggressive tactics, and leading from the front that became his hallmarks. In one notable patrol during September 20–30, 1932, he led 41 men of the Guardia Nacionale in the jungle northeast of Jinotega. The unit covered more than 150 miles, fought four engagements, destroyed 30 camps, and killed 30 insurgents, at a cost to themselves of 2 killed and 4 wounded.

Puller then held assignments in China, was an instructor at the Marine Basic School in Philadelphia, and during 1940–1941 served with the 4th Marine Regiment in Shanghai, where he was promoted to major and battalion commander. Assigned to the 7th Marine Regiment at Camp Lejeune, North Carolina, he became a pioneer in jungle warfare training.

During World War II (1939–1945), Puller distinguished himself with the 7th Marines on Guadalcanal in late 1942, then saw action on New Britain. In September 1944 he commanded the 1st Marine Regiment on Peleliu. In November he returned to the United States for training duty and was promoted to colonel.

When the Korean War (1950–1953) began, Puller led the 1st Marine Regiment in the Inchon Landing of September 1950 and then took part in the Changjin (Chosin) Reservoir Campaign, for which he was awarded his fifth Navy Cross, the most awarded to an individual in U.S. Marine Corps history. He was promoted to brigadier general in January 1951. That May, Puller returned to the United States to command the 3rd Marine Brigade, later redesignated the 3rd Marine Division. Promoted to major general in September 1953, he commanded the 2nd Marine Division. He retired due to disability in November 1955 as a lieutenant general.

Although a competent staff officer, Puller was first and foremost a warrior. During his long career, he won 53 decorations, probably the most in U.S. Marine Corps history. He was also perhaps the most colorful figure in U.S. Marine Corps history. Puller died in Hampton, Virginia, on October 11, 1971.

Spencer C. Tucker

See also Nicaragua Insurgency

Further Reading

Davis, Burke. *Marine! The Life of Lewis B. (Chesty) Puller, USMC (Ret.)*. Boston: Little, Brown, 1962.

Hoffman, Jon T. "Lieutenant General Lewis Burwell Puller." *Marine Corps Gazette* 82(6) (June 1998): 27–30.

Punitive Expedition.

See Mexican Expedition

Q

Qaboos bin Said al-Said

Birth Date: November 18, 1940

Sultan of Oman since 1970. Qaboos bin Said al-Said was born the son of Sultan Said ibn Tamir on November 18, 1940, in Salalah, Province of Dhofar. Qaboos spent seven years in Britain during his youth and attended the Royal Military Academy at Sandhurst. He returned to Oman in 1965, much influenced by Western ideas. As a result, his conservative father placed him under virtual house arrest.

On July 23, 1970, Qaboos, aided by loyal military forces, staged a coup d'état and deposed his father, who then went into exile in Great Britain. Sultan Qaboos then set about trying to modernize his country and bring it into the international political mainstream. As such, he built new roads, extended educational opportunities, and greatly improved medical care. He also defeated the insurgency known as the Dhofar Rebellion (1962–1976) that had been supported by the Soviet Union and its allies in South Yemen. That conflict was finally ended in 1976.

Qaboos maintained strong ties with the United States, sometimes alienating other Arab countries. Indeed, he was one of only two Arab leaders to support the 1978 Camp David Accords signed by Israel and Egypt and brokered by the United States. In 1985 Qaboos began to cultivate relations with the Soviet Union. He also attempted to assume a stronger stance in regional politics. Qaboos brought Oman into the Gulf Cooperation Council and worked hard to stabilize the region in the wake of the Persian Gulf War (1991), which he strongly supported and to which he dispatched troops.

In 1996 Qaboos issued a decree promulgating a new basic law that clarified royal succession, provided for a legislative council and a prime minister, and guaranteed basic civil liberties for Omani citizens. Qaboos, who still rules with an iron hand, holds the positions of prime minister and minister of foreign affairs, defense, and finance. His rule has been fairly progressive, however, especially vis-à-vis Persian Gulf standards, and since 1994 he has appointed numerous women to government posts. Qaboos has also been a cooperative partner in the U.S.-led war on terrorism since September 2001, allowing coalition forces overflight and basing rights. He was less supportive of the Iraq War (2003–2011).

In October 2004 as a result of many of the Qaboos's reforms, which included the institution of universal suffrage in 2003, Oman held its first free elections for the economic advisory council, known as the Shura Majlis Council. Still, Sultan

Qaboos continues to exercise absolute power, and government institutions operate merely in an advisory capacity.

Paul G. Pierpaoli Jr.

See also Dhofar Rebellion

Further Reading

Kechichian, Joseph A. *Oman and the World: The Emergence of an Independent Foreign Policy.* Santa Monica, CA: RAND, 1995.

Owtram, Francis. *A Modern History of Oman: Formation of the State since 1920.* London: I. B. Tauris, 2004.

Quadrillage and *Ratissage*

Key elements in the oil slick (*tache d'huile*) pacification method pursued by French forces during insurgencies in North Africa and Indochina as well as by other states in counterinsurgencies, such as the Americans during the Seminole Wars. The technique involved splitting up the territory to be pacified into grids or squares. Once this gridding (*quadrillage*) had been accomplished, each square was then raked (*ratissage*) by pacification forces familiar with the area. If carried out on a regular basis by a sufficient number of troops, *quadrillage* and *ratissage* could be successful, but French forces during the Indochina War lacked the numbers of men necessary to carry out the pacification technique.

Spencer C. Tucker

See also Algerian War; Indochina War; Seminole Wars; *Tache d'Huile*

Further Reading

Fall, Bernard. *The Two Viet Nams.* Revised ed. New York: Praeger, 1964.

R

Ratissage.

See *Quadrillage* and *Ratissage*

Reconcentrado System

System of population control instituted by Spanish governor-general of Cuba General Valeriano Weyler y Nicolau in February 1896 whereby some half million Cubans were rounded up and placed in *reconcentrado* (reconcentration) centers as part of the Spanish effort to end the Cuban War of Independence (1895–1898).

By 1896, Cuban insurgents, operating in small guerrilla units, were attacking the sugar industry, crippling the Cuban economy. Especially in western Cuba, the insurgents were burning sugarcane fields and mills and destroying railroads, telegraph lines, and other property. The rebels hoped that destroying the Cuban economy would force the Spanish to conclude that it was not worth retaining control of the island.

To check this upsurge in violence and end the rebellion, the Spanish government sent reinforcements to Cuba, but this step produced only limited results. The Spanish attempted to hunt down and confront the insurgents in traditional stand-up battles, but the insurgents refused to cooperate and began conducting irregular warfare. The Spanish Army was unable to adapt to these guerrilla techniques, and conservative Spanish premier Antonio Cánovas del Castillo dispatched Weyler to Cuba in January 1896 to bring an end to the conflict.

Weyler, a professional officer who had risen through the ranks of the Spanish military because of performance rather than politics, worried little about public relations. An attaché to Washington during the American Civil War (1861–1865), he became an advocate of the scorched-earth tactics employed in the Civil War by Major General William Tecumseh Sherman. Weyler set out to break the Cuban independence movement and eliminate popular support for the insurgency through a policy of population control. The program called for removing civilians from their homes and farms and concentrating them in highly fortified towns, thereby breaking the resolve of the detainees as well as the rebels, who relied on the civilians for moral as well as material support.

Gathering the villagers into fortified reconcentration centers would eliminate sources of food and other material support for the insurgents and would also deprive the insurgents of an efficient intelligence network, which had given them valuable information regarding Spanish troop movements. Also, relocating the peasants to the camps would protect them from exposure to insurgent propaganda and would seriously impede insurgent recruitment efforts. Finally, there was also a psychological component to Weyler's system. The insurgents were likely to have friends or relatives among the *reconcentrados,* so the fear that a relative could be targeted for special abuse by the Spanish might intimidate the insurgents and force them to end the fighting.

Upon arriving in Cuba in February 1896, Weyler issued the first of a series of reconcentration orders. Under these, some 500,000 people were removed from their homes and farms and herded into four fortified camps. As the villagers abandoned their homes, the Spanish troops swooped in to burn whole villages, raze crops, and kill livestock to eliminate the rebels' food supply. The economic tactics employed by both the Spanish and the Cubans seriously affected the Cuban economy, as foreign trade plummeted.

The camps were in most cases surrounded by high fences, and housing accommodations were extremely limited. More often than not, the detainees were jammed into abandoned warehouses, tents, or dilapidated buildings without the benefit of toilet facilities, running water, or food-preparation areas. Food and medicine were in very limited supply. Soon the detainees were suffering from malnutrition and communicable diseases. Not surprisingly, discontent was rampant. Many thousands died in the reconcentration centers, and before long news of the misery had begun to spread abroad, much to the chagrin of Madrid.

Indeed, reports of the deplorable conditions made headlines in American newspapers, evoking sympathy among the American people, who increasingly sided with the insurrectionists. By the summer of 1896, the plight of the Cuban detainees had become the favorite fodder for sensationalist journalism in the United States. In October 1897 a new Spanish government, headed by Premier Práxedes Mateo Sagasta, recalled Weyler and agreed to terminate the reconcentration system. Nonetheless, conditions in Cuba, combined with the explosion of the U.S. Navy battleship *Maine* in Havana Harbor (February 15, 1898), the publication of the Dupuy de Lôme-Canalejas Letter, and other contentious issues, finally pushed the William McKinley administration into war in April 1898.

In the longer term, the Spanish policy of reconcentration informed the British concentration camps of the South African War (Second Boer War) and the U.S. Strategic Hamlet Program during the Vietnam War.

Jeffery B. Cook

See also Resettlement; South African War; Strategic Hamlet Program; Weyler y Nicolau, Valeriano

Further Reading

Gould, Lewis L. *The Spanish-American War and President McKinley.* Lawrence: University Press of Kansas, 1982.

Trask, David F. *The War with Spain in 1898.* Lincoln: University of Nebraska Press, 1996.

Regulator Revolt

Start Date: 1768
End Date: 1771

Uprising in the British North American colony of North Carolina during 1768–1771 that is sometimes regarded as a harbinger of the American Revolutionary War (1775–1781). The Regulator Revolt (War of the Regulation, Regulator Movement) was mounted by inhabitants of the backcountry of North Carolina who had many reasons for complaint against their colonial government. The county assemblies were not democratic, with local offices bought and sold and many officeholders not even residents. In addition, taxation was patently unfair, land titles were difficult to obtain, and corruption was endemic.

Protests began in August 1766 when a mass meeting resulted in "Regulation Advertisement Number 1," an appeal to the people of the colony to end these various abuses. When royal governor William Tryon failed to address the grievances, in 1768 the Regulation was formally organized, with the protesters refusing to pay taxes until their grievances were met. Tyron warned the organizers to obey the law but, recognizing the justice of some of their complaints, ordered officials and lawyers to stop charging exorbitant fees. This failed to resolve the problem, and the situation worsened. In September 1770 riots occurred in several counties, the largest one at Hillsboro.

With protests mounting and the number of Regulators steadily growing, Tryon decided to act before the situation got out of hand and called out the militia to suppress the Regulators. Some 1,500 militiamen responded, most of them from the colony's eastern counties. Under Tryon's personal command, in mid-May 1771 the militiamen marched to Grand Alamance Creek, where some 2,000–3,000 unarmed and poorly disciplined Regulators were assembled to meet them.

The ensuing two-hour Battle of Alamance Creek (May 16, 1771) was the largest violent confrontation between opposing forces of Anglo-Americans in the colonial period. The militiamen dispersed the Regulators. Each side lost 9 men killed, while 61 militiamen and an unknown number of Regulators were wounded.

Following the battle, 6 Regulators were convicted of treason and hanged. Tryon offered clemency to the remainder if the Regulators would agree to lay down their arms and respect the law. More than 6,000 Regulators accepted these terms, but some 1,500 families left North Carolina and moved west into present-day Tennessee. Many of these so-called unredeemed Regulators would fight on the British side during the Revolutionary War.

While backcountry inhabitants of South Carolina and Virginia had similar and additional complaints and also drew up grievances, there was no violence in these two colonies similar to that of North Carolina.

Spencer C. Tucker

Further Reading

Ekirch, Roger. *Poor Carolina: Politics and Society in Colonial North Carolina, 1729–1776.* Chapel Hill: University of North Carolina Press, 1981.

Kars, Marjoleine. *Breaking Loose Together: The Regulator Rebellion in Pre-Revolutionary North Carolina.* Chapel Hill: University of North Carolina Press, 2002.

Lefler, Hugh T., and William S. Powell. *Colonial North Carolina: A History.* New York: Scribner, 1973.

Reid-Daly, Ronald Francis

Birth Date: September 22, 1928
Death Date: August 9, 2010

Rhodesian Army officer who established the Selous Scouts during the Rhodesian Bush War (Zimbabwe War of Liberation, 1964–1979). Ronald "Ron" Francis Reid-Daly was born on September 22, 1928, in Salisbury, the capital of British Southern Rhodesia. He joined the British Army in 1951 and was a member of the Rhodesian contingent of the Far East Volunteer Unit, intended for service in the Korean War (1950–1953). Diverted to service in the Malayan Emergency (1948–1960), the Rhodesian contingent became C Squadron of the British Special Air Service regiment, devoted to counterinsurgency operations there.

Following three years in Malaya, Reid-Daly returned to Rhodesia. Unhappy as a civilian, he joined the Southern Rhodesia Staff Corps and became an instructor at the School of Infantry. In 1961 he was the regimental sergeant major of the new Rhodesian Light Infantry (RLI). Commissioned in the RLI in 1964, he saw service in the Rhodesian Bush War. He was nearing retirement in 1973 as a lieutenant colonel when he was persuaded to establish a new counterinsurgency unit with a majority of blacks, many of them former insurgents. Known from March 1974 as the Selous Scouts, this unit was initially employed in tracking and intelligence duties but from 1977 was involved in hunter-killer activities. The Selous Scouts came to be recognized as one of the world's premier counterinsurgency units and operated with great success not only in Rhodesia (today Zimbabwe) but also in cross-border operations against insurgent bases in neighboring Mozambique and Zambia.

Many in the Rhodesian military looked askance at the Selous Scouts for its unorthodox methods, however. Allegations that its members had been engaged in trafficking in ivory led to an angry exchange between Reid-Daly and Rhodesian Army commander Lieutenant General John Hickman in January 1979, whereupon Reid-Daly was court-martialed for insubordination. Convicted, he faced only a reprimand but resigned his commission and unsuccessfully fought to legally clear his name.

Reid-Daly then left Rhodesia and settled in South Africa. He briefly headed military training in Transkei, the first of the South African homelands granted full independence, and then formed a private security firm before retiring completely. Reid-Daly died in Cape Town on August 9, 2010.

Spencer C. Tucker

See also Fire Force, Rhodesian; Frente de Libertação de Moçambique; Mugabe, Robert Gabriel; Nkomo, Joshua; Pseudoforces; Reid-Daly, Ronald Francis; Rhodesian Bush War; Special Air Service; Zimbabwe African National Union; Zimbabwe African People's Union

Further Reading

Baxter, Peter. *Selous Scouts: Rhodesian Counter-Insurgency Specialists.* Solihull, West Midlands, UK: Helion, 2011.

Moorecraft, Paul, and Peter McLaughlin. *The Rhodesian War: A Military History.* Barnsley, UK: Pen and Sword Military, 2008.

Reid-Daly, Ron, and Peter Stiff. *Selous Scouts: Top Secret War.* Alberton, South Africa: Galago, 2002.

Resettlement

Population resettlement has been a major tool of armies and states throughout history. An early and extreme example of this is the case of ancient Carthage. Following the capture of Carthage in the Third Carthaginian War (149–146 BCE), Rome destroyed the city and sold into slavery the 50,000 inhabitants, all that remained of a presiege population of 500,000 people.

In counterinsurgency, the goal of resettlement is to separate a susceptible population from insurgent influence. One means of accomplishing this is through a defensive barrier. The most outstanding example of such a barrier is the Great Wall of China, intended primarily to keep foreign invaders at bay. Other more recent examples are the French Army's Morice Line during the Algerian War (1954–1962), the U.S. military's McNamara Line during the Vietnam War (1957–1975), and the cordon sanitaire of minefields laid during the Rhodesian Bush War (Zimbabwe War of Liberation, 1964–1979).

Resettlement was also a major tool of colonial warfare. Examples of practitioners include the Spaniards during the Cuban War of Independence (1895–1898), the Americans in the Philippine-American War (1899–1902), the British in the South African War (Second Boer War, 1898–1902), the Soviet removal of the Crimean Tartars to Central Asia in 1944, the British in the Malayan Emergency (1948–1960), and the U.S. and South Vietnamese governments in the Strategic Hamlet Program of the Vietnam War.

The Spaniards were the first colonial power in modern times to experiment with what became known as reconcentration camps, relocating populations to areas where they might be separated from guerrilla influence and where the guerrillas would be unable to rely on friendly civilians for recruitment, financial support, and even food. Those outside the camps would be considered rebels, and Spanish troops made every effort to destroy the means of subsistence available to them. Conditions in the hastily constructed camps were poor, and little thought was given to the considerable logistical requirements. Bringing together large numbers of people in one small area abetted the spread of disease, leading to the deaths of many. The poor conditions in the camps became grist for the mill of the so-called yellow press in the United States and helped tilt American public opinion in favor of intervention.

Conditions in the British camps during the Second Boer War were no better. Indeed, there was even a two-tiered ration system in the camps where families with male members fighting on the Boer side received reduced rations. Meanwhile, British troops destroyed the Boer farms and killed the livestock. Following great public outcry over the practice, the British Army went over to an even more inhumane approach of releasing the families back into the devastated countryside where they were forced to fend for themselves.

Soviet leader Joseph Stalin, alarmed at the collaboration of many Crimean Tartars with the Germans in World War II (1939–1945), in 1944 simply decreed the removal of the entire population to Central Asia as a form of collective punishment. Given the nature of the Soviet Union, no criticism of this vast enterprise appeared in the Soviet press.

Modern population resettlement in counterinsurgency enjoyed perhaps its greatest success during the Malayan Emergency (1948–1960), when Lieutenant General Sir Harold Briggs moved ethnic Chinese squatters (the chief supporters of the Communist insurgency) into 509 so-called New Villages with new medical and educational facilities. The villagers also received title to land. Strict controls over its distribution kept food from assisting the guerrillas. The British established village councils, and responsibility for communal defense was ultimately passed to the inhabitants themselves. Resettlement was a major factor in the ultimate defeat of insurgency.

Large-scale population resettlement was also tried during the Vietnam War, where early on the Communist insurgents—the Viet Cong (VC)—relied heavily on rural support. The initial South Vietnamese Agroville Program gave way to the U.S.-supported Strategic Hamlet Program advocated by British counterinsurgency expert Sir Robert Thompson. The Strategic Hamlet Program was a vast effort. In July 1963 the government claimed 7,200 strategic hamlets with a population of 8.7 million. The program was also a failure. Villagers were uprooted, many of them from their ancestral homes, and often relocated to sites chosen primarily for defensive capabilities rather than agricultural potential. The villagers were ordered to construct defenses and then man these against attack. They were supposed to receive government benefits in the form of improved medical care, schools, and other advantages, but these rarely materialized in a program that was marked by wide-scale corruption. Many of the strategic hamlets were simply Potemkin villages. Awash in a sea of corruption, the program was finally abandoned.

Population resettlement programs in Portuguese Africa and during the Rhodesian Bush War were also largely failures, with inadequate benefits for the inhabitants and too little security for village crops, which at night were also subject to animal depredations. If resettlement programs are to enjoy success, as was the case in Malaya, there must be careful planning, a commitment of adequate resources, and careful oversight of implementation.

Spencer C. Tucker

See also Algerian War; Briggs, Sir Harold Rawdon; Concentration Camps in the Second Boer War; Malayan Emergency; Morice Line; Philippine Islands and U.S. Pacification during the Philippine-American War; *Reconcentrado* System; South African War; Thompson, Sir Robert Grainger Ker; Vietnam War

Further Reading

Beckett, Ian F. W. *Encyclopedia of Guerrilla Warfare.* Santa Barbara, CA: ABC-CLIO, 1999.

Beckett, Ian F. W., and John Pimlott, eds. *Armed Forces and Modern Counter-Insurgency.* New York: St. Martin's, 1985.

Resistance

Defined here as the act of opposing a foreign occupying power, resistance has existed since the beginning of warfare and conquest. There have always been some citizens of an occupied nation who refused to accept the military verdict and attempted to continue the fight against a victor, sometimes with success.

The term "resistance" may mean many things. The actual act of resistance runs the gamut from noncooperation to civil disobedience, conducting intelligence activities, carrying out sabotage and assassinations, running escape lines, and even carrying out hit-and-run raids against small enemy units. The term "resistance" is also applied to an organization or a particular movement, such as the Maquis in France during World War II (1939–1945) or the Partisans in Yugoslavia. Resistance may be undertaken by individuals or by groups of people organized to work clandestinely against an oppressor. To the occupied, people who engage in such activities are resisters and are often held up as heroes. To the occupying power, such people are considered bandits, criminals, and even terrorists.

Most nations have created myths concerning their resistance activities. As a consequence, we will never know, even approximately, the numbers of people actually involved in resistance activities. After World War II for quite understandable reasons, the governments of many countries, including France, sought to magnify the numbers of people involved in the resistance and their contribution to victory.

Resistance is most often associated with World War II. Resistance movements during that conflict were sharply fragmented along national lines, and there were bitter rivalries within the resistance groups of some nations that often led to bloodshed. These were the result of sharp ideological and religious differences, long-standing ethnic feuds, fiefdoms, and petty jealousies among the leaders themselves. In Czechoslovakia, the Defense of the Nation and the Falcon Organization vied with one another. In the Netherlands various religious and political groups emerged, but they did not work together until September 1944. In France, the resistance was at first sharply fragmented. Not until May 1943 did the National Council of the Resistance (CNR) unite all major French resistance groups. In Greece, infighting among the Ellinikos Laikos Apeleftherotikon (ELAS, Greek People's Liberation Army) and the Ethnikós Dimokratikós Ellinikós Syndesmos (EDES, National Republican Greek League) brought civil war. In Albania, royalist Zogists fought a prorepublican resistance group. The Yugoslavian resistance was polarized between the royalist Četniks under the leadership of Dragoljub "Draza" Mihailović and Communist Partisans led by Tito (Josip Broz). While the Četniks were promonarchial and conservative, the Partisans were antimonarchy and sought a postwar Communist state. The Četniks were also reluctant to embark on the types of operations, such as direct attacks on German troops, that would bring reprisals against the civilian population. The Partisans felt no such compunction. Inside the Soviet Union, many resisters sought not only freedom from the Germans but also freedom from Soviet control.

Often Allied agents parachuted into an occupied state had difficulty sorting out all these rivalries and making the appropriate determinations as to where Allied financial and military assistance should be directed. Throughout the occupied countries, the Communist resistance groups, although they were late to take the field (until the German invasion of the Soviet Union in June 1941, Stalin advocated close ties with Nazi Germany), tended to be highly effective. This was because they were better trained and organized, had strong ideological motivation, and had no reservations about employing force.

Geography impacted resistance activities and determined the levels of activity and participation. Mountainous, forested, or swampy terrain favored the guerrillas. It was thus easier to conduct resistance activities in Norway, Yugoslavia, Albania, and Greece, all countries with many hills, forests, and caves. In Asia, jungles often worked to the advantage of the resistance.

Resistance took many forms and was both passive and active. Passive resistance was generally nonconfrontational, a method of coping and asserting one's patriotism. Passive resistance involved many people in occupied Europe and in Asia, encompassed a wide range of activities, and might include nothing more than reading an illegal newspaper, selling or buying goods on the black market, or not handing in materials decreed necessary for the Axis war machine. Passive resistance might also mean secretly listening to church sermons, praying for a royal family or leaders in exile, listening to BBC broadcasts, leaving a public place when a German entered it, or other such activities. At the highest levels, passive resistance might include balking at anti-Jewish legislation, not handing over individuals sought by the occupier, or seeking to evade the occupying power's exactions.

Active resistance included intelligence gathering, acting as couriers or radio operators, disseminating information or Allied propaganda through such means as underground newspapers, printing false identification papers and ration cards, rescuing downed Allied pilots and assisting them in reaching neutral nations, sabotage, freeing prisoners, hiding Jews, and even carrying out assassinations of individuals and conducting military actions against small numbers of occupying troops. Active resistance was far more dangerous and often life-threatening to the individual involved as well as his or her family. For that reason, those who engaged in it were always a minority. Active resistance required considerable courage as well as clairvoyance for Frenchmen in 1940 to see that Germany might indeed lose the war and for one to be willing to risk all toward that end.

The British Special Operations Executive (SOE), established by Prime Minister Winston Churchill in 1940, helped finance and train agents from the nations of Axis-occupied countries to carry out active resistance activities. Its U.S. counterpart, the Office of Strategic Services (OSS), conducted similar activities. While the SOE and the OSS enjoyed some successes, they also experienced a number of failures leading to the death of a number of agents. The most dramatic failure resulted from Englandspiel, an elaborate German counterintelligence operation in the Netherlands that led to the death of many Allied agents. Resisters had to exercise constant vigilance and not only against the occupying forces. The governments of their own countries, working with the occupiers, often sent out forces, such as the Milice in France, to hunt them down.

One notable resistance success was the February 1943 strike executed by British-trained Norwegian resisters against the hydroelectric plant at Vermork, Norway. This raid and the subsequent sinking of a ferry delayed German production of so-called heavy water essential for the production of an atomic bomb.

The Poles, who suffered terribly at the hands of their German and Soviet occupiers during the war, immediately established active resistance. They provided immensely useful intelligence on the German development of V-weapons and also created the secret Home Army. Jews in the Warsaw Ghetto employed active resistance, rising up against the Germans and providing a heroic example of courage against impossible odds.

The French Maquis also fought the Germans. Resistance activities mounted from the Vercors Plateau in the Alps of eastern France provoked a strong reaction in the form of 20,000 German troops who in June 1944 decimated the Vercors Maquis and mounted savage reprisals against the civilian population. The Germans carried out ferocious reprisals against the Vercors and elsewhere. Often the Germans executed innocent civilian villagers or hostages at the rate of 20 or more for each of their own slain. Reprisals were especially fierce after British-trained Czech commandos assassinated the Reich protector of Bohemia and Moravia, Reinhardt Heydrich. His death led the Germans to kill most of the inhabitants of Lidice and level the town. Other communities in other parts of Europe suffered a similar fate.

Resistance activities sharply increased as the Axis powers suffered military reversals, especially when it became clear that the Axis would lose the war. Resisters had to be constantly on guard and regularly change their modus operandi. They also had to contend with double agents, of whom there were a substantial number. French resistance leader Jean Moulin, the leader of the CNR, for example, was betrayed to the Gestapo by an informant.

It is difficult to gauge the effectiveness of resistance activities during the war. They may not have greatly speeded up the end of the war, but they did affect events in that the occupiers were forced to divert large numbers of troops from the fighting fronts to occupation duties and to hunting down the resistance. Resistance in all its forms was a vindication of national identity and pride and a statement for freedom. Unfortunately, the bright and idealistic hopes of resistance leaders in many countries that the war would bring new political structures were for the most part left unfulfilled. In most countries, the resistance leaders were thanked politely and then shown the door as the old elites soon reestablished themselves in power.

Some resistance groups, of course, fought not only against the Axis powers but also against colonial forces. Thus in Vietnam, the nationalist Communist-dominated Viet Minh led by Ho Chi Minh fought both the Japanese and the French. As a consequence, in a number of countries the resistance continued after World War II ended, utilizing the methods and weapons supplied to fight the Japanese. This was the case in Vietnam but also in the Philippines and even in the Soviet Union.

Annette E. Richardson and Spencer C. Tucker

See also Ellinikós Laïkós Apeleftherotikós Stratós; Ho Chi Minh; Office of Strategic Services; Special Operations Executive; Tito; Viet Minh

Further Reading

Bennett, Rab. *Under the Shadow of the Swastika: The Moral Dilemma of Resistance and Collaboration in Hitler's Europe.* New York: New York University Press, 1999.

Haestrup, Jorgen. *European Resistance Movements, 1939–1945: A Complete History.* Westport, CT: Praeger, 1981.

Michel, Herni. *The Shadow War: Resistance in Europe, 1939–1945.* London: Andre Deutsch, 1972.

Semelin, Jacques. *Unarmed against Hitler: Civilian Resistance in Europe, 1939–1943.* Translated by Suzan Husserl-Kapit. Westport, CT: Praeger, 1993.

Resistência Nacional Moçambicana

Mozambique insurgent group formed in 1975 as a conservative political party and rival to the Marxist-Leninist and principal Mozambique insurgent group the Frente de Libertação de Moçambique (FRELIMO, Front for the Liberation of Mozambique), headed by Samora Machel. The Resistência Nacional Moçambicana

(RENAMO, Mozambique National Resistance) fought FRELIMO in the long Mozambican Civil War of 1975–1992.

RENAMO was established by the Rhodesian Central Intelligence Organization in 1975. André Matsangaisa, a former FRELIMO military commander, was RENAMO's first leader. With RENAMO, the Rhodesians hoped to undermine Machel's support for the Zimbabwe African National Union (ZANU) led by Robert Mugabe, then waging guerrilla warfare in Rhodesia. Following a violent successionist struggle after Matsangaisa was killed in 1979, Alfonso Dhlakama became the RENAMO leader.

When Rhodesia became independent as Zimbabwe, Mugabe committed forces to support Machel in Mozambique. The South African government then assumed support for RENAMO, forcing Machel to negotiate the Nkomati Agreement in 1984. Under its terms, South Africa agreed to end its support of RENAMO, and Machel agreed to expel the African National Congress, then headquartered in Mozambique.

RENAMO benefitted from the fact that Machel's FRELIMO drew most of its support from the Makonde people of northern Mozambique, who represented only about 3 percent of the total population. RENAMO was much more broadly based. It also benefitted from opposition to FRELIMO's Marxist-Leninist ideology and policies. Although RENAMO controlled perhaps 85 percent of the national territory, FRELIMO won the national elections that followed Mozambique's independence in June 1975.

RENAMO contested the election results, and from 1977 Mozambique was subjected to a violent civil war between the opposition forces of the anticommunist RENAMO militias and the Marxist FRELIMO regime. This conflict, combined with sabotage from the neighboring white-ruled state of Rhodesia and the apartheid regime of South Africa, ineffective FRELIMO policies, failed central planning, and economic collapse, characterized the first decades of Mozambican independence.

The Mozambique Civil War ended in 1992 with the Rome Peace Accord. As of 2013, FRELIMO continues as the governing party, while RENAMO, which espouses a center-right democratic political philosophy, remains the principal opposition.

Spencer C. Tucker

See also Frente de Libertação de Moçambique; Machel, Samora Moïses; Mozambique Insurgency; Mugabe, Robert Gabriel; Zimbabwe African National Union

Further Reading

Beckett, Ian F. W. *Encyclopedia of Guerrilla Warfare.* Santa Barbara, CA: ABC-CLIO, 1999.

Cann, John P. *Counterinsurgency in Africa: The Portuguese Way of War, 1961–1974.* St. Petersburg, FL: Hailer, 2005.

Rich, Paul, and Richard Stubbs, eds. *The Counter-Insurgent State: Guerrilla Warfare and State Building in the Twentieth Century.* New York: St. Martin's, 1997.

Rhodesian Bush War

Start Date: 1964
End Date: 1979

The Rhodesian Bush War, also known as the Zimbabwe War of Liberation, occurred during 1964–1979 when forces of Rhodesia's white minority government fought black nationalist insurgents serving with the military wings of the Zimbabwe African National Union (ZANU) and the Zimbabwe African People's Union (ZAPU). Settled by British and South African colonists beginning in the 1890s, Rhodesia remained a British possession until November 1965, when its white minority (some 250,000 people), led by Ian Smith, unilaterally declared independence. The move was intended to forestall British efforts to pressure Rhodesia to institute a government that was more responsive to the political and economic aspirations of the country's black majority of 4.5 million people. Led by Britain, the international community condemned the move and applied economic sanctions in hopes of compelling the Rhodesians to accept decolonization. With the sanctions slow to take effect and the white minority resistant to any form of meaningful political compromise, black nationalist leaders decided to resort to violence to attain their political goal of majority rule.

For much of the 1960s, the guerrilla campaign was ineffective. ZANU and ZAPU, though united by their overarching political goal and leftist orientation, remained bitter rivals throughout the conflict. Their hostility hampered the coordination of effort and was grounded in tribal, ideological, and strategic differences. ZANU, its ranks dominated by the Shona ethnic group, embraced a Maoist approach to insurgency that dictated a guerrilla war within Rhodesia. ZAPU professed the Soviet model of a national liberation struggle, with an emphasis on building up a conventional force in neighboring Zambia that would be capable of defeating the Rhodesian regime in open battle. Incapable of reconciling these differences, both organizations mounted a series of limited incursions by small guerrilla units into Rhodesia in the late 1960s. These infiltrators were easily detected and destroyed by Rhodesian security forces.

The collapse of Portugal's African colonial empire altered the strategic course of the war. ZANU now secured sanctuaries in Mozambique, the new government of which was sympathetic to ZANU's cause. Increasingly benefitting from the training and equipment obtained from the Soviet Union, China, Tanzania, Algeria, and Ghana, ZANU intensified its incursions into Rhodesia, attacking white farmsteads and establishing a base of political support among the rural black population in the northeastern part of the country.

The Rhodesians responded by creating operational sectors that integrated static defenses (free-fire zones and extensive mine belts), population control (food control, martial law, and resettlement programs), and innovative tactical and operational methods. The latter maximized the use of air and ground assets by fusing them into rapid-response Fire Forces that utilized light helicopters to provide fire support and mobility for light infantry units charged with tracking down and destroying guerrilla units. The Fire Forces benefitted from the Rhodesian military's superior intelligence-gathering apparatus. Elite formations such as the Rhodesian Light Infantry, the Selous Scouts, Grey's Scouts, and the Rhodesian Special Air Service specialized in patrolling the countryside, tracking down infiltrating guerrilla bands, and vectoring air and ground forces to destroy insurgent units. A joint military operations center, established in 1978, coordinated the efforts of the various branches of Rhodesia's security forces and functioned as a clearinghouse for intelligence collected in the field.

Rhodesian forces enjoyed a tactical advantage over the guerrillas throughout the war, but military successes alone could not produce a victory in what was fundamentally a political struggle. The Rhodesian regime failed to address the underlying political, social, and economic grievances exploited by the guerrillas in their efforts to gain legitimacy and to mobilize the support of the country's black population. Without a comprehensive strategy, the white government's position deteriorated throughout the late 1970s.

Following the collapse of Portuguese colonial authority in Mozambique and Angola, South Africa scaled back its assistance to Rhodesia, recalling the ground troops, helicopters, and air crews that it had loaned to the Smith regime. Concerned about the stability of their country's northern border, South African leaders now began to pressure Rhodesia to enter into a dialogue with the guerrillas. At the same time, the effects of the economic sanctions made deep inroads on Rhodesia's economy, constraining the ability of government forces to secure fuel and spare parts. Finally, the emigration of whites who could see no end to the war and who found the government's growing demands for military service increasingly burdensome created serious shortages of military manpower.

Rhodesian military action intensified in the final stages of the war, including a series of spectacular cross-border operations that targeted guerrilla camps in Zambia and Mozambique. These were a microcosm of the Rhodesian counterinsurgency effort. In tactical and operational terms, they attested to the Rhodesian security forces' ability to keep ZANU and ZAPU off balance through a deft combination of air assault and highly mobile motorized columns of light infantry. The operations resulted in the dispersal of hundreds of guerrillas, the destruction of insurgent supply stocks and weapons, and the erosion of the black nationalists' morale. Strategically and politically, however, the cross-border raids may have positively hurt the Rhodesians by highlighting their flagrant disregard for their neighbors' sovereignty and intensifying international condemnations of the white majority government. Exhausted by the war and unable to envision a successful end to the counterinsurgency effort, the Rhodesian government agreed to a cease-fire brokered by Britain in December 1979. Elections held the following year brought Robert Mugabe, head of ZANU, to the presidency. Rhodesia was no more, replaced by the new nation of Zimbabwe.

The Rhodesian Bush War remains a classic case study of a conflict that the counterinsurgents managed to win militarily but lost politically. Lacking the resources and the willingness to engage in civic action programs, Rhodesians made few serious attempts to win the hearts and minds of the rural black population. The failure to do so allowed the insurgents to win the one aspect of the struggle that mattered the most: the contest for political legitimacy.

Sebastian H. Lukasik

See also Fire Force, Rhodesian; Hearts and Minds; Mugabe, Robert Gabriel; Selous Scouts; Zimbabwe African National Union; Zimbabwe African People's Union

Further Reading

Abbott, Peter, and Philip Botham. *Modern African Wars: Rhodesia, 1965–80.* Oxford, UK: Osprey, 1986.

Cilliers, Jackie. *Counter-Insurgency in Rhodesia.* London: Croom Helm, 1984.

Hoffman, Bruce, Jennifer M. Taw, and David Arnold. *Lessons for Contemporary Counterinsurgencies: The Rhodesian Experience.* Santa Monica, CA: RAND, 1991.

Moorecraft, Paul, and Peter McLaughlin. *The Rhodesian War: A Military History.* Barnsley, UK: Pen and Sword Military, 2008.

Rhodesian Fire Force.

See Fire Force, Rhodesian

Riego y Nuñez, Rafael del

Birth Date: ca. April 9, 1784
Death Date: November 7, 1823

Spanish Army officer, insurgent leader, and liberal politician. Born on April 9, 1784 (some sources give November 24, 1785), in Tineo, Asturias, Spain, Rafael del Riego y Nuñez graduated from the University of Oviedo in 1807. He then moved to Madrid, where he joined the Spanish Army. During the early fighting against the French in the Peninsular War (1808–1814), he was taken prisoner but escaped.

Riego was again captured by the French on November 10, 1808, during the Battle of Espinosa de los Monteros and was sent to France. Eventually released, he dropped the "del" from his name and traveled in Britain and Germany before returning to Spain. Riego rejoined the army as a lieutenant colonel and took the oath to the Spanish Constitution of 1812 just before that liberal document was abolished in May 1814 by King Ferdinand VII, who had been restored to power on a pledge to maintain it. Six years of absolutist rule followed. Riego meanwhile became a Freemason and participated in several failed conspiracies with the opposition liberals to overthrow Ferdinand.

With the Spanish Crown deprived of valuable resources as a consequence of the Latin American independence movements, Ferdinand resolved to reconquer the New World colonies, and toward that end he assembled army units at the port of Cádiz. Disaffection among these brought a revolt on January 1, 1820, that was led by Riego, who had assumed command of the Asturian Battalion. The rebel forces marched on Madrid. With unrest spreading throughout Spain and revolt occurring in Madrid itself, Ferdinand agreed on March 10 to restore the Constitution of 1812.

The newly founded progressive government made Riego a field marshal and captain-general of Galicia. On January 8, 1821, he took command of Spanish forces in Aragon. Falsely accused of republicanism following a failed republican revolt, he was imprisoned but was released following popular demonstrations in Madrid and his election to the Cortes (parliament) in March 1822.

In December 1822 the Quintuple Alliance powers of Britain, France, Austria, Prussia, and Russia decided that a liberal Spanish government posed too great a threat to the now conservative and reactionary governments of the rest of Europe and dispatched forces to restore absolute monarchy. This task was given to France, the forces of which invaded Spain in April 1823.

Riego took command of the Spanish Third Army and fought both the invaders and Spanish absolutists. Having taken Madrid, French forces moved south. They then advanced on Cádiz, defeating Riego's forces in the Battle of the Trocadero on August 31, 1823. Riego escaped but was betrayed and taken prisoner near the village of Arquillos in Jaén on September 15. Ferdinand ignored French advice that he pursue moderate policies as well as his own pledge of amnesty and took harsh measures against the liberals and other opponents of his regime. Sent to Madrid, Riego was there tried and found guilty of treason for having voted in the Cortes in favor of a reduction in the king's powers. Riego was hanged in La Cebada Square in Madrid on November 7, 1823. He is today regarded by many Spaniards as a national hero.

Spencer C. Tucker

Further Reading

Bowen, Wayne H., and José E. Alvarez. *A Military History of Modern Spain: From the Napoleonic Era to the International War on Terror.* Westport, CT: Praeger Security International, 2007.

Mosquera, Alejandro. *Rafael del Riego.* A Coruña, Spain: Ateneo Republicano de Galicia, 2003.

Rif War

Start Date: 1920
End Date: 1926

Spain had held small coastal enclaves across the Straits of Gibraltar in North Africa since the 17th century. In the early 20th century, however, Spain and France reached an agreement to partition Morocco between them. German opposition to such a step brought two acute international crises in 1905 and 1911 that nearly resulted in a general European war, but in accordance with the Treaty of Fez (March 30, 1912), Sultan Mulay Hafid was forced to accept a protectorate. Spain assumed de facto control of strips of northern Morocco, while France secured the bulk of the country. Although the Moroccan sultan theoretically was sovereign, he reigned but did not rule. French general Louis H. G. Lyautey became French resident-general and held real power. His adroit diplomacy and pacification policies solidified French rule and extended it into the Atlas Mountains region.

Opposition to European control continued, however, notably from Berber tribesmen in the interior Rif Mountains region who in 1893 had threatened the Spanish enclave of Melilla and forced Spain to send substantial reinforcements to North Africa. Indeed, during World War I (1914–1918), both the French and Spanish governments continued to carry out counterinsurgency operations there. A new leader against foreign rule in Morocco arose after the war in 1920, however, in the person of Muhammad ibn Abd el-Krim al-Khattabi. In 1921 Abd el-Krim, joined by his brother, who became his chief adviser and commander of the rebel army, raised the standard of resistance against foreign control of Morocco. This marked the beginning of the Rif War (1921–1926), although some date the conflict from 1920.

In late July 1921, determined to destroy the rebels, Spanish general Fernandes Silvestre moved into the Rif Mountains with some 20,000 men. Silverstre failed to carry out adequate reconnaissance or take sufficient security precautions, and at Annual (Anual) on July 21, Rif forces fell on the Spaniards, killing as many as 12,000 and taking several thousand others prisoner. The rebels also seized important quantities of arms and equipment there as well as from Spanish regional outposts.

Some of the Rif forces now advanced on Melilla, the principal Spanish base in the eastern Rif region, held by 14,000 Spanish troops. Fearful that an attempt to take Melilla might lead to a widened war in consequence of the many citizens of other European states living there, Abd el-Krim ordered his troops not to attack. Later he characterized this decision as his biggest mistake of the war.

Meanwhile, news of the Spanish military disaster of Annual shook Spain to its core and led directly to the establishment of a virtual military dictatorship in Spain under General Miguel Primo de Rivera in 1923.

In 1923 Abd el-Krim proclaimed the Republic of the Rif, with himself as president. He endeavored to create a centralized Berber government that would respect traditional values but override tribal rivalries. Fighting continued, and by the end of 1924 the Spanish authority was reduced to the coastal enclaves of Melilla and Tetuán. At its peak, insurgent strength numbered some 80,000–90,000 men, although only about 20,000 rifles were available to them at any one time, and many of the modern weapons in Rifian hands were poorly maintained.

Aircraft played a key role in this war. During the fighting, the Spanish Army of Africa employed up to 150 planes, including British-built Airco DH-4s bombers, to drop conventional ordnance and also considerable quantities of German-developed mustard gas on Rifian villages. Targets included souks (markets), livestock, and Abd el-Krim's headquarters. The Spaniards also used their aircraft to resupply encircled posts. Rifian antiaircraft fire did bring down a number of low-flying Spanish planes, however.

On April 12, 1925, an overconfident Abd el-Krim opened a major offensive against the French part of Morocco in what many historians hold was a major miscalculation. Lyautey had only limited resources, and Abd el-Krim's forces were able to overrun 45 of 66 French posts on the Ouergha River Valley. Lyautey used French air assets to good effect, however, and in July he was able to halt the Berber advance short of Fez. Faced with the Rif threat, that same month the French and Spanish governments agreed to close cooperation against Abd el-Krim. The French contributed 150,000 men under Marshal Henri Philippe Pétain, while the Spanish assembled 50,000 under General José Sanjurjo.

Pétain abandoned Lyautey's population-centric methods in favor of a highly kinetic industrial approach to the war that employed infantry along with cavalry but also tanks, artillery, and attack aircraft. By late summer, Rifian forces were under attack by the French and Spanish from the north and south.

In September 1925, coalition forces carried out an amphibious landing at Alhucemas Bay near Abd el-Krim's headquarters. Within a month, 90,000 French and Spanish troops were ashore in what was the most significant operation of its kind in any irregular war during the interwar period.

The period November 1925–April 1926 saw both sides in winter quarters with only limited French and Spanish air operations occurring. Facing overwhelming force and technological superiority in the form of modern aircraft artillery and with his own weapons stocks dwindling and forces melting away, Abd el-Krim surrendered to the French on May 26, 1926. This action brought the Rif War to a close, although the French continued to fight various insurgent tribes in the Atlas Mountains until the early 1930s.

William T. Dean III and Spencer C. Tucker

See also Abd el-Krim al-Khattabi, Muhammad ibn; Annual, Battle of; Lyautey, Louis Hubert; *Tache d'Huile*

Further Reading

Alvarez, Jose E. *The Betrothed of Death: The Spanish Foreign Legion during the Rif Rebellion, 1920–1927*. Westport, CT: Greenwood, 2001.

Balfour, Sebastian. *Deadly Embrace: Morocco and the Road to the Spanish Civil War.* Oxford: Oxford University Press, 2002.

Woolman, David S. *Rebels in the Rif: Abdel Krim and the Rif Rebellion*. Stanford, CA: Stanford University Press, 1968.

Roberto, Holden Álverto

Birth Date: January 12, 1923
Death Date: August 2, 2007

Angolan insurgent leader and founder of the Frente Nacional de Libertação de Angola (FNLA, National Front for the Liberation of Angola). Holden Álverto Roberto was born on January 12, 1923, in São Salvador, Angola, then a Portuguese colony. He moved with his family to Léoipoldville (now Kinhasa) in the Belgium Congo (present-day Democratic Republic of the Congo) and in 1940 graduated from a Baptist missionary school. For the next eight years, Roberto worked for the Belgian Finance Ministry in the Congo. In 1951 he visited Angola, where he witnessed the mistreatment of an old man by the Portuguese authorities, which Roberto said aroused him politically.

In July 1956 Roberto and Barros Necaca founded the Union of Peoples of Northern Angola, subsequently renamed the Union of Peoples of Angola. In December 1958 Roberto represented Angola at the Ghana-sponsored All-African People's Congress, where he also met a number of future African leaders. In the 1950s the U.S. government paid Roberto a small stipend for intelligence collection.

António Agostinho Neto's Movimento Popular de Libertação de Angola (MPLA, Popular Movement for the Liberation of Angola) initiated the Angolan Insurgency in January 1961. That March, having organized militants among the Bakongo tribe of northern Angola, Roberto led some 4,000–5,000 men from Kinshasa during attacks against Portuguese border posts and farms in Angola, killing all the Portuguese they encountered. In March 1962 Roberto formed the FNLA. Jonas Savimbi, who had joined Roberto's movement the year before, became foreign minister in Roberto's self-proclaimed Revolutionary Government of Angola in Exile. Roberto received the support of president of Zaire (now the Democratic Republic of the Congo) Mobutu Sese Seko, when he divorced his wife and then married a woman from Mobuto's wife's village. Roberto also received some aid from Israel.

In 1964 Savimbi broke with Roberto when the latter refused to expand his movement beyond the Bakongo tribe. Savimbi founded the União Nacional para a Independência Total de Angola (UNITA, the National Union for the Total Independence of Angola). Thus, there were three groups—the MPLA, the FNLA, and UNITA—fighting the Portuguese in Angola. The FNLA largely operated from bases in Zaire into Angola and claimed to have some 10,000 men in 1972.

On the eve of Angolan independence in 1975, the FNLA and UNITA formed an alliance, and Mobuto sent Zairean forces into the country in a bid to block the leftist MPLA from taking power. He hoped thereby to establish a pro-Kinshasa government. This bid failed thanks to a Soviet airlift of Cuban troops, who defeated the FNLA, UNITA, and Zairean forces.

A Cold War proxy battle ensued with the Marxist MPLA government of Angola, which enjoyed the support of the Soviet Union and Cuba, while the allegedly anticommunist FNLA and UNITA received assistance from the United States, Zaire, and China. In 1991 both UNITA and the FNLA agreed to the Bicesse Accords, which allowed Roberto to return to Angola and permitted him to run for president, but he received only 2 percent of the vote. Roberto died in Luanda on August 2, 2007. Upon his death, the Angolan government recognized him as one of the leaders of the "national liberation struggle."

Spencer C. Tucker

See also Angolan Insurgency; Frente Nacional de Libertação de Angola; Movimento Popular de Libertação de Angola; Neto, António Agostinho; Savimbi, Jonas Malheiro; União Nacional para a Independência Total de Angola

Further Reading

Klinghoffer, Arthur Jay. *The Angolan War.* Boulder, CO: Westview, 1980.

Marcum, John A. *The Angolan Revolution.* 2 vols. Cambridge, MA: MIT Press, 1969 and 1978.

Roberts, Frederick Sleigh

Birth Date: September 30, 1832
Death Date: November 14, 1914

British general and one of the most capable officers to emerge from the British colonial campaigns in the second half of the 19th century. Born on September 30, 1832, in Cawnpore, India, Frederick Sleigh Roberts was the son of a general in the service of the British East India Company. Roberts was educated at Eton; the Royal Military Academy, Sandhurst; and the East India Company's training school in Addiscombe. He was commissioned in the Bengal Artillery in December 1851.

Roberts then served on the North-West Frontier as his father's aide-de-camp. During the Indian Mutiny of 1857, Roberts participated in the recapture of Delhi in September, where he was wounded, and in the recapture of Lucknow in November. He won the Victoria Cross for his actions in the Battle of Khudaganj (January 2, 1858).

After a short stint in Britain, Roberts returned to India in 1859 and saw action on the North-West Frontier. In 1868 he took part in the Abyssinian Expedition to rescue European hostages taken by Emperor Tewodros II. The campaign demonstrated Roberts's mastery of logistics, and he was made quartermaster general of the British Indian Army in 1875.

Roberts won fame during the Second Anglo-Afghan War (1878–1881). In October 1878 he led the Kurram Field Force into Afghanistan. Occupying the Khost Valley and threatening Kabul, Roberts destroyed an Afghan force at Peiwar Kotal and played an important role in the conclusion of a peace agreement. When fighting began anew in September 1879, he led the Afghan Field Force in another invasion of Afghanistan, capturing Kabul and defeating the Afghans near Shepur in December.

When the Afghans besieged the British garrison at Kandahar, Roberts cemented his military reputation by a 23-day march that covered more than 300 miles from Kabul and ended in defeat of the Afghans at Kandahar on September 1, 1880. His Afghan campaigns demonstrated his careful planning, excellent command of logistics, and mastery of tactics. Concerned for the welfare of his men and sparing of their lives in battle, Roberts was affectionately known by his troops as "Bobs."

In 1881 Roberts assumed command of British forces in Madras. During 1885–1893 he commanded the British Indian Army, and in 1892 he was made Baron Roberts of Kandahar. Returning to Britain, he was promoted to field marshal and took command of British forces in Ireland in 1895.

After early British defeats in the South African War (Second Boer War) of 1898–1902, in December 1899 Roberts was appointed to succeed British general Sir Redvers Buller. Roberts reorganized British forces and the logistics systems. Concentrating his resources, he captured Bloemfontein, lifted the siege of Kimberley, and took both Johannesburg and Pretoria, dispersing the Boer forces, who then went over to guerrilla warfare. Succeeded in command by his chief of staff General Herbert Kitchener in November 1900, Roberts returned to Britain and was rewarded by being made a viscount and then an earl.

Roberts was commander in chief of the British Army from 1901 to 1904, when he retired and devoted himself to an unsuccessful campaign for compulsory military service. Roberts fell ill and died at St. Omer, France, on November 14, 1914, while visiting Indian troops fighting in World War I (1914–1918).

Spencer C. Tucker

See also South African War

Further Reading

Beaumont, Roger. *Sword of the Raj: The British Army in India, 1747–1947.* Indianapolis: Bobbs-Merrill, 1977.

James, David. *The Life of Lord Roberts.* London: Casell, 1914.

Rogers, Robert

Birth Date: November 7, 1731
Death Date: May 18, 1795

American militia officer best known for his innovative military tactics and service in the French and Indian War (1754–1763). Born in Methuen, Massachusetts, on November 7, 1731, Robert Rogers was raised in New Hampshire, where he received only a rudimentary education but developed keen skills as a woodsman and hunter. Rogers served briefly as a scout for the New Hampshire Militia during King George's War (1744–1748) but did not win military distinction until the French and Indian War.

Following service with militia forces supporting British regulars in the expedition against Crown Point, New York (August–September 1755), and battles around Lake George (September), Rogers received promotion to captain. Ordered to raise a company of rangers in March 1756, he selected most of the men in the unit and equipped them from his own means. Promoted to major in 1758, Rogers was ordered to expand his rangers to include nine companies totaling roughly 200 men.

Rogers' Rangers, as his unit became known, specialized in scouting and reconnaissance missions. Working in small groups, the rangers often operated behind enemy lines gathering intelligence or engaging in raids and ambushes. All of the men were accomplished woodsmen, adept at moving swiftly through rough terrain and living off the land. They wore green jackets in an attempt at camouflage. The rangers demonstrated their unique mobility during the Battle on Snowshoes (March 13, 1758), when they employed snowshoes to launch raids against French and allied Native American encampments in the dead of winter. Rogers authored a manual, *Rogers' Ranging Rules,* detailing his tactical methodologies.

After taking part in British major general Jeffery Amherst's capture of Fort Ticonderoga (July 26, 1759) and Crown Point (July 31), Rogers achieved his greatest military exploit to date in a daring raid with his men far behind enemy lines against the Abenaki settlement at St. Francis (today Odanak), Quebec, Canada. After a three-week trek through the wilderness avoiding both the French and their native allies, Rogers and his men attacked St. Francis (October 6, 1759). There they killed some 200 natives, freed 5 English captives, and burned the town before returning to British lines. Undertaken in retribution for Abenaki raids and massacres of English colonists in New England, the attack greatly reduced that tribe's future raiding. Rogers' Rangers also supported Amherst's capture of Montreal (September 8, 1760).

After Montreal fell, Amherst reassigned Rogers to the Great Lakes region to seize the remaining French fortifications there. The rangers continued their success with several key victories, including the surrender of Fort Detroit (November 29, 1760), which added to Rogers's fame in the colonies. Rogers' Rangers returned to the Detroit territory again in 1763 to assist the British Army in suppressing Pontiac's Rebellion.

Rogers traveled to England in 1765 to compile his war memoirs and publish accounts of his heroics against the French and their native allies. He asked King George III for money to fund an expedition to explore the Mississippi River to the Pacific Ocean. Although the king refused the request, he did reward Rogers with command of Fort Michilimackinac in present-day Michigan. As commandant of the fort, Rogers followed a path of corruption and insubordination, mostly in trying to pursue his obsession of creating an expedition to find the elusive Northwest Passage. Arrested and tried for treason, he was acquitted in 1768. Rogers returned to England in hopes of securing another command but landed in debtors' prison.

At the outbreak of the American Revolutionary War (1775–1783), Rogers offered his services to Continental Army commander General George Washington, who refused the offer, as he did not trust Rogers's allegiance to the Patriot cause and suspected that he was a British spy. An embittered Rogers then accepted a commission as a British lieutenant colonel and raised his own two companies of Loyalist rangers outside New York City. He fought in several campaigns during 1776–1777 but did not experience notable success. Rogers returned to England in 1782, where he lived in poverty and obscurity until his death in London on May 18, 1795.

A resourceful leader of scouting forces, Rogers had a major impact on tactics employed in insurgency and counterinsurgency warfare. Present-day U.S. Army Rangers still operate along the principles that he espoused.

Bradford A. Wineman

See also Skulking Way of War

Further Reading

Cuneo, John R. *Robert Rogers of the Rangers.* New York: Oxford University Press, 1959.

Rogers, Robert. *The Annotated and Illustrated Journals of Major Robert Rogers.* Fleischmann, NY: Purple Mountain, 2002.

Smith, Bradford. *Rogers' Rangers and the French and Indian War.* New York: Random House, 1956.

Roguet, Christophe Marie Michel

Birth Date: 1800
Death Date: 1877

French Army general and guerrilla warfare theorist. Christophe Marie Michel Roguet was born in 1800 and was a page to French emperor Napoleon I in 1815. Commissioned in the engineers, Roguet subsequently transferred to the infantry and was promoted to general in 1845. He was an aide-de-camp to Emperor Napoleon III in 1851 and then served as a senator during the Second Empire. He died in 1877.

Roguet is best known for his studies of the Vendée Revolt (1793–1796) during the French Revolution. He produced three works on it for the French military. These were *L'Emploi de la force armée dans les émeutes* (The Employment of Force in Riots, 1832), *Guerres de l'insurrection* (Insurrectionary Wars, 1839), and *Répression des émeutes* (Suppression of Riots, 1848). He also published two books commercially: *De le Vendée militaire, avec carte et plans, par un officier supérieur* (On Military Vendée with Map and Plans, by a Superior Officer, 1834) and *L'Avenir des Armées Européene ou le soldat cityoen* (The Future of European Armies or the Citizen Soldier, 1850).

Roquet's view of the suppression of the Vendée Revolt was remarkably modern in that he recognized the primacy of political action, including the need to win the hearts and minds of the civilian population. He also drew on lessons advanced by French marshal Louis-Gabriel Suchet as a consequence of the 1808–1814 Peninsular War in Spain and endeavored to apply these to French pacification efforts in Algeria.

Spencer C. Tucker

See also Algeria, French Pacification of; Hearts and Minds; Vendée Revolt

Further Reading

Beckett, Ian F. W. *Encyclopedia of Guerrilla Warfare.* Santa Barbara, CA: ABC-CLIO, 1999.

Griffith, Paddy. *Military Thought in the French Army, 1815–1851.* New York: Manchester University Press, 1989.

Roguet, Christophe Marie Michel. *De le Vendée militaire, avec carte et plans, par un officier supérieur* [The Vendée Militaire, with Map and Plans, by a Senior Officer]. Paris: J. Coréardje, 1834.

Royal Irish Constabulary

The Royal Irish Constabulary (RIC) was the national police force of Ireland from 1822 to 1922. The British government's Peace Preservation Act of 1814 created the first organized police force in Ireland. The provincial constabulary was established under the Irish Constabulary Act of 1822. The RIC constituted the only police force in Ireland during the period of its existence with the exception of municipal police forces in Dublin, Belfast, and Londonderry. For most of its history, the RIC numbered some 10,000 members. Some 75 percent of the force was Roman Catholic, which allowed it to perform its functions throughout Ireland with little sectarian opposition.

Because of widespread poverty in Ireland, social unrest was common, and the RIC was regularly called upon to control protests, riots, and general lawlessness among the rural population. The RIC maintained law and order equitably if not always popularly. To ensure the perception of fairness in local administration and law enforcement, RIC constables were not permitted to serve in their family's home county.

In the second half of the 19th century, RIC capabilities were increasingly stressed by the Irish independence movements. The RIC was able to infiltrate the Fenian movement and frustrated that movement's revolt in 1867. However, the Easter Uprising of 1916 demonstrated RIC limitations in this area, and that uprising was put down only by the British Army.

With the end of World War I (1914–1918), the Irish Republican Army (IRA), the military wing of the Sinn Féin independence organization, made the RIC its particular target. The 9,700 RIC constables were widely dispersed in some 1,500 barracks throughout the country and were thus vulnerable to a well-organized insurgency. A campaign of murder and intimidation began in 1919 with the ambush and assassination of RIC constables but also the social ostracism of their families. The IRA program of terrorism and intimidation caused the RIC to abandon many of its isolated barracks, which essentially ceded much of rural Ireland to the IRA and Sinn Féin. In these circumstances many RIC members resigned (600 in a three-month span in 1920 alone), and the RIC found it difficult to recruit replacements.

The British government responded by recruiting English and Scottish World War I veterans for service in Ireland. Known as the Black and Tans because of their mixed military and police uniforms, they lacked the local knowledge and ties and careful training of the earlier RIC constables. The British also established the Auxiliary Division of the RIC. The Black and Tans and Auxiliaries responded to the increased IRA violence with their own campaign of retribution and intimidation, which further alienated many of the Irish regarding British rule. As the violence increased, British authorities increasingly relied on the army. The IRA destruction of the RIC was likely the most important military aspect of the Irish insurgency.

With the proclamation of the Irish Free State, in April 1922 the RIC ceased to exist. The Civic Guard took its place. In Northern Ireland, the RIC was reconstituted as the Royal Ulster Constabulary.

Louis A. DiMarco

See also Black and Tans and the Auxiliaries; Collins, Michael; Irish Republican Army; Northern Ireland Insurgency

Further Reading

Curtis, Robert. *The History of the Royal Irish Constabulary.* Dublin: McGlashan and Gill, 1871.

Hittle, J. B. E. *Britain's Counterinsurgency Failure: Michael Collins and the Anglo-Irish War.* Washington, DC: Potomac Books, 2011.

Leeson, D. M. *The Black and Tans: British Police and Auxiliaries in the Irish War of Independence, 1920–1921.* New York: Oxford University Press, 2011.

S

Salan, Raoul Albin-Louis

Birth Date: June 10, 1899
Death Date: July 3, 1984

French Army officer and bitter opponent of the dismantlement of France's colonial empire. Born in Roquecourbe (Tarn Department) near Toulouse on June 10, 1899, Raoul Albin-Louis Salan was admitted to the French Military Academy of Saint-Cyr in August 1917 during World War I (1914–1918) but was immediately sent to the front in France. He returned to Saint-Cyr after the war, graduating in August 1919. He then served in Algeria, Morocco, the Middle East, and Indochina.

At first loyal to the Vichy regime following the defeat of French forces by the Germans in June 1940, Salan rallied to the Free French Resistance in 1943 and, as a colonel in command of a regiment, took part in the liberation of metropolitan France. In 1945 Salan was posted to French Indochina, where he commanded French forces in the north, accompanying Vietnamese nationalist leader Ho Chi Minh to France and the July 1946 Fontainebleau Conference.

In April 1952 Salan assumed command of all French forces in Indochina, holding that post until January 1953, when he became inspector general of land forces in France. He accompanied French Army commander General Paul Ely on a fact-finding tour to Indochina in June 1954 and then returned there with Ely when the army commander was named high commissioner and commander in chief of French forces (July–October 1954). The French military defeat in the Battle of Dien Bien Phu in May 1954 was a clarion call for Salan, who believed that there could be no defeats for the French colonial empire, a conviction shared by many of his fellow professional officers.

During January–May 1955, Salan commanded the reserve army in France and was a member of the Supreme War Council. Front de Libération Nationale (FLN, National Liberation Front) insurgents had begun the Algerian War in late 1954, and in November 1956 Salan was dispatched as commander of French forces in Algeria with the rank of general of the army. Salan supported the coup d'état against the Fourth French Republic in May 1958 and the return to power of General Charles de Gaulle and establishment of the Fifth Republic. De Gaulle, who mistrusted Salan, removed him from command that December.

In 1959 Salan retired to Algeria. Realizing that de Gaulle was prepared to grant Algeria independence, Salan allied himself with the anti-Algerian independence movement known as Algérie Française (French Algeria). On April 22, 1961, Salan was one of four French generals to foment a military coup attempt in Algeria. Known as the Generals' Putsch, it failed after three days, and Salan went underground to lead the Organisation de l'Armée Secrète (OAS, Secret Army Organization) in a brutal campaign of terror against the French government both in Algeria and France. That July he was sentenced in absentia to death for treason.

Arrested in Spain in April 1962, Salan was returned to France and tried a month later. Found guilty, he was sentenced to life imprisonment. He was released in May 1968 under a governmental amnesty. In 1982 President François Mitterand restored Salan's military rank along with his pension. Salan died in Paris on July 3, 1984.

Cezar Stanciu

See also Algerian War; Indochina War; Organisation de l'Armée Secrète

Further Reading

Horne, Alistair. *A Savage War of Peace: Algeria, 1954–1962*. London: Macmillan, 1977.

Salan, Raoul. *Le Sens d'un Engagement, 1899–1946* [The Meaning of Commitment, 1899–1946]. Paris: Presses de la Cité, 1970.

Salan, Raoul. *Mémoires: Fin d'un Empire, "Le Viet-Minh Mon Adversaire," October 1946–October 1954* [Memoirs: End of an Empire, "My Adversary the Viet-Minh"]. Paris: Presses de la Cité, 1954.

Saloth Sar.

See Pol Pot

Sandinistas.

See Frente Sandinista de Liberación

Sandino, Augusto César

Birth Date: May 18, 1890
Death Date: February 21, 1934

Nicaraguan insurgent leader. Augusto César Sandino was born in Niquinohomo, Nicaragua, on May 18, 1890. The illegitimate child of a small business man, Sandino grew up in poverty surrounded by the social inequities of the coffee industry in which large landowners ensured that peasants did not own enough land to feed their families and were thus forced to labor on the coffee plantations. Sandino's mother was imprisoned for debt, and as a child he worked picking coffee. In 1906 he went to live with his father but was treated as a servant because of his birth. In 1910 Sandino was forced to work for his father's grain business, ending Sandino's formal education.

In 1916 Sandino left Nicaragua for Costa Rica, where he worked as a mechanic and saved money to return to Nicaragua in 1919 and start his own grain venture. When he shot a man during an argument, he was again forced to flee Nicaragua. During the next three years Sandino worked odd jobs, finally finding employment with a U.S. oil company in Tampico, Mexico. Here he became politicized. Embracing spiritualism and Freemasonry, he opposed government, the Catholic Church, and capitalism.

In 1926 Sandino returned to Nicaragua and worked for another American company operating a gold mine in Nueva Segovia. Here he joined the Liberals, who opposed the Conservative government. The Liberals and Conservatives had been fighting for decades. The U.S. government, seeking to establish a more stable business environment, supported the Conservatives and had sent marines there in 1912. In 1926, although the marines had been withdrawn, Washington pressured the outgoing president to yield his seat to his Conservative colleague. The Liberal opposition then formed a provisional government, and fighting began in the so-called Constitutional War.

General José María Moncada led the Liberal forces. Sandino, now one of Moncada's officers, pressured the general for more decisive action, but Moncada refused. U.S. marines landed in force in Nicaragua in January 1927, and in May U.S. envoy Henry Stimson negotiated a truce between Moncada and the Conservative government. Moncada agreed to let the Conservative president serve until the 1928 election and to disarm his troops. The marines then organized the Nicaraguan Guardia Nacionale (National Guard) to serve as a neutral police force. Sandino, convinced that the U.S. government was out to control Nicaragua, formed his own revolutionary army and took to the mountains. In September 1927 he issued his Articles of Incorporation of the Defending Army of the National Sovereignty of Nicaragua and launched attacks against both the U.S. marines and the National Guard.

Sandino's nationalistic fervor earned him heroic and mythic status among many Nicaraguans. From 1927 to 1933 he continued to reject calls for negotiation, even when the Liberal government came to power in 1928. Unable to defeat the marines or the National Guard in traditional combat, Sandino's forces became expert in guerrilla tactics. Despite nearly 4,000 marines and U.S. aircraft, the war dragged on, and the U.S. Congress withdrew funding. In early 1932 Stimson negotiated the withdrawal of the marines, with their task to be taken over by the National Guard with its new U.S.-appointed leader, Anastasio Somoza García.

Elections held in 1933 produced a new Liberal president, Juan Batista Sacasa, who invited Sandino to Managua in February 1934 for a peace conference. Sandino did not trust Sacasa or Somoza but had promised to lay down his arms once the marines had departed and he had retired to an agricultural commune under an amnesty. On February 21 Sandino departed after meeting with Sacasa and Somoza, only to be kidnapped along with his brothers and murdered by National Guardsmen under the orders of Somoza.

Sandino's fight for independence from U.S. interference in internal Nicaraguan affairs as well as his calls for social and political reform made him a national hero, inspiring the Sandinista National Liberation Front that triumphed over the U.S.-backed Somozas in the Nicaraguan Revolution of 1979.

Monica Orozco

See also Frente Sandinista de Liberación; Nicaragua Insurgency; Puller, Lewis Burwell

Further Reading

Macaulay, Neill. *The Sandino Affair.* Chicago: Quadrangle, 1967.

Nolan, David. *The Ideology of the Sandinistas and the Nicaraguan Revolution.* Coral Gables, FL: University of Miami Institute of Interamerican Studies, 1984.

Sandino, Augusto César. *Sandino: The Testimony of a Nicaraguan Patriot.* Edited by Sergio Ramirez. Princeton, NJ: Princeton University Press, 1990.

San Martín, José Francisco de

Birth Date: February 25, 1778
Death Date: August 17, 1850

South American independence leader. Born at Yopayú in the viceroyalty of Río de la Plata (northeastern Argentina) on February 25, 1778, José Francisco de San Martín was the son of a Spanish Army officer. San Martín returned to Spain with his family in 1785 and there joined the Spanish Army in 1790, serving for more than 20 years. He distinguished himself in fighting against the French during the Peninsular War and attained the rank of lieutenant colonel.

Despite his long service in the Spanish Army, San Martín believed that Spain's Latin American colonies should be independent. Learning of the independence movements in Latin America, he resigned his commission in 1812 and joined those supporting a war for Latin American independence. San Martín arrived in Buenos Aires in March 1812 and associated himself with the revolutionary government. His previous military experience secured him command of a mounted unit, and in December 1813 he joined the revolutionary army in northern Argentina.

Latin American revolutionary leaders believed that their success depended on securing Peru, a center of loyalist support. Royalists there had already defeated three Argentinian invasions of upper Peru (later Bolivia). San Martín planned a cross-Andean invasion to liberate Chile, which could then be used as a base for a seaborne invasion of Peru.

San Martín resigned from the revolutionary army in January 1817 and was appointed governor of Cuyo Province in western Argentina at the base of the Andes. Establishing a base at Mendoza, he conferred with Chilean exiles and built a military force of Argentinians, Chileans, and slaves who had been promised freedom in exchange for military service.

San Martín's Army of the Andes, numbering 2,500 infantry, 700 cavalry, and 21 guns, departed Mendoza and made its way north through the Andes passes into Chile during January 24–February 8, 1817, catching Spanish forces there completely by surprise. After defeating a small Spanish force in the Battle of Chacabuco (February 12–13) and occupying Santiago (February 15), San Martín then named his friend and ally Bernardo O'Higgins to direct political affairs in Chile. On the arrival of a large Spanish force from Peru under General Mariano Osorio in early 1818, San Martín engaged Osorio and was narrowly defeated by him in the Battle of Cancha-Rayada (March 16). San Martín then struck back and this time routed Osorio in the Battle of Maipo (April 5), securing Chilean independence. Chilean leaders then offered San Martín the position of supreme ruler of Chile, but he declined in order to continue the war against the Spanish in Peru.

For 18 months, San Martín carefully prepared an invasion force. Now actively supported by the Chilean and Argentinian governments and with a flotilla of ships commanded by Englishman Thomas Cochrane, Earl of Dundonald, to transport his men, San Martín set out for Peru by sea with 4,500 men in August 1820. He landed about 100 miles south of Lima, but because the Spanish forces in Peru were larger than his own, he refused to accept battle unless it was on favorable terms, hoping that his presence would spark popular uprisings. In the meantime, he planned to whittle down the Spanish through guerrilla warfare. Indeed, the Spanish soon evacuated Lima in June 1821. Entering Lima, San Martín declared Peruvian independence on July 21, 1821.

Peruvians were sharply divided politically, and San Martín was forced to take power as the protector of Peru. He instituted policies that angered the rich, including the imposition of taxes, an end to Indian tribute, and freedom for children of slaves. Threatened by unrest and the continued presence in Peru of the larger Spanish force, San Martín met with fellow Latin American revolutionary leader Simón Bolívar at Guayaquil (July 26–27, 1822). Although there is some disagreement on this (no record of the meeting was kept), it appears that San Martín agreed to hand over the liberation of Peru to Bolívar. Returning to Lima, San Martín resigned in September 1822 and departed for Argentina. He then began a self-imposed European exile and died in Boulogne-sur-Mer, France, on August 17, 1850.

Idealistic, selfless, and a sincere patriot and capable military leader, San Martín supported constitutional monarchies for Latin America, while Bolívar favored independent republics.

Spencer C. Tucker

See also Bolívar, Simón

Further Reading

Lynch, John. *The Spanish American Revolutions, 1808–1826.* New York: Norton, 1986.

Rojas, Richard. *San Martín: Knight of the Andes.* New York: Doubleday, 1945.

Santa Cruz de Marcenado, Marqués de.

See Navia-Osorio y Vigil, Álvaro de

Savimbi, Jonas Malheiro

Birth Date: August 3, 1934
Death Date: February 22, 2002

Angolan insurgent nationalist leader, founder of the União Nacional para a Independência Total de Angola (UNITA, National Union for the Total Independence of Angola) movement, and guerrilla tactician. Born on August 3, 1934, in Munhango, Bie Province, in the Portuguese colony of Angola, Jonas Malheiro Savimbi was purposely vague and evasive about his early life. He claimed that he had earned a PhD from the University of Lausanne, Switzerland, and he may have spent two years in Portugal as a medical student. Returning to Angola, he joined Holden Roberto's Frente Nacional de Libertação de Angola (FNLA, National Front for the Liberation of Angola), accepting the post of foreign minister in this movement that had initiated an insurgency against the Portuguese in 1961.

Savimbi broke with Roberto in 1964, however, when the latter refused to expand his movement into southern Angola, and in 1966 Savimbi founded UNITA. Whereas the FNLA base of support was among the Bakongo people, UNITA was centered in the south among the Ovimbundu and Chokwe people. Savimbi then waged a guerrilla war against the Portuguese.

The Angolan insurgents fighting Portuguese colonial rule were the left-wing Movimento Popular de Libertação de Angola (MPLA, Popular Movement for the Liberation of Angola), led by António Agostinho Neto; Roberto's FNLA; and Savimbi's UNITA. UNITA was the only one of the three guerrilla organizations permanently operating entirely from within Angola.

After Angola won independence in 1975, the MPLA and Neto came to power with the explicit support of the Soviet Union and Cuba. The FNLA dissolved, but Savimbi immediately turned UNITA against the pro-Soviet, Marxist Angolan government, plunging the new nation into a horrific civil war. Both South Africa and the United States supplied UNITA with arms and weapons. The Soviet Union and Cuba backed the MPLA, and Cuba provided troops.

Among the African leaders who openly supported Savimbi were Felix Houphouet-Boigny of Ivory Coast and Mobutu Sese Seko of Zaire. Others were more discreet in their aid but nevertheless maintained diplomatic and commercial ties with UNITA. Savimbi began to score victories against the MPLA in the late 1980s. By 1990, in fact, his forces controlled almost half of Angola.

The Angolan government negotiated a cease-fire with UNITA in 1991. The following year Savimbi lost a questionable presidential election, and the civil war was reinvigorated, with periodic breaks, for another decade. Despite United Nation condemnatory sanctions and embargoes and international recognition of the popularly elected government in Luanda, Savimbi persisted, financing UNITA mainly through illicit sales of diamonds.

The United States and the Soviet Union used Angola as a proxy during the Cold War, while Savimbi portrayed himself as a warrior against communism. With the end of both the Cold War and the apartheid regime in South Africa, he continued the civil war, becoming a virtual international pariah with no major patrons. Since 1966 Savimbi had survived more than a dozen assassination attempts, but he was killed in battle at Lucusse on February 22, 2002. Just six weeks after his death, UNITA rebels signed a cease-fire agreement, which ended the long civil war. Savimbi's struggle resulted in the death of more than 1 million people and the displacement of 2 million others.

John H. Barnhill and Spencer C. Tucker

See also Angolan Insurgency; Frente Nacional de Libertação de Angola; Movimento Popular de Libertação de Angola; Neto, António Agostinho; Roberto, Holden Álverto; União Nacional para a Independência Total de Angola

Further Reading

Bridgland, Fred. *Jonas Savimbi*. St. Paul, MN: Paragon, 1986.

Windrich, Elaine. *The Cold War Guerrilla*. Westport, CT: Greenwood, 1992.

Selous Scouts

An elite multiracial special forces regiment formed during the Rhodesian Bush War (1964–1979). Arguably among the best counterinsurgency forces in history, the Selous Scouts were organized by Lieutenant Colonel Ronald Reid-Daly during November 1973–January 1974 and incorporated many former guerrillas who had fought the white minority government of Rhodesia (today Zimbabwe). They were named in March 1974 for Frederick Courtney Selous, the renowned hunter, explorer, and soldier who had guided the first white settlers into what became Southern Rhodesia in 1890. The Selous Scouts were established as part of Operation HURRICANE, the Rhodesian counterinsurgency effort in the northeastern part of Rhodesia along the border with Zambia and Mozambique.

The Selous Scouts were modeled after the British experience with pseudoforces in the Malayan Emergency and the Kenya Emergency and the Flechas ("Arrows") of the Portuguese Army in Africa. Originally controlled by the British South Africa Police with the goal of tracking and intelligence collection, in 1977 the Selous Scouts passed under the control of the army and were involved in hunter-killer operations. Blacks made up a majority of the Selous Scouts, which also boasted the first Rhodesian commissioned black officers. As they included many turned rebels, the Selous Scouts were able to adapt to changing enemy tactics, and they claimed to have accounted for 68 percent of all guerrillas killed after their change in mission.

Each member was carefully screened not only for loyalty and physical stamina but also for initiative and intelligence. Training was very rigorous. Although often criticized for their unkempt appearance, the Selous Scouts were taught to act, live, and fight like rebel units. They operated in small independent teams, were well versed in many types of weapons, and were parachute qualified. Their motto was "Pamwe Chete" (Shona for "together as one" or "all together").

Because of their large number of black native speakers, the Selous Scouts were able to move easily around the countryside, work with the indigenous population, and even infiltrate the military arms of the insurgent Zimbabwe African National Union (ZANU) and Zimbabwe African People's Union (ZAPU). The Selous Scouts conducted missions into insurgent territory and carried out cross-border operations. In the Nyadzonya Raid of August 9, 1976, 72 Selous Scouts drove 60 miles inside Mozambique to attack the base camp of the Zimbabwe African National Liberation Army (ZANLA), ZANU's military wing, reportedly killing 1,100 insurgents, for no losses themselves.

Allegations that the Selous Scouts had been engaged in trafficking in ivory led to an angry exchange between Reid-Daly and Rhodesian Army commander Lieutenant General John Hickman in January 1979, Reid-Daly's conviction on a charge of insubordination, and his retirement from the army. The Selous Scouts were disbanded in 1980 on the beginning of majority black rule in Zimbabwe.

Donald A. MacCuish and Spencer C. Tucker

See also Fire Force, Rhodesian; Frente de Libertação de Moçambique; Mugabe, Robert Gabriel; Nkomo, Joshua; Pseudoforces; Reid-Daly, Ronald Francis; Rhodesian Bush War; Special Air Service; Zimbabwe African National Union; Zimbabwe African People's Union

Further Reading

Baxter, Peter. *Selous Scouts: Rhodesian Counter-Insurgency Specialists.* Solihull, West Midlands, UK: Helion, 2011.

Moorecraft, Paul, and Peter McLaughlin. *The Rhodesian War: A Military History.* Barnsley, UK: Pen and Sword Military, 2008.

Reid-Daly, Ron, and Peter Stiff. *Selous Scouts: Top Secret War.* Alberton, South Africa: Galago, 2002.

Seminole Wars

Event Dates: 1817–1818, 1835–1842, and 1855–1858

There were three 19th-century wars between the United States and Seminole Native Americans. Fought during 1817–1818, 1835–1842, and 1855–1858, the wars had valuable lessons for insurgency and counterinsurgency operations.

The Seminoles who inhabited southern Georgia and much of Spanish Florida had once been part of the Creek Confederacy. In the early 19th century, the Seminoles came into conflict with European Americans encroaching onto their lands and retaliated by launching occasional raids on frontier settlements. The Seminole practice of harboring fugitive slaves also increased friction with the settlers, and during the War of 1812 (1812–1815) the Seminoles sided with the British.

The First Seminole War began on November 21, 1817, when American troops, after Seminole raids, burned the Seminole settlement of Fowltown in southern Georgia. On November 30 the Seminoles attacked a boat on the Apalachicola River, killing 36 soldiers and 10 women and children. This led U.S. president James Monroe to order in troops under Major General Andrew Jackson. Jackson assembled more than 3,000 soldiers and some 1,500 allied Creeks and invaded Spanish Florida in March 1818. He destroyed several Seminole towns and forced the surrender of Pensacola on May 24 before withdrawing. Jackson's incursion led to the Spanish government's decision to sell Florida to the United States in 1819.

The Second Seminole War (1835–1842) resulted from President Andrew Jackson's policy of forced Native American relocation and the Indian Removal Act of 1830, by which the Seminoles and other southeastern Indians were to give up their homelands and relocate to the new Indian Territory (present-day Oklahoma). While some Seminoles agreed to move west, others refused and took refuge in the Everglades under the leadership of Osceola.

On December 28, 1835, the Seminoles ambushed a force of 108 U.S. soldiers and virtually annihilated it. Other U.S. forces suffered heavy casualties in inconclusive fighting in December. U.S. troop strength was steadily increased, and although the soldiers destroyed some settlements and crops, they accomplished little else. The army also employed flags of truce to lure Seminole parties into the open and then take them prisoner. Osceola was among those thus captured.

Despite these successes, U.S. battlefield victories remained elusive. On December 25, 1837, in the largest confrontation of the war, 1,000 troops under Colonel Zachary Taylor attacked 400 Seminoles near Lake Okeechobee and finally drove off the Native Americans; however, Taylor's loss of 150 was six times that of the Seminoles.

In 1838, new U.S. commander Brigadier General Thomas Jesup tried offering African Americans fighting alongside the Seminoles freedom in exchange for military service against the warring tribe. This led some 400 blacks to switch sides. Jesup resigned shortly afterward, having been harshly criticized for his use of a flag of truce to capture Osceola. Taylor assumed command in May 1838, and with the war seemingly over, the U.S. government ordered him to end the campaign even though Seminole raids continued. Taylor soon asked to be relieved, and in April 1839 Major General Alexander Macomb replaced him. By that time, the war had settled into a pattern of army forays and Seminole retaliatory raids, both of which accomplished little.

The government changed army commanders in Florida frequently, sending Brigadier General Walker Armistead to succeed Macomb and then sending Colonel William Worth as Armistead's replacement. Worth's aggressive forays drove the Seminoles into the Everglades, where he continued to assail them with navy assistance. Worth sought to destroy Seminole crops and dwellings and insisted on campaigning in the hot summer months, although this came at high cost to his own men in sickness and disease.

With the cost of the war approaching $20 million, in 1842 U.S. officials decided to make concessions to achieve peace. An August 1842 agreement granted the 600 Seminole survivors (those captured had already been sent west) a reservation in southern Florida and officially ended hostilities, although sporadic fighting continued into 1843.

The Third Seminole War began in 1855 after conflict between white settlers and the estimated 300–400 remaining Seminoles in the remote southern portions of Florida. Billy Bowlegs was the principal Seminole leader. He sought to maintain peace by avoiding contact with settlers. In 1850, however, Congress passed legislation under which all federal lands at least half covered with water and that might be drained were turned over to the states. In Florida, this amounted to about 20 million acres. Developers and land speculators soon rushed in with plans to drain the Everglades.

All efforts, including financial inducements, to persuade the remaining Seminoles to relocate west of the Mississippi failed. Bowlegs and the majority refused to go. Fighting began on December 20, 1855, when Seminole warriors attacked a survey party at the edge of the Big Cypress Swamp. The Seminoles employed guerrilla tactics, striking along the frontier and then quickly withdrawing into the Everglades, the massive swampy jungle-like wetland that occupied must of southern Florida. Command fell to Brigadier General William S. Harney. A veteran of the Second Seminole War, he realized that the only way to defeat the Seminoles was to invade and drive them from their territory. When negotiations failed, Harney began his offensive in January 1857. Outnumbered and with families to protect, the Seminoles were forced from one area to another. Those who were captured were sent west. In April 1857, command of southern Florida fell to Colonel Gustavis Loomis. Loomis continued the offensive into Seminole territory and developed the use of so-called alligator boats. These flat-bottomed craft more than 30 feet in length could operate efficiently in shallow water and transport up to 16 men. In them, companies of soldiers could move throughout the Everglades and attack the remaining Seminole camps.

Exhausted, on March 27, 1858, Bowlegs finally accepted a government offer of a separate reservation in Oklahoma and a $500,000 trust for the tribe, and on

Illustration depicting Seminole warriors attacking a blockhouse during the Third Seminole War (1855–1858). Fighting began when a Seminole band led by Billy Bowlegs attacked a U.S. Army patrol on December 20, 1855. The Seminoles employed highly effective guerrilla tactics but by the end of the war in May 1858 perhaps only 100 Seminoles remained in all Florida. (Library of Congress)

May 8 Loomis announced an end to all hostilities. The Third Seminole War marked the end of effective native resistance in Florida. There were then perhaps as few as 100 Seminoles left in the entire Florida peninsula.

Spencer C. Tucker

See also Taylor, Zachary; Worth, William Jenkins

Further Reading

Mahon, John K. *History of the Second Seminole War, 1835–1842.* Gainesville: University of Florida Press, 1967.

Missall, John, and Mary Lou. *The Seminole Wars: America's Longest Indian Conflict.* Gainesville: University Press of Florida, 2004.

Peters, Virginia Bergman. *The Florida Wars.* Hamden, CT: Archon Books, 1979.

Sendero Luminoso

Peruvian insurgent organization established by Abimael Guzmán Reynoso. Sendero Luminoso (Shining Path) took its name from a saying attributed to José Carlos Mariátegui, founder of Peru's first Communist Party: Marxism-Leninism will open the shining path to revolution.

Guzmán, a professor of philosophy at the University of San Cristóbal de Huamanga in southeastern Peru from 1962 until 1978, had become interested in the plight of the region's Quechua natives. In the late 1970s he organized his student followers into a clandestine and hierarchical structure in preparation for armed struggle. A strong believer in Chinese Communist leader Mao Zedong's theory of mobilizing the peasantry as opposed to the traditional Latin American approach of city dwellers, Guzmán eschewed evolutionary socialism and sought to bring about a dictatorship of the proletariat that would include cultural revolution and eventually lead to world revolution and the achievement of pure communism.

By 1980, Shining Path was ready to carry out terrorist activities against anyone associated with or supportive of the so-called bourgeois order. Shining Path's early campaigns greatly exacerbated the tensions between landless peasants in the highlands and giant coastal cooperatives supported by the government. The organization encouraged the peasants to invade these cooperatives in order to occupy or loot them. The Peruvian government launched a counterinsurgency effort in 1982, placing 19 provinces under a state of emergency. Although Shining Path was responsible for many casualties among peasants, government forces were responsible for many more. Guerrilla warfare between the group and the increasingly militarized government raged for the next decade.

Shining Path assassinated highly placed public figures and wounded or killed many members of the security forces. The insurgency also ruined efforts of Peruvian president Alan García to regenerate locally based capitalist development in Peru. To make matters worse, Shining Path revolutionaries had made an arrangement with the coca growers, providing them with protection in exchange for payment from the profits of the illicit trade.

Guzmán, or Chairman Gonzalo as he was known within the organization, developed a powerful cult of personality that attracted significant support from the nation's Andean Indians as well as from Spanish-speaking city dwellers. Guzmán not only championed a people's war against the government and the right wing, but by the early 1990s he also believed that any group on the Left that sought to use nonviolent methods to improve the plight of the poor was his enemy. Thus, in 1991 Shining Path terrorists killed four mothers and their children for their work with a committee that distributed free milk to children. Shining Path also killed the president of a local Catholic charity and two foreign relief workers from an evangelical agency and blew up a sophisticated agricultural experimental station sponsored by the Japanese government. With this kind of destruction, Shining Path made it impossible to get any kind of help to the poor people most affected by the nation's economic crisis. In Puno Province alone, the government estimated in 1991 that the insurgency put an end to more than $100 million worth of economic and developmental aid.

By 1992, Shining Path's activities had claimed an estimated 23,000 lives and resulted in property damage of some $22 billion. Most of the victims were peasants. Faced with a deteriorating situation, in April 1992 President Alberto Fujimori carried out what amounted to a coup against his own presidency. He dissolved the congress and the judiciary branch, suspended the constitution, and declared himself the head of the provisional government. These extreme measures did not arouse great opposition within Peru, as most citizens saw them as a necessary response to a desperate situation.

Fujimori's enhanced security efforts led to the capture of Guzmán on September 12, 1992. Brought before a military tribunal in October 1992, he was convicted of terrorist activities and sentenced to life imprisonment without parole. (In 2004, his first trial having been declared illegal, Guzmán was again tried and convicted, this time by a civilian court, and his previous sentence was upheld.) In 1994 from his cell, Guzmán offered peace terms to end the insurgency. This act had the effect of splintering Shining Path, some members of which continue insurgent activities in the countryside in hopes of reaching a peace agreement with the government, while others are now involved in the cocaine trade.

Spencer C. Tucker

See also Guzmán Reynoso, Abimael

Further Reading

Gorriti Ellenbogen, Gustavo. *The Shining Path: A History of the Millenarian War in Peru.* Chapel Hill: University of North Carolina Press, 1999.

Palmer, David Scott, ed. *Shining Path of Peru.* New York: St. Martin's, 1992.

Poole, Deborah, and Gerardo Rénique. *Peru: Time of Fear.* New York: Monthly Review Press, 1992.

Taylor, Lewis. *Shining Path: Guerrilla War in Peru's Northern Highlands.* Liverpool: Liverpool University Press, 2006.

Senussi and Sultan of Darfur Rebellions

Start Date: 1914
End Date: 1916

A number of North African desert tribes and traditional leaders resisted European colonial rule in the late 19th and early 20th centuries. The Senussis (Sanusyyias) were one such opponent of French colonialism. Originating as an Islamic reform movement, the Senussis inhabited parts of Tunisia and Algeria. Senussi adherents believed that they could oppose Western colonialism by returning to what they believed was the original purity of Islam in the Prophet Muhammad's day.

Muhammad ben Ali al-Sanusi founded the Senussi movement in western Algeria in 1837. To escape French rule, soon afterward he moved east into the mountainous interior of Cyrenaica. By 1900, the movement had spread along the Saharan caravan routes. The movement had 143 lodges (*zawiyas*) in oases and desert towns across thousands of miles of eastern Libya and the Sahara. The Senussis sent out trained members to teach and to arbitrate disputes. Although they were nominally under Ottoman rule, the Senussis were in fact an independent force in much of the Sahara.

With the beginning of the Italo-Turkish War (1911–1912), the Senussis sided with the Ottomans. The Senussis' early military successes increased their stocks of arms, and the Ottomans provided some military training. Nuri Pasha, half brother of Enver Pasha, and Ottoman Iraqi general Ja'far al-'Askar led the tribal levies against the Italians. Italy won the war, however, and took Libya from the Ottoman Empire.

At the same time, the French expanded their influence in the Sahara, and by 1914 most of the western Saharan region was under French and Italian control. Nonetheless, the Senussis resisted Italian rule, and on August 26, 1914, during World War I (1914–1918), they captured a major Italian supply column. Most of the Italians were killed, and the Senussis secured thousands of rifles, a few artillery pieces, and some supplies. By the time of their entry into World War I in May 1915, the Italians had been forced to abandon most of the Libyan interior.

In October 1914 the Ottoman Empire cast its lot with the Central Powers, and the sultan at Constantinople proclaimed a jihad (holy war). This led Grand Senussi Sayed Ahmed to go to war with the French and British in addition to continuing the fight against the Italians.

In November 1915 the Senussis invaded British-controlled Egypt. The exact reason behind this is obscure, but the move proved to be a disaster. At Aqqaqir, Egypt, on February 26, 1916, the British Army's Western Desert Force employed armored cars and superior firepower to defeat the Senussis. Ja'far al-'Askar, the Senussi commander, was wounded and captured, and the remaining Senussis were driven into Libya, where they continued to harass the Italians and the French to the west.

It was 1921 before the Italians began their reconquest of Libya. They utilized armored cars, motorized infantry, and aircraft. The Italians also slaughtered the sheep herds on which the Senussis relied, dropped mustard gas from the air, and poisoned water wells. In addition, the Italians erected a 200-mile fence to cut the Senussis off from Egypt and exploited Senussi tribal divisions. Some 12,000 Senussis were held in concentration camps. The capture and execution of Senussi leader Omar Mukhtar in September 1931 finally ended Senussi resistance.

In 1916 a Senussi ally had threatened the British. South of Libya, the sultanate of Darfur occupied roughly 150,000 square miles of territory, much of it mountainous. Darfur, bordered by present-day Chad to the west, had once been an independent kingdom but by the late 19th century supposedly became a tributary province of Sudan under Anglo-Egyptian rule. In practice, its sultan enjoyed substantial autonomy. Sultan Ali Dinar ruled the area and its peoples, some of whom spoke Arabic rather than tribal languages. In 1914, influenced by the Senussis, Ali Dinar refused to acknowledge Anglo-Egyptian suzerainty, instead declaring himself a subject of the Ottoman sultan.

In March 1916 the British moved against Ali Dinar. He had an army of perhaps 5,000 men, armed mostly with older small arms and a few small artillery pieces. Ali Dinar's attempts to turn his remote location and native desert terrain to advantage proved unsuccessful. Their overwhelming advantage in firepower gave the British victory in the chief battle at the village of Beringia on May 22, 1916. After a British aircraft bombed the sultanate's capital of Al Fasher, opposition collapsed. Ali Dinar was killed on November 6, 1916, after a short gun battle with Anglo-Egyptian troops, and the British secured the entire area.

The Ottomans had invested very little in the way of manpower and supplies in the fighting in Africa, but with the help of the Senussis and Sultan Ali Dinar, for two years they had tied down tens of thousands of French, Italian, and British troops who might have been employed on other war fronts. Darfur's relationship with the Sudan remained difficult, and in the late 1990s another rebellion developed there.

Andrew Jackson Waskey and Spencer C. Tucker

Further Reading

Spaulding, Jay, and Lidwien Kapteijns. *An Islamic Alliance: 'Ali Dinar and the Sanusiyya, 1906–1916.* Evanston, IL: Northwestern University Press, 1994.

Theobald, A. B. *'Ali Dinar: Last Sultan of Darfur, 1898–1916.* London: Longmans, Green, 1965.

Vikor, Knut S. *Sufi and Scholar on the Desert Edge: Muhammad b. 'Ali al-Sanusi and His Brotherhood.* Evanston, IL: Northwestern University Press, 1995.

Serong, Francis Philip

Birth Date: November 11, 1915
Death Date: October 1, 2002

Australian brigadier and counterinsurgency expert. Francis Philip Ted Serong was born on November 11, 1915, in Abbotsford, Australia. He attended St. Kevin's College, Melbourne, and graduated in 1937 from the Royal Military College, Duntroon. During World War II (1939–1945), he saw service as a staff and regimental officer in New Guinea with the Australian 6th Division.

Serong's talents in jungle warfare came to the attention of his superiors, who after the war reoriented army training to emphasize this area. In 1955 Serong assumed command of the new Jungle Training Centre at Canungra, Queensland, which he had begun the year before. The training center promoted a regimen of toughness and endurance and focused on the lessons of the Malayan Emergency (1948–1960).

In 1960 Colonel Serong was dispatched to Burma (today Myanmar). Its government had requested an adviser to assist in dealing with ongoing tribal and Communist-inspired insurgencies. Then in mid-1962 Serong was ordered to the Republic of Vietnam (RVN, South Vietnam) to head the 30-man Australian Army Training Team Vietnam (AATTV) attached to the U.S. Military Assistance Command, Vietnam (MACV), and to serve as senior counterinsurgency adviser to MACV commander General Paul Harkins.

In its decade-long existence, the AATTV became the most highly decorated Australian unit to serve in Vietnam. Unfortunately, neither Harkins nor his successor, General William C. Westmoreland, placed emphasis on counterinsurgency, and Serong's relationship with MACV was rocky from the start. Serong argued unsuccessfully that the Vietnam War would be unwinnable until a sound overall counterinsurgency strategy was in place.

In early 1965 with the war in South Vietnam about to assume a new character, Serong was seconded to the U.S. Department of State, with secret assignment to the Central Intelligence Agency (CIA). During the next two years, acting as a civilian, he headed a team charged with building a National Police Field Force (PFF). Serong sought to utilize such a force for forward patrolling on the British colonial policing model. However, the PFF proved stillborn because it was actively opposed by both Westmoreland and Robert Komer, who assumed control of American counterinsurgency operations in South Vietnam in mid-1967.

In 1968 Serong retired from the Australian Army but maintained his connection with the CIA, using work with think tanks such as the RAND Corporation and Batelle as his cover while continuing to advise the South Vietnamese government. Following the 1973 Paris Peace Accords and the sharp reduction in American aid, Serong became a direct adviser to the South Vietnamese government.

In late 1974 Serong, perceiving South Vietnam's vulnerability to the impending final offensive by the Democratic Republic of Vietnam (DRV, North Vietnam), recommended that the South Vietnamese government evacuate the two northern military regions of the country in order to consolidate its forces and reduce its overextended supply lines. This advice was rejected until March, when it was too late. Serong departed South Vietnam on April 29, 1975, the day before the fall of Saigon.

Serong subsequently returned to Australia, where he devoted the remainder of his life to promoting nationalist and anticommunist platforms. He also wrote extensively on defense issues, arguing for an Australian forward-defense strategy. Serong died in Melbourne on October 1, 2002.

George M. Brooke III

See also Komer, Robert William; Vietnam War; Westmoreland, William Childs

Further Reading

Blair, Anne. *Ted Serong: The Life of an Australian Counter-Insurgency Expert.* Melbourne, Australia: Oxford University Press, 2002.

Blair, Anne. *There to the Bitter End: Ted Serong in Vietnam.* Crow's Nest, New South Wales, Australia: Allen and Unwin, 2001.

Davies, Bruce, and Gary McKay. *The Men Who Persevered: The AATTV, the Most Highly Decorated Australian Unit of the Vietnam War.* Crow's Nest, New South Wales, Australia: Allen and Unwin, 2005.

Serong, Ted. *An Australian View of Revolutionary War.* London: Institute for the Study of Conflict, 1971.

Sétif Uprising

Event Date: May 8, 1945

On May 8, 1945, as much of the world celebrated the end of World War II (1939–1945) in Europe, riots broke out among the Berber population of the city of Sétif in the Department of Constantine in Algeria. The Sétif Uprising (Sétif Massacre) began as just another World War II victory parade, approved by the French authorities.

Because May 8 was a market day, it attracted many Berbers from around the city who nursed long-standing grievances with the European settlers over the seizure of their ancestral lands. While marchers carried posters proclaiming the Allied victory, there were also placards calling on Muslims to unite against the French, demanding the release of nationalist leader Messali Hadj, and calling for death for Frenchmen and Jews. Early in the parade, a French plainclothes policeman pulled a revolver and shot to death a young marcher carrying an Algerian flag. This touched off a bloody rampage.

Muslims attacked Europeans and their property, and the violence quickly spread to outlying areas. The French authorities responded with a violent crackdown that included Foreign Legionnaires and Senegalese troops, tanks, aircraft, and even naval gunfire from a cruiser off the Mediterranean coast. Settler militias and local vigilantes supported the authorities and seized a number of Muslim prisoners from jails and summarily executed them.

Major French military operations lasted two weeks, while smaller actions continued for a month. An estimated 4,500 Algerians were arrested; 99 people were sentenced to death, and another 64 received life imprisonment. Casualty figures remain in dispute. At least 100 Europeans died. The official French figure of Muslim dead was 1,165, but this is certainly too low, and figures as high as 10,000 have been cited.

In March 1946 the French government announced a general amnesty and released many of the Sétif detainees, including moderate nationalist leader Ferhat Abbas, although his Friends of the Manifesto and Liberty political party was dissolved. The fierce nature of the French repression was based on a perception that any leniency would be interpreted as weakness and would only encourage further unrest.

The Sétif Uprising and the fact that it was not followed by any meaningful French reform drove a wedge between the two communities in Algeria. Europeans now distrusted Muslims, and the Muslims never forgave the violence of the repression. The French authorities failed to understand the implications of this and were thus caught by surprise when rebellion began in Algeria in November 1954.

Thomas D. Veve and Spencer C. Tucker

See also Algerian War

Further Reading

Aron, Robert. *Les Origines de la guerre d'Algérie: Textes et documents contemporaine* [The Origins of the Algerian War: Contemporary Texts and Documents]. Paris: Fayard, 1962.

Gordon, David C. *The Passing of French Algeria.* London: Oxford University Press, 1966.

Smith, Tony. *The French Stake in Algeria, 1945–1962.* Ithaca, NY: Cornell University Press, 1978.

Tucker, Spencer C. "The Fourth Republic and Algeria." Unpublished doctoral dissertation, University of North Carolina at Chapel Hill, 1965.

Shamil, Imam

Birth Date: 1797
Death Date: March 1871

Political and religious figure who was the third imam of the Caucasian Imamate (1834–1859) and who led resistance to Russian rule in the Caucasus War (1817–1861). Born in 1797 in the small village of Gimry in present-day Dagestan, Russia, Shamil was a lifelong friend and confidante of first imam Ghazi Mollah. Both were leaders of the Murids (Sufi for "committed one"), a fanatical Islamic monastic order that battled the Russians during 1834–1859.

Gravely wounded in the Battle of Gimry (October 1832) in which Ghazi died, Shamil was one of only two people to escape and survive. He spent a year convalescing in the mountains and assumed power in 1834 following the assassination of the second imam. Shamil took part in the epic June–August 1839 Russian siege of the Murid stronghold of Akhoulgo. Some 3,000 Russians died in the siege, while nearly all of some 4,000 of Shamil's followers perished. Shamil was again among the few who escaped.

When not actually engaged in battle, Shamil focused on recruiting and enforcing a particularly stringent version of Sharia. Moving from town to town with the Qur'an and an executioner, he never established a formal capital. Leading as many as 20,000 men and employing hit-and-run tactics and ambushes, Shamil enjoyed some success against Russian supply trains, foraging parties, and small outposts. During the Crimean War (1853–1856), he allied with the Ottoman Empire but was unsuccessful in efforts to secure British aid. With the end of that war, the Russians pursued new tactics that included deforestation, improved roads, and military outposts. They also embarked on a political offensive to restore the power of tribal leaders usurped by the Murids. These policies helped reduce the Murid safe havens, and Russian prince Baryatinsky was able to secure Shamil's surrender in August 1859 in the siege of Gounib that ended the Caucasian War.

To his surprise, Shamil was treated leniently and exiled first to Kaluga near Moscow and then to Kiev. He died in Medina in March 1871 after receiving permission to perform the Hajj. Two of his sons became officers in the Russian Army, while two others became officers in the Ottoman Army. Shamil is revered as a Muslim warrior by Caucasian nationalists resisting Russian rule.

James K. Selkirk Jr. and Spencer C. Tucker

Further Reading

Griffin, Nicholas. *Caucasus: Mountain Men and Holy Wars*. London: Hodder Headline, 2001.

Smith, Sebastian. *Allah's Mountains: Politics and War in the Russian Caucasus*. New York: I. B. Tauris, 1998.

Shays' Rebellion

Start Date: 1786
End Date: 1787

Following the American Revolutionary War (1775–1783), the United States experienced a period of severe economic depression. To offset high war debts, many states, including Massachusetts, levied higher taxes. To make matters more difficult, taxes had to be paid in hard currency, which was in chronic short supply. Combined with low farm prices and a lack of readily available currency, the taxes pushed many farmers and small property owners heavily into debt. Those who could not pay their debts faced imprisonment and the loss of their farms. These conditions produced a growing discontent that flared into armed rebellion in western Massachusetts in 1786.

Daniel Shays, for whom Shays' Rebellion was named, was one of its leaders. During the Revolutionary War, he had fought with distinction in numerous battles, had been promoted to captain, and had been presented a ceremonial sword by the Marquis de Lafayette. Shays then settled in Pelham, Massachusetts.

The western farmers resented the political control of Massachusetts by those living in the eastern part of the state. They modeled their actions on the American Revolution, protesting the oppressive taxation and planning meetings to discuss their grievances and circulate petitions to be sent to their representatives in the state legislature. When their petitions were ignored and property seizures continued, the farmers turned to rebellion.

In the autumn of 1786, Shays was joined by nearly 2,500 men who gathered in front of the Springfield, Massachusetts, courthouse to prevent the court from meeting in order to foreclose on farms and imprison debtors. Later, Shays and his men forced the Massachusetts Supreme Court to adjourn after the state legislature failed to respond to the farmers' grievances.

The conflict escalated when Massachusetts governor James Bowdoin and Samuel Adams (once leaders of taxation protests against the British) characterized Shays's action as treasonous rebellion. In January 1787, three separate rebel forces—commanded by Shays, Eli Parsons, and Luke Day—marched on the federal arsenal at Springfield. A communication between Day and Shays was intercepted by the commander of the county militia, and the arsenal was defended by some 1,200 local militia under Brigadier General William Shepard. As the rebels approached, Shepard ordered the defenders to open fire with two artillery pieces, killing 4 of the rebels and wounding many others. Neither the rebels nor the militiamen fired their muskets. Not having believed that their neighbors and fellow veterans would fire on them, Shays's men withdrew.

Shays subsequently regrouped his troops at his hometown of Pelham and then headed toward Petersham. On the night of February 3–4, some 4,400 Massachusetts militiamen led by Major General Benjamin Lincoln marched from Hadley and on the morning of February 4 surprised the insurgents camped at Petersham, taking 140 prisoners, although most of the rebels, including Shays, escaped. Shays took refuge in Vermont. The skirmish at Petersham officially ended the rebellion, although some fighting and bloodshed occurred during the course of the next several months in the Berkshire hills to the west.

The impact of Shays' Rebellion was significant. Massachusetts dealt leniently with most of the rebels, who faced disqualification for up to three years from voting, holding office, and serving on juries. Leaders of the rebellion received stiffer penalties, and 18 were sentenced to death. But only 2 of the 18 (John Bly and Charles Rose of Berkshire County) were actually hanged (for banditry), and even Shays received a pardon once passions subsided. Ironically, some state leaders became political victims of the uprising. Hard-liners such as Adams and Bowdoin were voted out of office, and the more lenient John Hancock became governor.

Although the rural uprising was a failure, the demands for tax relief and postponement of debt payments did receive some redress. Nationally, Shays' Rebellion bolstered calls for constitutional reform. Since the inception of the Articles of Confederation of 1781, many critics had called for a more powerful federal government than that of the Articles of Confederation, particularly with respect to issues of national finance and the raising of an army to repel external attack or internal insurrection. These issues were clarified with the new U.S. Constitution of 1787, which empowered the new central government to raise taxes and armed forces.

William McGuire, Leslie Wheeler, and Mark Thompson

See also American Revolutionary War

Further Reading

Gross, Robert A., ed. *In Debt to Shays: The Bicentennial of an Agrarian Rebellion.* Charlottesville: University of Virginia Press, 1993.

Richards, Leonard L. *Shays's Rebellion: The American Revolution's Final Battle.* Philadelphia: University of Pennsylvania Press, 2002.

Szatmary, David P. *Shays' Rebellion: The Making of an Agrarian Insurrection.* Amherst: University of Massachusetts Press, 1980.

Shining Path.

See Sendero Luminoso

Simson, Hugh James

Birth Date: 1886
Death Date: 1941

British Army officer and author of a classic text on counterinsurgency. Born in 1886, Hugh James Simson was commissioned in the Royal Scots Regiment in 1906. During World War I (1914–1918), he served as an interpreter with Japanese forces in Qingdao, China; then served on the Western Front; and finally served as a trainer with the American Expeditionary Forces. After the war, Simson served with British forces stationed in Russia to keep war supplies from falling into the hands of the Bolsheviks during the Russian Civil War.

During 1924–1927, Simson was assigned to the Staff College, Aldershot. Promoted to lieutenant colonel in 1927, he served in China, and during 1930–1932 he was the British military attaché in Tokyo, after which he was assigned to the War Office. In September 1936 Simson was appointed brigadier general on the British staff in Palestine, although he served in the rank of colonel. He retired from the army in March 1937 and died in 1941.

Simson's book *British Rule and Rebellion,* published in 1937, was based primarily on the Arab Revolt in Palestine of 1936–1939, which he experienced firsthand. The book also made reference to turmoil in Ireland immediately after World War I. Simson identified what he called "subwar," the increasing use by those seeking to overturn existing governments of terrorism and propaganda to gain a psychological advantage and sway public opinion. In order to meet this threat, Simson stressed the need for close coordination of the activities of the civil, military, and police authorities, especially in the intelligence sphere. Simson called for prompt government action in the case of unrest, to include the imposition of martial law.

Spencer C. Tucker

See also Arab Revolt of 1936

Further Reading

Beckett, Ian F. W. *Encyclopedia of Guerrilla Warfare.* Santa Barbara, CA: ABC-CLIO, 1999.

Simpson, J. J. *British Rule, and Rebellion.* 1937; reprint, Salisbury, NC: Documentary Publications, 1977.

Skulking Way of War

A form of warfare in which attackers used stealth to surprise their enemies that was employed largely by Native Americans and later adopted by Europeans in North America. Ambushes were typical of the skulking way of war, as were raids on small isolated garrisons or settlements. Skulking tactics relied on detailed knowledge of local terrain and the cover of darkness to conceal movements and acquire positions from which to waylay foes. Attackers also exercised individual initiative, advancing or retreating in open order. Many times, individual combatants aimed and fired at specific targets on their own volition. Combatants usually did not press attacks against enemies who were well prepared to receive an assault, avoided pitched battles, and retreated if they were themselves ambushed.

Native Americans pursued skulking warfare throughout the era of the 19th-century Indian Wars. Although other forms of combat occurred in particular cases, skulking tactics prevailed among American Indian warriors throughout the period. Over time, Native American combatants also replaced indigenous arms (bow and arrows, edged weapons, etc.) with firearms of European and later American manufacture as their primary weapon.

In contrast to the skulking way of war, conventional European warfare of the colonial period emphasized the role of prescribed orderly battle. Infantry moved in unison in compact close-order formations, handling and discharging weapons together in volleys fired under the direction of officers. Europeans and their colonial descendants varied in their abilities to adapt to or cope with skulking warfare. Militiamen from New France were largely successful in employing these tactics, and they often joined with their American Indian allies in raiding the English colonial frontier during wars between the two countries.

English forces often had more difficulty coping with skulking foes, particularly in conflicts such as King Philip's War (1675–1676) in which effective military responses emphasized direct assaults on American Indian communities or employed native allies against other native foes. However, by the mid-18th century, some British colonial units such as Rogers' Rangers were primarily employing skulking tactics. Skulking tactics saw widespread use among both Native American and U.S. forces in most of the Indian wars that transpired from the 1790s to 1890.

Matthew S. Muehlbauer

See also Rogers, Robert

Further Reading

Hirsch, Adam J. "The Collision of Military Cultures in Seventeenth-Century New England." *Journal of American History* 74 (March 1988): 1187–1212.

Malone, Patrick M. *The Skulking Way of War: Technology and Tactics among the New England Indians.* Lanham, MD: Madison Books, 2000.

Otterbein, Keith F. "Why the Iroquois Won: An Analysis of Iroquois Military Tactics." *Ethnohistory* 11 (1964): 56–63.

Starkey, Armstrong. *European and Native American Warfare, 1675–1815.* Norman: University of Oklahoma Press, 1998.

Small Wars Manual, U.S. Marine Corps

Originally published in 1940, the U.S. Marine Corps *Small Wars Manual* was prompted by articles in professional journals by Marine Corps officers discussing the low-intensity conflicts in the Caribbean area involving the marines and known as small wars (e.g., the Banana Wars in Central America and the Caribbean). The Marine Corps was then thought of largely as a sort of international police force that could be rapidly deployed by sea to protect American overseas interests. Articles by Major Samuel Huntington about the particular nature of such interventions and counterinsurgency operations associated with them began appearing in the *Marine Corps Gazette* as early as 1921. Later articles in the same publication were written by Majors C. J. Miller and Richard Peard and Lieutenant Colonels W. P. Upshur and Harold Utley. Other articles appeared in the principal U.S. Navy journal, *Proceedings of the U.S. Naval Institute.*

Colonel Utley was a major figure in the study of counterinsurgency warfare. He taught a course at Quantico on low-intensity conflict that had grown to 45 hours of instruction by 1938. Utley and others compiled the *Small Wars Manual,* which appeared in 1940.

This 492-page publication examined the practical and philosophical aspects of low-intensity conflicts. Chapters included the introduction of forces, the organization of forces, logistics, training, initial operations, patrolling, mounted detachments, convoys, aviation, river operations, disarmament of the local population, armed indigenous organizations, military government, supervision of democratic elections, and withdrawal of forces.

The *Small Wars Manual* identifies a small war as one that does not involve regular warfare against a first-rate power, one that has been undertaken to suppress lawlessness or insurrection, and one involving the protection of American interests, lives, and property abroad. Small wars employ the minimum force necessary and differ greatly from major warfare. In small wars, diplomacy remains active, and the State Department exercises a constant and controlling influence over military operations.

The *Small Wars Manual* concludes that hostile forces in occupied territory will employ guerrilla warfare. The manual notes the difficulties that may arise from deceit by hostile sympathizers and agents or the intimidation of the native population upon whom reliance might be placed to gain information. In addition, the unrest sparking the military intervention may be primarily economic, social, or political in nature, and thus the application of military measures may not alone suffice to restore peace and orderly government. Military measures should be applied only to such an extent as to permit the continuation of peaceful corrective measures so as to restore peace. The manual emphasizes the need of the intervention force to be aware of the local culture, to include ethnic composition, religious makeup, class distinctions, political outlooks, mores, etc.

The *Small Wars Manual* notes that abuses by those in power, including the oppression of opposition political parties, are often the cause of revolution. Revolutionary forces may be poorly trained, organized, and equipped, but they often have high esprit and idealism, with individual fighters willing to sacrifice their lives for their strongly held beliefs. While the *Small Wars Manual* pays considerable attention to the underlying political, economic, and social causes of insurgencies, it does not prescribe actions to assist other governmental departments in addressing these causes.

Despite being published in 1940, the *Small Wars Manual* remains relevant today. Still recommended professional reading, it provides much useful information on the conduct of counterinsurgency warfare.

Biff L. Baker and Spencer C. Tucker

See also Utley, Harold Hickox

Further Reading

Bickel, Keith B. *Mars Learning: The Marine Corps' Development of Small Wars Doctrine, 1915–1940.* Boulder, CO: Westview, 2001.

U.S. Navy Department. *NAVMC Manual No. 2890: United States Marine Corps Small Wars Manual.* Washington, DC: U.S. Marine Corps, 1940.

Smith, Jacob Hurd

Birth Date: January 29, 1840
Death Date: March 1, 1918

U.S. Army general notorious for the severity of his campaign in Samar in 1901–1902 during the Philippine-American War (1899–1902). Born in Kentucky on January 29, 1840, Jacob Hurd Smith enlisted in the army at the onset of the American Civil War (1861–1865) and was commissioned a second lieutenant in 1862. Badly wounded in the Battle of Shiloh (April 6–7, 1862), on his recovery he spent the remainder of the war as a recruiting officer.

Smith secured a regular army commission as a captain in 1867, but controversy dogged him. Accused of involvement in illegal financial dealings with funds entrusted to him for enlistment bounties, he was removed from the post of temporary army judge advocate in 1869. He also encountered legal problems for his failure to pay debts.

Smith then fought in the Indian Wars in the American West. In 1885, however, he was court-martialed for failing to pay a sum he had lost playing cards. Found guilty, he was sentenced to confinement to post for 18 months and loss of half his pay. In 1886 he was again court-martialed for having made false statements in the case. Again found guilty, he would have been dismissed had not President Grover Cleveland intervened and reduced the sentence to a reprimand.

When the Spanish-American War began, Smith was a major. Following service in Cuba, he was assigned to the Philippines as a colonel in command of the 12th Infantry Regiment during the Philippine-American War. Following the Balangiga Massacre on the island of Luzon on September 28, 1901, when villagers and guerrillas attacked 74 American soldiers and killed 48 of them in what was the single worst U.S. military disaster of the war, commander of U.S. forces in the Philippines Major General Adna Chaffee placed Smith, now a brigadier general commanding the 6th Separate Brigade, in charge of a punitive campaign on Samar.

Chaffee's decision was based on Smith's reputation as a commander who was tough on guerrillas. Although Chaffee did not seem to realize Smith's willingness to resort to extralegal means to achieve his ends, he must have known that Smith had in the past shown a callous disregard for the lives of prisoners and had made statements condemning what he believed to be the tendency of officers involved in pacification duties to be too lenient. Typical of this was a letter to the *Manila News* in which Smith blamed the Balangiga Massacre on "U.S. officers who love 'little brown brother.'"

In ordering him to recapture the U.S. weapons taken at Batangas, Chaffee no doubt encouraged Smith to employ harsh methods, but it is by no means clear, as Smith later claimed, that Chaffee ordered him to turn Samar into "a howling wilderness." Clearly, Smith's orders regarding policies to be followed in Samar increased the violence there. Most notoriously, Smith allegedly gave verbal orders to U.S. Marine Corps major Littleton T. Waller, who commanded a marine battalion on loan to Smith, to "kill and burn," take no prisoners, turn the interior of Samar into "a howling wilderness," and regard every male over the age of 10 as a combatant who could be executed.

Although Waller did not take Smith's orders literally and insisted that the marines not make war on children, the resulting violence of the Samar Campaign attracted considerable unfavorable coverage in the American press. In March 1902 Major Waller was court-martialed for the execution of 10 civilian porters during the Samar Campaign. Waller tried to protect Smith by basing his defense on General Order No. 100 during the American Civil War that dealt with the treatment of guerrillas caught behind the lines. Smith was then called as a witness by the prosecution and, in an act of self-protection, perjured himself by denying that he had issued any special orders to Waller. The defense rebutted Smith's testimony with 3 witnesses who had heard the conversation between the 2 men in which Smith had told Waller not to take prisoners and to execute males above the age of 10. It was by this means that the order became public.

Waller was acquitted, forcing Secretary of War Elihu Root to order a court-martial for Smith in May 1902. Root sought to reduce the damage by claiming that Smith's orders had never been meant to be taken literally. Smith, however, contradicted Root and informed reporters that such a course was the only effective one when dealing with "savages." Root tried to have Smith declared temporarily insane, but this failed when two of three medical officers appointed by Chaffee to hear the case refused to agree to this.

In Smith's court-martial, the charge was not for his orders or for war crimes but rather for "conduct to the prejudice of good order and military discipline." The court found Smith guilty and sentenced him to a verbal reprimand. To mitigate the outcry in the United States over the affair and the lenient sentence, Root recommended that Smith be retired, which President Theodore Roosevelt accepted. Smith retired to Portsmouth, Ohio, and died in San Diego, California, on March 1, 1918.

Spencer C. Tucker

See also Philippine Islands and U.S. Pacification during the Philippine-American War

Further Reading

Fritz, David L. "Before the Howling Wilderness: The Military Career of Jacob Hurd Smith, 1862–1902." *Military Affairs* 34 (December 1979): 186–190.

Linn, Brian McAllister. *The Philippine War, 1899–1902.* Lawrence: University Press of Kansas, 2000.

Schott, Joseph L. *The Ordeal of Samar.* Indianapolis: Bobbs-Merrill, 1964.

Somaliland Insurgency

Start Date: 1889
End Date: 1920

In 1884 the British and French established protectorates on the coast of Somaliland on the Horn of East Africa. Although the region possessed scant resources, controlling the coast was strategically important as protection for the British sea route to India that now ran through the Suez Canal. Italy was also active in the region, with the border between British and Italian Somaliland established in 1894.

In 1899, however, British Somaliland was threatened by Sheik Sayyīd Muhammad Abd Allāh al-Hassan. Known to the British as the "Mad Mullah," the charismatic Hassan employed both religious and nationalist arguments to assemble a coalition of Ogaden tribes. His Dervish state was essentially organized for war, with Hassan alleging that the Christian Ethiopians and British were working in tandem to destroy both Islam and Somali freedom.

Hassan then led raids of Dervish warriors against neighboring British, French, Italian, and Ethiopian territory. Indeed, during 1901–1904, the Dervishes won a number of victories. The British soundly defeated Hassan's forces on the Jidaale (Jidballi) Plain in January 1904, when he mistakenly opted for a pitched battle in the open. Reportedly, Hassan suffered some 7,000 dead, and he and his followers were driven from British territory.

By 1913, however, Hassan's followers controlled much of the interior and had constructed a number of stone forts. On August 9 of that year, Hassan's Dervishes inflicted a costly defeat on the British Somaliland Camel Constabulary in the Battle of Dul Madoba, killing 57 members of the 110-man unit. British plans for a major military effort against Hassan were then interrupted by World War I (1914–1918).

After the war the British decided to employ airpower, and in January 1920 Royal Air Force bombers struck the Dervish settlements and a number of stone forts constructed around Taleex (Taleh), the capital of Hassan's Dervish state, in the Sool region of Somalia. The bombing damaged the forts and killed a number of members of Hassan's family. As a consequence of this and air attacks elsewhere accompanied by ground assaults, the Dervishes were forced back into the Ogaden. Hassan attempted to rebuild his army, but he died of influenza in December 1920, and without his leadership, the insurgency collapsed. The British success with airpower here encouraged them to try the same solution in other colonial locations, notably Iraq, that same year.

Spencer C. Tucker

See also Iraq Revolt

Further Reading

Abdi-Sheik, Abdi. *Divine Madness: Mohammed Abdulle Hassan (1856–1920)*. London: Zed, 1993.

Jardine, Douglas J. *The Mad Mullah of Somaliland*. London: Jenkins, 1923.

South African War

Start Date: October 11, 1899
End Date: May 31, 1902

The South African War (1899–1902), also known as the Second Boer War, followed more than a century of conflict between the British Empire and the Afrikaans-speaking Dutch settlers known as Boers, who had established in Southern Africa the independent republics of the South African Republic (Transvaal Republic) and the Orange Free State. The causes of the war are complex but were centered on the desire of the British in South Africa to control the gold mines and diamond fields in Boer territory. The British had recognized the two Boer republics, but the British attempt to annex the Transvaal led to the First Boer War (1880–1881). Following British defeats, especially the Battle of Majuba Hill (February 27, 1881), the independence of the two republics was upheld, although relations remained tense.

The discovery of diamonds at Kimberley in the Orange Free State in 1866 and of gold in the South African Republic in 1886 led to a massive influx of foreigners, known to the Boers as Uitlanders, to work the mines in the Transvaal. These discoveries also led to a determination on the part of British imperialists, most notably mining magnate and prime minister of the Cape Colony Cecil Rhodes, to take over the Boer Republics. Rhodes planned an invasion into the Transvaal timed with an uprising by Utilanders in Johannesburg. The ensuing Jameson Raid (December 29, 1895–January 2, 1896) saw a column of 600 men led by Leander Staar Jameson captured by the Boers and no Uitlander uprising.

The embarrassing Jameson Raid led to Rhodes's recall and greatly increased tensions between the British and the Boers. Negotiations centered on political rights of the Uitlanders, the majority of whom were British and whose numbers threatened to subsume the Boer population.

Much to the satisfaction of Lord Milner, the new British high commissioner for South Africa, negotiations in June 1899 failed. British colonial secretary Joseph Chamberlain demanded full voting rights for the Uitlanders, and South African Republic president Paul Kruger issued an ultimatum on October 9, 1899, giving the British government 48 hours to withdraw forces from the borders of both the Transvaal and the Orange Free State. When London rejected the ultimatum, the two Boer republics declared war.

The war divided into three phases. The first phase began on October 11, 1899, and lasted into December. In it, the Boers were on the offensive, with their large mounted columns known as commandos carrying out preemptive strikes into the British Natal and the Cape Colony, laying siege to the British garrisons and then winning a series of tactical victories over British forces under Lieutenant General Sir Redvers Buller attempting to relieve their forward garrisons. In the second phase (January–September 1900), a large British force commanded by Field Marshal Frederick Sleigh, Viscount Roberts, who replaced Buller, systematically captured the Boer capitals and major population centers. Roberts declared victory and returned to England. His chief of staff, Lieutenant General Horatio Kitchener, assumed command of the British and imperial forces. What were believed to be only mopping-up operations turned out to be anything but that, and the third phase of the war—from September 1900 to the end of hostilities on May 31, 1902—saw the Boers resort to guerrilla warfare and the British undertaking counterinsurgency tactics.

With the beginning of hostilities, the Boers enjoyed a clear numerical advantage. They were able to assemble an invasion force of 34,000 men within a week's time, leaving another 20,000 to keep watch on the Uitlanders and the Kaffirs (native

A Boer detachment at Spion Kop, Ladysmith, in 1900 during the South African War (Second Boer War) of 1899–1902. The Boers enjoyed success early in the fighting, employing their great mobility to advantage and laying siege not only to Ladysmith but to Kimberley and Mafeking. (Van Hoepen/Hulton Archive/Getty Images)

blacks), while the British had only 25,000 men in all of Southern Africa (10,000 in Natal). Most of the Boer troops were farmers who were excellent horsemen and marksmen. Many were armed with repeating Mauser rifles that fired smokeless powder and allowed the Boers to make excellent use of cover and concealment. The Boers also possessed some modern French (Creusot) and German (Krupp) artillery.

The Boers enjoyed a tremendous advantage in mobility. Almost all were mounted, whereas only one-eighth of the British forces were. The Boers were well suited to act as light cavalry although lacking in discipline. The top generals of the war were almost exclusively Boer. They included Louis Botha, Piet Joubert, Christiaan de Wet, and Jan Smuts.

British military leaders, long accustomed to war on the cheap in colonial conflicts, discounted Boer capabilities. The British had only about 70,000 troops available for deployment to Southern Africa, and these lacked equipment, supplies, and artillery. It took the British four months to assemble an expeditionary force, and during that time the Boers ran wild.

In the early fighting the British deployed largely infantry, often employing linear tactics with their artillery in the open. The British had placed the bulk of their forces in forward positions in anticipation that they would be soon taking the offensive. This allowed the more numerous Boers commandos to cut off the British garrisons and to lay siege to Ladysmith, Mafeking, and Kimberley.

The success of British conventional operations in the second phase of the war was due to overwhelming numbers, more cavalry, and the beginnings of an understanding by the British command of the importance of mobility and speed. The handling of the British mounted forces (cavalry, mounted infantry, and Afrikaners) as well as the addition of well-trained mounted Australian and New Zealand colonial units permitted the British to gain the upper hand in conventional operations. This resulted in several defeats of Boer units in the field and the capture of Bloemfontein, capital of the Orange Free State, on March 13, 1900, followed by that of Pretoria, capital of the Transvaal, on June 5, 1900.

The third phase of the war was the most difficult. The Boer leadership decided to continue the war but to employ guerrilla warfare. They sought to take the offensive into Natal and the Cape Colony, hoping to inspire an uprising in the Cape Colony. They also sought to harass the extended British supply lines. All of this was intended to create war weariness in Britain that would lead to peace terms favorable to Boer interests.

Boer forces kept constantly on the move, living off the civilian population and capturing British supplies. The British sent out flying columns, the coordinated movements of which were designed to trap the Boer field forces. Though containing mounted contingents, the British columns could not match Boer mobility. While the British were unable to pin down the elusive Boers, the Boers found it difficult to carry out decisive strikes, and the Afrikaner populations of Natal and the Cape Colony were unwilling to rise in rebellion. Thus, through the rest of 1900 and into 1901, the war was somewhat of a stalemate.

Recognizing that the Boers' mobility was due to their ability to support themselves through the local Boer population, Kitchener instituted a policy of population relocation and the destruction of the Boer farms. Boer families were forcibly removed from their farms on the Veldt and relocated into concentration camps. The empty farms were burned and livestock and crops were destroyed in order to deprive the Boer raiders of their logistics infrastructure.

Little thought had been given to logistics in the concentration camps. Rations were inadequate at best and even less for those Boer families who had male members in the field. Disease caused by poor facilities and sanitation and inadequate diet ravaged the Boer civilian population. The camps became a great embarrassment for the British government and helped garner much international sympathy for the Boer cause. Ultimately Kitchener abandoned the camps, only to institute an even more inhumane policy of forcing the Boer civilians back onto their ruined farmsteads.

Kitchener also instituted the construction of blockhouses. These prefabricated structures were first positioned along rail lines, in some places as close as every 200 yards, and manned with infantry. The blockhouses were proof against small-arms fire and were protected by barbed wire. Eventually barbed wire linked the positions, and the system was expanded to other areas. This cordoning off of the wide-open spaces limited the mobility of the mounted Boers. Such a program was both expensive and manpower-intensive, with British field forces having grown to some 250,000 men by late 1901. Eventually the blockhouse lines extended over 3,700 miles of territory and were manned by 66,000 infantry. Although this system could not stop the Boers, it significantly limited their operational mobility.

Finally, the British greatly improved their intelligence collection. This involved employing ex-Boers (about one-fifth of the Boers fought on the British side) but also large numbers of native Kaffirs. They knew both the terrain and Boer methods of operation. British mobile columns continued to operate, and more and more of the British forces were mounted. They now included regular British Army cavalry as well as troops from New Zealand, Australia, and Canada. Men and horses could be moved by rail and then leave the trains at strategic locations. Many of the columns operated at night. Still, Boer forces achieved several notable successes into 1902, including the October 1901 destruction of one of the most capable British units, under Colonel George E. Benson, who was mortally wounded, and the defeat of a major column under Major General Paul Methuen and the capture of the general and 600 of his men on March 7, 1902.

The suffering of their families, exhausted resources, and fears of a rising by the Kaffirs, however, prompted the Boer decision to sue for peace. The conflict was officially ended by the Treaty of Vereeniging, signed on May 31, 1902. If the British triumphed, it was only because they agreed to share political power. Under the treaty terms, the Boers accepted British sovereignty in return for representative institutions as soon as circumstances permitted. The British government also granted the Boers £3 million to rebuild their farms.

In 1907 the British allowed free elections, first in the Transvaal and then in the Orange River Colony (former Orange Free State). As a result, the Boer leaders again took the reins of political power. In 1910 following a constitutional convention, a Union of South Africa was created, binding the Cape Colony, Natal, the Orange River Colony, and the Transvaal together, with former Boer general Louis Botha as prime minister. The Boers now became one of the most stalwart supporters of the British Empire, as was seen in their loyalty during World War I (1914–1918).

The chief losers in the war were not the whites, who again ruled South Africa. At least 40,000 Kaffirs had served each side as noncombatants, and Kitchener even armed another 10,000, despite Boor protests, but the Kaffirs now found themselves worse off than ever before. The South African War also encouraged the German government in an adventurous foreign policy. Many foreign observers now saw Britain as a military paper tiger. This was a consideration in Germany's decision to declare war in 1914.

In the fighting during the South African War, British Empire forces sustained some 21,000 deaths, more than 13,000 of which were from disease and other non-battle causes. Boer losses were approximately 9,000, while some 28,000 civilians died, mostly in the concentration camps.

Louis A. DiMarco and Spencer C. Tucker

See also Kitchener, Horatio Herbert; *Reconcentrado* System; Roberts, Frederick Sleigh; South African War

Further Reading

Pakenham, Thomas. *The Boer War.* New York: Random House, 1979.

Farwell, Byron. *Queen Victoria's Little Wars.* New York: Norton, 1986.

South Sudan Insurgency

Start Date: 1983
End Date: 2005

During 1955–1972, there had been civil war in Sudan. Northern Sudan was overwhelmingly Arab and Muslim in religion and had long-standing ties with Egypt. Southern Sudan was predominantly non-Arab and animist or Christian. The fighting came to an end only in 1972 when, in the Addis Ababa Agreement, the northern Sudan agreed to self-government for the southern Sudan in what became known as the Southern Sudan Autonomous Region.

In 1983 Sudanese president Gaafar al-Nimeiry suspended the Southern Regional Assembly and introduced a federal state structure in violation of the 1972 Addis Ababa Agreement. In September 1983, unrest in the southern Sudan became outright rebellion when Nimeiry, pressed by the Muslim Brotherhood, imposed Sharia (Islamic) law throughout the country, including the largely Christian southern Sudan. Religious courts now imposed such penalties as the cutting off of a hand for theft.

These measures provoked a new round of fighting. The insurgency known as the Second Sudanese Civil War was led by the Sudan People's Liberation Army (SPLA), the military arm of the Sudan People's Liberation Movement, with Colonel John Garang commanding the southern antigovernment guerrillas. During the course of the next several years, government control in the southern Sudan was limited to the towns, while Garang's guerrillas controlled the countryside.

Against the insurgents, the Sudanese government employed Soviet-built military helicopters and cargo aircraft modified to act as bombers. These attacked indiscriminately, with devastating effect on this region's villages and population, most of whom were innocent civilians. Widespread food shortages brought both malnutrition and outright starvation.

The SPLA continued the insurgency, despite an April 1985 coup d'état that toppled Nimeiry. Then in May 1986 Sadiq al-Mahdi became prime minister. The insurgency continued, however, because the Muslim character of the government remained unchanged. In 1989 Colonel Omar al-Bashir seized power and proclaimed himself president of Sudan.

Meanwhile, Sudanese government-sponsored militias periodically attacked villages in southern Sudan. In 1995 former U.S. president Jimmy Carter negotiated a cease-fire to allow humanitarian aid into southern Sudan. The cease-fire held for six months. Sporadic fighting then resumed until the Nairobi Comprehensive Peace Agreement of January 9, 2005. Over its span of more than two decades, the fighting had claimed the lives of as many as 2 million people and brought the displacement of another 4 million.

Peace talks had made significant progress in 2003 and 2004, and the Nairobi Agreement of January 9, 2005, granted the southern Sudan autonomy for a six-year period, to be followed by a referendum on independence. The agreement also created a co–vice presidency position, allowed both northern and southern Sudan to split oil deposits equally, and left the armies in place.

Although sharp disagreements occurred between the two sides concerning territorial boundaries and oil sharing, with some additional fighting, and although the Sudanese government waffled on the matter of holding the referendum, the United Nations applied pressure, and the referendum went forward as planned. On January 9, 2011, the southern Sudanese voted nearly 99 percent in favor of secession. South Sudan became a sovereign independent state on July 9, 2011, although disagreements over precise territorial boundaries in the oil-producing areas continued, and there has been some bloodshed and threats by Sudanese president al-Bashir.

Spencer C. Tucker

Further Reading

Deng, Francis Mading. *War of Visions: Conflict of Identities in the Sudan.* Washington, DC: Brookings Institution, 1995.

Wai, Dunstan, M. *The African-Arab Conflict in the Sudan.* New York: African Publishing, 1991.

South-West Africa Insurgency

Start Date: 1966
End Date: 1990

The southwestern African nation of Namibia is a mineral-rich country on the Atlantic coast between Angola to the north and South Africa to the south. Namibia is home to at least a dozen ethnic groups, the largest of which is the Ovambo of eight tribes, representing some 45 percent of the population. As a consequence of the European scramble to divide up Africa in the last decades of the 19th century, a conference was held at Berlin during 1884–1885. The conference granted Germany the territory that today constitutes Namibia and was then known as South-West Africa. Following the defeat of Germany in World War I (1914–1918), South-West Africa passed to South Africa as a League of Nations mandate in 1920. In 1966, the United Nations (UN) General Assembly revoked the South Africa mandate, but South Africa refused to yield control and rejected subsequent appeals to do so, despite an International Court of Justice ruling in 1971 that declared it to be in "illegal occupation" of the territory.

Organized resistance began when the South African government endeavored to extend its apartheid policies to South-West Africa, with homelands for blacks that would have left 88,000 whites as the largest ethnic group in two-thirds of the territory while restricting some 675,000 blacks to the remaining third. On April 19, 1960, Andimba Toivo ya Toivo organized the South-West Africa People's Organization (SWAPO) and called for the independence of Namibia. SWAPO then commenced a guerrilla war, known in South Africa as the Border War. It began on August 26, 1966, in a clash between SWAPO and the South African police and air force. SWAPO's military wing, the People's Liberation Army of Namibia (PLAN), operated from bases in Angola.

The struggle over South-West Africa drew in the superpowers, with Marxist Angola supported by the Soviet Union, the United States supporting SWAPO, and the People's Republic of China supporting SWAPO's main domestic rival, the South-West Africa National Union (SWANU). SWANU's operations were based in Dar es Salaam, Lusaka, and Luanda.

SWAPO used its extensive external ties to became the dominant insurgent organization in South-West Africa. In 1973 the UN General Assembly declared SWAPO the "authentic representative" of the people of South-West Africa, and in 1977 the UN declared SWAPO the "sole and authentic representative of the Namibian people." The UN also extended SWAPO financial aid.

SWAPO's independence struggle took on a regional dimension when Portugal suddenly withdrew from Angola in 1974. The Soviets and Cubans intervened in Angola in support of the Marxist Movimento Popular de Libertação de Angola (MPLA, Popular Movement for the Liberation of Angola) regime there and subsequently developed close military ties with SWAPO. Before Angola's independence, SWAPO used the Angolan territory dominated by the MPLA's major rival, the Union for the Total Independence of Angola (UNITA), to support its insurgency. After independence, SWAPO could utilize MPLA-controlled territory. Thus, South Africa joined the United States in supporting UNITA.

The terrorist activity of the military wing of PLAN was limited to a few border areas. Approximately 85 percent of PLAN forces consisted of Ovambos. PLAN cooperated with the military wing of the MPLA in Angola and thus was able to use Angolan territory from which to launch attacks. But South African Defense Force counterinsurgency operations were able to contain the SWAPO insurgency, largely by pushing its bases deeper into Angola.

From September 1975 to October 1976, the six sessions of the Turnhalle Conference—a South African–brokered internal reform effort for South-West Africa that did not however include either SWAPO or SWANU—resulted in a draft constitution. It was overwhelmingly approved by a 95 percent vote in a whites-only referendum in May 1977 but, under pressure from the UN, never went into effect.

The United States, along with its British, French, West German, and Canadian allies, formed the Contact Group to negotiate Namibia's independence with South Africa and the so-called Front Line States (FLS), consisting of Angola, Botswana, Mozambique, Tanzania, Zambia, Zimbabwe. The FLS acted as patrons and advisers to SWAPO. In 1989 negotiations between the Contact Group and the FLS finally resulted in U.S.-mediated discussions involving Angolan, Cuban, and South African forces that brought the Angolan Civil Wars close to resolution. South Africa agreed to withdraw its troops from Namibia as the Cubans withdrew their forces from Angola. The South-West Africa Insurgency (Namibia Insurgency) came to an end. South-West Africa became independent as the new state of Namibia on March 21, 1990.

James J. Hentz and Spencer C. Tucker

See also Savimbi, Jonas Malheiro

Further Reading

Crocker, Chester. *High Noon in Southern Africa.* New York: Norton, 1992.

Larkin, Bruce. *China and Africa: 1949–1970.* Berkeley: University of California Press, 1971.

Seiler, John. "South Africa in Namibia: Persistence, Misperception, and Ultimate Failure." *Journal of Modern African Studies* 20(4) (December 1982): 689–712.

Tsokodayi, Cleophas Johannes. *Namibia's Independence Struggle: The Role of the United Nations.* Bloomington, IN: Xlibris, 2011.

South-West Africa People's Organization

The Marxist South-West Africa People's Organization (SWAPO) was the most important insurgent organization fighting for independence in South-West Africa, the colony under South African rule that became the independent nation of Namibia in 1989. During World War I (1914–1918), South African troops occupied what was then the German colony of South-West Africa. Following the war, South Africa continued to control the territory through a League of Nations mandate until after World War II (1939–1945), when the United Nations (UN), which had replaced the League of Nations, refused South Africa's request to annex South-West Africa. From 1946 onward, South Africa continued to rule the colony in spite of a variety of UN resolutions and an International Court of Justice ruling against it as well as increasing pressure from Pan-African groups.

Organized resistance from within South-West Africa arose when the South African government sought to create homelands for blacks similar to the ones it had created in South Africa itself. The planned legislation would have left 88,000 whites as the largest ethnic group in two-thirds of South-West African territory while confining some 675,000 blacks to the remaining third.

Sam Nujoma founded the Ovambo People's Organization in 1957 to represent the rights of contract workers among the Ovambo people, the largest ethnic group in South-West Africa. On April 19, 1960, he reorganized that group as SWAPO and responded to South African attempts to extend its apartheid policies by calling for the independence of Namibia. SWAPO then commenced a guerrilla war against South African occupation. Known in South Africa as the Border War, it is generally accepted to have begun on August 26, 1966, in a clash between SWAPO and the South African Air Force and police. SWAPO's military wing, the People's Liberation Army of Namibia, operated from bases in Angola.

SWAPO members working for political change within Namibia were subjected to great intimidation by South African military and police forces. One of the organization's cofounders, Andimba Toivo Ja Toivo, was imprisoned for 16 years. Meanwhile, Nujoma spent much of his time in exile working on the diplomatic front. In 1968 the Organization of African Unity recognized SWAPO as the sole legitimate authority within Namibia, and the UN declared in 1973 that SWAPO was the "authentic representative" of the South-West African people. Four years later, the UN endorsed SWAPO as the "sole and authentic representative of the Namibian people." The UN also furnished financial assistance to SWAPO.

SWAPO adopted a Marxist-Leninist program. This was in part a rejection of the European colonial economic system, a belief that the Soviet system of state control offered the best means for rapid industrialization, and the impact of communal tribal practices. SWAPO's 1976 political program was based on scientific socialism.

In spite of international support, progress toward independence was slow. Throughout the 1970s, the South African government proposed various administrative plans to grant greater autonomy to Namibians that would be acceptable to the whites living there. Those plans were always rejected by SWAPO leaders, who insisted that no arrangement could be legitimate without the withdrawal of South African troops. Negotiations were further complicated by the situation in Angola, where the South African government supported the insurgency of Jonas Savimbi and the União Nacional para a Independência Total de Angola (UNITA, National Union for the Total Independence of Angola) against the Cuban-backed government of António Agostinho Neto. During the 1980s, the support of the U.S. government for the South African troops in Angola undermined U.S. support for Namibia (which lies between South Africa and Angola).

Finally in 1989, U.S.-mediated discussions between Angolan, Cuban, and South African forces brought the Angolan Civil Wars close to resolution, and South Africa agreed to withdraw its troops from Namibia as the Cubans withdrew their forces from Angola.

The same year, SWAPO won 41 of 72 seats in the Constituent Assembly (redesignated as the National Assembly in 1990) and 57.3 percent of the popular vote in the February 1990 elections. Sam Nujoma, the head of SWAPO, was chosen president. SWAPO remains the governing party of Namibia.

Spencer C. Tucker

See also Angolan Insurgency; Neto, António Agostinho; Savimbi, Jonas Malheiro; União Nacional para a Independência Total de Angola

Further Reading

Banks, Arthur S., and Thomas C. Muller, eds. *Political Handbook of the World, 1998.* Basingstoke, UK: Macmillan, 1998.

Williams, Gwyneth, and Brian Hackland. *Dictionary of Contemporary Politics of Southern Africa.* New York: Macmillan, 1989.

Wiseman, John A. *Political Leaders in Black Africa: A Biographical Dictionary of the Major Politicians since Independence.* Brookfield, VT: E. Elgar, 1991.

Soviet-Afghan War

Start Date: 1979
End Date: 1989

The Soviet-Afghan War, one of the major events of the Cold War, marked the end of the 1970s' period of détente between the United States and the Soviet Union, severely weakened the Soviet regime and hastened its collapse, and remains an important example of a successful insurgency.

Afghanistan had long been fought over by the Great Powers. There had been two Anglo-Afghan wars, in 1838–1842 and 1878–1882. Then in 1885 a major clash occurred between Russian and Afghan forces at Panjdeh. The Treaty of Kabul of 1921, however, effectively established Afghan independence from British influence.

In July 1973, Afghan king Mohammed Zahir Shah was ousted in a coup. His brother-in-law and commander of the Afghan Army, Lieutenant General Mohammed Daoud Khan, established an authoritarian republic with himself as president. In August 1975 the Soviet Union pledged economic assistance. In early 1978 Daoud, alarmed over growing Soviet influence, reduced the number of Soviet advisers in Afghanistan from 1,000 to 200. Daoud, who was unpopular with many Afghans for his authoritarian rule, failed to move effectively against the Afghan Communists, however, and was overthrown and killed in a coup in April 1978.

In May 1978 Nur Mohammad Taraki assumed the presidency. He was also secretary-general of the People's Democratic Party of Afghanistan (PDPA, Afghan Communist Party). The country was renamed the Democratic Republic of Afghanistan. The PDPA meanwhile carried out an extensive modernization program that included freedom of religion and women's rights and also implemented an extensive land reform program.

The majority of Afghan city dwellers either welcomed or were ambivalent to these reforms, but their secular nature made them highly unpopular with religiously conservative Afghans in the villages and the countryside who favored traditionalist Islamic restrictions regarding women. Opposition to the so-called godless Communist regime quickly built, and in these circumstances the Jimmy Carter administration extended covert assistance through the U.S. Central Intelligence Agency (CIA) to the conservative Islamic antigovernment mujahideen (freedom fighters, holy warriors) who had begun battling the Afghan government. The U.S. assistance, which was channeled to the mujahideen through the Pakistan's intelligence agency, the Inter-Services Intelligence, resulted in steady mujahideen gains in rural Afghanistan.

In September 1979, meanwhile, Premier Hafizullah Amin overthrew President Taraki, who was slain in the coup. Carried out without Soviet approval, this change of power led to considerable friction with the Soviets, who were also increasingly concerned about the growth of the mujahideen insurgency. Soviet leader Leonid Brezhnev was committed in the so-called Brezhnev Doctrine to preventing the overthrow of established Communist governments and was also fearful of the possible impact of an Islamic fundamentalist Afghan regime on the Muslim populations of the republics of Soviet Central Asia. During the last months of 1979, Moscow dispatched some 4,500 advisers to assist the Afghan Communist regime and also authorized Soviet aircraft to attack mujahideen positions.

Soviet defense minister Dmitrii Ustinov now convinced Brezhnev to intervene in force, arguing that this was the only sure means of preserving the Afghan Communist regime. Ustinov also postulated a short, victorious intervention. Beginning in November, the Soviets increased the size of their garrisons at two air bases in Kabul and quietly began prepositioning forces just north of Afghanistan.

On December 24, 1979, Soviet troops invaded. Moscow cited the 1978 Treaty of Friendship, Cooperation and Good Neighborliness between the two countries and claimed that the Afghan government had invited them in. Soviet special forces seized control of Kabul Airport, and three airborne divisions were rushed in, while four motorized rifle divisions invaded overland. Deputy minister of internal affairs Lieutenant General Viktor S. Paputin had command. Despite resistance, the Soviets occupied Kabul. Amin died, either in the fighting or by execution; Paputin was also killed in the fighting. The Soviets then installed as president moderate former Afghan vice president Babrak Karmal.

During the next several months, Soviet forces occupied the major Afghan cities and secured control of the roads. Unable to meet the Soviets in conventional battle, the mujahideen resorted to protracted guerrilla warfare, ambushing Soviet road-bound convoys and laying siege to several Soviet-occupied towns. In February 1980, moreover, there was a popular Afghan uprising in Kabul, although it was quickly crushed by Soviet troops.

The Soviet invasion had immediate international consequences. It effectively ended the period of détente between the Soviet Union and the United States. President Carter expressed concern that the Soviets might thus be able to dominate the Persian Gulf and interdict at will the flow of Middle East oil. He enunciated what became known as the Carter Doctrine, that any effort to dominate the Persian Gulf would be interpreted as an attack on American interests to be met by force if necessary. Carter also ordered limits on technology transfers and the sale of agricultural products to the Soviet Union, and he canceled U.S. participation in the 1980 Moscow Summer Games.

Carter called on Congress to support increased defense spending and pushed for the creation of a Rapid Deployment Force capable of intervening in the Persian Gulf or other areas threatened by the Soviets. He also offered increased military aid to Pakistan, moved to improve ties with the People's Republic of China, and approved expanded covert assistance to the mujahideen. These steps, except for the last, had but limited impact.

The Soviet military strategy in Afghanistan called for, in order, relieving the besieged towns; driving the Afghan mujahideen from the towns, roads, and fertile agricultural regions back into the mountains; securing the frontier near the Khyber Pass to prevent the mujahideen from receiving weapons and other military supplies from Pakistan; and eliminating mujahideen mountain base camps. The first two phases enjoyed success. The Soviets employed jet aircraft to bomb rebel positions, followed by Mil Mi-24 Hind armored helicopter gunships firing rockets and machine guns. Mil M-26 Hook helicopters then brought in assault troops to attack the mujahideen in place.

Although the mujahideen inflicted significant casualties on the Soviets, they themselves suffered heavily and were driven from the towns and into the hills and mountains. The Soviets gradually increased the size of their forces in Afghanistan to some 105,000 men, but this was never sufficient to defeat the insurgents. Soviet forces were also unable to control the mountainous areas where the guerrillas established bases, nor did the Soviets always enjoy complete control of the fertile valleys, where the mujahideen continued to carry out hit-and-run attacks that yielded much-needed Soviet weapons and equipment. The Soviets also were never able to seal the porous frontier with Pakistan, which remained a source for both Pakistani and CIA-supplied arms and equipment.

The Soviets responded with wanton attacks on villages. They also employed numerous small land mines that maimed or killed numerous innocent civilians and, according to some sources, utilized biological and chemical weapons in violation of the 1925 and 1972 Geneva protocols. The mujahideen, meanwhile, remained divided among themselves, thanks to tribal and clan loyalties that prevented them from establishing a unified leadership. In May 1985, however, representatives of seven major mujahideen groups meet in Peshawar, Pakistan, and there established a united front organization.

Afghan resistance fighters, known as mujahideen, return to a village destroyed by Soviet forces, March 25, 1986. The long Soviet-Afghan War (1979–1989) was one of the major events of the Cold War and is a classic example of a successful insurgency. (Department of Defense)

On May 4, 1986, in a bloodless coup engineered by the Soviets, Mohammed Najibullah, the former head of the Aghan secret police, replaced Karmal as secretary-general of the PDPA and in November 1987 was elected president of Afghanistan. Meanwhile, in October 1986 after meeting with Soviet leader Mikhail Gorbachev, Najibullah offered the mujahideen a unilateral cease-fire agreement and limited power-sharing arrangement. They rejected the offer, and the war continued.

The United States had meanwhile increased its aid to the mujahideen. The most important weapon supplied by the CIA was the Stinger shoulder-launched ground-to-air missile. It and the similar British-supplied Blowpipe proved to be the key in defeating Soviet air-to-ground support and especially the deadly Soviet armored helicopter gunships. The Afghan fighters were able to blunt several Soviet offensives.

Finally, with costs in Soviet blood and treasure mounting, in April 1988 in Geneva, Gorbachev agreed to a United Nations–sponsored agreement for the withdrawal of Soviet forces from Afghanistan in two phases during May 15, 1988–February 15, 1989. Soviet military advisers remained in Afghanistan, however, providing assistance to the more than 300,000-man Democratic Republic of Afghanistan (DRA) Army, and Moscow also continued to support the DRA with weapons and equipment totaling some $500 million a month.

The Soviet-Afghan War had claimed some 15,000 Soviet dead, 54,000 wounded, and 417 missing. Afghan losses can only be approximated, but the best estimates are more than 1 million Afghan mujahideen combatants and civilians killed and more than 5.5 million civilians displaced, most of these to northwestern Pakistan.

Having helped inflict a major defeat on the Soviet Union with the withdrawal of its forces, the United States and its allies then lost interest in Afghanistan and extended little aid to assist the government or try to influence events there. In April 1992 the mujahideen seized Kabul, bringing finis to the DRA. Fighting continued between the rival mujahideen groups, however, and an extremist Islamist group known as the Taliban seized power in September 1996.

Spencer C. Tucker

See also Mujahideen in the Soviet-Afghan War

Further Reading

Borovik, Artyom. *The Hidden War: A Russian Journalist's Account of the Soviet War in Afghanistan.* New York: Grove, 1990.

Braithwaite, Rodric. *Afgantsy: The Russians in Afghanistan, 1979–89.* New York: Oxford University Press, 2011.

Feifer, Gregory. *The Great Gamble: The Soviet War in Afghanistan.* New York: Harper, 2009.

Spartacus

Birth Date: ca. 109 BCE
Death Date: 71 BCE

Roman soldier and insurgent leader. Little is known of Spartacus's early life. Most Roman sources have him born in Thrace and claim that he was a Roman soldier who deserted and was then captured and enslaved. He has been described as both intelligent and cultured. It has been established that Spartacus was trained at a gladiator school in Capua. He embraced the thought of Blossius of Cumae that "the first shall be last." Spartacus and some 70 others escaped from the gladiator school and led a slave revolt that became known in Roman history as the Third Servile War (73–71 BCE).

Overrunning much of southern Italy, the former slaves plundered the great estates of the region, freeing other slaves until their army had grown to as many as 120,000 men, perhaps including women and children who also joined. Spartacus defeated all Roman forces, including two legions, sent against him and devastated the great estates of southern Italy, although reportedly he tried to restrain his followers from acts of destruction. During the winter, Spartacus set his men to work making weapons.

Spartacus's army marched north, headed for Cisalpine Gaul in the spring of 72 BCE. The Senate dispatched consuls Gellius Publicola and Ginaeus Cornelius

Lentulus Clodianus, each with two legions, against Spartacus. Publicola defeated the Gauls and Germanic peoples, who had separated from Spartacus. But at Picenum in central Italy, Spartacus and the remainder of his followers defeated both Roman armies in turn. In Cisalpine Gaul (Gaul on the south side of the Alps), Spartacus triumphed over yet another legion under Roman governor Gaius Cassius Longinus.

Spartacus apparently planned to march the army into Gaul or to Spain, perhaps disbanding the army to allow its members to return to their homes, but his followers allegedly insisted on additional plunder, and he went along with this. There are some suggestions that perhaps 10,000 of his followers departed at this time to return home, however. In any case, Spartacus marched the army south again, plundering as it proceeded and defeating two legions under Marcus Licinius Crassus. The army spent the winter of 72–71 BCE near the Straits of Messina.

Spartacus's plans to have Cilician pirates transfer his army to Sicily collapsed, and Crassus, then the wealthiest man in Rome, raised eight legions and led them against the slave army, trapping it in Calabria in early 71 BCE. At the same time, the Senate recalled other Roman forces from abroad. Although Sparatcus managed to break through Crassus's lines and headed toward Brundisium (today Brindisi), Crassus pursued and caught up with the slave army in Lucania. Crassus was victorious, and Spartacus died in fighting near the Silarus River. Crassus ordered some 6,000 of Spartacus's followers crucified along the Via Appia (Appian Way), their bodies visible to travelers for sometime thereafter. Another 5,000 slaves escaped but were later defeated by Gnaeus Pompeius Magnus (Pompey the Great), recalled from Iberia. Both Pompey and Crassus later allied with Julius Caesar in the First Triumvirate.

A brave and resourceful leader, Spartacus remains a potent symbol of resistance to oppression and has been commemorated in film, dance, and music. The German Communists after World War I (1914–1918) called themselves the Spartacist League.

Spencer C. Tucker

Further Reading

Bradley, Keith R. *Slavery and Rebellion in the Roman World, 1490 B.C.–70 B.C.* Bloomington: Indiana University Press, 1989.

Plutarch. *Fall of the Roman Republic.* Translated by R. Warner. London: Penguin, 1872.

Trow, M. J. *Spartacus: The Myth and the Man.* Stroud, UK: Sutton, 2006.

Special Air Service

The Special Air Service (SAS) is a regiment of the British Army that was constituted in May 1950. Part of the United Kingdom Special Forces, the SAS has long been regarded as a model for the world's special forces. The SAS actually began in 1941 in the North African theater in World War II (1939–1945) when Lieutenant Colonel

David Sterling formed the L Detachment, 21st Special Air Service Brigade. The name of the original organization was specifically designed to confuse German intelligence regarding the nature of the unit and indicate the possible existence of a British parachute brigade in the theater. The organization's wartime mission was primarily raids against Axis airfields and headquarters deep behind enemy lines. The SAS employed a variety of transport, including land vehicles, aircraft, and watercraft. The SAS also executed missions to support, train, advise, and equip groups resisting Axis rule in France, Greece, and Yugoslavia. During the war, the unit underwent several reorganizations but ended in the SAS Brigade as the 1st and 2nd SAS Regiments, respectively.

After World War II, the SAS was temporarily disbanded. In January 1947 it was reformed as the 21st SAS Regiment, part of the British Territorial Army (reserves). The Malayan Emergency (1948–1960) led to the need for an SAS-type unit to assist in hunting down insurgents. The result was the formation of the active army 22nd SAS Regiment in 1952. In 1959 the 23rd SAS Regiment was formed as an additional regiment in the Territorial Army. Its members are experts in escape and evasion.

Since its return to active service, the SAS has played a key role in British counterinsurgency operations. After helping to end the Malayan Emergency, the SAS served in various active operations around the world, including in Borneo, Oman, Aden, Sierra Leone, Somalia, Gambia, Iraq, Afghanistan, the Falkland Islands, Bosnia, and Northern Ireland. The SAS specialties remain deep reconnaissance and raiding. The organization conducts these operations against conventional forces, such as the Iraqi military during the 1991 Persian Gulf War, and against insurgents in a wide variety of conflicts. The SAS played a key role in the last years of Operation banner, the British military operation against the Irish Republican Army (IRA) in Northern Ireland. In that campaign, SAS missions were often closely coordinated with the police of the Royal Ulster Constabulary. All three regiments of the SAS have executed reconnaissance and raiding missions in support of North Atlantic Treaty Organization (NATO) operations in the Afghanistan War (2001–present).

In 1975 the SAS added the new mission capability of hostage rescue. The SAS has exercised this capability in conjunction with larger British Army missions, such as in Sierra Leone in 2000 when the SAS rescued five British military peacekeepers taken prisoner during the Sierra Leone Civil War. The most famous SAS operation of this type was the 1980 rescue of hostages in the Iranian embassy in London, which was closely coordinated with the London police force.

Currently, the SAS remains organized in one active and two reserve regiments (22nd, 21st, and 23rd SAS, respectively). The 22nd SAS Regiment is commanded by a lieutenant colonel and is organized into four squadrons of some 60 men each. Each squadron is commanded by a major and contains 4 troops and a small headquarters section. Each troop is led by a captain and specializes in a particular tactical skill: air troop, parachute insertions; boat troop, amphibious operations; mobility troop, vehicle operations; and mountain troop, mountain and arctic warfare.

Louis A. DiMarco

See also Aden Emergency; Indonesia-Malaysia Confrontation; Malayan Emergency; Northern Ireland Insurgency; Special Operations Executive

Further Reading

Geraghty, Tony. *Who Dares Wins: The Story of the SAS, 1950–1992.* London: Warner, 1993.

McCrery, Nigel. *The Complete History of the SAS: The Story of the World's Most Feared Elite Fighting Force.* London: Carlton, 2004.

Special Operations Executive

British intelligence agency specializing in overseas sabotage and secret operations during World War II (1939–1945). British officials established the Special Operations Executive (SOE) in July 1940, impelled by a much-exaggerated belief that fifth-column activities in western Europe had contributed greatly to the successful German conquest of those countries. Intended in British prime minister Winston L. S. Churchill's words to "set Europe ablaze" by promoting resistance activities in occupied countries, the SOE initially combined sabotage, research, and propaganda functions. In August 1941, propaganda operations were transferred to the Political Warfare Executive, a separate agency under the Foreign Office; the SOE remained under the Ministry of Economic Warfare, headed by Hugh Dalton.

SOE operations focused primarily on delivering agents to European countries to work with and, where appropriate, inspire indigenous resistance movements. Because these activities frequently attracted attention from the German Gestapo and local police, they aroused the enmity of the British intelligence agencies, especially MI6, which focused primarily on gathering information and preferred obscurity to ensure the safety of its operations.

At its height, the SOE employed 10,000 men and 3,000 women. At least half of the men and some women spent periods as agents in hostile or neutral countries. The SOE was normally organized in country sections, although in France the SOE had six sections, each of which worked with a different faction of the French Resistance. Activities of the SOE sections eventually provided arms for half a million French opponents of Germany and thus facilitated the success of the June 1944 Allied landings.

Although its earlier efforts in Italy had proved fruitless, in 1943 the SOE took part in the unconditional surrender negotiations between General Dwight D. Eisenhower and Marshal Patrice Badoglio. Thereafter the SOE assisted Italian partisans who fought the remaining German occupation forces. The SOE's Scandinavian efforts were also largely successful, assisting Danish and Norwegian anti–German Resistance efforts, foiling German plans to use Norwegian heavy water to develop atomic weapons, gathering military intelligence in Denmark, and securing valuable seaborne supplies of special steels and ball bearings from Sweden. In Poland, SOE operatives assisted in extensive sabotage efforts by severely damaging 6,000 locomotives, which disrupted German railroad traffic to the Eastern Front. SOE agents in Czechoslovakia helped in the May 1942 assassination of German obergruppenführer Reinhard Heydrich, a propaganda coup that nonetheless provoked savage reprisals against Czech Jews and the town of Lidice. SOE efforts in the Netherlands, by contrast, proved disastrous. In 1942 and 1943, German intelligence secretly penetrated SOE communications networks, capturing more than 50 SOE agents, many of whom were executed.

Communist operatives penetrated the large SOE mission in Cairo, which supervised Balkan missions and helped to steer SOE assistance toward Communist resistance factions. In Greece, the SOE armed several thousand agents but found that Communist partisans often used this weaponry to eliminate rival Greek forces rather than the Germans. In Yugoslavia, the SOE initially supported General Drza Mihajlovié's Chetnik resistance fighters but later switched its support to the Communist forces led by Josip Broz (Tito), a decision that greatly aided the latter in winning control of Yugoslavia. In Albania, SOE operatives likewise tended to favor Communist over right-wing guerrilla groups.

Although SOE operatives were active in Africa and Latin America, the most significant non-European SOE operations were in Asia. Australian-based SOE agents of Force 136 clashed, sometimes bitterly, with their counterparts from the U.S. Office of Strategic Services (with whom, by contrast, they cooperated well in Europe). In Burma (present-day Myanmar), the SOE contravened its own charter by undertaking intelligence-collecting work. The SOE also helped to organize highly effective bodies of Karen guerrillas, who killed more than 17,000 Japanese troops in the war's final months. In April 1945 the SOE persuaded the Japanese-sponsored Burmese National Army to switch its loyalties to the Allies. In Malaya, Force 136 aided the Malayan People's Anti-Japanese Army (MPAJA) to fight the Japanese. Subsequently, the MPAJA, transformed into the Malayan Anti-Races Liberation Army, the military part of the Malayan Communist Party, put its training and weaponry to good use fighting Commonwealth forces in the Malayan Emergency (1948–1960). SOE operations in Thailand and French Indochina were limited and somewhat ineffective.

Although forbidden to operate in China, the SOE secretly sent two missions there. One mission undertook highly profitable foreign exchange and smuggling ventures that left SOE finances with a surplus when the agency disbanded in January 1946. The other mission instructed the Chinese Communists of the Eighth Route Army in SOE sabotage methods.

Although SOE personnel were relatively few and its resistance and guerrilla efforts in occupied countries during World War II could only supplement and not substitute for full-scale military invasions of those territories, SOE operations proved valuable in boosting Allied morale and dislocating Axis control of subjugated areas.

Priscilla Roberts

See also Malayan Emergency; Office of Strategic Services; Tito

Further Reading

Dear, Ian. *Sabotage and Subversion: The SOE and OSS at War.* London: Cassell, 1999.

Foot, Michael R. D. *SOE: An Outline History of the Special Operations Executive, 1940–46.* Frederick, MD: University Publications of America, 1994.

Mackenzie, W. J. M. *The Secret History of SOE: Special Operations Executive, 1940–1945.* London: St. Ermins Press, 2000.

Special Operations Forces, U.S.

U.S. Special Operations Forces (SOFs) are those active and reserve component forces of the military services specifically designated by the secretary of defense to conduct and support special operations. SOFs are organized, trained, and equipped specifically to accomplish 11 core activities: direct action, special reconnaissance, foreign internal defense, unconventional warfare, counterterrorism, civil affairs operations, counterproliferation of weapons of mass destruction, information operations, security force assistance, counterinsurgency, and military information support operations. Within the context of irregular warfare, SOFs focus on counterinsurgency, foreign internal defense counterterrorism, unconventional warfare, and stability operations.

Counterinsurgency consists of comprehensive civilian and military efforts taken to defeat an insurgency and to address any core grievances. Foreign internal defense involves participation by civilian and military agencies in action programs undertaken by another government or other designated organization to free and protect its society from subversion, lawlessness, insurgency, terrorism, and other threats to its security. Counterterrorism activities are actions taken directly against terrorist networks and indirect actions to influence and render global and regional environments inhospitable to terrorist networks. Unconventional warfare activities are those conducted to enable a resistance movement or insurgency to coerce, disrupt, or overthrow a government or occupying power by operating through or with an underground, auxiliary, or guerrilla force in a denied area. Finally, stability operations encompass a wide range of military missions, tasks, and activities conducted outside the United States in coordination with other instruments of national power to maintain or reestablish a safe and secure environment and to provide essential governmental services, emergency infrastructure reconstruction, and humanitarian relief.

The U.S. Special Operations Command (USSOCOM) is one of nine combatant commands directly responsible to the president and the secretary of defense. As a functional combatant command, USSOCOM has been given lead responsibility for waging war on terrorism, to include planning, directing, and executing special operations. USSOCOM also provides SOFs to support geographic combatant commanders' theater security cooperation plans. SOF operations usually require units with combinations of special equipment, training, people, or tactics that go beyond those found in conventional units. Army SOFs include rangers, special forces, military information support operations, and civil affairs units, both of the active and reserve components, and army special operations aviation.

Rangers are airborne light infantry capable of rapid deployment and are organized and trained to conduct highly complex joint direct-action operations in coordination with or support of other special operations units of all services. Rangers also can execute direct-action operations in support of conventional non–special operations missions conducted by a combatant commander. In addition, rangers can operate as conventional light infantry when properly augmented with other elements of combined arms. U.S. Army special forces are organized, trained, and equipped to conduct special operations with an emphasis on unconventional warfare capabilities.

Military information support operations, formerly called psychological operations units, plan operations to convey selected information and indicators to foreign audiences in order to influence their emotions, motives, and objective reasoning and ultimately to alter the behavior of foreign governments, organizations, groups, and individuals. The purpose of psychological operations is to induce or reinforce foreign attitudes and behavior favorable to the originator's objectives. Civil affairs units are the designated active and reserve component forces that are organized, trained, and equipped to conduct civil affairs activities and to provide specialized support to commanders responsible for civil-military operations.

The U.S. Army Special Operations Aviation Command provides rotary-wing aircraft tailored for special operations missions that may include insertion and extraction, armed attack, and deep penetration as well as providing command and control.

U.S. Air Force special operations forces consist of both active and reserve components (not including U.S. Air Force rescue/combat search-and-rescue units). They perform a variety of missions. Air force special operations forces' fixed-wing assets provide deep penetration, close air support, refueling, and resupply. Rotary-wing aviation units provide infiltration, exfiltration, and combat search and rescue. Special tactics assets provide key ground-to-air coordination. The Foreign Internal Defense Squadron consists of U.S. Air Force pilots who specialize in training foreign military personnel. Finally, combat weather personnel provide forecasts as well as data collection and analysis related to the area of operations.

U.S. Navy special operations forces consist of sea-air-land (SEAL), SEAL delivery vehicle, and special boat team units of both active and reserve components. SEAL teams are organized, trained, and equipped to conduct special operations in maritime, littoral, and riverine environments. Special boat teams conduct or support special operations with patrol boats or other specialized watercraft. SEAL delivery vehicle teams support SEAL infiltration and exfiltration via submarines, surface vessels, aircraft, or land vehicles.

U.S. Marine Corps special operations forces consist of three special operations line battalions, each with four companies. These latter may be task organized to conduct direct action, foreign internal defense, special reconnaissance, unconventional warfare, counterterrorism, and information operations missions. They may also provide tailored military combat skills training and adviser support for foreign forces.

A joint special operations task force is a temporary headquarters or joint task force that consists of special operations units from more than one service, formed to carry out a specific operation or to prosecute special operations in support of a theater campaign or other operations. The joint special operations task force may have conventional non–special operations units assigned or attached to support the conduct of specific missions.

Biff L. Baker

See also Special Air Service

Further Reading

U.S. Department of Defense. *Joint Publication 1–01: Dictionary of Military and Associated Terms.* Washington, DC: Department of Defense Joint Staff, 2012.

U.S. Department of Defense. *Joint Publication 3–05: Doctrine for Joint Special Operations.* Washington, DC: Depaertment of Defense Joint Staff, 2003.

Spinola, António Sebastião Ribeiro de

Birth Date: April 11, 1910
Death Date: August 13, 1996

Portuguese military officer and first president of Portugal's provisional government following the April 1974 revolution. António Sebastião Ribeiro de Spinola was born in Estremoz, Portugal, on April 11, 1910. He entered the army after graduating from the Colegio Militar (Military College) in 1928. Spinola served in the Portuguese intervention forces in the Spanish Civil War (1936–1939) and accompanied the German Army as an observer on the Eastern Front during World War II (1939–1945).

During 1961–1964, Spinola served in Angola in the beginning stages of the nationalist insurgency there. In 1968 he was named commanding general and high commissioner of Guinea-Bissau, where the Partido Africano da Independência de Guiné e Cabo Verde (Party for the Independence of Guinea and Cape Verde) was gaining strength, thanks in part to Soviet support. There Spinola applied aggressive leadership along with innovative counterinsurgency tactics in what he called a social counterrevolution that was designed to win the people's hearts and minds. He respected local institutions and had his men build schools and hospitals and endeavor to improve the quality of native crops and herds. Spinola also raised indigenous forces and carried out attacks on insurgent bases in neighboring states. Despite success, he became convinced of the ultimate futility of Portugal's African wars, which were consuming the lion's share of the national resources. Spinola was also disillusioned by Portuguese dictator Marcelo Caetano's refusal to allow any negotiations with the insurgents. Nonetheless, during Spinola's time in Guinea, his charisma and outspokenness had a considerable impact on the younger generation of officers, who later would topple Caetano.

Upon his return from Africa in 1973, Spinola was offered the post of minister of colonies but refused because he disagreed with Caetano's determination to hold on to the colonies. Spinola was then named vice chief of staff of the armed forces. In February 1974 without government approval, he published his influential book *Portugal e o Futuro* (Portugal and the Future). It called for liberalization and democratization at home and an immediate political solution to end the anticolonial wars in Africa. The book became a best seller and heralded the end of Caetano's Estado Novo. On April 25, 1974, in the Carnation Revolution, a group of young officers known as the Armed Forces Movement (MFA), many of whom had served under Spinola, toppled Caetano in a nearly bloodless coup and established the Second Republic. They first named Spinola head of the Junta of National Salvation and then provisional president of Portugal.

Spinola and the officers of the MFA disagreed, however, about the extent to which the coup should entail substantial social change and especially about how quickly and thoroughly Portugal should divest itself of its colonies. Spinola envisioned a gradual withdrawal and possibly a Portuguese federation to replace the empire; the more radical leaders of the MFA wanted unequivocal and immediate withdrawal of all forces. Spinola resigned in September 1974, and the next year he conspired with conservatives to overthrow the government but was forced into temporary exile. Following Spinola's departure, the establishment of the republic, and decolonization, some of Portugal's former colonies—especially Angola—attracted increased Soviet, Cuban, and American involvement. Spinola died in Lisbon on August 13, 1996.

Eric W. Frith and Spencer C. Tucker

See also Angolan Insurgency; Arriaga, Kaúlza de Oliveira de; Guinea Insurgency; Hearts and Minds; Mozambique Insurgency

Further Reading

Graham, Lawrence, and Harry M. Mlaker, eds. *Contemporary Portugal: The Revolution and Its Antecedents.* Austin: University of Texas Press, 1979.

Maxwell, Kenneth. *The Making of Portuguese Democracy.* New York: Cambridge University Press, 1995.

Spinola, António de. *Portugal and the Future.* Johannesburg: Perskor, 1974.

Sri Lankan Civil War

Start Date: 1983
End Date: 2009

The island nation of Sri Lanka, located just 20 miles off the southern tip of India, was known as Ceylon until 1972. In the 19th century the British, then ruling Ceylon, imported Tamil laborers from southern India to work on the Ceylonese plantations. While the Sinhalese Buddhists comprise 75 percent of the population, there is now a strong Tamil Hindu minority of some 20 percent in the north and east of the country.

In 1948 Ceylon became a self-governing dominion within the British Commonwealth of Nations. Solomon Bandaranaike, prime minister during 1956–1959, sparked conflict between the Sinhalese people and the Tamils by making Sinhalese the only official language and by other policies that exacerbated communal politics. The Tamils began a civil disobedience movement, and occasional violence erupted. In 1959 Bandaranaike was assassinated, not by Tamils but by a Buddhist radical who wanted the prime minister to do even more to establish Sinhalese dominance.

The 1960 elections were won by Bandaranaike's widow, Sirimavo Bandaranaike, the world's first female prime minister. She expanded her husband's foreign and domestic policies during two terms in office (1960–1965, 1970–1977). In 1972 she changed the country's name to Sri Lanka, Sinhalese for "resplendent land," and declared it a republic. She then promulgated a new constitution and made Buddhism the state religion, further alienating the Tamils. Bandaranaike also faced insurrection from the Maoist People's Liberation Front (MPLF) that prompted a state of emergency lasting six years (1971–1977).

In May 1983 the Sri Lankan Civil War officially began when the Liberation Tigers of Tamil Eelam (LTTE, or Tamil Tigers) militants, who demanded an independent Tamil state, killed 13 Sri Lankan soldiers. Ethnic violence rocked the country in July, prompting the government to declare a state of emergency. Attempts to crush the insurgents failed, and the LTTE was able to establish its control over the Jaffna Peninsula in northern Sri Lanka. Aided secretly by supporters in the southern Indian state of Tamil Nadu, the guerrillas were effectively organized and well-armed.

Agreements in 1987 brought Indian troops, ostensibly as peacekeepers, to diffuse the situation. They remained until 1990 but failed to arrest the violence. In fact, the unrest grew worse. Supporting the LTTE, the MPLF renewed attacks on the government in 1989. In 1990 Tamil guerrillas turned against Muslims who supported the Sinhalese. In 1991 the Indian government took over direct rule of the Indian state of Tamil Nadu, provoking an LTTE suicide bomb attack that killed former Indian prime minister Rajiv Gandhi that May. By 1992 nearly 20,000 people had been killed in the insurgency, including many senior military and government officials. Then in May 1993, the LTTE assassinated Sri Lankan president Ranasinghe Premadasa, bringing even more bloodshed.

In August 1994 Chandrika Kumaratunga became prime minister of a coalition government that bridged both Buddhist extremists and Marxist revolutionaries. In November 1994 she became the first woman elected president in Sri Lanka. Her government thereafter veered between military campaigns and peace negotiations, including one begun through Norwegian intermediaries in 2001.

In 2005 hard-line Sinhalese president Mahinda Rajapakse, a former labor activist, was elected president. He was determined to use the military to wipe out the LTTE. In early 2008, Sri Lanka's army significantly increased offensive operations against the LTTE in northeastern Sri Lanka, while Rajapakse banned reporters from the region, punished dissenters, and ignored foreign appeals for the safety of Tamil civilians who were caught up in the fighting. In May 2009 Sri Lankan forces overran the last LTTE stronghold, killing or capturing all LTTE combatants and bringing an end to the long civil war and to the LTTE itself. Since 1983, the fighting had claimed the lives of some 70,000–80,000 people.

Arne Kislenko and Spencer C. Tucker

See also Liberation Tigers of Tamil Eelam

Further Reading

Amato, Edward J. "Tail of the Dragon: Sri Lankan Efforts to Subdue the Liberation Tigers of Tamil Eelam." Unpublished master's thesis, U.S. Command and General Staff College, Fort Leavenworth, Kansas, 2002.

Bullion, Alan J. *India, Sri Lanka and the Tamil Crisis, 1976–1994: An International Perspective.* London: Pinter, 1995.

Hashim, Ahmed S. *When Counterinsurgency Wins: Sri Lanka's Defeat of the Tamil Tigers.* Philadelphia: University of Pennsylvania Press, 2012.

Stern, Avraham

Birth Date: December 23, 1907
Death Date: February 12, 1942

Fervent Zionist and founder and leader of the Lehi (Lohamei Herut Israel) terrorist group (the Stern Gang) who was known by the alias Yair. Avraham Stern

Avraham Stern, leader of the Lehi underground terrorist organization known as the "Stern Gang," who was killed by the British in Palestine in September 1942. (Israeli Government Press Office)

was born in Suwałki, Poland, on December 23, 1907. He attended Poland's Hebrew High School but immigrated to Palestine in 1925 and continued his education in Jerusalem. Stern then studied philosophy and classical languages at Jerusalem's Hebrew University. Fluent in Latin and Greek, he won a scholarship to study in Florence, Italy. There he was impressed by dictator Benito Mussolini as well as by Italian fascism.

With an academic career having lost its allure, Stern returned to Palestine. His attempts to make a living from writing failed. By the late 1920s he had embraced Revisionist Zionism, a movement founded by Ze'ev Jabotinsky that sought to establish a Jewish state in Palestine but envisioned armed struggle to achieve that end. Palestine was then ruled by Britain under a League of Nations mandate, and tensions between Jews and Arabs owing to increased Jewish migration and Jewish land purchases had led to violence. Stern became an active member of the Haganah Jewish self-defense organization that sought to protect Jewish settlements from Arab attack and took part in the defense of Jewish homes and shops in Jerusalem during the Arab Riots of 1929.

Sporadic violence continued throughout the next decade. London now sought to curb Jewish immigration and land purchases in Palestine. Stern set out to organize a more active defense of Jewish interests, and in 1931 he helped found the radical group known as Irgun, which advocated counterterrorist tactics against the Arabs and the military liberation of Palestine. Stern directed a training program that emphasized the use of small arms and explosives. He soon became Irgun's top field commander.

In 1937, however, Stern formed a splinter group, the Irgun Zevai Leumi (IZL, National Military Organization). By that time he had distanced himself from Jabotinsky and turned to Abba Achimeir, whose Brith Habiryonim faction was even more radical than the Revisionists. Achimeir and Stern sought a more aggressive approach, involving a campaign of terror. Stern's watchwords were "study, train, and think," but his emphasis was on force.

The formation of the IZL coincided with another Arab uprising, the Arab Revolt of 1936–1939. British authorities seemed unable or unwilling to end the violence. Stern organized a bombing campaign and instructed his IZL squads "kill, be killed, but do not surrender." Martial law brought a semblance of peace, but new British policies helped push Stern into a different strategy.

Recognizing the strong possibility of a world war, London opted to protect Britain's significant Middle Eastern holdings by placating the Arabs. Its May 17, 1939, White Paper declared that only 75,000 more Jews would enter Palestine. After that, local Arabs would decide immigration policy. Zionists in Palestine saw this as a dangerous blow against their future. Furthermore, few Western countries were willing to accept the growing numbers of Jewish refugees.

Stern returned to Poland, hoping to expand IZL operations and recruit fighters. Although he established a daily newspaper, *Die Tat* (Action), the German invasion of September 1, 1939, interrupted his mission. Returning to Palestine, Stern made a complete break with Jabotinsky and the IZL due to their argument for the need for cooperation with Britain, which had gone to war against Germany on September 3. Stern called instead for a campaign against Britain. A year later he formed the Lohamei Herut Israel (Fighters for Israel's Freedom, also known as Lehi for its Hebrew acronym). Recruited chiefly from the IZL, Lehi numbered about 200 dedicated men and women. Robbery, bombing, and assassination were its tactics. British authorities labeled Lehi the Stern Gang.

In a controversial action, Stern sent agents to contact Nazi Germany. Arguing that "the enemy of my enemy is my friend," he attempted to forge an alliance between Lehi and Abwehr, the German secret service. Nothing came of this, but word of Stern's activities caused most Jews to sever all ties with Lehi.

In January 1942 following a bomb explosion in Tel Aviv that killed three policeman, British authorities offered £1,000 for Stern's arrest. Cut off from support and now hunted, Stern went into hiding. He escaped several dragnets but was finally discovered in Tel Aviv on February 12, 1942, when six British policemen broke into his safe house and shot him dead. In 1978 an Israeli postage stamp was issued in his honor.

Spencer C. Tucker

See also Arab Revolt of 1936; Irgun Tsvai Leumi; Lohamei Herut Israel

Further Reading

Bell, J. Boyer. *Terror Out of Zion: Irgun Zvai Leumi, Lehi and the Palestine Underground, 1929–1949.* New York: St. Martin's, 1979.

Bethell, Nicholas. *The Palestine Triangle: The Struggle for the Holy Land, 1935–48.* New York: Putnam, 1979.

Brenner, Lenni. *The Iron Wall: Zionist Revisionism from Jabotinsky to Shamir.* London: Zed, 1984.

Stern Gang.

See Lohamei Herut Israel

Strategic Hamlet Program

Start Date: 1961
End Date: 1964

The Strategic Hamlet Program was the most ambitious and well-known effort by Ngo Dinh Diem, president of the Republic of Vietnamese (RVN, South Vietnam), to pacify the countryside and neutralize the Viet Cong (VC) Communist insurgents. The plan called for placing the rural population in protected hamlets, isolating the people physically and politically from the insurgents while providing them with security and a better life. Following in the wake of the Agroville Campaign of 1959 but on a wider scale, the Strategic Hamlet Program was inaugurated in 1962 and officially ended early in 1964. The program began to wane even before Diem was overthrown in November 1963.

The Strategic Hamlet Program grew out of British counterinsurgency expert Sir Robert Thompson's experiences in the Malayan Emergency (1948–1960), where a rural resettlement effort had enjoyed some success. Beginning in 1961, Thompson headed the British advisory mission in South Vietnam. The situation in Vietnam was more complex than in Malaya, however. The VC was well established throughout the countryside, and unlike in Malaya, where the vast majority of insurgents were ethnic Chinese, the VC were of the same ethnicity as the villagers.

Thompson's notion was to bring security to where the people already lived. Relocation was to be minimal. Thompson estimated at the start of the program that only some 5 percent of the hamlets, those in VC-controlled areas, would have to be moved to new sites. He proposed the plan in November 1961, and the first strategic hamlet was established in Binh Duong Province north of Saigon (now Ho Chi Minh City) in March 1962.

Although key American civilians favored the program, U.S. military leaders criticized it, believing that it tied military forces to a defensive posture. Lieutenant General Lionel McGarr, head of the U.S. Military Assistance and Advisory Group, thought that this role was more appropriate for police than for regular forces and urged military clearing operations instead.

Aware of the danger of being perceived by the Vietnamese as an American puppet, Diem undertook the Strategic Hamlet Program on his own without first informing the Americans. Diem and his brother Ngo Dinh Nhu, who had charge of implementing the program, significantly changed Thompson's concept. Thompson proposed surrounding existing hamlets with security forces, but Diem and Nhu decided that security should begin within the hamlets, and they embarked on an ambitious plan to build fortified hamlets, which in practice involved relocating villagers. Unfortunately for the success of the program, Nhu concentrated on securing territory rather than on efforts to win the hearts and minds of the peasants through improvements such as medical care and education.

Nhu wanted half of South Vietnam's 14,000 hamlets to be completed by early 1963 and another 5,000 by early 1964. His overly ambitious plans created far more hamlets than South Vietnam's forces could protect or its cadres could administer. Under pressure from Saigon to show results, province officials often appeased Nhu with meaningless data. By September 1962, the government claimed that 3,225 hamlets had been completed, with a population of 4.2 million, out of a planned 11,316 hamlets. But the definition of "completed" varied greatly. Pressure to meet unrealistic goals encouraged a focus on the superficial aspects such as erecting fences, which often sufficed to reclassify an existing settlement as a strategic hamlet.

The program also imposed onerous burdens on the people, such as restrictions on their movement and demands for guard duty. Most villagers saw the program as a security measure rather than as reform. The hamlets also proved to be highly vulnerable to VC attack because too many of them were poorly built and weakly defended. By July 1964, only 30 of the 219 strategic hamlets in Long An Province remained under government control. Yet by July 1963, the government claimed 7,200 strategic hamlets with a population of 8.7 million.

Faulty execution compromised the program. Not only did the Strategic Hamlet Program fail to halt the insurgency, but it also manifested the arbitrary and repressive aspect of Diem's rule and was plagued by corruption. The program's inadequacy served as a metaphor for the regime's failure to stem the insurgency, gain and hold the support of the people, and win the confidence of the John F. Kennedy administration, which acquiesced in Diem's overthrow.

The failure of the Strategic Hamlet Program had a larger significance in that pacification would be supplanted as a strategy for fighting the war. Two successor pacification efforts in 1964, Chien Thang and Hop Tac, were also poorly executed and failed to reverse Saigon's declining fortunes in the countryside. In late 1964 the emboldened Communists began to infiltrate conventional People's Army of Vietnam (PAVN, North Vietnamese army) units into South Vietnam to administer the coup de grâce. This was a situation that was beyond the scope of pacification to remedy, leading Washington to intervene with a bombing campaign and ground troops.

Richard A. Hunt and Spencer C. Tucker

See also Hearts and Minds; Malayan Emergency; Pacification; Thompson, Sir Robert Grainger Ker; Vietnam War

Further Reading

Hunt, Richard. *Pacification: The American Struggle for Vietnam's Hearts and Minds.* Boulder, CO: Westview, 1995.

Osborne, Milton. *Strategic Hamlets in Vietnam.* Data Paper 55. Ithaca, NY: Cornell University Southeast Asia Program, April 1965.

Thompson, Sir Robert. *Defeating Communist Insurgency.* New York: Praeger, 1966.

Suchet, Louis-Gabriel

Birth Date: March 2, 1770
Death Date: January 3, 1826

French marshal and one of the most successful French generals of the Peninsular War (1808–1814). Born in Lyon, France, on March 2, 1770, into the upper bourgeoisie as the son of a silk manufacturer, Louis-Gabriel Suchet was educated at Catholic schools. He entered his father's business but left it on the beginning of the French Revolution of 1789 and joined the army via the National Guard. As a chef de bataillon (major), he fought in the Siege of Toulon (1793) and in Napoleon Bonaparte's Italian Campaign of (1796–1797), when Suchet was wounded. During Bonaparte's Egyptian Campaign (1798–1799), Suchet served under General Guillaume Marie Anne Brune in Holland. In 1799 Suchet was promoted to general of division.

Suchet's skill in staff work kept him in the background, but he distinguished himself under General André Masséna in Italy (1800) and then was inspector of infantry. Suchet took part in the campaigns of Austerlitz (1805) and Jena-Auerstädt (1806). In 1808 he was made a count.

Ordered to Spain in 1808, Suchet earned a reputation as a highly effective counterinsurgency commander. He proceeded to establish French control over Aragon. As military governor of Aragon and later Valencia, Suchet instructed his men to respect the local population and their Catholic religion. He paid his own expenses and spent considerable effort reforming the local administration, for which he utilized Spanish officials. Following a population-centric approach to counterinsurgency, he worked to improve local conditions, such as schools and hospitals. Defeating the Spanish guerrillas, he captured their leader, Francisco Espoz y Mina, in March 1810.

Suchet's forces not only waged a successful counterinsurgency campaign in Spain but also battled conventional Spanish forces, defeating troops under Joaquin Blake in the Battle of Maria (June 15, 1809). Following a two-month siege (May–July 1811), he captured Tarragona in Catalonia, held to be impregnable, and for this accomplishment he was raised to marshal of France on July 8, 1811. Valencia fell in June 1812, for which Suchet was made Duc d'Albufera da Valencia.

At this point Napoleon was dramatically reducing his forces in Spain to feed his invasion of Russia, and Suchet was forced to send men to assist the emperor. Following King Joseph's defeat at Vitoria (1813), Suchet was obliged to withdraw his men into southern France.

When Napoleon abdicated in April 1814, Suchet swore allegiance to King Louis XVIII. When Napoleon returned to France in the Hundred Days (1815), however, Suchet rallied to him. With Napoleon's defeat, Suchet was stripped of his rank and became destitute. In 1819 his rank was restored, but he never returned to public life. His memoirs are a valuable source regarding the Peninsular War. Suchet died near Marseilles on January 3, 1826.

William T. Dean III and Spencer C. Tucker

See also Guerrilla; Peninsular War

Further Reading

Alexander, Don W. *Rod of Iron: French Counterinsurgency Policy in Aragon during the Peninsular War.* Wilmington DE: Scholarly Resources, 1985.

Bergerot, Bernard. *Le Marechal Suchet.* Paris: Tallandier, 1986.

Suchet, Louis-Gabriel, duc d'Albufera. *Memoirs of the War in Spain, from 1808 to 1814.* London: H. Colburn, 1829.

Suicide Bombings

Suicide bombings occur when an explosive is delivered and detonated by a person or persons who expect to die in the blast along with the intended target or targets. Suicide bombings are now often employed in insurgencies. In recent years, their numbers have risen exponentially and not just in the Middle East. The United States was struck by four hijacked aircraft piloted by Islamic fanatics associated with the Al Qaeda terrorist organization on September 11, 2001, resulting in the deaths of almost 3,000 people. This has been the worst and most dramatic example of suicide bombings. Suicide bombings have also been rife in Iraq following the Iraq War and in Afghanistan, among other places.

During World War II (1939–1945), Japanese pilots, known as kamikazes ("divine wind"), deliberately crashed their aircraft into Allied ships and exacted a heavy toll, especially in the Battle for Okinawa. Suicide bombers have also employed vehicles, while individual suicide bombers utilize explosive belts or vests filled with shrapnel and strapped to their bodies. Because military targets are often heavily defended, typically the targets are crowded shopping areas, restaurants, or buses. Suicide bombers may approach softer targets directly linked to the military or police, such as a line of recruits.

Detonating the explosives kills and injures people in the vicinity and can also be employed to destroy important property, such as religious shrines. An explosion in an enclosed area is more destructive than one in the open, and suicide bombers pick their targets accordingly. Forensic investigators at the site of a suicide bombing can usually identify very quickly the bomber and the general type of device that he or she used. A suicide vest decapitates the bomber, while an explosive belt cuts the bomber in two.

Such explosive devices are easily constructed. They might include an explosive charge, a battery, cable, a light switch detonator, and a custom-made belt or vest to hold the explosives. Scrap metal might be employed to act as shrapnel, which in the blast would kill or maim those nearby. Explosives can also be carried in a briefcase or bag. The bomber sets off the explosive device by flipping a switch or pressing a button, sometimes remotely. Muslim extremists might leave a written or video will and pronounce the Fatiha (opening verse of the Qur'an) and the words "Allahu akbar" ("Allah is great") as they detonate their bombs.

Suicide bombings have been commonplace in the Middle East since the 1970s, when they were employed in Syria by the Islamic resistance against the Baathist government. The belief among many Muslims that such attacks bring martyrdom has encouraged suicide bombings all over the world, including in Afghanistan, Chechnya, Croatia, Tajikistan, Pakistan, Yemen, Panama, Argentina, and Algeria, but such attacks were also employed prior to this period by the Tamil Tigers in Sri Lanka. Palestinians began suicide bombings in the early 1990s. It is obvious from the Japanese in World War II, the Tamils, and anarchist violence that the motivation is primarily nationalist, and in fact Islam strictly forbids suicide and engaging recklessly in jihad so as to obtain martyrdom. There are set rules regarding who may participate in jihad, and these exclude young people, those with dependents, and also traditionally women. The main religious justification is that jihad is really a defense of Islam and is required of believers who need not wait for jihad to be formally declared as under normal circumstances. To Muslims, there is a difference between an individual and a collectively incumbent religious duty. Religious authorities who decry the linkage of Islam with suicide and the killing of innocent people argue that the greater jihad, the striving to be a good Muslim, can substitute for jihad as armed struggle or that if armed struggle is necessary, it should not involve attacks of this type. Not all religious authorities take this position, of course, and unfortunately news reports of suicide bombers serve as a recruiting tool for other suicide bombers.

For many young Muslims, the temptation of martyrdom with its promise of rewards in paradise proves irresistible. They are taught that martyrdom cleanses them of sins and that they will have special powers to intercede on behalf of their relatives and close friends on the Day of Judgment. The families of suicide bombers are often extremely proud of their loved ones and can acquire higher status in the Muslim communities. Some have received financial payments. Certainly, successful suicide bombers believe that they will be remembered as popular heroes. Other motivations include revenge and hatred of the West and Westerners and religious fanaticism within Islam itself (Shiite against Sunni and vice versa).

Understandably, suicide bombings are enormously upsetting to potential civilian victims. Suicide bombers turn up when they are least expected as their victims go about their daily business, and victims and bystanders are taken completely by surprise. The victims are often civilians, and children make up a sizable percentage of those killed. Because the bomber has no concern for his or her own life, it is difficult to prevent such attacks. As with all acts of terror, the fact that such bombings spread fear is extremely valuable to the radicals' cause. Since 2003, suicide bombings in Iraq have claimed thousands of victims, most of them civilians. Indeed, in the summer of 2004, suicide bombers began to shift their target from coalition forces to civilians. Motivations include demonstrating the weakness of the government, coalition security, and the reconstruction apparatus; retaliatory action against those collaborating with the government; and increasingly to exact sectarian revenge. Suicide bombings are also being employed increasingly by the Taliban in Afghanistan. A growing number of the bombers are women.

Amy Hackney Blackwell and Sherifa Zuhur

See also Harakat al-Jihad al-Islami fi Filastin; Harakat al-Muqawama al-Islamiyya; Intifada, Second; Jihad; Terrorism

Further Reading

Aboul-Enein, Youssef H., and Sherifa Zuhur. *Islamic Rulings on Warfare.* Carlisle Barracks, PA: Strategic Studies Institute, 2004.

Friedman, Lauri S. *What Motivates Suicide Bombers?* Farmington Hills, MI: Greenhaven, 2004.

Khosrokhavar, Farhad. *Suicide Bombers: Allah's New Martyrs.* Translated by David Macey. London: Pluto, 2005.

Skaine, Rosemarie. *Female Suicide Bombers.* Jefferson, NC: McFarland, 2006.

Sumter, Thomas

Birth Date: August 14, 1734
Death Date: June 1, 1832

Prominent guerrilla leader operating in the South during the American Revolutionary War (1775–1783). Born to Welsh parents on August 14, 1734, near Charlottesville, Virginia, Thomas Sumter had little formal education and initially worked as a farmhand. Sumter joined the militia in 1755 during the French and Indian War (1754–1763) and fought in the Battle of the Monongahela against the French and allied Indians that same year. He also fought the Cherokees in 1760. The next year he and a friend were able to secure a peace treaty with three Cherokee chiefs in the Great Smoky Mountains region, and in 1762 Virginia sent Sumter and the chiefs to London to meet King George III.

Returning to Virginia, Sumter was imprisoned for debt but escaped and fled to North Carolina, where he received a financial reward for his services against the Cherokees, enabling him to pay off his debts. He then moved to South Carolina, settling in Eutaw Springs and opening a trading post. He married a wealthy widow in 1764 and acquired both property and local prominence. In 1773 Sumter was appointed a justice of the peace, and in 1775 he was elected to the provisional congress.

Following the beginning of the American Revolutionary War, in 1776 Sumter became a captain in the Rangers. Promoted to lieutenant colonel of the 2nd Rifle Regiment, he took part in the Patriot repulse of the British attempt in 1776 to capture Charleston and then distinguished himself in fighting Cherokees supporting the British and in the repulse of a Loyalist invasion of South Carolina from Georgia. Ill with malaria, Sumter returned home to recuperate, where he remained for the next two years.

Sumter returned to the fray in 1780. British forces were then attempting to pacify all of South Carolina, and Lieutenant Colonel Banastre Tarleton's legion burned Sumter's home. Sumter recruited a volunteer guerrilla force and began raiding British bases and supply trains. Appointed a South Carolina Militia brigadier general in October, he became known as "the Gamecock."

Because of the small number of Continental Army regulars in the South, militia played a greater role, and the new American commander in the South, Continental Army major general Nathanael Greene, made every effort to work with the militia commanders, of whom Sumter and Francis Marion were the most important. Whereas Marion cooperated effectively with Greene and was completely reliable, Sumter largely went his own way and only occasionally obeyed Greene's orders. For example, Sumter simply ignored Greene's order to join him for what would be the Battle of Hobkirk's Hill in April 1781, although Sumter did join Greene in the later Siege of Ninety-Six (May–June 1781).

Sumter had a number of successes in attacks on British outposts but also had many failures, most notably at Monck's Corner in July 1781 when he ordered a charge on a British position without having conducted a reconnaissance. He also drew much criticism for the so-called Sumter's Law, under which he paid his men with plunder. Angered by criticism, Sumter resigned his commission in June 1782.

Sumter served several terms in the South Carolina state legislature but was subjected to frequent lawsuits over his wartime property confiscations. Both South Carolina and North Carolina enacted legislation to protect him from court action. He engaged in land speculation, and he served in the U.S. House of Representatives (1789–1793 and 1797–1801) and the U.S. Senate (1801–1810). Sumter died near Stateburg, South Carolina, on June 1, 1832.

As a partisan commander, Sumter proved effective in minor engagements, but he was also a poor tactician who often failed to mount a proper reconnaissance. He was also a failure as a strategist, for he waged his own war, refusing to obey orders unless they suited his own purposes.

Spencer C. Tucker

See also American Revolutionary War; Marion, Francis

Further Reading

Bass, Robert D. *Gamecock: The Life and Campaigns of General Thomas Sumter.* New York: Holt, Rinehart, and Winston, 1961.

Hoffman, Ronald, Thad W. Tate, and Peter J. Albert. *An Uncivil War: The Southern Backcountry during the American Revolution.* Charlottesville: Published for the U.S. Capitol Historical Society by the University Press of Virginia, 1965.

Sun Tzu

Birth Date: ca. 544 BCE
Death Date: ca. 496 BCE

Sun Tzu (Sunzi) is an honorific name given Sun Wu, a sixth-century BCE Chinese general in the state of Qi. Little is known about his life. The earliest account of Sun Wu is from the second century BCE. Apparently he was a member of the landless Chinese aristocracy, with traditional accounts placing his birth in 544 BCE and his death in 496. He rose to be one of the major military commanders of King Wei of the state of Qi.

Sun Tzu's book *Bing Fa* (translated into English and published as *The Art of War*) is the only one of a half dozen Chinese military classics to have received wide study in the West. Although some scholars have questioned its authenticity, most recognize the book as China's oldest and most profound military treatise. First translated from Chinese into French in the 18th century, the book reportedly influenced Napoleon Bonaparte. The book is also said to have had a major impact on the dictums of Mao Zedong (Mao Tse-tung) in the 20th century.

Much of the book's appeal rests in the fact that it is a series of aphorisms rather than a long philosophical treatise. Although the terms "insurgency" and "counterinsurgency" did not exist at the time, Sun Tzu captured their essence. His writings emphasize the need for effective intelligence, speed, surprise, deception, flexibility, and deception. The book stresses techniques that will bring victory over an opponent, and such principles may be applied to any field of human endeavor. The book has thus been used as a text in business schools.

Sun Tzu articulates the need for cohesive action between political and military leaders, and he wrote extensively about direct and indirect attacks and the importance of spies to gather intelligence about the enemy. He argued that benevolent treatment of the population is an essential element in military success. Sun Tzu also identified the need for both direct (conventional) and indirect (special operations) attacks.

Biff L. Baker and Spencer C. Tucker

See also Mao Zedong

Further Reading

Sun Tzu. *The Art of War.* Translated by Lionel Giles. New York: World Spiritual Classics, 2011.

U.S. Department of Defense. *Joint Publication 1–01: Dictionary of Military and Associated Terms.* Washington, DC: Department of Defense Joint Staff, 2012.

Syrian Insurgency

Start Date: March 25, 2001
End Date: Ongoing

The Syrian Insurgency (also known as the Syrian Uprising and the Syrian Civil War) began on March 15, 2011, in the wake of the broader Arab Spring movement throughout the Middle East and North Africa. The insurgency started as a protest movement demanding reforms and action against corruption and escalated into an attempt to overthrow the Baathist regime of President Bashar al-Assad, who had been in power since 2000. By March 18, the Syrian Army was called in to suppress the protesters over concerns that they might get out of hand and lead to the overthrow of the regime, as occurred with President Hosni Mubarak in Egypt. The Syrian military employed harsh tactics against the demonstrations. Witnesses reported several dozen people killed in the city of Deraa in less than a week of the demonstrations. The military response in cities such as Deraa and Deir al-Zor, far from cowing the demonstrators, brought larger protests from civilians and from some defected members of the Syrian military, prompting even harsher attacks by the Assad regime. By the end of 2012, this civil strife had claimed an estimated 60,000 lives and showed little sign of abating.

In the wake of the uprisings, Assad attempted to address some concerns raised by protesters, such as formally ending the five decades of emergency law in the country and dissolving the security courts that had angered locals with unfair and corrupt adjudication. He also issued a decree legalizing political parties and indicated that he was even open to changing the constitution. However, such measures were offset by actions of the government security forces against the protesters, especially in Deraa and in Damascus, where in one day 100 people were killed, a 13-year old boy was tortured and killed, and 15 young students were arrested for writing antigovernment slogans on a wall. By late June, many Syrian cities witnessed massive antiregime demonstrations, which then encountered Assad's security forces.

Sunnis make up some 74 percent of the population of Syria, but the country has been ruled for half a century by the Alawite (Shia) sect, which numbers only about 13 percent and to which the Assads belong. The demonstrations brought to the fore long-standing resentments held by the Sunnis as well as by minority Christians, Druze, and others. Much of the fighting was along sectarian lines, with the Sunni areas experiencing the brunt of the government attacks. Thus, the Syrian people were not only fighting for fundamental governmental reform but were also revisiting historic rivalries. It was thus no surprise that cities such as Hama, Deraa, and Deir al-Zor, where there had been past sectarian violence, should see heavy fighting.

Establishing a united political and military front against Assad's forces proved challenging for the opposition. The United Nations (UN), the Arab League, and the international community long argued that intervening in the conflict without an established political and military opposition leadership in place would be disastrous. The Free Syrian Army, a conglomeration of the country's opposition forces and made up of defected members of Assad's military, had been formed by August 2011. The next month, the Syrian National Council and National Coordinating bodies were established in Turkey. Despite these bodies, opposition unity remained tenuous at best.

The Assad regime enjoyed the support of Iran (with Iranian weaponry passing through Iraqi air space). The regime also received at least diplomatic support from the Russian Federation, which was a major trading partner and maintained a Mediterranean naval base in the Syrian city of Tartus. The Syrian opposition looked to neighboring countries for assistance. Some Salafists and other jihadists joined the Syrian Insurgency. Fighters who had fought the Americans and security forces in Iraq transitioned to Syria and pushed an Islamist agenda. Concerns abounded that the uprising in Syria would disrupt the delicate Sunni-Shia balance in neighboring countries. Lebanon was particularly vulnerable to instability, and fighting triggered by the Syrian crisis occurred along sectarian lines in Tripoli and other cities. There was also some violence in Israel, Iraq, Turkey, and Jordan. Syrian Christians, fearing repression under a new Syrian regime, sought support from their coreligionists in Lebanon and Iraq. Turkey has played a critical role in the conflict by providing sanctuary to tens of thousands of Syrian refugees and also hosted the opposition leadership until September 2012, when the latter moved back into Syria.

Attempts by the UN, the Arab League, and the Gulf Cooperation Council to bring an end to the violence proved futile, as was Assad's prompting of parliamentary elections on May 7, 2012, which saw opposition forces rejecting the elections altogether. Russia, China, Iran, and even Hezbollah, an ally of Assad, offered assistance but to little avail.

Assad's forces shelled neighborhoods and cities and increasingly relied on airpower in an effort to defeat the opposition forces (which Assad referred to as terrorists). The cities of Homs and Bab Amr each endured more than a month of shelling, driving civilians out of the cities and forcing a temporary rebel withdrawal in March 2012. Opposition forces, albeit somewhat disorganized, mounted regular attacks against government targets such as the Damascus intelligence headquarters and military buildings. Suicide attacks increased during 2012, as did the use of roadside bombs.

During 2012, attacks by security forces against civilians and opposition forces increased dramatically. In the town of Daraya, an August battle between rebels and security forces brought the massacre of more than 300 people. Increasing government firepower against the Syrian civilian population brought major defections, including in July 2012 Brigadier General Manaf Tlas, a longtime close friend of Assad, as well as several Syrian ambassadors and legislators.

In July, Syrian rebels began to retake some of the towns they had been driven from earlier, capturing a military base near Aleppo. Their downing of military aircraft indicated improving weaponry and tactics. By November 2012, the military balance appeared to be tipping toward the opposition as its fighters edged closer to Assad's stronghold of Damascus. Concerns in December 2012 that Assad would employ chemical weapons in a last-ditch effort against the opposition brought warnings by the United States and West European countries that such a step would have serious consequences. In midmonth Syria for the first time employed Scud missiles against rebel concentrations, while the United States dispatched to Turkey Patriot missile batteries and 400 men to man them in a largely symbolic gesture designed to help protect the long Turkish border with Syria against possible missile or aircraft attack.

By July 2013, the UN estimated that the fighting had claimed some 100,000 dead and had displaced 1.7 million Syrians who have fled to other countries. The war, which had seemed to be going in favor of the rebels, turned in favor of government forces when on June 5 Assad's forces captured the key city of Qusair near the Lebanese border. The battle for Qusair was marked by the participation of fighters from the radical Lebanese Shiite Muslim organization Hezbollah. The participation of Hezbollah, which is strongly supported by Iran, angered many Sunnis and raised the prospect of a widened Middle Eastern war that would include at least Lebanon. On June 15, 2013, Egypt broke diplomatic ties with Syria and called for the overthrow of Assad.

Also on June 15, the U.S. government, following similar announcements by France and Britain, concluded that the Syrian government had indeed employed chemical weapons against its own people. This finding led the Barack Obama administration to declare that it would provide military support to the Syrian rebels. Representatives of 11 states, including the United States, then met in Qatar and pledged increased aid to the rebels. It was not clear what form this aid would take, but clearly the rebels—armed basically with small arms—were outgunned by Syrian government forces with tanks, artillery, and aircraft.

With Iran and Russia firmly supporting Assad—indeed Russian president Vladimir Putin announced that Russia intended to go ahead with the sale to the Syrian government of advanced antiaircraft missiles—peace seemed as elusive as ever.

Larissa Mihalisko

Further Reading

Ajami, Fouad. *The Syrian Rebellion.* Stanford, CA: Hoover Institution, Stanford University, 2012.

Lesch, David W. *Syria: The Fall of the House of Assad.* New Haven, CT: Yale University Press, 2012.

Starr, Stephen. *Revolt in Syria: Eye-witness to the Uprising.* New York: Columbia University Press, 2012.

Syrian Revolt.

See Great Syrian Revolt

T

Taber's *War of the Flea.*

See *War of the Flea*

Tache d'Huile

French term meaning "oil slick" or "oil spot" applied to the pacification technique of first securing key population centers and then expanding outward from them, much as an oil slick spreads on water. The *tache d'huile* process, pioneered by French Army officers Joseph Gallieni and Louis Hubert Gonzalve Lyautey during the French pacification of Madagascar (1895–1905) and Morocco in the 1920s, worked well in flat open areas where there were only a few watering holes, but it was not well suited to Indochina, with its heavily forested and rugged terrain. Nonetheless, the French attempted to utilize the method throughout the Indochina War (1946–1954), first securing the population centers and then attempting to expand their control into the countryside. In Vietnam, *tache d'huile* never had a chance of success because French forces were insufficient for the task.

Spencer C. Tucker

See also Gallieni, Joseph Simon; Indochina War; Lyautey, Louis Hubert; *Quadrillage* and *Ratissage*

Further Reading

Collins, William Frederick. "French Military Imperialism: The Conquest and Pacification of Madagascar, 1895–1905." Unpublished MA thesis, University of Maryland at College Park, 1987.

Gillet, Maxime. *Principes de pacification du maréchal Lyautey* [Marshal Lyautey's Principles of Pacification]. Paris: Economica, 2010.

Leopard, Donald Dean. "The French Conquest and Pacification of Madagascar, 1885–1905." Unpublished PhD dissertation, Ohio State University, 1966.

Maurois, André. *Lyautey.* New York: D. Appleton, 1931.

Taiping Rebellion

Start Date: 1851
End Date: 1864

The great Taiping Rebellion in southern China during 1851–1864 was rooted in spiritualism and based on the teachings of Hong Xiuquan and his quest for a period of Great Peace (Taiping). The Taiping Rebellion was one of a number of insurrections and conflicts with Western powers that challenged the Manchu rulers during the mid-19th century. After Britain's victory in the First Opium War (1839–1842) highlighted the ineffectual rule by the Qin dynasty, many ethnic Chinese groups such as the Han revolted against their Manchu overlords.

Hong Xiuquan, an aspiring civil servant turned seer, was the founder and spiritual leader of the Taiping Rebellion. Following a long illness and interaction with Western missionaries, Hong came to believe that he was the younger brother of Jesus Christ. Hong developed a religious ideology based on a mix of Christianity, Confucian thinking, and Chinese folklore in order to overthrow the Manchu "demons" and found a so-called egalitarian utopia. He held that he possessed divine authority to regulate all earthly affairs. The Taipings also banned gambling and the consumption of alcohol and opium.

In January 1851 Hong proclaimed a revolt against the Manchu Qing dynasty. The revolt began in Guangxi Province and expanded into Hubei and Hunan Provinces. The Taiping pledge to equally redistribute wealth and property garnered considerable popular support, as did the proclamation of equality for women, respect for education, and other socially progressive ideas. Large numbers of artisans, scholars, and craftsmen joined vast numbers of peasants in the movement. The Taiping ranks

A page from the *Illustrated London News* of February 25, 1855, with coverage of the Taiping Rebellion. The illustrations at the top are of various Taipings, while the panorama at the bottom is of the rebel capital of Nanking (Nanjing) and its defenses. (Mansell/Time & Life Pictures/Getty Images)

continually increased, with converts drawn by the promise of shared wealth and land. The Taiping armies eventually grew to as many as 1 million men.

Taiping strength rested not only on the size of the army but also in its high morale, strict discipline (the troops had to obey a set of 62 rules), and religious conformity. The Taipings also possessed effective military commanders, especially Yang Xiuqing, who led the rebel forces against the Imperial Army in the Changjiang (Yangzi River) Valley.

In order to combat the growing threat of the Taiping movement, the Qing initially called upon the Green Standard Army. Although designated an army, by 1850 this once effective imperial force amounted to little more than a national police force, the ranks of which consisted of generally low-quality, undisciplined, and undependable troops. The ideologically driven, dedicated, innovative, and disciplined Taiping forces stood in sharp contrast to and were generally victorious over the Green Standard armies during the first years of the rebellion. The Taipings captured Wuchang in January 1853, but instead of moving against Peking (today Beijing) in what was their best opportunity to take the imperial capital, they proceeded along the Changjiang Valley and captured Nanking (today Nanjing) on March 29, 1853. The Taipings then made Nanking their capital and there proclaimed a new dynasty, the Taiping Tianguo (Heavenly Kingdom of Great Peace), with Hong as ruler.

The Taipings, however, never rigorously implemented the egalitarian social programs that had drawn so many poor Chinese to their ranks. Furthermore, the revolutionary nature of the Taiping policies and religion were repugnant to the Chinese landholding elite, who now came to the aid of the Qing government. These factors and the endemic, bloody infighting within the ranks of the Taiping leadership doomed the regime to eventual failure.

The Taipings also suffered from internal strife. Although the Taiping forces seemed invincible when facing the Qing armies, their very success sowed the seeds for the eventual demise of the movement. Infighting among the leadership brought the execution of several individuals who had also been the most effective generals in the initial military campaigns, with Hong seeing them as threats to his supreme leadership. Other effective commanders died or were captured in battle.

With the end of the Second Opium War (*Arrow* War) in 1860, Imperial Viceroy Zeng Guofan and Li Hongzhang worked to reform and revitalize the imperial government. They also attempted to subdue the Taipings. Despite its promises of reform, the Taiping regime had become increasingly repressive, the key factor in its subsequent demise.

With the Taipings threatening Shanghai, in 1860 wealthy Shanghai merchants financed a mercenary army. It initially consisted of foreigners and was commanded by American soldier of fortune Frederick Townsend Ward. His so-called Foreign Arms Corps, which began with about 100 men, steadily grew in size and became known as the Ever Victorious Army for a series of successful military campaigns. After Ward was mortally wounded in battle in 1862, Englishman Charles "Chinese" Gordon replaced him.

Zeng Guofan meanwhile had reinvigorated the imperial forces. He attracted support because of his insistence on adherence to Confucian principles, including obligation to the welfare of the men and loyalty to one's superior. Soon this well-disciplined force of volunteers had grown into the Xiang Army, the chief military force against the Taipings. Zeng also created a naval force of hundreds of junks.

Hong Xiuquan died on June 1, 1864, probably of food poisoning. His death and Zeng's capture of Nanking a few days later marked the effective end of the Taiping Rebellion, which had nonetheless claimed the lives of some 20 million–30 million Chinese.

Thomas Crenshaw and Spencer C. Tucker

See also Gordon, Charles George; Zeng Guofan

Further Reading

Spence, Jonathan. *God's Chinese Son: The Taiping Heavenly Kingdom of Hong Xiuquan.* New York: Norton, 1996.

Tanner, Harold M. *China: A History.* Indianapolis, IN: Hackett, 2009.

Worthing, Peter. *A Military History of Modern China: From the Manchu Conquest to Tian'anmen Square.* Westport, CT: Praeger Security International, 2007.

Tamil Tigers.

See Liberation Tigers of Tamil Eelam

Taruc, Luis Mangalus

Birth Date: June 21, 1913
Death Date: May 4, 2005

Military leader of Philippine insurgents during World War II (1939–1945) and the Hukbalahap Rebellion (1946–1954). Luis Mangalus Taruc was born into a peasant family in San Luis, Pampanga, on June 21, 1913. By his own recollection, he became aware of the unfairness of the Philippine farming system at an early age. With frequent pauses to earn funds, Taruc worked his way through the first two years of college, finally becoming a tailor to support his family.

Taruc was influenced by Pedro Abad Santos, founder of the Socialist Party in the Philippines, who encouraged Taruc to become a peasant organizer and eventually the secretary-general of his party. As such, Taruc was repeatedly arrested for labor agitation. The Socialist Party merged with the Philippine Communist Party in 1938, but Taruc was not a dogmatic Marxist.

Some critics have disputed the importance of Taruc's role during the Japanese occupation of the Philippines (1942–1945). However, he became the military commander of the Hukbong Bayan Laban sa mga Hapon (People's Army against the Japanese), often referred to by the acronym Hukbalahap, or Huk. Taruc used his peasant unions to organize an insurgency that tied down Japanese troops and denied agricultural products to the occupiers.

The Hukbalahap refused to subordinate itself to the American-led insurgents in the Philippines and fought several skirmishes with rival groups. This plus their leftist beliefs prompted the U.S. Army to disarm the Huks in 1945. American authorities twice imprisoned Taruc on charges of banditry and supporting the Japanese occupation.

In 1946 Taruc was elected to the Philippine Congress, but he was denied his seat on charges of terrorizing voters. Similar actions drove the leftists to reestablish their insurgent organization, and Taruc resumed his role as field commander, leading as many as 14,000 active guerrillas by 1949. However, the Marxist political leaders of the movement disagreed with Taruc's Maoist, peasant-based approach to revolution. These disputes and improved government tactics decimated the insurgency, and Taruc surrendered on May 16, 1954. Despite a promise of amnesty, he was imprisoned for alleged crimes during World War II but was released on orders of President Ferdinand Marcos in 1968. He then continued to work for agrarian reform to benefit the agrarian poor. Taruc died in Quezon City in the Philippines on May 4, 2005.

Jonathan M. House

See also Hukbalahap Rebellion; Lansdale, Edward Geary; Magsaysay, Ramón del Fierro

Further Reading

Greenberg, Lawrence M. *The Hukbalahap Insurrection: A Case Study of a Successful Anti-Insurgency Operation in the Philippines.* Washington, DC: U.S. Army Center of Military History, 1987.

Kerkvliet, Benedict J. *The Huk Rebellion: A Study of Peasant Revolt in the Philippines.* Berkeley: University of California Press, 1979.

Taruc, Luis. *Born of the People.* New York: International Publishers, 1953.

Taruc, Luis. *He Who Rides the Tiger: The Story of an Asian Guerrilla Leader.* New York: Praeger, 1967.

Taylor, John Rodgers Meigs

Birth Date: 1865
Death Date: 1949

Author of a study of U.S. counterinsurgency operations in the Philippines during 1899–1902. John Rodgers Meigs Taylor was born in 1865. He graduated from the U.S. Military Academy, West Point, and was commissioned a second lieutenant in the 7th Infantry Regiment in 1889. In 1899 he was promoted to captain in the 14th Infantry.

During the Spanish-American War (1898), Taylor was assigned to the Philippines, where he headed the army's military information department. He was awarded the Silver Star for gallantry during his service there and two additional Silver Stars for his role in the Peking (now Beijing) Relief Expedition of 1900.

Taylor wrote a five-volume study of U.S. military operations in the Philippine-American War (1899–1902), then known as the Philippine Insurrection, and a study of Colonel James Franklin Bell's operations on Batangas during 1901–1902. The controversy surrounding Bell's military campaign led to the suppression of Taylor's work by governor-general of the Philippines William H. Taft. Taylor's work languished, as for some decades the U.S. Army gave scant attention to counterinsurgency warfare.

Taylor retired from the army in 1914 because of poor health and was then librarian at the U.S. Army War College until 1919. He was promoted to colonel on the retired list in 1918. Taylor died in 1949.

Spencer C. Tucker

See also Bell, James Franklin; Philippine Islands and U.S. Pacification during the Philippine-American War

Further Reading

Beckett, Ian F. W. *Encyclopedia of Guerrilla Warfare.* Santa Barbara, CA: ABC-CLIO, 1999.

Taylor, Zachary

Birth Date: November 24, 1784
Death Date: July 9, 1850

U.S. Army officer and president of the United States (1849–1850). Born near Barboursville in Orange County, Virginia, on November 24, 1784, Zachary Taylor moved as a boy to Kentucky and grew up on a plantation near Louisville. He received only a rudimentary education, but in May 1808 he secured a commission as a first lieutenant in the 7th Infantry Regiment.

Taylor's first duty assignment was New Orleans. He then commanded Fort Pickering near present-day Memphis, Tennessee. In November 1810 Taylor was promoted to captain and commanded Fort Knox, Vincennes, Indiana. Shortly before the beginning of the War of 1812, he assumed command of Fort Harrison (present-day Terre Haute) along the Wabash River in the Indiana Territory. In September 1812 Taylor and 50 men held off an attack on the fort by some 500 warriors allied with the British. For this rare American victory in the Northwest, Taylor was breveted major.

In the summer of 1814 Taylor led an expedition against Native Americans in the upper Mississippi River region (present-day Iowa and Wisconsin), but a British and

Indian force at Rock River, west of Lake Michigan, forced him to turn back that September. Taylor then withdrew south on the Mississippi River, near the mouth of the Des Moines River, and erected Fort Johnson, which he later ordered razed when he and his force withdrew to St. Louis in October 1814. In December 1814 as the war drew to a close, Taylor took command of Fort Knox in Kentucky.

After the war, Taylor reverted to his permanent rank of captain. Resigning his commission, he returned to the army in 1816 when President James Madison ordered Taylor's rank of major restored. Promoted to lieutenant colonel in 1819, Taylor relocated to Louisiana, where he served in recruitment and helped build a military road and fortifications. Reassigned to posts in present-day Minnesota and Wisconsin in the late 1820s, Taylor received promotion to full colonel in April 1832. He then led troops in the Black Hawk War (1832).

Taylor's experience fighting Native Americans proved helpful for his next combat assignment in the Second Seminole War (1835–1842), when he oversaw construction of a series of strongholds to support the army's advance into Indian country. On Christmas Day 1837, Taylor won the biggest engagement of the war in the Battle of Lake Okeechobee and was rewarded with a brevet to brigadier general. In May 1838 he assumed command of the Department of Florida and spent the next two years continuing the campaign against the Seminoles. His boldness in battle and indifference to etiquette and military dress (including sporting a wide-brimmed straw hat) earned him the affectionate nickname "Old Rough and Ready."

In July 1845 following the annexation of Texas, President James K. Polk ordered Taylor there to command the Army of Occupation of some 3,500 men. In March 1846, seeking a confrontation with Mexico, Polk ordered Taylor to cross the Nueces River and take up position along the Rio Grande, which Polk and Texans claimed as the southern border of Texas. On April 25, 1846, a Mexican cavalry unit crossed the river and attacked part of Taylor's force, inflicting American casualties. Polk used this incident as the catalyst for the Mexican-American War (1846–1848).

Taylor subsequently won the Battle of Palo Alto (May 8, 1848) and the Battle of Resaca de la Palma (May 9) and was breveted major general and named commander of the Army of the Rio Grande in July. He then occupied Matamoros, where his army remained until late summer as it struggled with logistical problems. In September 1846 Taylor advanced toward Monterrey, but logistical difficulties led him to conclude an armistice following the Battle of Monterrey (September 21–24) that allowed the Mexican garrison to depart, enraging Polk. The American public, however, saw Monterrey as a victory and made Taylor a national hero. Worried that Taylor would convert his growing popularity into political capital, Polk strove to keep the general from further combat and thus selected Major General Winfield Scott, commanding general of the army, to conduct the Mexico City Campaign, siphoning off much of Taylor's force toward that end.

Mexican president and general Antonio López de Santa Anna then marched against Taylor's weakened force in northern Mexico. In the ensuing Battle of

Buena Vista (February 22–23, 1847), Taylor with 4,700 men won a hard-fought victory over Santa Anna, who had some 15,000 men. Believing the war to be virtually over, Taylor departed Mexico that November, having developed a considerable dislike for both Polk and Scott.

Taylor ran for the presidency on the Whig ticket in November 1848 and won. His tenure as chief executive was consumed by the matter of slavery. President only for 16 months, Taylor died of acute gastroenteritis at the White House on July 9, 1850.

Jeffrey W. Dennis and Spencer C. Tucker

See also Black Hawk War; Seminole Wars

Further Reading

Bauer, K. Jack. *Zachary Taylor: Soldier, Planter, Statesman of the Old Southwest.* Baton Rouge: Louisiana State University Press, 1985.

Dyer, Brainerd. *Zachary Taylor.* New York: Barnes and Noble, 1967.

Tecumseh

Birth Date: ca. March 1768
Death Date: October 5, 1813

Shawnee chief and organizer of a Pan-Indian resistance movement. Tecumseh was born around March 1768 in a village along the Scioto River, near present-day Piqua, Ohio. His father was a war chief of the Kispoko band. At the time, the Shawnees were trying to resist white settlers flooding into the Ohio Territory, resulting in Lord Dunmore's War (1774). When the American Revolutionary War began in 1775, the Shawnees sided with the British in an attempt to retain their land. In 1777 Tecumseh's people were forced to flee westward to the Mad River and then farther west in 1780. These experiences instilled in Tecumseh a hatred for whites in general and for Americans in particular.

Beginning at age 16, Tecumseh participated in war parties and raided white settlements, but incursions by white settlers continued. In 1786 Kentucky militiamen burned Tecumseh's village, forcing his people to flee to a new location on the Maumee River. Under the leadership of his older brother Cheeseekau, Tecumseh earned a reputation as a brave and skillful warrior. After Cheeseekau was killed in 1792 in an attack on Nashville, Tecumseh succeeded him as war chief of the Kispoko band.

Tecumseh supported the loose confederacy of tribes organized by Blue Jacket and Little Turtle in 1790. When American forces under Brigadier General Josiah Harmar and then Brigadier General Arthur St. Clair marched against the tribes in Ohio, Tecumseh was among those who ambushed and defeated them. On August 20, 1794, Tecumseh took part in the Battle of Fallen Timbers, in which

Major General Anthony "Mad Anthony" Wayne decisively defeated Blue Jacket and broke the Pan-Indian confederacy.

Tecumseh refused to attend the signing of the Treaty of Greenville in 1795, in which Native Americans ceded most of Ohio to the United States. Instead, he led his followers into the Indiana Territory to escape white influence. In 1797 the band settled near present-day Anderson, Indiana. Tecumseh joined his brother Tenskwatawa (also known as the Prophet) in calling for a return to traditional values and a rejection of white influences. In 1805 Tecumseh moved his band back to Ohio, settling at Greenville. Tecumseh and Tenskwatawa began to exert growing influence among other tribes. Delegations visited Tecumseh and listened to his plan of an Indian confederacy to prevent further white encroachment.

While Tecumseh's message found favor among the younger warriors, older leaders opposed him. Whites were also uncomfortable with Tecumseh's presence so close to the border. Although he was careful to give no pretext for attacks by whites, Tecumseh realized that he was in danger in Ohio. To avoid possible conflict before he was ready, Tecumseh moved his band back to Indiana in the spring of 1808. The band settled along the Wabash River, just below the mouth of the Tippecanoe River. Tecumseh now grew more outspoken in his criticism of American expansionism.

In 1809 in the Treaty of Fort Wayne, Indiana territorial governor William Henry Harrison secured the cession of 3 million acres from tribes in Indiana. The outraged Tecumseh demanded that these land cessions halt, believing that the land belonged to all tribes and that none could be sold or given away without the consent of all. Realizing that only strength could stop American settlements, Tecumseh traveled widely to recruit for his confederacy. Although many favored his message, only the nativist Red Stick faction of the Creeks was willing to commit to joining his confederacy.

While Tecumseh was away in 1811, Harrison brought an American army to attack Tecumseh's village on the Wabash. Tenskwatawa launched an unsuccessful surprise attack on Harrison but was decisively defeated at the Battle of Tippecanoe (November 7, 1811). This event diminished Tecumseh's power and following among the Indians.

Tecumseh now turned to the British. When word reached him in July 1812 that war had been declared, he gathered a band of followers and led them into Canada, joining British major general Isaac Brock in defending Fort Malden against an invasion by Brigadier General William Hull from Detroit. There is a tradition that Tecumseh was commissioned a brigadier general in the British Army, the only Indian to be so recognized. Tecumseh then led his band into Michigan and destroyed a supply column in an ambush on August 5. He continued to harass American forces around Detroit, helping to convince Hull to withdraw from Canada and later to surrender Detroit.

The victory at Detroit caused large numbers of warriors to join Tecumseh. Brock then led a combined British and Indian force against Ohio. They fought a series of battles against American columns under Harrison, who sought to recapture Detroit. Tecumseh was in Indiana in January 1813 when an American force was destroyed on the Raisin River, with a massacre of the wounded. Tecumseh returned in time to join Brigadier General Henry Procter in an unsuccessful siege of Fort Meigs, destroying an American relief column on May 5. A second attempt to capture Fort Meigs in July also failed.

When Procter retreated to Canada after the American victory in the Battle of Lake Erie, Tecumseh was outraged. Nevertheless, he and a small group of warriors joined the British in their withdrawal eastward from Fort Malden. To pacify Tecumseh, Procter agreed to make a stand on the Thames River on October 5, 1813. Tecumseh was killed in the battle. After Tecumseh's death and the British defeat, the Native Americans lost heart and dispersed.

Tim Watts

Further Reading

Dowd, Gregory. *Spirited Resistance: The North American Struggle for Unity, 1745–1815.* Baltimore: Johns Hopkins University Press, 1992.

Edmunds, R. David. *Tecumseh and the Quest for Indian Leadership.* Boston: Little, Brown, 1984.

Sugden, John. *Tecumseh: A Life.* New York: Henry Holt, 1998.

Templer, Sir Gerald Walter Robert

Birth Date: September 11, 1898
Death Date: October 25, 1979

British field marshal. Born in Colchester on September 11, 1898, Gerald Walter Robert Templer was educated at Wellington College and at the Royal Military Academy, Sandhurst, from which he was commissioned in 1916 in the Royal Irish Fusiliers. He saw combat service in France during World War I (1914–1918). Between the world wars, Templer served in both the Middle East and Britain. He graduated from the Staff College in 1929.

At the outbreak of World War II (1939–1945), Templer was assigned to the intelligence section in the War Office. In November 1940 he was appointed to command a brigade, and in April 1941 he took command of the 47th Division as a temporary major general. In September 1942 he commanded II Corps, part of the British home defense, becoming the youngest lieutenant general in the army. Ten months later Templer requested command of a field division and reverted to major general. In October 1943 he was assigned command of the 56th Division in Italy, which he led in fighting at the Volturno River, Monte Camino, and Anzio. He was sent home the following August to recuperate after being wounded when his vehicle hit a mine.

In 1945 Templer was named director of civil affairs and the military government in the British occupation zone in Germany. The following year he returned to the War Office, where he served successively as director of military intelligence and vice chief of the Imperial General Staff. He was promoted to general in June 1950.

In 1952 following two years as chief of the Eastern Command, Templer was personally selected by Prime Minister Winston Churchill to become high commissioner in Malaya, then in the midst of the Malayan Emergency (1948–1960). To restore order, Templer selectively built on his predecessors' initiatives, most notably the Briggs Plan. He was also aided by changes that gave him virtually absolute power, with both political authority and military command of all federation forces. In exercising this responsibility, Templer emphasized that political development could not take a back seat to military operations.

Templer's instructions had been to emphasize to the people of Malaya that it was British policy that Malaya become a fully self-governing nation in due course. This would be dependent upon defeat of the Communist terrorists and the establishment of a clear partnership of all communities, an enormous challenge because communalism lay at the heart of the insurgency and because the ethnic Chinese (about 40 percent of the population) felt largely disenfranchised by the two other large communities, the Malays and Indians. Not surprisingly, the majority of insurgents were ethnic Chinese. To address this, Templer appealed directly to the Chinese and sought to show them that they would have a better future in a free Malaya.

Templer considered his primary initial task to restore order. To this end, he established three priorities: creating an effective intelligence process, reorganizing and retraining the police, and keeping the public informed. A key factor in his success was the creation of a separate elite Special Branch of the police, many of whose members were Chinese, to include former insurgents. He also streamlined government organization and emphasized initiative, timeliness, and accountability.

Templer's approach was closely associated with what became known as the hearts-and-minds approach in counterinsurgency. By the time of his departure in 1954, the insurgents had essentially been defeated. Templer subsequently served as chief of the Imperial General Staff from 1955 to 1958 and was promoted to field marshal in November 1956. Templer died in London on October 25, 1979.

George M. Brooke III

See also Hearts and Minds; Malayan Emergency

Further Reading

Cloake, John. *Templer, Tiger of Malaya.* London: Harrap, 1985.

Clutterbuck, Richard. *Conflict and Violence: In Singapore and Malaysia, 1945–1983.* Boulder, CO: Westview, 1985.

Nagl, John. *Counterinsurgency Lessons fom Malaya and Vietnam: Learning to Eat Soup with a Knife.* New York: Praeger, 2002.

Stubbs, Richard. *Hearts and Minds in Guerrilla Warfare: The Malayan Emergency, 1948–1960.* Oxford: Oxford University Press, 1989.

Ten Years' War in Cuba

Start Date: October 10, 1868
End Date: May 28, 1878

The Ten Years' War, the first in a series of three wars of Cuban independence during the 19th century, set the stage for the Little War (1879–1880) and the Cuban War of Independence (1895–1898) leading to U.S. intervention in Cuba's internal affairs and the Spanish-American War in 1898.

Although Christopher Columbus landed on Cuba in 1492, Spain did not conquer the island until 1515, following an expedition there led by conquistador Diego Velázquez in 1510. Cuba's fertile soil led to the cultivation of tobacco and sugarcane, while the discovery of gold in the interior brought the opening of a number of mines. To secure labor for the island's plantations and mines, the Spaniards enslaved most of the native population.

Exploitation of the natives and their susceptibility to European diseases brought their near extinction within a generation. The Spaniards then imported African slaves. Until the Haitian Revolution (1791–1804), the Cuban economy remained diversified, with tobacco, livestock, and shipbuilding as principal industries. Because sugar production in Haiti dropped precipitously, Cuban landowners secured concessions from the Crown to accelerate the sugar industry on the island.

Vast sugar plantations were established throughout the island. The harsh conditions of sugar cultivation and the labor-intensive methods of sugar farming led to a large slave population on Cuba. Ultimately, sugar cultivation enriched a small planter class along with the few who catered to the sugar plantation owners. The plantation system quickly dominated the island economically and politically.

Following the overthrow of Spain's Queen Isabella II in September 1868, Carlos Manuel de Céspedes, a wealthy plantation owner in eastern Cuba, spoke out against increased Spanish taxes and the lack of local autonomy. On October 8 the Spanish governor-general of Cuba, learning that Céspedes was plotting rebellion, telegraphed the provincial governor to arrest him, but the telegraph clerk warned Céspedes. The war began on October 10, 1868, when Céspedes assembled his slaves, announced their freedom (and conscription into his revolutionary army), and proclaimed Cuba independent from Spain.

The next day Céspedes and a small band of supporters attacked the nearby town of Yara. Although a failure, this attack, commonly known as the Grito de Yara (Shout of Yara), unleashed a war of independence and a slave revolt. Revolutionary sentiment quickly spread throughout the eastern half of Cuba, and by the end of the year the rebels numbered more than 10,000, many of them former slaves. Indeed, for many Cubans, emancipation was as important as independence.

Céspedes favored gradual independence. Hoping to win the support of plantation owners in the western half of the island, he proclaimed the death penalty for any revolutionary who attacked sugar estates or slave property. He also supported independence as a prelude to annexation to the United States, which many nationalists opposed.

Following the capture of Batamo on October 20, 1868, it became the seat of the new government. The rebels held Bayamo until January 11, 1869, when, faced with superior Spanish force, they burned it to the ground rather than surrender. Although the revolutionary forces enjoyed moderate success in the countryside, they were unable to capture population centers in the eastern half of the island, however.

On April 10, 1869, the rebels convened a constitutional assembly in Guáimaro. Two days later the assembly transformed itself into the Congress of Representatives. Céspedes was elected president, and his brother-in-law Manuel de Quesada was named chief of the armed forces.

In May 1869 Céspedes petitioned the U.S. government for diplomatic recognition. President Ulysses S. Grant refused to grant this, however. Focusing on Reconstruction, the U.S. government feared that recognition would undermine its legal case seeking economic damages from the United Kingdom for its involvement in the American Civil War. (Britain had recognized the belligerency of the Confederate States of America in 1861.) In addition, U.S. recognition of the Cuban rebels would absolve Spain from responsibility for damages to American property in Cuba inflicted by Cuban revolutionaries.

Regardless of their government's official position, many U.S. citizens and officials were openly sympathetic toward the revolutionary cause. In 1870 Quesada, with the collusion of American John Patterson, purchased the former Confederate blockade runner *Virginius* and employed it to supply the Cuban revolutionaries with weapons and other matériel. On October 31, 1873, however, the Spanish warship *Tornado* captured the *Virginius* off Jamaica and took it to Santiago, Cuba. In early November following Spanish legal proceedings, 53 men from the ship, many of them Americans, were executed as pirates. The action brought the United States and Spain to the brink of war. Tensions eased, however, after the Spanish government promised to indemnify the families of the executed Americans.

Meanwhile, the war dragged on. Spanish authorities caused construction of fortifications across the province of Camagüey, effectively dividing the island in half, and the inability of Céspedes to expand the war into the prosperous western half of the island cost him support. On October 27, 1873, the Congress of Representatives removed Céspedes from power, and Salvador Cisneros became president.

In 1875 Dominican-born Máximo Gómez launched an unsuccessful invasion of the western half of the island. The majority of the plantation owners there refused to support the revolution, however. Most of the fighting during the war was therefore confined to the eastern half of the island. Rebels burned loyalist plantations, and Spanish troops destroyed insurgent plantations.

Meanwhile, the end of the Third Carlist War (1872–1876) in Spain and the restoration of the Bourbons to the Spanish Crown allowed the Spanish government to dedicate greater resources to fighting the Cuban rebellion. By the end of 1876, King Alfonso XII had dispatched 100,000 troops to Cuba. On October 19, 1877, Spanish troops captured Cuban president Tomás Estrada Palma. In February 1878 as a result of repeated military misfortunes, the Congress of Representatives opened peace negotiations.

On February 10, 1878, the Cuban revolutionaries signed the Pact of Zanjón, effectively ending the Ten Years' War. Spain promised numerous administrative and political reforms. All revolutionaries were granted amnesty, and former slaves who served in the revolutionary army were granted their unconditional freedom. Revolutionary general Antonio Maceo Grajales, however, demanded complete emancipation and continued fighting for 10 more weeks, until May 28, 1878. Ultimately, the failure of the Spanish government to fulfill its promise of reform eventually led to the so-called Little War in 1879.

Michael R. Hall and Rick Dyson

See also Cuban War of Independence

Further Reading

Bradford, Richard H. *The Virginius Affair.* Boulder: Colorado Associated University Press, 1980.

Ferrer, Ada. *Insurgent Cuba: Race, Nation, and Revolution, 1868–1898.* Chapel Hill: University of North Carolina Press, 1999.

Knight, Franklin. *Slave Society in Cuba during the Nineteenth Century.* Madison: University of Wisconsin Press, 1970.

Pérez, Louis A., Jr. *Cuba: Between Reform and Revolution.* New York: Oxford University Press USA, 2006.

Terrorism

Acts of terror have long been a part of insurgencies, in part from the target government's ability to define the initial attacks as terrorism. As such, there is a decided tendency to equate counterinsurgency and counterterrorism, even though the techniques and strategies that lead to success in each tend to be radically different. In counterinsurgencies, emphasis is placed on co-opting the insurgent causes, addressing problems within the government, and reconciling with the citizenry. In counterterrorist campaigns, it is more important to neutralize the terrorists, separate them from the population, and expose the hypocrisy of the terrorists' actions and propaganda.

Part of the problem in separating terrorism and insurgency stems from the inherent difficulty of defining terrorism. Because there is no unilaterally accepted definition, the term "terrorism" becomes a convenient pejorative label to apply to any opposition that is certain to attract the contempt of civilized society. In general, most functional definitions of terrorism include violence or the threat of violence conducted by a nonstate actor or group and targeting a noncombatant population with the goal of creating a political change. Obviously, many insurgent attacks, particularly in the early stages of an insurgency, could fall within this definition, even if the end goal of the actor is not to instill fear so much as to fuel an insurgency.

During the French Revolution (1789–1799), radicals in Paris, whose spokesman was Maximilian Robespierre, embraced the idea that terror could be used to intimidate the opposition and therefore help to bring about a complete reorganization of society. Their Reign of Terror (1793–1794) created a backlash, however, that eventually consumed them and ended their attempt at social engineering. Such tactics were again applied, with more success, by the Bolsheviks after they seized power in Russia in November 1917.

By the end of the 19th century, anarchist organizations undertook attacks against symbols of oppression, often through assassinations, especially in Russia. Only in the 20th century did terrorism become associated with seemingly random attacks against civilians. By the 21st century, the most prominent terror organizations had shifted from targeted attacks against individuals to an emphasis on causing mass casualties. This approach naturally generates substantial media attention, spreading fear throughout the target population.

Because attacks fitting the definition of terrorism have long been a part of insurgencies, there is an extensive record of the overlap. Typically, most terror attacks linked to an insurgency occur in the earliest phases as the insurgents seek to amass resources, garner popular support, and draw attention to their cause. Successful early attacks often provoke government overreaction, which then leads to growing support for the insurgency. This overreaction may come in the form of oppressive restrictions on civilian activities under the guise of improved security or in the form of demonstrations of force that do a poor job of targeting terrorists, may injure or kill civilians, and result in extensive property damage. The tendency to provoke such responses, noted by both Chinese Communist leader Mao Zedong in his writings published as *On People's War* and French Army officer David Galula in *Counterinsurgency Warfare,* is one of the greatest tools for insurgents to employ in attempting to broaden their support.

Early American examples of attacks that could be classified as terrorism include Bacon's Rebellion of 1676 in colonial Virginia and John Brown's Raid of 1859. Terror campaigns in Algeria in the 1950s and in South Vietnam in the late 1950s and 1960s grew into full insurgencies and outright wars. Important in such actions is the selection by the attackers of carefully chosen symbolic targets and the avoidance of friendly civilian casualties. An effective propaganda campaign is also essential to their success. Ineffective and heavy-handed government responses provide motivation for others to join the insurgency.

The terror organization Al Qaeda, founded by Osama bin Laden, is considered a global insurgency against Western economic and social dominance. Al Qaeda's terror attacks reflect the desire to incite an uprising of Muslim fundamentalists, first against their own secularized governments and then against all foreign influence. Al Qaeda seeks to weld radical Islamic sectarianism into a reunified caliphate, a transnational Islamic state capable of standing against the Western powers on equal terms. As such, the fight against Al Qaeda is as much a counterinsurgency as a counterterrorism campaign. While Al Qaeda has garnered some sympathy in the Muslim world for its vision of a unified Islamic state, its methodology, the capricious nature of its terrorist activities, and its willingness to kill fellow Muslims has prevented it from obtaining the support necessary to advance its cause. Al Qaeda has also provoked a major military response, although not one characterized by a general attack against Islam, and thus has largely failed to win the support of the target population. Nevertheless, Al Qaeda offers a perfect example of the overlap between terrorism and insurgency on a scale never previously achieved by a terror organization and remains a threat around the globe.

Paul Joseph Springer

See also Afghanistan Insurgency; Algerian War; Galula, David; Iraq Insurgency; Mao Zedong; Viet Cong

Further Reading

Chaliand, Gerard, and Arnauld Blin. *The History of Terrorism: From Antiquity to Al Qaeda.* Berkeley: University of California Press, 2007.

Galula, David. *Counterinsurgency Warfare: Theory and Practice.* Westport, CT: Praeger Security International, 2006.

Hoffman, Bruce. *Inside Terrorism.* New York: Columbia University Press, 1998.

Mao, Zedong. *On People's War.* Peking: Foreign Languages Press, 1967.

Teutoburg Forest, Battle of the

Event Date: 9 CE

In 7 CE after subduing a number of tribes in Germania, the area north of the upper Danube and east of the Rhine, the Romans declared the region to be pacified. Germania seemed peaceful, and legate Publius Quinctilius Varus was assigned the task of integrating it into the empire. Varus had been governor in Syria, and his talents lay in administration rather than field command. His appointment to the German post strongly suggests that Emperor Augustus was unaware of the true state of affairs there.

The Romans did not understand the degree to which their rule—especially the taxes, which had to be paid in metal—was resented. Arminius, prince of the Cherusci tribe, who had commanded German auxiliaries under Rome and had been rewarded with Roman citizenship for his service, took leadership of the revolt, although he kept this secret from Varus. Arminius even suggested the route of march for the Roman legions to winter quarters, which he claimed would allow Varus to put down several small revolts along the way.

In the summer of 9 CE, Varus set out from near the Weser River with three Roman legions (XVII, XVIII, and XIX), all veterans of fighting in Germany and totaling 15,000–18,000 men, including some cavalry. Family members and camp followers accompanied them, as did German auxiliaries—perhaps another 10,000 people. Arminius then left the Roman column, allegedly telling Varus that he wanted to scout ahead. The attack occurred in the Teutoburg Forest (Teutoburger Wald), most probably near Osnabrück.

The Romans simply marched into an ambush. They and their wagons were strung out over a considerable distance. The German attackers numbered between 20,000 and 30,000 men and held the high ground on one side, with marshes on the other side. Traditional Roman tactics could not be applied in the difficult terrain, and the Roman position was made worse by strong wind and rain.

On the first day the Germans engaged in hit-and-run attacks, causing significant Roman casualties. Varus threw up breastworks, however, holding the Germans at bay for the night. He then ordered the wagons burned, hoping that this would increase the speed of the Roman march. However, burning the wagons had little effect, and the Romans then retreated to the original fortifications.

During several more days, the three legions were systematically destroyed. Only a handful of soldiers managed to escape to the nearby Roman base at Aliso. Varus and his officers preferred to commit suicide rather than be taken. Indeed, the Germans sacrificed those captured.

Although Artiminus brought Aliso under siege, he failed to take it and departed. The Roman garrison there then abandoned Aliso. Artinimus, however, made no attempt to follow up on his great victory by invading Italy or Gaul. This was impossible, as the tribes soon fell to quarreling among themselves. Prompt Roman action also secured their control of the Rhine bridges, but the loss of 3 legions with more than 10 percent of Roman military might (from 28 down to 25 legions) severely impacted Roman military options.

On learning of the Battle of the Teutoburg Forest, Emperor Augustus disbanded his German bodyguard, saying that no Germans could be trusted. He was also heard to cry "Quinctilius Varus, give me back my legions!" The numbers of these three legions never were resurrected, even after Roman operations in 14–16 CE and 41 CE recovered their standards.

The Battle of the Teutoburg Forest signaled the end of Roman efforts to expand northward. Augustus was now forced to rethink his entire suppositions about the military strength required to garrison the empire. He reintroduced conscription by the drawing of lots, using these levies to augment existing legions. He also concentrated eight legions—a third of remaining Roman strength—on the Rhine under his stepson Tiberius, who conducted punitive operations in Germany during 10–12 CE. Germanicus Caesar also campaigned there with four legions during 14–16 CE but made no real attempt at conquest and occupation.

Augustus abandoned plans for a German province between the Rhine and Elbe Rivers, thereby fixing Rome's northern boundary on the Rhine and Danube Rivers. North-Central and Northeastern Europe would not be brought within Latin cultural and legal systems for several hundred more years. Subsequent German leaders, including the Nazis, exploited the Battle of the Teutoburg Forest to build national consciousness and unity, presenting it as an example of Germans defending their "freedom" against foreign invasion.

Spencer C. Tucker

See also Arminius

Further Reading

Murdoch, Adrian. *Rome's Greatest Defeat: Massacre in the Teutoburg Forest.* Stroud, Gloucestershire, UK: Sutton, 2006.

Schlüter, W. "The Battle of the Teutoburg Forest: Archaelogical Research at Kalkriese near Osnabrück." *Journal of Roman Archaeology,* Supp. 32 (1999): 125–159.

Tacitus. *The Annals of Imperial Rome.* Translated by Michael Grant. London: Penguin, 1974.

Thompson, Sir Robert Grainger Ker

Birth Date: April 12, 1916
Death Date: May 16, 1992

British counterinsurgency expert. Born on April 12, 1916, in Charlwood, Surrey, England, Robert Grainger Ker Thompson was educated at Marlborough and Sidney Sussex College, from which he graduated in 1938. Later that same year he was posted as a Malayan Civil Service (MCS) cadet. Thompson was in Hong Kong attending Chinese-language school when the Japanese attacked in December 1941. He managed to escape, making his way across China to India, where he joined Brigadier Orde Wingate's Chindits as a Royal Air Force liaison officer. Thompson participated in both Chindit expeditions and became a devoted Wingate supporter, later vigorously defending him against his critics. By war's end, Thompson had been promoted to wing commander.

In 1946 Thompson returned to Malaya as assistant commissioner of labor in Perak. Perak was the center of the tin-mining industry, whose workers were predominantly recent Chinese immigrants and which also possessed a large number of Chinese squatters. Both groups became prime recruiting targets for the Malayan Communist Party, whose composition was approximately 90 percent Chinese.

In June 1948 the Malayan Emergency began. In mid-1949 Thompson was assigned to High Commissioner Henry Gurney's staff and the following year to the small personal staff of Lieutenant General Sir Harold Briggs, the director of operations. As the civilian member of Briggs's staff, Thompson participated in the drafting of what became known as the Briggs Plan, which is generally credited with laying the groundwork for the eventual insurgent defeat.

The centerpiece of the Briggs Plan was the rural resettlement of mostly Chinese squatters into what eventually numbered 480 secure "New Villages" and the regrouping of rubber estate and mine workers into secure areas. Security for these areas was achieved by creating a "police-military framework" around them. The guerrillas, known as the Malayan Races Liberation Army, could thereby be isolated from their essential base of support, the Communist underground in the villages, and both could then be destroyed separately. The government complemented the security framework with a variety of political, economic, and social programs, which the people could accept without fear of intimidation.

In mid-1951 Thompson was assigned as deputy commissioner of labor in Johore, one of the most heavily insurgent states in Malaya. His time here convinced him that to defeat an insurgency, it was essential to secure the least infested areas in the country first and then slowly work outward, thereby eventually isolating the most affected for final clearance.

Gurney was assassinated in October 1951, and Briggs departed soon thereafter due to ill health. The new high commissioner, General Sir Gerald Templer, unlike his predecessor, was given both political and military authority in Malaya. Templer built on the Briggs Plan with new initiatives, including closer cooperation among the civil, military, and police elements; placing priority on intelligence; overhauling the police, with emphasis on building up the Special Branch, notably with Chinese; developing an effective information and psychological warfare program; and lifting emergency regulations in areas once they were considered to be free of guerrillas. Thompson served as one of Templer's advisers during the latter's two years as high commissioner.

In 1955 Thompson became coordinating officer of security for the Malayan Federation. By this time the insurgency had essentially been defeated, although it would not be officially declared ended until 1960. In 1959, two years after Malaya achieved independence, Thompson was appointed permanent secretary of defense, the posting from which he would retire in April 1961.

During 1960, Thompson made his first trip to the Republic of Vietnam (RVN, South Vietnam), where at the behest of President Ngo Dinh Diem he made an assessment of the nascent Communist insurgency there. Thompson would later state that he was struck by what he perceived as great similarities between the Malayan and Vietnamese situations. In the autumn of 1961 following his retirement from the MCS, Thompson was sent by the British government to South Vietnam as head of a small British Advisory Mission (BRIAM) to "advise and assist" Diem. Soon after his arrival, Thompson submitted a counterinsurgency plan to Diem that incorporated many of the lessons of Malaya. Because it recommended that operations commence in the Mekong Delta, the plan became known as the Delta Plan. Diem chose to selectively adopt items from the plan to incorporate into his own

Strategic Hamlet Program, which was then implemented in a counterproductive manner.

Thompson established cordial relations with the Americans, but his influence with the Vietnamese remained limited, particularly following Diem's assassination in November 1963. In 1965 following BRIAM's dissolution, Thompson was hired as a consultant by the U.S. RAND Corporation. The following year he published *Defeating Communist Insurgency,* his most influential work, which compared the Malayan and Vietnamese insurgencies and established principles for dealing with similar conflicts. But by 1966 Thompson had become severely disillusioned with American strategy in Vietnam, which, he argued, showed a basic failure to understand the nature of the war. In *No Exit from Vietnam* (1968), he explained how this flawed strategy had led to the January 1968 Tet Offensive.

In 1969 on the advice of National Security Advisor Henry Kissinger, who had read and been impressed by the arguments in *No Exit,* President Richard Nixon appointed Thompson as an independent observer. Thompson remained in this capacity, making annual visits to Southeast Asia and reporting his findings either to the president or to Kissinger, until the final collapse of South Vietnam in April 1975. Thompson's disillusionment with the 1973 Paris Agreement led him to conclude that the lack of American will to enforce it was the ultimate cause of defeat. Thompson died on May 16, 1992, in Winsford, England.

George M. Brooke III

See also Malayan Emergency; Strategic Hamlet Program; Vietnam War

Further Reading

Brooke, George M. "A Matter of Will: Sir Robert Thompson, Malaya, and the Failure of American Strategy in Vietnam." Unpublished doctoral dissertation, Georgetown University, 2004.

Thompson, Robert. *Defeating Communist Insurgency: The Lessons of Malaya and Vietnam.* New York: Praeger, 1966.

Thompson, Robert. *Make for the Hills: Memories of Far Eastern Wars.* London: Leo Cooper, 1981.

Thompson, Robert. *No Exit from Vietnam.* New York: McKay, 1968.

Tito

Birth Date: May 7, 1892
Death Date: May 4, 1980

Yugoslav resistance leader and subsequent leader of Yugoslavia. Born on May 7, 1892, into a peasant family in the village of Kumrovec in Croatia, then part of the Austro-Hungarian Empire, Josip Broz (aka Tito) was apprenticed to a mechanic. He followed this trade, traveling throughout the Dual Monarchy. In 1913 he was drafted into the Austro-Hungarian Army. On the outbreak of World War I (1914–1918),

Broz, who was an excellent soldier, was a sergeant major commanding a platoon in a Croatian regiment. He fought on the Carpathian Front against the Russians until his capture in 1915. While a prisoner of war, he became fluent in Russian. Released following the March 1917 Russian Revolution, Broz joined the Bolsheviks at Petrograd but was then a political prisoner until the Bolsheviks took power in November 1917.

Broz fought in the Red Guard during the Russian Civil War but returned to Croatia in 1920 to take an active role in the Komunistička Partija Jugoslavije (YPJ, Yugoslav Communist Party). His underground work, often from jail, brought his rapid rise in the party apparatus as a member of the YPJ Politburo and Central Committee. He took the pseudonym "Tito" for security reasons.

Imprisoned from 1929 to 1934, in 1937 Tito became secretary-general of the YPJ. During World War II (1939–1945) following the German invasion of Yugoslavia in April 1941, Tito took command of the Communist Partisan movement with the twin goals of expelling the Germans and securing control of the government. Tito and the Partisans employed guerrilla tactics to compensate for their lack of advanced weaponry. Tito's Partisans were in competition with the Serbian-dominated Ćetniks (Chetniks) led by General Draza Mihailovic, minister of war in the exiled government. For the most part, the Ćetniks were unwilling to embark on the type of actions that would bring widespread reprisals by the Germans against the Yugoslav population, while the Partisans had no such inhibitions. In a controversial decision that had far-reaching repercussions for the political future of Yugoslavia, in 1943 the British government, which provided the Allied military support for the Yugoslav resistance, shifted all support to the Partisans.

Tito's Partisans grew to some 800,000 men and women by the end of the war, tying down a large number of Axis divisions. At the end of the war Tito was in full control of Yugoslavia, and he insisted that the Red Army ask permission to enter Yugoslavia in pursuit of the German. Tito's forces attempted to annex the southern provinces of Austria, moving into Carinthia. Yugoslav seizure of this territory was only prevented by the timely arrival of the British V Corps. The Yugoslavs were finally convinced by the threat of force to quit Austria in mid-May 1945.

Tito extracted vengeance on the Croats, many of whom had been loyal to the Axis, as had the Slovenes. The Partisans executed without trial perhaps 100,000 people who had sided with the Germans within weeks of the war's end. The majority of German prisoners taken in the war also perished in the long March of Hate across Yugoslavia.

With the support of the Red Army, Tito formed the National Front and consolidated his power. He nationalized the economy and built it on the Soviet model. Tito often went his own way in foreign policy matters, leading to a break with the Soviet Union in 1948. After this, he became more pragmatic in economic matters and allowed a degree of decentralization. Tito claimed that there might be "different paths to socialism," giving birth to what became known as polycentralism.

Tito traveled widely and became one of the principal leaders of the nonaligned nations. By 1954, however, he had ended reform. In the mid-1970s the Yugoslavian economy began to falter, and nationalist pressure from various ethnic groups threatened to break up the state. Tito died on May 4, 1980, in Lubljana. The complicated federated state system that he had decreed did not long survive his death, for the various ethnic groups then began to assert their independence.

Jeremy C. Ongley

Further Reading

Djilas, Milován. *Tito.* New York: Harcourt Brace Jovanovich, 1980.

Pavlowitch, Steven K. *Tito, Yugoslavia's Great Dictator: A Reassessment.* Columbus: Ohio State University Press, 1992.

West, Richard. *Tito and the Rise and Fall of Yugoslavia.* New York: Carroll and Graf, 1995.

Toussaint L'Ouverture, François Dominique

Birth Date: May 20, 1743
Death Date: April 7, 1803

Haitian insurgent leader. François Dominique Toussaint L'Ouverture was born on May 20, 1743, to slave parents on the Breda sugar estate outside of Cap Français on the French island colony of Saint-Domingue (Haiti) and became a domestic worker, probably a coachman. By 1779 Toussaint de Breda, as he was first known, was a free black growing coffee on rented property with a workforce of 12 slaves. He had also learned to read and write.

During Toussaint's youth, Saint-Domingue was the most prosperous of France's colonies. Its economy was based on the plantation and slavery system. Under the French mercantilist system, Saint-Domingue could not develop its own industries and was forced to purchase finished goods from France. All trade was carried by French ships. Although many planters became fabulously wealthy, they harbored some resentment against the French government for its strictures.

The population on Saint-Domingue consisted of three separate groups. Some 45,000 whites in 1789 held most of the power, while 30,000 free blacks or mixed-bloods occupied an intermediate position. Many members of this group were wealthy and owned slaves and plantations, but they were systematically discriminated against by the whites and excluded from real power. Most of the population of Saint-Domingue were slaves of African descent; they numbered about 450,000.

The French Revolution of 1789 quickly spread to the colonies. On Saint-Domingue, whites were divided between those supporting and those opposing the revolution. Free blacks and mulattos also took sides, and fighting—centered around the issue of racial equality, an obvious threat to the slave owners—began between the different factions.

On August 22, 1791, slaves of the Cap Français hinterland rose up in revolt. Toussaint apparently joined the revolt and is said to have saved the lives of the Breda plantation manager and his family early in the revolution. Toussaint's first recorded activity with the rebels, however, was on December 4, 1791, when he participated in negotiations between white and black leaders. These collapsed, and the revolt spread to other parts of the island.

Toussaint became chief lieutenant to slave general Biassou, and in 1793 they allied with the Spanish in Santo Domingo on the eastern side of the island. Following fighting in Europe between revolutionary France and the reactionary monarchies, both British and Spanish forces invaded French Saint-Domingue. In those circumstances, many blacks presented themselves as counterrevolutionaries, loyal to the French king and willing to fight with the Spanish.

François Dominique Toussaint L'Ouverture led the revolt in Haiti against France and proved a highly effective military commander. Although the revolt utimately failed and Toussaint was exiled, it was a major factor in Napoleon Bonaparte's decision to sell Louisiana to the United States. (Ridpath, John Clark, *Ridpath's History of the World,* 1901)

Tens of thousands of slaves were mobilized and armed to fight. In one month, more than 1,000 plantations were burned. In September 1793, however, the government in Paris abolished slavery.

Toussaint now changed sides, joining with the French against the Spanish and British who sought to continue the institution of slavery. Soon the leading black general for the French, Toussaint defeated those of his former colleagues still allied with the Spanish. Fighting continued until the Treaty of Bayle in 1795 ended the war between France and Spain.

By 1796, Toussaint was the leading figure and deputy governor on Saint-Domingue. The French-educated mulatto class now sought to replace the largely destroyed white class and take control themselves, but Toussaint limited this for the most part to the southern peninsula of the island. Many of his black officers took over the abandoned plantations and revived their production, using compulsory but paid labor of former slaves.

Toussaint employed his troops and influence with the free blacks to increase Saint-Domingue's autonomy. He engineered the return to France of various representatives of the central government and negotiated a trade agreement with the United States and an agreement with the British government to withdraw its troops and open trade between Saint-Domingue and the British colonies.

Supported by Great Britain and the United States, in July 1799 Toussaint launched a military campaign against his mulatto counterpart, André Rigaud. This so-called War of the South ended in complete victory for Toussaint. Yet the war drove a wedge between the blacks and mulattos. By the end of 1800, against orders from Paris, Toussaint had also conquered Spanish Santo Domingo. In this and other situations, he demonstrated increasing independence from the French government. Toussaint also promulgated a new colonial constitution that made him governor-general for life. He did not declare complete independence, however, for fear of alienating Britain and the United States.

In early 1802, French first consul Napoleon Bonaparte sent a military expedition to reassert French control over Saint-Domingue. In a brief but costly campaign, Toussaint was defeated and exiled to France. Many blacks had turned against him during the fighting. With the end of the campaign, however, they quickly realized that the French planned to reestablish slavery. Under general and future monarch of Haiti Jean-Jacques Dessalines, combatants of all colors united to expel the French. The colony was declared free on November 29, 1803, and given the name of Haiti in order to emphasize the break with European colonialism. Toussaint, meanwhile, died at Fort-de-Joux in the Doubs Department of France on April 7, 1803.

Tim Watts

Further Reading

Ott, Thomas O. *The Haitian Revolution, 1789–1804.* Knoxville: University of Tennessee Press, 1973.

Parkinson, Wenda. *"This Gilded African": Toussaint L'Ouverture.* New York: Quartet Books, 1978.

Tyson, George F., Jr., ed. *Toussaint L'Ouverture.* Englewood Cliffs, NJ: Prentice Hall, 1973.

Trinquier, Roger

Birth Date: March 20, 1908
Death Date: January 11, 1986

French Army officer and leading guerre révolutionnaire and counterinsurgency theorist. Roger Trinquier was born on March 20, 1908, in La Beaume, Hautes-Alpes Department, France. On graduation from the École Normale of Aix-en-Provence, he was called up for two years of compulsory military service. On its completion he decided to make the army a career. He graduated from the Officers' School at Saint Maixent in 1933 and was commissioned into the French colonial infantry. Trinquier's first assignment was to Indochina, where he led local colonial troops against pirates and opium smugglers in northern Tonkin (today northern Vietnam). After returning to France in 1936, in 1938 he was assigned to China, serving in Tianjin, Peking (Beijing), and Shanghai throughout World War II (1939–1945) and securing promotion to captain.

After World War II, Trinquier narrowly escaped being purged from the army as a Vichy collaborator. He served briefly in Indochina and then returned to France in 1946, charged with recruiting and training a colonial parachute battalion for service in Indochina. In November 1947 he returned to Indochina as second-in-command of the 2nd Colonial Commando Parachute Battalion. He assumed command of the battalion on the death of its commander in September 1948 and was promoted to major the next month. Among other innovations, Trinquier initiated a program of highly successful night ambushes. After some 30 airborne operations and numerous ground actions against the Viet Minh, in December 1949 he returned with his battalion to France.

In December 1952 Trinquier was again assigned to Indochina in the new Groupement de Commandos Mixtes Aéroportés (Composite Airborne Commando Group). He assumed command of that formation in early 1953 and achieved considerable success fighting behind Viet Minh lines in Tonkin and establishing a Montagnard guerrilla force that grew to some 20,000 men.

With the end of the war, Trinquier returned to France in January 1955 and was promoted to lieutenant colonel and assigned to the staff of the commander of French airborne forces. In August 1956 Tringuier was assigned to the 10th Parachute Regiment and made special assistant to division commander Brigadier General Jacques Massu for intelligence operations. Trinquier organized the intelligence-collection system that included paid Muslim informants and led to the creation of a database on the civilian population.

Trinquier thus played a key role in the success of the 10th Parachute Division in destroying the Front de Libération Nationale (FLN, National Liberation Front) insurgent network during the Battle of Algiers (January–March 1957). Trinquier also endorsed the harsh interrogation techniques, including torture, employed by Massu's division. Trinquier maintained that these were necessary in order to secure essential information.

Following a short assignment to France, Trinquier returned to Algeria in 1958 as commander of the 3rd Colonial Parachute Regiment, leading it in the field with great effectiveness. His regiment was able to effectively pacify its areas of operation and also captured a key FLN leader. In 1958 Trinquier was also a member of the Committee of Public Safety formed by army leaders in Algeria that toppled the French Fourth Republic and returned Charles de Gaulle to power.

In 1960 Trinquier was away from Algeria drawing up plans for French intervention in the Congo and thus missed the January 1961 attempted army putsch there against de Gaulle. Because Trinquier was so closely associated with those involved, however, he requested and was granted permission in 1961 to retire from the army.

Trinquier established himself in the wine business and helped found a French paratroop veterans' association. In 1961 he also published his ideas on counterinsurgency in *La Guerre Moderne* (The Modern Warfare), now regarded as a classic study of counterinsurgency warfare. Its thesis is that modern warfare will primarily involve insurgency and counterinsurgency rather than conventional warfare and that this requires a new approach that integrates political, military, economic, and psychological assets. Trinquier called for the formation of smaller and more mobile military units and a force that was politically astute and capable of integration with indigenous self-defense forces. He supported both the forced relocation of native populations and the torture of prisoners to secure essential intelligence information.

Trinqueir continued to write and publish extensively on his military experiences and on French politics and also expanded his ideas on counterrevolutionary warfare. These latter proved influential on U.S. military thinking during the Vietnam War and the Iraq War. Trinquier died in Vence, France, on January 11, 1986.

Louis A. DiMarco and Spencer C. Tucker

See also Algerian War; Algiers, Battle of; Front de Libération Nationale; Galula, David; Godard, Yves; Guerre Révolutionnaire; Indochina War; Massu, Jacques Émile; Organisation de l'Armée Secrète; Salan, Raoul Albin-Louis; Trinquier, Roger; Viet Minh

Further Reading

Paret, Peter. *French Revolutionary Warfare from Indochina to Algeria: The Analysis of a Political and Military Doctrine.* London: Pall Mall, 1964.

Shy, John, and Thomas W. Collier. "Revolutionary War." In *Makers of Modern Strategy: From Machiavelli to the Nuclear Age,* edited by by Peter Peret, 815–862. Princeton, NJ: Princeton University Press, 1986.

Trinquier, Roger. *Modern Warfare: A French View of Counterinsurgency.* Westport, CT: Praeger Security International, 2006.

Trocha

A defensive line system employed by the Spanish in their efforts to defeat insurgents in Cuba. Trochas were employed during the Ten Years' War (1868–1878) and again during the Cuban War of Independence (1895–1898). The first trocha was built to contain the anti-Spanish insurrection to the two most eastern provinces of the island. Beginning in 1895, trochas were also utilized to separate Cuban revolutionaries and insurrectionists from the general civilian population.

The Spanish word *trocha* means "trench," but the trochas employed in Cuba were far more than mere trenches. The first trocha was about 200 yards wide and featured fortified blockhouses located approximately every half mile along the line. Most trochas had a row of trees lining both sides. Between the blockhouses were stout barbed-wire fencing and smaller fortified redoubts. Where rebels were most likely to attack, the Spanish rigged the trocha with small explosives designed to go off when individuals tried to breach the line.

As originally constructed, the principal Spanish trocha bifurcated Cuba from north to south and ran for about 50 miles. The trocha began at Morón on the northern coast of Cuba and ended at Jucaro on the southern coast. Running roughly parallel to it was an already-existing railroad track. In 1895 when Spanish general Arsenio Martínez de Campos arrived in Cuba to contain the latest rebellion, he once again employed the trocha, ordering it additionally fortified. However, he was unable to quell the insurrection, so Madrid dispatched General Valeriano Weyler y Nicolau to the island in February 1896. Weyler ordered a new line constructed from Mariel to Majana as a means of confining the Cuban insurgents to the western part of the island. Manned by some 14,000 men, the trocha incorporated both electric lights and artillery and proved to be reasonably effective.

During the Ten Years' War, many rebels circumvented the trocha by employing clever tactics and ploys. During the period of Weyler's command the trochas were much more effective, and circumvention occurred chiefly by water, as rebels frequently employed small boats at night to bypass the trocha near the port city of Mariel. Many villages and towns were also surrounded by small trochas, little more than fortified rifle pits to deter rebels from entering the area. Most such trochas included a thick stand of barbed-wire fencing.

The trocha system and its link to Weyler's much-maligned *reconcentrado* policy created problems for the Spanish as the insurrection endured. Pictures and illustrations in the sensationalist and largely anti-Spanish U.S. press frequently focused on the barbed-wire fencing.

Paul G. Pierpaoli Jr.

See also Cuban War of Independence; *Reconcentrado* System; Ten Years' War in Cuba; Weyler y Nicolau, Valeriano

Further Reading

Foner, Philip S. *The Spanish-Cuban-American War and the Birth of American Imperialism, 1895–1902*. 2 vols. New York: Monthly Review Press, 1972.

Trask, David F. *The War with Spain in 1898*. Lincoln: University of Nebraska Press, 1996.

Trotha, Lothar von

Birth Date: July 3, 1848
Death Date: March 31, 1920

Imperial German Army general. Born on July 3, 1848, in Magdeburg in the Province of Saxony, Kingdom of Prussia, Lothar von Trotha entered the Prussian Army as an officer cadet in 1865. He fought in both the Austro-Prussian War (1866) and the Franco-Prussian War (1870–1871). In 1894 Trotha was appointed commander of the Schutztruppe (colonial troops) in German East Africa, where he ruthlessly suppressed native uprisings, including the Wahehe Rebellion (1891–1898). He then commanded the East Asian Expeditionary Corps, the German contingent in the international force sent to China during the Boxer Rebellion (Boxer Uprising) of 1899–1901.

In January 1904, led by Samuel Maherero, the Herero people of German South-West Africa (present-day Namibia) rebelled against German rule, killing as many as 150 Germans. In May, Trotha was given command of an expeditionary force of 14,000 men and ordered to crush the rebellion. After suffering some losses, Trotha soundly defeated the main Herero force in the Battle of the Waterberg Plateau on August 11. He then ordered his men to drive the Hereros into the barren Omaheke-Steppe, part of the Kalahari Desert, and to erect guard posts along the border and poison water holes. On October 2 Trotha also issued an order that any Herero encountered "inside the German frontier, with or without a gun or cattle, will be executed. I shall spare neither women nor children." Although Trotha subsequently ordered that women and children were not to be executed but instead would be driven from the territory, the result was devastating. Herero deaths are estimated at from 25,000 to 100,000. Trotha's men also routed the Nama people. Some 10,000 died, and another 9,000 were placed in makeshift camps and employed in forced labor.

Following a considerable public outcry, Trotha was relieved of his command. He returned to Germany in November 1905. Promoted to general of infantry in 1910, he retired from the army shortly thereafter. Trotha died in Bonn, Germany, on March 31, 1920.

Mark M. Hull and Spencer C. Tucker

See also Herero Revolt

Further Reading

Drechsler, Horst. *Let Us Die Fighting: The Struggle of the Herero and Nama against German Imperialism, 1884–1915.* London: Zed, 1980.

Kaulich, Udo. *Die Geschichte der ehemaligen Kolonie Deutsch-Südwestafrika (1884–1914): Eine Gesamtdarstellung* [History of the Former German Colony of South-West Africa (1884–1914): A Complete Presentation]. Frankfurt am Main: P. Lang, 2001.

Kiernan, Ben. *Blood and Soil: A World History of Genocide and Extermination from Sparta to Darfur.* New Haven, CT: Yale University Press, 2007.

Speitkamp, Winfried. *Deutsche Kolonialgeschichte* [German Colonial History]. Stuttgart: Reclam, 2005.

Troubles, The.

See Northern Ireland Insurgency

Trung Trac and Trung Nhi

Birth Dates: Unknown
Death Date: 43 CE

Sisters and Vietnamese heroines who were leaders of an insurgency against the Chinese. Also known as Hai Ba Trung (the Two Ladies Trung) or Trung Vuong or Trung Nu Vuong (the Trung Queens), they led the first uprising of Vietnamese against Chinese rule. Trung Trac and her sister Trung Nhi, who was the younger of the two, were daughters of the Lac *tuong* ("lord") of Me Linh in what is now Vinh Phu Province, Vietnam.

In 40 CE the two sisters led a revolt after To Dinh, the greedy and inept prefect of Giao Chi, killed Trung Trac's husband, Thi Sach, lord of Chu Dien. This triggered a general uprising against the unpopular Han Chinese regime. Angered by the Han's assimilation policy and the seizing of land and power from the local nobility in favor of Han immigrants who had just moved to Vietnam following Wang Mang's usurpation of the Han throne (9–23 CE), the uprising quickly spread throughout the Chinese colonies, from Cuu Chan (present-day Thanh Hoa) to Hop Pho (in present-day Guangdong Province, China). Chinese governors and colonial forces withdrew to China proper, and Trung Trac and Trung Nhi proclaimed themselves queens, choosing Me Linh as the capital.

After two years of intensive preparation, Han emperor Quangwu dispatched a Chinese army under Ma Yuan (Ma Vien), China's most famous general at the time. The queens were defeated at the Battle of Lang Bac. According to Vietnamese tradition, the two sisters refused to surrender and committed suicide in 43 CE by leaping into the Hat River.

Trung Trac and Trung Nhi are considered by many Vietnamese to be the most important and most revered heroines in Vietnam's history. Temples were erected in their honor, and the anniversary of their deaths has become Vietnamese Women's Day. Ceremonies are organized annually in their honor on the sixth day of the second month of the lunar calendar.

Pham Cao Duong

Further Reading

Bui Quang Tung. "Cuoc Khoi Nghia Hai Ba Trung Duoi Mat Su Gia" [The Two Trung Ladies' Uprising in Historians' Eyes]. *Dai Hoc* [publication of Hue University] 10 (July 1959): 1–16.

Nguyen Huyen Anh. *Viet Nam Danh Nhan Tu Dien* [Dictionary of Vietnamese Great Men and Women]. Houston, TX: Zieleks, 1990.

Pham Cao Duong. *Lich Su Dan Toc Viet Nam,* Vol. 1, *Thoi K Lap Quoc* [History of the Vietnamese People, Vol. 1, The Making of the Nation]. Fountain Valley, CA: Truyen Thong Viet, 1987.

Taylor, Keith Weller. *The Birth of Vietnam.* Berkeley: University of California Press, 1983.

Truong Chinh

Birth Date: February 9, 1907
Death Date: September 30, 1988

Secretary-general of the Indochinese Communist Party, Democratic Republic of Vietnam official, and secretary-general of the Dang Lao Dong Viet Nam Party

(Vietnamese Workers Party, Vietnamese. Communist Party). Born Dang Xuan Khu in Nam Dinh Province in Tonkin, northern Vietnam, on February 9, 1907, Truong Chinh (which means "Long March") was expelled from school for political agitation. He finished his secondary education in Hanoi at the Lycée Albert Sarraut and then studied at the Hanoi College of Commerce and taught for a time.

Truong Chinh joined Ho Chi Minh's Viet Nam Thanh Nien Cach Menh Dong Chi Hoi (Vietnam Revolutionary Youth Association), or Thanh Nien, and wrote articles for underground Communist publications. Truong Chinh was one of the founders in 1930 of the Dang Cong San Duong (Indochinese Communist Party [ICP]) and was valued for his propagandistic skills.

Seized by French authorities in 1931, Truong Chinh was convicted of subversion and consigned to Son La Prison. Released in 1936, he resumed ICP activities. As a cover in late 1936, he worked for a Hanoi newspaper under a pseudonym. Impressed with the activities of Mao Zedong (Mao Tse-tung) in China, Truong Chinh had already adopted the alias by which he is best known. In 1938 he published with Vo Nguyen Giap *The Peasant Problem, 1937–1938,* arguing that a Communist revolution could be both peasant based and and proletarian based, which formed the basis for ICP policies and later the policies of the Viet Nam Doc Lap Dong Minh Hoi (Vietnam Independence League), or Viet Minh.

When French authorities banned the ICP in 1939, Truong Chinh fled to safety in China. In 1940 he became head of the ICP's propaganda department, and in May 1941 he became the ICP's secretary-general. When in 1941 Ho Chi Minh organized the Viet Minh, a consortium of different nationalist parties under Communist leadership, Truong Chinh helped to portray it as an anti-French and anti-Japanese resistance movement dedicated to the overthrow of foreign dominance in Vietnam. He understood that this patriotic approach would win popular support for the Communists, who could later sweep aside the noncommunists. Truong Chinh played a leading part in the August Revolution in 1945 and helped draft the constitution of the Democratic Republic of Vietnam (DRV, North Vietnam). The next year he became a member of North Vietnam's first National Assembly.

Truong Chinh served as director of Viet Minh propaganda and oversaw intelligence and counterintelligence activities during the Indochina War (1946–1954). In 1946 he published *The August Revolution,* and the next year he published *The Resistance Will Win.* Truong Chinh stressed the teachings of Mao Zedong and the need for total mobilization of the masses. Unlike Mao, however, Truong Chinh emphasized the need for mobilizing international public opinion.

Truong Chinh was largely responsible for the new name of the Lao Dong, or Workers Party, adopted by the northern Communists in 1951. Within a short time he was secretary-general of the party, and by 1953 he was second only to Ho in the northern hierarchy.

Truong Chinh became suspicious of the meteoric rise in the party of Vo Nguyen Giap and his control of military forces. After a bitter struggle, Truong Chinh succeeded in having the army placed under the control of political commissars. As vice chairman of the Land Reform Committee in 1954, Truong Chinh implemented a draconian program of agrarian reform that included large-scale dispossession and numerous executions of alleged landlords, many of whom were no more than land-less peasants guilty only of being disliked by neighbors who accused them of being counterrevolutionaries. Truong Chinh's attempts to impose total collectivization of agriculture greatly diminished production and threatened famine. Dismissed from his positions as land reform vice chairman and as secretary-general of the Lao Dong Party, he was forced to make an official statement admitting "serious mistakes." Despite this, he retained his number three position within the politburo.

Truong Chinh's influence waned by 1968 as he urged a "Socialist construction" of the North, while some others (notably the first secretary, Le Duan) wanted the North Vietnamese government to concentrate on winning the war in the Republic of Vietnam (RVN, South Vietnam). Truong Chinh insisted that "military action can only succeed when politics are correct," adding that "politics cannot be fulfilled without the success of military action." Le Duan and his faction won the argument, thus paving the way for the 1968 Tet Offensive.

After the 1975 Communist victory in South Vietnam, Truong Chinh again rose in influence. In 1986 following the death of Le Duan, Truong Chinh served as interim secretary-general of the Vietnamese Communist Party from July until December 1986, when, probably as a result of the severe economic problems facing the Socialist Republic of Vietnam, the 6th National Party Congress elected a new secretary-general. However, Truong Chinh continued to serve as an adviser to the politburo until his death in Hanoi on September 30, 1988.

Cecil B. Currey

See also Ho Chi Minh; Indochina War; Le Duan; Mao Zedong; Propaganda; Vietnam War; Vo Nguyen Giap

Further Reading

Who's Who in North Vietnam. Washington, DC: Office of External Research, U.S. Department of State, 1972.

Who's Who in the Socialist Countries. New York: Saur, 1978.

Tseng Kuo-fan.

See Zeng Guofan

Tukhachevsky, Mikhail Nikolayevich

Birth Date: February 26, 1893
Death Date: June 12, 1937

Soviet marshal and military theorist. Born on the Aleksandrovkoye estate 150 miles southwest of Moscow on February 26, 1893, Mikhail Nikolayevich Tukhachevsky was the son of a nobleman and a servant girl. Debts forced the family to sell the estate and move to Moscow in 1909. There Tukhachevsky entered the Alexandrovsky Military College, studying military thought and history. During World War I (1914–1918) as an officer in the elite Semenovsky Guards, Tukhachevsky fought in Poland and was highly decorated before being taken prisoner in 1915. After three attempts, he escaped in 1917.

In 1918 Tukhachevsky joined the Red Army. A protégé of Leon Trotsky, Tukhachevsky became a prominent military commander during the Russian Civil War (1917–1920), commanding the First Army then the Eighth and Fifth Armies. Appointed commander in the west in April 1920, Tukhachevsky led the invasion of Poland in the Soviet-Polish War (1919–1921). Fighting here, however, laid the seeds for future conflict with Joseph Stalin and Kliment Voroshilov. At one point during the Battle of Warsaw, Stalin withheld vitally needed troops from Tukhachevsky's command.

Tukhachevsky brutally crushed the March 1921 anticommunist uprising at Kronstadt as well as the Antonov Revolt in Tambov Province in the Volga region (1920–1921) and the Basmachi Revolt (1918–1933) in Turkestan. During 1922–1924 he headed the Military Academy, and in May 1924 he became deputy to Marshal Mikhail Frunze, chief of the General Staff.

Tukhachevsky was a leading theorist of counterinsurgency. Indeed, some historians argue that he should be known as the father of counterinsurgency doctrine. His thoughts on this were expressed in an article, "Borba s Kontrerevoliutsionnim Vosstaniam" (Struggle with Counterrevolutionary Uprising) in *Voina I Revoliustsiia* (War and Revolution) in 1926. Tukhachevsky emphasized the need to take into account local customs and religious practices and the necessity for one individual to control both political and military efforts. The object of counterinsurgency operations was to break the opposing force into small guerrilla bands that could then be defeated in detail. Local forces should be employed where possible, turning those who were captured against their former comrades. Tukhachevsky noted the need for political concessions to break the insurgency; these could be rescinded once the insurgency had been ended. He also called for the confiscation and redistribution of "bandit" property and the relocation of hostile populations.

Following Frunze's death, Tukhachevsky became chief of staff of the Red Army (1926–1928). After disagreements with Defense Commissar Voroshilov, Tukhachevsky took command of the Leningrad Military District (1928–1931). There he developed his theories of deep operations, the application of mechanization and armor along with air support to warfare, and the use of airborne troops, carrying out actual maneuvers with these forces. Tukhachevsky saw clearly the nature of the German threat and called for forward areas to be lightly held, with large formations remaining back for subsequent reaction and deep-penetration operations.

Tukhachevsky returned to Moscow in 1931 as deputy commissar for military and naval affairs, chairman of the Revolutionary Military Council of the Soviet Union, and director of armaments. In 1936 he was named first deputy commissar for military-naval affairs and director of the Department of Combat Training. Foreign observers recognized his contribution in creating the most advanced armor and airborne divisions in the world. In November 1935 Tukhachevsky was promoted to marshal of the Soviet Union.

Tuckhachevsky believed strongly in the need to understand the defensive as a prerequisite for comprehending the operational level of war as a whole. Stalin, supported by Voroshilov and commandant of the Frunze Academy and marshal of the Soviet Union Andrei I. Yegorov, demanded unilateral adherence to the offensive in war. Tuckhachevsky also predicted that German leader Adolf Hitler would cooperate with Japan and that Germany would invade both Western Europe and the Soviet Union and argued for an end to cooperation with the Germans and a defense in depth.

Tukhachevsky's publication of these views early in 1935 in an article, "The War Plans of Germany in Our Time," angered Stalin, and that April Tukhachevsky was removed from his posts and assigned to command the Volga Military District. Arrested on May 26, 1937, he was secretly tried and condemned on charges of spying for the Germans. Tukhachevsky was executed by firing squad in the early morning hours of June 12, 1937, in Moscow. A 1956 Soviet investigation concluded that the charges against him had been fabricated, and he was formally rehabilitated in 1963.

A dedicated Russian patriot, Tukhachevsky was a brilliant military strategist. Stalin subsequently adopted Tukhachevsky's ideas during World War II (1939–1945), when they were proven correct.

Spencer C. Tucker

See also Basmachi Revolt; Pseudoforces

Further Reading

Alexandrov, Victor. *The Tukhachevsky Affair.* Englewood Cliffs, NJ: Prentice Hall, 1963.

Butson, Thomas G. *The Tsar's Lieutenant: The Soviet Marshal.* New York: Praeger, 1984.

Naveh, Shimon. "Mihail Nikolayevich Tukhachevsky." In *Stalin's Generals,* edited by Harold Shukman, 255–273. New York: Grove, 1993.

Tupamoros.

See Movimiento de Liberación Nacional

Tyrolean Revolt

Start Date: 1809
End Date: 1810

Uprising by Tyrolean peasants against the Bavarians and French during the Napoleonic Wars (1803–1815). Following its defeat by France in the War of the

Third Coalition (1805), Austria was forced to sign the Treaty of Pressburg (December 26, 1805). Among its provisions was Austria's cession of the Tyrol to France's ally Bavaria. Bavaria officially acquired the region in February 1806 and then instituted higher taxes and conscription and interfered in church matters. All of this angered the Tyrolean population. Austrian agents also actively encouraged opposition to Bavarian rule.

Taking advantage of France's involvement in Spain and general discontent in the Germanies concerning French rule there, Austria again declared war against France and Bavaria on April 9, 1809, citing as justification violation of the Treaty of Pressburg that had promised Tyrolean constitutional autonomy. Led by Andreas Hofer, as many as 20,000 Tyroleans drove the Bavarians from most of the Tyrol. Austrian emperor Francis I then pledged never to give up the Tyrol by treaty.

A combined Franco-Bavarian force retook Innsbruck, forcing Hofer and the rebels to retreat. Once the French redeployed troops against the Austrians, however, the insurgents returned, defeated Bavarian general Bernhard von Deroy, and recaptured Innsbruck. Tyrolese hopes were raised with the defeat of French emperor Napoleon I in the Battle of Aspern (May 22) but then were dashed by the emperor's decisive victory over the Austrians in the Battle of Wagram (July 5–6).

Napoleon meanwhile directed Marshal François Lefebvre to retake the Tyrol. Lefebvre led a multipronged advance into the region, but a number of the French and Bavarian columns were turned back, and Lefebvre, who had retaken Innsbruck, was forced to abandon it again, on August 14.

In the Treaty of Schönbrunn of October 14, 1809, Francis I again ceded the Tyrol. The rebels were defeated by the French and Bavarians in November, and many of them were executed. Despite little popular support, Hofer continued resistance. Betrayed in late January 1810, he was tried by a military court and executed on February 19. That same month, Napoleon forced Bavaria to cede part of the Southern Tyrol with the Trentino to the Kingdom of Italy and to cede the eastern Hochpustertal with Lientz to the newly created Illyrian Provinces. Following the defeat of Napoleon, the Congress of Vienna of November 1814–June 1815 restored the Tyrol to Austria.

Mark M. Hull

Further Reading

Harford, Lee S., Jr. "Napoleon and the Subjugation of the Tyrol." In *The Consortium on Revolutionary Europe, 1750–1850: Proceedings, 1989,* edited by Donald Horward and John Horgan, 704–711. Tallahassee: Florida State University, 1990.

Johnson, Otto W. "The Myth of Andreas Hofer: Origins and Essence." In *The Consortium on Revolutionary Europe, 1750–1850: Proceedings, 1989,* edited by Donald Horward and John Horgan, 720–728. Tallahassee: Florida State University, 1990.

U

Ung Lich.

See Ham Nghi

União Nacional para a Independência Total de Angola

Angolan insurgent organization led by Jonas Malheiro Savimbi. Savimbi established the União Nacional para a Independência Total de Angola (UNITA, National Union for the Total Independence of Angola) in 1966 after breaking with Holden Roberto's Frente Nacional de Libertação de Angola (FNLA, National Front for the Liberation of Angola) when Roberto refused to expand FNLA beyond northern Angola. Whereas the FNLA base of support was among the Bakongo people, UNITA was centered in southern Angola among the Ovimbundu and Chokwe peoples.

UNITA waged a guerrilla war against the Portuguese along with FNLA and the left-wing Movimento Popular de Libertação de Angola (MPLA, Popular Movement for the Liberation of Angola), led by António Agostinho Neto. UNITA was, however, the only one of the three guerrilla organizations operating entirely from within Angola.

When Angola won independence in 1975, the MPLA came to power. UNITA then allied with the FNLA and, supported by troops from Zaire (present-day Democratic Republic of the Congo), tried to oust the Marxist MPLA, only to suffer defeat by Cuban forces airlifted by the Soviet Union. Although the FNLA dissolved, Savimbi continued the struggle, initiating a horrific civil war. South Africa and the United States supplied UNITA with arms and weapons. The Soviet Union and Cuba backed the MPLA, with Cuba providing troops.

Claiming to be anticommunist, UNITA enjoyed the backing of a number of African leaders and by 1990 controlled nearly half of Angola. Following a cease-fire in 1991, in 1992 Savimbi lost a questionable presidential election, and the civil war resumed. The war continued off and on for the next decade, despite United Nations sanctions and international recognition of the popularly elected government in Luanda. Savimbi financed UNITA mainly through the illicit sales of diamonds. After Savimbi's death in battle in February 2002, UNITA agreed to a cease-fire, which ended the long civil war.

Spencer C. Tucker

See also Angolan Insurgency; Frente Nacional de Libertação de Angola; Movimento Popular de Libertação de Angola; Neto, António Agostinho; Roberto, Holden Álverto; Savimbi, Jonas Malheiro

Further Reading

Bridgland, Fred. *Jonas Savimbi.* St. Paul, MN: Paragon, 1986.

Klinghoffer, Arthur Jay. *The Angolan War.* Boulder, CO: Westview, 1980.

Marcum, John A. *The Angolan Revolution.* 2 vols. Cambridge, MA: MIT Press, 1969 and 1978.

United States Army School of the Americas

U.S. military facility that trained Latin American military and police forces in counterinsurgency techniques during the Cold War. Usually called the School of the Americas but formally known as the U.S. Army School of the Americas (USARSA), it opened in 1946 as the U.S. Army Caribbean School at Fort Amador in the Panama Canal Zone. The school was part of the larger U.S. Cold War containment strategy for Latin America that included the 1947 Rio Pact, the Organization of American States, and the Harry S. Truman administration's Point Four Program.

After World War II (1939–1945), Latin American militaries looked to the United States to supply the training for their national armed forces, replacing former French, Italian, and German military advisory groups. Particularly in the Caribbean region that included Central America, the Caribbean islands, and northern South America, the U.S. military sought to centralize its instruction of Latin American officers at a single location in the Panama Canal Zone. Initially, most of the training at the Caribbean Army School was in conventional warfare, unit exercises, and equipment maintenance. The school also taught police surveillance and antiriot techniques. Fear of Soviet subversion of Latin American labor movements and indigenous Socialist parties became a prime concern for U.S. policy makers in the 1950s. Thus, American instructors trained Latin American armies more for internal repression, the crushing of possible procommunist coups, and the monitoring and suppression of leftist dissenters.

Following the successful Cuban Revolution (1953–1959), American concerns over Communist penetration of the Western Hemisphere heightened, as did worries over the efficacy of leftist guerrilla movements championed by Ernesto "Che" Guevara and other Fidelistas. Guevara's activities unnerved U.S. military officials who had watched a ragtag group of Cuban radicals defeat a 50,000-man U.S.-trained and -equipped Cuban Army. Under the aegis of the John F. Kennedy administration, counterinsurgency doctrine received greater emphasis in U.S. military strategy. In

1963 Kennedy vastly expanded the U.S. Army Caribbean School, renaming it the U.S. Army School of the Americas, and deployed the 8th Special Forces Group to the Canal Zone to serve as instructors. The institution greatly increased the variety of its training programs that now concentrated on counterinsurgency, civic action, crowd control, psychological warfare, and anticommunist ideology.

Critics of the School of the Americas assert that during this period, the school began its policy of training officers in the techniques of interrogation, torture, kidnapping, assassination, and paramilitary terror tactics to be used in thwarting Communist insurgencies. From 1946 through the 1990s, the school graduated nearly 60,000 officers. The school became a target of attack from Panamanian nationalists who saw the facility as a violation of U.S.-Panamanian treaties that approved American military bases within the Canal Zone for canal defense only and not for the continental-wide repression of dissent. In 1967 Bolivian units trained at the School of the Americas helped track down and kill Guevara. During the 1960s, trainees from the school participated in six different counterinsurgency campaigns against leftist guerrillas in Latin America.

In the 1980s the School of the Americas came under even sharper scrutiny from human rights groups for its contribution to the U.S.-backed counterinsurgency wars in El Salvador, Guatemala, and Nicaragua. Human rights advocates such as Father Roy Bourgeois traced numerous atrocities committed against Central American civilians back to commanders and units trained by U.S. Green Berets at the School of the Americas. Links between graduates of the school and right-wing death squads also abounded. Critics increasingly referred to the institution as a "School for Assassins" and the "School for Dictators." Indeed, the school's alumni included Panamanian drug trafficker and dictator Manuel Noriega, Salvadoran death squad leader Roberto D'Aubuisson, Argentine military junta leader Leopoldo Galtieri, and Bolivian dictator Hugo Bánzer Suárez. Opposition to the school grew so vociferous that in 1984 the Pentagon agreed to withdraw it from the Canal Zone and transfer it to Fort Benning, Georgia. In 2001 it became the Western Hemisphere Institute for Security Cooperation.

Michael Donoghue

See also Guevara de la Serna, Ernesto; Western Hemisphere Institute for Security Cooperation

Further Reading

Barber, Willard Foster. *Internal Security and Military Power: Counterinsurgency and Civic Action in Latin America.* Columbus: Ohio State University Press, 1966.

Calvert, Peter. *Revolution and International Politics.* London: Pinter, 1996.

Gill, Lesley. *The School of the Americas: Military Training and Political Violence in the Americas.* Durham, NC: Duke University Press, 2004.

Nelson-Pallmeyer, Jack. *School of Assassins: The Case for Closing the School of the Americas and for Fundamentally Changing U.S. Foreign Policy.* Maryknoll, NY: Orbis, 1997.

United States Marine Corps Combined Action Platoons.

See Combined Action Platoons, U.S. Marine Corps

Urban Guerrilla Warfare

Urban guerrillas are those seeking to overthrow an existing government but using the urban environment as opposed to the traditional rural environment as their base of operations and support. Urban guerrilla warfare was especially utilized in the late 1950s and the 1960s as an alternative to rural operations among a largely peasant population. The major successful guerrilla movements in the decades after World War II (1939–1945) were predominantly rural-based. These included those led by Mao Zedong in China, Ho Chi Minh in Vietnam, and Fidel Castro in Cuba. However, this trend began to change in the late 1950s.

An early example of a rural insurgency shifting into an urban environment came during the Algerian War (1954–1962), when the leaders of the Front de Libération Nationale (FLN, National Liberation Front) fighting the French decided in late 1956 to take the offensive in the capital city of Algiers. This led to the Battle of Algiers (January–March 1957).

A number of factors make an urban environment appealing. Cities can provide cover for guerrillas and support for their operations. Urban areas also offer a fertile ground for publicity, where actions would be covered by national and international media. Insurgent strikes in rural areas might not attract the same notice, and the government might find it easier to control the news there.

Another factor leading insurgents into urban areas is the growing ability of conventional military forces to operate effectively in open terrain, thanks in large part to aircraft. Here counterinsurgent forces can track, identify, and attack guerrillas without much regard to collateral damage. Improvements in military technology such as aerial photography meant that even harsh terrain such as jungles and mountains provided less effective sanctuary.

Approaches to urban insurgent operations have differed sharply. Some insurgent groups such as the Brazilian Communist Ação Libertadora Nacional (ALN, National Liberation Action) and the German Rote Armee Fraktion (Red Army Faction) pursued a strategy designed to be the catalyst for a general uprising of the population against the government. The Brigate Rosse (Red Brigades) in Italy and the Provisional Irish Republican Army (PIRA) followed a long-term strategy that included guerrillas as well as a substantial effort to build a popular political base. The PIRA's war against the British government began in 1970 and continued for 28 years.

The tactics and strategy for a successful urban guerrilla revolution were spelled out by Spanish terrorist theorist Abraham Guillén (1913–1993) in *Estrategia de la guerrilla urbana* (Strategy of the Urban Guerrilla) in 1966 and by the better-known

Brazilian revolutionary Carlos Marighella's *Minimanual of the Urban Guerrilla* (1969). The objectives are to attack, discredit, and destroy the pillars of an allegedly corrupt government while simultaneously inspiring the urban population to support the insurgency. Among other actions, Marighella advocated kidnapping, assassination, bombings, and robbery. To him, there was little difference between the tactics of guerrillas and those of ordinary criminals except that the terrorist's motives are always ideological and never for personal gain. Also, guerrillas only targeted the government, foreigners, and the wealthy class supporting the government.

The great threat to urban guerrillas is that they operate in the urban environment. Although the population can provide cover and support, cities are the seats of local and national governments and home to the various classes and institutions supporting government. Thus, the urban guerrilla operates in an environment in which the government had a strong presence and support.

The strength of urban guerrilla operations lay in the ability to carry out operations that garner national and international media attention. Examples of this were the kidnapping of American ambassador Charles Elbrick by the Brazilian revolutionary ALN group in 1969, the kidnapping and assassination of former Italian prime minister Aldo Moro by the Red Brigade in 1978, and the capture and assassination of members of the Israeli Olympic Team by the Palestinian terrorist organization Black September in 1972.

The great flaw in a strategy of urban guerrilla warfare is the belief that violence against the government will inspire mass public support. In fact, each of the terrorist actions described above resulted in a diminution of support for the revolutionary movement.

National police forces are the best-equipped and best-trained organization for countering urban guerrillas. In South America, North America, and Europe, a variety of urban guerrilla organizations including the IRA (Great Britain), the Weathermen (the United States), and the Red Brigades were defeated primarily by police action. Police forces using traditional investigative methods were able to identify and locate key insurgents and could then employ special police tactical units or military antiterrorist units to capture or kill them. Urban guerrillas were well aware that police forces were the primary obstacle to their success, and for that reason, insurgent organizations such as the IRA made them a principal target.

During the 20th century, urban guerrilla operations were generally unsuccessful. Poor tactical decisions, the inability to connect ideologically with the urban population, and effective police operations all played a role. However, urban guerrilla warfare is still an attractive choice for many revolutionary movements. In the occupied West Bank and the Gaza Strip, various Palestinian groups have practiced urban guerrilla tactics against Israel. In Iraq, the various insurgent groups employed guerrilla tactics against the American and allied military forces, and some continue to mount terrorist actions in urban centers.

Louis A. DiMarco

See also Afghanistan Insurgency; Algerian War; Algiers, Battle of; Black and Tans and the Auxiliaries; Foco Theory; Front de Libération Nationale; Guillén, Abraham; Iraq Insurgency; Irish Republican Army; Libyan Civil War; Mao Zedong; Marighella, Carlos; Northern Ireland Insurgency; Police Role in Counterinsurgency

Further Reading

Joes, Anthony James. *Urban Guerrilla Warfare.* Lexington: University of Kentucky Press, 2007.

Marighella, Carlos. *The Minimanual of the Urban Guerrilla.* St. Petersburg, FL: Red and Black, 2008.

Utley, Harold Hickox

Birth Date: December 7, 1895
Death Date: July 8, 1951

U.S. Marine Corps officer and counterinsurgency theorist. Harold Hickox Utley was born in Springfield, Ohio, on December 7, 1895. He graduated from the U.S. Naval Academy, Annapolis, in 1906 and was commissioned in the Marine Corps. Utley served with U.S. occupation forces in Cuba in 1908 and in several shipboard marine detachments. He was in Haiti during 1915–1917 and briefly served with the Marine Brigade in the Dominican Republic. Promoted to temporary major in 1917, he was assigned to Washington before returning to Haiti as a member of its gendarmerie during 1919–1921. During 1928–1929, Utley commanded marine operations in eastern Nicaragua battling the forces of rebel leader Augusto C. Sandino and was awarded the Distinguished Service Order for his service.

Returning to the United States, Major Utley was assigned to Quantico, Virginia, as an instructor in the Field Officers Course, where he taught counterinsurgency tactics. He subsequently became the course director. At Quantico, on his own initiative Utley began an effort to gather information to establish counterinsurgency doctrine for the Marine Corps. He read extensively in existing works and wrote to Marine Corps officers who had participated in counterinsurgency operations to solicit information about their experiences. Because of his rank, Major Utley lacked great experience in field operations, and much of his information came from Captain Meritt A. Edson, who had also served in Nicaragua.

In 1933 Utley published the first three chapters of his "Tactics and Techniques of Small Wars" in the *Marine Corps Gazette,* the professional Marine Corps journal. The publication attracted the attention of commander of Marine Corps Schools Brigadier General Randolph C. Berkeley, leading to official approval for the publication of *Small Wars Operations* in 1936. The initial version of that Marine Corps manual bore Utley's clear imprint. *Small Wars Operations* identified five phases in small wars operations: initial landing; reinforcement and initial military operations; assumption of administration; policing leading to "free and fair" elections; and withdrawal, by which time a locally trained gendarmerie would be in place.

Utley retired from the Marine Corps in 1936 but was recalled to active service in 1940 to command the Marine Corps Detachment at Newport, Rhode Island. He retired permanently several years later due to poor health. Utley died at Newport on July 8, 1951.

Spencer C. Tucker

See also Nicaragua Insurgency; Sandino, Augusto César

Further Reading

Beckett, Ian F. W. *Encyclopedia of Guerrilla Warfare.* Santa Barbara, CA: ABC-CLIO, 1999.

Beede, Benjamin R., ed. *The War of 1898 and U.S. Interventions, 1898–1934: An Encyclopedia.* New York: Garland, 1994.

Utley, Harold H. "An Introduction to the Tactics and Techniques of Small Wars." *Marine Corps Gazette* 16 (May 1931): 50–53; 18 (August 1933): 44–48; 18 (November 1933): 43–46.

V

Vendée Revolt

Start Date: March 1793
End Date: March 1796

The Vendée Revolt in France occurred during the radical period of the 1789 French Revolution. The Vendée (today organized as the Department of Pays-de-la Loire) was a department organized in 1790 and located in west-central France that took its name from the Vendée River in southeastern France. The term "Vendée militaire" was used to describe the area south of the Loire River and northwest of the line formed from Saumur to Bressuire and Fontenay. During the French Revolution, the region was overwhelmingly rural, Catholic, and royalist.

The people of the Vendée overwhelmingly opposed the radical government in Paris that had proceeded against the Catholic Church in the Civil Constitution of the Clergy of 1790 and caused the death of King Louis XVI in early 1793. Class differences were not so much a factor in the Vendée as in the rest of France; indeed, lesser nobles and priests took leadership of the revolt. The uprising that began on March 11, 1793, was triggered, however, by implementation of a national military draft (the levée en masse) to raise 300,000 men nationwide. This led to revolts elsewhere in France against the ascendancy of radical Paris over the rest of the country. This so-called Federalist Revolt included the great cities of Marseille, Bordeaux, and Lyon.

Despite the War of the First Coalition (1792–1797), the French government lost no time in sending forces into the Vendée to crush the revolt there. The rebels, numbering some 60,000 men in all, chose Jacques Cathelineau as their leader, but they were poorly organized and had no real program apart from the desire to overthrow the Republicans. The rebels captured Saumur in June, but their subsequent effort to take the city of Nantes failed, and Cathelineau was killed.

Although other pressing concerns distracted the leaders in Paris, on August 1 the Committee of Public Safety in Paris decreed a scorched-earth policy in the Vendée and dispatched there additional manpower under General Jean-Baptiste Kléber. The troops established garrisons throughout the region, seized crops and livestock, and shot many suspected rebels out of hand. Others were guillotined, and many inhabitants were deported. Colonnes Infernales (Infernal Columns) made periodic sweeps that netted a number of rebel leaders.

With the overthrow of the radicals in Paris in July 1794, there was a general recognition among the successor Directory government that more humane measures would have greater success. General Lazare Hoche, dispatched to command in the Vendée in late August 1794, accomplished a great deal in completing the pacification there. He offered an amnesty and made such concessions as the free practice of religion and exemption from conscription. In February 1795 Hoche signed a cease-fire agreement with rebel leader François Athanase Charette de la Contrie, although it should be noted that Charette agreed largely to purchase time until the British could intervene.

In June 1795 the revolt began anew when British forces arrived. They occupied the small Île d'Yeu off the coast of Poitou and supplied arms to the rebels. In late July, however, Hoche defeated an émigré force landed by the British at Quiberon in Brittany. Hoche then proceeded against the remaining Vendéan bands. Charette was captured and executed on March 29, 1796. With the region again largely pacified, the state of siege was lifted that July.

Estimates of those killed in the Vendée Revolt range from 117,000 to as many as 450,000, out of a population of perhaps 800,000. The Vendée was not entirely pacified, however. There were brief revolts there again in 1799–1800, in 1815, and in 1832–1833.

Spencer C. Tucker

See also Hoche, Louis Lazare; Roguet, Christophe Marie Michel

Further Reading

Gabory, Émile. *Les guerres de Vendée: la Révolution et la Vendée, Napoléon et la Vendée, Les Bourbons et la Vendée, l'Angleterre et la Vendée* [The Vendée Wars: The Revolution and the Vendée, Napoleon and the Vendée, the Bourbons and the Vendée, England and the Vendée]. Paris: Laffont, 2009.

Tilly, Charles. *The Vendée.* Cambridge, MA: Harvard University Press, 1964.

Tilly, Charles, and Pierre Mantory. *La Vendée: Révolution et contre-révolution.* Paris: Fayard, 1970.

Venezuelan Insurgency

Start Date: 1963
End Date: 1965

The South American nation of Venezuela underwent an urban insurgency during 1963–1965. The Cuban Revolution (1953–1959) greatly impacted Latin America, including Venezuela, and in April 1960 leftist students there established the Movimiento de Izquierda Revolucionaria (MIR, Revolutionary Movement of the Left).

Rómulo Betancourt, who became president of Venezuela in February 1959, was a staunch opponent of the Cuban government of Fidel Castro and supported the expulsion of Cuba from the Organization of American States (OAS). Betancourt's positions led to several bloody uprisings in Venezuela, which were suppressed by the government. Betancourt then moved against the Venezuelan Left. His ruling Acción Democrática (AD, Democratic Action) Party largely disenfranchised the Partico Communista de Venezuela (PCV, Venezuela Communist Party).

In response, in January 1963 dissident military officers and members of the MIR, led by Douglas Bravo, organized the Fuerzas Armadas de Liberación Nacional (FALN, Armed Force of National Liberation). The FALN mounted a series of attacks, mostly in urban centers, with the intention of provoking a repressive response that would rally popular support against the government. FALN operations included the bombing of the U.S. embassy in Caracas, the destruction of a Sears Roebuck warehouse, and the sabotage of oil pipelines. These actions failed in their aim of rallying the urban poor against the government. Indeed, FALN attacks that killed innocent civilians, including a FALN assault on an excursion train in September 1963, turned the bulk of the Venezuelan population against the FALN and allowed Betancourt to introduce emergency legislation.

Betancourt went ahead with the scheduled December 1963 national elections. The FALN called for a boycott but was unable to disrupt the elections. More than 90 percent of eligible voters went to the polls, and Betancourt presided over an orderly transfer of power to his successor, Rómulo Gallegos.

Extensive aid from the United States greatly assisted the Venezuelan government in bringing an end to the insurgency. During Betancourt's presidency, military aid accounted for $64.5 million of the $180.1 million in U.S. assistance. U.S. police instructors also helped train the Venezuelan security services. In 1963, Venezuelan forces discovered a small cache of Cuban weapons hidden on an isolated stretch of coastline, prompting the OAS to apply economic sanctions against Cuba. The Venezuelan Insurgency was extinguished by 1965.

Spencer C. Tucker

See also Castro Ruz, Fidel Alejandro; Cuban Revolution; Fuerzas Armadas de Liberación Nacional of Venezuela

Further Reading

Alexander, Robert. *Rómulo Betancourt and the Transformation of Venezuela.* New Brunswick, NJ: Transaction, 1982.

Ewell, Judith. *Venezuela and the United States.* Athens: University of Georgia Press, 1996.

Kohl, James, and John Litt. *Urban Guerrilla Warfare in Latin America.* Cambridge, MA: MIT Press, 1974.

Levine, Daniel. *Conflict and Political Change in Venezuela.* Princeton, NJ: Princeton University Press, 1973.

Vercingetorix

Birth Date: ca. 75 BCE
Death Date: 46 BCE

Leader of a Gallic revolt against Rome. Vercingetorix, a member of the Arverni tribe in central Gaul (later France), was born around 75 BCE. Some contend that he was only in his late teens when he assumed leadership of the Gauls. His father, Celtillus, was an Arvernian noble who had been put to death for aspiring to the kingship. Gaul had only recently been conquered by Julius Caesar, but with Caesar away recruiting in Cisalpine Gaul and his legions scattered in garrison duty, a revolt broke out at Cenabum (Orléans) in the early winter of 53 BCE with the massacre of legionnaires.

In the Arvernian city of Gergovia, Vercingetorix led his dependents in joining the revolt, only to be expelled from Gergovia by its leaders, including his own uncle, who believed that a revolt against Rome was too risky. Vercingetorix and his followers, mostly the poor, then seized control of Gergovia, and Vincingetorix was proclaimed king. He quickly took leadership of the revolt, which soon spread throughout central and western Gaul. Vercingetorix hammered out treaties and imposed his will through the taking of hostages, and then he raised a large army and trained it to a degree not seen before in Gaul.

Caesar, returning from Italy, fought his way through the Gallic forces and rejoined his legions. He then retook Cenabum. Unable to compete with the better-armed and better-trained Romans in pitched battle, Vercingetorix adopted guerrilla tactics, harassing the Roman lines of communication and carrying out a scorched-earth policy to prevent the Romans from living off the land. Caesar laid siege to Avaricum (Bourges) in February 52 BCE. Vercingetorix was unable to relieve the city, and Caesar took it in March, putting to the sword its population of 40,000 people. Caesar then moved on to lay siege to the Arverni capital of Gergovia. Vercingetorix won the battle because Caesar chose to attack rather than lay siege to the city and starve it out.

When the Romans withdrew, Vercingetorix planned to attack them while they were drawn out on a march from the Saone Valley to the Seine. He assembled a large force of up to 95,000 men and might have been successful had not some of his force attacked prematurely. Both sides suffered heavily in the resulting battle, and in early July Vercingetorix withdrew to the stronghold of Alesia (Alise Sainte Reine, France), located on the top of Mount Auxois near the source of the Seine.

This time Caesar rejected an attack in favor of a protracted siege. Following one of history's most masterly siege operations (July–October 52 BCE), Vercingetorix was forced to surrender. Transported to Rome and imprisoned in the Tullianum there, he was led through the city in Caesar's triumph of 46 BCE and then put to death either by strangulation or beheading.

Resourceful, brave, and charismatic, Vercingeotrix was hampered by factionalism among the Gallic tribes and in any case could not overcome superior Roman discipline and training and Caesar's own adroit generalship.

Spencer C. Tucker

See also Caesar, Gaius Julius

Further Reading

Caesar, Gaius Julius. *Seven Commentaries on the Gallic War.* New York: Oxford University Press, 1996.

Rudd, Stephen, ed. *Julius Caesar in Gaul and Britain.* Austin, TX: Raintree Steck-Vaughn, 1995.

Viet Cong

The term "Viet Cong" (for Vietnam Communists, often given simply as VC) refers to Communist-led local insurgents in the Republic of Vietnam (RVN, South Vietnam) during the Vietnam War (1957–1975). The term was coined by the Ngo Dinh Diem regime in South Vietnam during the 1950s as a negative epithet intended to refute the claim of the insurgents that they were not Communists but instead represented a broad-based nationalist coalition. In fact, Vietnam now admits that the insurgency in South Vietnam had always been directed by the headquarters of the Dang Lao Dong Viet Nam (Vietnamese Workers' Party, that is, the Vietnamese Communist Party) in the Democratic Republic of Vietnam (DRV, North Vietnam) and that the VC simply represented the southern wing of the Vietnamese Communist Party and North Vietnam's armed forces.

Throughout the Vietnam War, U.S. order of battle lists maintained separate categories for VC and People's Army of Vietnam (PAVN, North Vietnamese Army) units, even though by 1968 most so-called VC units were made up almost entirely of North Vietnamese soldiers. The Communists made no distinction between VC and PAVN units, and all Vietnamese Communist military and political organizations were controlled through a single chain of command that ran directly back to Hanoi, the capital of North Vietnam.

The origin of the VC insurgency can be traced back to the war against France (1946–1954). Official Vietnamese histories view the wars against France and the United States as a single conflict and often refer to the two conflicts together as the Thirty-Year War (1945–1975).

Under the terms of the 1954 Geneva Accords that ended the Indochina War, more than 100,000 Communist military and political personnel regrouped to North Vietnam in 1955, but the Communists left behind tens of thousands of political cadres to continue the political struggle in South Vietnam, pending the national elections in 1956 that were called for by the Geneva Accords. The new government in South Vietnam refused to hold the elections and was supported in this stance by the United States. The South Vietnamese government now began hunting down the Communist cadres in South Vietnam. Fearful of possible U.S. military reaction, the North Vietnam's Communist leadership initially refused to allow the party in the South to conduct armed struggle, but in spite of these orders, the southern element of the party surreptitiously began forming small armed units and assassinating government officials.

In 1959 former southern party leader Le Duan, who was recalled to North Vietnam in 1957 to take over leadership of the Lao Dong Party, convinced its Central Committee to authorize military action to overthrow the government of South Vietnam. North Vietnam then began sending infiltrators, both military and political personnel, south to organize the struggle in South Vietnam.

In 1960 a wave of VC insurgent attacks swept across South Vietnam. These attacks were conducted largely without northern participation (only about 1,500 infiltrators plus a small quantity of weapons from North Vietnam had reached South Vietnam by the end of 1960). These attacks frightened the South Vietnamese and U.S. governments, resulting in a 1961 decision to increase U.S. military aid and advisory presence in South Vietnam. The growing number of infiltrators and weapons arriving from North Vietnam (a total of 40,000 infiltrators for the period 1959–1963) led to an explosion of insurgent activities that threatened the survival of the South Vietnamese regime. In 1960 the VC had some 10,000 full-time soldiers, but this figure grew to 25,000 in 1962 and then to 70,000 by the end of 1963.

In September 1964 the North Vietnamese Politburo decided to launch an all-out offensive to destroy the Army of the Republic of Vietnam (ARVN, South Vietnamese Army) and topple the South Vietnamese regime before the U.S. government had time to react. Four PAVN regiments were dispatched down the Ho Chi Minh Trail, together with PAVN general Nguyen Chi Thanh and a number of senior PAVN commanders. The Communist plan was thwarted by the arrival of U.S. ground troops in the spring and summer of 1965. As the United States and North Vietnam feverishly introduced large ground units and heavy firepower into South Vietnam, the character of the war changed. By 1966 the primary source of Communist manpower and supplies in South Vietnam was North Vietnam, supported by covert food purchases of food in allegedly neutral Cambodia.

In 1968 the Communist launched the Tet Offensive, an all-out attack on South Vietnam's cities aimed at provoking a nationwide insurrection to overthrow the pro-American government. The VC committed virtually all of its political cadres and guerrillas to this failed effort and suffered extremely heavy losses. These losses for all practical purposes spelled the end of the southern VC insurgency. According to Vietnamese documents, only 1,800 Communist soldiers were recruited inside South Vietnam during 1969, and a total of only 3,500 southern soldiers were recruited in the southern half of South Vietnam during the three-year period of 1969–1971. During that same three-year period, more than 270,000 North Vietnamese soldiers were sent to South Vietnam to fight.

Viewed in toto, the Vietnam War had quickly turned into a conventional war with only a small insurgent component. The southern VC played no significant role in the conflict during the final years of the war.

Merle L. Pribbenow

During the Vietnam War the Viet Cong constructed antipersonnel mines from such materials as artillery and mortar shells, and cartridge cases and pipe. U.S. forces sustained significant casualties from these weapons. (U.S. Army Center of Military History)

See also Le Duan; Ngo Dinh Diem; Vietnam War

Further Reading

Elliott, David W. P. *The Vietnamese War: Revolution and Social Change in the Mekong Delta, 1930–1975.* Armonk, NY: M. E. Sharpe, 2007.

Lien-Hang Nguyen. *Hanoi's War: An International History of the War for Peace in Vietnam.* Chapel Hill: University of North Carolina Press, 2012.

Military History Institute of Vietnam. *Victory in Vietnam: The Official History of the People's Army of Vietnam, 1954–1975.* Translated by Merle L. Pribbenow. Lawrence: University Press of Kansas, 2002.

Viet Minh

Communist front organization created to help the Indochinese Communist Party (ICP) achieve its overall objectives. The Viet Nam Doc Lap Dong Minh Hoi (Vietnam Independence League), commonly known as the Viet Minh, was established at the Eighth Plenum of the ICP in May 1941. The Viet Minh served as the organizational nexus for the development of a broad, national program. According to Viet Minh founder and leader Ho Chi Minh, the front was needed to organize the masses in resistance to French colonial rule and the occupying Japanese forces.

Viet Minh flexibility allowed the party to alter course quickly for current conditions. Perhaps the most important aspect of the front was its attention to the national question. By downplaying class revolution in favor of national liberation, the party attempted to involve all elements of society in the national struggle. Anticolonialism, patriotism, and nationalism were the only prerequisites for joining the national united front. The Viet Minh purposefully made temporary alliances with its enemies in order to achieve its more immediate objectives.

Following the Japanese occupation of 1940, the Viet Minh fought both the Japanese and the French. During World War II (1939–1945), the Viet Minh received assistance from the U.S. Office of Strategic Services in return for intelligence information and assistance in rescuing downed Allied pilots. With the war drawing to a close, the French planned to liberate Indochina themselves. The Japanese were well aware of this and on March 9, 1945, carried out a relatively bloodless coup against French colonial authorities and military forces. When Japan surrendered five months later, this left a political void in Indochina.

The Viet Minh exploited this situation, and on August 19, Ho's forces seized control of Hanoi. On September 2, 1945, in Ba Dinh Square in Hanoi, Ho proclaimed an end to French colonialism, Japanese occupation, and the Nguyen dynasty. Shortly after this declaration of independence, the ICP announced that it was dissolving, leaving the Viet Minh front as the only official party apparatus. In 1951 the ICP resurfaced officially with the formation of the Dang Lao Dong Viet Nam (Vietnamese Workers' Party, usually known as the Lao Dong Party). At this time, the Viet Minh was itself dissolved. According to revolutionary theory, the broad-based front was to be revised whenever historical circumstances changed drastically. The Communists therefore reconstituted the Viet Minh as the Lien Viet front (Lien Hiep Quoc Dan Viet Nam) during the Indochina War, and shortly after the 1954 Geneva Accords that ended that conflict, the Fatherland Front was born.

There is some question as to the actual date of the reconstitution of the Viet Minh front as the Lien Viet front. Some scholars have suggested that the Viet Minh lasted only until the war with France (1941–1946) began. One source gives April 1946 as the date for the reconstitution of the Lien Viet front. Others suggest, however, that it was the Viet Minh that battled the French from 1946 to 1954. In any case, the Viet Minh is popularly associated with the army that defeated the French in the Battle of Dien Bien Phu and that served the Democratic Republic of Vietnam (DRV, North Vietnam) so faithfully after its 1945 inception.

Robert K. Brigham

See also Ho Chi Minh; Indochina War

Further Reading

Duiker, William J. *The Rise of Nationalism in Vietnam, 1900–1941.* Ithaca, NY: Cornell University Press, 1976.

Marr, David G. *Vietnamese Tradition on Trial, 1920–1945.* Berkeley: University of California Press, 1981.

Woodside, Alexander B. *Community and Revolution in Modern Vietnam.* Boston: Houghton Mifflin, 1976.

Vietnam War

Start Date: 1957
End Date: 1975

The Vietnam War (1957–1975) grew out of the Indochina War (1948–1954). The 1954 Geneva Conference that ended the Indochina War between France and the nationalist-Communist Viet Minh provided for the independence of Cambodia, Laos, and Vietnam. Agreements reached at Geneva temporally divided Vietnam at the 17th Parallel, pending national elections in 1956. In the meantime, Viet Minh military forces were to withdraw north of that line, and the French forces were to withdraw south of the line. The war left two competing entities, the northern Democratic Republic of Vietnam (DRV, North Vietnam) and the southern French-dominated State of Vietnam (SV, South Vietnam), each claiming to be the legitimate government of a united Vietnam.

In June 1954, SV titular head Emperor Bao Dai appointed as premier Roman Catholic Ngo Dinh Diem, whom Bao Dai believed had Washington's backing. Diem's base of support was narrow but had been recently strengthened by the addition of some 800,000 northern Catholics who in 1954 relocated to the SV. In October 1955 Diem established the Republic of Vietnam (RVN, South Vietnam), with himself as president. The United States then extended Diem aid. The vast majority of the aid went to the South Vietnamese military budget. Little was allocated to education and social welfare programs, with the result that the aid seldom touched the lives of the preponderantly rural populace. As Diem consolidated his power, U.S. military advisers also reorganized the South Vietnamese armed forces. Known as the Army of the Republic of Vietnam (ARVN, South Vietnamese Army) and equipped with American weaponry, it was designed to fight a conventional invasion from North Vietnam rather than deal with an insurgency.

Fearing a loss, Diem refused to hold the scheduled 1956 elections. This jolted veteran Communist North Vietnamese leader Ho Chi Minh. Ho had not been displeased with Diem's crushing of his internal opposition but was now ready to reunite the country under his sway and believed that he would win the elections. North Vietnam was more populous than South Vietnam, and the Communists were well organized there. Fortified by the containment policy, the domino theory, and the belief that the Communists, if they came to power, would never permit a democratic regime, the Dwight D. Eisenhower administration backed Diem's defiance of the Geneva Agreements.

Diem's decision led to a renewal of fighting, which became the Vietnam War. Fighting resumed in 1957 when Diem proceeded against the 6,000–7,000 Viet Minh political cadres who had been allowed to remain in South Vietnam to prepare for the 1956 elections. The Viet Minh then began the insurgency with the full support of the North Vietnamese government. The insurgents came to be known as the Viet Cong (VC), for Vietnamese Communists. In December 1960 they established the National Liberation Front (NLF) of South Vietnam. Supposedly independent, the NLF was controlled by Hanoi. Indeed, Hanoi controlled the VC and the NLF throughout. The NLF called for the replacement of the Saigon government by a "broad national democratic coalition" and the "peaceful" reunification of Vietnam.

In September 1959, North Vietnamese defense minister Vo Nguyen Giap established Transportation Group 559 to send supplies and men south along what came to be known as the Ho Chi Minh Trail, much of which ran through supposedly neutral Laos. The first wave of infiltrators were native southerners and Viet Minh who had relocated to North Vietnam in 1954.

VC sway expanded, spreading out from safe bases to one village after another. The insurgency was fed by the weaknesses of the central government, the use of terror and assassination, and Saigon's appalling ignorance. By the end of 1958, the insurgency had reached the status of conventional warfare in several provinces. Guerrilla units also attacked ARVN regulars, overran district and provincial capitals, and ambushed convoys and reaction forces.

By mid-1961, the Saigon government had lost control over much of rural South Vietnam. Infiltration was as yet not significant. Diem meanwhile rejected American calls for meaningful reform until the establishment of full security. He failed to understand that the war was primarily a political problem and could be solved only through political means. Diem practiced the divide-and-rule concept of leadership. Isolated from his people and relying only on trusted family members and a few other advisers, he resisted U.S. demands that he promote his senior officials and officers on the basis of ability and pursue the war aggressively.

The John F. Kennedy administration was reevaluating its position toward the war, but increased U.S. involvement was inevitable, given Washington's commitment to resisting Communist expansion and the widely held belief that all of Southeast Asia would become Communist if South Vietnam fell. Domestic political considerations also influenced the decision.

In 1961 the Kennedy administration supported implementation of the Strategic Hamlet Program as part of a general strategy emphasizing local militia defense and also dispatched additional U.S. manpower. In February 1962 the United States also established a military headquarters in Saigon, the Military Assistance Command, Vietnam (MACV), to direct the enlarged American commitment. The infusion of

U.S. helicopters and additional support for the ARVN probably prevented a VC military victory in 1962. The VC soon learned to cope with the helicopters, however, and again the tide of battle turned.

Meanwhile, Diem's crackdown on the Buddhists led to increased opposition to his rule. After Diem rejected reforms, the United States gave tacit support to ARVN generals plotting a coup. On November 1, 1963, the generals overthrew Diem, murdering both him and one of his brothers. Within three weeks Kennedy was also dead, succeeded by Lyndon B. Johnson.

A military junta now took power in Saigon, but none of those who followed Diem had his prestige. Turmoil prevailed with coups and countercoups. Not until General Nguyen Van Thieu became president in 1967 was there a degree of political stability.

Both sides steadily increased the stakes, apparently without foreseeing that the other might do the same. In 1964 Hanoi made three decisions. The first decision was to send to South Vietnam units of the People's Army of Vietnam (PAVN, North Vietnamese Army). The second decision was to rearm its forces in South Vietnam with modern Communist-bloc weapons, giving them a firepower advantage over the ARVN, still equipped largely with World War II–era U.S. weaponry. The third decision was to order direct attacks on American installations, provoking a U.S. response.

On August 2, 1964, in the Gulf of Tonkin Incident, North Vietnamese torpedo boats attacked the U.S. destroyer *Maddox* in international waters in the Gulf of Tonkin. A second claimed attack on the *Maddox* and another U.S. destroyer, the *Turner Joy,* two days later probably never occurred, but Washington believed that it had, and the Johnson administration ordered retaliatory air strikes against North Vietnamese naval bases and fuel depots. The Gulf of Tonkin Incident also led to a nearly unanimous vote in Congress for the Gulf of Tonkin Resolution, authorizing the president to use whatever force he deemed necessary to protect U.S. interests in Southeast Asia.

Johnson now dramatically escalated the war. At the same time, he refused to mobilize the reserves and commit the resources necessary to win, concerned that this would destroy his cherished Great Society social programs at home.

Taking their cue from Johnson's own pronouncements to the American people, Ho and his generals mistakenly believed that Washington would not commit ground troops to the fight. Yet Johnson did just that. Faced with Hanoi's escalation, in March 1965 U.S. marines arrived to protect the large American air base at Da Nang. A direct attack on U.S. advisers at Pleiku in February 1965 brought a U.S. air campaign against North Vietnam.

Ultimately, more than 2.5 million Americans served in Vietnam, and nearly 58,000 of them died there. At the height of the Vietnam War, Washington was spending $30 billion per year on the war. Although the conflict was the best-covered war in American history (it became known as the first television war), it was also the least understood by the American people.

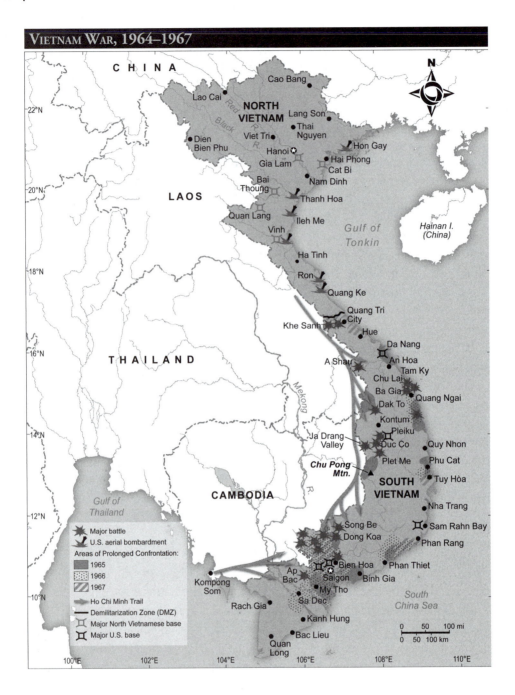

VIETNAM WAR, 1964–1967

CHINA

Cao Bang

Lao Cai

NORTH VIETNAM

Lang Son

22°N

Thai Nguyen

Viet Tri

Dien Bien Phu

Hon Gay

Hanoi

Hai Phong

Gia Lam

Cat Bi

Bai Thoung

Nam Dinh

20°N

LAOS

Thanh Hoa

Quan Lang

Ileh Me

Vinh

Gulf of Tonkin

Hainan I. (China)

Ha Tinh

18°N

Ron

Quang Ke

Quang Tri City

Khe Sanh

Hue

Da Nang

16°N

THAILAND

A Shau

An Hoa

Tam Ky

Chu Lai

Ba Gia

Quang Ngai

Dak To

Kontum

Pleiku

Ia Drang Valley

Duc Co

Quy Nhon

14°N

Plet Me

Phu Cat

Chu Pong Mtn.

SOUTH VIETNAM

Tuy Hòa

Nha Trang

Gulf of Thailand

CAMBODIA

12°N

Sam Rahn Bay

Song Be

Dong Koa

Phan Rang

Kompong Som

Ap Bac

Bien Hoa

Phan Thiet

Saigon

Binh Gia

My Tho

South China Sea

10°N

Rach Gia

Sa Dec

Kanh Hung

Bac Lieu

Quan Long

	Major battle
	U.S. aerial bombardment
	Areas of Prolonged Confrontation:
	1965
	1966
	1967
	Ho Chi Minh Trail
	Demilitarization Zone (DMZ)
	Major North Vietnamese base
	Major U.S. base

0   50   100 mi
0   50 100 km

100°E   102°E   104°E   106°E   108°E   110°E

Johnson hoped to win the war on the cheap, relying heavily on airpower. Known as Operation ROLLING THUNDER and paralleled by Operation BARREL ROLL (the secret bombing of Laos, which became the most heavily bombed country in the history of warfare), the air campaign would be pursued in varying degrees of intensity. Its goals were to force Hanoi to negotiate peace and to halt infiltration into South Vietnam. During the war, the United States dropped more bombs than in all of World War II, but the campaign failed in both its objectives.

In the air war, Johnson decided on graduated response rather than the massive strikes advocated by the military. Gradualism became the grand strategy employed by the United States in Vietnam. Haunted by the Korean War (1950–1953), at no time would Johnson consider an invasion of North Vietnam, fearful that the People's Republic of China would openly enter the war.

In 1965 with PAVN forces destroying ARVN units, MACV commander General William Westmoreland appealed for U.S. ground units, which Johnson then committed. Yet heavy personnel losses on the battlefield were entirely acceptable to the North Vietnamese leadership. Ho remarked at one point that North Vietnam could absorb an unfavorable loss ratio of 10 to 1 and still win the war. Washington never did understand this and continued to view the war through its own lens of what would be unacceptable in terms of casualties. From 1966 on, Vietnam was an escalating military stalemate, as Westmoreland requested increasing numbers of men from Washington. By the end of 1966, 400,000 U.S. troops were in Vietnam. In 1968, U.S. strength was more than 500,000 men. Johnson also secured some 60,000 troops from other nations (most of them from South Korea), surpassing the 39,000-man international coalition of the Korean War.

Westmoreland was not interested in pacification. His goal was to destroy the PAVN. Terrain was not judged important. Success was measured in terms of body count, which led to abuses. During 1966, MACV mounted 18 major operations, each resulting in more than 500 supposedly verified VC/PAVN dead; 50,000 Communist combatants were supposedly killed in 1966. By the beginning of 1967, the PAVN and VC had 300,000 men versus 625,000 ARVN troops and 400,000 Americans. Meanwhile, the VC continued its insurgency operations. Throughout, the war remained a mosaic of conventional and insurgency operations, with the latter prevailing in much of South Vietnam.

Hanoi meanwhile had reached a point of decision, with casualties exceeding available replacements. Instead of scaling back as some of the leadership urged, Hanoi prepared a major offensive that would employ all available troops to secure a quick victory. Hanoi believed that a major military defeat for the United States would end its political will to continue.

Giap prepared a series of peripheral attacks, including a modified siege of some 6,000 U.S. marines at Khe Sanh near the demilitarized zone (DMZ), beginning in January 1968. With U.S. attention riveted on Khe Sanh, Giap planned a massive offensive to occur during Tet, the Lunar New Year holidays. The North Vietnamese government believed that this massive General Offensive-General Uprising would see the population in South Vietnam rising up to overthrow the South Vietnamese government and bring an American withdrawal. In a major intelligence failure, U.S. and South Vietnamese officials misread both the timing and strength of the attack, finding it inconceivable that it would occur during Tet, sacrificing public goodwill.

The Tet Offensive began on January 30 and ended on February 24, 1968. Poor communications and coordination plagued Hanoi's plans, with attacks in one province occurring a day early. The attacked destroyed half of the city of Hue, the former imperial capital.

Hanoi's plan failed. ARVN forces generally fought well, and the South Vietnamese generally did not support the attackers. News that the Communists had executed some 3,000 people during their occupation of Hue caused many Vietnamese to rally to South Vietnam. Half of the 85,000 VC and PAVN troops who took part in the offensive were killed or captured in the worst military setback for North Vietnam in the war.

Paradoxically, the Tet Offensive was also the Communist side's most resounding victory. The intensity of the fighting came as a profound shock to the American people, following claims by the Johnson administration and Westmoreland that the war was being won. Americans now turned against the war, and at the end of March, Johnson announced a partial cessation in the bombing of North Vietnam and withdrew from the November presidential election. All sides now opted for talks in Paris in an effort to negotiate an end to the war.

Hanoi persisted, however. In the first six months of 1968, Communist forces sustained more than 100,000 casualties, and the VC was virtually wiped out; 20,000 Allied troops died in the same period.

American disillusionment with the war was a key factor in Republican Richard Nixon's razor-thin victory over Democrat Hubert Humphrey in the November 1968 presidential election. With no plan of his own, Nixon embraced Vietnamization, actually begun under Johnson, that turned over more of the war to the ARVN. U.S. withdrawals began. Peak U.S. strength of 550,000 men occurred in early 1969; there were only 157,000 men at the end of 1971. Massive amounts of equipment were turned over to the ARVN, including 1 million M-16 rifles and sufficient aircraft to make the South Vietnamese Air Force the world's fourth largest. Extensive retraining of the ARVN was begun, and training schools were established. The controversial counterinsurgency Phoenix Program also operated against the VC infrastructure, reducing the insurgency by 67,000 people between 1968 and 1971, but PAVN forces remained secure in sanctuaries in Laos and Cambodia.

Nixon sought to limit outside assistance to Hanoi and pressured it to end the war. In March 1970 a coup in Cambodia ousted Prince Noradom Sihanouk. General Lon Nol replaced him, and secret operations against the PAVN Cambodian sanctuaries soon began. During a two-month span, there were 12 cross-border operations in the so-called Cambodian Incursion. Despite widespread opposition in the United States to the widened war, the incursions raised Allied morale, allowed U.S. withdrawals to continue on schedule, and purchased additional time for Vietnamization. PAVN forces now concentrated on bases in southern Laos and on enlarging the Ho Chi Minh Trail.

In the spring of 1971, ARVN forces mounted a major invasion into southern Laos, known as Operation LAM SON 719. There were no U.S. advisers, and ARVN units took heavy casualties. The operation exacted a heavy toll on the ARVN's younger officers and pointed up serious command weaknesses.

By 1972, PAVN forces had been substantially strengthened with new Soviet weapons, including heavy artillery and tanks. Believing that the United States would not interfere, Hanoi decided on a major conventional invasion of South Vietnam. Giap commanded 15 divisions. He left only 1 division in North Vietnam and 2 divisions in Laos and committed the remaining 12 divisions to the invasion.

Known as the Spring Offensive and the Easter Offensive, the attack began on March 29, 1972, with a direct armor strike across the DMZ at the 17th Parallel that caught the best South Vietnamese troops facing Laos. Allied intelligence misread both its scale and precise timing. Hanoi risked catastrophic losses but hoped for a quick victory before ARVN forces could recover. At first it appeared that the PAVN would be successful. Quang Tri fell, and rain limited the effectiveness of airpower.

But in May, President Nixon authorized B-52 bomber strikes on Hanoi's principal port of Haiphong and the mining of its harbor. This new air campaign was dubbed Operation LINEBACKER and involved the use of new precision-guided munitions bombs (smart bombs). The bombing cut off much of the supplies for the invading PAVN forces. Allied aircraft also destroyed 400–500 PAVN tanks. In June and July, the ARVN counterattacked. The invasion cost Hanoi half its force—some 100,000 men died—while ARVN losses were only 25,000.

With both Soviet and Chinese leaders anxious for better relations with the United States to secure Western technology, Hanoi gave way and switched to negotiations. Finally, an agreement was hammered out in Paris that December, but South Vietnamese president Thieu balked and refused to sign, whereupon Hanoi made the agreements public. A furious Nixon blamed Hanoi for the impasse, and in December he ordered a resumption of the bombing, dubbed Operation LINEBACKER II. Although 15 B-52s were lost, Hanoi had fired away virtually its entire stock of surface-to-air missiles and agreed to resume talks.

After a few cosmetic changes, an agreement was signed on January 23, 1973, with Nixon forcing Thieu to agree or risk the end of all U.S. aid. The United States recovered its prisoners of war and departed Vietnam. The Soviet Union and China continued to supply arms to Hanoi, however, while Congress constricted U.S. supplies to Saigon. Tanks and planes were not replaced on the promised one-for-one basis as they were lost, and spare parts and fuel were both in short supply. All of this had a devastating effect on the ARVN.

In South Vietnam both sides violated the cease-fire, and fighting steadily increased in intensity. In January 1975, Communist forces attacked and quickly seized Phuoc Long Province on the Cambodian border north of Saigon. Washington took no action. Emboldened, the Communists next took Ban Me Thuot in the Central Highlands, then in mid-March President Thieu decided to abandon the northern part of his country. Confusion became disorder and then disaster, and soon PAVN forces controlled all of South Vietnam. Saigon fell on April 30, 1975, and was renamed Ho Chi Minh City. Vietnam was reunited but under a Communist government. An estimated 3 million Vietnamese, military and civilians, had died in the struggle. Much of the country was devastated by the fighting, and Vietnam suffered from the effects of the widespread use of chemical defoliants.

The effects were also profound in the United States. The American military was shattered and had to be rebuilt. Rampant inflation occurred as a result of the failure to face up to the true costs of the war. Many observers questioned U.S. willingness to embark on such a crusade again, at least to go it alone. In this sense, the war forced Washington into a more realistic appraisal of U.S. power.

Spencer C. Tucker

See also Abrams, Creighton Williams, Jr.; Cambodia, Vietnamese Occupation of; Ho Chi Minh; Ho Chi Minh Trail; Indochina War; McNamara Line; Strategic Hamlet Program; Viet Minh; Vo Nguyen Giap; Westmoreland, William Childs

Further Reading

Karnow, Stanley. *Vietnam: A History.* New York: Viking, 1983.

O'Ballance, Edgar. *The Wars in Vietnam, 1954–1960.* New York: Hippocrene, 1981.

Palmer, Bruce, Jr. *The 25-Year War.* Lexington: University Press of Kentucky, 1984.

Tucker, Spencer C. *Vietnam.* Lexington: University Press of Kentucky, 1999.

Villa, Francisco

Birth Date: June 5, 1878
Death Date: July 20, 1923

Mexican insurgent leader, bandit, and revolutionary. Francisco "Pancho" Villa was born Doroteo Arango on June 5, 1878, on a hacienda in San Juan del Río, Durango, to sharecropper parents. Doroteo's father died shortly thereafter, leaving his mother to raise five children. Much of Arango's early life is obscure. Illiterate, he worked as a ranch hand, experiencing the abusive labor practices of the landowner class. Legend has it that in 1894, Arango discovered his mother trying to prevent the rape of his younger sister by a landowner. After wounding the assailant, Arango fled to the Durango Mountains, becoming a bandit and cattle rustler.

In January 1901, Arango was arrested and forcibly inducted into the Mexican Army. He deserted a year later and settled in Parral, Chihuahua, near the Durango border, taking the name of Francisco Villa. During the next eight years, he lived as an outlaw while working intermittently as a laborer for foreign companies. In 1910, Chihuahuan authorities sought Villa's arrest for the killing of a former bandit companion who had become a police informant.

In 1910 on the beginning of the Mexican Revolution, Villa offered his services to liberal politician Francisco Madero, whose victory in presidential elections had been annulled by long-standing Mexican president and dictator Porfirio Díaz. Soon the revolutionary forces drove Díaz into exile, and Madero became president.

Villa continued in the Mexican Army under Mexican general Victoriano Huerta, but Huerta charged Villa with insubordination. Sentenced to death, Villa escaped to the United States, where his military exploits had attracted attention. In fact, some advisers to U.S. president Woodrow Wilson urged him to support Villa as the potential "George Washington of Mexico."

In 1913 Madero was assassinated, and Huerta seized control of the Mexican government. Villa returned to Mexico, allying with other revolutionary contingents in northern Mexico in an effort to topple Huerta. Venustiano Carranza, a politician from Sonora, proclaimed himself the first chief of the Constitutionalists, and for some time Villa and his División del Norte were allied with Carranza.

Villa was a charismatic leader, and many men flocked to his banner. Unlike guerrilla forces in southern Mexican led by Emiliano Zapata, the División del Norte was organized as a regular army. Mounted troops formed an important element of his forces in the vast arid expanse of the Sonoran Desert, but Villa also made use of the railroad for troop transport and for hospital services. He financed his forces and purchased arms by confiscating cattle from the large haciendaas and then selling them across the border in the United States.

With the defeat and exile of Huerta in 1914, the revolutionary leaders fell to quarreling among themselves. By 1915, Villa had grown impatient with Carranza's growing conservatism and claim to lead the country. After his largely cavalry force was defeated by Carranza's general Álvaro Obregón in the Battle of Celaya (April 13, 1915), Villa withdrew to Chihuahua.

In the autumn of 1915, the Wilson administration recognized Carranza as president of Mexico and ordered an arms embargo. Villa believed that Carranza would grant concessions that would enable the United States to control the Mexican economy. In hopes of undermining ties between the U.S. government and Carranza, on March 9, 1916, Villa led some 600 men across the border and attacked the town of Columbus, New Mexico. Eighteen U.S. citizens died in the raid.

In response, Wilson called out the National Guard and sent it to the Mexican border. He also ordered the Mexican Expedition (also known as the Punitive Expedition), a U.S. military incursion into northern Mexico led by U.S. brigadier general John J. Pershing charged with capturing Villa and bringing him to justice. Carranza protested the invasion, which in any case failed to capture Villa.

Ultimately when the United States declared war on Germany in April 1917, the troops were withdrawn.

Villa found himself a national hero. In 1920 after the assassination of Carranza, Villa struck a deal with the new government under new president Obregón. In exchange for a 25,000-acre hacienda in Durango, Villa ended his armed struggle and retired from politics. His men also received land and a year's military pay. As a landowner, Villa instituted a number of progressive agrarian measures. He also established a bank that made loans to farmers at low interest rates. Villa also provided a school for the children living on the hacienda.

On July 20, 1923, Villa was en route to a christening in Parral when he and five companions were shot to death by seven gunmen. Several days later Jesus Salas Barraza, a local politician, said that he had planned the killing in retaliation for Villa's "many crimes." Most Mexicans believed, however, that the order had come from high-level government officials. In 1976, Villa's remains were transferred from Durango to the Monument of the Revolution in Mexico City.

Lisa McClatchy

See also Mexican Expedition; Pershing, John Joseph

Further Reading

Herrera, Celia. *Pancho Villa Facing History.* New York: Vantage, 1993.

Katz, Frederick. *The Life and Times of Pancho Villa.* Stanford, CA: Stanford University Press, 1998.

O'Brien, Steven. *Pancho Villa.* New York: Chelsea House, 1994.

Vo Nguyen Giap

Birth Date: August 15, 1911

Vietnamese general and minister of defense. Vo Nguyen Giap was born in An Xa, Quang Binh Province, in central Vietnam on August 15, 1911. He attended the Lycée Nationale in Hue but was labeled an agitator and expelled. He then worked for a time as a journalist and joined the secret Revolutionary Party for a New Vietnam.

Arrested by the French in 1930, Giap was sentenced to two years of hard labor. Upon his release from prison, he studied at the Lycée Albert Sarraut at Hanoi, graduating in 1934. Giap then taught history and French at the Lycée Thuong Long. He also published a number of journals and newspapers, most of which were shut down by the authorities. He then earned a law degree from the University of Hanoi in 1938.

In 1937 Giap joined the Indochinese Communist Party, which ordered him to southern China in 1940. He was forced to leave behind his wife and daughter. The French arrested his wife in 1941; she was subsequently tortured to death. In China, Giap met Ho Chi Minh. Under Ho's orders, Giap returned to northern Tonkin, where he organized opposition to the French and became a leader of the Viet Nam Doc Lap Dong Minh Hoi (Vietnam Independence League, or Viet Minh), formed in 1942.

Giap formed 34 men into the Vietnam Armed Propaganda and Liberation Brigade in December 1944, the beginnings of the People's Army of Vietnam (PAVN, North Vietnamese Army). His troops underwent strict political indoctrination and military training. Giap was responsible for refining the rural revolutionary warfare theories of Mao Zedong that combined political and military activity into revolutionary warfare. At the end of World War II (1939–1945), Giap became minister of interior in the new government in the Democratic Republic of Vietnam (DRV, North Vietnam), formed in September 1945. He was then named senior general in the PAVN (1946–1972) and minister of defense of North Vietnam (1946–1986).

Giap led the Viet Minh against the French in the long Indochina War (1946–1954), in the course of which he built an army of nearly 300,000 men. He suffered heavy losses when he went over prematurely to major pitched battles against the French Army in the Red River Delta area, but he achieved victory in the most important battle of the war at Dien Bien Phu (March 13–May 7, 1954).

Giap also led PAVN forces in the fighting in the Republic of Vietnam (RVN, South Vietnam) following South Vietnamese president Ngo Dien Diem's refusal to hold the elections called for in 1956 by the 1954 Geneva Accords. Giap often engaged in intense debates with military commanders and political leaders concerning strategy. He generally cautioned patience, while others sought more aggressive action against South Vietnamese and U.S. forces. Giap opposed the Tet Offensive of January 1968. He was proven correct, as the offensive failed, producing high casualties for his own troops and no popular uprising in South Vietnam. However, the Tet Offensive was an unexpected psychological victory for Hanoi and led Washington to seek a way out of the war.

In 1972 Giap reluctantly ordered a massive invasion of South Vietnam in what became known as the Easter Offensive. Once again, Giap was proven correct when the South Vietnamese, supported by massive U.S. airpower, blunted the attack and inflicted heavy casualties on the North Vietnamese. Still, when the offensive was over, PAVN forces occupied territory that they had not previously controlled, and the subsequent 1973 peace agreement did not require their removal.

Sharp disagreements within the North Vietnamese leadership regarding Giap's military judgment led to him being stripped of his command of the PAVN, although he retained the post of minister of defense until 1986. Although Giap supported the final offensive in 1975 that resulted in the defeat of South Vietnam, his protégé, General Van Tien Dung, directed the offensive. Appointed to head the Ministry of Science and Technology, Giap opposed the Vietnamese invasion of Cambodia in 1978. In 1991 he was forced to give up his last post as vice premier in charge of family planning. After his retirement, the government designated Giap a national treasure.

Giap was certainly one of the great military commanders of the second half of the 20th century and an important figure in the reunification of Vietnam. With scant military knowledge at the start, he learned from his early mistakes and proved to be a remarkably adroit strategist.

James H. Willbanks

See also Ho Chi Minh; Indochina War; Viet Minh; Vietnam War

Further Reading

Currey, Cecil B. *Victory at Any Cost: The Genius of Viet Nam General Vo Nguyen Giap.* Washington, DC: Brassey's, 1997.

Davidson, Phillip B. *Vietnam at War: The History, 1946–1975.* Novato, CA: Presidio, 1988.

Tucker, Spencer C. *Vietnam.* Lexington: University of Kentucky Press, 1999.

Van Tien Dung. *Our Great Spring Victory.* New York: Monthly Review Press, 1977.

Vo Nguyen Giap. *Unforgettable Days.* Hanoi: Foreign Language Publishing House, 1978.

W

Walker, Sir Walter Colyear

Birth Date: November 11, 1912
Death Date: August 12, 2001

British Army general who played an important role in the Malayan Emergency (1848–1960) and commanded British forces during the Malayan-Indonesian confrontation over Borneo (1962–1966). Born into the family of a British tea planter in Assam on November 11, 1912, Walter Colyear Walker moved with his family to Britain after World War I (1914–1918). He was educated at Blundell's School in Devon and at the Royal Military Academy, Sandhurst.

Assigned to India upon commissioning, Walker served with the Gurkha Rifles in Quetta, in Assam, and on the North-West Frontier. In 1942 he studied at the Staff College at Quetta, after which he served on the staff of the Burma Corps against the Japanese. After serving as an instructor at the Quetta Staff College, Walker fought in the Imphal and Irrawaddy River campaigns in Burma (present-day Myanmar). Commanding the 4th Battalion, 8th Regiment, Gurkha Rifles, he was known as a rigorous trainer and a strict disciplinarian. He was subsequently assigned to the staff of the 7th Indian Infantry Division.

After World War II (1939–1945), Walker served in the General Headquarters in Delhi. After Indian independence in 1948, he was assigned to Malaya. With the proclamation of the Malayan Emergency, Walker created and trained the highly effective irregular jungle patrol unit known as the Ferret Force. At the end of 1948 he assumed command of the Far East Training Centre at Jahore Bahru, which prepared British Army units arriving in Malaya for jungle warfare. After attending the Joint Services Staff College in Britain, in 1950 he assumed command in Malaya of the 1st Battalion, 6th Regiment, Gurkha Rifles, which he built into a superb fighting force with a distinguished record against the Communist insurgents. He also wrote an important manual on counterinsurgency warfare, *The Conduct of Anti-Terrorist Operations in Malaya* (1952).

In 1954 Walker returned to Britain. Assigned to the Eastern Command as a colonel, he helped plan the 1956 Suez Expedition, carried out in concert with the French and Israelis. Promoted to brigadier in 1957, he assumed command of the 99th Gurkha Brigade in Malaya and the challenging task of defeating remaining insurgent forces in Jahore. Walker established an excellent relationship with the police and achieved success by dint of his leadership and enthusiasm, rigorous training and discipline, intelligence collection, and frequent ambushes.

In 1959 Walker's brigade assumed responsibility for the security on Singapore Island prior to the elections there. Facing a new challenge in urban security, Walker developed a training manual, *Internal Security in a City,* that became the standard work on the subject. Following attendance at the Imperial Defence College in London, in 1961 he was promoted to major general and assigned command of the 17th Gurkha Division.

In December 1962 Walker assumed command of all British forces in the colonies of North Borneo and Sarawak and the protectorate of Brunei, taking charge of the British effort in what became known as the Indonesia-Malaysia Confrontation (1962–1966), also known as the Borneo/Brunei Insurgency. Unable to prevent the infiltration of Indonesian military units into Malaysian territory, Walker established strong points and made effective use of helicopters. He also insisted on strict cooperation among the security forces and the establishment of joint headquarters as well as the protection of British base areas, control of the jungle, rigorous intelligence collection, and speed and mobility of field forces.

Walker also developed a comprehensive program to win the hearts and minds of the natives, many of whom were well disposed toward the British. This effort included the use of the Special Air Service (SAS) and police to advise village leaders as well as the use of medical and agricultural assistance. These steps made it difficult for the Indonesian insurgents to operate in Malaysian territory. Walker established a permanent British military presence in contested areas and in Operation CLARET sent SAS units led by native trackers in secret cross-border raids into Indonesia.

The conflict had been virtually won by March 1965, when Walker yielded command to his successor, Major General George Lee. Slated for retirement by the Army Board in 1967, in large part because of his overly vigorous defense of retaining the Gurkhas in the British Army, Walker was able to get the decision reversed and secure promotion to lieutenant general and assignment as deputy chief of staff for North Atlantic Treaty Organization (NATO) forces in Central Europe. Knighted in 1968 and promoted to full general the next year, Walker commanded NATO forces in Northern Europe during 1969–1972 but attracted criticism for his bellicose anti-Soviet statements.

Following his retirement in 1970, Walker came under further criticism for his strident and public anticommunism (he claimed that Prime Minister Harold Wilson was a Communist), antiunionism, and right-wing views as well as for his efforts to establish a private volunteer force in the event of a general strike. Two botched hip operations left him in considerable pain. Walker published two books on Soviet expansionism as well as his autobiography. He died in Yeovil, Somerset, England, on August 12, 2001.

Spencer C. Tucker

See also Hearts and Minds; Indonesia-Malaysia Confrontation; Malayan Emergency

Further Reading

Mockaitis, Thomas. *British Counterinsurgency in the Post-Imperial Era.* Manchester, UK: Manchester University Press, 1995.

Pocock, Tom. *Fighting General: The Public and Private Campaigns on General Walter Walker.* London: Collins, 1973.

Walker, Walter. *Fighting On.* London, 1997.

Wallace, William

Birth Date: Unknown
Death Date: August 23, 1305

Scottish nationalist and insurgent leader. Perhaps the best-known hero of medieval Scotland, Sir William Wallace was one of several leaders for Scottish independence, a cunning strategist, and a formidable warrior. The year of Wallace's birth is unknown, and his early years remain obscure. He was the son of Malcolm Wallace, a knight and small landowner from Renfrew, Scotland. William Wallace apparently had some education, since as a younger brother he may have been intended for service in the church.

Wallace came to prominence soon after 1296, when King John Balliol of Scotland, supported by many prominent nobles who resented English demands on Scotland, asserted his independence from his English overlord, King Edward I; concluded a treaty with France; and rashly invaded England. Edward marched north and defeated Balliol in the Battle of Dunbar (April 27), and in July Balliol surrendered, handing his kingdom over to Edward and departing for exile in France. Edward appointed John de Warenne, the Earl of Surrey, lord over the Scots. Edward's humiliation of Scotland and his widely detested governor roused Scottish nationalism and brought rebellions. Revolts led by Andrew de Moray and Wallace did the most to disrupt the English hold on Scotland.

The more powerful nobles, such as the Bruce family, were unable to organize a wider revolt, but Wallace and Moray had success. Wallace attacked Lanark and slew its sheriff. This success brought more support, and Wallace then combined his forces with those of Moray. Together, the two managed to free much of Scotland from English rule.

The English were quick to regroup, however, and in September 1297 an English army marched from Berwick to meet the Scots. Wallace's clever dispositions and rashness on the part of the English resulted in a great Scottish victory in the Battle of Stirling Bridge (September 11, 1297), and Wallace found himself a hero. Robert the Bruce knighted him and named him guardian of the kingdom of Scotland.

King Edward now raised a new army, marched north, and defeated Wallace in the Battle of Falkirk (July 22, 1298). Wallace avoided capture and may have fled to France, but not for long. He continued his attacks on the English, though with far less support, until he was betrayed and handed over to the English in 1305. Edward had him paraded through London, after which Wallace was publicly tortured and executed on August 23, 1305. In 1306, however, Robert the Bruce proclaimed himself king of Scotland; he spent the next several years at war with the English.

Although his career was short, Wallace had given the Scots hope that they might throw off the English yoke. His leadership, tactical skill, and personal bravery inspired his countrymen and gave them a symbol around which to fight. Wallace's victory at Stirling Bridge proved that the Scots could beat a numerically larger and technologically superior enemy, a lesson that Robert the Bruce put to good effect on June 24, 1314, when he defeated the English in the Battle of Bannockburn.

James Emmons

Further Reading

Goldstein, R. James. *The Matter of Scotland: Historical Narrative in Medieval Scotland.* Lincoln: University of Nebraska Press, 1993.

McNamee, Colm. *The Wars of the Bruces: Scotland, England and Ireland, 1306–1328.* Edinburgh, UK: John Donald, 2006.

Morton, Graeme. *William Wallace: Man and Myth.* Stroud, Gloucestershire, UK: Sutton, 2004.

Walls, Peter

Birth Date: 1927
Death Date: July 20, 2010

Commanding general of the Rhodesian Army and briefly of the Zimbabwe Army. Born in Rhodesia in 1927, Peter Walls attended Plumtree School in Rhodesia. He volunteered for the British Army during World War II (1939–1945) and attended the Staff College at Camberley, which welcomed students from the Commonwealth. After the war he joined the Black Watch and was appointed assistant adjutant in the Highland Brigade Training Centre.

Walls resigned his British Army commission when he was about to be transferred, choosing to return to Rhodesia. Soon he joined the Southern Rhodesian Staff Corps as a corporal. He was rapidly promoted and again commissioned. Walls served in Malaya during 1951–1953 during the Malayan Emergency (1948–1960), commanding what became known as the Far Eastern Volunteer Group, which became the C Squadron of the British Special Air Service. C Squadron consisted entirely of Rhodesians, who thereby gained considerable experience in counterinsurgency warfare. Walls developed a reputation as a man of action who led from the front.

In 1964 Walls took command of the 1st Battalion of the Rhodesian Light Infantry. He shared the opposition of the majority of whites in Rhodesia to majority rule in the colony. Walls and his men performed effectively against the insurgents in the Rhodesia Bush War (Zimbabwe War of Liberation, 1964–1979), and in 1972 Rhodesian prime minister Ian Smith, who was preparing to announce Rhodesian independence, appointed Walls to the post of general officer commanding the Rhodesian Security Forces.

Walls understood that a declaration of Rhodesian independence and white minority rule would bring an intensification of the insurgency mounted from neighboring countries by the Zimbabwe People's Revolutionary Army (ZIPRA), the armed force of the Zimbabwe African People's Union (ZAPU), operating from Zambia and Botswana, as well as the Zimbabwe African National Liberation Army (ZANLA), the military arm of the Zimbabwe African People's Union (ZAPU), in Tanzania and Mozambique.

Walls understood from his time in Malaya that a key element in any sound counterinsurgency strategy would be timely intelligence collection. He therefore charged Lieutenant Colonel Ron Reid-Daly with the formation of the Selous Scouts, ostensibly for tracking guerrillas but in effect to operate clandestinely behind and within the guerrilla ranks.

Guerrilla action intensified with the Portuguese departure from Angola and Mozambique, leaving Rhodesia's eastern and western borders open to infiltration by African nationalist forces trained and equipped by the Soviet Union and Cuba. In 1977 Smith named Walls to the post of commander of Combined Operations, in effect the head of the Rhodesian Army.

Rhodesian Army numbers proved insufficient to halt the guerrilla incursions from the neighboring African states. In 1977 Walls received reliable intelligence reports of a ZANLA concentration at Mapai in Mozambique. Smith gave permission, and on May 30, 1977, Walls sent 500 men 60 miles into Mozambique to Mapai to take control of the base camp under cover of Rhodesian aircraft. Although they soon withdrew, the Rhodesian forces continued operations beyond the national borders. On February 12, 1979, in an attempt to assassinate Walls, ZIPRA militants shot down a civilian Vickers Viscount airliner with a SAM-7 surface-to-air missile, killing all 59 passengers. Walls was not aboard.

The long military odds and international opposition to white minority rule in Rhodesia led to negotiations between the Rhodesian government and ZANU and ZAPU beginning in November 1979 and finally to majority black rule. Rhodesia became Zimbabwe. New prime minister Robert Mugabe kept Walls on as commander of the army, charging him with integrating ZIPRA, ZANLA, and the Rhodesian Army. Tensions soon developed, abetted by several assassination attempts on Mugabe.

In August 1980 Walls said in a BBC interview that he had asked British prime minister Margaret Thatcher to annul the results of the 1980 general election because Mugabe had employed intimidation to win. Mugabe fired Walls that September and secured legislation exiling him from Zimbabwe for life.

Walls settled at Plettenburg Bay on the Western Cape coast of South Africa. He died on July 20, 2010, in George, Western Cape, South Africa, while on his way to a holiday in the Kruger National Park. Walls did not leave any memoirs.

Spencer C. Tucker

See also Malayan Emergency; Mugabe, Robert Gabriel; Reid-Daly, Ronald Francis; Rhodesian Bush War; Selous Scouts; Special Air Service; Zimbabwe African People's Union

Further Reading

Cilliers, Jakkie. *Counter-Insurgency in Rhodesia.* London: Croom Helm, 1985.

"Lieutenant-General Peter Walls." Special Forces Obituaries, *Telegraph* (London), July 27, 2010.

Goodwin, Peter, and Ian Hancock. *Rhodesians Never Die: The Impact of War and Political Change on White Rhodesia, c1970–1980.* New York: Oxford University Press, 1993.

War of the Flea

In 1964 American journalist Robert Taber published *War of the Flea,* which is widely regarded as a classic study of the theory and practice of guerrilla warfare. Born in Illinois, Taber worked at various manual jobs before serving as a merchant seamen in World War II (1939–1945). He then became a journalist and worked for CBS News. His book, which has been through many editions, was based in part on interviews with Fidel Castro and on Taber's own experience of Cuba.

Taber supposedly sought to school the U.S. military regarding the dangers of insurgency in the Republic of Vietnam (RVN, South Vietnam), but his book instead became a guide for guerrilla warfare based on the principles enunciated by Chinese Communist leader Mao Zedong (Mao-Tse-tung).

Taber uses the analogy of a flea on a dog to describe the relationship between guerrillas and the military forces of established government seeking to defeat them. The flea on the dog is too small and agile and has a large area in which to operate. Eventually weakened, the dog succumbs to exhaustion, unable to defend himself from a veritable plague of fleas. Lengthy conflicts help the guerrillas both in the field—where it is extremely expensive for governments to attempt to defeat them—and in the politico-economic arena.

Taber identifies insurgency as the agency of radical social or political change and identifies counterinsurgency as the process by which revolution is resisted. Using examples of Cuba, China, Vietnam, North Africa, the Philippines, and Malaya, Taber provides a detailed analysis of the factors leading to the success or failure of guerrilla campaigns and the lessons learned from them.

Taber concludes that the key to victory is winning the loyalty of the population; a determined indigenous population will never lose to foreign occupiers in the long run. Insurgencies cannot succeed in well-functioning societies. However, if a nation's resources are controlled by a small elite and the majority of the population is poor or oppressed, then the guerrilla leaders will secure the support of a growing number of the people, which is the greatest asset in the guerrilla arsenal.

Biff L. Baker

See also Castro Ruz, Fidel Alejandro; Mao Zedong

Further Reading

Taber, Robert. *War of the Flea: The Classic Study of Guerrilla Warfare in Theory and Practice.* Washington, DC: Brassey's, 2002.

War of the Regulation.

See Regulator Revolt

Wat Tyler's Rebellion.

See Peasants' Revolt in England

Western Hemisphere Institute for Security Cooperation

Established in 2001, the Western Hemisphere Institute for Security Studies (WHIN-SEC) grew out of the United States Army School of the Americas (USARSA), the principal training school in counterinsurgency for Latin American military and police personnel. Established in Panama in 1946, the USARSA schooled more than 64,000 people in counterinsurgency techniques, sniper training, commando and psychological warfare, and military intelligence techniques. The school was moved to Fort Bragg, North Carolina, in 1984, but charges of human rights abuses committed by some graduates of the school led the U.S. Congress to close the facility in 2000.

The WHINSEC was established by the National Defense Authorization Act for Fiscal Year 2001 and opened on January 17, 2001. The U.S. Army's Training and Doctrine Command is the WHINSEC's controlling headquarters through its Combined Arms Center. The WHINSEC mission is to provide professional education and training supporting the democratic principles set forth in the Charter of the Organization of American States.

The WHINSEC faculty and staff number some 200 military, law enforcement, and civilian personnel. The staff offers some 40 different courses to military officers, noncommissioned officers, law enforcement officials, and civilians. Attendees can number more than 1,000 people at any one time from as many as 22 countries. Most courses are in Spanish, which allows participating countries to base student selection on professional credentials rather than English-language proficiency. WHINSEC personnel work closely with the U.S. Army North (USARNORTH) and U.S. Army South (USARSO) commands to develop curriculum in support of their security cooperation programs.

Each student is required to take at least 8 hours of instruction on human rights, the rule of law, due process, civilian control of the military, and the role of the military in a democratic society. WHINSEC's model Democracy and Human Rights Program goes beyond the 8 hours of human rights training mandated by U.S. law, since most courses include at least 10 hours of instruction in this area. Thus, the 51-week intermediate-level education course, designed for midlevel career officers (majors and lieutenant colonels) and the longest WHINSEC course, provides a minimum of 50 hours of human rights instruction, while the 18-week captains' career course offers a minimum of 24 hours in this area. WHINSEC augments the democracy and human rights class with a 2-hour block of instruction on ethical decision making.

Extensive practical application is provided in the classroom and in field exercises. The Field Studies Program augments human rights classroom training with exposure to U.S. culture, government, and places of business. While at WHINSEC, students and guest instructors and their families experience democracy in action living in the local Fort Benning and Columbus community.

WHINSEC values its transparency and is open to the public. Journalists, researchers, and others routinely visit throughout the year and can observe classes, talk with students and faculty, and review instructional materials.

WHINSEC's 13-member Board of Visitors includes the USARNORTH and USARSO commanders and four members of Congress as well as representatives from the State Department and the Defense Department and six individuals from academia, the clergy, or other nongovernmental organizations. The Board of Visitors is charged with ensuring that the WHINSEC curriculum complies with applicable U.S. laws and regulations, is consistent with U.S. regional policy goals, adheres to current U.S. doctrine, and emphasizes human rights, the rule of law, due process, civilian control of the military, and the role of the military in a democratic society.

Biff L. Baker

See also United States Army School of the Americas

Further Reading

Gill, Lesley. *The School of the Americas: Military Training and Political Violence in the Americas.* Durham, NC: Duke University Press, 2004.

U.S. Department of Defense. "Directive 5111.12: Western Hemisphere Institute for Security Cooperation." Washington, DC: 2002.

Western Sahara War

Start Date: 1973
End Date: 1991

Spain acquired the Western Sahara in the 1880s and then in 1958 joined the district of Saguia el-Hamra (in the north) with the Rio de Oro (in the south) to form the province of Spanish Sahara. In 1971 Sahrawi (an Arabic term for those from the Sahara) students in Moroccan universities formed the Sahrawi Frente Popular de Liberación de Saguía el Hamra y Río de Oro (Popular Front for the Liberation of Saguia el-Hamra and Río de Oro, better known as POLISARIO) with the goal of securing control of the Spanish Sahara.

After trying and failing to win support from various Arab governments, including those of Morocco and Algeria, the Sahrawi students relocated to Spanish Sahara. First led by El-Ouali Mustapha Sayed, on May 20, 1973, POLISARIO carried out an attack on a Spanish post at Khanga manned by Tropas Nomadas (Sahrawi auxiliary forces), seizing arms. POLISARIO soon controlled wide swaths of the desert and gained the support of the vast majority of the population, and a number of the Tropas Nomidas deserted to POLISARIO, bringing with them their weapons and military training.

With the end of the Francisco Franco regime in Spain, the Spanish government entered into negotiations for a handover of power but in the Madrid Accords of November 14, 1975, ended up reaching agreement with Morocco and Mauritania rather than POLISARIO. Spain agreed to divide the Spanish Sahara between Morocco and Mauritania. Morocco was to absorb the northern part of the Spanish Sahara (the Saguia el-Hamra), while Mauritania obtained the southern part (the Rio de Oro).

POLISARIO meanwhile proclaimed the establishment of the Sahrawi Arab Democratic Republic on February 27, 1976, and commenced guerrilla warfare against both Morocco and Mauritania. POLISARIO never had more than 10,000 fighters, while Morocco alone ultimately committed as many as 120,000 men to control the northern region. Algeria provided modern weaponry and other military assistance to POLISARIO, whose ranks swelled as a consequence of large numbers of refugees from the fighting who had relocated to camps in Algeria. POLISARIO was soon mounting highly effective hit-and-run attacks against both Moroccan and Mauritanian forces in the Western Sahara.

The weak Mauritanian government of Ould Daddah was never able to make a major effort to control the southern Sahara and committed there only about 3,000 men. When POLISARIO guerrillas attacked Mauritania's chief source of income, its iron mines, in 1978, army officers overthrew the Daddah government. The new leaders then entered into negotiations with POLISARIO and reached agreement on August 5, 1979, to quit the southern Sahara altogether and recognize the Sahrawi Arab Democratic Republic. Morocco responded by immediately claiming for itself the area of Western Sahara evacuated by the Mauritanians. Since 1979, however, the United Nations has recognized POLISARIO as the legitimate representative of the people of Western Sahara.

Fighting was most intense during 1979–1981, with POLISARIO fielding heavy weapons. In the mid-1980s, Morocco managed to largely keep the guerrillas at bay by building the Morocco Wall (a large berm, or sand wall) to surround the most economically important areas of the Western Sahara. This was manned by roughly as many Moroccan troops as there were Sahrawis. At the same time, Algeria largely withdrew its support for POLISARIO following formation in February 1989 of the Arab Maghreb Union, which included both Morocco and Algeria. The result was a stalemate, but maintaining the wall and its troops in Western Sahara proved to be a tremendous economic burden for Morocco.

On September 6, 1991, both sides agreed to a cease-fire and a referendum to be held in 1992. The cease-fire was monitored by the United Nations Mission for the Referendum in Western Sahara (MINURSO), which remains in place to the present. The referendum has not occurred, however, stalled largely over the issue of who will be eligible to vote. An uneasy peace continues, with POLISARIO threatening on numerous occasions to resume the war.

Spencer C. Tucker

Further Reading

Hodges, Tony. *Western Sahara: The Roots of a Desert War.* Westport, CT: Lawrence and Hill, 1983.

Jensen, Erik. *Western Sahara: Anatomy of a Stalemate.* Boulder, CO: Lynne Rienner, 2005.

Pazzanita, Anthony G. *Western Sahara.* Santa Barbara, CA: ABC-CLIO, 1996.

Westmoreland, William Childs

Birth Date: March 26, 1914
Death Date: July 18, 2005

U.S. Army general, commander of U.S. forces in Vietnam during 1964–1968, and U.S. Army chief of staff during 1968–1972. Born in Spartanburg County, South Carolina, on March 26, 1914, William Childs Westmoreland graduated from the U.S. Military Academy, West Point, in 1936 and was commissioned a lieutenant of field artillery. As a major, he served with distinction in the Battle of Kasserine Pass (February 1943). He fought in North Africa, Italy, France, and Germany and ended the war as a colonel. Westmoreland saw service in the Korean War (1950–1953) and was promoted to brigadier general in November 1952 as commander of the 187th Airborne Regimental Combat Team.

Promoted to major general in December 1956, Westmoreland commanded the 101st Airborne Division during 1958–1960 at Fort Campbell, Kentucky. During 1960–1963 he was superintendent of the U.S. Military Academy. Promoted to lieutenant general, he returned to Fort Campbell to command the XVIII Airborne Corps in 1963. In June 1964 he was named commander of the U.S. Military Assistance Command, Vietnam (MACV), as a full general.

Westmoreland subsequently presided over the steep escalation of the Vietnam War (1957–1975) and eventually commanded more than half a million American troops there. He embarked on an effort to seek out and engage Communist forces, defeating them in a war of attrition in search-and-destroy operations. Westmoreland had little interest in pacification programs, which arguably were more important. He and planners in Washington never did understand the extent to which leaders of the Democratic Republic of Vietnam (DRV, North Vietnam) were prepared to sacrifice manpower to inflict American casualties and influence opinion in the United

States. Casualty rates heavily unfavorable to Communist forces, taken as proof by Westmoreland that the war was being won, were nonetheless acceptable to Hanoi.

Westmoreland's overly optimistic predictions regarding the war in late 1967 helped feed public disillusionment in the United States following the heavy casualties of the January 1968 Communist Tet Offensive, which was nonetheless lost by the Communist side. Westmoreland interpreted the situation after the offensive as an opportunity and proposed the dispatch of additional troops to Vietnam. President Lyndon Johnson denied Westmoreland's request but did send some emergency reinforcements,.

In June 1968 Johnson recalled Westmoreland to Washington as chief of staff of the army. Westmoreland held that post until his retirement in July 1972, with much of his energies devoted to planning the transition to an all-volunteer force. Following retirement, Westmoreland continued to speak out on the Vietnam War, published his memoirs, and ran unsuccessfully for governor of South Carolina. He remained a major and controversial figure in the postwar debate over U.S. involvement in Vietnam. Westmoreland died in Charleston, South Carolina, on July 18, 2005.

James H. Willbanks

See also Vietnam War

Further Reading

Sorley, Lewis. *Westmoreland: The General Who Lost Vietnam.* Boston: Houghton Mifflin Harcourt, 2011.

Westmoreland, William C. *A Soldier Reports.* New York: Doubleday, 1976.

Zaffiri, Samuel. *Westmoreland: A Biography of General William C. Westmoreland.* New York: William Morrow, 1994.

Weyler y Nicolau, Valeriano

Birth Date: September 17, 1839
Death Date: October 20, 1930

Spanish Army general and governor-general of Cuba. Valeriano Weyler y Nicolau was born in Palma de Majorca, Spain, on September 17, 1839. At age 16 he entered the Spanish Army as a cadet at the Infantry College at Toledo. Attending the staff college as a lieutenant, he graduated at the top of his class in 1861. Assigned to Cuba as a captain in 1863, Weyler subsequently took part in the Spanish military expedition to reconquer Dominica.

During 1868–1872, Weyler was again in Cuba, this time taking part in crushing insurgent forces during the Ten Years' War (1868–1878). He returned to Spain in 1872 as a brigadier general, marked as an officer of great promise but known for brutal methods. He saw service against the Carlists and was rewarded by promotion to general of division, ennobled as marqués of Tenerife, and appointed to the Spanish Senate. During 1878–1883, he was captain-general of the Canary Islands and in the latter year became captain-general of the Balearic Islands.

In 1888 Weyler secured appointment as governor-general of the Philippines, a post he held until 1891 and during which he reportedly became wealthy. There he also orchestrated military operations to suppress uprisings on Mindanao and other islands. Returning to Spain in 1892, he took command of the Spanish Army's VI Corps, quelling unrest in Navarre and in the Basque areas of Spain. He was then captain-general of Barcelona, where he took an active role in suppressing Socialists and anarchists in this increasingly industrial city.

With Cuba again in the midst of an insurgency and with liberal pacification policies having failed, conservative Spanish premier Antonio Cánovas del Castillo appointed Weyler as captain-general there. Weyler served in this post during February 1896–October 1897. Arriving on the island with 50,000 Spanish reinforcements, he retained his reputation as a stern and uncompromising officer. Weyler soon ordered the arrest and expulsion from Cuba of American journalists, who had been reporting negatively on Spanish rule.

In order to isolate the insurgency, Wyler ordered the construction of trochas (fortified lines) across Cuba. More important, he sought to separate the insurgents from the civilian population in the countryside with his *reconcentrado* (reconcentration) system, whereby peasants were removed to fortified towns. The forerunner of the British concentration camps of the South African War (Second Boer War) and of the U.S. Strategic Hamlet Program during the Vietnam War, this program uprooted some 500,000 peasants and resettled them in hastily constructed and often inadequate communities, where they were prey to unsanitary conditions, disease, and even starvation. Thousands died. Meanwhile, Weyler's troops laid waste to the countryside, destroying crops and livestock and anything else that might be of use to the rebels. These policies, while they had some success against the insurgency, earned Weyler such American press epithets as "the Butcher," "the Beast," "the Mad Dog," and "the Hyena." They also greatly aroused general American opposition to Spanish rule in Cuba.

Sensitive to this criticism and to the sharp deterioration in U.S.-Spanish relations, the government of Premier Práxedes Mateo Sagasta recalled Weyler in October 1897 and replaced him with General Ramón Blanco y Erenas. On Weyler's return to Spain, he was approached about joining a military plot to overthrow the government but rejected it because he believed that it would divide the army.

When the Spanish-American War began, Weyler was optimistic, publicly talking about how an army of 50,000 Spanish troops might invade the United States. Elected to the Spanish Cortes (parliament), he blamed the subsequent Spanish defeat on the politicians. He defended both the army and his Cuban policies in his 1906 memoir *Mi mando en Cuba: História militar y política de la última guerra serpartista* (My Command in Cuba: The Military and Political History of the Last Separatist War).

Weyler was military governor of Madrid in 1900 and served as minister of war in several Spanish cabinets (March 1901–December 1902, July–December 1905, and December 1906–January 1907). In 1909 he was again governor-general of Barcelona and helped put down an anarchist rebellion there. During 1921–1923, he was commanding general of the army. Promoted to field marshal, he nonetheless retained his rank after participation in the plot in 1926 to overthrow the regime of Miguel Primo de Rivera. Weyler died in Madrid on October 20, 1930.

Spencer C. Tucker

See also Cuban War of Independence; *Reconcentrado* System; Ten Years' War in Cuba; Trocha

Further Reading

Ferrer, Ada. *Insurgent Cuba: Race, Nation, and Revolution, 1868–1898.* Chapel Hill: University of North Carolina Press, 1999.

Pérez, Louis A., Jr. *Cuba between Empires, 1878–1902.* Pittsburgh, PA: University of Pittsburgh Press, 1983.

Tone, John L. *War and Genocide in Cuba, 1895–1898.* Chapel Hill: University of North Carolina Press, 2006.

Whiskey Rebellion

Event Date: 1794

Antitax revolt in the United States. The Whiskey Rebellion occurred in the trans-Appalachian regions of Pennsylvania, Maryland, Virginia, North Carolina, and South Carolina and entered its armed confrontational phase in the summer of 1794, centered in western Pennsylvania. The insurrection essentially grew out of the need for the federal government to pay off the staggering national debt incurred during the American Revolutionary War (1775–1783). Under a plan devised by Treasury Secretary Alexander Hamilton, a federal excise tax of up to 25 percent was imposed on distilled spirits manufactured in the United States.

The tax went into effect on March 3, 1791. All distillers were now ordered to keep records of their production and set aside the appropriate amount of sales revenue for collection by federal tax collectors. Under the law, federal agents were empowered to search private property for illegal stills and contraband whiskey.

The tax was especially unpopular among farmers along the western frontier. Their major cash crops were corn, wheat, and rye, which could be easily distilled into whiskey. Furthermore, barrels of whiskey were much more transportable than grain. A packhorse, for example, could carry 2 bushels of grain or two barrels of whiskey distilled from 24 bushels of grain. Whiskey could be sold or used as currency for barter among the frontier settlers. Farmers in more settled areas, especially in the East, were less likely to distill whiskey. The tax also aggravated the already inflamed sensibilities of those people who lived in the trans-Appalachian West

Illustration depicting irate Pennsylvania farmers protesting the excise whiskey during the 1794 Whiskey Rebellion by tarring and feathering a tax collector. The revolt tested the principles of representative government and powers of taxation in the new nation. (Library of Congress)

and who believed that their interests were being subjugated to those of wealthier easterners.

As federal agents began searching farms and serving arrest warrants, opposition to the whiskey tax grew. The situation was most explosive in the four westernmost counties of Pennsylvania. On July 16, 1794, 40 armed men surrounded the home of John Neville, inspector of revenue for western Pennsylvania, and demanded his resignation. After shots were exchanged, the rebels withdrew. The following day, an estimated 500 rebels returned. A gun battle with 10 federal soldiers from Fort Pitt followed. The rebel leader, James McFarlane, was killed before the defenders withdrew, but Neville's home was burned. On August 1, the rebels massed near Pittsburgh. They threatened to burn the city, but the Pittsburgh representatives were able to convince them to settle for a protest march through the city instead.

On August 4, Supreme Court justice James Wilson certified that the federal courts could not meet because of armed insurrection. The certification gave President George Washington the legal authority to issue a proclamation on August 7. He invoked a federal statute, part of the Militia Act of 1792, that gave the president authority to call state militias into federal service when federal law was being obstructed by combinations too powerful for the courts and their marshals to suppress.

Washington realized, however, that sympathy for the rebels was widespread. He did not want to use federal troops because of preexisting fears that a standing army could be an instrument of oppression by the federal government. Instead, the president called for militias from Pennsylvania, Maryland, Virginia, and New Jersey to quell the uprising. Militiamen from Pennsylvania and Virginia had to be drafted for federal service, causing further disorder. Eventually 12,900 soldiers were raised and designated the Army of the Constitution. Democratic-Republicans who opposed a strong national government, such as Thomas Jefferson and James Madison, tried to negotiate a settlement without the use of force but to no avail.

After negotiations with the rebels broke down, on September 24 Washington appointed Continental Army veteran Henry Lee to command the army. Meanwhile, Washington himself traveled to western Pennsylvania to observe the situation, which reassured many Americans that the situation would not spiral out of control.

Marching in two wings, the federalized army converged on Bedford, Pennsylvania, crossing the Allegheny Mountains and arriving in Pittsburgh on November 2. Faced with overwhelming force, the rebellion simply collapsed. Up to 1,000 rebels, including the leaders, fled to Ohio. Twenty rebels were arrested and brought back to Philadelphia, which was then the national capital. They were paraded through the city on Christmas Day and placed on trial. Only 2 were convicted of rebellion and sentenced to death. Recognizing that the executions could have troublesome political consequences, Washington pardoned both men. Most of the militiamen were sent home, but some 1,500 remained in Pittsburgh during the winter of 1794–1795 to ensure public order.

The Whiskey Rebellion marked the first use of military force by the U.S. government to suppress domestic resistance to new federal laws. The rebellion clearly demonstrated the ability of the new government created by the Constitution of 1787 to keep order but also made clear the political limits that would be placed on using military forces to put down domestic dissent. One result of the Whiskey Rebellion, however, was to strengthen the power of the Democratic-Republicans, who opposed more centralized national power and had largely opposed the imposition of the tax, which was repealed in 1802.

Tim Watts

Further Reading

Boyd, Steven R., ed. *The Whiskey Rebellion: Past and Present Perspectives.* Westport, CT: Greenwood, 1985.

Hogeland, William. *The Whiskey Rebellion: George Washington, Alexander Hamilton, and the Frontier Rebels Who Challenged America's Newfound Sovereignty.* New York: Scribner, 2006.

Slaughter, Thomas P. *The Whiskey Rebellion: Frontier Epilogue to the American Revolution.* New York: Oxford University Press, 1988.

Wingate, Orde Charles

Birth Date: February 26, 1903
Death Date: March 24, 1944

British Army general. Born on February 26, 1903, in Naini Tal, India, Orde Charles Wingate was educated at Charterhouse School and the Royal Military Academy, Woolwich, from which he was commissioned in 1923. In 1927 he was posted to Khartoum, where he served with the Sudan Defence Force until 1933.

In 1936 Captain Wingate was sent to Palestine, then in the throes of the Arab Revolt. Despite his Arabist training and the pro-Arab sentiment of Palestine's British rulers, he became a fanatical Zionist. Wingate convinced his commanders to permit him to arm and train Jewish volunteers to counter increasing Arab raids and guerrilla attacks. In 1938 he formed, trained, and commanded the Special Night Squads (SNS), which consisted of the Jewish volunteer defense forces known as the Haganah and a cadre of British regulars.

To this point, the Haganah had relied almost exclusively on passive defensive tactics, waiting until a settlement was attacked and then defending from inside the perimeter. Wingate's SNS took the offensive, mounting active defenses of the settlements using night patrols and ambushes near the exits to Arab villages to stop the attackers even before they could get started. Wingate stressed speed, surprise, imagination, and psychological leverage. However, his outspoken public support for a Jewish state in Palestine led to his transfer back to England in 1939.

In 1940 Wingate returned to the Sudan to help organize the effort to drive the Italians from Ethiopia and restore Haile Selassie to his throne. The troops whom Wingate raised, known as Gideon Force, ultimately played a key role in achieving success, but Wingate's outspokenness angered his superiors. Exhausted and ill with malaria, Wingate unsuccessfully attempted suicide in June 1941.

In early 1942 General Archibald Wavell, who had high regard for Wingate, requested his transfer to the Far East. In India, Wingate raised the Chindits, an irregular force designed for operations in the enemy rear in Burma. The First Chindit Operation was conducted between February and April 1943 by a brigade-sized force. The operation achieved limited success but raised morale in a theater that heretofore had seen only Japanese victories. Wingate, now a major general, secured the personal support of Prime Minister Winston Churchill for additional operations. The Second Chindit Operation was conducted between March and July 1944 by three brigades and was supported by an American air contingent, but its results were also mixed, in part because of Wingate's untimely death in a plane crash on March 24, 1944.

Despite his extreme opinions and eccentricity, Wingate was a soldier of great determination and mental and physical toughness whose innovations in irregular warfare left a far-reaching legacy.

George M. Brooke III

See also Arab Revolt of 1936

Further Reading

Bierman, John, and Colin Smith. *Fire in the Night: Wingate of Burma, Ethiopia, and Zion.* New York: Random House, 1999.

Royle, Trevor. *Orde Wingate: Irregular Soldier.* London: Weidenfeld and Nicholson, 1995.

Sykes, Christopher. *Orde Wingate.* London: Collins, 1959.

Wolseley, Garnet Joseph

Birth Date: June 4, 1833
Death Date: March 26, 1913

One of Great Britain's most successful and experienced generals of the late Victorian age and arguably its greatest proponent of colonial warfare. Garnet Joseph Wolseley was born on June 4, 1833, in Golden Bridge House, County Dublin, Ireland. Only seven years old when his father, a retired British Army major, died, Wolseley and his family lived in genteel poverty. After attending local schools in Dublin, he worked as a surveyor.

In 1852 Wolseley joined the army as a second lieutenant. At a time when most commissions were purchased, Wolseley advanced by dint of ability. He saw service in the Second Burma War (1852–1853), when he was wounded; in the Crimean War (1854–1856), when he was again wounded, losing sight in one eye; in the Indian Mutiny (1857); and in the Third China War (1860), when he was breveted lieutenant colonel.

With war threatening between the United States and Britain in 1861, Wolseley secured a posting in Canada. He visited both the North and the South during the American Civil War (1861–1865) and wrote *The Soldier's Pocket Book* (1869), which became the template for future British Army field service regulations. In 1870 he commanded the successful Canadian Red River Expedition that ended the effort by Louis Riel to establish an independent republic in present-day Manitoba. This campaign in difficult terrain established Wolseley's reputation for organizational efficiency. Increasingly Wolseley was associated with the reform movement in the British Army, which included an effort to abolish the purchase of commissions.

Wolseley's reputation was made in his conduct of the Second Ashanti War (1873–1874), for which he also produced the army's first manual on jungle warfare. In 1875 he was dispatched to Natal. In 1878 he led the British occupation of Cyprus, and in 1879 he was back in Natal to end the Zulu Wars. Wolseley suppressed both the Pedi and Basotho peoples.

Returning to Britain in 1880, Wolseley was appointed army quartermaster general. By now the most popular active general in the British Army, he had also proven to be one of the most successful, having won all of his colonial campaigns with minimal expense and loss of life. During his extensive campaigning, he had gathered around him a group of young, capable officers. Known as the Wolseley Ring, they sought to reform army administration and tactics.

In 1882 Wolseley assumed the post of adjutant general, responsible for military training. In this capacity, he sought to update army tactics. That same year he was dispatched to Egypt to quell rebellious Egyptian Army units. His victory at Tel-el-Kabir on October 13, 1882, brought promotion to full general.

In 1884 the British government again sent Wolseley to Egypt, this time in a belated effort to rescue his friend, General Charles George Gordon, and British forces besieged at Khartoum. Wolseley's relief force proceeded slowly up the Nile and reached Khartoum in January 1885, only to find that the Mahdi's forces had captured the city and killed Gordon a few days earlier. Nevertheless, for his efforts Wolseley was made a viscount.

From 1890 to 1895 Wolseley was commander in chief in Ireland, during which time he sought to modernize the army's tactical doctrine. Raised to field marshal in 1894, the next year he became commander in chief of the British Army. Although he accomplished a number of reforms, poor health and political opposition prevented him from realizing all that he wanted. His last years in office were marred by the early British reverses in the South African War (Second Boer War) of 1899–1902, although these were the responsibility of field commanders. Retiring in 1901, he entered a prolonged mental decline. Wolseley died in Mentone, France, on March 26, 1913.

Hubert Dubrulle and Spencer C. Tucker

See also Gordon, Charles George; Mahdist Uprising in Sudan; South African War

Further Reading

Lehman, Joseph. *The Model Major General: A Biography of Field-Marshal Lord Wolseley.* Boston: Houghton Mifflin, 1964.

Maurice, Sir Frederick. *The Life of Lord Wolseley.* London: W. Heinemann, 1924.

Worth, William Jenkins

Birth Date: March 1, 1794
Death Date: May 7, 1849

U.S. Army general and successful commander of counterinsurgency forces. William Jenkins Worth was born in Hudson, New York, on March 1, 1794. Worth worked briefly as a clerk before the start of the War of 1812, when he joined the army as a private. He was commissioned a first lieutenant in the 23rd U.S. Infantry in March 1813 and served as an aide to Brigadier General Winfield Scott, who became both a mentor and a friend for 30 years. Worth's war service won him brevets to captain and to major.

During 1820–1821, Worth was commandant of cadets at the U.S. Military Academy, West Point. Promoted to colonel in 1835, he commanded the 8th U.S. Infantry. During the Second Seminole War (1835–1842), Worth distinguished himself under Major General Zachary Taylor. By 1841, Worth had charge of U.S. forces in the war. His strategy of carrying the war to the Seminoles by the destruction of their crops and dwellings and campaigning in the hot summer months, even at high cost to his own men in sickness and disease, helped bring the war to a conclusion.

Worth's accomplishment brought a brevet to brigadier general. In 1845 he was assigned to Taylor's Army of Occupation in southern Texas on the Mexican border but resigned his commission when President James K. Polk refused to confirm him as Taylor's second-in-command based on his brevet. Learning of the outbreak of hostilities with Mexico in May 1846, Worth withdrew his resignation and returned to service, although he missed the first battles of the war.

Brigadier General Worth commanded a division in Taylor's army and was his second-in-command. For his important role in the capture of Monterrey on September 24, 1846, Worth was breveted major general and was then that city's military governor. He quickly established order, instituted a curfew, and guaranteed the rights and property of Mexican civilians. Worth took Saltillo on November 17.

In January 1847 Worth was assigned to forces under Major General Winfield Scott preparing to land at Veracruz and march on Mexico City. Worth helped plan the campaign, and he led the first troops ashore on March 9, 1847. He was, however, critical of Scott's siege of three weeks, favoring instead an assault, which would have been more costly in terms of casualties. Appointed military governor, Worth instituted the same effective occupation policies as at Monterrey.

During the march to Mexico City, however, Worth fell out with Scott over a succession of perceived slights. The feud between Scott and Worth continued after the end of the fighting, when both Worth and Major General Gideon Pillow sought to downplay Scott's role in the capture of Mexico City. Published accounts and Worth's appeal to President Polk—no friend of Scott—led Scott to order the arrest of both Worth and Pillow. Scott and Worth subsequently resolved their difficulties, and Worth oversaw the withdrawal of U.S. troops from Mexico City in June 1848.

Worth then commanded the Department of Texas. He died in San Antonio, Texas, on May 7, 1849. The city of Fort Worth, Texas, is named in his honor.

Robert W. Malick and Spencer C. Tucker

See also Seminole Wars; Taylor, Zachary

Further Reading

Bauer, K. Jack. *The Mexican War, 1846–1848.* New York: Macmillan 1974.

Johnson, Timothy D. *A Gallant Little Army: The Mexico City Campaign.* Lawrence: University Press of Kansas, 2007.

Wallace, Edward S. *General William Jenkins Worth: Monterrey's Forgotten Hero.* Dallas, TX: Southern Methodist University Press, 1953.

Z

Zapata, Emiliano

Birth Date: August 8, 1879
Death Date: April 10, 1919

Mexican insurgent leader. Emiliano Zapata was born on August 8, 1879, in Anenecuilco, Mexico, to poor parents of Spanish and indigenous Indian background. In his youth, Zapata was a tenant farmer on a sugar plantation and was witness to the injustice of the wealthy landowners continuously expanding their holdings by confiscating peasant land. He organized the peasants in his village to protest, resulting in his arrest and imprisonment. Zapata then served briefly in the army before training horses for a wealthy landowner. In 1909 he led a group of peasants to forcibly occupy land claimed by an owner of a hacienda.

Mexico was then in crisis. The economic gulf between a wealthy few and the impoverished masses produced unrest and led to the Mexican Revolution of 1910, characterized by disjointed rebellions in the countryside. That year, one of the rebel leaders, Francisco Madero, overthrew the dictatorship of Porfirio Díaz. During the fighting, the charismatic Zapata raised a force to support Madero, a moderate democratic reformer.

Madero soon disappointed Zapata, rejecting his call that land be returned to the peasants. Indeed, Madero insisted that Zapata and his followers lay down their arms. Zapata declined after Madero's forces attacked his own. Zapata then led attacks on haciendas and government offices, winning a large following among the peasants. In 1911 he issued the Plan de Ayala, calling for Madero's overthrow and promising democracy and a redistribution of land. The slogan was "Tierra y libertad" ("Land and Liberty"). Two years later Madero's regime collapsed, partly because of the disorder promoted by Zapata and other rebel leaders, including Francisco "Pancho" Villa and Victoriano Huerta.

In February 1913 Huerta secured the presidency and established a dictatorship. A conservative, he had no desire to carry out reforms. Zapata now fought Huerta, securing control of the area south of Mexico City. Zapata confiscated the haciendas, redistributed land to the poor, and established an organization to provide farmers with credit. He enjoyed widespread peasant support, and order prevailed.

In July 1914 Huerta's government fell, and Venustiano Carranza became president. Carranza rejected Zapata's agrarian reform and soon was battling both Zapata's Revolutionary Army of the South and Villa's forces in the north. In November, representatives of Carranza, Villa, and Zapata met in Aguascalientes but failed to reach agreement. Carranza soon fled Mexico City for Veracruz, and Villa and Zapata alternately occupied the capital.

Mexican revolutionary and insurgent leader Emiliano Zapata fought to break up the large haciendas in northern Mexico, where wealthy landowners continued to expand their holdings at peasant expense. (Library of Congress)

In late 1914 Zapata agreed to cooperate with Villa. Carranza's generals, however, gradually gained the upper hand, and his reform programs appealed to the disadvantaged. Government decrees distributed unused lands owned by the national government and provided for the protection of industrial workers. By the spring of 1915, both Villa and Zapata were on the defensive.

In late 1916, Carranza oversaw a constitutional convention that was closed to Villa and Zapata. In part because of Zapata's influence, the Constitution of 1917 gave the government the right to restrict private property in order to more equitably distribute the nation's wealth. The constitution also outlawed child labor and stipulated the eight-hour workday. Carranza saw the document as a means to consolidate his power. Indeed, the document deflated Zapata's revolutionary movement.

Meanwhile, Carranza sent Pablo González, his most trusted general, to end the threat from Zapata. The ruthless González employed a scorched-earth policy, destroying villages and killing all those suspected of supporting Zapata. Finally, González arranged a fake defection by his loyal lieutenant, Colonel Jesús Guajardo. Zapata agreed to a meeting on April 10, 1919, at the Hacienda de San Juan in Chinameca, there to be ambushed and killed. Following Zapata's death, the Liberation Army of the South collapsed, and the rebellion in southern Mexico came to an end. Regarded as a martyr by many Mexicans after his death, Zapata's influence continues to this day, especially in southern Mexico.

Spencer C. Tucker

See also Villa, Francisco

Further Reading

Brunk, Samuel. *Emiliano Zapata: Revolution and Betrayal in Mexico.* Albuquerque: University of New Mexico Press, 1995.

Parkinson, Roger. *Zapata: A Biography.* New York: Stein and Day, 1975.

Womack, John. *Zapata and the Mexican Revolution.* New York: Vintage Books, 1970.

Zeng Guofan

Birth Date: November 26, 1811
Death Date: March 12, 1872

Chinese general who ended the Taiping Rebellion (1850–1864). Zeng Guofan (Tseng Kuo-fan) was born to a scholar farming family in Xiang District, Hunan, China, on November 26, 1811. He studied for the traditional scholarly examinations that were the route to civil service position. Passing the highest academic examination for the *jinshi* (doctoral degree) on his second attempt in 1838, Zeng was appointed to the Hanlin Academy in Peking (now Beijing) for 13 years. He concentrated on interpreting the Confucian classics. By the 1850s, however, he had spoken out against government policies.

Following the death of his mother in 1852, Zeng took the then-customary three-year leave at home for mourning but broke off the mourning to raise a military force in Hunan against Taiping forces that had entered the province during what became known as the Taiping Rebellion against the Qing dynasty. One of the major events in Chinese history, it ultimately claimed the lives of some 20 million–30 million Chinese.

Zeng attracted a wide following to his army because of his insistence on observance of Confucian principles, including obligation to the soldiers and loyalty to one's superior. Soon his well-disciplined force of volunteers had grown into the Xiang Army, the chief military force against the Taipings. Zeng also created a naval force of some 240 junks to operate on the region's rivers.

Zeng's forces were victorious in the Battle of Xiangtan (May 1, 1854) and also recaptured Hubei in October. The rebels retook Hubei the next year, and Zeng could do little during the next two years, although he secured the position of viceroy of Liangjiang, comprising the provinces of Jiangxi, Anhui, and Jiangsu, during 1860–1864 and also secured the right to finance his army through the collection of customs duties. Zeng's army grew to a force of 120,000 men with a number of capable generals, such as Li Hongzhang and Zuo Zongtang. Again defeated at the Battle of Qimen in Anhui Province in mid-1861, Zeng nonetheless continued to campaign and won the loyalty of the peasants. He was finally victorious, capturing the Taiping capital of Nanjing and ending the rebellion in 1864. For this he was awarded the title of marquis. Thereafter an administrator, Zeng served as viceroy of Zhili during 1865–1870 and again as viceroy of Liangjiang during 1870–1872. He resumed military command during May 1865–October 1866 against the Nian Rebellion in northern China but then resigned in favor of his protégé, Li Hong-zhang.

Zeng was responsible for a number of reforms and supported a program of modernization in China. This included the creation of the Jiangnan naval arsenal at Shanghai that built several modern warships. He strongly supported the study of Chinese classical literature, but it was at his recommendation that the Chinese government first sent students to be educated abroad. Zeng died in Nanjing on March 12, 1872. After his death, the government accorded him the name of Wenzheng, the highest title possible under the Qing dynasty.

Although not a great field commander, Zeng was certainly the leading Chinese general and civil leader of 19th-century China. His efforts ensured the continuation of the Qing dynasty into the 20th century.

Spencer C. Tucker

See also Taiping Rebellion

Further Reading

Jen, Yu-wen. *The Taiping Revolutionary Movement.* New Haven, CT: Yale University Press, 1973.

Porter, Jonathan. *Tseng Kuo-fan's Private Bureaucracy.* China Research Monographs. Berkeley: Center for Chinese Studies, University of California Press, 1972.

Spence, Jonathan. *God's Chinese Son: The Taiping Heavenly Kingdom of Hong Xiuquan.* New York: Norton, 1997.

Zimbabwe African National Union

One of the two nationalist insurgent organizations engaging in military operations against the minority white government of Rhodesia (today Zimbabwe) in the Rhodesian Bush War (Zimbabwe War of Liberation) of 1964–1979. The Reverend Ndabanigi Sithole was the principal founder of the Zimbabwe African National Union (ZANU), established in August 1963 in a split from Joshua Nkomo's Zimbabwe African People's Union (ZAPU). Whereas ZAPU drew its strength chiefly from the minority Ndebele people in western Rhodesia, ZANU was based chiefly on the majority Shona people of eastern Rhodesia. ZANU's military wing was the Zimbabwe African National Liberation Army (ZANLA). ZANLA operated from Mozambique after the Portuguese withdrawal from that country in 1974.

ZANU was heavily dependent on assistance from the People's Republic of China. ZANU's leaders sought to follow Chinese Communist leader Mao Zedong (Mao Tse-tung) in basing their insurgency largely on guerrilla warfare in the countryside. ZAPU, which drew its support chiefly from the Soviet Union, favored mobilizing urban workers and sought direct military confrontation with Rhodesian forces.

ZANU grew more radical and underwent a split when Sithole, who favored discussions with the Rhodesian government, was challenged by Robert Mugabe on the latter's release from detention by the minority white Rhodesian government of Prime Minister Ian Smith in 1974. ZANLA posed by far the greatest military threat to the Rhodesian government, and by the time of the cease-fire in December 1979, most of some 122,000 guerrillas inside Zimbabwe were from ZANLA, which also counted another 16,000 outside the country. ZAPU's military force, known as the Zimbabwe People's Revolutionary Army (ZIPRA), had few fighters within Rhodesia.

Both ZANU groups continued to use that name following their split. In 1979 Sithoe played a key role in the establishment of the transitional short-lived Zimbabwe-Rhodesia, led by Bishop Abel Muzorewa, but Mugabe's group dominated. In the Zimbabwe independence elections of 1980, Mugabe's ZANU registered as ZANU-PF (PF standing for Patriotic Front) and was swept into office. Sithoe's organization, which campaigned as ZANU, failed to win any seats. Mugabe continues to hold power in Zimbabwe in 2013.

Spencer C. Tucker

See also Mugabe, Robert Gabriel; Nkomo, Joshua; Rhodesian Bush War; Zimbabwe African People's Union

Further Reading

Moorcraft, Paul, and Peter McLaughlin. *Chimurenga.* New York: Macmillan, 1982.

Sibanda, Eliakim. *The Zimbabwe African People's Union 1961–87: A Political History of Insurgency in Southern Rhodesia.* Trenton, NJ: Africa World, 2005.

Zimbabwe African People's Union

One of the two nationalist insurgent organizations engaging in military operations against the minority white government of Rhodesia (today Zimbabwe) in the Rhodesian Bush War (Zimbabwe War of Liberation) of 1964–1979. The Zimbabwe African People's Union (ZAPU) was formed in December 1961, and its principal leader was Joshua Nkomo. ZAPU's military wing, the Zimbabwe People's Revolutionary Army (ZIPRA), commanded by General Lookout Masuku, operated from Zambia and Botswana.

There were several splits in ZAPU. Thus in 1963, the Reverend Ndabaningi Sithole led a group that formed the rival Zimbabwe African National Union (ZANU), which became the largest Zimbabwean insurgent organization. ZAPU drew its support chiefly from the minority Ndebele peoples in western Zimbabwe, while ZANU was based on the majority Shona peoples in the eastern part of the country. Whereas ZANU replied heavily on the People's Republic of China for military support and operated chiefly in rural areas of Rhodesia, ZAPU was aligned with the Soviet Union and followed its revolutionary ideology of mobilizing urban support and then waiting for the right moment to launch a Soviet-style military assault on the Rhodesian Army. Thus, virtually all of ZAPU's 22,000 fighters were outside Rhodesia at the time of the cease-fire in December 1979, giving ZANU an immense advantage in the subsequent struggle for political power.

ZAPU contested the 1980 elections in Zimbabwe that followed independence but lost to ZANU, headed by Robert Mugabe. ZAPU merged with the ZANU political party (ZANU-PF, with "PF" standing for "Patriotic Front") in 1987, but a number of its members voted to withdraw again in December 2008.

Spencer C. Tucker

See also Mugabe, Robert Gabriel; Nkomo, Joshua; Rhodesian Bush War; Zimbabwe African National Union

Further Reading

Moorcraft, Paul, and Peter McLaughlin. *Chimurenga.* New York: Macmillan, 1982.

Sibanda, Eliakim. *The Zimbabwe African People's Union 1961–87: A Political History of Insurgency in Southern Rhodesia.* Trenton, NJ: Africa World, 2005.

Zimbabwe War of Liberation.

See Rhodesian Bush War

Chronology of Selected Insurgencies through History

168–142 BCE	Maccabean Revolt. Uprising in Judea against the Seleucid Empire that is also a civil war between urban, hellenized Jews and those in the countryside who believe strictly in the Torah.
73–71 BCE	Third Servile War. Slave revolt against Rome led by the Thracian gladiator Spartacus. The revolt overruns much of Italy before it is crushed.
66–70	Jewish revolt against Roman rule, put down by Roman legions dispatched by Emperor Nero. The siege and sack of Jerusalem brings widespread loss of life and destruction of the Temple.
132–136	Bar Kokhba Revolt. The third major Jewish revolt against Rome, the Bar Kokhba Revolt is put down by Roman legions sent by Emperor Hadrian.
1358	Jacquerie. A peasant uprising in France in reaction to the heavy taxes levied for the expenses of the Hundred Years' War (1337–1453) and the ransom of nobles as well as the pillaging of the countryside by discharged mercenary troops.
1381	Peasants' Revolt in England. Perhaps the most extensive popular uprising in English history, the Peasants' Revolt in England is prompted by the unfair application of a new poll tax.
1524–1525	Peasants' Revolt in Germany. One of the largest upheavals in Europe before the French Revolution, the Peasants' Revolt in Germany is sparked by the success of the religious revolt known as the Protestant Reformation, fueled by widespread demands for social and economic justice.
1676–1677	Bacon's Rebellion. Violent uprising in the English North American colony of Virginia led by planter Nathaniel Bacon against the colonial government and its Native American policies.

1680	Pueblo Revolt. Native uprising in present-day New Mexico in North America against brutal Spanish rule, bringing temporary expulsion of the Spanish.
1763–1766	Pontiac's Rebellion. Rebellion, prompted by a change in policy, carried out by Native Americans in British North America against English rule.
1768–1771	Regulator Revolt. Occurring in the British North American colony of North Carolina, the Regulator Revolt is a revolt of the rural counties against unfair practices and the political dominance of the eastern part of the colony.
1773–1774	Pugachev's Rebellion. A largely disorganized peasant uprising led by a Russian peasant falsely claiming to be the czar that is nonetheless easily crushed by government forces. However, Pugachev's Rebellion has widespread political and social repercussions.
1775–1783	American Revolutionary War. A war that begins as an insurgency sparked by what the British colonists perceive as unfair government regulations and taxes imposed by a government in which they believe they are not represented.
1786–1787	Shays' Rebellion. A revolt in the United States by debt-ridden New Englanders seeking redress from the Massachusetts state government. Shays' Rebellion is easily crushed by state militia.
1793–1796	Vendée Revolt. A regional revolt in western France against the French Revolution. The Vendée Revolt is ended by a mix of force and toleration of traditional Catholic religious practices.
1794	Whiskey Rebellion. Revolt in the western counties of Pennsylvania in the United States against an excise tax on whiskey. The Whiskey Rebellion is easily ended by federalized state militias.
1808–1814	Peninsula War. Spaniards, aided by the Portuguese and British, overthrow the rule of their country by the French under Napoleon I.
1809–1810	Tyrolean Revolt. Uprising by those in the Tyrol region seeking to remain part of Austria as opposed to rule by Bavaria and France.
1817–1858	Seminole Wars. Three wars fought by the Seminole Indians of Florida in the United States against encroachments of their ancestral lands by white settlers.
1832	Black Hawk War. Conflict in the United States between Sauk and Fox Native Americans led by Chief Black Hawk against white settlers moving onto their ancestral lands in northern Illinois and southern Wisconsin.

1832–1847	French Pacification of Algeria. French forces, having invaded and conquered Algiers in 1830, seek to extend French rule.
1846–1848	Mexican-American War. Mexican insurgents during the war seek to disrupt American lines of communication.
1850–1864	Taiping Rebellion. A great uprising in China against inefficient government rule and corruption that is finally put down by the Manchu Qing dynasty but not before the fighting has claimed some 20 million–30 million lives.
1861–1865	American Civil War. Insurgent operations occur throughout the war, especially in Missouri.
1866–1890	American Indian Wars in the West. Native Americans west of the Mississippi fight to prevent settlers from moving onto and fencing off what they consider to be their ancestral lands, on which they hunt buffalo.
1868–1878	Ten Years' War. Cuban nationalists fight to end Spanish rule on the island.
1878	Bosnia-Herzegovina Insurgency. Muslims, content under the Ottomans, rise up to resist the imposition of Austro-Hungarian rule.
1881–1898	Mahdist Uprising in the Sudan. Religious fanatics rally to expel Egyptian and British forces from the Sudan.
1889–1920	Somaliland Insurgency. Charismatic sheikh Sayyīd Muhammad Abd Allāh al-Hassan, known as the "Mad Mullah," wages a religious war against British Somaliland.
1895–1898	Cuban War for Independence. Cuban nationalist forces again rise up against Spain, seeking independence for the island. The fighting merges into the Spanish-American War (1898).
1899–1902	South African War (Second Boer War). The Boer republics of the Transvaal and Orange Free State go to war against Britain to prevent their absorption into the British Empire.
1899–1902	Philippine-American War. Filipino nationalists go to war with the United States in an effort to achieve independence.
1904–1907	Herero Revolt. Natives in German South-West Africa, protesting increasing German settlement and harsh colonial rule, go to war and are ruthlessly crushed by German forces.
1905–1907	Maji Maji Rebellion. Tribal insurgency in German East Africa brought on by German rule, famine, and economic, political, and religious differences.

1912–1923	Ireland Revolutionary Era. Irish nationalists undertake a long-running effort to achieve independence from Britain.
1914–1916	Senussi and Sultan of Darfur Rebellions. After the Ottoman Empire joins the Central Powers in 1914, Grand Senussi Sayed Ahmed leads North African desert tribes against the French and British in addition to continuing to battle the Italians.
1915–1934	Haiti Insurgency and U.S. Intervention. Unrest in Haiti sparks a military intervention by the United States to protect its economic interests there.
1916–1917	Mexican Expedition (Punitive Expedition). Following an attack led by Mexican revolutionary Pancho Villa against Columbus, New Mexico, President Woodrow Wilson orders U.S. forces into northern Mexico.
1916–1919	Arab Revolt. Middle Eastern Arab leaders, encouraged and supported by the British, take up arms against the Ottoman Empire in expectation of establishing an Arab state after the defeat of the Central Powers in World War I.
1916–1934	Dominican Republic Insurgency. Chaotic conditions in the Dominican Republic prompt the United States to send marines.
1918–1933	Basmachi Revolt. A Central Asia Muslim insurgency beginning against Czarist Russia and continuing with the Soviet Union.
1920	Iraq Revolt. Iraqi nationalists revolt against the British League of Nations mandate government. The Royal Air Force plays a key role in putting down the revolt.
1921–1922	Moplah Rebellion. An Islamic revolt in the heavily Muslim Malabar region of southwestern India that is put down by the British.
1921–1926	Rif War. Muslim nationalists in Morocco revolt against Spanish and French rule.
1825–1927	Great Syrian Revolt. Syrian nationalists take up arms against the French League of Nations mandate government.
1927–1933	Nicaragua Insurgency. Unrest in Nicaragua and the threat to its economic interests prompts the United States to dispatch marines.
1936–1939	Arab Revolt. Muslim uprising in Palestine against both Jews and the British authorities that is sparked by growing Jewish immigration into this League of Nations mandate.
1940–1944	Chechnya Insurgency. Nationalists seek to establish independence from the Soviet Union and gain some assistance from the Germans following their invasion.

1946–1949   Greek Civil War. Greek Communists, fearful of the consequences of rightist control of the government and supported by neighboring Communist states, attempt to seize power.

1946–1954   Hukbalahap Rebellion. Communist guerrillas, upset with unfair land practices, take up arms against the Philippine government.

1946–1954   Indochina War. Revolt of Vietnamese nationalists against French colonial rule.

1947–1948   Madagascar Revolt (Malagasy Uprising). Uprising on the island of Madagascar against French rule.

1948–1960   Malayan Emergency. Communists in Malaya, principally Chinese squatters, try to seize power but are defeated by the British.

1949–1955   Karen Revolt. Revolt by the ethnic Karen minority in Burma (today Myanmar) against the exclusionary racial policies of the Burmese majority in control of the government.

1952–1960   Kenya Emergency. Revolt by nationalists, known as the Mau Mau, against British rule.

1953–1959   Cuban Revolution. Cuban rebel fighters, led by Fidel Castro, overthrow the dictatorial regime of Fulgencio Batista.

1955–1959   Cyprus Insurgency. Nationalists do battle with the British. The rebels are divided, however, between those who seek independence and those desiring union with Greece.

1956   Hungarian Revolution. Revolt against the Communist regime demanding reform that balloons into demands for democracy and withdrawal from the Warsaw Pact, prompting Soviet military intervention.

1957–1975   Vietnam War. A continuation of the 1946–1954 Indochina War, the Vietnam War is prompted by the desire of the leaders of Communist North Vietnam to secure the reunification of Vietnam, which had been divided in 1954 pending national elections. The fighting draws in the United States.

1960–1996   Guatemala Insurgency. A revolt led by junior military officers and supported by Communist Cuba against the military dictatorship ruling the country.

1961–1974   Guinea (Portuguese) Insurgency. Guinean nationalists, seeking independence, do battle with Portugese military forces.

1961–1975   Angola Insurgency. Angolan nationalists, seeking independence, do battle with Portugese military forces.

1962–1976	Dhofar Rebellion. Rebellion in which conservative Islamists in southern Oman seek independence from Oman.
1962–1981	Eritrean War for Independence. Eritrean nationalists wage a successful military struggle to achieve independence from Ethiopia.
1962–1966	Borneo/Brunei Insurgency. Indonesia supports an insurgency against eastern Malaysia, aided by the British, on the island of Borneo.
1960s–1975	Cambodia Insurgency. The Communist Khmer Rouge does battle with and topples the Cambodian government, installing a genocidal regime there.
1963–1965	Venezuelan Insurgency. Effort by radical junior army officers and the Communists to topple the government of staunch anticommunist Rómulo Betancourt.
1963–1967	Aden Emergency. Insurgents seek to topple the government of this British crown colony.
1964–1975	Mozambique Insurgency. Mozambique nationalists do battle with the Portuguese Army in an effort to achieve independence from Portugal.
1964–1979	Rhodesian Bush War (Zimbabwe War of Liberation). Black African nationalists seek to end white minority rule in Rhodesia.
1964–Present	Colombia Insurgency. Rural leftist guerrillas, a number of whom are linked with powerful drug cartels, do battle with the government.
1966–1990	South-West Africa (Namibia) Insurgency. Nationalists fight to achieve independence for this former League of Nations mandate ruled by South Africa and then do battle among themselves.
1968–1998	Northern Ireland Conflict (The Troubles). Members of the Irish Republican Army among the minority Catholics wage a terrorist campaign against the Protestant majority and the British Army in Northern Ireland in an effort to bring about union with Ireland.
1969–2012	Philippines Insurgency. Moro Muslim insurgents in the southern Philippine islands seek autonomy or independence from the Philippines.
1973–1991	Western Sahara War. Sahrawi insurgents do battle with Morocco, which had secured control of much of the Sahara from Spain.
1979–1989	Soviet-Afghan War. Afghans wage war against Soviet forces sent into the country to maintain a Communist regime in power.

1979–1991   Vietnamese occupation of Cambodia. Disparate nationalist Cambodian forces supported by China and the United States battle with the Vietnamese forces occupying Cambodia.

1980–1982   El Salvador Insurgency. Rural uprising against the conservative military-dominated government.

1981–1990   Nicaragua Insurgency. Leftist Sandinista guerrillas do battle with the family-run Somoza government. Following the Sandinista victory, U.S. president Ronald Reagan's administration supports anti-Sandinista Contra forces.

1982–   Peru Insurgencies. Guerrilla organizations, most notably the rural-based Maoist Sendero Luminoso (Shining Path), do battle with the Peruvian government.

1983–2005   South Sudan Insurgency. Predominantly non-Arab and animist or Christian South Sudan seeks independence from predominantly Arab and Muslim North Sudan.

1983–2009   Sri Lankan Civil War. Minority Tamils do battle with the Sri Lankan government in an effort to secure a Tamil state in the northern part of the island.

1987–1993   First Intifada. Muslim Palestinians contest Israel's control over the West Bank and demand the creation of a Palestinian state.

1987–Present   Kashmir Insurgency. Pakistani nationalists contest Indian control of most of the state of Kashmir, with its largely Muslim population.

1996–2006   Nepal Maoist Insurgency. Communist Maoist guerrillas seek to topple the Nepalese monarchy.

1999–2009   Second Chechnya War. Chechnyan nationalists wage an unsuccessful effort to achieve independence from the Russian Federation.

2000–2005   Second (al-Aqsa) Intifada. Palestinian nationalists contest Israeli's control of the West Bank and demand the creation of a Palestinian state.

2001–Present   Afghanistan War. U.S.-led coalition forces battle the Al Qaeda terrorist organization and Taliban insurgents seeking to topple the Afghanistan government installed following U.S. military intervention in 2001.

2003–2011   Iraq Insurgency. Insurgents, chiefly Sunni Muslims, battle the U.S.-led coalition forces and the new Shiite-dominated Iraqi government.

2011   Libyan Civil War. Insurgents, assisted by the North Atlantic Treaty Organization, overthrow longtime dictator Muammar Gaddafi.

2011–Present   Syrian Civil War. Insurgent forces, largely drawn from the majority Sunni Muslim population, seek to overthrow the long-standing al-Assad family dictatorship supported by some Sunnis and the vast majority of the minority Alawaite Shiite Muslims, backed by Shiite Iran.

Bibliography

Abbott, Peter, and Philip Botham. *Modern African Wars: Rhodesia, 1965–80.* Oxford, UK: Osprey, 1986.

Akehurst, John. *We Won a War: The Campaign in Oman, 1965–1975.* Wiltshire, UK: M. Russell, 1982.

Allen, Calvin H., and W. Lynn Rigsbee. *Oman under Qaboos: From Coup to Constitution, 1970–1976.* London: Routledge, 2000

Anderson, David. *Policing and Decolonization: Nationalism, Politics, and the Police, 1917–1965.* Edited by David Killingray. New York: Manchester University Press, 1992.

Anderson, John Lee. *Che Guevara: A Revolutionary Life.* New York: Grove, 1997.

Asprey, Robert B. *War in the Shadows: The Guerrilla in History.* Garden City, NY: Doubleday, 1975.

Aussaresses, Paul. *The Battle of the Casbah: Terrorism and Counter-Terrorism in Algeria, 1955–1957.* New York: Enigma Books, 2010.

Beckett, Ian F. W. *Encyclopedia of Guerrilla Warfare.* Santa Barbara, CA: ABC-CLIO, 1999.

Beckett, Ian F. W. *Modern Insurgencies and Counterinsurgencies: Guerrillas and Their Opponents since 1750.* London: Routledge, 2001.

Beckett, Ian F. W., ed. *The Roots of Counterinsurgency: Armies and Guerrilla Warfare.* New York: Blandford, 1988.

Beckett, Ian F. W., and John Pimlott, eds. *Armed Forces and Modern Counter-Insurgency.* New York: St. Martin's, 1985.

Bell, J. Bowyer. *The Irish Troubles: A Generation of Violence, 1967–1992.* New York: St. Martin's, 1993.

Bender, Gerald J. *Angola under the Portuguese: The Myth and the Reality.* Berkeley: University of California Press, 1978.

Bickel, Keith B. *Mars Learning: The Marine Corps' Development of Small Wars Doctrine, 1915–1940.* Boulder, CO: Westview, 2001.

Bigeard, Marcel-Maurice. *Pour une parcelle de gloire* [For a Bit of Glory]. Paris: Plon, 1975.

Blaufarb, Douglas S. *The Counterinsurgency Era: U.S. Doctrine and Performance, 1950 to the Present.* New York: Free Press, 1977.

Boot, Max. *Invisible Armies: An Epic History of Guerrilla Warfare from Ancient Times to the Present.* New York: Liveright, 2013.

Bracamonte, José, Angel Moroni, and David Spencer. *Strategy and Tactics of the Salvadoran FMLN Guerrillas.* Westport, CT: Praeger, 1995.

Budiardjo, Carmel, and Soei Liong Liem. *The War against East Timor.* London: Zed, 1984.

Byrne, Hugh. *El Salvador's Civil War: A Study of Revolution.* Boulder, CO: Lynne Rienner, 1996.

Cabrita, João M. *Mozambique: The Tortuous Road to Democracy.* New York: Palgrave, 2000.

Callwell, Charles. *Small Wars: Their Principles and Practice.* 1896; reprint, Lincoln: University of Nebraska Press, 1996.

Cann, John P. *Brown Waters of Africa: Portuguese Riverine Warfare, 1961–1974.* St. Petersburg, FL: Hailer, 2007.

Cann, John P. *Counterinsurgency in Africa: The Portuguese Way of War, 1961–1974.* St. Petersburg, FL: Hailer, 2005.

Carruthers, Susan. *Winning Hearts and Minds: British Governments, the Media, and Colonial Counter-Insurgency, 1944–1960.* New York: Leicester University Press, 1995.

Chabal, Patrick. *Amílcar Cabral: Revolutionary Leadership and People's War.* New York: Cambridge University Press, 1983.

Chaliand, Gérard. *Les Guerres irrégulières, XXe–XXIe siècles: Guérillas et terrorismes* [Irregular Wars, 20th–21st Centuries: Guerrillas and Terrorism]. Paris: Gallimard, 2008.

Chandler, David. *Brother Number One: A Political Biography of Pol Pot.* Boulder, CO: Westview, 1992.

Charters, David. *Squalid War: The British Army and Jewish Insurgency in Palestine, 1945–1947.* London: Macmillan, 1989.

Charters, David, and Maurice Tugwell, eds. *Armies in Low-Intensity Conflict: A Comprehensive Analysis.* Washington, DC: Brassey's Defence, 1989.

Christian, Shirley. *Nicaragua: Revolution in the Family.* New York: Random House, 1985.

Cilliers, Jakkie. *Counter-Insurgency in Rhodesia.* London: Croom Helm, 1985.

Clausewitz, Carl von. *On War.* Translated by Howard Michael and Peter Peret. Princeton, NJ: Princeton University Press, 1976.

Clayton, Anthony. *Counter-Insurgency in Kenya.* Nairobi: Transafrica Publishers, 1976.

Clayton, Anthony. *The Wars of French Decolonization.* New York: Longman, 1994.

Cloake, John. *Templer, Tiger of Malaya.* London: Harrap, 1985.

Close, David H. *The Greek Civil War, 1943–1950: Studies of Polarization.* New York: Routledge, 1992.

Clutterbuck, Richard. *Conflict and Violence: In Singapore and Malaysia, 1945–1983.* Boulder, CO: Westview, 1985.

Clutterbuck, Richard. *Guerrillas and Terrorists.* London: Faber and Faber, 1997.

Coates, John. *Suppressing Insurgency.* Boulder, CO: Westview, 1992.

Cobban, Helena. *The Palestine Liberation Organization: People, Power, and Politics.* New York: Cambridge University Press, 1984.

Cohen, A. A. *Galula: The Life and Writings of the French Officer Who Defined the Art of Counterinsurgency.* Santa Barbara, CA: Praeger, 2012.

Coogan, Tim Pat. *The IRA: A History.* 11th ed. New York: Praeger, 1998.

Corbett, Robin. *Guerrilla Warfare: From 1939 to the Present Day.* London: Orbis, 1986.

Cornwall, Barbara. *The Bush Rebels: A Personal Account of Black Revolt in Africa.* New York: Holt, Reinhardt, and Winston, 1972.

Corum, James S. *Training Indigenous Forces in Counterinsurgency: A Tale of Two Insurgencies.* Carlisle, PA: Strategic Studies Institute, 2006.

Corum, James S., and Wray R. Johnson. *Air Power in Small Wars: Fighting Insurgents and Terrorists.* Lawrence: University of Kansas Press, 2003.

Crawshaw, Nancy. *The Cyprus Revolt: An Account of the Struggle for Union with Greece.* London: Allen and Unwin, 1978.

Currey, Cecil B. *Edward Lansdale: The Unquiet American.* Boston: Houghton Mifflin, 1988.

Currey, Cecil B. *Victory at Any Cost: The Genius of Viet Nam General Vo Nguyen Giap.* Washington, DC: Brassey's, 1997.

Curtis, Robert. *The History of the Royal Irish Constabulary.* Dublin, Ireland: McGlashan and Gill, 1871.

Dalloz, Jacques. *The War in Indo-China, 1845–1954.* Savage, MD: Barnes and Noble, 1990.

Debray, Régis. *Revolution in the Revolution? Armed Struggle and Political Struggle in Latin America.* New York: Monthly Review Press, 1967.

Dederer, John Morgan. *Making Bricks without Straw: Nathanael Greene's Southern Campaign and Mao Tse-tung's Mobile War.* Manhattan, KS: Sunflower University Press, 1983.

Dewar, Michael. *The British Army in Northern Ireland.* London: Arms and Armour, 1985.

DiMarco, Louis A. *Concrete Hell: Modern Urban Warfare from Stalingrad to Iraq.* Oxford, UK: Osprey, 2012.

Dixon, Paul, and Eamonn O'Kane. *Northern Ireland since 1969.* New York: Longman, 2011.

Doherty, Richard. *The Thin Green Line: The History of the Royal Ulster Constabulary GC, 1922–2001.* South Yorkshire, UK: Pen and Sword Books, 2004.

Duiker, William J. *Ho Chi Minh*. New York: Hyperion, 2000.

Dupuy, R. Ernest, and William H. Baumer. *The Little Wars of the United States*. New York: Hawthorn Books, 1968.

Edgerton, Robert B. *Mau Mau: An African Crucible*. New York: Free Press, 1989.

Elliott, David W. P. *The Vietnamese War: Revolution and Social Change in the Mekong Delta, 1930–1975*. Armonk, NY: M. E. Sharpe, 2007.

Ellis, John. *From the Barrel of a Gun: A History of Guerrilla, Revolutionary, and Counter-Insurgency Warfare, from the Romans to the Present*. Mechanicsburg, PA: Stackpole, 1995.

Ellis, John. *A Short History of Guerrilla Warfare*. New York: St. Martin's, 1976.

Eyck, F. Gunter. *Loyal Rebels: Andreas Hofer and the Tyrolean Uprising of 1809*. Lanham, MD: University Press of America, 1986.

Fairbaim, Geoffrey. *Revolutionary Guerrilla Warfare*. Baltimore: Penguin, 1974.

Farwell, Byron. *Queen Victoria's Little Wars*. New York: Norton, 1986.

Fellman, Michael. *Inside War: The Guerrilla Conflict in Missouri during the American Civil War*. New York: Oxford University Press, 1989.

Foot, M. D. R. *Resistance: European Resistance to Nazism, 1940–1945*. New York: McGraw-Hill, 1977.

Fuller, Stephen M., and Graham A. Cosmas. *Marines in the Dominican Republic, 1916–1924*. Washington, DC: History and Museums Division, Headquarters, U.S. Marine Corps, 1974.

Furedi, Frank. *The Mau Mau War in Perspective*. Athens, OH: Ohio University Press, 1989.

Gall, Carlotta, and Thomas de Waal. *Chechnya: Calamity in the Caucasus*. New York: New York University Press, 1998.

Galula, David. *Counterinsurgency Warfare, Theory and Practice*. Westport, CT: Praeger Security International, 1964.

Galula, David. *Pacification in Algeria, 1956–1958*. Santa Monica, CA: RAND, 2006.

Gann, Lewis H. *Guerrillas in History*. Stanford, CA: Hoover Institution Press, 1971.

Gardiner, Ian. *In the Service of the Sultan: A First-Hand Account of the Dhofar Insurgency*. London: Pen and Sword, 2007.

Gates, David. *The Spanish Ulcer: A History of the Peninsular War*. New York: Norton, 1986.

Gates, John Morgan. *Schoolbooks and Krags: The United States Army in the Philippines, 1898–1902*. Westport, CT: Greenwood, 1973.

George, T. J. S. *Revolt in Mindinao: The Rise of Islam in Philippine Politics*. New York: Oxford University Press, 1880.

Geraghty, Tony. *Who Dares Wins: The Story of the SAS, 1950–1992*. London: Warner, 1993.

Girling, J. L. H. *People's War: Conditions and Consequences in China and South East Asia*. New York: Praeger, 1969.

Giustozzi, Antonio. *Koran, Kalashnikov, and Laptop: The Neo-Taliban Insurgency in Afghanistan, 2002–2007*. New York: Columbia University Press, 2009.

Gott, Richard. *Rural Guerrillas in Latin America*. Harmondsworth, Middlesex, UK: Penguin, 1973.

Greenberg, Lawrence M. *The Hukbalahap Insurrection: A Case Study of a Successful Anti-Insurgency Operation in the Philippines, 1946–1955*. Washington, DC: U.S. Army Center of Military History, 1987.

Grivas, Geōrgios. *General Grivas on Guerrilla Warfare*. New York: Praeger, 1965.

Guevara, Ernesto. *Reminiscences of the Cuban Revolutionary War*. New York: Monthly Review Press, 1968.

Guillén, Abraham. *Estrategia de la guerrilla urbana* [Urban Guerrilla Strategy]. Montevideo: Manuales del Pueblo, 1966.

Guillén, Abraham. *The Philosophy of the Urban Guerrilla: The Revolutionary Writings of Abraham Guillén*. Edited by Donald Clark Hudges. New York: Morrow, 1973.

Gwynn, Sir Charles William. *Imperial Policing*. London: Macmillan, 1934.

Hamilton, Donald W. *The Art of Insurgency: American Military Policy and the Failure of Strategy in Southeast Asia*. Westport, CT: Praeger, 1998.

Hashim, Ahmed S. *When Counterinsurgency Wins: Sri Lanka's Defeat of the Tamil Tigers*. Philadelphia: University of Pennsylvania Press, 2012.

Haycock, Ronald, ed. *Regular Armies and Insurgency*. Totowa, NJ: Rowman and Littlefield, 1979.

Haythornthwaite, Philip J. *The Peninsular War*. London: Brassey's 2004.

Healy, David. *The U.S. Occupation of Haiti, 1915–1934*. Washington, DC: Center for Strategic and International Studies, 1995.

Heggoy, Alf Andrew. *Insurgency and Counterinsurgency in Algeria*. Bloomington: Indiana University Press, 1972.

Henderson, W. O. *The German Colonial Empire, 1884–1919*. London: Frank Cass, 1993.

Henissart, Paul. *Wolves in the City: The Death of French Algeria*. New York: Simon and Schuster, 1970.

Henriksen, Thomas H. *Revolution and Counterrevolution: Mozambique's War for Independence, 1964–1974*. Westport, CT: Greenwood, 1983.

Hewitt, Christopher, and Tom Cheetham. *Encyclopedia of Modern Separatist Movements*. Santa Barbara, CA: ABC-CLIO, 2000.

Hittle, J. B. E. *Britain's Counterinsurgency Failure: Michael Collins and the Anglo-Irish War*. Washington, DC: Potomac Books, 2011.

Hodges, Tony. *Western Sahara: The Roots of a Desert War*. Westport, CT: L. Hill, 1983.

Hoffman, Bruce, Jennifer M. Taw, and David Arnold. *Lessons for Contemporary Counterinsurgencies: The Rhodesian Experience*. Santa Monica, CA: RAND, 1991.

Hossington, William A. *Lyautey and the French Conquest of Morocco*. New York: St. Martin's, 1995.

Howard, Michael. *Clausewitz*. New York: Oxford University Press, 1983.

Hunt, Richard A. *Pacification: The American Struggle for Vietnam's Hearts and Minds*. Boulder, CO: Westview, 1995.

Jacobs, Walter D. *Frunze: The Soviet Clausewitz*. The Hague: Nijoff, 1969.

Jeapes, Tony. *SAS Secret War*. London: HarperCollins, 1996.

Jeffrey, Keith. *The British Army and the Crisis of Empire, 1918–1922*. Manchester, UK: Manchester University Press, 1984.

Joes, Anthony James. *Urban Guerrilla Warfare*. Lexington: University Press of Kentucky, 2007.

Jones, Gregg R. *Red Revolution: Inside the Philippine Guerrilla Movement*. Boulder, CO: Westview, 1989.

Jones, Virgil Carrington. *Gray Ghosts and Rebel Raiders*. New York: Henry Holt, 1956.

Kaplan, Fred. *The Insurgents: David Petraeus and the Plot to Change the American Way of War*. New York: Simon and Schuster, 2013.

Katz, Samuel M. *Israeli Special Forces*. Osceola, WI: Motorbooks International, 1993.

Kelly, George Armstrong. *Lost Soldiers: The French Army and Empire in Crisis, 1947–1992*. Cambridge, MA: MIT Press, 1965.

Kerkvliet, Benedict J. *The Huk Rebellion: A Study of Peasant Revolt in the Philippines*. Berkeley and Los Angeles: University of California Press, 1977.

Kessler, Richard J. *Rebellion and Repression in the Philippines*. New Haven, CT: Yale University Press 1989.

Kiernan, Ben. *Blood and Soil: A World History of Genocide and Extermination from Sparta to Darfur*. New Haven, CT: Yale University Press, 2007.

Kilcullen, David. *Counterinsurgency*. New York: Oxford University Press 2010.

Kitson, Frank. *Gangs and Counter-Gangs*. London: Barrie and Rockliff, 1960.

Kitson, Frank. *Low Intensity Operations: Subversion, Insurgency, Peace-keeping*. London: Faber, 1971.

Klare, Michael T., and Peter Kornbluh, eds. *Low Intensity Warfare*. New York: Pantheon, 1988.

Kohl, James, and John Litt. *Urban Guerrilla Warfare in Latin America*. Cambridge, MA: MIT Press, 1974.

Krepinevich, Andrew F. *The Army and Vietnam*. Baltimore: Johns Hopkins University Press, 1986.

Lacoutre, Jean. *Ho Chi Minh: A Political Biography*. New York: Random House, 1968.

Langley, Lester D. *The Banana Wars: United States Intervention in the Caribbean, 1898–1934*. Lexington: University of Kentucky Press, 1985.

Lansdale, Edward G. *In the Midst of Wars: An American's Mission to Southeast Asia.* New York: Harper and Row, 1972.

Laqueur, Walter. *Guerrilla: A Historical and Critical Study.* Boston: Little, Brown, 1976.

Ledger, David. *Shifting Sands: The British in South Arabia.* London: Scorpion Communications and Publications, 1983.

Lee, Chong-sik. *Counterinsurgency in Manchuria: The Japanese Experience.* Santa Monica, CA: RAND, 1967.

Leeson, D. M. *The Black and Tans: British Police and Auxiliaries in the Irish War of Independence, 1920–1921.* New York: Oxford University Press, 2011.

Lewy, Gunther. *America in Vietnam.* New York: Oxford University Press, 1978.

Lien-Hang Nguyen. *Hanoi's War: An International History of the War for Peace in Vietnam.* Chapel Hill: University of North Carolina Press, 2012.

Linn, Brian McAllister. *The Philippine War, 1899–1902.* Lawrence: University Press of Kansas, 2000.

Mackay, James A. *Michael Collins: A Life.* London: Mainstream, 1996.

Mack Smith, Denis. *Garibaldi.* Englewood Cliffs, NJ: Prentice Hall, 1957.

Magnus, Philip. *Kitchener: Portrait of an Imperialist.* New York: Dutton, 1959.

Mahon, John K. *History of the Second Seminole War, 1835–1842.* Gainesville: University of Florida Press, 1967.

Maloba, Wunyabari O. *Mau Mau and Kenya: An Analysis of a Peasant Revolt.* Bloomington: Indiana University Press, 1998.

Mao Tse-tung [Mao Zedong]. *On Guerrilla Warfare.* New York: Praeger, 1961.

Mao Zedong. *Problems of Strategy in Guerrilla War against Japan.* Peking: Foreign Languages Press, 1965.

Marighella, Carlos. *The Minimanual of the Urban Guerrilla.* St. Petersburg, FL: Red and Black, 2008.

Marks, Thomas A. *Maoist Insurgency since Vietnam.* Portland, OR: Frank Cass, 1996.

Marlowe, Ann. *David Galula: His Life and Intellectual Context.* Carlisle, PA: United States Army War College, Strategic Studies Institute, 2010.

Marston, Daniel, and Carter Malkasian. *Counterinsurgency in Modern Warfare.* New York: Osprey 2010.

Martin, George. *The Red Shirt and the Cross of Savoy: The Story of Italy's Risorgimento (1748–1871).* New York: Dodd, Mead, 1969.

Massu, Jacques. *La vraie bataille d'Alger* [The Real Battle of Algiers]. Paris: Plon, 1971.

May, Glenn A. *Battle for Batangas: A Philippine Province at War.* New Haven, CT: Yale University Press, 1991.

McClintock, Cynthia. *Revolutionary Movements in Latin America: El Salvador's FMLN and Peru's Shining Path.* Washington, DC: United States Institute of Peace Press, 1998.

McCormick, Gordon H. *From the Sierra to the Cities: The Urban Campaign of the Shining Path*. Santa Monica, CA: RAND, 1992.

McCrery, Nigel. *The Complete History of the SAS: The Story of the World's Most Feared Elite Fighting Force*. London: Carlton Publishing Group, 2004.

McCulloch, Jock. *In the Twilight of the Revolution: The Political Theory of Amílcar Cabral*. Boston: Routledge and Kegan Paul, 1983.

Military History Institute of Vietnam. *Victory in Vietnam: The Official History of the People's Army of Vietnam, 1954–1975*. Translated by Merle L. Pribbenow. Lawrence: University Press of Kansas, 2002.

Missall, John, and Mary Lou. *The Seminole Wars: America's Longest Indian Conflict*. Gainesville: University Press of Florida, 2004.

Mockaitis, Thomas. *British Counterinsurgency, 1919–1960*. London: Macmillan, 1990.

Mockaitis, Thomas. *British Counterinsurgency in the Post-Imperial Era*. New York: Manchester University Press, 1995.

Mohan, Ram. *Sri Lanka: The Fractured Island*. New York: Penguin, 1989.

Mondlane, Eduardo. *The Struggle for Mozambique*. Baltimore: Penguin, 1969.

Moorecraft, Paul, and Peter McLaughlin. *The Rhodesian War: A Military History*. Barnsley, UK: Pen and Sword Military, 2008.

Moss, Robert. *Urban Guerrilla Warfare*. London: International Institute for Strategic Studies, 1971.

Moyar, Mark. *Phoenix and the Birds of Prey*. Annapolis, MD: Naval Institute Press, 1997.

Moyar, Mark. *A Question of Command: Counterinsurgency from the Civil War to Iraq*. New Haven, CT: Yale University Press, 2010.

Mumford, Andrew. *The Counter-Insurgency Myth: The British Experience of Irregular Warfare*. Hoboken, NJ: Taylor and Francis, 2011.

Nagl, John A. *Counterinsurgency Lessons from Malaya and Vietnam: Learning to Eat Soup with a Knife*. Westport, CT: Praeger, 2002.

Nalty, Barnard C. *The United States Marines in Nicaragua*. Washington, DC: Historical Branch, G-3 Division, Headquarters, U.S. Marine Corps, 1968.

Nasution, Abdul Haris. *Fundamentals of Guerrilla Warfare*. New York: Praeger, 1965.

Neizing, Johan. *Urban Guerilla: Studies on the Theory, Strategy and Practice of Political Violence in Modern Societies*. Rotterdam, Netherlands: Rotterdam University Press, 1974.

Newitt, Marilyn. *Portugal in Africa: The Last Hundred Years*. London: Longman, 1981.

Newsinger, John. *British Counterinsurgency: From Palestine to Northern Ireland*. London: Palgrave Macmillan, 2002.

O'Ballance, Edgar. *The Kurdish Revolt, 1961–1970*. Hamden, CT: Archon Books, 1973.

Odhiambo, E. S. Atieno, and John Lonsdale, eds. *Mau Mau & Nationhood: Arms, Authority and Narration.* Athens: Ohio University Press, 2003.

Omissi, David. *Air Power and Colonial Control: The Royal Air Force, 1919–1939.* Manchester, UK: Manchester University Press, 1990.

O'Neill, Brad E., William R. Heaton, and Donald J. Alberts, eds. *Insurgency in the Modern World.* Boulder, CO: Westview, 1980.

Osterling, Jorge P. *Democracy in Colombia: Clientlist Politics and Guerrilla Warfare.* New Brunswick, NJ: Transaction, 1989.

Paget, Julian. *Last Post: Aden, 1964–1967.* London: Faber and Faber, 1969.

Pakenham, Thomas. *The Boer War.* New York: Random House, 1979.

Palmer, Bruce, Jr. *The 25-Year War.* Lexington: University Press of Kentucky, 1984.

Palmer, David Scott, ed. *The Shining Path of Peru.* New York: St. Martin's, 1992.

Paret, Peter. *French Revolutionary Warfare from Indochina to Algeria: The Analysis of a Political and Military Doctrine.* London: Pall Mall, 1964.

Paret, Peter, ed. *Makers of Modern Strategy: From Machiavelli to the Nuclear Age.* Princeton, NJ: Princeton University Press, 1986.

Paul, Christopher, Colin P. Clarke, and Beth Grill. *Victory Has a Thousand Fathers: Detailed Counterinsurgency Case Studies.* Wichita, KS: RAND, 2010.

Peterson, John. *Oman's Insurgencies: The Sultanate's Struggles for Supremacy.* London: Saqi, 2007.

Pike, Douglas. *Viet Cong: The Organization and Techniques of the National Liberation Front of South Vietnam.* Cambridge, MA: MIT Press, 1966.

Pimlott, John, ed. *Guerrilla Warfare.* New York: Military Press, 1985.

Pool, David. *Eritrea: Africa's Longest War.* London: Anti-Slavery Society, 1982.

Pool, David. *From Guerrillas to Government: The Eritrean People's Liberation Front.* Oxford: James Currey, 2001.

Porch, Douglas. *The Conquest of Morocco.* New York: Knopf, 1983.

Porch, Douglas. *The Conquest of the Sahara.* New York: Knopf, 1984.

Porch, Douglas. *The French Foreign Legion: A Complete History of the Legendary Fighting Force.* New York: HarperCollins, 1991.

Porzecanski, Arturo C. *Uruguay's Tupamaros: The Urban Guerrilla.* New York: Praeger, 1973.

Ray, Brian. *Dangerous Frontiers: Campaigning in Somaliland and Oman.* London: Pen and Sword, 2008.

Reid-Daly, Ron, and Peter Stiff. *Selous Scouts: Top Secret War.* Alberton, South Africa: Galago, 1982.

Rich, Paul, and Richard Stubbs, eds. *The Counter-Insurgent State: Guerrilla Warfare and State Building in the Twentieth Century.* New York: St. Martin's, 1997.

Rochlin, James Francis. *Vanguard Revolutionaries in Latin America: Peru, Colombia, Mexico.* Boulder, CO: Lynne Rienner, 2003.

Rooney, David. *Guerrilla: Insurgents, Patriots, and Terrorists from Sun Tzu to Bin Laden.* London: Brassey's 2004.

Roy, Olivier. *Islam and Resistance in Afghanistan.* New York: Cambridge University Press, 1986.

Rubin, Barry. *Revolution until Victory? The Politics and History of the PLO.* Cambridge, MA: Harvard University Press, 2003.

Sarkesian, Sam C. *Revolutionary Guerrilla Warfare: Theories, Doctrines, and Contexts.* New Brunswick, NJ: Transaction, 2010.

Sarkesian, Sam C. *Unconventional Conflict in a New Security Era: Lessons from Malaya and Vietnam.* Westport, CT: Greenwood, 1993.

Seely, Robert. *Russian-Chechen Conflict, 1800–2000: A Deadly Embrace.* Portland, OR: Frank Cass, 2001.

Selser, Gregorio. *Sandino.* New York: Monthly Review Press, 1981.

Sherman, Richard. *Eritrea: The Unfinished Revolution.* New York: Praeger, 1980.

Short, Anthony. *The Communist Insurrection in Malaya, 1948–1960.* London: Muller, 1975.

Shrader, Charles R. *The First Helicopter War: Logistics and Mobility in Algeria, 1954–1962.* Westport, CT: Praeger, 1999.

Shy, John. *A People Numerous and Armed: Reflections on the Military Struggle for American Independence.* New York: Oxford University Press, 1976.

Simpson, J. J. *British Rule, and Rebellion.* Salisbury, NC: Documentary Publications, 1977.

Smith, Bradley F. *The Shadow Warriors: O.S.S. and the Origins of the C.I.A.* New York: Basic Books, 1983.

Smith, Martin J. *Burma Insurgency and the Politics of Ethnicity.* Atlantic Highlands, NJ: Zed, 1991.

Smithers, Alan J. *The Kaffir Wars, 1779–1877.* London: Leo Cooper, 1973.

Smythe, Donlad. *Guerrilla Warrior: The Early Life of John J. Pershing.* New York: Scribner, 1973.

Spinola, António de. *Portugal and the Future.* Johannesburg: Perskor, 1974.

Stubbs, Richard. *Hearts and Minds in Guerrilla Warfare: The Malayan Insurgency, 1948–1960.* New York: Oxford University Press, 1989.

Sun Tzu. *The Art of War.* Edited by Samuel B. Griffith. New York: Oxford University Press, 1971.

Tabor, Robert. *The War of the Flea: A Study of Guerrilla Warfare Theory and Practice.* New York: L. Stuart, 1965.

Tanham, George. *Communist Revolutionary Warfare.* Santa Monica, CA: RAND, 1961.

Thomas, Hugh. *The Cuban Revolution.* New York: Harper and Row, 1977.

Thompson, Sir Robert. *Revolutionary War in World Strategy.* New York: Taplinger, 1970.

Towle, Philip. *Pilots and Rebels: The Use of Aircraft in Unconventional Warfare, 1918–1988*. London: Brassey's, 1989.

Townshend, Charles. *Britain's Civil Wars: Counterinsurgency in the Twentieth Century*. London: Faber and Faber, 1986.

Trevelyan, George M. *Garibaldi and the Thousand*. London: Longmans, Green, 1909.

Trinquier, Roger. *Modern Warfare: A French View of Counterinsurgency*. New York: Praeger Security International, 1964.

Tucker, Spencer C. *Vietnam*. Lexington: University Press of Kentucky, 1999.

Turner, John W. *Continent Ablaze: The Insurgency Wars in Africa, 1960 to the Present*. London: Arms and Armour, 1997.

U.S. Department of the Army. *Field Manual No. 3–24 and Marine Corps Warfighting Publication No. 3–33.5: Counterinsurgency*. Washington, DC: U.S. Army, Training and Doctrine Command, 2006.

U.S. Department of Defense, *Joint Publication 3–24: Counterinsurgency Operations*. Washington, DC: U.S. Defense Department Joint Staff, 2009.

U.S. Navy Department. *NAVMC Manual No. 2890: United States Marine Corps Small Wars Manual*. Washington, DC: U.S. Marine Corps, 1940.

Utley, Robert M. *Frontier Regulars: The United States Army and the Indian, 1866–1891*. New York: Macmillan, 1974.

Valeriano, Napoleon D., and Charles T. R. Bohannan. *Counter-Guerrilla Operations: The Philippine Experience*. New York: 1962.

Vo Nguyen Giap. *People's War, People's Army: The Viet Công Insurrection Manual for Undeveloped Countries*. New York: Praeger, 1968.

Westmoreland, William C. *A Soldier Reports*. New York: Doubleday, 1976.

Woolman, David. *Rebels in the Rif: Abd el Krim and the Rif Rebellion*. Stanford, CA: Stanford University Press, 1968.

Zaffiri, Samuel. *Westmoreland: A Biography of General William C. Westmoreland*. New York: Morrow, 1994.

Editors and Contributors

Volume Editor

Dr. Spencer C. Tucker
Senior Fellow
Military History, ABC-CLIO, LLC

Introduction

Dr. Conrad C. Crane
Director
U.S. Army Military History Institute
Carlisle Barracks, Pennsylvania

Contributors

Dr. Biff L. Baker
Director of ICSOF and Professor of
    Intercultural Studies
USAF Special Operations School

Ralph Martin Baker
Independent Scholar

Dr. John H. Barnhill
Independent Scholar

Walter F. Bell
Information Services Librarian
Aurora University

Scott E. Belliveau
Department of International Studies
    and Politics
Virginia Military Institute

Dr. David M. Berman
School of Education
Department of Curriculum and
    Education
University of Pittsburgh

Andrew J. Birtle
Independent Scholar

Amy Hackney Blackwell
Independent Scholar

Dr. Anna Boros-McGee
Independent Scholar

Dr. Robert K. Brigham
Department of History
Vassar College

Jessica Britt
Independent Scholar

Colonel George M. Brooke III, USMC
    Rtd., PhD
Virginia Military Institute

Gates Brown
Independent Scholar

Robert M. Brown
Assistant Professor
U.S. Army Command and General
    Staff College

Dr. Jon L. Brudvig
Dickinson State University

Peter W. Brush
Librarian
Vanderbilt University

David M. Carletta
Department of History
Michigan State University

Dr. Barry Carr
History Department
La Trobe University

Jonathan Alex Clapperton
Department of History
University of Victoria, Canada

Dr. David Coffey
Associate Professor and Chair
Department of History and Philosophy
University of Tennessee at Martin

Dr. Justin P. Coffey
Associate Professor of History
Quincy University

Dr. Jeffery B. Cook
North Greenville University

Major Thomas Crenshaw, USAF
Instructor
Air Command and Staff College
Maxwell Air Force Base, Alabama

Dr. Cecil B. Currey
University of South Florida

Dr. Paul S. Daum
Department of History
New England College

Dr. William T. Dean III
Associate Professor of Comparative
    Military Studies
Air Command and Staff College
Maxwell Air Force Base, Alabama

Professor Phillip Deery
School of Social Sciences
Faculty of Arts
Victoria University

Jeffrey W. Dennis
Independent Scholar

Marcel A. Derosier
Independent Scholar

Dr. Louis A. Dimarco
Associate Professor
Department of Military History
U.S. Army Command and General
    Staff College
Fort Leavenworth, Kansas

Dr. Arthur J. Dommen
The Indochina Institute
George Mason University

Dr. Michael Donoghue
Department of History
Marquette University

Dr. Alan C. Downs
Department of History
Georgia Southern University

Hubert Dubrulle
Independent Scholar

R. Blake Dunnavent
Department of History
Lubbock Christian College

Rick Dyson
Information Services Librarian
Missouri Western State University

Dr. Richard M. Edwards
Senior Lecturer
University of Wisconsin Colleges and
Milwaukee School of Engineering

Dr. James Emmons
History Instructor
Social and Behavioral Sciences
    Division
North Idaho College

Dr. Will E. Fahey Jr.
Independent Scholar

Chuck Fahrer
Assistant Professor of Geography
Georgia College

Dr. Gregory Ference
Department of History
Salisbury University

Dr. John C. Fredriksen
Independent Scholar

Captain Eric W. Frith
Department of History
U.S. Air Force Academy

Dr. Michael R. Hall
Department of History
Armstrong Atlantic State University

Professor Philippe Haudrère
Faculté des Lettres,
Langues et Scies Humaines
l'Université d'Angers

Dr. William Head
Historian/Chief, WR-ALC Office of
    History
U.S. Air Force

Melissa Hebert
International Associate of Fire Chiefs

Dr. James J. Hentz
Department of International Studies
Virginia Military Institute

Jonathan M. House
William A. Stofft Professor
Department of Military History
U.S. Army Command and General
    Staff College
Fort Leavenworth, Kansas

Dr. Harry Raymond Hueston II
Associate Professor of Criminal Justice
West Texas A&M University

Dr. Mark M. Hull
Associate Professor
Department of Military History
U.S. Army Command and General
    Staff College
Fort Leavenworth, Kansas

Dr. Richard A. Hunt
Center for Military History

Dr. Arnold R. Isaacs
Independent Scholar

Dr. Jonas Kauffeldt
Assistant Professor of History
Gainesville State College

Dr. William H. Kautt
Associate Professor
Department of Military History
U.S. Army Command and General
    Staff College
Fort Leavenworth, Kansas

Jerry Keenan
Independent Scholar

Martin Kich
Professor of English
Wright State University–Lake Campus

Dr. Arne Kislenko
Department of History
Ryerson University

Dr. Ken Kotani
The National Institute for Defense
    Studies
Japan Defense Agency
Junior Research Fellow, Military History
Tokyo, Japan

Alan K. Lamm
Professor of History
Mount Olive College

Dr. Clayton D. Laurie
Intelligence Historian

Center for the Study of Intelligence
Central Intelligence Agency

Dr. William M. Leary
Department of History
University of Georgia

Keith A. Leitich
North Seattle Community College

Dr. Jan Martin Lemnitzer
London School of Economics and
    Political Science

Dr. Lucian N. Leustan
Senior Lecturer in Politics and
    International Relations
Associate Dean for Postgraduate
    Taught Programmes
Aston University, England

Dr. Irving W. Levinson
Assistant Professor
The University of Texas–San Antonio

Dr. Daniel Lewis
History Department
California State Polytechnic
    University

Arturo Lopez-Levy
PhD Candidate
University of Denver

Dr. Sebastian H. Lukasik
Assistant Professor of Comparative
    Military Studies
Department of Leadership
    and Strategy
Air Command and Staff College
Maxwell Air Force Base, Alabama

Dr. Donald A. MacCuish
Associate Professor of Comparative
    Military Studies
Air Command and Staff College
Maxwell Air Force Base, Alabama

Robert W. Malick
Adjunct Professor of History
Harrisburg Area Community
    College

Dr. Robert G. Mangrum
Professor of History
Howard Payne University

Dr. C. Kevin Matthews
Independent Scholar

Dr. Thomas D. Mays
Associate Professor
Humboldt State University

Lisa McClatchy
Independent Scholar

William McGuire
Independent Scholar

Larissa Mihalisko
Political Officer, Afghanistan
U.S. State Department

Dr. Sarah E. Miller
Assistant Professor of History
University of South Carolina,
    Salkehatchie

Wesley Moody
Florida Community College at
    Jacksonville

Dr. Jerry D. Morelock
Colonel
U.S. Army, Retired
Editor in Chief, *Armchair General*
    Magazine

Matthew S. Muehlbauer
Independent Scholar

Dr. Jaime Ramón Olivares
Professor of American History
Houston Community College–Central

Jeremy C. Ongley
Virginia Military Institute
Lexington, Virginia

Dr. Monica Orozco
Visiting Scholar and Professor of
    History
Westmont College, Santa Barbara, CA

Dr. Vernon L. Pedersen
Associate Dean for Academic Affairs
Montana State University,
    Great Falls

Dr. Pham Cao Duong
Independent Scholar

Dr. Paul G. Pierpaoli Jr.
Fellow
Military History, ABC-CLIO, LLC

Abel Polese
Hannah Arendt Institute
Dresden, Germany

Merle L. Pribbenow
Independent Scholar

Joseph Ratner
Department of History
New England College

Steven J. Rauch
Signal Corps Historian
U.S. Army Signal Center

Dr. Michael D. Richards
Department of History
Sweet Briar College

Dr. Annette E. Richardson
University of Alberta

Dr. Priscilla Roberts
Associate Professor of History,
School of Humanities
Honorary Director,
Centre of American Studies
University of Hong Kong

Dr. Rodney J. Ross
Senior Professor of History
    /Geography
Harrisburg Area Community College,
    Pennsylvania

Harve Saal
MACV, Studies and Observations
    Group
MACV-SOG History Project

James K. Selkirk Jr., CDR/USN
Academic Instructor and Adviser
Air Command and Staff College
Maxwell Air Force Base, Alabama

James E. Shircliffe Jr.
Principal Research Analyst
CENTRA Technology, Inc.

Dr. David J. Silbey
Department of Humanities
Alvernia College

Dr. Udai Bhanu Singh
Institute for Defence Studies and
    Analyses
New Delhi, India

Carina Solmirano
University of Denver

Dr. Lewis Sorley
Independent Scholar

Dr. Daniel E. Spector
Independent Scholar

Dr. Paul Joseph Springer
Associate Professor of Comparative
    Military Studies
Air Command and Staff College
Maxwell Air Force Base, Alabama

John Spykerman
U.S. State Department

Dr. Cezar Stanciu
University Valahia

Major Brian J. Tannehill
USAF Instructor
Department of Leadership
    and Strategy
Air Command and Staff College
Maxwell Air Force Base, Alabama

Mark Thompson
Associate Professor
University of North Carolina,
    Pembroke

Dr. Spencer C. Tucker
Senior Fellow
Military History, ABC-CLIO, LLC

Dr. Peter C. J. Vale
Department of Politics
Rhodes University

Dr. Bruce Vandervort
Department of History
Virginia Military Institute

Dr. Thomas D. Veve
Associate Professor of History
Dalton State College

Hieu Dinh Vu
Independent Scholar

Dr. Andrew Jackson Waskey
Division of Social Sciences
Dalton State College

Dr. William E. Watson
Associate Professor of History
Immaculata University

Tim Watts
Content Development Librarian
Kansas State University

Dr. Simon Wendt
John F. Kennedy Institute for North
    American Studies
Free University of Berlin

Leslie Wheeler
Independent Scholar

Dr. James H. Willbanks
Director
Department of Military History
U.S. Army Command and General
    Staff College, Fort Leavenworth

Dr. Bradford A. Wineman
U.S. Marine Corps Command & Staff
    College
Marine Corps University
Quantico, Virginia

Dr. David T. Zabecki
Major General
Army of the United States, Retired

Dr. Sherifa Zuhur
Director
Institute of Middle Eastern, Islamic,
    and Strategic Studies

Index